Politics in
Southern Africa

SECOND EDITION

Politics in Southern Africa

Transition and Transformation

Gretchen Bauer
Scott D. Taylor

LYNNE
RIENNER
PUBLISHERS

BOULDER
LONDON

Published in the United States of America in 2011 by
Lynne Rienner Publishers, Inc.
1800 30th Street, Boulder, Colorado 80301
www.rienner.com

and in the United Kingdom by
Lynne Rienner Publishers, Inc.
3 Henrietta Street, Covent Garden, London WC2E 8LU

Library of Congress Cataloging-in-Publication Data
Bauer, Gretchen, 1959–
    Politics in southern Africa : transition and transformation / Gretchen
Bauer, Scott D. Taylor. — 2nd ed.
        p. cm.
    Previous ed. (2005) has subtitle: State and society in transition.
    Includes bibliographical references and index.
    ISBN 978-1-58826-794-8 (pbk. : alk. paper)
    1. Africa, Southern—Politics and government.   I. Taylor, Scott D.,
1965– II. Title.
    JQ2720.A58B38 2011
    320.968—dc22

                                                    2011011361

British Cataloguing in Publication Data
A Cataloguing in Publication record for this book
is available from the British Library.

Printed and bound in the United States of America

        The paper used in this publication meets the requirements
 ∞   of the American National Standard for Permanence of
        Paper for Printed Library Materials Z39.48-1992.

    5   4   3   2   1

Contents

Acknowledgments

We would like to acknowledge the important contributions of many people who helped to make this second edition possible. At the University of Delaware, three undergraduate students—Regine Adrien, Corrie Bonham, and Ami Patel—provided helpful research assistance at different stages of the project. In bringing the book to completion, the contributions of University of Delaware graduate student Lauren Balasco and Georgetown University graduate student Ikepo Oyenuga proved invaluable. We would also like to thank our home institutions for financial and other support: the University of Delaware Department of Political Science and International Relations and the College of Arts and Sciences and the School of Foreign Service at Georgetown University.

The book benefited from the input of many individuals. In particular, we are indebted to many southern African friends and colleagues who have given generously of their time and insights during our numerous research trips to the region over the years. We would like to thank Lynne Rienner for encouraging us to revise the first edition and Claire Vlcek, assistant to Lynne Rienner, and Shena Redmond, senior project editor, for seeing the second edition through the production phase. Finally, we owe the greatest debt of gratitude to our families for their forbearance and patience while we worked on this project. Without their support, we could not have brought this book to fruition.

Southern Africa

1 Introduction

From June 10 to July 11, 2010, the eyes of the world were on South Africa. At the peak, some 700 million people sat in front of television and computer screens around the world, transfixed by events unfolding at the southernmost tip of the African continent. This unprecedented attention stemmed not from some human or natural catastrophe but from the International Federation of Association Football (FIFA) World Cup, the quadrennial contest to determine the world soccer champion. The attention was nearly universally positive. And for South Africa, it marked an international validation of that country's dramatic transformation: from international pariah to regional leader; from developing country to major emerging economy.

The fact that the World Cup competition was held in South Africa was itself a signal event and the first time the prestigious international tournament had been held on African soil. South Africa, which six years earlier had won the competitive international bidding process to host the games against considerable odds, spent roughly US$4 billion to prepare for the games, including expanding roads, highways, and ports; developing new interurban rail service; constructing new lodging facilities and telecommunications infrastructure; and, of course, building state-of-the-art sports venues. The world saw a picture of Africa that was thoroughly modern, technologically adept, remarkably unified, and above all, peaceful and secure.

This image of Africa revealed during the World Cup was in sharp contrast to common Western depictions of Africa that emphasize death, disease, poverty, dictatorship, war and conflict, exotic wildlife, and primitive "traditional" cultures. Although some of these aspects may persist to varying degrees, even in South Africa, they capture, at best, only a portion of the reality of contemporary Africa.

The FIFA World Cup thus focused a vital and refreshingly positive spotlight on Africa. And the expectations were lofty if not unrealistic: not merely to host the games successfully but also to build infrastructure designed to attract new investment and development over the long term. As such, the decision to

1

host the games also involved significant opportunity costs, given the enormous pressure on the state to spend not on stadiums and infrastructure but on the country's more immediate social welfare needs. The results of this gamble will not be clear for many years.

The other countries of southern Africa imagined that the World Cup might also have an immediate positive impact on them, such as through increased tourism, as well as be a catalyst for their own long-term development. Throughout the region, expectations were raised. Many people in governments, the hospitality sector, and investment agencies as well as the general public anticipated that their countries could capitalize on the games. A program called, appropriately enough, "Boundless Southern Africa" neatly captured this regional dynamic of optimism surrounding the World Cup. Initiated in 2008, the program was oriented around a rather new concept: transfrontier ecotourism. Moreover, Boundless Southern Africa was itself a direct response to a South African government initiative known as the African Legacy Programme, which was created in 2006 with the explicit aim of leveraging the *regional* benefits of the World Cup. Indeed, among its goals were to "improve Africa's global image and combat Afro-pessimism," to ensure that "the legacy benefits are not to be confined to the host country," and, together with the African Union, to make certain "that the 2010 World Cup legacy agenda is owned continent-wide."[1] In few places outside of South Africa was this African Legacy—and ownership—more apparent than among South Africa's southern Africa neighbors, who also sought to capture some of the world's attention and largesse.

To be sure, the countries of the southern African region did not reap the immediate rewards they anticipated, and even for South Africa, economists will long debate the return on its staggering combined World Cup–related expenditure of close to US$4 billion (28 billion rand) (see Fisher-French 2010). But not to be underestimated is the nonfinancial impact, articulated by the African Legacy Programme and others, "to improve Africa's image and combat Afro-pessimism."[2] In that respect, the World Cup appears to have succeeded, by conveying to the world a region at peace; a region in which prosperity is possible, if not universally shared; and a region that is populated by capable and resourceful people who have the ability to create and maintain functioning economic and political institutions.

Just a generation ago, such a benign, even upbeat, assessment of the socioeconomic, political, and institutional fabric of southern Africa would have been unthinkable. In 1990, southern Africa was plagued by collapsing economies, long-standing single-party authoritarian regimes in some countries, and protracted warfare and social conflict in the others. Angola and Mozambique had not yet emerged from decades of civil war, dating from before independence. Zambia and Malawi were suffering under the exhausted nationalism of three decades of authoritarian rule by presidents-for-life. Namibia, which had won its independence only in 1990, was emerging from a complex internationally brokered negotiation following a long liberation struggle. South Africa, though far more developed economically than its neighbors, was convulsed in the final throes of apartheid, the repressive and violent system that denied the black majority citizenship rights in the land of their birth, among other things.

The 2010 World Cup took place in a radically transformed environment. Growth in gross domestic product (GDP) in southern Africa had averaged over 4.5 percent per year since 2000, exceeding a combined $800 billion in 2009 (at purchasing power parity [PPP]). Before the global economic downturn in 2009, Angola's oil-based economy had expanded by more than 15 percent since 2000, whereas Mozambique's figure was about half that. Democratic elections have become the norm in South Africa, Malawi, Mozambique, Zambia, and Namibia as well as Lesotho. Long-delayed parliamentary elections were finally held in Angola in 2008. Botswana remains one of Africa's most stable democracies and has also benefited from robust economic growth. Indeed, among the countries of the region, only Zimbabwe and Swaziland have not seen marked improvement in democratic politics or economic performance, or both, since the transitions of the 1990s.

Thus, when measured by a host of international indicators, from GDP, foreign direct investment, freedom, transparency, governance, peace, or business climate,[3] to more subjective assessments of "modernity" and development, such as those captured in the World Cup snapshot, southern Africa is unique among Africa's regions. This distinctive character also firmly establishes southern Africa as a worthy geographic area for inquiry. Analyzing the domestic and regional bases for southern Africa's economic and political performance, and the specific challenges faced by the region, is the principal aim of this book.

In pursuing this line of inquiry, we resist clear preference in policy and popular circles, and among some scholars, for painting all of Africa with one undifferentiated brush. Thus, chronic violence in Somalia or Democratic Republic of Congo (DRC) becomes a quintessentially African archetype; the corruption plaguing Nigeria and Kenya becomes a metaphor for the condition of states and societies across the continent. This is done, for example, through provocative and often damning titles, though fortunately the content occasionally belies the cover and allows for some variation. One such example is Martin Meredith's *The Fate of Africa: A History of Fifty Years of Independence.* Although Meredith is a superb author, and his book not devoid of nuance, the overriding message that most readers will take away is that Africa is in terrible shape and its prospects are unremittingly dim (Meredith 2006). Other authors eschew nuance altogether and effectively condemn an entire continent.[4]

Although it is often journalists, responding to their editors' need to sell copy, who regularly produce the dramatically titled "Afropessimist" accounts, scholars have been guilty of such overgeneralizations as well. This is particularly the case when it comes to assessments of the African state, which has been variously described as "criminal" (Bayart, Ellis, and Hibou 1999), as being "in chaos" (Ayittey 1998), or as having achieved a condition of "instrumentalized disorder" (Chabal and Daloz 1999). Although a number of these analyses suggest that African states that have failed due to a combination of internal corruption, depraved leadership, and a hostile external environment can be restored (see Zartman 1995), one line of analysis suggests that the origin of African state dysfunction in the contemporary period is rooted in geography and dates to the *pre*colonial era, thus conforming to a centuries-old pattern of neglect of the countryside. According to Jeffrey Herbst (2000), precolonial political authorities lacked the incentive and capacity to project power beyond central cities; colonialism exacerbated the phenomenon, and hence the scope of the contemporary African state is limited geographically. As a result, sovereignty—indeed "stateness" itself—remains elusive. Patrick Chabal and Jean Pascal Daloz (1999) go so far as to portray Africa's predicament as normal, whereby "vacuous and ineffectual" states characterized by endemic corruption and neopatrimonialism predominate, liberal democratic state models and forms of government are fundamentally incompatible with African culture, Western notions of civil society are inapplicable, and the state is merely an instrument for depraved elites.

We regard this Afropessimist literature as deeply problematic, inasmuch as it typically sweeps aside any empirical observations from this vast continent that might challenge its dismal assumptions and their equally dire conclusions. At the same time, it is hard to argue that pessimistic views of African state and society are not based at some level on observable realities. Indeed, genocide in Rwanda, gruesome civil wars in Liberia and Sierra Leone, resource-driven violence in DRC, state collapse in Somalia, embedded corruption in Nigeria, and state-sponsored terrorism in Sudan certainly warrant condemnation, perhaps even pessimism; though even some of these are things of the past. Our point, however, is that the writings in what has been labeled the "Afropessimist tradition" all tend to obscure important regional and subregional distinctions and confirm Western preconceptions—and misconceptions—about the African continent (see Keim 2008). The message of these works is that what applies in one country or region of Africa obtains throughout the entire continent. Southern Africa, by contrast, is a region whose states have largely, albeit not completely, escaped the dire depictions that seem to dominate the Afropessimist narrative.

The African continent represents a vast area of the globe. Africa is three times the size of the continental United States. Its population of 1 billion people exceeds that of the Americas; after Asia, Africa is the second most populous continent. Its people reside in fifty-four countries and speak over a thousand different languages, corresponding to hundreds of distinct cultures. African history—ancient and medieval—is exceedingly rich and remarkably diverse, and its contemporary political and economic stories also vary widely.

Quite simply, as is often argued, "there are many Africas." Yet the impulse of both those unfamiliar with Africa and many scholars and practitioners is to treat Africa as a monolith. This use of "Africa" as convenient shorthand becomes particularly destructive and misleading, especially in the hands of Afropessimists, who attempt to extrapolate from a few countries a theory of African politics.

Even many African politics textbooks, which tend to be more evenhanded in their appraisal of Africa's problems and prospects, struggle to strike a balance between targeted analyses of specific countries and overgeneralizations of conditions on the continent.[5] Such texts that examine Africa as a whole are quite useful in providing a broad introduction to a continent unfamiliar to many audiences, and to be fair, authors are not accorded limitless pages to counter every myth about Africa or to engage in detailed analyses of every country and issue. Certain common factors do exist, such as the universality of colonialism and the preponderance of underdevelopment or maldevelopment, yet these have fostered a monolithic, undifferentiated approach to the study of African politics and society,[6] an approach that tends to obscure important regional distinctions.

Southern Africa as a Region

Southern Africa is one of the areas of the African continent that warrants systematic treatment as a region.[7] As Sandra MacLean (1999, 947) observes, "regions are almost always more than geopolitical divisions; they are also 'social constructions,' i.e., processes based on shared interests and intersubjective understanding." And although both political boundaries and identities can shift over time, "it is well established that the region of southern Africa does exist empirically. As Peter Vale states, 'the notion of Southern Africa—like the notion of Europe—is a single and indivisible one.' To be thus identified, a particular area or group of states must, over time, develop a sense of 'regionness.' There are various levels of this quality, determined largely by the degree to which the empirical and socially constructed attributes are entrenched and combined" (MacLean 1999, 947, citing Vale 1997, 73).[8]

Building on this notion of regionness, it is possible to identify a number of common empirical and socially constructed characteristics within and across states and societies in southern Africa. Indeed, given the many shared attributes and experiences, analysis of the countries as part of a regional bloc is a fruitful and revealing exercise.

First, many of the contemporary states of southern Africa share a common colonial and early postcolonial history. The region was initially settled by the Portuguese on both coasts, in what is now Mozambique and Angola, and by the Dutch in South Africa. However, with the exceptions of Angola, Mozambique, and Namibia (which was under German rule), much of the territory had fallen under British imperial domination by the end of the nineteenth century. Although Portuguese, Afrikaner (Dutch), and German influences continue to play a role in one or more of the states of the region today, the Anglo linguistic, legal, political, and economic heritage remains a common feature for most.

Moreover, for nearly all of southern Africa, colonialism lasted far longer than elsewhere on the continent. In five countries—Angola, Mozambique, Zimbabwe, Namibia, and South Africa—liberation movements were forced to resort to armed struggle to attain independence. Each of these movements was marked by at least a rhetorical commitment to socialism. In the context of the Cold War, the stated commitment to socialist principles generated intense interest in the region among external actors. It also fueled apartheid South Africa's campaign of regional destabilization against neighboring countries, the effects of which were borne by all the countries in southern Africa. This extended colonialism—and the resort to war to obtain independence—has had profound and lasting effects on social, political, and economic developments in the region, which are elaborated in the country chapters of this book.

Second, the presence of large white settler populations, or at least settler interests, emerges directly from the region's unique history and represents a key feature of many of its states. Each of the five aforementioned states that endured violent struggles for liberation had an expansive settler population. Although whites fled Angola and Mozambique on the eve of independence, their continued prominence in many countries, including South Africa, Zimbabwe, and Namibia and to a considerably lesser extent Botswana and Zambia, has been a double-edged sword. These states face severe and potentially destabilizing disparities of wealth and resources between rich and poor. Of course, there are wealthy black elites, and this class has expanded markedly since the 1990s; however, where a disproportionate share of wealth and productive capacity is owned and controlled by a "nonindigenous" white minority, tensions have lingered. In Zimbabwe, for example, the white population was demonized and targeted by the government of President Robert Mugabe in the first decade of the twenty-first century, leading to widespread violence, dislocation, and economic decline. There are also significant numbers of other "nonindigenous" groups, particularly Asians, who occupy important economic strata. How these countries incorporate racial and ethnic minorities affects their prospects for long-term stability.

At the same time, paradoxically, it can be argued that the white presence, and particularly the retention of a considerable percentage of "settler capital," in southern Africa have improved the development prospects for the region. Whereas some settler regimes in Africa, such as in Kenya and Algeria, abandoned the continent in the 1960s, their southern African counterparts held on much longer. White-ruled regimes in Zimbabwe (until 1980), Namibia (until 1990), and South Africa (until 1994) used their tight control over resources and their international access to provide a strong infrastructure and relatively sophisticated international economies that were inherited by black governments at independence.[9] By and large, these economies were more diversified and performed better than those in the region and elsewhere on the continent that experienced massive capital flight upon transition to multiparty rule.

Third, southern Africa is politically and socially interconnected and interdependent. Although the region cannot be described as culturally homogeneous, the peoples of southern Africa are interrelated to a significant degree. The first inhabitants of the region were the Khoisan, whose descendants still live in parts of Namibia, South Africa, and Botswana. In the early centuries of the common era the Khoisan were joined, and substantially displaced, by successive waves of peoples from the north, as the Bantu migrations dispersed peoples throughout Africa. These Bantu-speaking peoples were agriculturalists, as well as pastoralists, who brought with them techniques of smelting iron and other metals. Their descendants are found today throughout southern Africa—for example, the Chewa in Malawi, the Bemba in Zambia, and the Xhosa and Zulu in South Africa, among many other groups. In the nineteenth century the accelerated arrival of Europeans and the formal onset of colonialism in southern Africa and elsewhere meant the imposition of arbitrary boundaries that typically divided ethnic groups across colonial borders. With few exceptions, the colonial-era map of Africa is unchanged, and therefore connections remain between peoples across those same borders: there are Batswana in Botswana and South Africa, Basotho in Lesotho and South Africa, Ovambo in Namibia and Angola, Shona in Zimbabwe and Mozambique, and so on.

Connections among the peoples of southern Africa are also fostered by a regionwide migrant labor system, which is another artifact of European settlement and colonialism. With the discovery of diamonds and gold in the future South Africa in the late 1800s, there emerged a migrant labor system that brought workers from throughout the region to the mines in South Africa. Before and after independence, foreign migrant workers also crossed borders to work in mines in Namibia, Botswana, Zambia, and Zimbabwe. As they crisscrossed the region, mineworkers participated in a cross-fertilization of ideas and experiences across national borders, leading in some cases to an early organization of workers or the rise of nationalist movements. Southern Africans also crossed regional borders in search of educational opportunities. During the colonial period, for example, a number of southern African leaders (as well as other privileged elites) attended Fort Hare College in South Africa, the first university for blacks in the region. Much later, many black Namibians, with no tertiary-level educational opportunities in their own country, would flock to South African universities—and then return home imbued with tactics gleaned from South Africa's liberation struggle.

Liberation struggles also fostered interconnectedness among peoples and states of the region. Many of those fighting for independence in their own countries were forced to spend long periods of exile in neighboring countries. Countries like Angola, Mozambique, and Zambia, which gained their independence first, became havens in the 1970s and 1980s for rebel movements that were attempting to end minority rule in South West Africa (Namibia), Rhodesia (Zimbabwe), and South Africa. Thus, tens of thousands of Namibians spent decades in Angola, many South Africans flocked to Zambia, and Zimbabwean rebels established staging areas in Mozambique, to cite but a few examples.[10] In the process, these young exiles were also able to compare experiences from home and contemplate a common southern African future. Moreover, throughout these same years of struggle, the independent countries of the region were united in a political body known as the Frontline States (FLS), formed in an effort to isolate apartheid South Africa and bring an end to white minority rule in the country.[11]

Fourth, as in much of the rest of Africa, countries in southern Africa underwent processes of political and economic transition in the 1990s, during which significant political and economic liberalization took place—more or less successfully in some countries than in others. Although nearly every state in the region today claims to be democratic, the degree of democracy varies widely, in part reflecting the varied experiences of transition and the difficulty of inculcating and consolidating democratic regimes. Botswana, with a history of peace and stability and democratic elections since independence in 1966, was in no need of political transformation on the scale of the other countries. Namibia and South Africa, since their respective transitions in 1990 and 1994, have by and large abided by their widely acclaimed democratic constitutions and respected the rule of law. Zambia and Malawi, following a pattern familiar to much of the rest of Africa, made transitions in the early 1990s from decades of single-party rule by presidents-for-life (de facto in Zambia, de jure in Malawi) to fairly vibrant multiparty political systems. Zimbabwe, by contrast, has gone in the reverse direction, and, significantly, is the only country featured in this book that has experienced an erosion of democracy since the 1990s. There, President Robert Mugabe, in office since 1980, has employed ruinous and often violent strategies to undermine the opposition and continue his tenure in office by authoritarian means. Finally, the Lusophone states took divergent paths in the 1990s. In Mozambique, a successful transition from three decades of war to peace in 1992 made way for a vibrant period of reconstruction and development. In Angola, an end to decades of war was only accomplished after the death of rebel leader Jonas Savimbi in early 2002. An initially cautious cease-fire at the beginning of the decade, followed finally by elections in 2008 and a new constitution in 2010 may signal movement, albeit halting, toward economic and political transition in that country.

In addition to the nearly regionwide turn to more democratic modes of governance, the states of southern Africa share a unique feature in Africa: none has been the victim of a military coup. In fact, even coup *attempts* are rare, making southern Africa truly exceptional on the continent in this regard.[12] This may suggest a level of stability or at least a respect for and expectation of civilian rule that does not prevail throughout Africa. Moreover, the region is also characterized today by relative peace, including manageable levels of social conflict and internal security and cohesion—again, a factor that differentiates the south from nearly every other zone in Africa. Even the regime-initiated violence in Zimbabwe abated in the wake of a fragile postelection power-sharing arrangement initiated in 2008. This peace and stability should bode well for future economic development and the sustainability of social and political movements attempting to achieve greater democracy.

Economically, there is considerable variation among southern African countries. That variation stems from a host of factors, such as population size, resource endowment, location, and a legacy of decades of war versus peace and stability. Botswana and Namibia have around 2 million people; South Africa has almost 50 million. Botswana, Namibia, and South Africa have diamonds and other valuable minerals; Angola has diamonds and oil. In contrast, Malawi grows tobacco, and Mozambique, until fairly recently, was largely reliant on production of cashews and prawns. Botswana, Malawi, Zambia, and Zimbabwe are landlocked, whereas the others have ample access to the sea. Recent developments, however, including a rebound in global prices of commodities such as copper (Zambia's main export) since 2002, the discovery of vast diamond deposits in Zimbabwe, and the expansion of aluminum smelting and natural gas and hydroelectric resources in Mozambique, have had a salutary impact on regional economies. Yet whereas growth has been impressive, substantial disparities continue to characterize the region. For example, in 2009, estimated per capita gross domestic product (at purchasing power parity) in the region ranged from US$12,700 in Botswana to less than US$100 in Zimbabwe.[13] Nonetheless, taken together, the economies of southern Africa are among the strongest on the continent, and the potential for future collective growth and development is enormous.

Despite this relative economic strength, however, all of the countries of southern Africa (with the exception of Botswana and Namibia) adopted some form of neoliberal economic reform, often referred to as structural adjustment programs (SAPs), in the 1980s and 1990s. Designed and implemented by the World Bank and International Monetary Fund,[14] these programs were intended to spur a process of fundamental economic transformation. SAPs were imposed across the continent beginning in the 1980s, when African states proved unable to recover from the collapse of global primary commodities prices, declining terms of trade, and rising debt levels. When they were introduced, however, adjustment programs were envisioned as a short-term series of measures that would restore Africa's economic health (World Bank 1981). By the time adjustment programs entered their third decade, in the guise of Poverty Reduction Strategy Papers, the flaws in the initial rosy projections were glaringly apparent. Over the years, intense criticism and a lack of tangible and sustainable success led to substantial modifications in SAP programs themselves (Mkandawire and Soludo 1999); the World Bank even dropped the name SAP, replacing it with "development policy lending" in the lexicon. Notwithstanding such rebranding, and the elevation of "poverty reduction" as a priority in development policy rhetoric, the predominant development prescription remains a substantially neoliberal one. (In the contemporary period, perhaps only Angola, with its oil wealth and access to Chinese loans, can avoid the model.) This economic model regards state involvement in the economy negatively. However, given the outsized economic role played historically by southern African states, this process of transformation has proved particularly unsettling and painful for many. The interconnectedness of this region has meant that any economic difficulties in one country are keenly felt in neighboring states.

Indeed, regional proximity and economic interconnectedness have produced harmonies as well as tensions. A formal institution through which states attempt to mitigate conflict and promote economic and political cooperation is the Southern African Development Community (SADC). The SADC itself underwent a notable transition in the 1990s when it transformed itself from the Southern African Development Coordination Conference (made up of the members of the Frontline States grouping), into the Southern African Development Community, with South Africa at its core. Owing partly to South Africa's membership and its ability to play a hegemonic role given its far more developed economy, the SADC is widely regarded as the most viable regional economic community in Africa (McCarthy 1999).[15] Although one of three (somewhat redundant) bodies concerned with regional trade relations, SADC also represents a forum for regional cooperation on a large range of nontrade issues including politics, transport, gender, and health.

In sum, the histories and the prevailing political, social, and economic conditions, as well as the fates of each of the countries of southern Africa, are profoundly linked. This book attempts to regard them as such.

Theory and Southern Africa

Southern Africa has been examined through multiple theoretical lenses, each of which offers some insight on the politics of the region as a whole or of its constituent parts. International relations theories are particularly suited to the former, and scholars have employed variations on realist, liberal, and Marxist approaches to the study of the region (Vale 2001). Operating at a lower level of abstraction, scholars of comparative politics have relied generally on related theoretical tools, such as the modernization, dependency, and statist approaches, as well as on pluralist models that emphasize societal actors

(Chazan et al. 1999). Each of these theories and their various permutations has been employed to explain political and economic phenomena in independent Africa as a whole, though they have often come to conflicting conclusions about the nature of the politics in and of Africa.

Dependency and underdevelopment, for example, which have their intellectual origins in Marxism, were particularly helpful in conceptualizing the world as a system of states, in which the less-developed regions, including Africa, were unalterably relegated to the global periphery (Rodney 1974; Wallerstein 1974). Such perspectives, which elevate the notion of structure, had some validity: surely the marginal position from which African states entered the world stage—namely as economically backward, primary commodity exporters—helped to explain the late-twentieth-century African predicament (Leys 1994). These approaches, however, neglected too many factors. Like the structuralist theories within the international relations subfield, such as neorealism, which regarded the position of states as a result of power relations, the dependency tradition tended to ignore that power may also reside in states of the so-called periphery (as well as being vested in actors other than states).

In short, structural theories rely on material capacity and suggest that material attributes or endowments (whether wealth or power) determine political behavior (Finnemore and Sikkink 2001). In this view, African states are at the mercy of more powerful states in the developed North. Yet this is not consistently the case, and structuralist approaches are largely incapable of explaining the variation and change that define political life, at both the international and national levels. An emphasis on *agency,* by contrast, can help offset several of these shortcomings.

Depending on whether the level of analysis is international relations or at the state level, individual states or individual economic or political actors may be considered agents. If we examine first the role of the *state* as agent, the power that southern African states project in an international system is far more nuanced than structuralism allows. Structuralist theories are hard pressed to explain, for example, how South Africa has used its "middlepowermanship" to effectively negotiate international accords to its benefit and at the expense of both its less-developed neighbors and of *developed* countries (I. Taylor 2002). In a different way, Zimbabwe—and its neighbors—have resisted multiple forms of pressure from far more conventionally powerful developed states to remove President Robert Mugabe. The international community cheered a 2008 power-sharing arrangement between the ruling party and the embattled opposition party, but President Mugabe and his party have used both guile and control of the country's security apparatus to maintain control. Throughout the 1990s, chronically poor Zambia was able to play its various donors and lenders off one another to its advantage, practicing what some scholars labeled "partial reform syndrome" (Rakner, van de Walle, and

Mulaisho 2001). Botswana has defied many of the neoliberal tenets of "globalization" by successfully enacting and adhering to a state-centric, "developmentalist" model. Finally, the emergence of China as a major economic player throughout the region means that the structurally weak states of southern Africa are increasingly able to extract bargains by playing their traditional trade, development, and security allies against the ever more active Chinese— or by rejecting them altogether (Bräutigam 2010).

Moving more squarely into the realm of comparative politics, statist approaches reassert African (state) agency by proclaiming a greater role for the state, particularly concerning development questions and domestic affairs. They regard the state "as a primary motor force behind social and economic occurrences on the continent" (Chazan et al. 1999, 21). Of course, many African states lack bureaucratic capacity, or even legitimacy; yet whereas the state may be "weak by any conventional measure of institutional capacity . . . it remains the most prominent landmark on the African institutional landscape" (Bratton 1989, 410). In the statist view, African states are themselves actors, and their attributes, behaviors, and shortcomings help to explain problems of development and democracy.

Another theoretical framework frequently employed by Africanists is one that emphasizes the preeminent role of "one individual (the strongman, 'Big Man,' or 'supremo')" in African politics (Bratton and van de Walle 1997, 62). In this category, Robert Jackson and Carl Rosberg's *Personal Rule in Black Africa* (1982) was a prominent early example. Analyses that emphasize the ubiquity of neopatrimonial rule in Africa and the neopatrimonial nature of the state are certainly part of this tradition (Clapham 1982; Bratton and van de Walle 1997). More recently, scholars have argued that the neopatrimonial framework has been subject to such a high degree of conceptual stretching and has been employed to explain such a vast array of negative outcomes in Africa that its utility has been called into question (deGrassi 2008; Pitcher, Moran, and Johnston 2009). We certainly welcome these developments.

Nevertheless, such "personalist" approaches retain a prominent position in Africanist scholarship; hence they warrant attention briefly here. Certainly, they are difficult to categorize using the agent-structure dichotomy introduced above. In fact, such approaches fit rather uncomfortably in an agent-structure framework: on one hand, they *reduce* African politics and economy to the individual—the "big man"—claiming that he is responsible for political outcomes, attitudes, and behaviors. Hence they are in one sense the ultimate expression of agency. On the other hand, such approaches *deny* Africans in general any agency, by suggesting that neopatrimonial behaviors are immutable, deeply culturally embedded, and in effect *genetic,* thus giving them a structural quality. Such determinism is fundamentally at odds with our approach, which regards politics in southern Africa as dynamic rather than preordained.

The diversity of African politics demonstrates the necessity of utilizing different theoretical lenses to analyze political, economic, and social phenomena on the continent. We argue for balance, though, not for conceptual muddling. Neopatrimonialism, for example, may offer theoretical parsimony, but as Naomi Chazan and colleagues (1999, 23) point out, "politics in Africa (as elsewhere) cannot be reduced so easily to the activities of actors on the national scene." Quite simply, despite his significance, Mugabe does not *define* Zimbabwe, nor did Nelson Mandela, who practically embodied the first five postapartheid years, define South Africa. Thus, such reductionist emphasis on the "big man" (and arguably the culture of corruption he inspires) is inadequate to understanding contemporary Zimbabwe and President Robert Mugabe without reference to structural variables as well. Likewise, women's participation in southern African politics is constrained by what we might label *structural* biases against women, but reliance solely on structural factors denies women the agency they so obviously possess, evidenced by the gains of women politicians and activities of women's movements throughout the region. As Alexander Wendt argues, "it is impossible for structures to have effects apart from the attributes and interactions of agents" (1999, 12). At bottom, the lesson to be drawn is that agency and structure, and how they interact, are important in the study of African politics.

Agents not only shape their environment, but they are shaped and constrained by domestic and international influences as well. Thus there are clear limits to exclusively agent-based approaches, which tend to treat "collective understandings as simply epiphenomena of individual action and deny that they have causal power or ontological status" (Finnemore and Sikkink 2001, 393). This is the basis of constructivist approaches, which may offer a corrective to prevailing theories (Ba and Hoffman 2003, 21); indeed, we find a number of helpful insights in this literature.[16] Among the most helpful contributions of the constructivist research program is its emphasis on learning.

Southern Africa has been shaped by agents and structural forces. External practices are not always simply imposed without adaptation on an African tabula rasa. Exogenous ideas are "endogenized" when they encounter "local" African norms and traditions (Magnusson 2002). Hence the influences on southern Africa are broadly international (for example, neoliberalism, globalization, democratization) and domestic (local norms and traditions, including those of both democracy and authoritarianism) as well as regional (states, their leaders, and societies observe and are affected by one another in the regional context). Politics, economics, and society in the region are explained, therefore, as Bruce Magnusson (2002, 2) argues, "by the work (the practice) involved in the articulation of ideas, norms, and context among communities within the territorial state and across territorial lines." Martha Finnemore and Kathryn Sikkink (2001, 407) describe this practice as "learning": "The mechanisms that lead to learning include interaction (with domestic and international actors), comparison (with prior national experiences and with other countries' experiences), reflection (including internal debates and self-criticism) and personnel change."

The case study chapters reveal that in southern Africa, as elsewhere, there is learning across a range of social, political, and economic issues as regional norms and ideas shift in response to various exogenous—and endogenous—stimuli, continuing the process that MacLean (1999), in the vernacular of constructivism, labels the "social construction" of southern Africa. Examples of such learning include emerging regional ideas about the symbolic and practical role of land, what it means to be African or southern African, and evolving norms of constitutionalism and presidentialism, to name a few. As Chazan and colleagues (1999, 23) suggest in endorsing their "political interaction framework," "by looking at the interaction of social forces, economic activities, formal institutions, and prevalent values, we may better grasp the meaning and direction of the diverse patterns that have evolved in Africa since independence."

Like Chazan and colleagues, we apply an eclectic theoretical approach in this book and attempt to capture the diversity—and consistency—within the region. Indeed, whereas we employ a common framework for analyzing the countries, the research questions, and hence the emphases, in the chapters are varied. Nonetheless, each of the chapters explores the relationship among history, ideas, and institutions, broadly emphasizing economic development and democratization and seeking to identify the variables that enhance or retard the opportunities for their realization in the region. On the whole, the chapters serve to illuminate the tension between agent-based and structural explanations in Africa. Therefore, we draw on the theoretical literatures that privilege structure, state, and individual agents to inform the analysis of southern Africa's political, social, and economic transformations.

Country Case Studies

States of southern Africa could be analyzed in several possible ways. One example would be to classify them on the basis of trade relations, such as those that are Southern African Customs Union members and those that are not. Another would be to divide the states by degree of democracy or level of economic development. They might also be categorized by European language and cultural influences: predominantly Anglophone versus predominantly Lusophone. An alternative approach to analyzing the region might not privilege states at all and might instead weigh its *people* more heavily (Vale 2001, 28). Clearly, myriad other possibilities exist, and the choice of grouping or organization depends on which factors are emphasized. Thus, while recognizing the value of other possible criteria, this book divides the countries of southern

Africa largely according to historical experience, with attention to recent political transitions. As such, we have grouped them in the following way.

Malawi and Zambia were the first states in the region to gain their independence from colonial rule and are distinct in the region for the way in which their economic and political trajectories, after independence, mirror closely those of the rest of sub-Saharan Africa rather than southern Africa. Like other countries in sub-Saharan Africa, Malawi and Zambia experienced significant political transitions in the early 1990s. Botswana also achieved independence in the 1960s from Britain and, like its counterparts, emerged under conditions that were both optimistic and uncertain. Yet in many ways, Botswana defies categorization, given its unique position in southern Africa and indeed in Africa as a whole. Botswana is one of the very few countries in Africa to have experienced both stable multiparty democracy and relative economic prosperity since independence.

The Lusophone countries, Mozambique and Angola, form a logical pairing based on historical criteria, although their paths diverged in the early 1990s. Each attained its independence in 1975, only to plunge immediately into protracted war. Mozambique and Angola struggled bitterly to achieve first their independence from Portugal and then the peace that would allow them to develop and possibly catch up to some of their more developed neighbors. The postsettler societies of Zimbabwe, Namibia, and South Africa are the final grouping of states. These were the last countries in the region to attain their independence, and only after years of heightened struggle. All three countries contend still with the legacies of decades of oppressive white minority rule.

Malawi and Zambia are the subjects of Chapters 2 and 3. Both countries were colonized by the British, or British interests, beginning after 1889. As colonial possessions, they were eventually referred to as Nyasaland and Northern Rhodesia, respectively, and for the last ten years of colonial rule were part of the Central African Federation (together with Southern Rhodesia). Following the emergence of nationalist movements, the two countries gained their independence, largely peacefully, with the majority of other African countries in the early 1960s. Shortly after independence, moreover, both countries became one-party states led by presidents with a seemingly unbreakable hold on power: Malawi's Hastings Kamuzu Banda, as self-proclaimed president-for-life, and Zambia's Kenneth Kaunda, who faced no competition when he went to the polls every five years. While Malawi was clearly the more repressive of the two polities, Zambia was also intolerant of political dissent and permitted little autonomous societal organization. One significant difference between the two regimes was their stance toward apartheid South Africa and, by extension, the region. While President Kaunda in Zambia was one of the founders of the Frontline States organization, established to unite the region against South Africa, the Banda regime in Malawi was one of the very few friends of the apartheid state. Moreover, Zambia also allowed regional liberation movements fighting the South African regime to locate exile camps within its borders.

More recently, however, the two countries' political and economic paths have again converged. By the late 1980s both countries were experiencing economic crisis, though of somewhat different origins. Economic deprivation combined with the long-standing political repression led, in both countries, to calls for political liberalization. First in Zambia, and just a few years later in Malawi, the once all-powerful executives bowed to domestic and international pressure and agreed to an opening of their political systems. Transition elections were held first in Zambia in 1991 and then in Malawi in 1994, in both cases bringing new political parties and new leaders to power. In the years since, however, the optimism and promise of those transitions were first replaced by the emergence of "electoral authoritarian" regimes, but subsequently settled back into the vicissitudes of normal politics: economic growth remains stubbornly tied to international commodity prices; incumbents have been elected and left office as scheduled; each country is noticeably but shallowly democratic.

Yet in a paradoxical way, Zambia and Malawi are in many respects further advanced along the democratic path than their southern African neighbors. Whereas all of the other countries profiled in this book are still led by first-generation liberation movements cum governments, Zambia and Malawi represent a noteworthy, if flawed, second generation. Their liberation governments were replaced in 1991 and 1994, respectively; while this has not resulted in flourishing democracies per se, it has seen the flourishing of opposition parties in these countries and the maturation of civil societies that have diminished tolerance for authoritarian politics. Thus, even though the immediate democratic future is uncertain, the longer-term political development of these states has much to commend it. In sum, these two countries form an important part of the region. Although their politics sometimes conforms to the rest of Africa, their experience may provide a blueprint—to be followed or avoided—for the rest of southern Africa.

Chapter 4 examines Botswana, considered by many observers to be an exceptional case in Africa, albeit as other countries become more democratic it becomes less the exception. Like Zambia and Malawi, Botswana was also colonized by the British, though many argue that British colonial rule in Botswana was particularly mild and allowed for a significant degree of continuity of traditional rule, in particular the institution known as *kgotla* (an assembly of all adult males in the community). Moreover, like Zambia and Malawi, Botswana achieved independence relatively peacefully, in the case of Botswana under the leadership of the Botswana Democratic Party (BDP). Despite regular elections every five years and smooth leadership transitions, the BDP has remained in power ever since 1965, an outcome that has implications for the robustness of Botswana's "model" democracy. Botswana has also been a singular economic success story in Africa; its economic growth rates have been among the world's highest after diamonds and other minerals were discovered in the late 1960s and early 1970s. Moreover, revenues generated from the country's mines and cattle ranches (the primary source of wealth accumulation before diamonds were discovered) have been used judiciously to invest in the country's infrastructure and human resource base, earning Botswana the distinction of being one of the few "developmental" states—or at least a state with developmental characteristics—in Africa. In one way, however, Botswana is all too much like its neighbors in the region, having the second highest human immunodeficiency virus (HIV) infection rate in the world in 2010. Still, Botswana stands out for its progressive response to the HIV/AIDS (acquired immunodeficiency syndrome) crisis, among other things making antiretroviral drugs available to all Batswana who need them. Like many other countries in Africa, Botswana has also seen a most welcome decline since 2009 in the HIV prevalence rate.

The two Lusophone countries, Mozambique and Angola, are analyzed in Chapters 5 and 6. Although much joins these two countries to their southern African neighbors, Mozambique and Angola are appropriately considered apart. Both were colonized by Portugal, a backward European power that imposed a particularly harsh colonial rule and refused to quit when other European powers were abandoning their colonial empires. Indeed, liberation movements in both countries fought for more than a decade until a military coup brought down the regime in Portugal and independence was finally granted to Portugal's African colonies. But the fighting continued in both countries, as rebel movements challenged new governments: in Mozambique until 1992 and in Angola until 2002. In both countries there was substantial sponsorship of hostilities and combatants by a host of external players, including Rhodesia (Zimbabwe) and South Africa, the United States, the Soviet Union, Cuba, and others. In a more constructive international role, the United Nations sought to broker peace agreements in the early 1990s and to facilitate transitions to peace in both countries. In Mozambique they were successful. In Angola they were not; lasting peace was only achieved in Angola nearly a decade later in 2002. The economies of the two countries have always diverged significantly, and by 2009 Angola, with all of its tremendous resources, had a per capita income (at purchasing power parity) ten times that of Mozambique.

Chapters 7, 8, and 9 address the postsettler societies of Zimbabwe, Namibia, and South Africa. These countries share one of the most significant features of the region, namely enduring and recalcitrant settler regimes; as a result, independence or black majority rule was only obtained decades after the rest of the sub-Saharan African countries had achieved it. In all three, liberation movements were forced to resort to armed struggle, even war, to gain independence. Namibia and South Africa are particularly closely related; indeed, Namibia was the de facto colony of South Africa for seventy-five years. Many of these linkages, economic and sociocultural, continue to the present. Zimbabwe, meanwhile, differs in some important ways from the rest of southern Africa, but it also shares many characteristics within this trio of states. The similar legacies include the ascension to power of the leader of the independence movement (who has proved astonishingly resilient in the Zimbabwe case), gross and lasting disparities in land and resources, and the promotion of reconciliation without accountability. Each legacy has profound consequences for the future trajectories of these states. Zimbabwe's method of belatedly facing these challenges has proved aggressive, corrupt, and ultimately immensely destructive. Nonetheless, Zimbabwe's decline serves as a warning, as all three countries face some common challenges in the twenty-first century, although Zimbabwe must also confront the challenge of reconstruction.

Organization of the Book

In order to facilitate comparison across cases, this book adheres to a similar format for each of the country chapters. First, the chapter identifies the key themes that help to define contemporary politics and society in the country. Then it provides some historical background, from the precolonial period, through colonialism and the struggle for independence, until final decolonization was achieved. What follows is an examination of enduring racial and ethnic cleavages, an important, often defining characteristic in a region where all states are multiethnic and where six of eight experienced significant white settlement. Each chapter also offers a careful delineation of the different branches of government and the extent to which they act as a check on one another. After covering the realm of formal politics and institutions, the chapter turns back to the role of civil society actors, before turning to the fundamentals of the political economy. Each country chapter concludes with an examination of the most pressing challenges to state and society in the first decade of the twenty-first century and those they will likely confront in the years to come.

Chapters 10, 11, and 12 treat issues that transcend state boundaries in southern Africa: HIV/AIDS, women and politics, and southern Africa's international relations with Africa and the world. AIDS and gender are also subnational issues that relate to "deep politics." Although these issues are, or should be, of concern to states, these chapters offer at least a partial corrective to Vale's indictment of approaches that neglect people (2001). Southern Africa's international relations, meanwhile, speak to supranational issues and also move beyond the limitations of the state and state-centric analyses.

Chapter 10 examines what was a few years ago regarded as an existential threat to the countries of the region, namely the AIDS epidemic. Indeed, the countries with the highest HIV infection rates in the world continue to be the countries of southern Africa, at the same time that rates of new HIV infection and adult HIV infection prevalence rates are falling in the region as elsewhere in Africa. The rapid spread of HIV throughout southern Africa resulted in setbacks to decades of development progress; for example, life expectancy and infant mortality rates plummeted to below preindependence levels in some countries. At the same time, remarkably, at the end of the first decade of the twenty-first century, both prevention and treatment efforts appear to be working. As noted, new infection rates are falling, due in part to changes in behavior and in part to simple measures like enhanced access to nevirapine for pregnant women to prevent mother-to-infant transmission. As for treatment, whereas in 2003 only 2 percent of sub-Saharan Africans had access to antiretroviral drugs, by 2008 44 percent of Africans (and 48 percent of southern Africans) had such access, leading to an increase in those living with HIV/AIDS across Africa and the region (UNAIDS 2009a, 25). Although HIV/AIDS continues to threaten southern African polities and societies at multiple levels, it has become a disease for which people have developed an array of successful coping strategies. Today the people and countries of southern Africa are *living* with HIV/AIDS.

Chapter 11 investigates women and politics in the region. Gender intersects nearly every other issue, from political participation to social organization, and women have long filled much of the space created by weak state capacity in the region. Indeed, permeating gender relations in the region and enlisting the support of women has been essential to stemming the HIV/AIDS tide. More broadly, this chapter touches upon the way in which women have transformed their role over the decades in the region—from the precolonial period, through colonialism, and into the independence period. In particular the chapter focuses on how women are remaking politics in contemporary southern Africa. Indeed, several countries in the region—Angola, Mozambique, Namibia, and South Africa—are among world leaders in women's representation in national legislatures and national executives; these and other countries in the region, such as Lesotho, lead in women's representation at the local level as well. Vibrant women's movements across the region have been at the forefront of efforts to institutionalize national gender machineries and ensure that women politicians respond to the agendas of the women activists. In this arena, southern Africa sets a clear example for the rest of the continent.

Chapter 12 explores southern Africa's international relations by analyzing economic and political linkages within the region and strategic interactions between the region and the rest of Africa and between the region and the world. Thus the chapter focuses on such regional institutions as the SADC, pan-African structures such as the African Union and the New Partnership for African Development initiative, and international relationships centered on trade, debt, and aid regimes. Southern Africa is not yet "boundless," as its leading advocates would like, but it has arguably made far greater inroads than comparable institutions across the continent. Southern Africa, principally through the efforts of South Africa, has taken a leadership role in these regional and continental processes.

Chapter 13 concludes the book. Although the countries of southern Africa face entrenched problems and challenges—both individually and collectively—southern Africa is in many ways the most dynamic and most promising region on the African continent. Although the positive World Cup spotlight was welcome, it was fleeting; its glare nevertheless obscured the finer detail of the region. In this concluding chapter we outline the lessons derived from explicit study of southern Africa, and we outline avenues for future research and analysis, which the region deserves, and social science demands.

Notes

1. Http://www.sa2010.gov.za/. Note that works representative of the Afro-pessimist approach include Ayittey 1998; Chabal and Daloz 1999; Kaplan 1994; and Kaplan 2000.

2. Http://www.sa2010.gov.za.

3. Many such indicators are provided by the World Bank, Freedom House, Transparency International, United Nations Development Programme, the Economist Intelligence Unit, and others.

4. See, for example, Schwab 2002. In fairness, the relatively scarcer Afro-*optimist* books are not immune to overgeneralizing either, although most do strive at least to account for the negative. See, for example, Dowden 2010 and Hunter-Gault 2006.

5. See, for example, Tordoff 2002; Khapoya 2009; Chazan et al. 1999; Schraeder 2003; Gordon and Gordon 2001; Thompson 2001. Soyinka-Airewele and Edozie 2009 is a partial exception in that it is as much about the *study* of African politics as it is about the politics of Africa.

6. One text that does not take an explicitly regional approach, but nonetheless succeeds in capturing the diversity of the continent by categorizing African regime types, societies, and the like, is Chazan et al. 1999.

7. This book focuses exclusively on continental southern Africa and therefore ignores the island states of Madagascar, Mauritius, and Seychelles. Neither do we engage in any systematic examination of Lesotho or Swaziland, although references occasionally are made to these states. Lesotho and Swaziland are surrounded by South Africa geographically as well as politically and economically. Although the systems differ—Swaziland has become increasingly authoritarian, whereas Lesotho maintains its fragile democracy—these enclave states are ultimately tied to South Africa. Though Tanzania is a member of the Southern African Development Community (SADC) and is occasionally included among southern African countries, we regard its connection to East Africa as far more significant. Democratic Republic of Congo, a relative newcomer to SADC, is also not part of southern Africa's geography.

8. East Africa, North Africa, the Horn of Africa, West Africa, and arguably Central Africa also warrant attention on a regional basis. The specific countries one might include in any one of these regions, however, is to some degree a matter of interpretation, and overlapping affinities are clearly possible.

9. Ironically, in what some have described as "the new white trek to the north," white South African farmers have been offered land in neighboring countries (and as

far away as Nigeria) in return for teaching agricultural and other skills to rural peasants (Legum 2000).

10. Wars in the region may have had a similar impact. As a result of Mozambique's civil war, nearly 1 million Mozambicans became refugees, for nearly a decade, in neighboring Malawi. Over the years, war in Angola similarly drove many Angolans to neighboring Namibia.

11. The Frontline States comprised Angola, Botswana, Mozambique, Zambia, and Zimbabwe as well as Tanzania. Malawi, which supported the apartheid regime in South Africa, was not part of the Frontline coalition.

12. Patrick McGowan (2003, 339) reports that between January 1956 and December 2001 there were 80 successful coups d'état in sub-Saharan Africa, 108 failed coup attempts, and 139 reported coup plots.

13. Https://www.cia.gov/.

14. Zimbabwe's program was suspended in 1997 due to noncompliance. South Africa designed its program internally, albeit following substantially on the International Monetary Fund and World Bank model (Padayachee 1997).

15. The SADC is not without a number of problems, however, including South Africa's reluctance to play the role of regional hegemon (see Oden 2001 and Chapter 12 in this book).

16. As Finnemore and Sikkink (2001, 393) maintain, constructivism is simply "a framework for thinking about the nature of social life and social interaction, but makes no claims about their specific content. . . . Agents and structures are mutually constituted in ways that explain why the political world is so and not otherwise." It does not provide "substantive explanations or predictions of political behavior until coupled with a more specific understanding" of structures and agents; thus we need to consider it alongside other approaches. See also Wendt 1999 for applications to international politics.

2 Malawi: Institutionalizing Democracy

In southern Africa, Malawi and Zambia stand out for being more like the countries in the rest of Africa. Both British colonies, Malawi and Zambia gained their independence in the mid-1960s. Within years, both were one-party states under the rule of self-declared presidents-for-life. Deteriorating economic conditions that made life unbearable by the end of the 1980s, coupled with a loss of international support for the single-party model, led to demands for greater political liberalization by 1990. In the early 1990s both countries experienced democratic transitions, although the details were different. Both countries have since confronted the many challenges of simultaneous economic and political transition in a new world order in which Africa figures only marginally. In both countries the difficulties of democratic transition and consolidation have been compounded by the region's staggering AIDS epidemic.

Though Malawi and Zambia were both a part of the Central African Federation (with Zimbabwe) during the colonial period, Malawi has always been the poorer country. In 2009 Malawi had an estimated per capita gross domestic product (at purchasing power parity) of only US$800. Malawi's economic woes were made worse in the postindependence period by rule by an autocratic tyrant known in the region and beyond for his brutality and his predatory and corrupt rule. That tyrant, Hastings Kamuzu Banda, was finally challenged in the early 1990s by a combination of church groups, trade unionists, students, and political exiles who paved the way for the country's democratic transition.

Now, like other countries in the region, Malawi confronts the daunting challenges of democratic consolidation, including institutionalizing a robust multiparty political system. In May 2009 Malawi held its fourth presidential and parliamentary elections since the first multiparty elections in 1994. The elections were deemed free and fair by national and international election observers, in some contrast to the presidential and parliamentary elections five years earlier. Bingu wa Mutharika was reelected president of Malawi, but as the presidential

---

Malawi: Country Data

Land area   94,080 km²
Capital   Lilongwe
Date of independence   July 6, 1964
Population   15,447,500, 19% urban (2008)
Languages   English and Chichewa (official), other languages important region-
   ally: Chinyanja 12.8%, Chiyao 10.1%, Chitumbuka 9.5%, Chisena 2.7%,
   Chilomwe 2.4%, Chitonga 1.7%, other 3.6% (1998 census)
Ethnic groups   Chewa, Nyanja, Tumbuka, Yao, Lomwe, Sena, Tonga, Ngoni,
   Ngonde, Asian, European
Religions   Christian 79.9%, Muslim 12.8%, other 3%, none 4.3% (1998 census)
Currency   Malawian kwacha (MWK); Malawian kwachas per US dollar: 159.16
   (2009)
Literacy rate   62.7% (male, 76.1%; female, 49.8% [2003 estimate])
Life expectancy   50.92 years (male, 50.22 years; female, 51.64 years)
Infant mortality   83.5 per 1,000 live births
GDP per capita (PPP)   US$800
GDP real growth rate   7.6%
Leaders since independence
   Hastings Kamuzu Banda, prime minister, 1964–1966
   Banda, president, 1966–1971
   Banda, "president-for-life," 1971–1994
   Bakili Muluzi, president, 1994–2004
   Bingu wa Mutharika, president, 2004–
Major political parties
   Ruling party   Democratic Progressive Party (DDP)
   Other parties   Alliance for Democracy (AFORD), Malawi Congress Party
   (MCP), Malawi Democratic Party (MDP)
Women in parliament (lower/single house)   20.8% (2009 election)

Sources: Data derived from https://www.cia.gov; http://www.ipu.org/.
Note: Data from 2009 unless otherwise noted.

---

candidate not of the United Democratic Front (UDF) as in his election in 2004 but of the subsequently formed Democratic Progressive Party (DPP). Moreover, the DPP won a majority of seats in parliament, the first time in Malawi's multiparty era that a single party had done so. And, because the DPP is the president's party, for the first time in the multiparty period, Malawi is experiencing a united executive and legislature. The advent of the DPP and the 2009 election results represent a notable turn of events in Malawian politics.

This chapter examines in greater detail Malawi's precolonial past, the colonial period, the postindependence period, and, more recently, the posttransition period. The chapter highlights the ways by which a president-for-life was able to wield power for so long, the factors leading up to the country's democratic transition in the early 1990s, the meaning of ethnicity and region in Malawi politics, recent developments in multiparty and presidential politics, and continuing challenges of the political economy.

Historical Origins of the Malawian State

As in so much of southern Africa, the original inhabitants of the area around Lake Malawi were peoples who resembled the Khoisan peoples of Botswana, Namibia, and South Africa. In Malawi these people were known as Akafula, and they were also hunter-gatherers. These people were displaced or absorbed by later Bantu groups that moved into the region, leaving behind few distinctive traces beyond the cave wall paintings found in Malawi and elsewhere in southern Africa (Pachai 1973, 1–2). Around the ninth century, the Karanga moved into what is contemporary Malawi from the shores of Lake Tanganyika. These were agriculturalists and pastoralists who, as farmers, led a more settled existence. Between the thirteenth and sixteenth centuries most of central and southern Malawi was settled by Bantu-speakers. These Bantu-speakers were at first a collective part of the vast and widely settled community of Maravi peoples (Pachai 1973, 4). What started off as the Maravi, however, ended up as many of the ethnic groups in Malawi today, including the Chewa, Mang'anja, Nyanja, Chipeta, Nsenga, Chikunda, Mbo, Ntumba, and Zimba (Pachai 1973, 6). In the middle of this same period the Tumbuka came to inhabit northern Malawi, paying allegiance to the Maravi to the south. Two other groups, the Tonga and Kamanga, managed to remain independent of Maravi influence (Sindima 2002, 8). The nineteenth century witnessed a number of significant invasions into Malawi, of the Ngoni peoples from the south and the Yao, affluent traders, from the southeast. The most recent African group to enter Malawi were the Lomwe, who fled into Malawi in the late nineteenth century, attempting to escape harsh treatment by the Portuguese in neighboring Mozambique (Sindima 2002, 9).

Most of the inhabitants of precolonial Malawi were farmers, although over time more specialized skills developed as people began to work with iron, make cotton cloth, and produce salt. Malawi was also well integrated into an extensive network of trade and commerce that linked central and eastern Africa. Ivory was a prized commodity and traded by the Maravi empire to European and Arab traders. In the eighteenth century, however, the coastal slave trade came to eclipse the trade in ivory, iron goods, and salt. This trade in slaves continued until the end of the nineteenth century.[1] The main slave capturers, buyers, and traders in Malawi were the Yao, who collaborated with the Arabs and the Portuguese, and before the slave trade ended at least two major slave stations had been established in the territory. The principal centers of the central African slave trade were Zanzibar and the Portuguese ports of Quelimane and Inhambane in Mozambique. The greatest demand for slaves at the time came from Arab enclaves on Africa's east coast and European-owned sugar and coffee plantations on the islands of Mauritius and Reunion (Williams 1978, 29–30). According to Harvey Sindima (2002, 13), it was through ivory and slaves that Malawi was integrated into the world economy, but with clearly deleterious effect—displacing people, destroying villages, undermining the agrarian economy, and producing entrepreneurs who, when they became agents of foreign powers, weakened indigenous political authorities.

Three groups of Europeans—the Portuguese, Germans, and British—in addition to Arabs were interested in Malawi before the territory eventually became a British colony. The Portuguese were the first to arrive, via Mozambique in the seventeenth century; they were followed by the Germans, who entered from the north from Tanganyika. When the British arrived they had to contend with the Portuguese and the Germans, as well as Arabs still engaged in a lively trade in ivory and slaves in the middle to late nineteenth century (Sindima 2002, 15). During the mid-1800s significant missionary activity also commenced inside Malawi. In 1891 the British declared a protectorate over the region, calling it the British Central Africa Protectorate, and a year later began to establish the bureaucracy to administer it. In 1907 the name of the protectorate was changed to Nyasaland. In the same year executive and legislative councils were established, for European residents only. (African interests were represented by a Scottish missionary appointed by the governor.) In Malawi, as in their other colonies, the British followed a policy of indirect rule. This was implemented most concretely in 1933, when two ordinances were put into place. The Native Authority Ordinance recognized the place of traditional authorities, the chiefs, in the colonial administration and acknowledged their role in appointing "native authorities" in their jurisdiction. The Native Courts Ordinance did two things—it put into place a system of local government, and it introduced a new court system that involved setting up "native courts" that would rely largely upon customary law (Sindima 2002, 35–36). But according to Sindima (2002, 36), as in all colonies, "the politics of the colonial administration in Malawi was that of exclusion. It was characterized by non-representation, centralized authority, hierarchical, and ruled by the bureaucratic elite—civil servants."

As in South Africa, the African population in Malawi organized itself very early in response to the imposition of colonial rule. Beginning in 1912 native associations were formed around the country, on a regional basis, usually with a twofold aim: first, to inform the colonial authorities of African opinion, and second, to inform the African populace of laws passed by the colonial state and provide forums for the discussion of those and other matters relevant to them. The native associations were largely formed from among the African elite: teachers, district clerks, and chiefs (Sindima 2002, 54). While the formation of the associations was initially sanctioned by the colonial state, by 1930 they were considered a nuisance that should be eliminated. Indeed, in 1933 when the above-mentioned ordinances were passed, district commissioners sought to abolish the native associations, but failed (Sindima 2002, 54). In 1944 the regional associations came together to form the Nyasaland African Congress (NAC). At the organization's inaugural meeting President Levi Mumba called for political representation and economic and social development for the African population as well as for racial equality in the territory (Sindima 2002, 37). One of the overriding goals of the new organization was to provide a unity that had been sorely lacking when the associations were local-level bodies dispersed throughout the colony. In 1946 the colonial government officially recognized the NAC as a body representing the native associations; moreover, the chiefs in the territory also endorsed the NAC as a body representing the African population.

Soon after its formation, the NAC confronted an issue long sought after by the European settlers in Malawi and nearby territories, namely the formation of a federation with neighboring Southern and Northern Rhodesia. Europeans in Nyasaland favored the creation of a Central African Federation, fearing otherwise that they and their needs would be overlooked by the larger British colonies around them.[2] Europeans in the Rhodesias favored such a federation as a way of ensuring access to Nyasaland's major labor reserves. Indeed, if such a federation were not formed, they worried that much of Malawi's migrant labor force would be lost to mines in South Africa. The election of the Nationalist Party to power in 1948 in South Africa further spurred Europeans in the three territories toward closer union, as a means of forestalling any move north of Afrikaner influence and racist views (Sindima 2002, 44–46). The African population in Malawi, meanwhile, as represented by the NAC, vehemently opposed federation, predicting that it would benefit only the European population. As Sindima (2002, 61) notes: "Africans everywhere knew that the Federation was intended to secure the position of Europeans in the three countries." Moreover, African populations were more interested in pressing ahead for self-government than in a greater aggrandizement of European power in the region. In Nyasaland, African leaders also feared that some of the more racist policies followed in Southern Rhodesia would be transferred to Nyasaland. Indeed, missionaries in Nyasaland opposed federation for the same reason (Sindima 2002, 48–49, 61). Nyasaland chiefs traveled to Britain to express their strong opposition to the idea of federation and even sent a petition to the United Nations, but all to no avail. In 1953 the Central African Federation was formed from the three colonies and remained in place until 1963, when independence was imminent. In the end, the formation of the federation did much in Malawi to unite the African population and create the beginnings of a national consciousness.[3]

The failure to prevent the formation of the federation and the disputes that emerged over strategies for doing so represented a temporary setback for Malawi's incipient nationalist movement. But nationalist sentiments were soon reinvigorated as a result of constitutional changes in 1955 that provided, for the first time, for elected (as opposed to appointed) African representation on the legislative council. The first elected members were a group of young, university educated, highly articulate, confident, and outspoken NAC members who very effectively represented African views and demands. At the same time, these "young militants" recognized that a more senior person was needed to lead the nationalist movement, in particular one who could "win the allegiance of senior members of Congress or . . . be accepted as national leader by the more conservative rural elders" (Williams 1978, 173). It is in this context that these same young men were successful in persuading Hastings Banda to return to Malawi from Ghana in 1958 to lead the nationalist struggle. Banda was both highly educated and more senior (in his fifties); therefore it was hoped that he would unite modern and traditional elements in the nationalist movement (Forster 1994, 488). According to David Williams: "On 6 July 1958, Dr. Banda arrived at Chileka airport, Blantyre, to a tumultuous welcome. The young militants had done their job well; the nationalist movement had found not merely a leader but a Messiah, and it was soon to become apparent that Dr. Banda, intoxicated by the adulation, was delighted to be cast in that role" (1978, 176). One month later Banda was elected president-general of the NAC. Within the year, however, rioting broke out in Malawi over continued African resistance to federation, a state of emergency was declared, and Banda and other nationalist leaders were detained by colonial authorities in early 1959. During 1959, while Banda was still in detention, the by-then-banned NAC was transformed into the Malawi Congress Party (MCP). When Banda and others were released from detention in 1960, Banda was made president of the MCP. By this time, the principal MCP demand was for self-government, and the British government began to take steps in that direction. In 1961 the first general elections held in Malawi were won overwhelmingly by the MCP. In late 1962 a constitutional conference was held in London to discuss arrangements for granting complete self-government to Nyasaland, henceforth to be called Malawi (Williams 1978, 203). One immediate implication of the talks was the withdrawal of Malawi from the Central African Federation, announced in 1962 (prompting the demise of the federation). Plans for self-government proceeded apace. In 1963 the executive council was replaced by a cabinet and the legislative council transformed into a legislative assembly. Banda, meanwhile, was sworn in as prime minister. Formal political independence from British rule, under Banda, followed on July 6, 1964.

Society and Development: Regional and Ethnic Cleavages and the Politics of Pluralism

The system of political rule in Malawi under Hastings Kamuzu Banda has variously been described as authoritarian, repressive, tyrannical, neopatrimonial, predatory, and corrupt, among other monikers. Indeed, within months of independence the country was rocked by a "cabinet crisis" that set the tone for the years to come. In short, some of the founding members of the NAC—the "young militants" described above—were dismissed from the cabinet by Banda "for opposing his policy direction and his pretensions to absolute rule. Some fled the country, and some were pursued by MCP special branch officers who targeted them for assassination or abduction. This proved the first episode of what became a fixed feature of state politics: namely, the banning, detention, maiming, and murder of Banda's rivals within government and his critics outside it" (Kaspin 1995, 603).

Daniel Posner (1995, 134–135) has identified three broad trends that came to characterize politics in Malawi after the 1964 "cabinet crisis." The first was the centralization of political and economic power in the hands of President-for-Life Banda. On the political side, within two years of independence, Banda had taken over the Ministries of Agriculture, Foreign Affairs, Justice, and Public Works and established a one-party state. In 1971 he was designated president-for-life. "Parliament became a rubber stamp institution filled with Banda's sycophants. The British-model judiciary was emasculated by the creation of a parallel system of 'traditional courts,' controlled by the MCP, to which all political and serious criminal cases were referred." On the economic side, Banda wielded considerable power as well. "By virtue of his ownership—ostensibly 'in trust on behalf of the people of Malawi'—of Press Trust, a massive conglomerate of companies responsible for tobacco production, petroleum marketing, banking, insurance, and most of the country's manufacturing, Banda exerted a strong measure of personal control over more than 50 percent of the entire national economy" (Posner 1995, 134–135). Banda used his economic power for patronage and to support a grandiose lifestyle.

The second trend of the Banda years was "the ruthless treatment of political opponents and the total control of public life by the MCP and its appendages. Political dissenters were routinely detained and tortured in Banda's notoriously horrific prisons" (Posner 1995, 134–135). Opponents who had fled Malawi to neighboring countries were abducted and tried for treason, as with the Chirwa brothers in 1981, or assassinated in exile, as with Attati Mpakati in 1983 and Mkwapatira Mhango in 1989. Dissident cabinet ministers and members of parliament (MPs) were murdered, as happened in 1983 in the so-called Mwanza incident. Malawian poet Jack Mapanje, accused of seditious poetry, was detained in 1987 and imprisoned for five years (Kaspin 1995, 603; Posner 1995, 135). The cabinet was routinely reshuffled so as to prevent the emergence of any political rivals. The media were heavily censored and used for propaganda purposes. Civil society organizations were proscribed or co-opted by the ruling party. MCP appendages included the Malawi Young Pioneers, which became the armed wing of the MCP, and the Women's League, whose primary function seemed to be dancing for President Banda whenever he made public appearances (Mchombo 1998, 24). According to Posner (1995, 135), "so pervasive was the system of informers in Malawi, so loose was the definition of disloyalty, and so draconian were the penalties for appearing to be at odds with the president that fear and suspicion came to permeate society."

The third trend of the postindependence period was "the crystallizing of regional identities." Though regional and ethnic allegiances were officially discouraged in independent Malawi, both had deep roots in the country (Chirwa 1994b, 96). Indeed, clear differences among regions—northern, central, and southern—were evident already from the colonial period. Less well endowed with resources and less well developed, the north was always more sparsely populated and during the colonial period functioned as a labor reserve for plantations in southern Malawi and mines and farms in South Africa and the two Rhodesias. At the same time, Scottish Presbyterian missionaries established a small number of superior schools in the north that provided important educational opportunities for some northerners. Together these two differences—higher educational attainment and exposure to the outside world through migrant labor—enabled northerners to take the lead in politics during the colonial period and also to move into good positions in the colonial and postcolonial civil service (Chirwa 1994b, 97).

The central region, by contrast, was an early center of smallholder tobacco production (from the early 1920s on) and later became the center of plantation tobacco production (from the late 1960s on). The region serves as the country's breadbasket, producing most of the maize, the staple food, as well as most of the tobacco, the major export crop and foreign exchange earner. The central region is more densely populated than the north, though relatively behind in terms of educational achievement. The south, meanwhile, was the center of the colonial economy. European settlers experimented with coffee, cotton, and tobacco in this region between 1890 and 1920, finally settling upon tobacco as the primary product until the 1930s, when they turned to tea. The south was also "the colonial commercial hub, partly to cater to the white settlers, and partly also because of its proximity to Mozambique, which provided access to the outside world" (Chirwa 1994b, 98). As the colonial commercial center, the south attracted people from throughout Malawi, as well as from Mozambique, who worked on the settler plantations and other establishments—and often remained permanently in the country. Among other things, this has meant that many southern Malawians are second- or third-generation Malawians and that the south is home to a significant mix of ethnolinguistic communities. The south is also Malawi's most populous and most urbanized region. Malawi's small manufacturing base is located in the south, as is a significant Asian business community (Chirwa 1994b, 98–99).

As in most of southern Africa, ethnic identities have figured prominently in postcolonial politics in Malawi. Continuing the colonial tradition after independence, all official documentation in Malawi contained information on one's ethnic group and region (Posner 1995, 136). While President Banda suggested in his speeches that the people of Malawi were Malawians and not members of individual ethnic groups, he usually went on to remind his listeners that he himself was a Chewa (the largest ethnic group in Malawi).[4] Deborah Kaspin (1995, 604) suggests that a process of "Chewa-ization" of Malawi was instituted under the Banda regime. According to Posner:

> From the beginning of Banda's rule, Malawian culture was made synonymous with Chewa culture. In 1968, the Chewa language was adopted as the sole national language; the use of other African languages in the press or on the radio was declared illegal. The relocation of the capital from Zomba in the south to Lilongwe in the central region was only the most notable instance of a broader pattern of shifting development expenditure and investment from the south and north to the Chewa heartland. (1995, 136)

Not only did President Banda privilege his own Chewa ethnic group—pouring development money into the central region and new capital city, imposing Chewa as the national language, and so on—but he also discriminated against others.[5] Kaspin (1995, 609) writes of a "politics of exclusion" with regard to the north and the south. The north was allowed to stagnate economically while its people, teachers, civil servants, and politicians were vilified by the president and his ruling party. In the south, the situation was not quite as bad: "Although southern politicians were also vulnerable to Banda's relentless search for the enemy within, they were not subjected to repeated accusations of tribalism nor to any other stereotype as southerners. Nor was there a palpable lack of interest in the development potential of the south. . . . Nevertheless, the regime did generate a pervasive experience of cultural marginalization in the south" (Kaspin 1995, 609). In the end, of course, these policies served to ensure that both regions became significant sources of opposition to the Banda regime.

Indeed, that opposition began to coalesce by the end of the 1980s and beginning of the 1990s. Like so many other countries in sub-Saharan Africa, Malawi experienced a democratic transition in the early 1990s. Several factors have been cited as contributing to this transition, despite President Banda's best efforts to avoid it, indeed to reject the clear global trend in the direction of political liberalization (Ihonvbere 1997, 194–201). First, replicating a key factor in many political transitions in southern Africa, the Malawian economy had deteriorated markedly by the early 1990s. In 1980 the country had entered into a structural adjustment program (SAP) sponsored by the International Monetary Fund; as with SAPs across the region, the costs of adjustment were being borne by those who could least afford them. More than a million refugees from neighboring war-torn Mozambique further strained the Malawian economy. Drought in the early 1990s only exacerbated matters, driving many people from the rural to the urban areas. By the end of 1993 inflation was running at more than 20 percent, and unemployment, crime, and hunger had reached unprecedented levels (see Kamkwamba and Mealer 2009). As living standards fell throughout the land, the Malawian people held the government responsible for their worsening situation.

Second and somewhat related, international donors played a role in Malawi's transition by refusing further economic assistance until human rights in Malawi were respected and a political liberalization was initiated. This included the World Bank and all of the major donors on whom Malawi had depended heavily for years. At a meeting of donors in Paris in 1992, Malawi received an unprecedented shock when the donors suspended "all new aid, except for drought and refugee relief, expressing deep concern about the lack of progress in the area of basic freedoms and human rights and linking new aid to 'good governance'" (Ihonvbere 1997, 196). Such conditionalities were encouraged by reports by Amnesty International and the Southern African Human Rights Foundation, which provided "chilling accounts of the brutality of Banda's government." While Western donor countries had supported Malawi and the Banda regime for years, due to its strongly anticommunist stance, once the Cold War ended in the early 1990s the rationale for such support was gone. Instead, Malawi and other African countries were suddenly called upon to demonstrate good governance and a host of other democratic attributes. Others have identified the key role played by a demonstration effect, namely the effect on Malawi of the political liberalization process that unfolded in neighboring Zambia just before Malawi's commenced.

Third, again as in other countries in southern Africa, the church played a significant role in Malawi in forcing Banda to recognize the need for change. A pastoral letter released by the country's eight Catholic bishops in March 1992 "denounced corruption, indiscipline, repression and human rights abuses in the country, and noted that 'academic freedom is seriously restricted, exposing injustices can be considered a betrayal, revealing some evils of our society is seen as slandering the country, monopoly of mass media and censorship prevent the expression of dissenting views'" (Ihonvbere 1997, 196). The pastoral letter was the first of its kind in Malawi and is reported to have stunned Banda. Moreover, it also unleashed a rash of protests across the country, one of which, in Zomba, was met with gunfire from the police. More important, however, the letter had the effect of emboldening the people of Malawi. As Julius Ihonvbere (1997, 197) writes: "People began to realize that Banda's regime was not God-ordained and once the religious leaders had condemned it, ordinary citizens had a spiritual responsibility to work for change."

Fourth, a foreign-based opposition also contributed to the political liberalization in Malawi in the early 1990s. This included a variety of groups that had varying agendas but that shared at least one common goal, namely getting rid of Banda's dictatorship. The Socialist League of Malawi operated first from Zambia and later Zimbabwe and even had intentions of creating a military wing to be trained in Cuba. In the United Kingdom, the Malawi Support Committee had the active support of trade unionists and Labour Party parliamentarians. The Malawi Freedom Movement attempted a guerrilla attack in northern Malawi in the late 1980s but not much activity after that. Another group, the Congress for a Second Republic, frequently issued criticisms of the Banda government, calling attention to the crisis of governance in Malawi.

Finally, an opposition existed inside Malawi as well, and by the early 1990s it took to Malawi's streets. Opposition forces included students at the University of Zomba, who after the release of the pastoral letter demanded the introduction of multiparty politics in Malawi. In late 1993 civil servants and utility workers went on a strike in protest over worsening economic conditions; workers in the sugarcane plantations set the fields on fire in support of the strike. When striking civil servants won significant pay increases as a result of the strikes, workers throughout the country followed suit. While these activities did not lead immediately to the emergence of a strong labor movement, "the strikes reflected a new bold attempt at challenging Banda's dictatorship" (Ihonvbere 1997, 198). Most important, however, these two forces—external and internal—came together. At a meeting in March 1992 in Lusaka, Zambia, eighty opposition activists gathered and declared a renewed commitment to operating inside Malawi and "pushing the struggle for political liberalization to its maximum" (Ihonvbere 1997, 199). Called the Interim Committee for Democratic Alliance, the organization was also instructed to create a broad-based movement within the country to challenge the Banda regime. The first challenge came when exiled trade unionist and prodemocracy activist Chakufwa Chihana returned to Malawi in March 1992 to take on Banda. After reading a speech upon his arrival at the airport, Chihana was arrested and detained by the police. This prompted immediate riots and demonstrations that turned violent in many places. In response, Banda dissolved the parliament and held elections in June 1992 for 91 of the 141 parliamentary seats. These elections recorded the lowest voter turnout in the country's history and also the defeat of almost half the MPs, including those nominated and endorsed by Banda. The 1992 riots and demonstrations, clearly of a political nature, continued until President Banda finally capitulated in January 1993 and agreed to the holding of a referendum on March 15, 1993, on the introduction of multiparty democracy.

Organization of the State

The referendum was actually held in June 1993, in order to allow United Nations monitors to participate. President Banda was confident that he would prevail, citing the typical arguments against a multiparty political system in Africa—"that he was 'father' of the nation, that democracy would increase tribalism and regionalism and [that] it would lead to waste and intolerance" (Ihonvbere 1997, 200). In the event, an overwhelming majority of Malawians, 63.5 percent, voted in favor of multiparty politics. Within weeks of the referendum the constitution was amended to provide for a multiparty political system.

Within a year, in May 1994, national elections were held for president and parliament. Eight political parties contested the parliamentary elections, though only three—the Alliance for Democracy (AFORD), the MCP, and the UDF—won seats. Five candidates contested the presidential race, though only three—AFORD's Chakufwa Chihana, the MCP's Banda, and the UDF's Bakili Muluzi—were serious contenders. In the parliamentary election, the UDF received the largest number of votes, 46.4 percent, followed by the MCP with 33.7 percent and AFORD with 19.0 percent. The presidential results were remarkably consistent with those of the parliamentary election. Bakili Muluzi, a Muslim businessperson from the south, won the election with 47.2 percent of the vote. Former president-for-life Banda placed second with 33.4 percent of the vote, compared to northern trade unionist and former exile Chakufwa Chihana, who came in third with 18.9 percent of the vote (Wiseman 2000, 643–644).

Constitution

In February 1995 a national constitutional conference was held in Malawi for the purpose of recommending a permanent constitution to the National Assembly.[6] On May 17, 1995, a democratic constitution was adopted by the National Assembly (Mutharika 1996, 205). A major task of Malawi's constitution, according to Peter Mutharika (1996, 209), was "to address the excesses of the Banda regime while at the same time creating a document that gives a democratically elected government sufficient power to rebuild the country and to create a new political order." For example, the constitution provides that "state power is founded on the principles of accountability and transparency; require[s] the state to respect the fundamental human rights of all persons within the country; provide[s] that all persons are equal before the law; and provide[s] that no institutions or persons shall stand above the law" (Mutharika 1996, 217). Moreover, the constitution also mandates that the state provide for the welfare and development of the people of Malawi. The constitution also provides for the creation of an independent electoral commission as well as an office of ombudsman and a human rights commission, both of which are meant to protect individual Malawians against misconduct by public officials. Both bodies have extensive investigative powers (Mutharika 1996, 217). Other bodies provided for in the constitution include an anticorruption bureau and a law commission. According to Peter VonDoepp (2010, 5) several of these bodies played visible roles early in the first decade of the twenty-first century during President Bingu wa Mutharika's first term; at the same time, they have also been hampered somewhat by a lack of funding, a lack of staff, and some government interference in personnel matters.

The basic governmental structure of Malawi, as laid out in the constitution, "is neither parliamentary nor presidential." Mutharika (1996, 206) calls it a "hybrid system" that provides for a directly elected president able to appoint his or her own cabinet, while final legislative power is vested in a parliament. Moreover, after thirty years of one-man rule under President-for-Life Banda, the constitution also seeks to "structure a delicate system of checks and balances between the three branches of government." So, for example, under the new constitution, the power to appoint the chief justice is shared: the president makes the appointment, subject to a two-thirds affirmative vote by the National Assembly. There are other areas, as well, in which deliberate attempts have "been made to intersect the power of the executive and the legislative" (Mutharika 1996, 207).

Executive

The constitution provides for a president, first vice president, and second vice president; the second vice president may be appointed by the president if he or she decides it is in the national interest to do so, but may not be from the party of the president. According to the constitution, all three positions are limited to a maximum of two consecutive five-year terms, a direct response to Banda's life presidency (Mutharika 1996, 210). Like some other presidents in southern Africa, President Muluzi, toward the middle of his second term, attempted to extend his term of office. First, he and the UDF tried to amend the constitution to remove the term limit altogether. When that effort failed, they moved to amend the constitution to extend the presidential term from two terms to three; according to VonDoepp (2010, 1), the efforts to amend the constitution "consumed Malawian politics" in the early 2000s. The second effort also failed, with the result that President Muluzi was not the UDF's candidate in the 2004 presidential election; instead Muluzi chose Bingu wa Mutharika as the candidate for the UDF ticket but remained leader of the party. Relations quickly soured between Mutharika and Muluzi, with Mutharika making clear he would not be subservient to the former president. Thus, within a year of winnng the 2004 election, Mutharika left the UDF and formed his own political party, thereby thrusting the UDF into the political opposition. In 2009 Muluzi tried again to contest the presidential poll (hoping that the constitution only prohibited more than two *consecutive* terms) but was prevented from doing so when the Malawi Electoral Commission (and a subsequent court ruling) rejected his candidacy due to the *maximum* of two consecutive terms for one president as stated in the constitution (Smiddy and Young 2009; VonDoepp 2010).

As elsewhere in the region, the powers of the president in Malawi are quite extensive. They include the power to "convene and preside over meetings of the cabinet, confer honours, appoint ambassadors and other diplomatic representatives, negotiate, sign, enter into and accede to treaties, appoint commissions of inquiry, refer constitutional disputes to the High Court, and proclaim referenda and plebiscites as required by the Constitution or an Act of

Parliament." At the same time, there are certain limitations on the president's powers—for example, the president is required to address the parliament on the state of the nation and may be called before the parliament to answer questions (Mutharika 1996, 212). Since the first multiparty election in 1994, two men have served as president of Malawi—Muluzi from 1994 to 2004 and Mutharika since 2004.

Judiciary

In Malawi the judiciary has played a particularly significant—and positive— role in posttransition politics. VonDoepp (2001b, 235) suggests that since the transition, "the judiciary has emerged as a primary locus of political activity, deciding numerous cases relevant to the political and personal interests of the opposition." For example, opposition leaders have "turned to the courts for injunctions to halt government actions antithetical to their interests—whether state efforts to go ahead with poorly managed by-elections, extralegal state attempts to block opposition rallies, or plans to strip assets from MCP elites. They have also used the courts to challenge the results of electoral contests that they feel were rigged or inappropriately conducted" (2001b, 237). In general VonDoepp (2010, 11–12) suggests that the judiciary has distinguished itself "for relative competence and independent decisionmaking"—so much so that the judiciary's bold decisions have invited "harassment and interference from the government, mostly in the form of verbal badgering and threats to individual judges."

According to Mutharika (1996, 215), since the judiciary was "subverted" under the Banda regime, the new constitution pays particular attention to it. In an effort to emphasize the independence of the judiciary, for example, "the constitution provides that all courts shall exercise their powers independent of any person or authority." Moreover, Malawi's High Court and Supreme Court of Appeal are empowered to "review any law, and any action or decision of the government, for conformity with the constitution" (VonDoepp 2001b, 236). Further, the constitution abolishes the traditional courts established during the Banda era that were used to try (and invariably convict) political opponents of the Banda regime.[7] In keeping with legal systems throughout southern Africa, however, Malawi's new parliament is empowered by the constitution to establish new traditional courts "presided over by lay persons or chiefs with jurisdiction limited exclusively to civil cases at customary law and to such minor common law and statutory civil cases as prescribed by an Act of Parliament" (Mutharika 1996, 215).

Despite its important role in enabling a balance of power, the judicial system in Malawi, as in other countries in the region, remains "inefficient and handicapped by serious weaknesses, including poor record keeping, a shortage of attorneys and other trained personnel, heavy caseloads, and a lack of resources." In 2009, the judiciary's budgetary and administrative problems "effectively denied expeditious trials for most defendants, although improvements were made due to increased staffing" (US Department of State 2010c).

Military

Malawi has a relatively small military force, totaling 5,300 active personnel in 2002. This included an air force of 80 and a navy, which patrols Lake Malawi, of 220. The country also has a well-armed and well-trained mobile police force of 1,500, which is often deployed in internal security operations (EIU 2003e, 11). Malawi has not been involved in an external conflict since independence—remaining neutral in the regional conflicts of the past fifty years.[8] Some Malawian armed forces were deployed in Democratic Republic of Congo, but only as part of an African Union peacekeeping force, not as a party to the conflict (EIU 2003e, 10). Malawi has good relations with its immediate neighbors, none of which is involved in a military conflict. VonDoepp (2010, 12) observes that although Malawi's military has historically restrained itself from involvement in politics, "it has become more visibly involved in recent years," with some high ranking army officers among those accused of plotting to overthrow the president in 2008. In 2007 the army and police were deployed to break up an opposition political rally.

Representation and Participation

Legislature

The new constitution originally provided for a bicameral parliament consisting of a directly elected national assembly and an indirectly elected senate. The primary function of the National Assembly was stated to be legislative, and the Senate's was to be deliberative. Moreover, the Senate was to represent "special interest groups" such as chiefs, women's organizations, disabled groups, religious associations, and others.[9] In the event, a senate was not established in Malawi (in keeping with the majority of African countries, which have only unicameral legislatures), with cost being given as the reason (EIU 2003e, 7). The number of seats in the National Assembly is determined by the electoral commission before each general election. Malawi's first National Assembly, following the 1994 elections, had 177 members. Before the 1999 election, the number of seats was increased to 193, and that number remained the same for the 2004 and 2009 elections. Members of the National Assembly are elected for five-year terms that coincide with the term of the president. The new constitution confers more powers upon the National Assembly than under the Banda regime, including a role in approving certain high-level government appointments and certain financial management responsibilities (Mutharika 1996, 213–215).

After six years with no local-level legislatures, elections for local authorities (mayor, city councils, and rural district councils) were finally held in 2000. Local authorities have the power to levy taxes, spend money at their own discretion, and run social services. In early 2005, however, local authorities were dissolved with the expectation that constitutionally mandated local elections would be held later in the year. In the event, local government elections were not held in 2005, with the government citing budgetary constraints as the reason. In November 2009 the constitution was amended to make the timing of local elections the prerogative of the president (US Department of State 2010c). As of mid-2011, local government elections still had not been held in Malawi.

Forty women were elected to the National Assembly during the 2009 election, such that women comprised nearly 21 percent of members in early 2011. This represents a steady improvement in electoral results for women in the years since the democratic transition, with women accounting for 5.65 percent of seats in 1994, 9.38 percent in 1999, 14.44 percent in 2004, and 20.83 percent in 2009. National legislative elections are conducted using a plurality-majority electoral system, the type that is typically less friendly to women candidates. Still, Malawi's 2009 election results for women were better than recent election results in the other southern African countries, such as Botswana or Zambia, that use the first-past-the-post electoral system. There are no legal or constitutionally mandated electoral gender quotas in place in Malawi, nor have political parties adopted gender quotas for national legislative elections; though the constitution does make the attainment of gender equality a principle of state policy.[10] According to Gender Links (2010a), Malawi was able to increase women's legislative representation to 21 percent in 2009 as a result of a well-orchestrated 50/50 campaign. Following the 2009 presidential election, Joyce Banda was sworn in as the first woman vice president in Malawi, but she was abruptly dismissed by Mutharika in early 2011. A continuing challenge for women in Malawi remains the widespread perception of their "traditional" role as dancers and praise singers in support of political parties (Gilman 2004); where once this activity was coerced now it is paid.

Elections

Since the democratic transition in the early 1990s, presidential and national assembly elections have been held simultaneously every five years in Malawi. For the most part, the 1994 and 1999 elections were considered free and fair, although the 1999 election was somewhat problematic. John Wiseman (2000, 645) describes the 1999 election as having been "relatively free but not wholly fair" in that the ruling party had certain advantages over the other parties, namely "the UDF's control of radio broadcasting, use of state funds for campaigning, and the bias of the Electoral Commission's Chairman." In 2004 the UDF's advantage as the incumbent continued. Moreover, amid cries of vote rigging and fraud, even international observers conceded that the 2004 elections lacked transparency. Indeed, VonDoepp (2010, 3) observes that elections in Malawi "typically produce periods of heightened political tension" including violence during campaigns, accusations of bias in the state-owned media, and charges of voting irregularities followed by legal challenges. In that regard, according to VonDoepp (2010, 3), the 2009 elections stand out for having avoided many of these problems; they were the freest and fairest since multiparty polls were first held in 1994.

A distinctive feature of Malawi's first three elections (though less so in 2004) was the decisive impact of region upon the election outcome. Indeed, every analyst of the early elections observed the regional trend in voting in Malawi, namely that people voted for candidates not because of the policies their parties stood for but because of the region a party leader hailed from (Chirwa 1994a, 17).[11] The main political parties in the country had clear regional bases—AFORD predominated in the north, MCP in the central region, and UDF in the south. With 11 percent of the population in the north, 39 percent in the central region, and 50 percent in the south, the UDF would always win. In the 1994 and 1999 legislative elections the parties received almost the exact same percentages of the vote as the population percentages of the regions in which they were based. This was not the case in the 2004 election, in which the UDF and AFORD ran as electoral partners, and numerous smaller parties and one large coalition also contested the presidential and parliamentary races.

The 2009 election was completely unlike previous elections in Malawi. As noted, within a year of being elected president in 2004, Bingu wa Mutharika had left the UDF over leadership tensions with former president Muluzi and formed his own political party—the Democratic People's Party. For the 2009 election Muluzi and the UDF joined forces with the MCP and John Tembo, creating a "formidable bloc" to compete against Mutharika and the DPP (VonDoepp 2010, 2). In strong contrast to previous elections, according to VonDoepp (2010, 2), "Mutharika ran a highly effective cross-regional campaign focused on his administration's record of providing public goods and economic growth. Mutharika ultimately emerged victorious, bucking long-standing regional voting patterns." Indeed, for the first time a political party with apparent national appeal had won the parliamentary elections; the DPP won 59 percent of the vote overall and at least 50 percent of the vote in each of the three regions. The UDF and MCP, meanwhile, retained their status as regional political parties. Similarly, Bingu wa Mutharika won 66 percent of the vote, the first time in posttransition Malawi that a presidential candidate had won such a significant victory; Mutharika's significant victory was helped in part by the fact that there were only two major-party candidates—Mutharika and the MCP's John Tembo. The UDF's Muluzi was barred in the days before the election from running for a third, even nonconsecutive, presidential term (Smiddy and Young 2009, 663–664).

Political Parties

The state of party politics in Malawi since the transition in the early 1990s reveals some of the many challenges of institutionalizing multiparty political systems wherein presidents-for-life and single parties have ruled for decades. Party politics in Malawi in the first posttransition decade were marked by rivalry, factionalism, shifting alliances, changing coalitions, and complete U-turns by party leaders. A few larger parties existed alongside many smaller parties of lesser significance. Much of the public, meanwhile, had little trust and confidence in the country's political parties and leaders. Some of that began to change in the second posttransition decade with the emergence of Bingu wa Mutharika as president and the DPP as a national party.

Even before the 1993 referendum was held in Malawi, new parties had emerged—for example, the UDF and AFORD launched in 1992. Until 2005, the UDF was the dominant party in Malawi. The UDF has drawn most of its support from the populous south, home of former president and party leader Bakili Muluzi. AFORD's stronghold had been in the north, home to party leader Chakufwa Chihana. Shortly after the 1994 election, AFORD joined the UDF in a ruling coalition, receiving six positions in the cabinet for AFORD MPs. In 1996 Chihana decided to end AFORD's alliance with the UDF, though not all party members, including some of the AFORD cabinet members, left with him. For the 1999 elections AFORD joined the MCP in the presidential race, though in late 2001 Chihana renounced AFORD's alliance with the MCP and renewed his backing of the UDF. Indeed, AFORD contested the 2004 elections as the electoral partner of the UDF. In the run-up to the 2004 election, moreover, significant divisions emerged within the UDF over the issue of a third term for President Muluzi. In January 2001 some members of the UDF formed the National Democratic Alliance (NDA), intended as a pressure group opposed to President Muluzi's bid for a third presidential term. The NDA was led by Brown Mpinganjira, a former transport minister who was for many years the UDF's second in command. In the 2009 election Mpinganjira was the vice presidential candidate for the MCP's John Tembo.

The largest opposition political party in Malawi has been the MCP, the ruling party for nearly thirty years under Hastings Banda. Historically, the MCP has drawn its greatest support from the central region of Malawi and continues to do so. The MCP came in second, after the UDF, in the 1994 and 1999 presidential and parliamentary elections and won the most seats in the 2004 parliamentary election.[12] In the 2009 election, the MCP won the third most seats in the National Assembly after the DPP and independent candidates. After Banda's death in 1997, the MCP suffered a factional split between those aligned with John Tembo, a longtime associate of Banda, and those allied with Gwanda Chakuamba, the party's new president at the time. In the months before the 2004 elections Chakuamba left the MCP and formed a new party, the Republican Party, from among disaffected MCP members. The MCP still polled the most votes in the 2004 legislative election, leaving the UDF to scramble for legislative partners in order to remain the ruling party.

Numerous attempts were made to unite the country's fractured opposition in advance of the 2004 elections. Indeed, shortly before the election seven parties came together to form the Mgwirizano (Unity) Coalition, whose presidential candidate, Gwanda Chakuamba, placed third just behind the MCP's Tembo. Two larger parties, the MCP and the NDA, decided not to join the coalition, thereby weakening its prospects in the view of most Malawians. Malawi's churches, in particular the Central African Presbyterian Church, the Catholic Church, and the Anglican Church, were at the forefront of the effort to unite the opposition in a coalition to defeat the UDF. In the 2009 election the unsuccessful alliance of political parties was between the MCP and the UDF. The inability of highly fragmented oppositions to come together to unseat incumbents has been a signpost of politics in the posttransition period in southern Africa.

The formation of the DPP in the wake of the 2004 election and its significant victory in the 2009 election is surely the most intriguing development in Malawi's posttransition politics. As noted above, the DPP, for the first time in Malawi's democratic politics, represents a political party without a regional base; rather in 2009 it garnered substantial support from all three regions, thus making it a national party. In addition to gaining support in all three regions, Mutharika and the DPP did very well in the country's two major urban areas, Blantyre and Lilongwe. Kimberly Smiddy and Daniel Young (2009, 663) observe that "whereas opposition candidates in other African countries often win most of their support from disgruntled urbanites, Mutharika was able to make significant inroads in the cities." Moreover, the fact that Mutharika and the DPP presided over a period of remarkable economic growth for the country appears to have enhanced their standing among the populace—and contributed to their electoral successes. Mutharika had become popular during his first term for his management of the economy; this included high economic growth rates, improved food security, debt relief, a targeted fertilizer subsidy program, and higher tobacco prices (Smiddy and Young 2009, 663–664). The question for the future is whether Malawi now edges toward the politics of single-party dominance as in most other countries in the region or remains one in which a few parties split the allegiance of the people.

Civil Society

Not surprisingly, after being "the most tightly controlled and highly personalized one-party state in Africa," Malawi could not claim to have a very deeply rooted civil society in the early posttransition years (Wiseman 2000, 641; VonDoepp 2001b, 232). Indeed, as in many countries in the region, most civil society organizations in Malawi (with the exception of the churches) have a very limited presence in the rural areas—where 80 percent of the population lives—and are concentrated mainly in the major urban areas. Still, they are contributing to Malawi's new democracy, "voic[ing] important challenges against questionable government actions" (VonDoepp 2001b, 233). Moreover, the number and vibrancy of civil society organizations grew during the first decade of the twenty-first century (VonDoepp 2010, 6).

As noted earlier, churches in Malawi were at the forefront of the democratization effort that began in Malawi in the early 1980s, and according to VonDoepp (2001b, 233) they "have not wholly retreated from the political sphere." Indeed, "church leaders have been primary contributors to national political discourse—raising important issues such as the spread of corruption and the fractious behavior of political elites. They have also intervened to foster discussions among opposing elites whose disagreements have aggravated political tension in the country." And they were pivotal in trying to bring together the opposition in the months before the 2004 election. At the same time, VonDoepp (2002, 42–43) also argues that at the local as opposed to the national level in Malawi, "most clergy have been disinclined to engage in extensive grassroots civil society activism." Reasons for this include "the kinds of religious ideas that inform their work and their relationships to other actors in communities who might frown on such activism." A third reason is the clergy's desire to enhance their class position in Malawi society. VonDoepp's work on local-level clergy in Malawi serves as a reminder of the many factors constraining the democratizing potential of civil society in Africa. Still, the churches in Malawi have a huge following and are considered to wield a significant influence over the population at large. They are more trusted than most politicians and for this reason may continue to play an important role in party politics in Malawi (EIU 2003i, 2).

In many countries in the region, youth or student organizations have been an important sector in an emerging civil society. In Malawi, university students also participated, through strikes and demonstrations, in the call for a democratic transition in the early 1990s. But youth organizations in Malawi in general have a more troubling heritage. Under the government of Hastings Banda and the MCP, youth organized as "the Malawi Young Pioneers and the MCP Youth League had the notorious task of safeguarding discipline and obedience, often resorting to physical violence if there was any reason to suspect dissidence." Unfortunately, in the new Malawi, according to Harri Englund (2002, 13), this pattern is being repeated, as "the UDF's youth wing, confidently referring to itself as 'Young Democrats,' has been implicated in acts that have been anything but democratic." Indeed, the fact alone that the UDF has an official youth wing is a clear holdover from an earlier era. During the Muluzi years, the UDF's Young Democrats were implicated in acts of violence against those who uttered public statements construed to be critical of the Muluzi/UDF government.

A new type of organization to emerge in posttransition Malawi is the voluntary association that promotes a particular language or ethnic identity. One in particular, the Chitumbuka Language and Culture Association, from previously marginalized northern Malawi, has been especially resilient, according to Englund (2002, 23). In Malawi, these language associations can fulfill some of the democratic functions attributed to civil society organizations, according to Gregory Kamwendo (2002, 149). For example, they can complement government efforts, hampered by lack of resources, to raise the status of languages marginalized during the years of Malawi's "Chewa-ization" under Hastings Banda. Further, according to Kamwendo, the language associations can help "in changing negative popular attitudes towards indigenous languages" (2002, 149). Finally, the language associations, like other civil society organizations, can act as watchdogs—in this case of language rights. The greatest danger with such associations, according to Kamwendo, is that they will be manipulated by politicians to attain their own political ends—for example, to mobilize communities around particular ethnocentric or parochial interests. And yet if language rights are to be understood as part and parcel of broader human rights, then their assertion and protection is potentially beneficial to a new democracy.

Nandini Patel and colleagues (2007, xix) suggest that even after nearly two decades of more democratic rule, "the government and civil society have not yet established a partnership in the process of governance," rather that relationship has been tenuous and conflictual. Not surprisingly, civil society organizations have been accused by government of being partisan and in the service of their funders while civil society organizations often feel marginalized and sidelined by government. Patel and colleagues (2007) argue that civil society organizations have been reactive rather than proactive in the years since the democratic transition.

The media is potentially another important civil society actor in most southern African countries. Indeed, foreign media, in particular, played a significant role in Malawi's early 1990s transition. When Chakufwa Chihana returned from exile to challenge the Banda regime (and was arrested, upon arrival, at the airport), the British Broadcasting Corporation provided in-depth international coverage and "made Chihana a hero in the eyes of his countrymen" (Posner 1995, 139). But it was other media formats that really turned the tide in the struggle for political liberalization during those years. According to Posner, the fax machine, photocopier, and personal computer played crucial roles in turning the tide against the Banda regime. Indeed, under the Banda regime the media were tightly controlled. Since the transition, however, this has changed. Malawi's new constitution provides for freedom of speech and of the press, and this has been unevenly respected by the government. By 2008, eleven independent newspapers were available, including two daily newspapers, one triweekly, seven weeklies, and one monthly (VonDoepp 2010), representing a broad spectrum of political viewpoints. Most of them are privately owned, though several are owned by individuals and interests associated with particular political parties. Newspapers have been publicly condemned by government politicians for irresponsible journalism for reporting statements by citizens critical of government.

As for the broadcast media, in 2009 there were twenty-two private radio stations in Malawi but broadcasting only in urban areas; indeed, radio service is otherwise dominated by the state-owned Malawi Broadcasting Corporation (MBC), which provides the main source for news in the rural areas. News coverage and editorial content of MBC programming was reported by the US Department of State to be clearly progovernment in 2009. The only national television station, Television Malawi, was launched in 1999 and is, again, government owned and operated. The US Department of State (2010c) reported that in 2009 journalists in Malawi were subjected to arrest, harassment, and intimidation due to their reporting. VonDoepp (2010) reports that while most media operate without substantial interference, those associated with the political opposition are more likely to be harassed or censored. In early 2011 Sevenzo (2011) reported that university students, civil society organizations, and the media were all under attack from an increasingly autocratic Mutharika.

Fundamentals of the Political Economy

Malawi is a slender, small, landlocked country, formed largely out of territory to the west and south of Lake Malawi, the third-largest lake in Africa. Three more lakes are to be found in southern Malawi, as is the Shire River, which runs from Lake Malawi into the Zambezi River, which flows into the Indian Ocean. Malawi has fairly rich soils and grows cash crops such as tea, tobacco, and sugar as well as some staple food crops, though it has very little in the way of valuable minerals. Despite being such a small country, Malawi had an estimated population of 15.4 million in 2010, making it one of the more densely populated countries in Africa. An estimated 45 percent of Malawians were under the age of fifteen in 2010; indeed, Malawi had one of the highest population growth rates in Africa: 2.8 percent. This population growth rate, combined with the fact that more than 80 percent of the population remains in the rural areas, puts tremendous pressure on land in Malawi. The land problem is particularly acute in southern Malawi, where about half of the population lives (Peters and Kambewa 2007).

Malawi's postindependence economy may be divided it into three periods: the period before 1979, when nearly every sector of the economy experienced rapid growth; the period after 1979, when almost every sector experienced rapid decline followed by erratic recovery trends (Chinsinga 2002, 29); and the period from 2005 on, when the economy again showed significant economic growth. From independence until 1979 the country experienced annual economic growth rates of 6 percent, compared to annual population growth rates of about 3 percent. Exports rose nearly sixfold in the same period. A number of factors are cited as contributing to the country's early growth: "favourable world demand, favourable climatic conditions, rapid expansion of large-scale agriculture, high levels of gross domestic investment, and low and declining real wages and labour costs in the agricultural sector" (Chinsinga 2002, 29). By 1981, however, like many African countries, Malawi was registering a negative economic growth rate. A number of factors can be identified as contributing to the country's rapid economic downturn after 1979 and into the early 2000s, some global and some quite specific to Malawi. These included the oil shock in the late 1970s, which affected the whole world; serious drought in the early 1980s; a sharp decline in terms of trade; the rise in interest rates on international financial markets; the closure of the Beira-Nacala trade corridor due to the war in Mozambique; the influx of refugees from war-torn Mozambique (ultimately totaling 1 million people); and declining levels of development assistance (Chinsinga 2002, 29–30). These factors were compounded by several "structural rigidities that underpinned the country's economy," such as a narrow export base and heavy reliance on tobacco, a reliance on imported fuel and declining stock of domestic fuel wood, and an inflexible system of government-administered prices and wages (Chinsinga 2002, 30).

Malawi's early sharp economic downturn meant that it was the first country in southern Africa to sign on to a structural adjustment program, which it did in 1981. And yet as Blessings Chinsinga noted, Malawi gained very little from being the first country in the region to adopt an SAP:

> Despite being the pioneering country within the sub-region, Malawi is yet to show off the benefits for taking the lead in adopting the SAPs. The overall outcome has been disappointing. Several reviews emphasise that the SAPs have laid heavy social burdens on the vulnerable segments of the society, particularly women and children. The popular view in this regard is that the design of the SAPs did not take into account the potentially adverse effects on the poor in the short and medium terms. (2002, 30)

As a result of the economic hardships generated by the SAPs, the poor in Malawi adopted certain coping strategies to survive (Chinsinga 2002, 31). For example, in the face of declining health services, people turned to traditional medicine and treatment at home. In the face of a falling and unaffordable housing stock, people were forced to seek refuge in crowded and unsafe squatter settlements. Some people resorted to selling off household goods and farm assets, or migrating to urban areas, even other countries. The negative impact of the SAPs on a wide swathe of vulnerable people (not a problem unique to Malawi) prompted the adoption in 1990 of a special program known as the Social Dimension of Adjustment. In Chinsinga's view (2002, 32), the adoption of this program led directly to the adoption, after the political transition, of Malawi's poverty alleviation program in 1994. The intention of the poverty alleviation program was to address a number of features of poverty in the country, such as household food insecurity, low productivity among smallholders, a weak small-business sector, and limited access to essential social services, among others.

That poverty is widespread in Malawi is indisputable. A number of socioeconomic indicators and trends reveal the depths of Malawi's challenges.[13] For example, the country had an estimated life expectancy of fifty-one years in 2010, among the lowest in the world, attributable to the cumulative effects of poverty, the HIV/AIDS epidemic, chronic malnutrition, and substandard health services. Malawi's infant mortality rate, estimated at 83.5/1,000 was also among the worst in the world in 2010, better only than Mozambique and Angola in southern Africa. (A country's infant mortality rate is often used as an indicator of the level of health in a country.) Malawi continues to have a high illiteracy rate, even by African standards, with significant discrepancies between men and women. Estimates for 2003 suggested that only about 50 percent of females over age fifteen and 75 percent of males over age fifteen could read and write. In 2007 the school life expectancy (total number of years of schooling from primary to tertiary levels) in Malawi was 9 years for girls and boys as compared to 12 years in Botswana or Namibia or 13 years in South Africa. High school failure and dropout rates are blamed on child malnutrition and long distances to schools.

Further, as Chinsinga noted (2002, 38) "any tangible attempt at poverty alleviation [in Malawi] has to address the challenge of agrarian reform." This is because 80 percent of Malawi's population depends on agriculture for their livelihood. The staple crop, maize, is grown by most of Malawi's smallholders. Cash crops grown by smallholders include tobacco, groundnuts, rice, cotton, and maize. The country's large commercial estates also grow tobacco, the country's most important export earner, as well as tea, sugar, coffee, rubber, and nuts. During the Banda years, the land area occupied by the large estates expanded rapidly; indeed, the 1967 Land Act allowed only a "one-way transferability" of land—from the customary or smallholder sector to the estate sector. In 1990 this was halted, as a condition for further World Bank development assistance. In January 2002, meanwhile, the cabinet approved a new land policy for Malawi. Among other things, the policy protects customary land against conversion to public land, thereby providing some measure of land tenure security for smallholders. And yet the policy does not address the issue of the tremendous pressure on land in Malawi as a result of the extremely high population density in the country. Chinsinga (2002, 39) suggests that this is because of self-interest on the part of Malawi's elite: "Politicians, top policy-makers and prominent businessmen own vast tracts of land which they are not prepared to give up." Without a genuine redistribution of land, poverty alleviation will not be achieved, Chinsinga contends.

The more recent period in Malawi's political economy coincides with President Mutharika's first term beginning in 2004. As VonDoepp (2010, 3) notes, "growth rates, economic management and relations with donors improved considerably during Mutharika's first term." Annual economic growth rates ranged from more than 5 to nearly 10 percent. In 2006, Malawi was approved for debt relief under the Heavily Indebted Poor Countries (HIPC) initiative, and in 2007 Malawi was granted eligibility status to receive financial support under the US Millennium Challenge Corporation initiative. During Mutharika's first term, Malawi also signed a three-year Poverty Reduction and Growth Facility worth US$56 million with the International Monetary Fund (IMF). As is often the case, improved relations with the IMF led bilateral and other multilateral donors to resume assistance as well.[14]

Challenges of the Twenty-First Century

At the beginning of the twenty-first century Malawi faces daunting socioeconomic and political challenges. Poverty and its associated conditions remain a tremendous challenge for Malawi. Poverty is greater in rural areas and the southern region of the country and among female-headed households and households whose head has no formal education. As one indicator of widespread poverty, Malawi is characterized by a heavy burden of disease as evidenced by high levels of child and adult mortality and a high prevalence of diseases such as malaria, tuberculosis, and HIV/AIDS. Malawi's high population density contributes to a greater spread of communicable diseases. Malawi's heavy disease burden is exacerbated by a brain drain of medical professionals; in 2000 about 59 percent of Malawian-born doctors and 17 percent of Malawian-born professional nurses practiced outside Malawi. It should be noted, though, that Malawi, like other countries in the region, has experienced substantial improvements in the availability of antiretroviral therapy for those living with HIV/AIDs.[15] In Malawi too, the HIV prevalence rate had fallen dramatically by 2009.

Malawi is also characterized by a largely rural population (80 percent) that is urbanizing rapidly (6.3 percent per year)—three times the global rate and nearly two times the African rate—making it one of the most urbanizing countries in Africa. In Malawi rapid urbanization also contributes to poverty, as the resulting urban settlements are characterized by poor access to physical infra-structure such as roads and electricity; poor access to social services such as health, education, water, and sanitation; and insecure tenure and poor housing conditions. The United Nations estimated that by 2005, 90 percent of Malawians living in urban areas lived in slum conditions, with poverty and poor housing being mutually reinforcing.[16] For those in the rural areas, access to land and the challenges of rain-fed agriculture remain. In 2005 President Mutharika began a program of subsidizing fertilizer and high-yielding seeds for small farmers in Malawi, with a near doubling of Malawi's harvest in 2006 and an increase again in 2007, such that Malawi was able to sell a surplus to the United Nations and to surrounding countries. While the program is immensely expensive, it is seen by some as a model for other African countries.[17]

In the political realm, Malawi has been at the forefront of some of the recent trends in southern Africa. Since ousting one of Africa's most tyrannical and predatory leaders in 1994, the people of Malawi have experienced a multiparty political system for nearly two decades. While one party, the UDF, dominated for the first decade or so, that changed with President Mutharika's dramatic withdrawal from the party in 2005 and the formation of a new party, the Democratic People's Party. In elections in 2009 the DPP proved itself to be a national party—something no other party has achieved since the 1994 transition—and President Mutharika initially proved to be a more popular leader than his predecessor. Two years into his second term, however, Mutharika appeared to be transitioning from "talented technocrat . . . to intolerant autocrat," arbitrarily dismissing those who would challenge him and cracking down on any signs of political dissent (Sevenzo (2011). It remains to be seen how the DPP will fare in the next presidential and parliamentary elections and how the next presidential succession will transpire. As elsewhere in the region, then, the challenges of crafting and consolidating enduring democratic politics remain.

Notes

1. As elsewhere in Africa, for the most part the slave trade had a devastating impact upon those it touched, although there were some groups who benefited. As David Williams (1978, 31) notes, "Vast areas were devastated and societies terrorized, and most people found themselves in a situation even worse than they had been when the perennial threat of starvation and disease and the erratic, but ever present, threat of war had put their lives constantly at risk. However, some individuals and some groups were able to seize advantage, sometimes very considerable advantage, from the changed situation."

2. According to Williams (1978, 129): "The remoteness of Nyasaland, its lack of mineral resources, the sparseness of its revenue, and the presence there of a small but relatively powerful and articulate European community had all contributed in their var-

ious ways to a belief among Europeans that considerable advantages would be gained from association with other territories."

3. Peter Forster (1994, 483) suggests that the emergence of a national identity in Malawi was aided by certain historical processes. For example, "the inhabitants had a long record of travelling outside the country as labour migrants or as soldiers: this had helped to create a collective identity because many came to be known as 'Nyasas' regardless of tribal origin."

4. As Wiseman Chirwa (1994b, 95) notes, there was a contradiction: on the one hand the Banda regime tried hard to forge a unified nation-state; on the other hand there were strong tendencies toward regionalism and ethnic discrimination.

5. According to Chirwa (1994b, 95), "we have ample evidence that Dr. Hastings Kamuzu Banda's regime 'pursued a policy of systematic exclusion of people from the Northern Region, as well as Yaos (and especially Lomwe) from the Southern Region, from political power.'"

6. One day before the 1994 election the National Assembly had adopted a provisional constitution, effective for a period of one year.

7. The judges in those traditional courts were traditional leaders who had no legal training. Moreover, in those courts "there was no right to legal representation and . . . the rules of evidence did not apply" (Mutharika 1996, 215).

8. Troops from Malawi's army were deployed in Mozambique from 1985 to 1993, on six-month rotations, to protect the Nacala rail line that provides Malawi with access to the sea. A clear result of that deployment, according to John Lwanda (2002, 158), was high death rates from HIV/AIDS among members of the Malawi military and their wives and girlfriends from 1989 onward.

9. According to Mutharika (1996, 214), "second chambers have usually been adopted in countries with disparate regional, ethnic, linguistic or religious groups to ensure that the interests of small groups are adequately protected. Doubts were raised at the Constitutional Conference as to the need for a second chamber in Malawi and whether the country had enough resources to support such a chamber."

10. Http://www.eisa.org.za/. Retrieved December 2010.

11. See, among others, Chirwa 1994b; Kaspin 1995; Van Donge 1995; Posner 1995; and Wiseman 2000.

12. President Muluzi won the 1999 presidential election with 52.2 percent of the vote, compared to his main rival, Gwanda Chakuamba, the candidate for the MCP/AFORD alliance, who gained 45.2 percent of the vote. In the 1999 parliamentary election the UDF's vote was nearly unchanged, 47.3 percent, as was the MCP's with 33.8 percent. The AFORD, by contrast, gained only 11 percent of the vote, with 6.7 percent going to independent candidates (Wiseman 2000, 643–644). In 2004 the UDF retained its hold on the presidency; with 35 percent of the vote, Bingu wa Mutharika beat the MCP's John Tembo (27 percent) and Gwanda Chakuamba (26 percent) of the Mgwirizano Coalition. In the parliamentary race the MCP won 60 seats, the UDF 49 seats, and the Mgwirizano 27 seats, a considerable change from the 1999 electoral outcome ("Malawi President Gains Majority" 2004).

13. Https://www.cia.gov/. Retrieved December 2010.

14. Https://www.cia.gov/. Retrieved December 2010.

15. Http://www.who.int/. Retrieved December 2010.

16. Http://www.unmalawi.org/. Retrieved December 2010.

17. Http://www.un.org/. Retrieved December 2010.

3 Zambia: The Uncertainties of Political Pluralism

On October 24, 1964, Zambia celebrated its independence from Great Britain. Unlike many neighbors in the region that endured protracted liberation struggles, Zambia enjoyed a relatively peaceful transition to independence, although it was hardly without the tensions, machinations, and political protests that characterized the struggles of other states. Zambia's relatively rapid transition from British rule was condensed into a three-year period, which itself followed three years of intensified nationalism that had begun in 1958. By the end of 1961, independence and majority rule—once distant aspirations—were irreversible. Free of much of the controversy of other southern African states, and free of the debilitating effects of war, Zambia embarked upon its independence with great promise under the guidance of its first president, Kenneth Kaunda. Shortly after independence it could be asserted that "the country starts . . . with a vision of whither it should go, a method of approach suitable to its circumstances and resources potentially sufficient to raise its standards. It is more favoured than most of its contemporaries" (Hall 1966, 299).

Indeed, in the early 1960s, Zambia was considered to have great potential for development. The country was blessed with mining infrastructure, bequeathed by the colonial regime; favorable international conditions for its principal export, copper; a viable foundation for industrial infrastructure; and a small but expandable base in commercial agriculture. Politically speaking, Zambia entered independence with a multiparty system, although one party— Kaunda's United National Independence Party (UNIP)—predominated. Moreover, unlike in other states in the region, the small settler population that remained in Zambia following its transition adjusted to black rule and was largely committed to the development project of the country (Roberts 1976, 242).

By 1975, just over a decade after independence, much of Zambia's initial promise had been squandered, however, as the economy entered a protracted decline and the state slid into one-party authoritarianism. It was not until the

Zambia: Country Data

Land area   743,398 km²
Capital   Lusaka
Date of independence   October 24, 1964
Population   13,460,305 (July 2010 estimate), 35% urban (2008)
Languages   Bemba 30.1% (official), Nyanja 10.7% (official), Tonga 10.6% (official), Lozi 5.7% (official), Chewa 4.9%, Nsenga 3.4%, Tumbuka 2.5%, Lunda 2.2% (official), Kaonde 2% (official), Lala 2%, Luvale 1.7% (official), English 1.7% (official), other 22.5% (2000 Census)
Ethnic groups   African 99.5% (includes Bemba, Tonga, Chewa, Lozi, Nsenga, Tumbuka, Ngoni, Lala, Kaonde, Lunda, and other African groups), other 0.5% (includes European, Asian) (2000 Census)
Religions   Christian 50%–75%, Muslim and Hindu 24%–49%, indigenous beliefs 1%
Currency   Zambian kwacha (ZMK); kwachas per US dollar: 5,237.4
Literacy rate   80.6% (male, 86.8%, female, 74.8% [2003 estimate])
Life expectancy   52.03 years (male, 50.81 years; female, 53.28 years [2010 estimate])
Infant mortality   44.63 per 1,000 live births
GDP per capita (PPP) $1,400 (2009 estimate)
GDP real growth rate   6.3% (2009 estimate)
Leaders since independence
   Kenneth Kaunda, president, 1964–October 1991
   Frederick Chiluba, president, November 1991–January 2002
   Levy Mwanawasa, president, January 2002–August 2008
   Rupiah Banda, president, August 2008–
Major political parties
   Ruling party   Movement for Multiparty Democracy (MMD)
   Other parties   National Democratic Focus (NDF), National Restoration Party (NAREP), Patriotic Front (PF), United Party for National Development (UPND), United National Independence Party (UNIP), United Liberal Party (ULP)
Women in parliament (lower/single house)   14.0% (2006 election)

Sources: Data derived from https://www.cia.gov; http://www.ipu.org/.
Note: Data from 2009 unless otherwise noted.

beginning of the twenty-first century that this situation finally began to improve. Despite recent growth, however, Zambia has remained poor, ranking among the bottom half of countries as measured by gross domestic product (GDP). Within the region, in 2008 Zambia stood at fifth among the twelve states in southern Africa as measured by GDP (EIU 2008).

By the 1990s, Zambia's economy had substantially collapsed in the wake of inappropriate and poorly specified development strategies, which were both socialist and neoliberal; weak integration with the international marketplace; and a substantial decline in the global price of Zambia's principal commodity export, copper. The economy came back, literally from the brink, as a result of a dramatic rebound in global commodity prices, including copper, beginning in 2002. In large part, this copper revival was due to demand from China, whose rapid economic growth continues to fuel its appetite for raw materials. Even though this gives the Zambian state considerable breathing room, every government has repeatedly failed to diversify the economy, which remains substantially dependent on copper as its principal source of foreign exchange earnings. Thus, the country remains highly susceptible to inevitable future commodity price fluctuations.

In the aggregate, Zambia's political trajectory since 1964 has followed a similar path. Although Zambia began independence as a multiparty democracy, President Kaunda and UNIP gradually restricted political competition, culminating in a constitutional change that established a de jure one-party state in 1972. Kaunda was virtually impervious to challenge for the next two decades, despite ever-worsening standards of living and reports of political abuse. When, as a result of domestic and international pressures, Kaunda finally consented to multiparty elections in 1991, he was roundly defeated by the upstart Movement for Multiparty Democracy (MMD) and its presidential candidate, former trade union leader Frederick Chiluba.

Coming to office amid economic collapse but with enormous domestic and international goodwill, Chiluba in many ways turned out far worse than his predecessor (Bratton and Posner 1999; Chan 1999; Rakner 2001). If Kaunda had brought Zambia to the brink, politically and economically, then Chiluba can be (dis)credited with overseeing Zambia's descent into an antidemocratic kleptocracy in the 1990s. In many respects the country was in a much worse position at the end of Chiluba's rule than it had been a decade earlier, thus continuing the pattern of decline begun in the 1970s.

However, political developments since 2001 provide some basis for cautious optimism regarding Zambia's democratic future. Chiluba's successor, President Levy Mwanawasa, presided over a much more plural political environment in which opposition parties gained a substantial presence in parliament. Moreover, Mwanawasa appeared to take a much firmer stand against corruption, even going so far as to target Chiluba and members of his cabinet. When Mwanawasa died in 2008 before the completion of his second term, his vice president, Rupiah Banda, came to office, pledging to continue the reformist policies of his predecessor.

Zambia under the administrations of Mwanawasa and Banda is more democratic—certainly more competitive—than under past regimes. Moreover, a decade of economic growth potentially enables further political strengthening. Yet several caveats are also necessary. First, Mwanawasa's presidency was something of a paradox. He was regarded as a visionary by some in the international community as well as in Zambia and widely eulogized around the world as a committed democrat and anticorruption crusader (Malupenga 2009; Kalungu-Banda 2009). Yet, in reality, his positions often seemed to alternate between democratic and autocratic, bold and status quo. Second,

Rupiah Banda now presides over a highly pluralist, often divided polity. Banda has not commanded the same adulation as his predecessor, and as a result the Zambian political milieu is increasingly fragmented ethnically, regionally, and along urban and rural lines.

Third, there are many structural constraints on Zambia's economy and the way in which Zambia encounters the global economy. Although Zambia's economy grew at an unprecedented annual average of 4.8 percent between 1999 and 2009 (ADB and OECD 2011), its continued reliance on copper means that the country will continue to be at the mercy of global markets and, in particular, Chinese appetites for industrial metals. Such problems defy "easy" policy solutions designed and imposed by political agents. Moreover, the country's landlocked geography vastly increases the cost of imports, such as fuel and raw materials, and drives up the cost of everything Zambia produces, thus diminishing its competitiveness. This is exacerbated in a region of competing rather than complementary economies, not to mention external competition with Asian economies. In addition, although HIV prevalence rates have fallen, the AIDS crisis continues to sap the country of human and material resources. Yet whereas these dilemmas are structural in nature, the solutions to certain problems are in the purview of agents; hence, individual actors and organizations, in the presidency, political parties, and civil society, are vital to understanding Zambia's future trajectory.

Taking all these factors into consideration, this chapter addresses problems of both agency and structure in Zambia and examines the ability of the country's political and social institutions to confront its myriad development challenges. The case of Zambia, one of the first countries in the region to gain independence, undergo a democratic transition, attempt economic structural adjustment, and experience competitive party politics, provides a series of critical signposts for other countries in southern Africa.

Historical Origins of the Zambian State: Context, Key Actors, and Issues

The country known today as Zambia was established in 1890 and 1891, initially as a territory of the British South Africa Company (BSAC) under charter from the British crown. Shortly before, representatives of the same company had extracted concessions from African rulers in Southern Rhodesia, now Zimbabwe (Hall 1966). The name "Rhodesia," after BSAC head Cecil Rhodes, came into common use in 1895, initially to describe both territories. By 1897 the two regions, whose intertwined histories are well chronicled (Leys and Pratt 1960; Franklin 1963; Gann 1964), formally became known as Southern and Northern Rhodesia, respectively.

Although initial European incursions into the southern African region began with Portuguese trade, exploration, and limited settlement as far back as the early sixteenth century, the area occupied by contemporary Zambia did not garner much European attention until the 1850s, through the exploits of Scottish missionary and explorer David Livingstone, who visited the area as early as 1851 (Wills 1964). It was not until 1890 that measurable numbers of whites arrived in the region, mainly pushing out from South Africa in search of mineral wealth. Initially, those arriving in Northern Rhodesia were employed mainly by the BSAC, but within a decade other settlers began to trickle in (Hall 1966). Even so, when the period of BSAC "company rule" in the territory ended in 1923 and administration of Northern Rhodesia was formally ceded to the colonial office in London, the settler population numbered fewer than 5,000. Nonetheless, a legislative council, which asserted a high degree of autonomy from Britain, was established in the colony to provide Northern Rhodesia's small white population with representative government (Hall 1966, 182).

Given their common origins and dominant English-speaking settler populations, some combination of the two Rhodesias—either amalgamation into one territory or a form of federation—was long considered. The prospect was discussed between representatives of the Rhodesias and the colonial office in London as early as the 1930s. However, questions over sovereignty, "native policy," and other disputes prevented consensus for two decades (Leys and Pratt 1960). Finally, in 1953, Northern and Southern Rhodesia were linked, together with Nyasaland (modern-day Malawi), in the Central African Federation. Officials from Northern Rhodesia and Nyasaland believed that federation would allow them to immediately benefit from economic diversification by joining with the more industrialized southerners. They would also get the benefit of a larger white population, thus offering greater autonomy from London. For its part, Southern Rhodesia gained access to the human and natural resources of its two partners. The powers of the federal government centered on defense, trade, communications, industry, and finance, whereas national powers extended to local government, African education, health, agriculture, and land policy. This left the individual governments a considerable degree of autonomy in determining "native policy," always the most contentious issue.

As in Nyasaland, blacks in Northern Rhodesia had been the most resistant to federation, believing that racial policy would fall to the lowest common denominator: that of Southern Rhodesia, where blacks had been thoroughly dispossessed and pass laws were in effect. Despite the setback that federation signaled for blacks, it was nonetheless the case that by the mid-1950s, when the federation was at its peak, the colonial era had already begun to pass in Africa and elsewhere. In this period, fledgling African nationalist movements jelled. The nationalist movement in Northern Rhodesia was led by Harry

Nkumbula and Kenneth Kaunda, first via the Northern Rhodesia African National Congress, which was renamed the African National Congress (ANC) in 1953. Nationalist activity began to reach peak levels of agitation in 1958, but a split emerged in the movement, and Kaunda established a more radical faction, the Zambia African National Congress.[1] In 1959, the Zambia African National Congress was banned by the colonial government and Kaunda was imprisoned, but he emerged from incarceration in 1960 at the helm of the newly established United National Independence Party.

Despite the colonial government's reaction to African nationalism, Northern Rhodesia had always maintained a relatively more liberal set of social and political policies toward the African population, partly because of its smaller settler population, than had Southern Rhodesia—or, for that matter, than had the other settler states in the region. Thus, coupled with the retreat of empire internationally, domestic unrest in Zambia prompted constitutional negotiations rather than violence. These negotiations took place in 1961 and 1962, although an outright transfer to majority rule was not effected immediately (Northern Rhodesia Constitutional Conference 1961; Sklar 1975). Similarly, the federal government also began to make minor concessions to blacks at the same time.[2] However, the prospect of black rule was anathema to the larger and more autonomous settler population in Southern Rhodesia. Hence the dissolution of the federation became inevitable once an African majority was elected to the Northern Rhodesian legislative council in the 1962 elections.[3] This also paved the way for Northern Rhodesia's independence, which formally came in October 1964, and the country became known officially as the Republic of Zambia. Following an overwhelming electoral victory by UNIP (which occurred prior to official independence), Kenneth Kaunda became Zambia's first president.

The First Republic, which lasted from independence until 1972, was a multiparty, if not entirely democratic, system. In the early years of independence, the ANC provided a modicum of parliamentary competition, having won ten seats (to UNIP's fifty-five) in the sixty-five–seat assembly. Several other parties born in the First Republic arose out of internal conflicts within UNIP. One, the United Party, existed briefly between 1966 and 1968, but was then banned by the ruling party, which had grown increasingly sensitive to competition over time. The most significant UNIP splinter group, the United Progressive Party (UPP), was formed in August 1971 by Kaunda's former vice president, Simon Kapwepwe. The UPP posed potential problems for UNIP because it attracted support from traditional UNIP strongholds in Copperbelt and Northern provinces, particularly among ethnic Bemba (Zambia's most numerous group). When interparty violence emerged, it provided justification for UNIP to act on its calls for a one-party state in order to prevent future violence and curb "disunity" (Beveridge and Oberschall 1979; Gertzel 1984).

In February 1972, the UPP was banned, Kapwepwe and 123 leading members of the party were detained, and the UNIP cabinet announced its intention to establish a "one party participatory democracy" (Gertzel 1984). Subsequently, the leadership of the longtime opposition party, the ANC, was co-opted, and a constitutional amendment was passed in December 1972 making Zambia a de jure one-party state. Kaunda was then sworn in as president of Zambia's Second Republic,[4] which would endure for another eighteen years. Although fraught with problems, including systemic constraints on political competition,[5] the Second Republic in fact was fairly successful at restraining ethnic competition among Zambia's seventy-three ethnic groups.

Society and Development:
Zambia's Ethnic and Racial Cleavages

Racial and ethnic pluralism has profoundly, if differently, impacted development in all of the southern African countries. In marked contrast to Namibia, South Africa, and Zimbabwe, where race remained a major social cleavage, the centrality of race diminished in Zambia following its independence. Zambia's white population peaked at 73,000 in 1960, and the numbers declined thereafter.[6] Importantly, because Zambia was never completely a "settler state," it avoided a postcolonial crisis in which nationalists resorted to guerrilla warfare in order to bring about majority rule. Unlike the situation in Zimbabwe, for example, the white settlers who remained in Zambia following independence were by and large those who demonstrated a willingness to live amicably under a black government (Roberts 1976, 249).

Besides the lower initial population and the low density of settler farmers and industrialists, several factors can be identified that have rendered race less significant and far less divisive in Zambia historically than in Zimbabwe and South Africa. The first two, the relatively better treatment of blacks throughout colonialism and the swiftness and relative tranquility of the transition to majority rule, have been addressed above. The third factor is the predominance of multinational corporations (MNCs) present from the colonial era. These displaced or prevented the establishment of a sizable local white bourgeoisie that might compete directly with black economic interests after independence.[7] Nevertheless, certain latent racial hostilities persist, and it is inaccurate to suggest that racial discrimination against Africans (and a corresponding resentment on the part of Africans of whites and Indians[8]) has disappeared in Zambia. As in other countries in the region, whites are heavily represented in the light manufacturing and large-scale commercial farming sectors. In recent years, the government, seeking investment and agricultural expertise, has encouraged immigration of mostly white commercial farmers from South

Africa and Zimbabwe. Although some analyses raise concerns that these migrants could import racial conflict to Zambia, it is unlikely that they will reach sufficient numbers to incite great opposition. Possibly of greater importance is the arrival of large numbers of Chinese, a phenomenon that accelerated markedly in the first decade of the twenty-first century, with the entrenchment of Chinese mining, construction and, increasingly, retail interests. These developments are discussed in more detail below.

Perhaps to a greater degree than race, ethnicity might be expected to be a major fault line in contemporary Zambian society, given the sheer number of ethnolinguistic groups; among these, the Bemba-, Tonga-, Lozi-, and Nyanja-speaking peoples are the most numerous and together account for over 50 percent of the population.[9] Various forms of ethnic management were practiced in the colonial era. Some ethnic groups were subjected to direct British interventions and others to forms of British "indirect rule." Examples of the former include the Bemba in Zambia's north and northeast, who provided much of the labor for the copper mining industry and saw their traditional political structures disrupted severely. Similarly, the Tonga people in the south were transformed into a "rural proletariat," as their rich farmland was appropriated by white settlers and the colonial state. Conversely, the Lozi, claimants of a precolonial kingdom concentrated in the western part of the country, were largely left alone and governed via indirect rule using traditional structures (Gertzel 1984).

One of the few arguable advantages conferred by direct rule was a semblance of "development." Populations subject to direct rule, particularly those proximate to settlement, gained access to a degree of modern infrastructure, a modicum of formal education, and a labor force more acquainted with a Western capitalist economy. Those groups in closest contact with the colonial enterprise frequently were its heirs following independence. Such uneven development precipitated lasting ethnic conflicts in other postcolonial states, such as Kenya and Nigeria. However, although Zambia's ethnic pluralism was a factor in a number of clashes, these tensions never erupted, into wholesale ethnopolitical conflict. This resulted partly from demographics: given ethnic pluralism, no single group has the numerical superiority to allow it to dominate the others. President Kaunda helped to quell nascent ethnic tensions by balancing ethnic representation and support in his cabinet, particularly in the Second Republic.[10] Despite its antidemocratic character, Zambia achieved a semblance of unity through the one-party state; "One Zambia, One Nation," Kaunda's clarion call for national unity, was thus more than simply a political slogan.

The Third Republic administration of President Chiluba, himself of Bemba lineage, faced numerous accusations that the cabinet was increasingly dominated by the Bemba, although its actual composition did not appear disproportionately skewed toward that group. Nevertheless, this perception fostered resentment from some quarters and helped give rise to opposition parties in non-Bemba areas where MMD support was weakest. As early as the

1992–1993 period, this was seen in Western province, a Lozi stronghold, and in Eastern province, where Kaunda and UNIP maintained their greatest support.[11] By the late 1990s, the phenomenon was perhaps most pronounced in Zambia's Southern province, where Tonga voters overwhelmingly flocked to the United Party for National Development (UPND), which was established in 1998 by Anderson Mazoka, a prominent businessman of Tonga descent. Mazoka made concerted and modestly successful efforts to nationalize UPND's appeal, but following his death in 2006, the contested selection of Hakainde Hichilema, himself also Tonga, cemented perceptions of UPND as a "Tonga party." It is also important to point out that in spite of similar efforts to promote a national agenda with a national audience, most opposition parties have been unable to expand beyond regional and largely ethnic bases of support. Even the MMD, which was dominant virtually nationwide in the 1991 and 1996 elections, saw its support dwindle outside of Copperbelt, Northern, and Luapula provinces in Zambia's north in the 2001 election.[12] By the 2008 election, MMD's ethnic base had again clearly shifted. As other parties took on an increasingly regional cast, so too did MMD, which gained more influence in Eastern and Central provinces while substantially ceding its position in the three northern territories to the ascendant Patriotic Front (PF) party, which is widely viewed as dominated by ethnic Bemba and Bemba speakers.[13]

In sum, ethnic and regional origins are important markers of cultural and linguistic identity for most Zambians. Moreover, it is apparent that ethnic identity has become more rather than less *politically* salient since the demise of UNIP's hegemony from the 1980s and 1990s and the denouement of MMD's national dominance in 2001 (see Posner 2005). Renewed ethnic salience notwithstanding, ethnic-based conflict remains rare in contemporary Zambia. In addition, notwithstanding regular accusations that the ruling party favors this or that group, Zambia's cultural pluralism has historically tended to be reflected in its government, and for the most part President Kaunda's successors have tended to follow his practice of ethnic and regional balancing (Posner 2005).

Organization of the State

Zambia is organized into three main branches of government: the executive, the legislative, and judicial branches.

Executive

Zambia utilizes a presidential system, adopted at independence, in which the executive is the head of state and head of government. Much like his counterpart Hastings Banda in Malawi, President Kaunda was essentially a "president-for-life," although elections were held every five years from 1968 to 1988. After the 1972 declaration of a one-party state, candidates for parliament faced off against one another in what Michael Bratton and Nicolas van de Walle (1997) label a "competitive one-party system" under UNIP. Presidential elections, however, were merely a plebiscite on Kaunda's rule, since he was unopposed. Requiring all Zambians to unite under the UNIP banner seemed to fulfill Kaunda's credo, "One Zambia, One Nation." Rather than ushering in a new era of unity and tolerance, however, Zambia's Second Republic gave rise to new political restrictions and rising authoritarianism. UNIP hegemony was constitutionally guaranteed, and Kaunda's authority was greatly enhanced. Proposals for a dual executive—with certain powers, such as ministerial appointments, vested in the prime minister—were rejected by UNIP officials; proposals to limit presidential terms were also rejected ("Chona Report" 1972). Thus, although power began to be concentrated in the person of the president as early as 1964, this phenomenon accelerated markedly in the Second Republic, as Kaunda increasingly conformed to the characteristics of the neopatrimonial "big man" in which "one individual . . . dominates the [bureaucratic] state apparatus and stands above its laws" (Bratton and van de Walle 1997, 62).

As with many other presidents of his generation, Kaunda, the independence leader, came to see himself as indispensable to his country; surrendering power was not considered. UNIP's constitutionally protected political hegemony from 1972 was accompanied by economic collapse, particularly following the oil crisis in 1973. By 1980, Zambia's economy was in free fall. Following disastrous experiences with economic structural adjustment programs in 1986, 1990, and 1991, which led to sharp price hikes for staple foods, the UNIP regime faced substantial popular unrest. Although Kaunda suspended the programs in both cases, he failed to placate society, and once he lost the support of Zambia's crucial urban populations, Kaunda's demise was assured (Martin 1993). Coupled with international pressure and the spillover effects of the "third wave" of democracy in Africa and worldwide, Kaunda acquiesced to multipartyism in 1990. A new constitution was enacted, clearing the way for multiparty elections in October 1991, the first since 1968.

The opposition coalesced into a broad movement, the Movement for Multiparty Democracy, which contested the 1991 elections as a political party. In spite of the considerable benefits of incumbency, the MMD routed UNIP, and former labor leader Chiluba was elected president with over 80 percent of the vote in a contest widely regarded as legitimate and fair. The 1991 constitution restricted the president to two terms of five years each. It failed to address many of the institutional perquisites of the president's position. Presidential power was undiminished under Chiluba, who wielded his authority sometimes ruthlessly.

In addition, the 1991 constitution left intact the presidential entitlement to appoint up to eight additional MPs. Common throughout the region, this provision gives the president power to add to his majority—or to create one where parliament reflects a closely divided electorate. Not surprisingly, these appointed seats increase *presidential* power because loyalty of these MPs lies as much with the president himself as with the ruling party (Bratton and van de Walle 1997). Cabinet appointments, which may include the eight appointed seats, also boost executive power by co-opting loyalties. "The government is made up of the President and cabinet ministers and other ministers and deputy ministers—a total number approaching 70—appointed by the President from members of the House" (Burnell 2002, 293).[14] The appointment of nearly 50 percent of sitting MPs to political positions provides an important patronage tool for the executive and helps to co-opt potential dissenting voices in the legislature. Prospective cabinet ministers are not vetted before parliament, and this lack of consultation has caused rifts between the president and the National Assembly.[15] Further, although the cabinet is collectively accountable to the parliament, the parliament has little means of enforcing that accountability, and individual cabinet officials answer only to the president (Burnell 2002, 293).

Technically, the parliament can check executive authority by enacting (with a two-thirds majority) legislation to which the president withholds his assent, or by introducing an impeachment motion. However, neither of these avenues has been successful in Zambia. Another existing (but unused) leveling mechanism is that, whereas the president has the power to dissolve the parliament, the parliament can also dissolve itself, by two-thirds majority, thereby triggering elections for both parliament and the presidency. "Thus, unlike purely presidential systems, the two branches are not mutually independent" (Burnell 2002, 293). In practice, where the MMD controlled 125 and 131 of the elected seats following the 1991 and 1996 elections, the loyalty of the vast majority of the legislative body was to President Chiluba, as it was to Kaunda in the UNIP era. The MMD parliamentary monopoly was broken in 2001, and since that time, the structure of parliament and the constellation of parties are actually quite competitive, at least on paper. Nevertheless, considerable power continues to accrue to the executive, who not surprisingly "has monopolised the introduction of new legislation" (Burnell 2002, 293). The fact that the MMD has fashioned a strong party structure (in a universe of weak parties) also contributes to the president's control.[16] As leader of the party, as well as the state, the president can impose considerable discipline. Floor crossing is not permitted in Zambia, and therefore anyone expelled or resigning from his party loses his seat in parliament. Given this confluence of factors, it is clear that historically the Zambian parliament has been subordinate to the president.

In 2001, however, there was a major revolt that originated in the cabinet and spread to the wider parliament. Early that year, President Chiluba began to backtrack on earlier pledges to serve only two terms, and his supporters began to openly promote a constitutional change that would allow him to serve a third term in office, a maneuver requiring a two-thirds majority vote in parliament. The initial and most vociferous calls to block this cynical attempt to manipulate the constitution came from civil society, which appeared to lack the capacity to thwart the MMD ("Opposing Chiluba's Encore" 2001). However, by late April 2001, 22 ministers and deputy ministers, joined by a number of MMD and opposition MPs, *publicly* opposed their president; eventually, 74 of the 158 MPs signed a petition vowing to vote against a constitutional amendment bill.

The breakdown in party discipline and personal loyalty was as stark as it was unprecedented. Three factors explain this unlikely outcome. First, civic organization and protest reached its greatest level since 1991, as resistance to Chiluba spread nationwide. Civil society's clearest expression came through the Oasis Forum, which is addressed later in the chapter. Second, the security forces notified Chiluba that they would not intervene if protest turned violent. These two factors helped to shift many MMD insiders' perception of self-interest. Similarly, third, some senior members felt betrayed by the third-term bid and felt that the advancement of their own political careers was being hijacked to accommodate Chiluba's. Hence, the notion that "it was our turn" appeared to figure prominently in the thinking of those who opposed Chiluba from within the MMD.[17] By July 2001, Chiluba recognized he could not win and announced he would not attempt to stand again for the presidency, although Levy Mwanawasa, who was selected by the MMD's forty-member national executive committee, was not announced as the party's candidate until August 2001 ("Presidential Candidate's Adoption" 2001).[18]

The December 2001 national elections signaled the possibility of unprecedented changes in legislative-executive relations. Mwanawasa, the former lawyer and onetime MMD and national vice president, narrowly won the presidential election with just under 29 percent of the vote. The MMD was unable to secure a majority of the elected seats in parliament, however, raising the possibility that henceforth laws would be passed through interparty negotiation, compromise, and coalition building, rather than simply by executive fiat as in the past. Instead, as president, Mwanawasa not only forced out many of the MMD old guard but also moved to co-opt even opposition parties into his cabinet and engineered an alliance with UNIP, which by then held a small but majority-making thirteen seats in parliament.[19] In the process, Mwanawasa skillfully constructed a new base upon which to build loyalty—to him rather than to the office per se.

One other important feature of presidential power in Zambia warrants mention. Historically, the president has had great discretion over financial resources, both through official and illicit transactions. Chiluba maintained a multimillion-dollar slush fund for use by his office (Rakner, van de Walle, and Mulaisho 2001).[20] For his part, President Mwanawasa exercised particular control and influence over the Ministry of Finance. In itself, this is unsurprising, as the finance ministry is typically the most important in Africa, given its powerful fiscal role and its unparalleled international access and connections. As is the case elsewhere in Africa, institutional oversight of presidential accounting tends to be weak, at best, and this invariably raises concerns. As president, Levy Mwanawasa seemed to alleviate some of these concerns. His first appointee as finance minister, Emmanuel Kasonde, was a status quo pick: a former insider, much like the president himself, Kasonde had served in the MMD government as President Chiluba's first finance minister. In 2003, however, President Mwanawasa appointed Ng'andu Magande, a former banker and international civil servant, to the role. Magande quickly earned kudos, particularly in the donor community, and a reputation as a reformer. Certainly, Mwanawasa's economic team also had the benefit of a more auspicious global economic environment, including the salutary impact of high copper prices.

President Mwanawasa came to be regarded as an anticorruption reformer in some circles, particularly internationally. Yet Mwanawasa also faced accusations of both procedural and financial improprieties that resulted in a brief unsuccessful (and highly partisan) impeachment attempt. Moreover, corruption was scarcely eradicated in his government, which witnessed the emergence of several large financial scandals. Thus, the generally upstanding reputation Levy Mwanawasa came to enjoy was, in part, a reflection of the stark contrast with his predecessors.

Under President Chiluba especially, Zambia's track record regarding financial rectitude was unambiguously poor. Indeed, in Mwanawasa's first year in office, he took the step—unprecedented in democratizing Africa—of targeting his erstwhile benefactor, Chiluba, by prevailing on the parliament to lift his immunity from prosecution.[21] In 2003 Chiluba was formally charged with sixty-five counts of "public theft" totaling more than US$29 million, although in separate criminal prosecutions in Zambia he was accused of stealing more than US$40 million in total (van Donge 2009, 76–77). The cases dragged on for years and the amount of theft the state sought to prove was regularly adjusted downward; yet it helped to establish Mwanawasa's bona fides.

Mwanawasa's reformist gestures reveal both the power and shortcomings of agency. He improved Zambia's reputation along with his own, and some capacities of the Zambian state were strengthened.[22] On the other hand, Mwanawasa ultimately could be described as a personalist ruler, albeit a far more positive one than the Jackson and Rosberg (1982) caricature of the 1980s. Thus, when Mwanawasa died in August 2008 from complications of several strokes, his failure to establish durable *institutions* meant that several of his putative reforms did not survive him.

His anticorruption crusade is a case in point. In a curious twist of international jurisprudence, Chiluba was found guilty of stealing US$46 million in public funds by a *London* court in 2007. Yet in Zambia, Chiluba was actually acquitted in August 2009, and Banda's government declined to appeal. The ad hoc prosecutorial apparatus that Mwanawasa had spearheaded to pursue the case against Chiluba, namely the Task Force against Plunder and Corruption, also did not survive Mwanawasa and was disbanded shortly after the Zambia verdict.[23] And, by 2010, a newly exonerated Chiluba was enlisted to help campaign for MMD candidates. (It is important to note as well that corruption hardly ceased under the Mwanawasa administration, and several scandals emerged within the ministries of lands, agriculture, and health. Though the latter was uncovered in 2009, nearly a year after Mwanawasa's death, the embezzlement of millions of dollars of international aid to the ministry had apparently gone on for some time (Usher 2010).

Nonetheless, like Mwanawasa, the current incumbent president, Rupiah Banda, does not enjoy an entirely free hand. Zambia is a much more watchful and transparent polity than it was under the administrations of Kaunda or Chiluba. Civil society is more vigilant, aided by the Internet and the proliferation of mobile technology. Admittedly, too, the abortive prosecution of Chiluba does suggest to current and future executives that they no longer have the ability to act with total impunity, immune to parliamentary or public scrutiny. More important, the *practice* of two decades of democracy and of successive peaceful, if frequently flawed, elections has helped (see Lindberg 2006). Although party turnover has been rare in Zambia, from 1990 through 2011 the country has known four different civilian presidents. Hence the idea that presidents are merely *temporary* occupants of the State House has now been firmly ingrained in the public consciousness.

Constitution

The Zambian constitution has undergone several revisions since independence. The 1972 constitution established the one-party state; the 1991 constitution dissolved the one-party monopoly and introduced presidential term limits; and the 1996 constitution, which was highly controversial but remains in force, placed restrictions on citizenship and presidential candidates, among other things. As noted in the previous section, Chiluba attempted to change the constitution again in 2001 to allow himself to contest a third term. President Mwanawasa initiated a constitutional review process in August 2003 that followed the model of each of the previous constitutional changes, which also were preceded by the establishment of a constitutional review commission (CRC), albeit with differing functions and mandates. Expected to last twelve months, the process dragged on for several years, finally culminating in a controversial National Constitutional Convention (NCC) in 2010.

The 1996 constitution was derived in part from the input of the Mwanakatwe Commission, which solicited submissions and participated in town hall–type meetings throughout Zambia in 1993 and 1994. In theory, this is an admirable example of grassroots democracy, and the commission, named for its chairman, John Mwanakatwe, submitted its report in June 1995. However, the MMD-dominated parliament ignored numerous recommendations of the commission, when the constitutional amendment bill was debated in 1996 (Bratton and Posner 1999, 393). The Economist Intelligence Unit (EIU 2003k, 15) claims that Chiluba's government rejected "70 percent of [the CRC's] submissions and instead authorise[d] a text custom-made in key respects for the president." Differing with this claim, but not with its consequences, Michael Bratton and Daniel Posner (1999, 393) note that the government actually agreed with many of the CRC's proposals, but that by cutting off intense public debate and ratifying the changes in parliament, the government committed a "gross violation of the spirit of democratic discourse that President Chiluba claimed to champion." Indeed, the government ignored a key recommendation of the Mwanakatwe Commission—and a civil society and donor demand—"that any new constitution should be ratified by a national referendum and a constituent assembly, rather than by parliament" (Bratton and Posner 1999, 393). This approach, however, permitted the MMD-dominated parliament to adopt constitutional provisions that proved grossly partisan.[24]

Many expected that Mwanawasa's CRC (formally, the Mung'omba Commission, after its chairman Wila Mung'omba) would also lead to a constitution adopted behind closed doors. Yet this time, the government proceeded with a constituent assembly, the NCC, which many of the Mung'omba Commission's 41 members had demanded. Yet even the way in which this NCC was adopted drew considerable criticism. It was regarded as overly partisan, and numerous civil society organizations were excluded from its deliberations; however, various groups were able to make written submissions to the body.[25]

Judiciary

Zambia has a multitiered judicial system. The Supreme Court is the highest court and serves as the final court of appeal. It is headed by the chief justice and deputy chief justice and seven other judges who are nominated by the president and ratified by parliament. Below the Supreme Court is the High Court, which is defined in the Constitution of Zambia as having "unlimited and original jurisdiction to hear and determine any civil or criminal proceedings under any law" (pt. 6, art. 94, para. 1), including, of course, appeals from lower courts. The High Court holds regular sessions in all nine provincial capitals. Judges on both the Supreme and High Courts serve until the mandatory retirement age of sixty-five. At the next level are the magistrate courts, which have original jurisdiction in some civil and criminal cases. There is also an Industrial Relations Court, charged with hearing labor matters, and an extensive, if ill-defined, system of local courts, which adjudicate principally customary and family law. "The local courts are today the busiest courts in Zambia. Some urban courts hear between 30 and 50 cases in a day" (Afronet 1998). Yet these courts are without even the most basic facilities—paper, pens, transport—and are routinely neglected by higher courts and the country's political institutions (Afronet 1998). Indeed, at all levels, the twin problems of resource constraints and judicial independence have plagued Zambia's court system, as they have other countries in the region. A Freedom House survey (1999) noted that "some of Zambia's jurists retain a stubborn independence while others are subservient to Chiluba and the MMD." In addition, the survey decried the overburdened court system, detentions lasting years without trial in some cases, and arbitrary and often unconstitutional rulings in civil cases by customary courts of "variable quality."

While many of the systemic problems—insufficient resources, overcrowding, unrelieved dockets, and inadequate representation—continue to plague Zambia's judicial system, the more competitive politics prevailing since 2001 may have a salutary impact on judicial independence in Zambia's courts. As Jennifer Widner (2001, 100) notes, party competition gives "politicians a material incentive to check executive encroachment on judicial functions. Without competition, politicians' individual attitudes toward the courts mattered much more." Fortunately, President Kaunda's stance toward the courts was relatively benign.[26] According to Peter VonDoepp (2001a), despite the lack of competition in Zambia's Second Republic, Kaunda generally eschewed interference in the judiciary, and his government followed suit. However, Kaunda did intervene indirectly, by appointing supportive jurists, and none were permitted to challenge the premise of one-partyism. On the other hand, judges occasionally issued politically unpopular decisions that challenged the ruling UNIP elites.

Ironically, pressure on the judiciary to conform to political interests may have increased under the ostensibly "democratic" rule of the MMD. Recall that genuine multiparty competition, though no longer illegal after 1991, was virtually nonexistent in the first decade of the Third Republic. Therefore, following Widner's (2001) logic, MMD elites were little concerned with executive interference in the judiciary, demonstrating hostility toward legal rulings and jurists unfavorable to the ruling party (VonDoepp 2001a). By 2003, political intimidation appeared to have waned, however, perhaps fostering an environment of increased judicial independence. *Country Profile Zambia* (EIU 2003g, 17) suggests that "despite some questionable judgments in high-profile cases, the spirited judiciary has managed to preserve its independence from the executive and legislature." Paradoxically, some of the most politically sensitive cases on the docket involve President Mwanawasa and his government.

Mwanawasa led a massive anticorruption campaign that targeted a number of extremely powerful and high-profile former members of President Chiluba's cabinet, including Chiluba himself, whose trial began in August 2003. At the same time, however, Mwanawasa was effectively a *defendant* before the High Court, where opposition parties filed a petition to invalidate the December 2001 election immediately after the new president was inaugurated in January 2002.[27] The case charged Mwanawasa with electoral fraud and illegal (and unconstitutional) use of state resources during his 2001 campaign. In 2005, the petition against Mwanawasa was dismissed. In a lengthy decision, the court found that despite numerous irregularities, Mwanawasa had been duly elected. It was not established whether Mwanawasa was aware of these alleged violations at the time they occurred, or whether he merely unwittingly benefited from the MMD's formidable political machine. If the court had found against Mwanawasa, however, the constitution would have required that a new election be called.

In 2003, then chief justice Matthew Ngulube was compelled to resign following the determination that he accepted more than US$10,000 in gifts from former president Chiluba between 1998 and 2000 (Simon 2005). This case had a distinctly political cast, however, as did the appointment of Ngulube's successor, Ernest Sakala, which left Mwanawasa's critics convinced of presidential tampering in the judiciary.

These cases reveal that despite Zambia's relative judicial independence, the capacity of the courts to act as impartial arbiters is sometimes constrained. Indeed, Peter VonDoepp (2006, 396) argues that "the Zambian case suggests that judges act strategically in response to case-specific political factors. . . . [T]hey tend to defer to the government in high interest cases, while engaging in assertive behavior in other, lower-profile cases." He also finds that institutional rules in Zambia offer only limited protection to jurists, noting that "the president has the authority to dismiss a judge on grounds of incompetence or misbehavior, albeit only with the advice of a special tribunal that must investigate the case" (VonDoepp 2006, 397). Such institutional weakness clearly undermines horizontal accountability by potentially subjecting jurists to the whim of the executive. This contrasts with other polities, such as Malawi, for example, where "the president must obtain majority support from parliament, then consult with the Judicial Service Commission before removing a judge" (VonDoepp 2006, 397).

Notwithstanding these challenges, however, the judiciary remains one of the most trusted institutions in Zambia. The 2008 Afrobarometer survey found that 62 percent of respondents trust the courts "somewhat" or "a lot," exceeding the trust Zambians place in any other institution (in some cases quite dramatically) except that of traditional leaders (*Afrobarometer* 2010, 22–23).

Representation and Participation

Legislature

Zambia has a 158-member unicameral legislature, which serves as the principal law-making body, and a House of Chiefs, which has advisory functions. President Mwanawasa reconstituted the latter in 2003, after it had been moribund under his predecessor. Although in some countries the House of Chiefs may serve as an upper chamber, in Zambia its functions are limited to those of an advisory body on traditional practices and matters of customary law; this body includes 27 of the country's 286 traditional rulers, who retain considerable influence in their communities. The House of Chiefs remains largely at the margins of Zambian politics, though it can claim a symbolic role as the venue for debate about the role of traditional authorities in contemporary life. Thus, President Mwanawasa both co-opted and earned the goodwill of the traditional authorities, without allowing them a formal legislative role.[28]

In the more politically salient National Assembly, 150 MPs, representing single-member constituencies, are directly elected for five-year terms, and up to eight additional members are appointed by the president. Under both the UNIP and MMD governments, at least through the 1990s, the parliament served essentially as a rubber stamp for executive decisionmaking. As noted earlier, the executive exercises disproportionate authority, notwithstanding a constitutional nod to a balance of power among the branches, and his power is enhanced by control over spending, access to unbudgeted funds, and the ability to make ministerial appointments from among sitting MPs. Following the 2001 elections, however, the MMD lost its majority, creating the prospect of divided government in Zambia for the first time. And while divided government can lead to legislative gridlock, it also can yield new alliances and unique compromises and cooperation. Indeed, the 2001 election presented a genuine opportunity for opposition parties, despite their diversity, to form an opposition alliance that would offset the executive power of the presidency.

But during its first year in office the Mwanawasa government was able to establish a working majority in parliament, co-opting members of opposition parties and using the latter's own disunity to its advantage. Consequently, the lion's share of political power in Zambia remained vested in the president. As an experienced governing party, the MMD took advantage of its ten-year tenure as the majority party and the incumbency it still enjoyed in the presidency to woo both legislators and voters back into its camp. By-elections and defections thus helped MMD regain the parliamentary majority. By-elections are required within ninety days from the date a parliamentary seat becomes vacant, or whenever a sitting MP switches parties (including independents). By October 2003, two years after the 2001 election, the MMD had increased its presence in the National Assembly by 5 seats to 74 seats, whereas the UPND, at that point still the leading opposition party, had just 46. Several of the new MMD members came at the expense of the UPND, which suffered a number of defections in the period. However, the MMD's parliamentary supremacy was secured, ironically, by its old rival UNIP, with which it formed a loose governing coalition.[29] The advantage of this arrangement is that it was not necessary to put a seat at risk by holding a by-election.

In sum, whereas Zambia's parliament became substantially more competitive after 2001, institutional structures continue to favor the party of the president, given the disproportionate power of the executive branch. Moreover, despite the fact that all parties produce dense manifestos, they tend to differ little on substance; personalities and, to an increasingly greater degree, regional origin therefore emerge as central factors for voters. Unsurprisingly, therefore, another hallmark of Zambian multipartyism is that party identities are incredibly fluid. Since the reintroduction of multipartyism in 1991, an MP's switch from the opposition to the ruling party has neither been unexpected nor likely to lose him or her a seat.[30] Interestingly, the reverse is also true: notwithstanding the benefits enjoyed by the ruling party, the fragmentation—in the electorate, parties, and parliament—in recent years especially has boosted the candidacies of local favorite sons and daughters, regardless of party.

Party System and Elections

In 1991, democratic, multiparty elections were a rarity in sub-Saharan Africa. Zambia's transition from authoritarian to more democratic rule—critical elements of which included President Kaunda's willingness to allow multipartyism, the "free and fair" conduct of elections, and the peaceful transfer of power—was greeted with great enthusiasm both inside and outside the country. Indeed, because of this remarkably smooth process and apparently democratic outcome, Richard Joseph (1992) declared Zambia a "model for Africa," and other scholars were similarly impressed by the achievement (Baylies and Szeftel 1992; Bratton 1992). Zambia, therefore, was seen as something of a bellwether case, in that it was at the forefront of a democratic wave on the African continent. To its credit, Zambia has also held regular elections at the national level under the MMD, as it had under the UNIP. Elections, of course, are only one part of democratic governance, albeit a critical part. Staffan Lindberg (2006) argues that the iterative process of holding periodic, regular elections itself can help to inculcate democratic practices in a polity. Whereas a deepening of democracy since 2001 is apparent, national elections in 1996 and 2001 did little to inspire confidence.

After 1991 Chiluba was able to quickly consolidate his control over the party structure and the pliant parliament. The MMD's enormous parliamentary majority in 1991 (128 seats to UNIP's 22) left it in virtually the same position of UNIP in the First Republic: it achieved supermajority status, with very few checks on political decisionmaking as a result. The MMD's overwhelming dominance fueled growing authoritarianism and unchallenged policy choices, many of which proved disastrous in the 1990s. The party showed progressively less tolerance of opposition activities as the decade wore on, a stance that was a reflection of its own growing insecurities.[31]

Thus, notwithstanding the celebratory mood in 1991, Zambia was only nominally democratic throughout the decade that followed. The propensity toward single-party dominance and the precarious nature of Zambian democracy were actually first signaled by President Chiluba's declaration of a state of emergency in March 1993 on spurious claims that UNIP was plotting to overthrow the government through a clandestine operation code-named "Zero Option." Several UNIP leaders were detained, and civil liberties were suspended for two months. When the charges turned out to be unsupportable and evidence of a coup conspiracy nonexistent, it became apparent that the MMD was merely attempting to consolidate power by undermining UNIP, then the only viable opposition party (Ihonvbere 1995; Bratton and Posner 1999). The hastily imposed state of emergency marked the beginning of Zambia's slide into renewed authoritarianism, although relative quiescence prevailed until 1996, the year MMD was required to go to the polls to renew its mandate.

In March 1996 the regime harassed and eventually incarcerated three independent journalists (employed by *The Post* newspaper), following controversy arising from their publication of articles critical of Chiluba (Bratton and Posner 1999). The arrests, officially on "contempt of parliament" charges, were spurious and were immediately condemned by international and local human rights groups, resulting in the reporters' eventual release. The crackdown on the press was followed in quick succession in May 1996 by the promulgation of the widely criticized constitution; the explosion of a series of bombs, reportedly by a shadowy group called "Black Mamba"; and the arrest of eight senior members of UNIP, again on specious charges of treason.[32] Finally, in November 1996 the MMD went ahead with the national elections under highly suspicious conditions, including allegations of voter registration fraud, a divisive constitution, and an atmosphere of intimidation. In response, UNIP and several other parties decided to boycott the elections, which the MMD then won in a landslide (Baylies and Szeftel 1997; Bratton and Posner 1999).

An actual coup attempt occurred in October 1997, although it was led by a small band of disgruntled soldiers, who were not only disorganized but also reportedly drunk at the time. The coup attempt amounted to little more than a half-day takeover of a broadcast station, but it led to a second state of emergency declaration two months later. Although their links to the coup attempt were tenuous at best, several opposition leaders, this time including former president Kaunda, were jailed along with seventy-eight soldiers. Most were held without charge for several months, and the trial did not begin until June 1998, reflecting the weakness of the government's case (particularly against the handful of accused civilians). Kaunda, whose ties to the coup were never supported by the evidence, was released just prior to the commencement of the trial. South African president Nelson Mandela and former Tanzanian president Julius Nyerere appealed to Chiluba for Kaunda's release; at the urging of his nationalist-era contemporaries, Kaunda agreed to give up active politics, thereby diminishing the perceived threat to Chiluba.[33]

The failure to fulfill the political and economic promise of 1991 reflects the inability of the MMD and its leadership to even begin to address the Herculean problems facing the country in the 1990s. More broadly, however, this failure highlights the enormous difficulty of instituting genuine democracy after brief political openings that merely allow challengers to become incumbents and act like their predecessors. The rise of such "virtual democracies" has been an all too common occurrence following the democratic wave earlier in the decade (Joseph 1997). Zambia's virtual democracy was epitomized by the regime's authoritarian tendencies, but it was also aided by certain institutional features. The first-past-the-post, majoritarian electoral system favors large parties and particularly the incumbent party. Similarly, the Electoral Commission of Zambia (ECZ), which is charged with overseeing elections, voter registration, voter education, and the like, had scant autonomy from the government throughout the 1990s (European Union 2001; Carter Center 2002). Although considered more independent under the Mwanawasa government (ironically, since the ECZ was believed instrumental in his 2001 victory), the ECZ continues to be funded and influenced by the government, and its five commissioners are appointed by the president.

Despite a political and institutional environment after 1991 that was substantially inhospitable to political opposition, Zambian opposition parties proliferated. One explanation for this surely lies in the desire for electoral alternatives. However, the requirements for party registration are minimal (just 200 signatures), so a number of the thirty or more parties that surfaced at any given time in the 1990s foundered quickly or existed almost entirely on paper, having little substance behind them. Since 1991, several parties have been able to gain seats in parliament, although, as noted, most had only regional support: UNIP in the east; the National Party and, later, Agenda for Zambia, both predominantly supported by the Lozi community in Western province; and the UPND, with its strongest support in the south among the Tonga community. The Forum for Democracy and Development (FDD) emerged mainly as an MMD spin-off in mid-2001, accommodating the MMD cabinet members and parliamentarians who refused to support Chiluba's third-term bid. However, the multiplicity of parties seldom translated into measurable parliamentary seats.[34] Indeed, of the seventeen parties that contested the 2001 parliamentary elections, only five gained more than a single seat. Of those, only UPND retained its electoral relevance throughout the decade.

By the 2006 election, UPND, the FDD, and UNIP had entered a short-lived electoral alliance, the United Democratic Alliance (UDA), which collectively won twenty-six seats. Such alliances are purely for expediency, however, as demonstrated by their fluidity in recent years. Indeed, the UDA barely remained intact through the 2006 election. With its national support dwindling, UNIP itself switched sides, aligning with its former archrival, the ruling MMD. Although UPND remains a force in Southern province, the death of its popular founder, Anderson Mazoka, and his replacement as party leader by businessman Hakainde Hichilema appear to have sharply diminished the party's national fortunes.

Meanwhile, former MMD government minister Michael Sata led his PF party from obscurity in 2001 to near victory in 2006 and in the 2008 special presidential election. The PF's support surged, particularly among the charismatic leader's base among Bemba speakers in the north and as a result of his populist, urban-centered, movement.[35] In 2009, UPND and the PF joined in an electoral arrangement they called the Pact. Yet whereas their numbers might be collectively sufficient to dislodge the MMD, disagreement over whether Hichilema or Sata would stand as the Pact's presidential candidate in the 2011 election led to the Pact's dissolution in March of that year.[36]

In short, in the twenty-first century the party system in Zambia is more fluid and dynamic (even unsettled) than ever. Incumbency still had some power for the MMD, but other parties' support was driven more by personality and region than by any coherent ideological position. Nic Cheeseman and Marja Hinfelaar (2010, 53) argue that in Zambia the "continual repositioning of party platforms on major issues of economic policy and campaign style reveals that not all African elections take place in an ideological vacuum." Yet it is precisely this inconstancy that reveals Zambia's barren ideological landscape. In fact, parties that sought to appeal to Zambian class identities (such as a short-lived Labor Party and the farmer-oriented National Lima Party in the 1990s) failed to gain any traction.

Zambia has held four national elections since 1991, including the special 2008 presidential election necessitated by the death of Levy Mwanawasa. Although its margins have narrowed, the MMD has won every one. Tables 3.1,

Table 3.1   Presidential Election, 2008

Candidate	Party	Number of Votes	Percentage of Votes Cast[a]
Rupiah Banda	MMD	718,359	40.09
Michael M.C. Sata	PF	683,150	38.13
Hakainde Hichilema	UPND	353,018	19.70
Godfrey K Miyanda	HP	13,683	0.76
Total		1,768,210	98.68

Source: Electoral Commission of Zambia.

Notes: Registered voters: 3,944,125. Voter turnout: 45.43 percent. MMD = Movement for Multiparty Democracy; PF = Patriotic Front; UPND = United Party for National Development; HP = Heritage Party.

a. Percentage of total votes cast, including 23,596 invalid or spoiled ballots.

3.2, and 3.3 indicate the results in three of these elections. The 2001 and 2011 contests are in many ways the most interesting: 2001 because Chiluba was blocked from pursuing a third presidential term, and 2011 because conditions are auspicious for the first transfer in executive and legislative control in a generation.

Even without Chiluba in the competition, the 2001 elections were marred by allegations of voter fraud, intimidation, and harassment of opposition politicians and their supporters and of errors by the ECZ. Unchastened by Chiluba's failed attempt to gain a third term, the ruling MMD used all the perks of incumbency to ensure victory for its candidates. The party's overwhelming financial advantages, control of a politicized police force, and unfettered access to the public media made the party a formidable opponent. Moreover, the government postponed the elections until late December, ordinarily the height of the rainy season in Zambia, in an apparent attempt to depress turnout. Given these tactics, it was surprising that on election day nearly 70 percent of registered voters arrived at polling stations. People waited in line for hours on end—in some cases as many as twenty hours—usually

Table 3.2   Presidential Election, 2006

Candidate	Party/ Coalition	Number of Votes	Percentage of Votes Cast[a]
Levy Mwanawasa	MMD	1,177,846	42.98
Michael M.C. Sata	PF	804,748	29.37
Hakainde Hichilema	UDA	693,772	25.32
Godfrey K Miyanda	HP	42,891	1.57
Winright Ken N'gondo	APC	20,921	0.76
Total		2,740,178	100.00

Source: Electoral Commission of Zambia.
Notes: Registered voters: 3,941,229. Voter turnout: 70.77 percent.
a. Excluding rejected votes of 1.75 percent.

Table 3.3   National Assembly Elections, 2006

Party	Number of Seats	Percentage of Seats
Movement for Multiparty Democracy (MMD)	73	50.00
Patriotic Front (PF)	43	28.67
United Democratic Alliance (UDA)	26	17.33
Independents	3	2.00
United Liberal Party (ULP)	2	1.33
National Democratic Focus (NDF)	1	0.67
Not contested (postponed)	2	
Total	150	100.00

Source: Electoral Commission of Zambia.

without food, water, or shelter from the hot sun; fortunately, the rains held off until after the elections. Citizens expressed an unyielding resolve to voice their opinions, and many reported that they were "voting for change"—that is, an end to what they regarded as ten years of failed, corrupt MMD rule.[37] Many observers had predicted a win by presidential candidate Anderson Mazoka, a prominent businessman and head of the United Party for National Development. The UPND was perhaps the best organized party among the opposition and had considerable momentum. In the end, although the UPND won forty-nine seats in the National Assembly, the MMD won sixty-nine and, of course, the presidency.[38] While the MMD clearly enjoyed continued support in many parts of the country, the questionable conduct of the election by the party and the ECZ were important factors in securing the MMD's plurality of the parliamentary vote and Mwanawasa's narrow victory.

In 2006, the PF supplanted the UPND as the MMD's leading political opposition. Although an increasingly popular President Mwanawasa was able to increase his percentage of the vote to 43 percent, Michael Sata and his PF party were able to make remarkable gains, capturing just over 29 percent of the vote (see Table 3.2). With the advantages of incumbency, Mwanawasa's increased national popularity, and his abilities as a politician more savvy than his 2001 detractors realized, it is likely that MMD would have remained the odds-on favorite entering the 2011 national elections. However, Mwanawasa's death in 2008 significantly altered the electoral landscape in Zambia.

Sata dampened his anti-Chinese populism and repositioned himself as a centrist in order to challenge Mwanawasa's former vice president, Rupiah Banda. Banda, who had assumed the role of acting president and was constitutionally required to call for elections within three months, was not popular nationally but emerged atop an internally divided MMD (Cheeseman and Hinfelaar 2010). In the 2008 special presidential election, Sata's "strategy of moderation" and Banda's unpopularity resulted in a more than 450,000 vote reduction from the MMD's 2006 total, although Banda squeaked by with the victory (Cheeseman and Hinfelaar 2010, 71). Some analysts privately suggested that the Electoral Commission of Zambia delayed the release of results from two remote areas in order to tip the final tally in MMD's favor.[39] In any event, had the UPND and the PF been able to combine their resources, it appears a consensus candidate would have emerged victorious. The electoral map is even more favorable to the opposition in 2011.

Civil Society

That MMD's electoral hegemony was challenged at all in the these elections in the first decade of the twenty-first century stems significantly from what can best be labeled a popular *revolt* by civil society. In February 2001, civil society organizations came together under the aegis of the Oasis Forum, whose principal mission was to prevent a Chiluba third term. The Oasis Forum, named after Lusaka's Oasis Restaurant, in which the first meeting was held, developed into a mass campaign that eventually forced Chiluba to capitulate. This was a prominent example of the periodic vibrancy of civil society in Zambia and represents one of the four key junctures in state-society relations.

The first juncture that warrants examination centers on the role of civil society in the 1990–1991 transition. The Movement for Multiparty Democracy was established in July 1990 "as an umbrella committee of interest groups whose principal demand was, as its name suggested, the restoration of competitive politics. To form an opposition front, Frederick Chiluba led the trade union movement into a coalition with business, professional, student, and church groups. As well as bridging class and status divides, the urban-based MMD skillfully used the far-flung teachers' and civil servants' unions to mobilize support in the countryside" and drew in "a diverse set of ethnoregional groups as well" (Bratton and van de Walle 1997, 199). The interest groups that arrayed against Kaunda and the one-party state had depth as well as breadth. Thus the sheer number of actors involved and the national reach of their organizations—as represented in the MMD, which of course became a political party—brought considerable pressure to bear on President Kaunda to permit competitive elections.

The role of civil society in the transition has been the subject of considerable research (Baylies and Szeftel 1992; Bratton 1992; Ihonvbere 1995; Rakner 1998). This research is unanimous in its conclusion that civil society played an instrumental role in channeling popular discord into a formidable, organized social movement and later into a party. Diverse and contradictory societal interest groups (for example, business and labor) engaged in a robust and cooperative effort, ultimately compelling Kenneth Kaunda to allow elections—and to stand down when he lost (Baylies and Szeftel 1992).

The second period, roughly from 1993 through the end of the decade, was nearly the converse of the first. It was characterized by the relative quiescence of civil society, which was in part a result of the authoritarian backlash of the Chiluba government. In the brief honeymoon period immediately following the 1991 election, associational life blossomed, particularly since the lawyers, churches, students, businesspeople, laborers, and the other actors who established MMD had reason to believe their interests would be well represented in the new government (Rakner 2001). Ironically, what transpired instead was a curtailment of civil liberties under the rubric of two hastily imposed (if short-lived) states of emergency, sustained harassment of the small independent press, and the marginalization of the labor, business, and nongovernmental organization (NGO) communities that aided the MMD's ascension to power (Rakner 2001; Bräutigam, Rakner, and Taylor 2002). Commenting on this period, Bratton and Posner (1999, 392) observed that "although rhetorically committed to openness and transparency, Chiluba's government [proved] to be intolerant of criticism, slow to react to allegations of corruption within its ranks, and disturbingly willing to exploit its command over government resources and institutions (including the police and parliament) to undermine the opposition and favor its own party members."

During this time, far narrower segments of civil society played a watchdog role than might have been anticipated based on the 1991 transition. Only the independent print media, notably the *Post* newspaper, joined by a handful of NGOs, remained regular critics of the government. Other civic organizations, such as those representing the business community, offered more tailored criticism and attempted to attract donor support for their activities (Taylor 2007). Local NGOs, like the Foundation for Democratic Process, the Zambia Independent Monitoring Team (ZIMT), and the Committee for a Clean Campaign (CCC), developed expertise in issues of voter education and election monitoring. However, the cost of speaking out against government abuse of power proved high after 1993. As Bratton and Posner (1999, 397) report, the *Post* "was the target of 20 separate acts of harassment by the government or its supporters between January 1994 and October 1996." Similarly, when ZIMT and the CCC "called press conferences to announce their opinion that the [1996] elections had been flawed, their offices were raided, their bank accounts were frozen, and their chairmen were detained by the police" (Bratton and Posner 1999, 401).

Such actions had a predictably chilling effect on societal discourse. Although public criticism of the government never stopped (the *Post,* for example, was unrelenting and occasionally over the top), interest groups were naturally fearful of the repercussions of speaking out. The Zambia National Farmers Union, for example, was ostracized by the government and forced to conciliate (Taylor 2007). The Chiluba government skillfully marginalized (or worse) those groups that showed any discernible hostility toward it. At the same time, it proved adept at cultivating new support bases in society through co-optation and patronage in the classical neopatrimonial pattern. Chiluba's multimillion-dollar slush fund was instrumental in this regard.

The quiescence of civil society at the end of the 1990s makes its resurgence in 2001 all the more noteworthy. Thus, at the third juncture lies the Oasis Forum, the initially spontaneous consortium of interest groups that arose to challenge Chiluba's third term. The Oasis committee formally included the leaders of key groups in the legal, church, and NGO communities. Specifically, five organizations were represented: the Law Association of Zambia; three church umbrella bodies representing each of the major Christian faith traditions in the country, namely the Evangelical Federation of Zambia, the Christian Council of Zambia, and the Zambian Episcopal Conference; and finally the Nongovernmental Organizations Coordinating Committee, itself an umbrella of major NGOs operating in Zambia. Meeting in February 2001, the

Oasis Forum wrote the Oasis Declaration, which was submitted to President Chiluba. The brief declaration recounted the Zambian people's desire, expressed repeatedly in constitutional review commissions in 1972, 1991, and 1996, to limit the president to two five-year terms. It specifically called on the president to respect the constitution and to resist calls for a third term, noting "that the ongoing debate is not only costly and counter-productive but is an ill-considered attempt at legitimizing an *illegitimate* or unlawful objective and desire to subvert the Constitution" (Oasis Forum 2001, n7).

The Oasis Forum helped to focus a growing popular campaign to prevent Chiluba and the parliament from rewriting the constitution for narrow political gain. Moreover, the reach of the Oasis constituent groups, particularly the churches, was significant, thereby enabling opponents of the president's effort to reach a vast swath of Zambian society. Using Chiluba's own past statements, which condemned African leaders—including his predecessor, Kaunda—for clinging to power, critics throughout Zambian society became more vocal in their protest. In defiance of government efforts to block public protest against the third term, a popular "hooting" demonstration also emerged, in which those opposed to the third term sounded their car horns in unison. In this and more substantive ways, Zambian civil society united in the face of Chiluba's brazen grab for power. Members of Chiluba's cabinet, though self-interested, also recognized the formidable resistance to the third term and abandoned Chiluba, who in turn was forced to abandon his bid.

Oasis's successful effort leads us to wonder where civil society was between 1991 and 2001. While at first glance it would appear that Zambians' greatest expression occurs in decennial cycles, in fact the middle years of the 1990s did not find all Zambian civil society organizations in the doldrums. Indeed, a number of organizations, including some of those that participated directly and indirectly in the Oasis Forum, found a way to take advantage of the pluralist environment after 1991. Although access to the state was often limited or nonexistent (Rakner 2001), certain groups were able to build capacity and capabilities (almost invariably with donor assistance), notwithstanding the state's occasionally stark authoritarian methods. In the process, NGOs expanded indigenous capacity for everything from election monitoring to political and civic education to combating AIDS. This more "mature" civil society, prominently in evidence in the anti–third-term campaign of 2001, would appear to provide a bulwark against future authoritarian impulses by the state.

A fourth juncture pertains to state-society relations broadly, and thus arguably is unrelated to "civil" society in the conventional sense, though it did lead to the mobilization of labor and other traditional civil society groups. Moreover, these developments tended to be localized in urban areas of Lusaka and the Copperbelt; however, their ramifications were both national and international.

A series of riots took place in the Copperbelt and Lusaka in 2006, sparked by worker protests over labor practices at Chinese-owned mining facilities. These protests were themselves related to a deadly explosion at a Chinese-owned factory servicing the mine at Chambishi. By early 2006, there was growing public restiveness over real and perceived employment discrimination, particularly at the mines, and an abiding sense that Zambian resources were benefiting foreigners rather than Zambians.

Evaluations of the Chinese record on this front vary. Some scholars urge a more nuanced appreciation for the complex role of "China" in Africa, pointing out that Chinese interests are actually a diverse mix of state and private businesses, small and large. One proponent of this view, Deborah Bräutigam (2009), argues that the Chinese have already moved substantially in a positive direction continent wide. Yet Chinese investors have been astoundingly tone deaf to Zambia's sociocultural conditions: for example, initially disallowing union activity at Chambishi and subsequently maintaining unsafe conditions; flaunting Zambian labor law by employing Chinese expatriates in excess of permissible limits; and establishing Special Export Zones (SEZs—tariff-free zones designed to facilitate value-added exports) that have been both slow to materialize and have served *Chinese* business interests rather than facilitated the technological spillover to African firms that proponents of the SEZs anticipated.

The resentments such maneuvers generated and the social reaction that followed were astutely, if xenophobically, marshaled by Michael Sata in his 2006 campaign. The PF captured significant vote majorities in urban centers, partly by playing on popular ambivalence about economic reforms and urban unemployment. But Sata also tapped into and fomented the widespread disaffection with Chinese investors and labor unrest in the wake of the Chambishi explosion.

Importantly, state actors recognized that their economic partnership with the Chinese raised their political vulnerability with the urban constituencies. Indeed, the MMD's political response was a 2008 windfall profits tax on the mines. Though repealed when copper prices dropped in 2009, this significant increase in the tax was an act of economic populism designed to win back disaffected urban voters. Likewise, the hasty creation of the Citizens Economic Empowerment Commission (CEEC) in 2006 was a political reaction to a restive public that perceived that the benefits of Zambia's renewed economic growth were accruing mainly to non-Zambians. The CEEC, essentially a vehicle for affirmative action in Zambia, is intended to promote business and job creation among historically disadvantaged Zambians. Yet the establishment of CEEC can also be interpreted as an effective maneuver by the MMD government to hijack and quiet the radical rhetoric of "indigenization" threatened in 2006 by Sata. In this regard, and somewhat encouragingly, the formation of CEEC reveals that the state can at least attempt to be responsive to social developments— especially if they have a potential political payoff.

Fundamentals of the Political Economy

Although the first decade of the twenty-first century saw impressive GDP growth, Zambia's main economic engine remains little changed since independence in 1964: it is still dependent on copper and its mining sector for nearly 90 percent of its foreign exchange earnings. At independence, Zambia was just emerging from ten years of federation in which the benefits flowed to Southern Rhodesia.[40] Yet despite the disadvantages of federation, the 1960s marked a period of great optimism for Zambia's future. Its small population of slightly over three million, low population density, fertile agricultural base, and existing copper resources held great development promise. Unlike Southern Rhodesia, Zambia at independence had few whites in industrial enterprises outside of the mining sector, and just 400 white commercial farmers (Hall 1966). An indigenous African industrial or commercial agricultural base was practically nonexistent. Thus in terms of economic development, the country had to start virtually from scratch.

As in much of independent Africa, the state was regarded as the guarantor of economic security for the newly empowered black majority, and it assumed a leading role; the private sector was dominated by MNCs, especially in the critical mining sector.[41] Zambia quickly adopted a program of import substitution industrialization (ISI), similar to those of other developing countries at that time, calling for local production of manufactured goods. The economic foundation of President Kaunda's policies was laid in the Mulungushi reforms, which were launched in 1967 and signaled the desire to put the economy in the hands of the black majority. Importantly, within Kaunda's worldview of "humanism," with its socialist undertones, Africanization meant a state-owned economy, not the development of an indigenous private sector. The Mulungushi initiative therefore called for massive acquisition by the state of locally and internationally owned enterprises. As in most African countries where nationalization took place, with the notable exception of Mozambique and more recently Zimbabwe, acquisition was part of a negotiated process for which firms were compensated; Zambia even borrowed internationally to fund the program, thereby adding to its debt burden (Kayizzi-Mugerwa 2003).

However, with the exception of the copper-mining firms Anglo-American Corporation and American Metal Climax Company, from which the state acquired a majority shareholding (subsequently consolidated under Zambia Consolidated Copper Mines [ZCCM]),[42] most of the nationalized firms produced solely for local markets.[43] Thus the key policy error by Kaunda and UNIP was not nationalization per se, but the fact that little effort was made to diversify the country's export revenue stream beyond copper, which accounted for approximately 90 percent of exports during the Kaunda regime and a similar percentage thereafter. Nationalization greatly hindered state flexibility, especially the ability to restructure the economy and bureaucracy, as the state became too dependent on the copper sector (Shafer 1994). Nevertheless, Zambia enjoyed relative prosperity for its first five years. World copper prices were high, enabling the government to pursue nationalization with vigor and to grant cheap credit that fueled the growth of an emergent petty bourgeoisie (Gertzel 1984).

The dependence on copper revealed profound weaknesses in the economy, however, when prices began to soften by 1970 (Gertzel 1984). Even then, the Zambian government took few steps to diversify beyond the country's traditional copper export base. Cherry Gertzel (1984) suggests that a rebound in prices the following year may have contributed to the continued delusion that the copper boom was a permanent fixture of the international economy. It was not. The international oil crisis of 1973 and 1974, prompted by drastic cuts in production by the Organization of Petroleum Exporting Countries cartel, sharply reduced global demand for copper. As a result, world copper prices fell sharply in 1974 and 1975, reducing Zambia's 1975 copper export revenues by over 43 percent.[44] Copper prices remained virtually stagnant for nearly *a quarter century,* and Zambians felt the impact profoundly. During those years Zambia had the dubious distinction of being "one of only three countries in the world with a worse development indicator index in 2001 than in 1975" (EIU 2003g, 36). (It is worth noting, however, that while Zambia remains a low human development country, ranking 150 of 169 in 2010, its Human Development Index [HDI] has improved since 2000 such that it was above the sub-Saharan African average in 2010 [Human Development Report 2010a, 3–5].)

In 1979 and 1980, the second international oil crisis raised costs immeasurably for oil-dependent states like Zambia and precipitated a global recession that made matters worse. In the 1980s, Zambia was compelled to seek relief from the International Monetary Fund (IMF) and later the World Bank, marking the beginning of two decades—and counting—of dependence on loans from the international financial institutions (IFIs) and the donor community.

Structural Adjustment and Donor Dependence

Zambia actually had signed its first standby agreement with the IMF in 1973, availing itself of the IMF's Oil Facility (Ihonvbere 1995). However, the 1980s marked a sharp decline in the Zambian economy: copper prices did not recover, per capita GDP declined 3 percent per year, and the country faced a rising debt burden. As Julius Ihonvbere (1995, 78) observes, the government agreed to a 1983–1985 adjustment package with the Bank and the IMF to "restore financial stability," but by 1986 the Zambian government was over US$100 million in arrears to the IMF and the program was suspended. Zambia briefly tried a "homegrown" structural adjustment strategy, but this too failed, and neoliberal reforms were discontinued until the Chiluba government reinstated a structural adjustment program (SAP) under the auspices of the

World Bank and the IMF in 1991 (Martin 1993). Contrary to UNIP, the MMD had a popular mandate to implement SAPs, since the party had made it clear that fixing the economy would require austerity (Bratton 1992).

Encouraged to return to Zambia by the economic and political promises of the Chiluba government, with its professed commitment to governance, the donor community and the IFIs engaged the regime. Indeed, through much of the 1990s, more than 40 percent of the budget was donor dependent, a level that continued into the following decade. In the 1990s the donors frequently praised the MMD's commitment to the SAP, including its liberalization of foreign exchange, pledges to reduce inflation and public expenditure, and the country's aggressive approach to privatization (Rakner, van de Walle, and Mulaisho 2001). But the conditions in Zambia continued to worsen in the 1990s, and analysts variously point to donors' lack of clear goals and government's lack of long-term strategy and waning commitment to reform (Rakner, van de Walle, and Mulaisho 2001) or to the programs themselves (Mkandawire and Soludo 1999)—or all three (Bräutigam, Rakner, and Taylor 2002)—for the explanation. At bottom, Lise Rakner, Nicolas van de Walle, and Dominic Mulaisho (2001, 563) noted that "after almost a decade of uninterrupted policy reforms, the record in terms of economic growth, employment creation, investments, and poverty reduction remains weak."

In response, donor support was actually withheld on multiple occasions. For example, reacting to the constitutional changes and the flawed elections in 1996, bilateral donors froze aid between 1996 and 1998. The delayed privatization of ZCCM after 1997 led to further suspensions by lenders. In the first full year of Mwanawasa's administration, the IMF withheld a US$100 million poverty reduction and growth facility loan—the low-interest loan program launched by the IMF in 1999—and a World Bank loan in the amount of US$342 million was also delayed, as were several bilateral commitments. However, in the past, donor conditionalities proved difficult to enforce because, as Rakner, van de Walle, and Mulaisho (2001) point out, the IFIs and the bilateral donors were seldom in accord, particularly over political matters in the 1990s, thereby reducing the international leverage on the Chiluba government. In any event, donor uncertainties about Mwanawasa, lingering fears about corruption, and concerns about fiscal spending were assuaged, aided by renewed economic growth.

From State-Led to Private Economy

The Mulungushi reforms in the First Republic stifled much of the potential for an indigenous private sector. Even after the Mulungushi reforms, however, "foreign and state capital constituted overwhelmingly the dominant actor within the economy, holding virtually all of the large-scale private enterprises and dwarfing the participation of private Zambian capital. Indeed, even resident non-Zambian individuals probably remained more economically important than private Zambians" (Baylies and Szeftel 1984, 69). Under Kaunda, the state exercised hegemony in virtually every economic sector, forming a massive state holding company, the Zambia Industrial and Mining Corporation. The state invested heavily in manufacturing industries, including paint, chemicals, textiles, and sugar. In addition, the agricultural sector was controlled, with a state monopsony on the marketing of many crops, particularly the national staple, maize. Government indirectly subsidized maize consumption by offering a low price ceiling to farmers, who had no other legal outlet for their produce. This was intended to placate potentially restive urban consumers by offering them the staple at low cost; however, such "urban bias" had the effect of driving producers out of the market, creating shortages and unsustainable economies (Bates 1981).

In those few sectors that the state did not operate, some multinational firms, such as Colgate Palmolive, Reckitt and Colman, and Dunlop, among others, stepped in to supply goods to the local market. Thus, outside the state and MNCs, there was limited space occupied by small and medium-scale manufacturers, commercial traders, and about 400 predominantly white commercial farmers; in short, the local private sector was small, weak, and vulnerable as a result of UNIP policies. Interestingly, it largely remained so in the 1990s, despite changes in the economic and political regime that accompanied the ascension of the promarket MMD (Bräutigam, Rakner, and Taylor 2002). In the 1990s, in place of a state antithetical to domestic private interests was an environment in which international firms, chiefly from South Africa, were able to swamp Zambian markets and overwhelm uncompetitive Zambian-owned enterprises. Zambia thus underwent substantial deindustrialization as uncompetitive firms faced the regional and wider international marketplace following trade liberalization in 1992 (Bräutigam, Rakner, and Taylor 2002).[45]

Despite the marginality of most Zambian-owned firms, especially those owned by black Zambians, privatization has been a major feature of the Zambian economy since 1992. That year, the Zambia Privatization Agency (ZPA) was set up, and by 1997 the professionally managed entity had sold 224 of the 275 formerly government-owned companies that had been listed for sale. International observers, including the World Bank, hailed Zambia's privatization, attributing the "success of the privatization program to the fact that the process through the [ZPA] was predominantly private sector–driven, with little interference from the government" (Rakner, van de Walle, and Mulaisho 2001, 562). Yet these cheerful assessments were clearly based on the *quantity* of Zambia's privatizations rather than the quality. For example, the 200-plus transactions (some of them suspect) yielded a relatively small sum—less than US$100 million in proceeds. Moreover, the transaction that dwarfed all the others combined, the privatization of Zambia Consolidated Copper Mines, was botched, perhaps deliberately. Offers were made in 1997 and 1998 by an international consortium of mining companies and, quite inexplicably, were rejected by the government. "The view among the donors in Lusaka is that the negotiations failed because of a combination of incompetence and corruption on the part of the MMD government" (Rakner, van de Walle, and Mulaisho 2001, 563).

In 2000, the sale of ZCCM was finally completed—as an "unbundled" entity to a number of buyers, principally the longtime minority shareholder, the South Africa–based Anglo-American Corporation. However, the condition of the mines had declined in the intervening period, and the global price of copper had softened, resulting in a far lower final price for the ZCCM assets. Indeed, the delay alone may have cost Zambia hundreds of millions of dollars in forgone revenue (Rakner, van Walle, and Mulaisho 2001). In an uncharacteristic display of parliamentary oversight, the National Assembly conducted a massive investigation into what went wrong. It discovered that the otherwise efficient ZPA was circumvented, and instead the sale was handled by political insiders without any transparency ("Report of the Committee on Economic Affairs and Labour"). In addition, Peter Burnell (2002, 299) writes that the report found "evidence not simply of procrastination but illegal conduct, procedural irregularities and corruption, all of them costing the treasury and the country dearly in a number of ways." To make matters worse, in 2002, Anglo-American ceased its mining operation in Zambia, including two of the largest mines, writing off its investment because it could not make the enterprise financially viable. Fortunately for Zambia, new buyers were found just as global copper prices began to reach historical highs.

As economic policy, privatization was always publicly defended by Chiluba's government, but behind the scenes it was contested; some elites had ideological objections to surrendering national assets and industries so dearly acquired (Rakner, van Walle, and Mulaisho 2001). "National pride," coupled with corruption, surely explains much of the fiasco surrounding ZCCM. Mwanawasa initially appeared less interested in privatization than his predecessor. His second finance minister, Ng'andu Magande, who was appointed in July 2003, was also resistant, despite pressure from the donors and IFIs to privatize the major assets that remained in the state's portfolio. These included the national telephone company, Zamtel; the electrical utility, Zesco; the Zambia State Insurance Company; and the Zambia National Commercial Bank (Zanaco). The Dutch institution Rabobank finalized its purchase of a 49 percent share in Zanaco in April 2007, and a Libyan firm bought Zamtel in June 2010, suggesting that resistance to privatization within the Mwanawasa government was hardly insurmountable.

Debt Forgiveness and Economic Growth: A New Start?

The embrace of IFI- and donor-sponsored neoliberal reform, including privatization, produced mixed results; however, given its aid dependence, Zambia enjoyed little maneuvering room. Although Zambia's structural constraints, and the resulting dependence on the IFIs and donor countries, persist, three factors fundamentally altered Zambia's political economy in the early twenty-first century: the rebound in copper prices mentioned earlier; the vastly expanded Chinese role and presence; and major reductions in Zambia's international debt load.

Zambia debt relief was initiated under the poverty reduction strategy paper (PRSP). The PRSP process became the critical step for countries to qualify for debt relief under the advanced highly indebted poor countries initiative (Advanced HIPC) led by the World Bank and IMF. Zambia's overhang of external public debt stood at US$6.1 billion in 2003, proving a substantial drain on the country's resources and policy flexibility. Two years later, however, the country qualified for debt relief under HIPC, resulting in approximately US$6 billion in multilateral debt relief. Similarly, most of Zambia's bilateral donors also eliminated or restructured their debt after 2006.

Although one of the principal goals of the PRSP exercise was diversification of the Zambian economy beyond copper, this scarcely happened. Copper and to a lesser degree cobalt remain the overwhelming source of Zambia's foreign exchange earnings. In addition, the economy remains substantially driven by the minerals sector, with copper and cobalt still constituting more than four-fifths of Zambian exports in the first decade of the twenty-first century. China's demand for copper and other metals, necessary to fuel its own industrialization, has helped keep global prices high and has lessened the immediacy of diversification in commodity-based economies such as Zambia's.

Owing to the problems of loss-making state-owned enterprises and only partially successful privatization, ecological setbacks, and poor integration with the global economy, the Zambian economy shrank in real terms throughout the first half of the 1990s. As seen in Table 3.4, GDP declined precipitously from 1991 to 1995, partly as a result of debilitating droughts, before rebounding in 1996. With the rebound in the all-important copper sector, combined with favorable agricultural conditions and the effects of debt relief, Zambian GDP grew at an impressive 5.7 percent, even in 2008 amidst the global economic downturn. In fact, Zambia's growth has been consistently robust from 2002 on. Thus the country was at last able to see downward pressure on the country's debilitating poverty levels; Zambia improved to 108 out of 192 countries ranked by poverty level in 2010 (World Bank 2011). Zambia's economic growth potential, however, remains deeply susceptible to structural imbalances as well as climatological forces. In addition to its copper dependence, for example, the region faced another drought from 2001 to early 2003 that forced the importation of relief maize and agricultural sector declines of 2.6 percent and 4.1 percent in 2001 and 2002, respectively (EIU 2003k,12). Through 2010, drought had not recurred, however, and Zambia has received above average rainfall since 2002. Moreover, Zambia's trade rela-

Table 3.4   Real GDP Growth in Zambia, 1991–2009

	1991	1992	1993	1994	1995	1996	1997	1998	1999	2000
Percent	0.0	(1.7)	6.8	(8.6)	(2.8)	6.9	3.3	(1.9)	2.2	3.6

	2001	2002	2003	2004	2005	2006	2007	2008	2009
Percent	4.9	3.3	5.1	5.4	5.2	6.3	6.2	5.7	6.3

Source: World Bank Databank, http://databank.worldbank.org.
Notes: Parentheses indicate negative growth. Measured as a percentage of constant 2000 prices.

tions are nearly as undiversified as its economic production. Although Zambia has reduced its dependence on South African imports, 51 percent were sourced from there in 2009 (down from two-thirds in 2003 [EIU 2003k]). On the export side of the ledger, Zambia now finds itself reliant on its two leading mining investors, Switzerland and China, which together account for 58 percent of Zambian exports, principally minerals and metals.[46]

Challenges of the Twenty-First Century

By the late 1990s, it was clear to all that Chiluba and the MMD had overseen the unraveling of a once-promising democratic experiment. The MMD leaders were just as authoritarian as their predecessors and fantastically more corrupt. Leading intellectuals and technocrats, people who had been essential to the MMD's foundation, had either bolted the party or been dismissed (Rakner, van de Walle, and Mulaisho 2001). The economic renewal that many expected to accompany the MMD's tenure was not forthcoming, as a result of exogenous shocks, lack of adequate planning by both the Zambians and the donors, an inability to attract trade and investment due to global competition, and outright corruption. Against this backdrop, 2001, the ten-year anniversary of the first multiparty elections, marked a clear opportunity to reclaim Zambia's democratic promise, reinvigorate civil society, and renew international interest and attention on Zambia.

Mwanawasa's 2001 election was tainted to be certain, and it was widely assumed that the new president would merely be a stooge for Chiluba, who would pull the strings behind the scenes. To the surprise of many, Mwanawasa quickly demonstrated his independence, in part by pursuing criminal investigations against Chiluba and his cohorts. Having endured a decade of democratic disintegration and kleptocracy under Chiluba's rule, the initial public skepticism about Mwanawasa declined rapidly. Restoring a trademark characteristic of the MMD's first year in 1991, he appointed individuals who were well regarded for their competence, rather than their loyalty to the party. However, not long after this quite unexpected honeymoon period, Mwanawasa's image was tarnished by his renewed political alliances with some of the Chiluba cabinet members who were facing charges, including several of those he had accused. In the end, Mwanawasa had both his devoted admirers and staunch detractors, though many Zambians choose to recall him fondly (Malupenga 2009). His legacy may be aided most, however, by comparison to his successor, Rupiah Banda. Banda, an accidental president, tends to be held in much lower esteem by donors and the Zambian electorate. After a generation in power, the MMD is experiencing much of the same electorate fatigue that UNIP generated prior to 1991. The party's constituency has shrunk considerably, and it has lost the urban areas and many of Zambia's provinces. Thus, however unwittingly, Rupiah Banda ultimately may preside over party change. With change, inevitably, comes uncertainty but also the potential for greater democratization in Zambia through peaceful turnover.

Like Mwanawasa, Banda has availed himself of Zambia's unambiguously strong presidential system. Unlike their two predecessors, however, both Mwanawasa and Banda have been constrained by parliamentary opposition. But in Africa's dominant-party democracies, the power of incumbency is not to be underestimated. The MMD is threatened, but is in a formidable position to use its control over electoral bodies, instruments of state, and access to increased economic rent flows in order to maintain its rule after the 2011 national elections. Should the MMD maintain control of the government until the 2016 election, it will preside over an increasingly skeptical and perhaps even hostile electorate. Alternatively, should any of the current opposition parties emerge victorious, they will have perhaps even more work cut out for them to prove their legitimacy to other sections of the country. How these political questions are resolved may determine whether Zambia can continue to enjoy the growth and economic stability that characterize many of its southern African neighbors.

Notes

1. Nkumbula wanted to participate in the Northern Rhodesian elections, whereas Kaunda believed the process to be antithetical to black interests (Roberts 1976, 220).

2. At the federal level, pressure from London and rising African nationalism in both northern territories prompted the governing United Federal Party to make at least superficial steps toward African representation. For example, in 1961 a new federal constitution was adopted that offered blacks fifteen out of sixty-five seats in the federal legislature and a "Bill of Rights" (Sklar 1975).

3. As a result of the 1961–1962 negotiations, African representatives were permitted to form a majority, "provided some of them were also supported by a minimum percentage of white voters." This allowed whites to control, to a degree, the *type* of African elected. Additional constitutional changes in 1963 allowed for universal adult suffrage. UNIP won fifty-five seats and the ANC ten; an additional ten seats were reserved for whites until formal independence in October 1964 (Sklar 1975, 17).

4. The Second Republic constitution was passed in August 1973. The first elections under the one-party constitution were held in December 1973 (Gertzel 1984).

5. Zambia's one-party state was characterized by participation and competition, though the latter, limited to a choice between two candidates of the same party, was a source of rising frustration among the electorate (Bratton and van de Walle 1997, 141–142).

6. The European population was 3,000 in 1920, 36,000 in 1950, and 73,000 by 1960 (Sklar 1975, 9, 16). The 1995 census revealed a total population of 10.2 million, of whom 30,000 were of European descent and 20,000 of Asian (primarily Indian) descent.

7. Since many MNCs were nationalized or forced into joint ventures with the state, "Africanization" generally did not come at the expense of *local* private sector actors. Refer to "Fundamentals of the Political Economy" later in this chapter.

8. For example, Indian merchants in the southern city of Livingstone were the targets of well-publicized violence in 1997, and several prominent businessmen and politicians of Indian descent were the targets of racist statements from several black politicians in the run-up to the 2001 elections.

9. Twenty-five percent of the population speaks Bemba as its first language, followed by Nyanja (11.7 percent), Tonga (11.7 percent), and Lozi (5.6 percent), based on the 1990 census. However, since these tongues serve as regional lingua francas, actual ethnic identification is lower (see http://www.ethnologue.com).

10. Interestingly, shortly after independence, UNIP was regarded, particularly by the ANC, as a "Bemba party," despite its representation from all over Zambia (Roberts 1976, 242). Kaunda himself is not Bemba; his parents were Nyasa missionaries from Malawi to Zambia's Northern province, where the younger Kaunda was raised among Bemba speakers (Hall 1966, 124). In the First Republic, Nkumbula's ANC had strong support among the Tonga (Hall 1966, 227). See also Sklar 1975, 9.

11. In the west, Lozis predominate, and Chiluba's treatment of Lozi officials fostered considerable resentment.

12. Although these three provinces have the largest Bemba populations, they were also long-standing MMD strongholds.

13. President Mwanawasa hailed from the Lenje ethnic group, a minority indigenous to Central province, whereas his successor, Rupiah Banda, not only was a lifelong devotee of the UNIP and Kenneth Kaunda but also is identified with his Eastern province roots. Absent a strong centralizing party and charismatic president, opposition politicians and their (intentionally or unintentionally) ethnoregional parties can be seen as viable options for voters in the provinces. The PF, under the leadership of Michael Sata, and the UPND, now led by Hakainde Hichilema, were beneficiaries of the substantial Bemba and Tonga abandonment, respectively, of the MMD in the first decade of the twenty-first century.

14. In 2003 the government briefly debated reducing the number of ministries from twenty-one to fourteen, but President Mwanawasa rejected the idea in early 2004.

15. In May 2003, President Mwanawasa unexpectedly dismissed his vice president, Enock Kavindele, whom he accused of corruption. Kavindele was replaced by Nevers Mumba, an evangelical Christian pastor and a minor-party presidential candidate in 2001. The appointment was controversial, and apparently unconstitutional, since Mumba was not an MP at the time of his promotion, and as a candidate for office in the prior election he should have been disqualified under Article 68. This helped motivate opposition MPs to launch an unsuccessful impeachment motion against Mwanawasa (EIU 2003k, 13).

16. Peter Burnell (2001, 241) labels Zambia a dominant-party system "where one party commands, alone and over time, the absolute majority of seats." The possibility of alternation exists, even if it is unlikely.

17. Author interview with Ackson Sejani, Forum for Democracy and Development party secretary and former MMD minister, Lusaka, October 26, 2001. It is worth noting, however, that despite this rather remarkable revolt, President Chiluba and his cohorts were able nonetheless to cajole the vast majority of MMD members into changing the *party* constitution to allow Chiluba a third term as party leader ("Zambia's Ruling Party" 2001). The MMD party rules then stipulated that the leader of the party stand as the MMD presidential candidate in the general election.

18. In addition to bringing in cabinet members from opposition parties—UNIP, the Zambia Republican Party, and the Forum for Democracy and Development—in February 2003, the MMD eventually gained a majority through by-elections and defections and the formation, in May 2003, of a loosely defined alliance with UNIP.

19. Chiluba briefly retained his role as MMD party president after leaving national office in 2001 but was forced to relinquish the party post in 2002 in order to access certain retirement benefits from the state.

20. "In 1998 the Zambian parliament approved a discretionary fund of approximately US$5 million for the president of the republic, and in 1999 the government refused to announce the amount allocated to the presidential fund," which had no "system of accountability in place to ensure it is used for legitimate purposes" (Rakner, van de Walle, and Mulaisho 2001, 570).

21. Under the law, former presidents are entitled to immunity from prosecution for alleged crimes committed in office. However, Mwanawasa persuaded the parliament to lift Chiluba's immunity in July 2002. Some human rights and anticorruption advocates applauded, although other observers feared it might become a dangerous precedent that would backfire because other incumbent authoritarians would refuse to relinquish office rather than risk prosecution. This may be the case, but executive prosecution has not been adopted as an anticorruption tool in other African polities (Taylor 2006).

22. The national reputation of the government of the Republic of Zambia improved markedly with the donors early in Mwanawasa's tenure, although certain measures, such as the Corruption Perceptions Index (CPI), actually worsened slightly. Additionally, there was some strengthening of the state's investigative and prosecutorial capacity, through existing institutions such as the Office of the Auditor General and the Anti-Corruption Commission and through the creation of the Task Force Against Corruption and some enhanced capacity of the tax collection entity, the Zambia Revenue Authority (ZRA), for example.

23. One last effort by the anticorruption forces sought to utilize international law to enforce the London judgment within Zambia. However, the Lusaka High Court ruled that the London verdict could not be enforced in Zambia. Although the Zambian state actually applied to the High Court to have the judgment registered in Zambia, the government's decision not to appeal the judge's controversial finding reignited doubts about its commitment to the anticorruption agenda established by Mwanawasa (EIU, 2010a).

24. Among the most controversial provisions of the 1996 constitution was a restriction in Article 34—the "citizenship clause"—on who could contest the presidency; the new document barred any individual whose parents, like those of former president Kaunda, were not also born in Zambia. This was a transparent attempt to bar Kaunda from rechallenging Chiluba for the presidency. By 1995, Kaunda had begun to make a political comeback, and Chiluba was clearly threatened by Kaunda's ascendancy. The new document also imposed the two-term limit retroactively, a move that was also aimed at Kaunda (Bratton and Posner 1999, 393–394).

25. Author interview, Peter Henriot, Jesuit Centre for Theological Reflection (JCTR), Lusaka, August 11, 2010.

26. President Kaunda clashed with some members of the then all-white higher courts early in the Second Republic, leading several jurists to resign from the bench (Roberts 1976).

27. Zambia's electoral laws require that the president be sworn in within forty-eight hours following the certification of election results. Thereafter, any challenge to the poll results must be done through the legal system.

28. It is worth noting that Article 129 of the 1996 amended constitution, with the backing of then president Chiluba, explicitly banned political activity, especially the contesting of elections, by chiefs. It states: "A person shall not, while remaining a chief, join or participate in partisan politics." Chiluba feared that chiefs would make formidable political opponents. Thus, Mwanawasa's revival of the House of Chiefs can be seen as a partial effort to both placate and co-opt this community and their followers. (See Lewis Mwanangombe, "Let Our Chiefs Govern," Inter-Press Service, December 21, 2009, http://ipsnews.net/.)

29. The distinction between UNIP and MMD later became almost completely obscured when Rupiah Banda, a prominent lifetime member of UNIP, became Mwanawasa's vice president in 2006 and subsequently state president upon Mwanawasa's death in August 2008. Because Banda only joined MMD upon his cabinet appointment, some MMD stalwarts regarded his ascent to the presidency as a UNIP "takeover" of MMD.

30. Typically "he" will win a seat, as fewer than 15 percent of MPs in Zambia are women, among the lowest rate in southern Africa and below the sub-Saharan average of 19 percent in early 2010 (http://www.ipu.org/).

31. Although only UNIP, the MMD, and a handful of insignificant parties contested the 1991 elections, opposition parties multiplied thereafter: some forty-one were registered by late 1997.

32. The "UNIP eight" were jailed on suspicion of their involvement with the bombings, despite the fact that there was no evidence linking them to the explosions or to the Black Mamba organization. Most observers suspect that the bombings were actually orchestrated by the MMD as a pretext to marginalize UNIP by paralyzing its leadership. The UNIP leaders were freed after nearly six months in prison (Bratton and Posner 1999; Rakner, van de Walle, and Mulaisho 2001).

33. Kaunda's eldest son, the popular Major Wezi Kaunda, was seen as heir to the family political mantle and was poised to assume the leadership of UNIP and perhaps of the country when he was assassinated in 1999. Another Kaunda son, Tilyenji, subsequently emerged as leader of UNIP, but he was unable to restore the party to its former glory.

34. There was also a growing tendency in the 1996 election and after for individuals to be elected to parliament as independents, some of whom had previous party affiliations. Ten won seats in 1996. However, only one independent was elected in 2001.

35. In the 2006 parliamentary and presidential election, Sata adopted a staunchly anti-Chinese message in his campaign. Given the unpopularity of Chinese investors among labor groups and the poor, due to perceptions of unfair and unsafe working conditions in their facilities, this message resonated with the public (Negi 2008).

36. This mirrored an earlier attempt in 2008 to forge a party alliance between UPND and PF, which also failed because Hichilema and Sata and their parties could not agree on a consensus candidate. Predictably, the opposition split its vote in 2008, though Hichilema and Sata collectively garnered 57.8 percent of the vote (Simutanyi 2010). Note that at the time of writing the date for the 2011 election had not been set.

37. Reflected in author interviews with voters, Lusaka and Chongwe district, December 27, 2001.

38. International and domestic observers alike criticized the conduct of the election and electoral process. Opposition parties used the statements of delegations from the Carter Center, the European Union, the Southern African Development Community Parliamentary Forum, and others, which pointed out numerous irregularities. Armed with the international evaluations and comprehensive reports from domestic monitors, Mazoka and the other losing candidates lodged the court challenge to have Mwanawasa's victory overturned.

39. Personal communication to the author, Lusaka, August 5, 2010.

40. According to Richard Sklar (1975, 16), it "is generally thought that as a result of the redistribution of revenues following the establishment of the federation, Northern Rhodesia lost about £7 million per year to Southern Rhodesia—a total of £70 million during the federation's ten-year life span." Moreover, "there can be no question that the [Zambian] Copperbelt [was] the financial backbone of the federal fiscal structure" (Sklar 1975, 16). Indeed, William Tordoff (1980, 2) argues that "for a period of almost 10 years Northern Rhodesia became the milch cow of predominantly Southern Rhodesian white interests."

41. This situation was not appreciably different from the role the state had played for whites in the colonial era, in which subsidies were made available for white commercial enterprises, especially farming (Roberts 1976).

42. The two foreign firms retained minority shareholdings of just over 34 percent after nationalization.

43. Import substitution industrialization was expensive and inefficient to maintain: most of the finished goods produced required the importation of expensive raw material and intermediate inputs of goods that Zambia did not produce.

44. Although prices rebounded somewhat in 1979–1980, production peaked in 1976 at 745,700 tons and generally declined in the years thereafter (Mulemba 1992). By way of contrast, 336,700 tons were produced in 2002 (EIU 2003k) and 680,000 tons were produced in 2009 (www.chinamining.org 2010).

45. One of the many types of factories that were closed down during this period were 85 textile firms driven out of business by the massive importation of cheap used clothing, known in Zambia as *salaula,* which came primarily from the United States (see Tranberg Hansen 2000).

46. World Trade Organization, Trade Profiles, October 2010. Available at http://stat.wto.org/.

4 Botswana: Still the Exception?

By most accounts Botswana is a remarkable exception in southern Africa, indeed in Africa as a whole. Of little interest to European settlers, Botswana experienced a relatively mild colonization by the British, one that relied more heavily than most on indigenous leaders and long-standing political practices. The territory experienced a peaceful transfer of power from British to indigenous rule in 1966, avoiding any resort to arms to gain its independence, or any hint of civil strife or war afterward. Since that independence in 1966, Botswana has been a stable, multiparty democracy (though clearly a party system in which one party has dominated) with a military that has largely eschewed involvement in the regional conflicts that have entangled neighboring countries over the years or in civilian rule at home. National elections have been held every five years beginning with the first preindependence elections in 1965, and all have been considered free and fair. Though there has been no alternation of power, in terms of a change in ruling party, there have been three successful leadership transitions since independence. While Botswana does not boast a thriving civil society, organizational activity increased considerably in the 1980s and 1990s, and a political opposition has grown (if also faltered), indicating a potentially maturing political culture.

Landlocked, with a harsh arid climate and small population (just over 2 million in 2011), at its independence Botswana was one of the poorest countries in the world. With an estimated per capita gross domestic product (GDP) of US$12,700 (at purchasing power parity) in 2009, the country was already designated a middle-income country in the early 1990s. Indeed, since diamonds and other minerals were discovered in the 1960s and 1970s, Botswana has experienced enviable economic growth rates; its sustained real gross domestic product growth rate, averaging 6.1 percent from 1966 to 1991, was among the highest in the world—matched only by the East Asian newly industrialized countries in the same period. Botswana has not been spared the global economic downturn of the first decade of the twenty-first century, however; indeed, economic growth fell below 5 percent in the middle of that decade and

---

Botswana: Country Data

Land area   566,730 km^2
Capital   Gaborone
Date of independence   September 30, 1966
Population   2,029,307, 60% urban (2008 estimate)
Languages   English 2.1% (official), Setswana 78.2%, Kalanga 7.9%, Sekgala-gadi 2.8%, other 8.6%, unspecified 0.4% (2001 census)
Ethnic groups   Tswana 79%, Kalanga 11%, Basarwa 3%, other (including Kgalagadi and European) 7%
Religions   Christian 71.6%, Badimo 6%, other 1.4%, unspecified 0.4%, none 20.6% (2001 census)
Currency   pula (BWP); pulas per US dollar: 7.4632
Literacy rate   81.2% (male, 80.4.%; female, 81.8%) (2003 estimate)
Life expectancy   60.93 years (male, 61.1 years; female, 60.75 years) (2010 estimate)
Infant mortality   11.79 per 1,000 live births
GDP per capita (PPP)   US$12,700
GDP real growth rate   –5.4%
Leaders since independence
   Seretse Khama, president, September 1966–July 1980
   Quett Masire, president, July 1980–April 1998
   Festus Gontebanye Mogae, president, April 1998–April 2008
   Ian Khama, president, April 2008–present
Major political parties
   Ruling party   Botswana Democratic Party (BDP)
   Other parties   Botswana Alliance Movement (BAM), Botswana Congress Party (BCP), Botswana Movement for Democracy (BMD), Botswana National Front (BNF)
Women in parliament (lower/single house)   7.9% (2009 election)

Sources: Data derived from https://www.cia.gov; http://www.ipu.org/.
Note: Data from 2009 unless otherwise noted.

---

fell sharply again in 2009. While much of the first three decades of growth is attributable to the postindependence exploitation of diamonds, Botswana has also sought to diversify its economy. Among other things, it has carefully cultivated a high-end tourism industry. Many in the country continue to rely upon the long-standing source of wealth accumulation—cattle raising—while many more are subsistence farmers in the rural areas. Although income disparities remain great in the country, ordinary Batswana[1] have benefited from the postindependence economic growth, especially in terms of access to social services and infrastructure.

Indeed, Botswana has been described as the only clear example of a "developmental state" in Africa (Wiseman 1998). And like the developmental states of East Asia, Botswana has been labeled an African "miracle" by some observers (Samatar 1999). More recently, however, Ellen Hillbom (2008) has argued that, in fact, Botswana has experienced economic growth without development, thereby allowing for significant poverty and unequal resource and income distribution to exist alongside considerable wealth. All the same, Botswana is consistently rated the least-corrupt country in Africa by Transparency International and among the best credit risks in Africa by major investment firms. The gains from Botswana's considerable economic growth have been invested in the country's infrastructure and human resource base. Where once there were dirt roads, there are now high-quality tarred roads. Free universal education has been provided for all, and Botswana has one of the highest literacy rates in Africa. Botswana has also experienced one of the fastest rates of urbanization in the world since independence. As of 2007, however, Botswana also had the second highest HIV/AIDS adult prevalence rate of any country in the world (after Swaziland). The emergence of HIV/AIDS in Botswana was a devastating development that threatened to undo the impressive accomplishments of the postindependence period. Fortunately, Botswana has also been a leader in the region in terms of confronting the AIDS crisis.

Challenges to Botswana's future include ongoing tensions emanating from Zimbabwe's continued economic and political instability and a recent political instability of its own stemming from significant factionalism within political parties, in particular the ruling party. Among other things, this factionalism contributes to a proliferation of opposition parties. Additionally, since 2008, power has been ever more centralized in the executive branch of government. Indeed, Kenneth Good and Ian Taylor (2008) ask whether, given these developments and democratization in other countries in the region, Botswana's exceptionality has not become less remarkable (see also Molutsi 2005). Growing poverty, income inequality, and unemployment, especially in the rural areas, also threaten Botswana's future.

With such a distinctive position on the African continent, Botswana has attracted widespread attention from academics and others eager to understand the sources of its apparent success. Explanations for Botswana's accomplishments are varied and focus on a range of factors both structural and agent based, including the colonial practice of "parallel rule" and retention of the *kgotla* and other traditional legal institutions after independence, a relative ethnic homogeneity, remarkable leadership skills on the part of early presidents and a largely (at first) expatriate civil service, the discovery of diamonds after independence, and the wise and judicious use of diamond revenues by a developmental state.

Historical Origins of the Botswana State: Context, Key Actors, and Issues

One of the factors that distinguishes Botswana enormously from other African countries is its relative ethnic homogeneity. Indeed, 80 percent of the population is Tswana, although the Tswana people are further divided into eight important subgroups, often referred to as separate *merafe* or "tribes." These eight subgroups hail from eight Tswana chiefdoms that emerged in the late eighteenth and early nineteenth centuries from a number of smaller groups in what is today eastern Botswana and northern South Africa.[2] Of the eight groups, the Bamangwato are the largest; three other groups—the Bakwena, Bangwaketse, and Bakgatla— once rivaled the Bamangwato, though today each represents a much smaller percentage of the population. The last four groups—the Barolong, Batlokwa, Bamalete, and Batawana—were, and remain, quite small. The remaining 20 percent of Botswana's population consists of Bakalanga, different Basarwa groups, and Europeans.

According to John Holm (1988, 181–183), three factors accounted for the growth of the four larger chiefdoms during the late precolonial period: war, trade, and strong leadership by *dikgosi* or chiefs. In order to withstand attacks by Zulu armies coming from the southeast in the early 1800s, and later incursions by Afrikaner trekkers seeking to escape British rule in the Cape colony, the four groups were forced to become strong militarily.[3] This need to defend against outside attack also promoted development of a more autocratic leadership style within these groups. During the same period the Tswana chiefdoms were a locus for regional trade, "strategically placed to control movements of goods to African peoples north and east of their area" (Holm 1988, 181). These Tswana chiefdoms also became heavily involved with European traders once they moved into the area—granting licenses and otherwise manipulating the transit of goods to their own benefit.

The Tswana chiefs' successes in war and trade, which enabled their expansion during this period, were attributable in part to the fact that the chiefs were already powerful rulers (Holm 1988, 181). These were hereditary rulers who had little need to rely upon "public support" in making their decisions. The chiefs played key roles in local economies, allocating all land within their chiefdoms and controlling or owning all the cattle, the primary form of wealth. Chiefs were also the religious leaders, not only practicing various forms of traditional healing but also supervising others in the community who "worked with the world of the spirits" (Holm 1988, 182). Not surprisingly, chiefs dominated decisionmaking as well. However, in so doing they relied upon a mechanism that exists to this day in Botswana, the *kgotla*, an assembly of all adult males in the community (eventually expanded to include women). The *kgotla*, which was convened when pressing matters needed to be discussed, provided a measure of popular discussion and consultation. Moreover, though chiefs theoretically had the authority to make laws unilaterally, the *kgotla* served as a check on chiefly authority, since its principal goal was to gain approval of the members of the chiefdom for a given course of action (Samatar 1999, 42). There were more direct constraints on the power of a chief as well. For example, "immediate relatives might usurp his authority by deserting to another tribe with followers, refusing to follow orders in a military campaign, assassinating him, or in the last resort, establishing a new chiefdom" (Holm 1988, 182). In addition, the chiefs had to abide by traditional law. This law was largely determined by a group of elder advisers who, under threat of insurrection, expected the chief, like everyone else, to comply with its dictates.

Cattle provided the primary form of wealth accumulation in precolonial Botswana—not surprising in an arid country, a good part of which is taken up by the Kalahari Desert.[4] As such, the potential for agriculture was not a significant draw for European settlers in the colonial period; nor were minerals, which were only discovered after independence. Still, as in other parts of southern Africa, European traders and Christian missionaries arrived in the territory in the early nineteenth century. According to Christiaan Keulder (1998, 98), by 1870 relatively permanent trading and missionary settlements had been established as well as the beginnings of a migrant labor system that would send Batswana men to the new diamond and gold mines in South Africa. Among other things, the early traders and missionaries facilitated the granting of concessions to European companies during this period, so much so that colonialism in Botswana, unlike that in most other parts of Africa, occurred almost entirely through concessions.

Indeed, the colonization of Botswana was fairly unique in Africa in that the indigenous rulers, the Tswana chiefs, invited a European power, the British, to declare a protectorate over their territory, which the British called Bechuanaland (Holm 1988; Keulder 1998). The chiefs did this out of fear of a worse subjugation by the Afrikaners, who continued to make incursions into their territory from the Transvaal, and of rumblings from the Germans in Namibia about linking that territory with German Tanganyika (never mind the Germans' brutal suppression of the indigenous population). Thus in 1880 an informal protectorate relationship was secured between the Tswana chiefs and the British government in Cape Town, and in 1885 this agreement was formalized, and Bechuanaland was made a crown colony of the British (du Toit 1995). The British agreed, in part out of concern to protect road links with its Rhodesian colonies to the north but also to avoid the territory's incorporation into what were then the Boer republics in South Africa. As such, the colonization of Botswana was much less violent than that of Namibia, South Africa, or Zimbabwe.

There were significant consequences of Botswana's route to colonization—first by concession and then by invitation. According to Keulder:

First, fewer Europeans settled in the Bechuanaland Protectorate than in South Africa, Namibia or Zimbabwe. This meant that less pressure was placed on the colonial government to protect European interests at the cost of indigenous ones, and that racism was not so institutionalized as in the other colonies mentioned. Second, the colonial government could leave much of the day-to-day administration to the traditional leaders. Traditional power configurations were less distorted, and the leaders retained much of their legitimacy as they were allowed far more freedom to perform their functions to the benefit of their subjects. Traditional leaders thus remained prominent during the colonial period (even though their powers were substantially reduced). (1998, 99)

Thus colonial rule in Botswana has been described as "so mild that even the term 'indirect rule' [used elsewhere in Africa by the British] would be an exaggeration" (Holm 1988, 183). Most historians refer instead to a system of "parallel rule" that emerged in the colony, whereby "the colonial government regulated the affairs of the European population while the tribal authorities managed tribal affairs with very little interference" (Keulder 1998, 100). Magistrates acted as a link between the colonial authorities and the traditional leaders. By and large, the chiefs continued to rule with only a few constraints: "They could no longer make war; they were supposed to collect a small hut tax to support the colonial administration; and they had to curb certain practices that offended British sensibilities, like slavery and polygamy" (Holm 1988, 183). British administrative headquarters, meanwhile, were not even set up in the Bechuanaland protectorate, but rather across the border in Mafikeng in South Africa.

Nonetheless, for much of the colonial period, the Bechuanaland protectorate faced an uncertain future. For some time after the formation of the Union of South Africa in 1910, South Africa sought to incorporate Botswana, an effort it only abandoned when South Africa became a republic and left the Commonwealth in 1961. During much of the same period until the 1950s, Southern Rhodesia (Zimbabwe) also sought to incorporate Bechuanaland into its territory (du Toit 1995, 23). This uncertainty provides a "partial explanation (as well as an excuse) for the lack of a British commitment to the educational, social and physical infrastructure development of the territory" (Picard 1985, 11).

Meanwhile, events in neighboring South Africa prompted the emergence of a nationalist movement in Botswana, although much later than in other parts of Africa.[5] Following the Sharpeville massacre and the banning of the African National Congress (ANC) and the Pan-Africanist Congress (PAC) in 1960, an estimated 1,400 South Africans fled into Bechuanaland over a four-year period. As Holm (1988, 185) argues, this "infusion of the politically aware" South Africans led directly to the founding of the first nationalist party in Botswana, the urban-based Botswana People's Party (BPP). Indeed, so great was the South African connection that five of the party's twenty-two branches in 1961 were located in Johannesburg (serving Batswana migrant workers there). While the BPP did not last for long, its attacks on colonial rule sent a clear message to colonial authorities that independence would soon have to be granted. Eventually this group split into two and the Bechuanaland [Botswana] Democratic Party (BDP) emerged to carry the nationalist torch more successfully (Nengwekhulu 1979; Ramsay 1993).

The BDP was organized by a number of activists—Seretse Khama, Quett Masire, and others—based in the rural areas. Seretse Khama embodied the powerful social groups that came to form the support base for the BDP, while Masire's origins among a family of farmers and teachers were more ordinary (Parsons, Henderson, and Tlou 1995; Masire 2006). Khama was the first-born son of a Bamangwato chief and should have become Bamangwato chief himself when he returned home from his university studies in the United Kingdom (UK) in the late 1940s. He was prevented from doing so, however, by pressure from the Nationalist Party government in South Africa, which was greatly displeased by his example of racial mixing—he had married a white woman while in Britain and was returning with her to Botswana (Williams 2007).[6] The Bamangwato people were outraged that they were being denied their rightful chief and quickly rallied around Khama's nascent organization, the BDP. Indeed, it has been suggested that in not becoming Bamangwato chief, Khama was ultimately able to broaden his appeal as a truly national leader and to avoid the encumbrances of the day-to-day duties of chieftaincy (Wiseman 1998). Upon his return from the UK, Khama had also taken up cattle ranching—the only major productive sector of the Botswana economy before independence. In so doing, Khama carefully cultivated relations with commercial farmers in the country—both black and white—and was able to ensure a reliable financial base for his party. To the colonial authorities, meanwhile, the BDP was a much more attractive group than the more radical BPP. In 1961 Khama was named as one of two Africans to serve on the territory's executive council, thereby gaining valuable administrative experience (Fawcus and Tilbury 2000). Thus, within a relatively short period of time, Khama secured the support of four influential groups who helped propel the BDP into power: traditional authorities, the educated elite, cattle ranchers, and the colonial civil service (Holm 1988). When the first elections were held in Botswana in March 1965, the BDP won 80 percent of the vote. On September 30, 1966, Botswana gained its independence, and Seretse Khama became the new country's first president.

Organization of the State

Constitution

Botswana is described in its constitution as a unitary state and a parliamentary republic. The constitution provides for an executive presidency in which the president is both head of state and head of government. The constitution also provides for a unicameral legislature: a national assembly based on the Westminster parliamentary system. The National Assembly consists of 57 elected members (increased, with each new population census, from 31 in the first election), the president, the speaker, the attorney general, and 4 members appointed by the president. The constitution further provides for a 15-member (nonelected) House of Chiefs, which advises government on traditional and customary issues; that body was expanded to 35 members in 2005 and renamed with its Setswana name, Ntlo ya Dikgosi. Finally, the constitution provides for an independent judiciary that is able to enforce the code of human rights contained in the constitution and may also interpret the constitution (du Toit 1995; Lekorwe et al. 2001; Morton, Ramsay, and Mgadla 2008).

According to the US Department of State (2010b), the government of Botswana has generally abided by its 1966 constitution, respecting the human rights and freedoms of its citizens. However, there have been some infractions. During 2009, for example, there were reports of abuses by security forces, poor prison conditions, lengthy delays in the judicial process, restrictions on press freedom, and restrictions on the right to strike. The government has been accused of human rights abuse with respect to the already marginalized Basarwa (or San) people once living in the Central Kalahari Game Reserve (CKGR). The Botswana government's continued narrow interpretation of a 2006 High Court ruling means the majority of San originally relocated from the CKGR have not been able to return to or hunt in the CKGR, thereby putting the lives and livelihoods of Botswana's original inhabitants in danger.

In still abiding by its 1966 constitution, Botswana is unlike all of the other countries discussed in this book that have experienced political transitions in the 1990s and early twenty-first century (minus Zimbabwe) and in so doing have adopted new constitutions. In late 2010 in Gaborone, opposition Botswana Congress Party (BCP) MP Dumelang Saleshando raised the idea of undertaking a constitutional reform process in Botswana. Among other issues, Saleshando cited the need to revisit the use of a plurality electoral system and its negative impact on women's representation in parliament (not to mention the way in which it also leads to the overrepresentation of the ruling party in parliament) (Saleshando 2010). In a recent comparison of gender provisions in the constitutions of Botswana and South Africa, Druscilla Scribner and Priscilla Lambert (2010) show that equality rights in Botswana's constitution are minimal to nonexistent, thereby limiting the ability to pursue policies that advance women's (and other groups') equality.

Executive

The president of Botswana is not popularly elected by the people; rather, in advance of parliamentary elections, each political party nominates a candidate for president, and the candidate of the party with the majority in the National Assembly becomes president following the election. The president, moreover, selects the vice president, and the pattern to date has been for the vice president to succeed his president, making for an automatic succession to the presidency. Moreover, in 1998 presidential terms of office were limited to two five-year terms, and since that time the president has ascended to office in advance of parliamentary elections (Lekorwe 2005; Maundeni 2005; Molomo 2005).

The president heads the cabinet, which is appointed from among members of the National Assembly. The president is required only to consult with the cabinet, which acts in an advisory capacity to him or her (Barei 2008; Maundeni 2008). In a cabinet reshuffle in September 2002, the number of cabinet members was increased from sixteen to twenty, the largest number in Botswana's history. As in Namibia then, the cabinet completely dominates the country's National Assembly and effectively blunts any trend toward parliamentary autonomy.

By late 2010 there had been four presidents of Botswana, all members of the BDP. Seretse Khama, who led the country to independence, was the first and was reelected as president in 1969, 1974, and 1979 before dying in office in 1980. He was succeeded by his vice president and BDP cofounder Quett Masire, who was reelected in 1984, 1989, and 1994 before retiring from the presidency in 1998. Masire was succeeded by his vice president, Festus Mogae, who was then reelected by parliament in 1999 and 2004. President Mogae chose Ian Khama, the son of Seretse Khama and previously head of the armed forces, as his vice president. Ian Khama became Botswana's fourth president in early 2008 when Mogae finished two terms in office; he was indirectly elected president in the late 2009 parliamentary elections. Some observers, such as Good (2010, 315), describe an "escalation in the militarization and personalization of power" in Botswana since Ian Khama, with his military background and predisposition, came to power in early 2008.

Botswana has avoided the kind of divisive constitutional maneuvers orchestrated by some regional presidents and their parties to extend presidential terms; indeed, a two-term limit was one of a few electoral reforms adopted as recently as 1998. Still, there are many in academia, the media, and politics who would like to see the president directly elected by the people. Thus, while Botswana has an established tradition of executive turnover marked by a smooth transfer of power between presidents, the mechanism is not without its critics.

Judiciary

As in other countries in the region, Botswana retained a dual legal system at independence in which customary law, albeit in a clearly subordinate position, was institutionalized alongside a judicial system based on Roman Dutch law. The dual legal system consists of modern courts, which apply Roman Dutch common and statutory law in the country, and customary courts. The modern courts are composed of magistrate courts at the lowest level, an industrial court, a court of appeal, and the High Court. Alongside these, more than 200 customary courts deal with the civil and penal laws of the country. These customary or traditional courts are presided over by local chiefs and their representatives and headmen (du Toit 1995, 28–29). There are four categories of customary courts, with the category determining the powers of the court (for example, whether they may engage in reconciliation only or may impose punitive rulings).

As in most of southern Africa, most people in Botswana first encounter the legal system through the traditional or customary courts. Most civil cases are tried in customary courts, under the authority of a traditional leader. These courts handle matters such as land, marital, and property disputes. In such courts, defendants have no legal counsel, and there are no precise rules of evidence. However, rulings may be appealed through the civil court system. Perhaps not surprisingly, the quality of decisions reached within the traditional courts tends to vary considerably; among other things, customary courts do not afford the same due process as the other courts (US Department of State 2010b). At the same time, as Pierre du Toit (1995, 59–60) argues, Botswana's dual legal system is a source of strength to the Botswana state: "By protecting the customary courts of the *lekgotla* assemblies after independence, the state effectively merged the established rules of social control with those of the modern constitutional system. This merging has had the effect of making traditional, established, indigenous survival strategies largely compatible and congruent with those prescribed by the modern legal state."

More recently, according to Onkemetse Tshosa (2008, 48), a norm since independence—the independence of the judiciary—has suffered "serious setbacks." One indicator of this, according to Tshosa, has been several resignations by High Court judges in the face of pressure from the executive. The independence of the judiciary is further compromised, according to Tshosa, by the fact that the chief justice and the president of the Court of Appeal are appointed solely by the president. Moreover, there are no clear-cut recruitment procedures for members of the judiciary as a whole.

Military

As Mpho Molomo (2001) notes, Botswana's security and defense situation is determined in large part by its location—it shares long borders with Namibia, South Africa, and Zimbabwe and just touches upon Zambia. In the past, Botswana suffered the spillover effects of armed liberation struggles in neighboring countries and of South African–sponsored regional destabilization. During the early 1970s, for example, Botswana experienced frequent incursions by Rhodesian security forces, allegedly in pursuit of Zimbabwean liberation fighters. These forces "wreaked havoc in Botswana by carrying out acts of kidnapping, abduction, arson, and murder of innocent civilians" (Molomo

2001). Indeed the entire Botswana-Zimbabwe border became a war zone from which residents were forced to flee, leaving behind homes and fields.

Botswana experienced similar destabilization from South Africa during the same period. Following the Soweto uprising in 1976, many South African youth sought political asylum in Botswana, prompting still more raids by the South African Defense Force (SADF). South Africa's "total strategy," deployed from 1977 onward, had clear regional implications. Among them were the repeated incursions by the SADF into Botswana throughout the remainder of the 1970s and into the 1980s, allegedly in pursuit of ANC combatants. In that period Botswana was defended only by the Police Mobile Unit (PMU), a group of paramilitary police responsible for internal security. With the PMU overwhelmed by the task and calls for greater defense by the opposition, the government established the Botswana Defense Force (BDF) in 1977 (Molomo 2001). Despite this, raids and incursions continued from across both borders until those respective internal conflicts were settled. Interestingly, Scott Beaulier and Robert Subrick (2006) suggest that Botswana's lack of a military until 1977 is one reason that it avoided what they term the "African Growth Tragedy." By not expending resources on the military in the first decade of independence, the government was able to accumulate resources and deploy them in other critical sectors; in addition, without a military in the early years, the government avoided a common opportunity for corruption.

Since 1986 the military budget in Botswana has increased steadily and, according to Thomas Ohlson and Stephen John Stedman (1994, 220), "the military has tried to exempt itself from the bureaucratic openness that characterizes other sectors of the state." This was particularly evident in the early 1990s, when the Botswana military refused to discuss plans to build an extensive air base in the country, reportedly also to be used by the US Air Force. Those plans were later abandoned, but the military buildup has continued, despite the relative peace and stability that have been achieved in southern Africa. By 2006 there were nearly 15,000 troops in the BDF; most of them were in the army, with far fewer in an air force and a police mobile unit (still well below the size of other militaries in the region).

The BDF is known for a high level of professionalism among its members and "has attracted a rich pool of talent," according to Fred Morton, Jeff Ramsay, and Themba Mgadla (2008, 54). External security—patrolling Botswana's borders—remains its primary mission, although it devotes considerable time and resources to antipoaching efforts, monitoring urban crime, controlling livestock and animal disease, and participating in peacekeeping missions across Africa. In 2007 about 7 percent of the national budget was allocated to the military, still far less than the 25 percent allocated to education and 12 percent allocated to health (Morton, Ramsay, and Mgadla 2008).

By the early twenty-first century, some observers expressed concern that "if you build up a large military without a purpose, it becomes a threat to the country" (Molomo 2001). Indeed, there has been strong reaction to the buildup of the BDF inside and outside the country, with some charging that expanding Botswana's military could be a government response to the growth of a more significant internal political opposition. Objections to the expansion of the military have also come from Botswana's neighbors, in particular Namibia, with which Botswana has experienced some conflict over border issues and the repatriation of refugees. At the same time, the military remains firmly under civilian control in Botswana, reporting to the minister of presidential affairs and public administration, and accountable to parliament on budget matters.

There was a general consternation of a slightly different nature when, in the very month that Ian Khama succeeded Festus Mogae as president—April 2008—Khama created a Directorate of Intelligence and Security (DIS) in the office of the president. Among other things, the DIS is able to enter premises and make arrests without a warrant if the DIS suspects that a person has committed or is about to commit a crime. Civil society organizations have lamented the formation of the DIS, arguing that it is not subject to sufficient oversight and poses a threat to citizens' civil liberties (US Department of State 2010b). Just a year after its formation, one opposition politician likened the DIS to a terror squad of the type common in other African countries (Piet 2009). Within two years, the DIS was considered "an instrument of political suppression and impediment to civil liberties," taking orders from individuals rather than following the strictures of the parliamentary act that created it (Motshipi 2010). Good (2010, 315) refers to a "militarization of the Botswana 'miracle'" since Lieutenant-General Khama ascended to power.

The Bureaucracy

At independence in 1966 Botswana was woefully unprepared for the challenges that lay ahead. As a colony, Bechuanaland, along with the other two High Commission territories of Swaziland and Basotholand, had been drawn into the economic ambit of South Africa, utilizing the South African currency, belonging to a single customs union, and sharing road, rail, and communications networks. The benefits from this arrangement accrued to South Africa but worked to the disadvantage of the other three, since industry and investment were most attracted to South Africa as the most developed of the areas. Investment in social and economic infrastructure was meager during the colonial period in Bechuanaland, with the combined result that at independence "Botswana showed a distinctive profile of underdevelopment" (du Toit 1995, 26–27). In a huge country, only 25 kilometers (15.5 miles) of road were tarred, only one government secondary school existed (opened in 1965), and only a handful of Batswana had attended university. Moreover, most of the retail trade in the territory was controlled by foreigners, and most of the population survived as subsistence cattle farmers, with a significant minority of men traveling to the mines of South Africa as migrant laborers. The capital city of Gaborone was under construction as independence loomed.

Not surprisingly, Botswana was also bequeathed an underdeveloped public bureaucracy at independence. That bureaucracy was rapidly transformed in the years after independence, however, and many observers credit the bureaucracy with helping to achieve Botswana's multiple postindependence gains (Samatar 1999). One characteristic of this transformation was the rapid expansion of the central government service in the years after independence, leading to a significantly increased public sector employment. Moreover, a striking feature of this institutional expansion, according to du Toit (1995, 33), was "the extent to which the colonial pattern of expatriates holding crucial public service positions endured." Thus, rather than proceed with a rapid indigenization of the public service, Botswana opted for a gradual replacement of expatriates.[7] (At the same time, training of Batswana in significant numbers at home and abroad to join the bureaucracy was an integral part of this strategy and may have helped diffuse any pressures for more rapid, politically driven Africanization [Samatar 1999, 95].) Du Toit (1995, 35) argues that "this expatriate sector of the public work force contributed a vital ingredient to the quality of the statehood that evolved in post-independence Botswana"—adding not only to the strength of the state but also to its autonomy. That autonomous bureaucracy, according to du Toit (1995, 47),

> in coalition with the BDP, has succeeded, through its technocratic priorities of growth and stability (at the expense of participation and equity), in establishing a solvent state that can deliver public goods (roads, schools, watering facilities, clinics, etc.) on a nontribal, nonregional basis. . . . Consequently the state is seen as neutral, not as an ethnic body, and the legitimacy of the state, the regime, the constitution, and the parliamentary system is enhanced.

Indeed, this is one of the explanations often put forward for Botswana's political and economic successes since independence—that Botswana is one of the few African states with the characteristics of a developmental state (Tsie 1996, 601; Osei Hwedie 2001b). According to Balefi Tsie (1996, 601), "since independence Botswana's bureaucratic and political elites have pursued a series of policies calculated to promote economic growth and development. In the process, both elites acquired a developmental orientation. The bureaucratic elite in Botswana is powerful and generally effective in formulating and executing development policy." The epicenter of the development process is the Ministry of Finance and Development Planning, which Abdi Ismail Samatar (1999, 96) likens to the Japanese Ministry of Trade and Industry, the centralized, meritorious, and autonomous agency that oversaw Japanese industrial development. As evidenced by the ministry's bureaucratic capacity, "much of the development in Botswana has been state-sponsored and directed. It is in this sense," according to Tsie (1996, 601), "that one can speak of a developmental state in Botswana." It is important to note the degree of Botswana's exceptionalism in this regard. Whereas Botswana's strong, centralized state has been instrumental in its ability to transform the economy, its counterparts in the region have experienced enormous pressure from the international financial institutions for more than a decade to decentralize their states (Samatar 1999, 96).

Representation and Participation

Legislature

There are only two tiers of government in Botswana—national and local. At the national level, a mostly elected National Assembly exists alongside a mostly indirectly elected House of Chiefs (that only has advisory powers). In the National Assembly, members of parliament are elected to five-year terms on the basis of a first-past-the-post or winner-take-all electoral system. Mogopodi Lekorwe and colleagues (2001, 2) note that the first-past-the-post electoral system in Botswana has produced a dominant-party political system in which the ruling Botswana Democratic Party has won each and every election by a landslide victory (at least in terms of seats in parliament). So, for example, with 65 percent of the vote in the 1989 election, the BDP won 31 of 34 seats in the National Assembly (91 percent); in 1999, with only 54 percent of the popular vote, the BDP won 33 of 40 seats (82 percent); and in 2009, with only 54 percent of the vote, the BDP won 45 of 57 seats (79 percent) (see Tables 4.1 and 4.2). The ruling party's numbers in the National Assembly are further enhanced by the postelection appointment of four "specially" elected members of parliament. According to the constitution, individuals are nominated by the president and elected by the National Assembly to these seats, though they are commonly perceived to be appointed by the president. In essence, these four additional MPs, who have always been drawn from the ruling party, help to cement the president's and the ruling party's control over the National Assembly. According to John Holm and Staffan Darnolf (2000, 127–128), these MPs owe a special loyalty to the president for their appointment and, with a few exceptions, have been among the most articulate in pushing the president's positions within the National Assembly. More recently, women's organizations have demanded that the president nominate women to all four of the specially elected seats in the National Assembly, though this demand has not been met.

Indeed, despite its long-standing multiparty political system, political stability, and high socioeconomic indicators for women (compared to many of

Table 4.1   Number of Seats Directly Elected in Parliament, 1965–2009

Party	1965	1969	1974	1979	1984	1989	1994	1999	2004	2009[a]
BDP	28	24	27	29	28	31	27	33	44	45
BNF	b	3	2	2	5	3	13	6	12	6
BPP	3	3	2	1	1	0	0	b	0	0
BIP/IFP	0	1	1	0	0	0	0	b	b	b
BCP	b	b	b	b	b	b	b	1	1	4
BAM	b	b	b	b	b	b	b	0	0	1
MELS	b	b	b	b	b	b	0	0	0	0
Total seats	31	31	32	32	34	34	40	40	57	57

Source: http://www.eisa.org.za/WEP/bot2009presults.htm.
Notes: a. In 2009 one independent member of parliament was elected, so 56 of the 57 total seats were party seats.

b. Ran no candidates or party did not exist.

BDP = Botswana Democratic Party; BNF = Botswana National Front; BPP = Botswana People's Party; BIP/IFP = Botswana Independence Party/Independence Freedom Party; BCP = Botswana Congress Party; BAM = Botswana Alliance Movement; MELS = Marx, Engels, Lenin, and Stalin Movement of Botswana.

Table 4.2   Party Support, 1965–2009 (percentage of popular vote)

Party[a]	1965	1969	1674	1979	1984	1989	1994	1999	2004	2009
BDP	80	68	77	75	68	65	55	54	51	54
BNF	b	14	12	13	20	27	37	25	25	22
BPP	14	12	6	8	7	4	4	b	2	2
BIP/IFP	5	6	4	4	3	2	4	b	b	b
BCP	b	b	b	b	b	b	b	11	16	19
BAM	b	b	b	b	b	b	b	5	3	2
MELS	1	0	1	0	2	2	0	0	1	1
Rejected	b	b	b	b	b	b	b	5	2	b
Total	100	100	100	100	100	100	100	100	100	100

Source: http://www.eisa.org.za/WEP/bot2009presults.htm.
Notes: a. See Table 4.1 notes for full forms of acronyms.

b. Ran no candidates, party did not exist, or data not collected (rejected).

the other countries in the region), Botswana had the lowest representation of women in its national legislature in southern Africa—barely 8 percent following the late 2009 election (Gender Links 2010b). For a time, women's representation was on the increase, reaching 17 percent with the 1999 election, but it has fallen steadily since. This may be attributed to a number of factors, including the lack of a political transition leading to the adoption of electoral gender quotas for parliamentary elections; the "usual barriers" to women's political participation, especially to standing for office in the context of a first-past-the-post electoral system; limited commitment from the main political parties to women's increased political representation; diminished women's movement mobilization in the first decade of the twenty-first century; and an unsupportive executive (Bauer 2010).

In general, executive influence over the legislature runs deep in Botswana, as it does throughout southern Africa. Candidates for National

Assembly elections are nominated by their parties. They must pledge themselves to the party's presidential candidate in advance of the election. Further, in appointing cabinet members, the president is not required to consult with parliament. At the same time, it is suggested that most MPs would like to become cabinet ministers and therefore seek to remain in the president's good graces (Holm and Darnolf 2000, 127). Moreover, just as in Namibia, the small size of the national legislature ensures that more than a majority of MPs from the ruling party are either ministers or deputy ministers. Thus, once the president has attained cabinet approval for a policy, he or she can be confident that cabinet members will be able to determine the ruling-party vote in parliament on the matter (Holm and Darnolf 2000, 127).

A formal role has been established for chiefs at the national level, in the form of participation in a house of chiefs. As noted, the House of Chiefs was expanded from 15 to 35 members in 2005 and renamed Ntlo ya Dikgosi. The 35 members consist of 8 hereditary chiefs from the eight major Tswana groups (the paramount chiefs), 22 indirectly elected chiefs from other groups and areas, and 5 chiefs specially elected or appointed by the president. The 8 paramount chiefs are members of the House of Chiefs for life, while the other 27 elected and selected chiefs serve five-year terms. The first election to the expanded House of Chiefs was held in 2006. Early in the twenty-first century royal women in Botswana began asserting their right to accede to the chieftaincy of their respective groups. While women in Botswana had frequently served as regents in the past, they had never served as chiefs (Matemba 2005). By 2010 four members of the House of Chiefs were women.

The House of Chiefs has no capacity to make laws; indeed it has only an advisory function, in particular on any matters related to provisions of the constitution and powers of chiefs, subchiefs or headmen, customary courts, customary law, or tribal organization or property. Initially, according to Keulder (1998, 109), even that advisory function was limited because of the lack of participation of House of Chief members "and the fact that only five were literate enough to read and comment on the bills that were forwarded to them." Subsequently, it was required that members of the House of Chiefs be proficient in English; in any event this is not an issue in contemporary Botswana.

In establishing a formal role for traditional leaders at the national level, the government of Botswana accrued certain benefits, according to Keulder (1998, 109). First, the government secured expert advice on traditional institutions and life in the rural areas. Second, an acceptable channel was established through which grievances could be articulated and channeled. Third, by providing a formal means for chiefs to participate in government, the government avoided severing an important link with the rural areas. Fourth, it was expected that the chiefs could be relied upon to assist in the modernization of the rural areas.

Finally, at the local level in 2010, Botswana was divided into ten rural districts and six urban districts. Local government institutions include district (rural) councils and town (urban) councils that are elected every five years, at the same time that members of the National Assembly are elected and using the same electoral system. Other institutions of local government include land boards that are responsible for the allocation and administration of land under the jurisdiction of district councils, district administration that is "a high profile agency representing the central government in a local authority area," and tribal administration, the oldest local government institution that today has jurisdiction primarily over the administration of justice through customary law and practice (Mogotsi 1995, 55). The most significant contribution of the tribal administration is the provision of the *kgotla*. Indeed, a *kgotla* is used by all of the local-level institutions. The main functions of the district councils include primary education, collection of local taxes and licensing fees, control of the brewing and sale of traditional beer, sanitary services and water supplies, construction and maintenance of local public roads, and supervision of local markets (Keulder 1998, 115).

Holm (1988, 187) considers the local council system in Botswana to be the "centerpiece" of its democracy. The local councils act as intermediaries between the central government and local communities, though Adam Mfundisi (2008, 63) suggests more recently that local government structures have been "constantly altered and demeaned" by national political leaders and senior civil servants. Still, Holm argues that local councils have democratized local government—essentially replacing hereditary leaders with elected representatives. Indeed, the councils and other institutions, such as the land boards, have assumed many of the powers formerly held by chiefs and other traditional authorities. In the early twenty-first century, Botswana was one of several countries found in Afrobarometer research to be practicing a form of hybrid democracy at the local level in which people viewed their selected chiefs and elected councilors in a similar favorable light and of a piece of the same local government system (cited in Logan 2009).

Party System and Elections

As noted, Botswana has a multiparty political system, but one in which one party, the BDP, has dominated thoroughly. Indeed, the BDP has won every national election since 1965, although the percentage of the popular vote won by the BDP has dropped in recent elections (to 54 percent in 2009), suggesting an increasingly competitive political arena. With the exception of concern over one ballot box in one election (1984), elections in Botswana have been considered free and fair. Three changes affecting elections followed from a national referendum in 1997; these were lowering the voting age from 21 to

18, creating an Independent Electoral Commission, and providing for the use of an absentee ballot.

Up to and including the 1994 election, the BDP was challenged at each election by three parties—the Botswana National Front (BNF), the Botswana People's Party (BPP), and the Botswana Independence Party (BIP). In 1999 the challenge came from two other parties, the Botswana Congress Party (created from a split with the BNF) and the Botswana Alliance Movement (BAM), as well as the BNF. In mid-2004 the BNF, BAM, and BPP formed an alliance—known as the Election Pact—to oppose the BDP in the late 2004 election. In 2009 the primary contenders were again the BDP, BNF, and an alliance of the BCP and BAM.

In the mid- to late 1990s it appeared as if Botswana might be moving away from a dominant-party system (Wiseman 1998; Holm and Darnolf 2000). During the 1994 National Assembly election, for example, the BDP received its first serious threat from another political party, when the BNF won 13 seats in an expanded parliament, far more seats than it or any opposition party had won before (see Table 4.1). According to John Wiseman (1998), the BNF had been increasingly successful at the local level for even longer, beginning with the 1984 election, in which it gained control over the Gaborone town council. In 1989 and 1994 the BNF won control over several more town councils, including Selebi-Phikwe, and its first district (rural) council. In several other town and district councils the BNF became a serious contender for power, even though it did not win the election.

In the late 1990s Wiseman (1998) identified a number of reasons for the apparent drop in support for the BDP. Founded in 1961, the BDP was the party that had led the country peacefully to independence. More important, however, was Seretse Khama's leadership of the BDP. Wiseman describes Khama as the BDP's "most politically valuable asset." Once Khama was elected president, his personal prestige "virtually guaranteed" the BDP's repeated election victories up until his premature death in office in 1980. Further, according to Wiseman (1998, 248–249), because of the groundwork laid by Khama, the political succession by his vice president Quett Masire "passed off remarkably smoothly and without acrimony." Under Masire, and his successors, Festus Mogae and Ian Khama, however, the BDP has been less ably led and has been increasingly riven by factionalism and disunity.

In addition to its association with Seretse Khama and its status as the party of independence, the BDP derived considerable electoral benefit from having presided over the dramatic growth and development of the country's economy (Wiseman 1998, 249–250). For decades, the BDP steadfastly warned that the election of opposition parties would jeopardize Botswana's economic successes. At the same time, with the knowledge that mineral resources are finite, and some indication that the country's boom years might be coming to an end by the early 1990s, the BDP's ability to benefit from the country's economic successes was waning. In addition, during the early 1990s the BDP's reputation for financial efficiency and rectitude was undermined by successive scandals involving the sale of land and provision of houses in and around Gaborone and by problems at the National Development Bank. These corruption scandals surely contributed to the BDP's poor showing in the 1994 election.

Paradoxically, these very issues may have resulted, in part, from Botswana's growth and development under the BDP. For example, rapid urbanization and economic growth greatly enhanced the value of urban land and demand for housing, thereby creating preconditions in which corruption could occur. Further, the government's massive road-building program also had the effect of "democratizing" travel, thereby eroding advantages the BDP may have enjoyed as the party in power in reaching the rural areas. Moreover, the massive improvements in education and literacy have also meant a better informed and more discriminating electorate able to take advantage of national political reports to be found in an increasingly independent press (Wiseman 1998).

By the same token, while the BNF had been weakened by disunity and leadership problems until the mid-1980s, by the mid-1990s these were decidedly less pronounced. Moreover, the BNF increasingly sought support from among non-Tswana groups in the country. At the same time, the primary support base for the BNF in the 1990s was to be found in the urban areas, in particular the urban working class and unemployed, both of which were growing, as were the urban areas generally.

In the aftermath of the 1994 election, according to Lekorwe and colleagues (2001), the BDP sought outside assistance in developing a strategy for the future. Among other things, it was recommended that the party should honorably retire some of its older leaders and at the same time should bring into the party a dynamic new leader who was "untainted" by factional fights. It was in this context that Seretse Khama's eldest son, Ian, was made Festus Mogae's vice president when Mogae assumed the presidency in 1998. By the time of the 1999 election, however, the BNF had imploded, as a result of a leadership struggle within the party; a new party, the Botswana Congress Party, formed from one faction of the BNF. In the 1999 election the BNF won only six seats, less than half the number it had won in 1994. For the 2004 election the BNF was back up to 12 MPs, but the overall number of directly elected MPs had been expanded from 40 to 57, meaning that the BNF's representation was about the same as in 1999. By the time of the 2009 election the BNF, still riven by intense factional battles, managed to win only 6 seats in parliament, hardly more than the BCP and BAM alliance, which won 5 seats. The story by the time of the 2009 election, meanwhile, was one of intense factional battles within the ruling BDP. While the BDP held its own during the 2009 election, it suffered a split in the aftermath of the election when, in 2010, one faction broke away to form a new political party, the Botswana Movement for Democracy.

Civil Society

The general consensus around civil society in Botswana is that it has been "historically absent" in the country, only showing some signs of life from the early 1990s onward (Good 1996; Tsie 1996; Holm and Darnolf 2000; Lekorwe et al. 2001). Holm and Darnolf (2000, 129–130) write that a few interest groups did emerge during the colonial period, primarily among the educated class that, as all over colonial Africa, found itself marginalized by colonialism. These included groups such as the Botswana Teachers Union, the Botswana Civil Servants Association, the Red Cross, the Botswana Council of Women, and the Young Women's Christian Association. By and large those early groups were primarily interested in apolitical welfare issues, rather than playing a more active advocacy role (Wass 2004; Mokomane 2008, 158).

Since independence, according to Holm and Darnolf (2000), the government has in some respects monitored the growth of civil society, mandating that organizations register with the government, but only after meeting certain requirements. Other challenges to civil society organizations in Botswana mirror those of other countries in southern Africa: they lack sufficient funding (especially once Botswana was declared a middle-income country), stable staffs, and large memberships. In trying to affect government policy, moreover, organizations often find themselves co-opted (by access to resources, employment opportunities, and so on) by the very ministries they are seeking to influence. In Holm and Darnolf's view (2000, 133), "civil society exists as an extension of the bureaucracy rather than as a set of independent actors confronting politicians and civil servants."

Although civic organizations in Botswana tend to lack the vibrancy and visibility of their counterparts elsewhere in the region, Holm and Darnolf's assessment may be overstated, at least in the case of the women's movement for a period of about two decades. Indeed, from about the mid-1980s until the early twenty-first century, women's organizations were at the forefront of civil society activism in Botswana. As Agnes Ngoma Leslie (2006) describes, a significant women's rights movement emerged in Botswana in the late 1980s and early 1990s, initially as a result of an intensive mobilization around a single initiative, namely the challenge to Botswana's citizenship law otherwise known as the Unity Dow case. Whereas at independence citizenship in Botswana had been determined by birth, this was changed in the early 1980s to birth by descent, and for married women the citizenship of the father only determined the citizenship of a child. Within a few years of the new law's passage a women's rights organization, Emang Basadi, emerged to challenge it. Though it took ten years, the challenge was eventually victorious.

The 1980s and 1990s were a period of heightened women's mobilization in Botswana. In its early days, consistent with its origins around the Unity Dow case, Emang Basadi focused on legal reform and led a legal awareness campaign. It held workshops, seminars, and conferences in an effort to mobilize women, to make them aware of discriminatory laws, and to advocate for reform of these laws (in which they were successful). It carefully cultivated the collaboration of other new women's organizations, such as the Metlhaetsile Women's Information Center, Ditshwanelo, and the Botswana chapters of Women in Law in Southern Africa and Women in Law and Development in Africa, seeking to create a women's movement in the country (Leslie 2006). With the establishment in 1993 of a political education project, Emang Basadi shifted its agenda from a mainly law reform and legal education strategy to a political education and political empowerment program (Selolwane 2000). The shift was brought about by women's continued marginalization in politics and society, a reluctance on the part of authorities to respond to women's needs, and government passiveness and inaction (indeed intransigence) on the Unity Dow case—not finally resolved until 1995 (Emang Basadi 1999; Selolwane 2000). Among other things, Emang Basadi issued electoral manifestos in 1994 and 1999 in the hopes of influencing the manifestos of political parties contesting elections in those two election cycles. Just as importantly, Emang Basadi held multiple workshops to train women candidates in an effort to elect more women to parliament and local councils. Indeed, the 1999 and 2004 elections were the most successful for women candidates. Good (1996) and Judith Van Allen (2001), among others, suggest that Emang Basadi's work was responsible not only for increasing women's representation in parliament but also for broadening Batswana's understanding of democracy and democratizing (somewhat) elections and politics in the country overall. By 2010, however, there were only traces of the once vibrant women's movement in Botswana (Bauer 2010).

Other types of civil society organizations in Botswana include human rights organizations and indigenous rights organizations, with some overlap among them. Ditshwanelo, the Botswana Center for Human Rights, was formed in 1993 and has focused, among other things, on the government's failure to ratify a number of international conventions and protocols—for example, on the rights of children or women—or its failure to adhere to the provisions of those documents already signed. Another concern of human rights activists inside (and outside) Botswana has been the treatment of the Basarwa, or San, people, mentioned earlier. By the 1990s a number of San "self-help" organizations had emerged in Botswana. For example, a group called the First People of the Kalahari works on the dispossession of land among the San. Their plight has worsened since independence, as wealthy cattle farmers have sought more land for themselves or as mineral prospecting has expanded. Much such activity takes place at the local level, with protests lodged at district councils and land boards, with some few San even venturing into elected office at the local level in order to advance their cause (Good 1996, 59–60; Saugestad 2001). At the same time, and much to the dismay of the government of Botswana, concerns of the San, in particular around the CKGR, have attracted the attention and involvement of international organizations such as Survival International.

In many parts of southern Africa, trade unions have been particularly powerful actors in civil society—for example, helping to topple the apartheid regime in South Africa and initiate a democratic transition in Zambia. Though initially powerless in Zimbabwe, in the late 1990s unions in that country emerged to challenge the state as well. In Botswana, by contrast, trade unions have been notoriously weak. Indeed, only in 1977 did the labor movement in Botswana come together to form the Botswana Federation of Trade Unions (Tsie 1996, 606). Balefi Tsie provides a number of reasons for the weakness of organized labor in the country. First, Botswana suffers a low level of industrialization—a vestige of its colonial-era role as a labor reserve for South African mines and a source of beef exports to South Africa. Second, and related, until the 1980s there was only a low level of formal sector wage labor in the economy. Third, what labor movement has existed has always been plagued by poor organization and lack of effective leadership. Fourth, strikes, an important tool of labor organizers, have effectively been prohibited in Botswana; indeed, by the mid-1990s there had never been a legal strike in the country (Tsie 1996, 607).

While civil society in Botswana may be weaker than in other countries in the region, it is not because civil society organizations have not learned from their counterparts elsewhere in southern Africa. Indeed, it is important to note that civil society organizations in Botswana have extensive ties with similar groups in the region. For example, the founders of many of the trade unions in Botswana first learned about labor mobilization as migrant laborers in South Africa and Zimbabwe—and continue to consult with more experienced trade unionists in South Africa today. Similarly, women activists in Botswana have been involved in research and publication projects with other women activists across the region and have exchanged ideas and best practices, including the idea of a women's manifesto, subsequently adopted in Namibia (Holm, Molutsi, and Somolekae 1996, 51). All in all, however, the assessment would have to remain that civil society in Botswana is weak (Sebudubudu and Osei Hwedie 2006, 37).

Fundamentals of the Political Economy

Botswana's economic transformation since independence has been quite stunning. At independence it was considered a very poor developing country that would likely remain dependent upon foreign assistance to finance its national budget and upon beef exports to Britain and South Africa for foreign exchange earnings. Yet by the 1980s it had the highest economic growth rate in the world, averaging about 10 percent per year—and this despite six years of drought that negatively affected the country's cattle industry (Osei Hwedie 2001b). Botswana did not escape the worldwide economic downturn and experienced a dramatic recession in 2009. But with recovery in the mining sector by 2010, real gross domestic product was predicted to grow by 5 percent in 2011 (Lute 2011).

Much of Botswana's economic good fortune rests on the discovery of diamonds in the early 1970s; luckily for Botswana, this was after independence rather than before. By 2003 Botswana was the largest producer of diamonds by value in the world. And since the cost of diamond production in Botswana is low compared to the diamonds' overseas sale value, diamond sales are extremely profitable to the country. Moreover, in 1975 the government successfully negotiated with the De Beers diamond company for a fifty-fifty share ownership in all of the country's diamond mines (Taylor and Mokhawa 2003, 263). Unlike other host governments in Africa that effectively surrender their natural resources to exploitation by multinational corporations, the Botswana government pressed De Beers for a number of conditions on its investment (Samatar 1999, 19–20). The result was that the government retains considerable influence over the national diamond-mining company, known as Debswana, in areas such as wage policies and production levels. By 1981 diamonds had replaced beef as the country's leading foreign exchange earner (Taylor and Mokhawa 2003, 263). With the revenue from the diamond mines, the government was able to invest in other mineral industries as well, including copper and ash.

At the same time, mining is capital- rather than labor-intensive. Therefore, diamond mining has not greatly increased employment, nor has it expanded the formal sector of the economy. "This has had the knock-on effect," according to Ian Taylor and Gladys Mokhawa (2003, 263), "of maintaining high levels of income inequality and poverty." One of the government's strategies for increasing employment has been to try to expand its manufacturing sector, though this has met with limited success. Some of its initiatives in this realm include the establishment of a regional development project that used special incentives to attract foreign industry, in the copper- and nickel-mining town of Selebi-Phikwe, and the location of a Hyundai assembly plant in Gaborone for the manufacture of Hyundais to southern Africa's transport hub, South Africa. Neither of these efforts was successful, in the first instance because of the government's failure to adequately assess the quality of the companies seeking to locate in Selebi-Phikwe and in the second case because of deep hostility on the part of the South African government and trade unions to the competition created by the Hyundai plant in Gaborone (and the government's failure to negotiate directly with the Hyundai corporation, rather than a shaky subsidiary) (Good and Hughes 2002). Indeed, these two failures were a serious blow to Botswana's attempts to attract quality investment and to diversify more significantly its manufacturing sector.

Moreover, Botswana's diamond industry has, somewhat ironically, become embroiled in the worldwide campaign against conflict diamonds. Also called blood diamonds and dirty diamonds, these are diamonds that have been illegally excavated and traded from conflict-ridden places such as Angola, Sierra Leone, Liberia, and Democratic Republic of Congo and then also used to fund (and so exacerbate) the conflicts in those same places (Taylor and Mokhawa 2003, 264). The anti–conflict diamond campaign has sought to "stem the sale of diamonds that originate from areas under the control of forces opposed to elected and internationally recognized governments, or are in any way connected to those groups." The campaign was ultimately successful in that in 2001 the World Diamond Council agreed to the development, implementation, and oversight of a tracking system for the export and import of diamonds in order to prevent conflict diamonds from entering the global market.

Botswana's role in the campaign has in many ways backfired. Botswana has been very concerned that the campaign would not impugn the reputation and product of "clean diamond" countries such as itself and Namibia. Thus, while it has supported international restrictions on conflict diamonds, the Botswana government has worked hard to assert that its own diamonds are clean (Taylor and Mokhawa 2003, 271).[8] But this assertion came under intense scrutiny when Botswana found itself in its own controversy over diamonds. In brief, the government expedited its plan to remove the San people from the Central Kalahari Game Reserve, which was established in 1961 on the ancestral lands of two San groups as a home for them. The reasons given for the removal of the San from the reserve are related to the government's plan to develop the area for tourism—and possibly diamonds (Taylor and Mokhawa 2003, 276). In late 2002, in its effort to relocate the Basarwa, the government went so far as to seal boreholes, which provide water for the Basarwa, and destroy the property of inhabitants of the reserve. One London-based nongovernmental organization, Survival International, led the outcry over the Botswana government's moves against the Basarwa (allegedly in search of diamonds). The government response was, according to Taylor and Mokhawa (2003, 279), "intransigent, illiberal and chauvinistic." Of course Botswana's diamonds are still not conflict diamonds, officially defined, but they have certainly been tarnished by association with the forced removal of the San from the game reserve.

Challenges of the Twenty-First Century

Botswana faces many challenges in the twenty-first century, including the second highest HIV/AIDS adult prevalence rate of any country in the world—close to 24 percent of adult population. There was a time, according to multiple sources, that the nation spent its weekends at funerals, though this had abated noticeably by the first decade of the twenty-first century. This is in part because unlike the situation in some other parts of Africa, the government of Botswana has openly acknowledged HIV/AIDS and is working vigorously to combat it. While he was president, Festus Mogae provided aggressive leadership, "warning his people [and others around the world] in fiery speeches that they are 'threatened with annihilation,' chairing his country's AIDS council and badgering his health officials with questions about condom distribution in prisons and construction timetables for clinics" (Grunwald 2002). Since leaving office, Mogae has campaigned tirelessly across Botswana and Africa to stop the spread of HIV (UNAIDS 2008a). In 2000 Botswana embarked upon a five-year "African Comprehensive HIV/AIDS Partnership" involving the Bill and Melinda Gates Foundation and the pharmaceutical company Merck. Each pledged US$50 million over the five-year period, with Merck also offering an unlimited supply of antiretroviral drugs. Among other things, this allowed Botswana to be the first country in Africa to offer free antiretrovirals to anyone who needed them. Other elements of the five-year plan were a training program for health care workers and a new research laboratory in Gaborone, both established by Harvard University (UNAIDS 2007).

So far those Batswana who have opted for the antiretroviral therapy have shown very high adherence rates—an initial fear about the antiretroviral therapy in the developing world had been that because of impoverished circumstances, people would not be able to adhere to the often difficult drug regimens (and drug-resistant strains might result). Moreover, Botswana's program is not only about treating those who are already infected but also about preventing further infections. Condoms are widely available, and prevention messages are being disseminated over the airwaves, on billboards, in classrooms, and more. In 2007 UNAIDS executive director Piet Piot praised Botswana for showing an "exceptional response to AIDS at the highest levels." By 2009, Botswana was one of several countries in southern Africa to report a dramatic decline in its HIV/AIDS prevalence rate (UNAIDS 2009a, 27).

An additional challenge is one faced by many other countries in the region and continent, namely how to deepen democracy. A 2000 survey of Batswana (Lekorwe et al. 2001, iv) indicates that democratic attitudes run deep in the country: "The results reflect long-standing democratic values and the firm entrenchment of democratic institutions. Batswana demonstrate their satisfaction with democracy and the legitimacy of the state by claiming that the government exercises power within legal means and equally represents the interests of all citizens." At the same time, a changing array of opposition political parties has failed to wrest power from the ruling party in Botswana, though they have managed, over time, to lure significant support away from the BDP. But many would argue that until there is an alternation of power at the national level in Botswana, democracy remains elusive. By 2010 the ruling party itself was fraught with a debilitating factionalism that eventually led to a splinter party, the Botswana Movement for Democracy, only to see some members and politicians return within months, though the party remains. Many continue to be troubled by what appears to be an increasing centralization—and in the view of some a militarization—of power within the executive since Ian Khama became president. On balance, a consensus seems to exist among many observers that deepening democracy in Botswana will require a stronger parliament, stronger opposition political parties, stronger civil society, and stronger media.

Like other countries in the region, Botswana is challenged by the need to further diversify its economy, lest it find itself one day without diamonds and once again reliant upon cattle and migrant labor. In general, the government of Botswana seems cognizant of the need to plan for 2040, when diamonds are forecast to run out. A strategy, branded Vision 2016, elaborates where Botswana would like to be fifty years after independence. Vision 2016 calls for a continued average growth rate of 8 percent, a trebling of per capita incomes, and the elimination of poverty. This is to be achieved through diversification into manufacturing and services, in particular financial services. To that end the country is investing massively in the education of its young people and has established an international financial services center and a booming stock exchange and has welcomed a growing number of foreign banks (Johnson 2003). Botswana's historical neglect of industry (in favor of large-scale cattle ranching and diamonds) and the concentration of existing industrial assets in non-Batswana hands may make its industrial objectives more difficult in the competitive international environment of the early twenty-first century, however (Samatar 1999, 133). At the same time, given Botswana's developmental characteristics, the state's capacity to realize its vision would appear to be among the strongest on the continent.

A final challenge for Botswana reflects its geographic position in southern Africa—it shares long borders with three countries and close proximity to others. Indeed, the challenges of the 1970s and 1980s, when Botswana faced considerable danger due to its warring neighbors, in some respects reemerged in the first decade of the twenty-first century. In particular, Botswana suffered from an influx of refugees as a result of the political instability and economic turmoil in Zimbabwe through most of that decade. Outside Francistown a new prison was erected in 2002 just to accommodate the massive influx of illegal immigrants, primarily from Zimbabwe. Additionally, outbreaks of foot and mouth disease, a result of ineffective control measures in Zimbabwe and the spread of the disease across the border, threatened lucrative contracts with the European Union for the country's beef exports. President Ian Khama has been alone among presidents in southern Africa in challenging Robert Mugabe's more than thirty years of uninterrupted rule. Indeed, some scholars have argued that Botswana should take a more proactive role in promoting democracy in southern Africa and the world (Molutsi 2005, 28).

The potential spillover effects from the situation in Zimbabwe, and the repercussions already experienced, provide a solemn reminder of the interconnectedness of the region. Yet Botswana's history augurs well for its ability to prosper regardless of the troubles of its neighbors. After all, Africa's developmental state achieved that status in part because it was able to establish and maintain policy rationality, domestic security, political stability, and economic growth in an often hostile regional environment.

Notes

1. The people of Botswana are referred to in the plural as Batswana (singular is Motswana).

2. See Holm 1988. The earliest inhabitants of what is today Botswana, and the only inhabitants until Bantu-speaking groups arrived in the sixteenth century, were the Basarwa, otherwise known as the San or bushmen.

3. This was the period of the *mfecane,* during which the Zulu kingdom under Shaka Zulu was created. "The resultant process of conquest, warfare, population flight, and social dislocation affected the people of the entire subcontinent from the Fish River in southern Africa to the southern shores of Lake Victoria. These events directly affected the demographic features of the populations of what eventually became the independent states of Botswana, South Africa, and Zimbabwe" (du Toit 1995, 20).

4. Indeed, about 80 percent of the population lives in one 80-mile-wide strip of eastern Botswana. The population is concentrated along the railroad line that travels through the eastern part of the country (Picard 1985, 4).

5. Neil Parsons (1985, 37) calls this idea of the delayed nationalist movement one of "the most cherished myths about Botswana's history." According to him, the origins of modern nationalism in Botswana can be traced to the 1920s and two branches of an intellectual nationalist movement, one among "progressive [though still autocratic] chiefs" and another more democratic nationalist tradition.

6. According to Wiseman (1998, 248): "Although the marriage was approved by the Bamangwato at a huge public meeting of the tribe it ran into serious opposition from the British colonial authorities who, under pressure from the South African government (which at the time was constructing the apartheid system of strict racial segregation), stripped Seretse of his hereditary rights to the chieftaincy and, for a time, banned him from the territory." See also Williams 2007.

7. Du Toit (1995, 58) quotes President Khama as saying in 1967: "We would never sacrifice efficiency on the altar of localization."

8. Indeed, as many others have done, the government has gone so far as to assert that "Botswana's diamonds had been fundamental in bringing about social and economic development. The gist of the campaign was to assert that diamonds in Botswana have been used to provide health care, build houses, educate Batswana and, most importantly, create a politically sound environment that, so the argument goes, has contributed to the country's longstanding liberal democracy and relative stability" (Taylor and Mokhawa 2003, 272).

5 Mozambique: Institutionalizing Dominant-Party Politics

On May 8, 2001, President Joachim Chissano of Mozambique announced to a meeting of the Central Committee of the ruling party, Front for the Liberation of Mozambique (Frente de Libertação de Moçambique; Frelimo), that he would not be the party's candidate for the presidential elections due in December 2004. Chissano, who won the presidency in the country's first multiparty elections in 1994 and was reelected in 1999, actually had served as head of state since 1986, when he assumed the presidency upon the death of Samora Machel. Despite Chissano's long tenure in office, his withdrawal was extraordinary at the time, both within Mozambique and the region. Indeed, there was considerable initial doubt among supporters and critics alike that the president would actually abide by his decision (Marshall and Jaggers 2001), and the skepticism was justified. The list of state presidents in the region who had made similar pledges to retire from office, but had subsequently sought ways to preserve their grip on the presidency, was a long one. In addition, Chissano himself had said once before, in 1999, that he would not stand for reelection before ultimately choosing to run (reportedly because no suitable alternative could be found within Frelimo [MNA 2001]).

Another reason Chissano's decision was unexpected lay in its "legal voluntarism." The 1990 Mozambican constitution, which established the institution of direct, popular elections for the office of president, expressly states in Article 118 that "the President of the Republic may only be re-elected on two consecutive occasions." While this is regarded by some as a flaw of constitutional design, it nonetheless would have permitted Chissano to stand in 2004, since he was elected in 1994, and reelected only once, five years later (MNA 2001). Nevertheless, unlike his regional counterparts Frederick Chiluba of Zambia, Bakili Muluzi of Malawi, Sam Nujoma of Namibia, and Robert Mugabe of Zimbabwe, Chissano appeared genuinely anxious to relinquish the reins of the presidency, notwithstanding the existence of this convenient constitutional loophole. In May 2001 a senior member of the Frelimo Central Committee sought to allay lingering doubts, suggesting that "president

---

Mozambique: Country Data

Land area   786,380 km²
Capital   Maputo
Date of independence   June 25, 1975
Population   22,061,451, 37% urban (2008)
Languages   Emakhuwa 26.1%, Xichangana 11.3%, Portuguese 8.8% (official;
   spoken by 27% of population as a second language), Elomwe 7.6%, Cisena
   6.8%, Echuwabo 5.8%, other Mozambican languages 32%, other foreign
   languages 0.3%, unspecified 1.3% (1997 census)
Ethnic groups   African 99.66% (Makhuwa, Tsonga, Lomwe, Sena, and others),
   European 0.06%, Euro-African 0.2%, Asian 0.08%
Religions   Catholic 23.8%, Muslim 17.8%, Zionist Christian 17.5%, other
   17.8%, none 23.1% (1997 census)
Currency   metical (MT); meticais (MZM) per US dollar: 27.4
Literacy rate   47.8% (male, 63.5%; female, 32.7% [2003])
Life expectancy   41.37 years (male, 42.05; female, 40.68 years [2010 estimate])
Infant mortality   103.82 per 1,000 live births
GDP per capita (PPP)   US$900
GDP real growth rate   6.3%
Leaders since independence
   Samora Moisés Machel, president, 1975–1986
   Joachuim Alberto Chissano, president, 1986–2004
   Armando Guebuza, president, 2005–
Major political parties
   Ruling party   Front for the Liberation of Mozambique (Frelimo)
   Other parties   Democratic Movement for Mozambique (MDM), Mozam-
   bique National Resistance (Renamo), Party for Peace, Development, and
   Democracy (PDD)
Women in parliament (lower/single house)   39.2% (2009 election)

Sources: Data derived from https://www.cia.gov; http://www.ipu.org/.
Note: Data from 2009 unless otherwise noted.

Chissano believes that standing for the presidency again would violate the spirit, if not the letter, of the Mozambican constitution. President Chissano believes that, were he to stand again, in reality he would be asking for a fourth term. For he was already president when the 1990 constitution, establishing limits on terms of office, was approved. President Chissano had then been elected in 1994 and 1999, so he now regarded himself as already in his third term" (Fernando Ganhao, quoted in MNA 2001).

Although hardly universally popular, Chissano held considerable power within both the party and the state and enjoyed substantial benefits of incumbency. Given these resources, a Chissano victory in 2004, while not ensured, was perhaps very likely. Hence, even the official Frelimo explanations for his unexpected recusal appear credible. Indeed, in June 2002, Chissano ensured his retirement when Armando Guebuza, leader of the Frelimo Parliamentary

Group, was elected as the party's new secretary-general and its candidate for the 2004 election.

We cite Chissano's decision to step down from the presidency as an important, albeit symbolic step in the inculcation of democratic practices in Mozambique. While certainly not a panacea for Mozambique's myriad problems—including deep poverty, growing corruption, lingering political violence, and overcentralization of power by the regime—Chissano's departure was a potential harbinger of democratization in the country and the region as a whole. First, it marked an important reversal of the trend in the region in which presidents attempted to subvert constitutional term limits and nascent democratic institutions by using, in effect, extraconstitutional means to extend their terms in office. While these efforts undermined the rule of law and threatened fragile political institutions elsewhere, Chissano was apparently willing to buck the trend and step down, despite his preeminent role in the Frelimo party hierarchy.[1]

The Mozambican precedent undoubtedly had a regional impact. Indeed, it may have emboldened anti–third-term activists in Zambia and Malawi, where bids by incumbent presidents Frederick Chiluba and Bakili Muluzi were thwarted in 2001 and 2002, respectively. At the same time, however, care should be taken not to overstate the regional demonstration effect of Chissano's decision: after all, Robert Mugabe's power in Zimbabwe has continued since 1980; Malawi's Muluzi continued to explore the third-term possibilities, albeit ultimately without success, long after Mozambique discarded the idea; and Namibia's Sam Nujoma is rumored to have considered a fourth term before handpicking his successor instead. Thabo Mbeki wanted to retain the ANC party presidency, which would have resulted in the continuation of his authority. Mozambique in the first decade of the twenty-first century thus represented an important incremental step toward instilling a regional norm of presidential term limits and constitutional governance.

Second, Chissano's departure from the scene briefly introduced, however unwittingly, the prospect for alternation of political parties in Mozambique. Although Frelimo has enjoyed a strong monopoly on elected office, the polity was quite competitive in its first three national elections and at the local level. The 1999 national election revealed this close divide, as Afonso Dhlakama, the candidate of the principal opposition party, Mozambique National Resistance (Resistência Nacional Moçambicana; Renamo), came within 5 percent of victory in a disputed presidential election, and Renamo actually won a majority of the votes in six provinces. Moreover, it was widely believed that Frelimo's selection of Armando Guebuza, also a controversial and polarizing figure, as Chissano's successor would provide a singular opportunity for Renamo and its longtime leader, Dhlakama, to at last capture the presidency. Alternation of power, although not an end in itself, is an important aspect of democratic deepening. At the same time, however, the prospect of alternation—at least a Dhlakama/Renamo victory—posed its own risks in Mozambique.

Ultimately, however, Chissano's departure may have had a more positive impact at the level of international symbolism than it did in Mozambique itself. Contrary to expectations in 2004, the election of Guebuza actually began a period of *less* political competition. The elections in December that year saw Frelimo not only retain control over the reins of government but also expand it substantially. Mozambique's democratic experiment has scarcely failed, and part of the uncompetitive climate is due to fragmentation within the opposition, but as Frelimo has become more secure, it has also become more insular. In the aftermath of the 2004 contest, Frelimo has consolidated its hold over the state. In most of the country's three decades of independence, politics has been a zero-sum game, in which Frelimo has been little interested in any semblance of power sharing or even national representation of Renamo's views, and many of the institutional structures discussed below reinforce the ruling party's monopoly. In retrospect, then, the five years between 1999 and 2004 marked the most competitive period in Mozambique's modern political history. The capacity of Mozambique's democracy to deepen, despite this recent uncompetitiveness and despite its fragile institutions, is a central concern in this chapter.

Mozambique experienced tremendous change in the 1990s, beginning a positive, albeit sometimes halting trajectory toward stability and democracy. The country emerged from fifteen years of civil war to achieve a negotiated peace in 1992. As the de jure one-party state gave way to political pluralism, founding multiparty elections were conducted in 1994; three national multiparty elections have been held at regular five-year intervals since. As it prepares to enter its third decade of peace and democratic rule, however flawed, Mozambique has substantially put behind it the designation "postconflict country." Positive developments are also apparent on the economic front. Although still a desperately poor country, Mozambique averaged impressive GDP growth of nearly 10 percent annually in the 1990s, and high growth rates continued at an average of 7.5 percent per year in the first decade of the twenty-first century.

Despite these auspicious signs, however, political and economic challenges in Mozambique should not be underestimated. Frelimo's consolidation of state power has signaled an emergent electoral authoritarianism. Corruption among party elites, particularly concerning budgetary transparency and the privatization of state assets, has emerged as a major issue and has threatened state and government legitimacy (Astill-Brown and Weimer 2010). Tensions persist between former combatants Frelimo and Renamo and, increasingly, other parties, as alluded to above. Social problems such as HIV/AIDS and income inequality have multiplied. And notwithstanding economic gains, poverty remains pervasive, helping to precipitate severe riots in 2010.

The legacy of four centuries of Portuguese colonialism and, thereafter, state socialism still complicate modern Mozambique. The experience of Portuguese colonialism distinguishes Mozambique from the rest of the region, save Angola, and left Mozambique with precious few resources and an illiteracy rate among the highest in Africa. The economic destruction wrought by the rapid and unexpected decolonization in 1974 and 1975, the civil war that followed, and inappropriate development policies left the economy in shambles by the 1990s (Pitcher 2003). Today, although Mozambique has moved beyond prawns and cashew nuts as sources of foreign exchange, it is, like all countries of the region, overwhelmingly dependent on the vagaries of primary commodity exports for its development: energy, such as hydropower and natural gas; aluminum; and commercial fishing. It is also deeply reliant upon foreign aid.

The scale of the challenges raises a number of questions. Most important among these concerns is the durability of the political and economic institutions Mozambique has created in the past decade. On the political front, especially, are Mozambique's democratic-institutional structures sufficiently robust to withstand the consolidation of power under Frelimo and Guebuza? Will the significant political opening and competition seen under Chissano be revived, or does Mozambique continue to entrench single-party dominance? In fairness, such questions are not fully answerable with the evidence now available. Yet this chapter's examination of a range of developments in Mozambique helps us to move in that direction.

Historical Origins of the Mozambican State

The Portuguese established one of the first permanent trading posts in southern Africa in the contemporary Mozambican province of Inhambane in 1534. Most of the European activity was initially centered on coastal trade, including trade in slaves. It later expanded to include trading and mining activity in the interior. The Portuguese granted large concessions to foreign companies (principally British) to help finance the colony; however, only one, Sena Sugar Estates, which like the other companies was given near-complete control over African labor and administration, had any measurable success (Alden 2001, 2). Indeed, since most of "these commercial activities were not tremendously successful," Mozambique became a transit and service-based economy almost from the outset (Rupiya 1998, 10).

Most of the peoples initially subjugated by the Portuguese were in the northern "cultural band," comprising significantly the Macua-Lowme, who today make up some 47 percent of the population. In the south, the Tsonga people (23 percent of the contemporary population) were part of the Gaza empire, which put up intense resistance to Portuguese rule through the nineteenth century (Weinstein 2002, 144). It was not until 1914 that the whole of the indigenous population was subjugated by the Portuguese (Alden 2001, 2).

Subsequently, thousands of indigenous people were forced into the colonial wage economy. Mozambican labor was made available for the South African mining industry by formal agreement in 1901; a similar agreement was later made with Southern Rhodesia. Of course, these were completely unconcerned with the conditions of labor or the rights of workers, and the bulk of remittances were paid to the Portuguese colonial state rather than to the miners themselves. Thus, "for all intents and purposes, the Mozambican economy was under foreign (non-Portuguese) control" until the 1930s (Alden 2001, 3). In 1932 the Portuguese government sidelined the trading companies and imposed direct rule over Mozambique for the first time.

Substantial Portuguese settlement did not begin until the late nineteenth and early twentieth centuries and only accelerated after World War II. Still, by the 1940s, there were only around 33,000 Portuguese living in Mozambique (Alden 2001, 4), and several thousand Indians who worked in the trades. As with French colonialism in Africa, there was never an expectation in Lisbon or among Portuguese settlers in Africa that control would be ceded to the indigenous population. Moreover, with a settler population numbering 100,000 in 1960, there was also a vested self-interest opposing majority rule among resident whites. Thus Mozambique actually bears considerable resemblance to other settler colonies in southern Africa, namely Namibia, South Africa, and Zimbabwe, where emergent African nationalism encountered settler resistance and precipitated a violent struggle for independence. Indeed, Mozambique's peak European population of around 200,000 by 1973 (Alden 2001, 4) is also quite comparable to the peak white population levels in Zimbabwe and Namibia.

Black nationalism coalesced within Frelimo, which was formed in 1962 under the leadership of Eduardo Mondlane, an anthropologist and onetime United Nations (UN) employee. In September 1964, the first shots of revolution were fired in the northern province of Cabo Delgado. Frelimo, which later adopted Marxism-Leninism, was not at the time explicitly Marxist, but it was eventually the recipient of "radical African, Arab, Eastern European and Chinese aid" (Rupiya 1998, 11). Mondlane "from the outset found himself mediating between two opposing perspectives within the organization": one nationalist and concerned with Mozambican liberation, the other committed to scientific socialism (Alden 2001, 4–5). However, Mondlane was assassinated in Dar es Salaam, Tanzania, where the movement had set up its exile headquarters in 1969, prompting escalating conflicts within the party (Rupiya 1998).[2] Following Mondlane's death a three-person leadership council briefly ran the movement. When one of the members, Una Sinango (who was accused of taking part in Mondlane's assassination), was forced out of the movement, Samora Machel, one of the remaining two leaders, moved to the forefront and quickly consolidated his control over the party and its military operations (Weinstein 2002, 146).

The remaining years of Portuguese colonialism bear many similarities to the dying days of settler rule in Zimbabwe. As in Zimbabwe's guerrilla war, Frelimo advances, though probably incapable of toppling the colonial government, nonetheless constituted "a major psychological blow to the Portuguese" (Rupiya 1998, 11). The Portuguese response was extreme and included such tactics as the use of napalm, scorched earth policies, forced removals of rural poor, and internment camps. Again, as in Zimbabwe, noncombatant civilians were not spared the effects of the colonial regime's attempts to crush the rebel movement. In April 1974, however, the military coup in Portugal toppled the fascist Salazar regime headed by Marcelo Caetano and paved the way for independence in the former colonies. Immediately thereafter, Portugal withdrew its 60,000 troops (Rupiya 1998, 11).

Interestingly, white colonists in Lourenco Marques (now Maputo) briefly considered a unilateral declaration of independence following the Rhodesian example of 1965, but decided against it (Rupiya 1998, 12). The Lusaka Accord of September 1974 officially ended colonial rule and gave power to a provisional government dominated by Frelimo. The People's Republic of Mozambique became independent on June 25, 1975.

Independent Mozambique was extremely ill suited to the achievement of democracy and development. As noted above, Portuguese colonialism had very shallow roots and very limited investment in human or physical infrastructure. Ninety percent of the population was illiterate, and Frelimo was ill prepared to govern. Most settlers with needed skills fled the country, and many departing colonists destroyed much of the limited economic base (Rupiya 1998, 12). The white population fell to 30,000 by 1977, and international capital flight also occurred as a reaction to the new government's Marxist rhetoric (Alden 2001, 5). In terms of a policy agenda, nationalization of productive assets and the provision of public health were among Frelimo's early concerns. However, economic policies, including "white elephant" industrial projects and Soviet-style collectivization of agriculture, forced resettlements, and the establishment of inefficient state farms, proved disastrous (Alden 2001, 7; Bowen 2000, 10–12). From the beginning, independent Mozambique was a one-party state under the strict control of Frelimo, which formally transformed itself into a Marxist-Leninist "vanguard party" at its 1977 party congress. Links were established to the Soviet Union and Eastern Europe for political and military support (Rupiya 1998).

The death of Mondlane in 1969 contributed to the ascendance of the radical faction within Frelimo (Alden 2001, 5–6). Nonetheless, Frelimo's Mozambique appears to fit rather uncomfortably with more doctrinaire Afro-Marxist regimes of the period, and in any event the commitment to Marxism proved fairly short lived. For example, while allegiances were established with the Eastern Bloc, Mozambique also maintained significant economic relationships with the United Kingdom and even South Africa. Moreover, in 1981, the

Council for Mutual Economic Cooperation (COMECON), the institution that managed trade and assistance among the communist countries, rejected Mozambique's appeal for membership, effectively cutting off the country. Thereafter, Mozambique's only economic recourse was the West, and the "capitalist road" was formally, if not rhetorically, embarked upon by 1983 with the adoption of initial liberalization measures under the direction of the international financial institutions (Alden 2001, 8–9). Indeed, in the 1980s, even the US government, under the staunchly anticommunist administration of Ronald Reagan, regarded Frelimo as only superficially Marxist (see Crocker 1992). Hence, in the global support for anticommunist insurgencies funded by the US government under the so-called Reagan Doctrine, the Mozambican rebel movement Renamo was unable to secure US government support at all, although plenty of support flowed from right-wing think tanks in the United States. In this sense, Frelimo's rhetorical commitment to Marxism throughout the 1980s—like Robert Mugabe's avowed "socialism" in neighboring Zimbabwe—was more an effort to maintain "radical" bona fides than a genuine ideological commitment. In any event, the retreat from this weakly expressed Marxism accelerated in the 1980s, so that by Frelimo's July 1989 party congress, Marxism-Leninism had been officially abandoned (Rupiya 1998, 14).

Mozambique's postcolonial stability and economy were also undermined by military conflict. Renamo, known until 1981 as the Mozambique National Resistance (MNR), was established in 1977 by the Rhodesian Central Intelligence Organization. The MNR was designed to serve as a destabilizing force within Mozambique that would sabotage communities, as well as government economic and military installations, in an effort to punish Machel's government and to undermine Zimbabwe's National Liberation Army guerrillas who were using Mozambique as a staging area for attacks on Rhodesian forces (Vines 1996, 15–20). Although the MNR was a Rhodesian creation (supported by apartheid South Africa after Zimbabwe's independence) and engaged in massive human rights abuses, it was able nonetheless to tap into substantial anti-Frelimo sentiment in the central and northern provinces of Mozambique. However, according to Martin Rupiya (1998, 13), the MNR was not a serious threat to the Frelimo government until around 1982, when, with South African support, its fighting strength was dramatically increased. South Africa's interests in destabilizing Mozambique were multiple and complex; its principal objectives were to increase regional dependence on South Africa, and to undermine Frelimo and its support for African National Congress (ANC) operations in Mozambique.

In 1984, the Frelimo government signed the Nkomati Accords, a nonaggression pact with apartheid South Africa. The parties agreed that Frelimo would shut down ANC bases and that the South African military would halt its support for Renamo. The South Africans violated the pact, however, and continued to arm and support Renamo, albeit indirectly, thus ensuring the continuation of war in Mozambique (Rupiya 1998, 13). After 1984, Renamo supported its activities through civilians, whom it routinely brutalized and mutilated (Rupiya 1998; Minter 1994). "In seeking to control and instil fear in rural populations, [Renamo] became particularly well-known for mutilating civilians, including children, by cutting off ears, noses, lips and sexual organs. These tactics were part of a standard terrorist strategy intended to advertise the rebels' strength, to weaken symbolically the authority of the government and to undermine the rural production systems on which Mozambique depended" (Rupiya 1998, 13; see also Vines 1996).

By the late 1980s, it had become clear that the war was reaching a stalemate and that the conflict was increasingly "ripe" for negotiation. Unlike Angola, Mozambique lacked the natural resources and fungible commodities like oil and diamonds that would have allowed the combatants to sustain the war. Moreover, the changing global and regional environment—the end of the Cold War, the transition in Namibia, and the initiation of dialogue in South Africa—meant that fewer external actors were interested in sponsoring or prolonging the conflict. Thus, after several years of negotiations at various levels and brittle cease-fires, a lasting general peace agreement (GPA) finally was signed in Rome in October 1992. The United Nations Operation in Mozambique (ONUMOZ), a force of 6,800 troops, was assigned to monitor the peace agreement, demobilize nearly 100,000 troops, create a new unified national army, resettle up to 6 million internally displaced persons, and organize elections (Rupiya 1998, 15).

At independence in 1975, Frelimo had formal military units numbering around 10,000 troops in the Popular Forces for the Liberation of Mozambique, which later became known as the Armed Forces of Mozambique (FAM, derived from the Portuguese acronym) (Berman 1996, 43). FAM was not a formidable, disciplined military force, and it was unable to completely counter Renamo after about 1980, when the latter gained South African support. Of course, the government's forces were entirely incapable of confronting the South African Defense Force (SADF), which attacked Mozambican-based ANC targets "with impunity" in the 1980s. By 1990, in response to the Renamo threat, the total armed forces of the government numbered 72,000 troops, some 60,000 of whom were in the army. Renamo's guerrilla forces, by contrast, started quite small—in the dozens—but reached several thousand by 1979. Once the South Africans took over as Renamo's sponsors, the number of fighters escalated, apparently to 16,000 by 1984 and 20,000 by the time the GPA was signed in 1992 (Berman 1996, 45–46, 48).

The government received almost all its weaponry from the Soviet Union, but "the relationship was never that close" and the size of the arsenal was limited. Moreover, the Soviets were unwilling to supply the weapons that Frelimo sought, and replacement parts were scarce (Berman 1996, 49–50). Light arms, on the other hand, were provided to the government not only by the Soviets and the Eastern Bloc, but also by the United Kingdom and Portugal. Renamo also had a significant number of small arms (but almost no mechanized weapons), which were supplied by the South Africans and purchased with contributions from anticommunist organizations in the West (Berman 1996, 52).

As Carrie Manning (2001, 146) points out, Renamo was "best known to the world for its grotesque campaign of terror against Mozambican civilians," although recent analyses reveal that during the war, government forces also committed atrocities. Nonetheless, the scale of "brutality and savagery" practiced by Renamo guerrillas is widely believed to have been much greater, including the destruction of villages, rape, mutilation, murder, forced conscription, and the use of child soldiers (Berman 1996, 55; Minter 1994; Vines 1996). At war's end, the enormous task of reintegrating these competing factions into a single society, including into a combined military, fell largely to the United Nations. Following the signing of the GPA, the process of implementing demobilization began. However, it was not until December 1993 that troops began to register (Berman 1996, 67).

Forces from each of the armies were required to register at separate assembly points and indicate their willingness to join the new combined army, renamed the Armed Forces for the Defense of Mozambique (FADM), or reenter civilian life (Berman 1996, 60). The expectation was that the new FADM would number 30,000 (mostly army), and that 50 percent of these troops would come from each side (Berman 1996, 69). Astoundingly, however, only 5–6 percent of FAM troops and 10 percent of Renamo soldiers were willing to join the new force. War weariness and fairly generous pensions to former combatants provided strong disincentive to join the FADM. Thus some 78,078 soldiers (57,540 from government and 20,538 Renamo) were demobilized by August 1994 (Vines 1996, 155).[3]

The transitional elections were delayed by mistrust between the parties, but were ultimately held on October 27–29, 1994. In the 250-seat National Assembly, Renamo got 112 seats, while Frelimo won an absolute majority of 129; a small coalition party, the Democratic Union, won 9 seats. In the presidential race, Chissano convincingly defeated his rival, Renamo leader Afonso Dhlakama, by a margin of 53.3 percent to 33.73 percent, with some ten other candidates splitting the remainder. The 88 percent turnout among 6.2 million registered voters and peaceful transition to pluralist politics revealed the deep frustration with war shared by Mozambique's population, which numbered 16 million at that time. The peace negotiations in the early 1990s, culminating in the 1994 elections, laid the groundwork for marked economic advances and the relative stability and "normal politics" in Mozambique that have ensued. However, these processes did not eliminate the cleavages that often reinforced the support for parties in the conflict. Though the cleavages persist, the consolidation of power under Frelimo has foreclosed key political outlets for the expression of differences.

Society and Development: Enduring Cleavages

Like many other countries in the region, Mozambique underwent a protracted liberation struggle, from 1962 to 1974, and like its Lusophone counterpart Angola, it was subsequently ravaged by civil war. Thirty years of violent conflict destroyed much of the fabric of the country and undermined its development potential. Not surprisingly, then, by the 1990s Mozambique was one of the poorest, most economically backward states in the world.

Renamo, for its part, was an externally created insurgency, which often relied on gruesome tactics meant to sow terror and compel obedience (Vines 1996). Thus, in one sense, Renamo was an illegitimate actor. However, it would be wrong to suggest that the movement did not also cultivate its own constituency by tapping into anti-Frelimo sentiments. The bases of these grievances were multiple. As noted above, the economic policies of the Frelimo government alienated the rural peasantry and created deep resentments of the collectivization program (Bowen 2000). Moreover, Frelimo's use of incarceration to "reeducate" political dissidents created a wellspring of ill-will against the party. The Frelimo government's hostility toward the Catholic Church also fostered divisions (Baloi 1996), as did Frelimo's targeting of chieftaincy structures, which the party saw as vestiges of Portuguese colonialism; these were important institutions to Renamo and its predominantly rural supporters (Harrison 1996). Finally, the overwhelmingly southern bias of the Frelimo leadership contributed to ethnolinguistic tensions and turned many residents of Mozambique's central provinces in particular—where the party's support was always tenuous—away from Frelimo (Weinstein 2002).

To some extent, then, several of Mozambique's important social cleavages correspond to divisions in the historical support bases for Frelimo and Renamo—as well as other minor parties. Even though support for opposition has waned in recent elections, recent developments suggest *exclusion* of opposing views rather than homogenization under the ruling party or the diminution of pluralism.

Mozambique is ethnically diverse as well as religiously plural.[4] Catholicism tends to be national and is represented in each of Mozambique's nine provinces, whereas Protestant churches are more concentrated regionally. Catholic clergy have offered criticisms of both parties, but Catholic lay people have tended to support Renamo. Other religious identities, as with ethnic identities, tend to correspond to regional bases and were reflected in Renamo and Frelimo voting patterns historically. Luis de Brito notes a severe regional split in parties' support bases in the 1994 elections. Frelimo's leaders historically come from the southern provinces (de Brito 1996, 470), and Frelimo's main areas of support came from those four southern constituencies and in the far north. In the 1994 election, for example, Frelimo won three provinces, plus Maputo city in the south, and two in the northern region, Cabo Delgado and

Niassa. The central area of the country was the site of the greatest activity by the Portuguese in their efforts to combat Frelimo, as well as the site where the Rhodesian government first established Renamo. Thus, this is a region both distrusted and disaffected historically by the regime. Likewise, people in Manica, Sofala, and Zambezia provinces in particular felt marginalized by the Frelimo state, not only as a result of their neglect during the war but also due to long-standing policies of state socialism that effectively punished the peasantry (de Brito 1996, 472).

The Frelimo-Renamo divisions were more regional, social, and historical than ethnic, which may partially explain Frelimo's ability, with the passage of time, to make substantial inroads among some former Renamo supporters in recent elections. Yet whereas Mozambique does not have the degree of fractious ethnic-based politics seen elsewhere on the continent, the perception of a southern, urban bias in Frelimo was reinforced in the 2004 campaign. The fact that presidential candidate Guebuza also represented the "old guard" of Frelimo sent a signal as well to the electorate that little had changed in the party's orientation. On the other hand, the leadership hierarchy of Renamo has historically been predominantly Ndau, and "Ndau chauvinism" has been a defining feature of Renamo's existence (Vines 1996, 130)—so much so that the Ndau language became a lingua franca during the war (versus Portuguese in Frelimo) (Vines 1996, 83). Yet this Ndau chauvinism did not prevent Renamo from developing a national profile.

Importantly, as memories of the war receded, the zone of conflict between Renamo and Frelimo and their supporters became increasingly entrenched in the *political* arena. The stakes became more about political power and policy delivery and, not inconsequentially, control over resources. Writing in 1996, Alex Vines observed that "Renamo has entered a new chapter in its history, its artificial origins and brutal reputation increasingly forgiven, though not forgotten, by communities across the country. . . . If Renamo exploits Frelimo's mistakes . . . and succeeds in transforming its election votes into grass-root support it stands a chance of becoming a future government" (1996, 193). This assessment certainly proved premature, as Renamo made a series of tactical missteps in the intervening years, and Frelimo enjoyed the benefits of prolonged incumbency. As a result, Renamo lost the electoral war far more convincingly than the armed struggle. Indeed, Renamo's share of the national vote fell precipitously in the first decade of the twenty-first century, trends that are discussed below in the section on political parties. Nonetheless, elections as recently as 1999 revealed that Renamo and especially Dhlakama were seen by a large segment of the populace as viable alternatives to continued Frelimo rule.

Renamo, and specifically Dhlakama, has long believed that they have been denied their rightful national political representation by Frelimo, both by fraudulent electoral practices and through malfeasance in various commissions. These concerns are now shared by other political parties, such as the Democratic Movement of Mozambique (MDM), many of which emerged from splits within Renamo in 2008 and 2009. Frelimo, for its part, has regularly dismissed such concerns and resisted accommodation (Manning 2001, 163). Consequently, the relationship among the parties is increasingly zero-sum, even though the electoral system theoretically protects minority party representation and positive-sum outcomes should be feasible. Whereas most opposition leaders stopped far short of inciting violence, Renamo's unexpectedly large defeat in the 2004 elections prompted claims of massive electoral fraud and raised the specter of unwillingness to abide the results ("Frelimo Wins" 2004).

A return to interparty factional violence on a measurable scale is unlikely. Nonetheless, several fundamental structural conflicts and societal cleavages were not sufficiently addressed in the 1990s. The cleavages in Mozambique certainly transcend the old Frelimo-Renamo dichotomy. Indeed, the challenges that minority parties and interests face in accessing the political sphere are formidable. Mozambique's proportional representation electoral system in fact fails to accommodate minority interests because of a 5 percent electoral threshold. The twenty-first century consolidation of political power by Frelimo reduces the opportunities for formal institutions, namely politics and parliament, to serve as an outlet for expression by disaffected groups. Frelimo's centralization of state authority, therefore, does more to inflame than diffuse conflicts.

Organization of the State

Mozambique is divided into ten provinces, plus the capital city, Maputo, which has the status of a province. Each province has a capital, which serves as the headquarters of the provincial government. The provinces in turn are subdivided into districts and localities. Despite this multitiered political architecture, Mozambique is a highly centralized polity with administrative power and functions vested in the national government in Maputo (Orre 2001). At the apex of this structure is a president, who is head of state. The president appoints a prime minister, who serves as head of government, and he also appoints the ten provincial governors.

Executive

Directly elected by separate ballot in 1994, 1999, 2004, and 2009, a president with accountability to the voters (via the ballot at least) is still relatively new in Mozambique. When the Portuguese departed in 1975, no elections or national referenda were held: as head of Frelimo, Samora Machel became president of independent Mozambique, and Frelimo was designated as the country's only legal party. Following President Machel's death in 1986, the Frelimo Central Committee designated Joachuim Chissano as his successor;

only in 1994 did constitutional changes take effect permitting direct presidential election. International observers to the 1994 election certified the results as relatively free and fair, and Renamo and its presidential candidate Afonso Dhlakama accepted the results and agreed to cooperate with the Frelimo government in the new democratic order (Marshall and Jaggers 2001). Chissano, however, resisted calls for a government of national unity, designed on the South African model, and instead appointed an all-Frelimo government.

The Mozambican presidency is invested with substantial powers, and while Chissano was not widely suspected of abusing that authority, skeptics suggested that his pledge to step down was hollow and that he was planning a third term in office (Marshall and Jaggers 2001). Hence, when the veracity of Chissano's pledge was confirmed commensurate with the ascendance of Armando Guebuza as his successor in 2002, this no doubt strengthened Chissano's legacy as a democratic leader. Ironically, however, it may have weakened his own presidency by making him a lame duck with a full two years remaining in office. The selection of Armando Guebuza, who was not preferred by Chissano, as "president-in-waiting" undermined President Chissano's authority, according to some sources (EIU 2002a, 7). Further, although Chissano was something of a darling of the international community, Guebuza is regarded as secretive, a hard-liner, and a micromanager by both foreign and local observers. Indeed, as early as 2002, some observers suggested that a Guebuza presidency would have "negative implications for the quality of governance and political pluralism in the country. He is closely associated with Frelimo's more authoritarian instincts and has been involved in human rights violations and other abuses in his previous positions in government" (EIU 2002a, 7).

In his tenure thus far, Guebuza has consolidated power, but appears to have governed within the constitution (which, after all, favors executive power). Arguably, prior to the 2004 election, parliament served as something of a bulwark against abuse of executive authority because seats were closely divided between Frelimo and an alliance of Renamo and several minor parties. Frelimo's overwhelming majority in parliament (76 percent) after 2009, however, certainly lessens the constraints. Armed with its supermajority, parliament launched a committee in December 2010 to draft amendments to the constitution. Both Guebuza and parliamentary leaders, however, were adamant that they had no interest in altering the constitution to remove the president's two-term limit; instead leaders suggested court system reforms would play a prominent role ("Mozambique Launches" 2010).

Legal Institutions and Constraints on State Power

Judiciary. Mozambique's judicial system has been characterized by outside observers as stricken with "paralysis and incompetence," and much of the responsibility for this state of affairs is believed to rest with the president, although it is not clear whether this results from neglect or a deliberate effort to undermine the judiciary (EIU 2002a, 13, 17). Even Mozambique's own Ministry of Justice described the judicial system as "sick," though it blamed this illness not on political interference but on "obsolete laws" that lead to "'a frightful absence of ethics, zeal, and dedication' in entities charged with administering justice" (cited in Freedom House 2002). In any event, the massive backlog of judicial cases has "led to near impunity for criminal activity" (EIU 2002a, 13).[5] In the early twenty-first century Freedom House (2002) noted overcrowded jails, excessively long detentions, and "rampant corruption," including frequent bribery of judges. In addition, the legal system was critically understaffed: just 170 judges and approximately 200 defense lawyers served a population of 19 million. Perhaps more worrying, "many observers consider that the judicial paralysis is not accidental, but is encouraged to facilitate criminal activity and complicity at the highest level" (EIU 2002a, 18). The possible court-related amendments to be considered by the parliament's constitution committee therefore would be most welcome—to the extent that they aim to reduce administrative delays and opportunities for political interference.

The 1975 constitution made little pretense of separation of powers and subjugated the courts to the government. After promulgation of the 1990 constitution, however, such political interference was supposed to be eliminated. Yet both interference with and neglect of the judicial branch were commonplace in the 1990s. Indeed, the lack of judicial independence and the excessive burdens on the system were each revealed in the aftermath of the 1999 elections.

According to the constitution the Supreme Court is intended to be the nation's highest court (having both appellate and original jurisdiction). In regard to constitutional matters and supervisory authority over the electoral process, however, a Constitutional Council, similar to South Africa's Constitutional Court, is supposed to have special jurisdiction that supersedes that of the Supreme Court (Article 181). Yet even by 1999 a Constitutional Council had not been formally established. Thus when Renamo alleged fraud in the 1999 election, the Supreme Court had to perform the duties of the nonexistent council. Acting in this expanded capacity, the court ruled in favor of Frelimo and failed to address a number of issues raised by Renamo concerning the transparency and credibility of the count (Manning 2001, 157). These issues were unlikely to change the result, but the actions of the court failed to engender wider support for the legitimacy of the electoral process and for the courts (Carter Center 2000, 27). At bottom, by 2011, a culture of judicial autonomy, or even competence, had yet to materialize.

Constitutionalism. The 1990 constitution was accepted by the all-Frelimo parliament in January 1990, and after substantial public debate it was formally signed in November of that year. It was promulgated without any formal inclusion of Renamo and other nascent opposition parties, which then called for the formation of a constituent assembly, but Frelimo rejected the idea (Alden 2001, 20). Renamo members were permitted to contribute to the constitutional debate as individuals, however. Moreover, since some of the provisions of the GPA, signed two years later, were incorporated into the constitution by amendment—notably provisions about the formation of political parties, freedom of association and expression, and details on the electoral process (which were later codified in a separate electoral law)—the final constitution was not objectionable to Renamo (Carrilho 1996, 129). The 1990 constitution superseded the 1975 constitution, which had established a one-party "people's republic," and the post of president was held by the party president of Frelimo (Carrilho 1996, 130).

In November 2004 parliament adopted a new constitution, which took effect in 2005 (following the 2004 elections). In a rare show of unanimity, all 250 deputies (members of parliament) in parliament voted in favor of the new constitution. Among its major provisions, Article 166 of the 2004 constitution of Mozambique provided for the establishment of a Council of State comprising former presidents, the chair of parliament and former chairs, the prime minister, the head of the Constitutional Council, seven eminent citizens, and an ombudsperson. This body is charged with advising the president on a range of issues, including the dissolution of parliament, declaration of states of emergency or war, the holding of elections, and so on ("Mozambique Adopts" 2004). As such, the Council of State was regarded in some circles as weakening, or at least constraining, presidential power, but the council has met only sporadically, suggesting that this role has not been actualized.

Among the key provisions of Mozambique's 2004 constitution are separation of powers; presidential term limits; the freedom to create political parties as the expression of political pluralism "and the fundamental instruments for the democratic participation of citizens in the governing of the country" (as stated in Chapter IV, Article 74 of the 2004 constitution of Mozambique); pluralism of opinion and the freedoms of expression and the press; the right to meet, associate, and demonstrate; and the establishment of legal equality of all citizens before the law (Article 11) as well as between men and women "in all spheres of political, economic, social and cultural life" (Article 36). As a matter of practice, however, many of these impressive liberal dimensions of both the 1990 and 2004 versions of the constitution have been erratically applied and sporadically enforced. For example, the judiciary has not escaped executive interference, as discussed above. Other individuals have also called into question the right of habeas corpus and freedom to demonstrate, rights enshrined in the constitution (Orre 2001).

Lacking a strong constitutional tradition, Mozambique faces the challenge of living up to its constitution rather than having a poor-quality document. However, two prominent features constrained constitutional manipulation, at least until 2009. As with other countries in the region, constitution alteration requires approval by a two-thirds majority in the National Assembly. The rough balance of power between Renamo and Frelimo in the legislature in the 1990s precluded abuse of the constitution by the ruling party.

This balance disappeared in 2004 when Frelimo's victory gave it 160 of 250 seats in the assembly—barely 7 seats short of a two-thirds majority. However, according to Article 292 of the 2004 constitution, a feature not seen in other countries moves the debate from the partisan parliamentary realm to the population at large and provides a vital institutional safeguard against frivolous or politically driven constitutional changes: "If the proposed amendment implies fundamental changes in the rights of citizens or in the organization of public powers, the proposal, after adoption by the Assembly of the Republic, shall be submitted to public debate and to a referendum." This important provision would appear to safeguard the integrity of the constitution, insulating it from the type of political meddling witnessed elsewhere in the region. Importantly, however, no such referendum is required to alter the presidential term limit clause.

Representation and Participation

Legislature

Under the 1975 constitution, the ten provincial assemblies, plus the Maputo City Assembly, elected the National Assembly of the Republic (Carrilho 1996, 132–133). With effect from the first multiparty elections in 1994, however, the populace has a much greater role in political life, directly electing members of the 250-seat unicameral parliament. Still, constituency representation remains weak. As in South Africa, elections to parliament are conducted on a party list system with proportional representation. However, an important distinction is Mozambique's 5 percent threshold, which bars any party receiving less than 5 percent of the national vote from gaining a seat in the assembly. As discussed below in the section on political parties, this leads to considerable exclusion; in 1999, minor parties that collectively received nearly 13 percent of the vote gained no seats in parliament. Independent candidates are also barred from contesting parliamentary seats under the electoral law.[6] The combination of the threshold and the importance of parties privileges larger parties at the expense of smaller parties and their supporters.

The number of seats allotted to each constituency is based not on population but on the number of registered voters in each constituency (Carrilho 1996, 137). This feature of the electoral law places extremely high importance on the voter registration exercise, yet because Mozambique engages in annual voter registration, this practice may actually result in more equitable and accurate distribution of deputies in the assembly. At the same time, however, it poses the risk that the most populous provinces may be underrepresented simply because of inadequate registration. It is necessary to point out that in the 1999 elections, however, this apparently was not the case: the most heavily populated provinces, Zambezia, Nampula, and Sofala—then Renamo strongholds—did receive the highest number of seats. Nevertheless, lingering questions about the neutrality and independence of the National Electoral Commission (CNE) and delimitation bodies have also raised concerns about the possibilities for illicit gerrymandering of parliamentary seats (Carter Center 2000).

Renamo rejected the idea of a majoritarian, single-member constituency system in the course of the Rome peace negotiations in 1992 (Carrilho 1996, 136). In the 1994 election, using the proportional representation system Renamo favored, it won 112 seats to Frelimo's 129. Political science research on electoral models in divided societies suggests that a proportional representation system facilitates positive-sum outcomes: various parties and their constituencies can gain seats in parliament proportional to their share of the vote (Lijphart 1977; Horowitz 1985; Sisk 1995). In the fragile context of postwar Mozambique, the application of a "winner-take-all" model might have risked reigniting the conflict. Renamo's deep discontent over its minority status since 1994 aside, it is a particular irony that, had the 1994 election been held under a majoritarian system, Renamo would have emerged with an absolute majority in parliament, 152 seats to just 98 for Frelimo (assuming the same provincial constituencies); in fact, Renamo would have swept the elections in Tete, Manica, Sofala, Zambezia, and Nampula provinces (Carrilho 1996, 139).

In the second legislative elections, held in December 1999, Frelimo again gained a majority, increasing to 133 seats, and Renamo, in partnership with several smaller parties under the banner Renamo-UE (Electoral Union), won 117 seats. Although no other party or coalition gained a seat because they failed to win 5 percent of the vote nationwide, Renamo-UE's significant presence in the assembly gave it a platform. Renamo was therefore able to influence national legislative debates, though it remained incapable of effecting meaningful legislative change as the minority. The Mozambican system is strongly presidentialist, which makes it impossible for parliamentarians, particularly in opposition, to gain a platform to challenge presidential authority. Certainly the Frelimo majority has not impeded executive branch initiatives, and with its 76 percent majority from 2009, this would appear unlikely in the extreme.

National Elections and Electoral Institutions

Until the adoption of the new constitution in 1990, National Assembly deputies were elected indirectly by the provincial assemblies. "There was a direct vote only in electing deputies at the grassroots level, namely to the popular assemblies in localities, villages and neighborhoods. In the election of district and provincial assemblies, the votes were cast by delegates at electoral conferences," rather than directly by voters (Carrilho 1996, 132–133). Hence, absent meaningful authority and voting at the popular level, there was scant need for an electoral infrastructure.

The Electoral Law of Mozambique (Law no. 4 of 1993) established the National Electoral Commission. The CNE consists of an unwieldy nineteen members, appointed to five-year terms by the president, although some are proposed by opposition parties. In the 1999 elections, the CNE was viewed as partisan toward Frelimo. This is not surprising; indeed, questions about electoral commission independence, frequently justified, have proved endemic in Africa's transitional democracies. Many CNE procedures were ad hoc, largely because of ambiguities in the 1999 electoral law, and there was a lack of transparency in the critical final stages of vote tabulation (Carter Center 2000, 30). Yet these are precisely the elements an opposition needs to trust the integrity of the process and the legitimacy of the final result: well-defined electoral laws and an independent commission. Indeed, Renamo members of the CNE refused to validate the results in 1999 and filed the complaint with the Supreme Court.

The 1999 elections were the first in the era of "normal politics." Whereas the number of registered voters climbed from 6.2 million in 1994 to 7.1 million in 1999, turnout among registered voters fell from 5.4 million (88 percent) in 1994 to 4.8 million (just over 68 percent) in 1999. Although still an impressive level for the region, the lower turnout in 1999 reflects the lower stakes—peace was no longer on the ballot—and diminished popular expectations. (Local government elections in 1998, discussed below, may have also depressed enthusiasm for the 1999 election. Renamo boycotted the local elections in 1998, and turnouts ranged between just 6 and 15 percent.) In any event, the election was close, and unexpectedly so at the presidential level, where Chissano defeated Dhlakama by a margin of just 52.3 percent to 47.7 percent.

In January 2000 the Supreme Court found in favor of Frelimo. Although the court acknowledged that about 377,773 potential valid votes had been excluded in the vote-tallying process, it did not provide any further information about their provincial distribution, their probable impact on the election outcome, or the fact that this figure significantly exceeded Chissano's margin of victory (205,593 votes) (Carter Center 2000, 27). As noted earlier, Dhlakama would have had to receive the overwhelming majority of these excluded votes, which was unlikely, to alter the final result (Manning 2001). Yet the lack of transparency damaged the integrity of the electoral system.

Denied recourse through the courts, Dhlakama announced initially that Renamo would refuse to take its seats in parliament but subsequently reconsidered (Manning 2001, 163–164). Although its parliamentary boycott backfired,

Renamo was joined by other political and civic groups, as well as international observers, in calling for revisions to the electoral law and removal of its apparent contradictions. Also demanded was a restructuring of electoral institutions, namely the CNE and the Technical Secretariat for Electoral Administration (STAE), the administrative arm of election management institutions, which operates only during elections. A multiparty Parliamentary Advisory Commission was established to revise both parliamentary procedures regarding elections and the structure of the CNE and to make needed changes to the electoral laws at the local and municipal and national levels. However, this body was beset by partisanship and was unable to reach consensus between its Frelimo and opposition members on the extent of reforms. Manning (2001, 164–165) suggests that much of the blame for the failure of various such commissions lies with Renamo, which often seemed to prefer the spoiler role to that of partner.

The 2004 and 2009 National Elections

The December 2004 elections for the National Assembly of the Republic and the presidency resulted in a decisive victory for Frelimo and for its presidential candidate, Armando Guebuza. In the legislative contest, Frelimo garnered some 62 percent of the vote, whereas Renamo could muster only 29.7 percent; the remainder went to minor parties, all of which failed to reach the 5 percent threshold for representation. As a result, Frelimo was awarded 160 seats, whereas Renamo's parliamentary representation fell to 90 seats from its previous level of 117. Guebuza, for his part, amassed more than double the votes of Afonso Dhlakama: approximately 2 million (63.7 percent) to 998,000 (31.7 percent) ("Frelimo Wins" 2004). Given the closeness of the 1999 election, at the parliamentary and especially the presidential level, the magnitude of the Frelimo victory is striking. Moreover, although overall voter turnout fell precipitously from 5.3 million in 1999 to just 3.5 million in 2004 (approximately 45 percent of registered voters), this redounded chiefly to the detriment of Dhlakama, who "has lost more than 1 million supporters in the past five years" (Mozambique Political Process Bulletin 2004).

Perhaps not surprising, the electoral process was marred by allegations from Renamo and the minor opposition parties of massive fraud on the part of Frelimo and the electoral administration. Although such charges had by this time become a familiar Renamo tactic, they were not entirely without merit. Indeed, there was evidence of a number of irregularities, as reported by domestic and international observers. These included flawed voter registration, inflated turnouts in favor of Frelimo, wrongfully invalidated ballots, and police intimidation of opposition supporters in some areas ("Frelimo Wins" 2004). In addition, there were logistical problems associated with poor data collection techniques and "computer chaos" by the STAE office in Maputo, resulting in a delayed vote count (Mozambique Political Process Bulletin

2004). Nevertheless, whereas these and other problems raised justifiable concerns, many of the broader accusations could not be substantiated by independent observers; most concluded therefore that the irregularities were not of such a systematic and national scale that they would measurably alter the outcome.

The 2009 contest showed perhaps less improvement in electoral administration on the part of the CNE than expected. International observers criticized the CNE for its lack of transparency, its rationale for rejection of some candidate lists, and other irregularities (Commonwealth Observer Group 2009, 19–20; "EISA and SADC Join Chorus of Critics" 2009).[7] Domestic observer groups, meanwhile, decried CNE's failure to investigate the many reports of irregularities. Like the observers from the Commonwealth, Mozambican groups criticized the apparent discrimination against MDM under the leadership of Daviz Simango. Despite MDM's pledge to advance candidates for every constituency, Simango's new party was barred by the CNE from contesting elections in five of the ten provinces. These shortcomings in administration and other irregularities aside, no groups concluded that they were sufficient to undermine the validity of the Frelimo victory.

Prior to the election, the perennial Renamo candidate Dhlakama claimed that if he lost, he would not run again. In the event, Guebuza soundly defeated Dhlakama by a margin of 75 percent to 16.4 percent. Simango garnered only 8.6 percent, which appears to have been won at the expense of his former party, rather than Frelimo. The ruling party also won nearly 75 percent of the parliamentary vote and swept the Provincial Assembly elections with 703 of the 812 seats contested.

A number of questions thus emerge in the wake of the 2004 and 2009 elections. As we have discussed throughout the chapter, a major concern remains: what Frelimo and President Guebuza will do with their vastly expanded mandate, and what this unambiguous one-party dominance will mean for the future of constitutionalism, presidential term limits, corruption, and a host of other risks associated with such imbalance (Astill-Brown and Weimer 2010, vii). Conversely, how do Renamo, MDM, and other aspiring opposition parties adjust now that their opportunities to govern are foreclosed, at least for the foreseeable future?

Additionally, while the margin for the ruling party was impressive and suggests a high level of popularity of and satisfaction with Frelimo among actual voters, turnout was again low. The low turnout in both 2004 and 2009 of approximately 43.6 and 44 percent of registered voters raises several concerns. The 2004 turnout, which was a third lower than in 1999, was beset by numerous problems with voter registries and at least partly affected by the onset of the rainy season in Mozambique (EISA 2005, 34). But the 2009 election was deliberately held well before the onset of the rainy season, to avoid such problems. Hence low turnout may also reflect, more worryingly, voter apathy. Frustration with the available political alternatives, and perhaps with the political process itself, on the part of its citizenry presents serious challenges to Mozambique's ongoing democratization.

Political Parties: Accommodation or Exclusion?

From two-party to dominant-party system? Until fairly recently, the principal political cleavage in Mozambique was between Frelimo and Renamo and their supporters, although this occasionally took on regional, ethnic, and religious overtones. Historically, the president of Frelimo was also its presidential candidate. Chissano retained this top leadership post in the party until 2005, however, leaving Armando Guebuza to contest the 2004 presidential election from the position of Frelimo secretary-general, to which he was appointed in June 2002. In one sense, this was a healthy development, since it suggested greater separation of party from government. At the same time, the division of offices exposes Frelimo to internal divisions based on conflicting loyalties and competition between the two leaders.[8] In any case, Chissano relinquished the post following the election.

Dhlakama faces no such dilemma in Renamo, where his leadership has remained unchallenged for three decades, especially after expulsion or departure of other senior members of the party. In fact, the unwillingness of Dhlakama to step aside helps explain the fragmentation of Renamo and the party's inability to attract new voters, though he remained sufficiently popular with remaining party stalwarts to win the nomination in 2008 (Commonwealth Observer Group 2009). The forty-five-year-old Simango broke away from this old guard to form MDM in early 2009.

The future of Renamo as a national party certainly cannot be taken for granted. As a militia movement founded and promoted by external actors to destabilize independent Mozambique, Renamo had no covering ideology or, initially, much grassroots support (Vines 1996; Minter 1994). Not until the mid-1980s did Renamo begin to articulate a position loosely favoring a market economy and political democracy, though more a reaction to Frelimo than a clearly defined ideology (Minter 1994). However, Frelimo itself was changing in the mid-1980s, becoming increasingly capitalist in orientation and accepting multipartyism. In 1987, Frelimo adopted a structural adjustment program, which entailed a "fundamental rethinking of [its previous] economic model," and in 1989 dropped Marxism-Leninism as the official state ideology (Simpson 1993, 329). A year later the multiparty constitution was adopted. In short, Renamo's principal means of differentiating itself was as being anti-Frelimo. In fact, according to some observers, a dearth of ideology and a limited political platform continue to characterize Renamo, whose raison d'être largely remains its opposition to that of Frelimo, personalized in Dhlakama himself.[9] The departures of some of the top leaders in Renamo, including, prominently, former number-two Raul Domingos in 2000 and younger leaders like Simango in 2008, has further concentrated power in the hands of Dhlakama.

Nonetheless, until the 2004 election Mozambique looked very much like a two-party state, which the 5 percent electoral threshold system helped to preserve. Yet the depiction of Mozambican politics solely as a two-party competition between Frelimo and Renamo was always somewhat misleading. For example, at least ten minor parties allied with Renamo in 1999 in order to secure some parliamentary seats in the UE. Fourteen other parties contested the parliamentary elections in 1994, and twelve did so in 1999. In 2009, for example, Daviz Simango gained 8.59 percent as a third-party candidate; in the parliamentary poll, his MDM and sixteen other minor parties collectively garnered 7.6 percent of the vote. These continue to represent a not inconsequential percentage of the electorate, despite having scant official representation in the assembly.

Yet the third-party support has fallen sharply from years past. In 1994, almost 18 percent of the electorate chose parties other than Renamo or Frelimo; however, the 5 percent threshold denied all these voters representation except those who voted for the Democratic Union. The share of votes for minor parties dropped to about 13 percent in the 1999 election, but this still amounted to over half a million people. Despite its increased share of parliamentary seats, Frelimo was stung by its performance, particularly the six provinces in the central part of the country that it lost to Renamo. Hence it quickly began to focus its energies out in the districts and the municipal areas in preparation for the 2004 national elections. It redoubled these efforts in the prelude to 2009, with visible success. Hence the diminution of the overall third-party share of the vote has also redounded to the benefit of Frelimo.

For its part Renamo was ill prepared to build on its gains in the 1999 election or take advantage of Frelimo changes at the presidential level. At one point, the emergence of a so-called third force (in addition to the two major parties) of united new and existing opposition groups was thought to hold electoral promise, but it has not materialized. One such party, the Party for Peace, Development, and Democracy (PDD) (formerly a nongovernmental organization known as the Institute for Peace and Democracy [IPADE]), led by former Renamo leader and member of parliament Raul Domingos, contested the December 2003 local and municipal elections and the 2004 national election but fared quite badly. Domingos, who ran as a presidential candidate himself, spoke of a need to "fill up a vacuum between Renamo and Frelimo" ("Mozambique's Former Rebel" 2003); in fact, only Frelimo has filled up this "vacuum." It remains to be seen if MDM has greater viability and longevity than PDD.[10]

Division and exclusion. In July 2000, President Chissano appointed ten provincial governors, all from Frelimo. Dhlakama had insisted that Renamo be awarded the positions in the six central provinces in which it won majorities in 1999. The presumed benefits of proportional representation at the national parliamentary level were thus offset by the lack of provincial autonomy. Combined with Frelimo's domination of the local and municipal spheres, discussed in greater detail below, the party obtained a virtual monopoly on power at all levels of government (becoming even more pronounced after 2009). Not surprisingly, dialogue between the parties was extremely difficult in an atmosphere of mutual recriminations and Renamo's quite public frustration. After failing to make headway on the governorships, Dhlakama announced in July 2000 that "the Renamo Electoral Union and Dhlakama will no longer cooperate in the maintenance of peace in this country. . . . I will no longer appeal to the people to avoid violence. That is to say, from today, people can start acts of violence as they have wanted to do since January. I am not calling on anyone to be violent, but I will no longer stop my supporters from demonstrating against the despotism of Chissano" ("Renamo Boycotts" 2000).

Frelimo appeared to send mixed messages to its chief rival. On the one hand, Frelimo policies were hardly conciliatory. Following both the 1994 and 1999 elections, it governed as if the polity were not deeply divided, which of course it was. Yet, Chissano himself suggested that Frelimo's attempts to negotiate with Renamo in good faith on a range of political and economic initiatives were routinely greeted with suspicion by Dhlakama and quickly rejected.[11] Indeed, Renamo confirmed that it was suspicious of Chissano's motives and resentful of his apparent disrespect for the party.[12] Chissano's retirement presented few opportunities for rapprochement: Guebuza, whose view of Renamo is even less charitable, has only limited incentive to conciliate. With Renamo's clout diminished and a "Third Force" failing to materialize, Frelimo has ruled without oppositional constraint since 2004.

Local Elections and (De-)Centralization

The first elections for control over municipal governments (municipal assemblies and municipal presidents), in 1998, were boycotted by Renamo. This left Frelimo with overwhelming majorities, which it maintained in the 2003 municipal elections despite Renamo's participation. Given its strong electoral support in more than half the provinces (notwithstanding its record in the municipalities),[13] Renamo endorsed greater decentralization while objecting to the ill-defined boundaries between "municipal" and "provincial" authority. Indeed, this ambiguity was the principal justification for its 1998 boycott: since Frelimo controlled the gubernatorial posts already, municipal governments could exercise little autonomy, "simply adding more to Frelimo's plate."[14]

Renamo's indictment of Mozambique's centralized state remains a reasonable one. Subnational governance structures are quite weak in Mozambique, and municipal as well as provincial governments are dependent on the national government for resources. Moreover, despite some efforts at decentralization, the effective delivery of services by these local governments to the communities they serve has been erratic, a situation not unlike local governments in other countries. The state president appoints all of the provincial governors, who in turn control appointments to every other administrative level down to the district, and the municipal structures are few in number. Consequently, national elections, particularly presidential, take on added importance; rather than diffusing competition, such a system concentrates it.

Civil Society

Given years of war and statist control, as in Angola, civil society appears less mobilized in Mozambique than in much of the rest of the region. In the post-conflict milieu of the 1990s, empowerment of labor unions, human rights organizations, and the media was delayed by the need to recover from a protracted war and by state elites initially unaccustomed to pluralism. In Mozambique, civil society organizations (CSOs) remain less prominent than in neighboring states. However, there are a number of NGOs operating in the fields of human rights, such as the Mozambican Human Rights League, and of democracy, such as the Mozambique Association for the Development of Democracy, that criticize government. In addition, organizations operate in the areas of gender, health, and development, for example, as well as under the auspices of Christian or Muslim bodies. Several independent media outlets have also emerged since the mid-1990s. And bodies such as the Electoral Observatory, which represents numerous domestic election monitoring groups, have experienced growth in capacity.

As the sociopolitical climate liberalized, groups have become less inhibited about critiques of government policy. They criticize a lack of consultation by the government, particularly on development initiatives. Although admonishing Frelimo for trying to claim credit for its various development initiatives smacks of naiveté, some CSO criticisms of Frelimo's exclusive approach do raise red flags. For example, the national development program, Agenda 2025; Mozambique's participation in the African Union; the decision to join the British Commonwealth; and the World Bank–funded Poverty Reduction Strategy Paper (PRSP) each necessitated wide consultation but received little, according to the government's critics.[15] Yet whereas civil society has been adjusting to expanded opportunities and an altered role since the constitutional changes of the 1990s, so too has the state. Its history is one of top-down, hierarchical decisionmaking.

The small independent media has faced challenges as a watchdog. A 1990 press law for the first time allowed privately owned media companies and guaranteed press freedoms (da Silva 1996, 58). In response, a number of privately owned newspapers emerged prior to the 1994 election. In addition, two major government-owned newspapers, the daily *Noticias* and the weekly *Domingo*, were privatized in 1993 under a holding company, Noticias SRL. However, the two major shareholders in Noticias SRL are the Bank of Mozambique and the National Insurance Company, both parastatals. Predictably, these newspapers are still beholden to the state, if indirectly, and have shown obvious bias toward Frelimo, particularly in election periods (Carter Center 2000, 16). State-owned television, which is not widely available throughout the country, and state radio, which is, both display similar partiality toward the ruling party while demonizing Renamo.

Independent media outlets include a number of private radio stations, catering to various audiences, such as those with a religious orientation. Two private television stations are also operational, though they have limited reach. The International Telecommunications Union (ITU) estimates that Mozambique has 200,000 Internet users; however, some estimates place the number at more than 600,000. Although even the larger figure represents less than 3 percent of the population, the number of users is nonetheless growing at a fantastic rate as costs decline and access improves, such as through handheld devices (Internet World Stats 2010). This medium is an increasingly important source of information throughout Africa, and especially southern Africa. Yet Internet and cellular technology are hardly immune from government interference. In fact, in a widely criticized maneuver, the government reportedly ordered cellular phone companies to shut down short message service (SMS) text messaging in September 2010 in an effort to quell the riots in Maputo ("Mozambique Govt Suspends SMSes" 2010).

Private print media outlets face a number of constraints, not least of which are the cost of print and distribution, high levels of illiteracy, and a history of harsh libel laws that can carry criminal penalties. Nevertheless, independent journalists have persevered despite a difficult climate. Notably the private newsletters *Metical* and *Mediafax* both began as news sheets that were faxed to subscribers. Although the latter were limited by the reports' method of distribution and widespread illiteracy, especially in rural areas, they became highly successful. Today *Mediafax* is distributed by e-mail to a large subscriber base in Mozambique, the region, and internationally. *Mediafax* was formed in 1992 out of a cooperative called Media Coop. The highly regarded editor of *Mediafax*, Carlos Cardoso, was assassinated in November 2000 while investigating a scandal related to the privatization of the Commercial Bank of Mozambique in which several Frelimo elites were implicated. Cardoso's death had a chilling effect.

Political Economy and Development

Elite Interests

After it was rejected by COMECON in 1981, Mozambique increasingly looked to the West for assistance in securing the country's economic future. In

1984 it joined the World Bank and International Monetary Fund (IMF) and in 1985 it received its first International Development Assistance (IDA) loan. For all intents and purposes, Mozambique had by this time moved away from its always tenuous commitment to Marxism-Leninism. Indeed, US economic assistance also increased greatly in the 1980s. In 1987, Mozambique committed itself firmly to the neoliberal path when it adopted an IMF structural adjustment program, which it called the Economic Rehabilitation Program (PRE) (Berman 1996, 57). The PRE legitimized pursuit of individual profit and, in so doing, undermined much of the legitimacy of Frelimo party leaders, who took advantage of market-based opportunities, like privatization, to enrich themselves (Bowen 2000, 198; Pitcher 2003). This opportunism and use of political office for economic gain accelerated in the 1990s and fostered growing popular resentment. As Merle Bowen (2000, 198) argues, the economic transition begun in the 1980s markedly increased the scope for corruption, which had been "prevalent but petty in the past." The new economic regime has been accompanied by rampant corruption. For example, one study found that US$805 million was lost in untaxed exports due to corruption among customs officials. One of the most publicized scandals involved the Commercial Bank of Mozambique, from which US$11.5 million disappeared before the institution was privatized in 1996 (Alden 2001, 118). Investigation of this theft, as noted above, led to the murder of journalist Carlos Cardoso.

Frelimo appears to lack the crises of conscience or of identity revealed in the occasional populism of its Marxist-turned-capitalist counterparts in Zimbabwe and South Africa. However, whereas those countries at least had long-standing historical linkages to peasants (Zimbabwe) or workers (South Africa) that could be reinvigorated if politically necessary, Frelimo's "abandonment of Marxism-Leninism [in 1989] only ended its 'official' alliance with peasants and workers. In practice, this alliance had been fraudulent for decades" (Bowen 2000, 200). The election of Guebuza, holder of an expansive business empire and one of the richest men in Mozambique, hardly signaled that Frelimo will attempt to run on anything but a globalist, neoliberal agenda— regardless of the abject poverty suffered by most of the electorate. (These conditions, of course, contributed to violent protests in the country, most notably in the September 2010 riots in Maputo, which erupted over price increases and a reduction in food subsidies. Although these were later restored, the riots were brutally put down by the government and represent an indelible stain on Mozambican political economy under the Guebuza government.)

In addressing what they label the "state-party-business nexus" that now defines much of Mozambique's political economy, Jeremy Astill-Brown and Markus Weimer (2010, 7) offer a fairly damning assessment:

> Mozambique's transition is not yet complete. However, compared to the rather slow and difficult evolution of the democratic forces, the capitalist

instinct seems to have been catapulted out of its historical stranglehold and is flourishing. This means that opportunities for enrichment abound but access to them is limited to a small group. It is very much tied to being part of the political elite, which usually means having access to or being a high-ranking member of FRELIMO. This is a factor that increases economic freedom for the elite and stifles democracy. Such a strategy of exclusive enrichment is not necessarily deliberate, but is in danger of becoming so, since vested economic interests mean some party members and public office holders have no stake in strengthening democratic forces in Mozambique. This force should not be underestimated as a hindrance to reform and democratization in the country.

The Macroeconomy

From a global perspective, Mozambique's economy has grown at a phenomenal rate since the early 1990s and has been labeled in some quarters an "African newly industrializing country" (Nordas and Pretorius 2000). Indeed, the economy grew at over 9 percent per year from 1997 through 2001 in real terms. Although it experienced only 1.1 percent growth in 2000 due to damaging record floods, growth rebounded to 11.9 percent in 2001 and averaged a robust 7.51 percent per year between 2002 and 2009 (World Bank Databank). The country has also seen benefits from debt relief schemes, such as the enhanced Highly Indebted Poor Countries (HIPC) initiative and the Multilateral Debt Relief Initiative (MDRI). The first of these resulted in a nearly 75 percent (more than US$4.5 billion) reduction in Mozambique's debt load as early as 2000; subsequent programs provided further relief, although the country has continued to borrow to finance imports. This afforded the government a degree of fiscal flexibility previously unknown to it and the ability to invest in human development: education, health (particularly childhood immunizations), and water.

The government published its PRSP in October 2001, the goals of which are "to achieve high rates of sustainable, poverty-reducing growth, consolidate macroeconomic stability, and achieve a quantitative and qualitative increase in the delivery of social service" (EIU 2002a, 8). As in other countries such as Zambia and Malawi, the PRSP program was undertaken as a prerequisite for the advanced HIPC initiative. A locally owned version, the Action Plan for the Reduction of Absolute Poverty (PARPA), was under way before the PRSP process began, which suggested that poverty reduction strategies were actually being taken seriously.[16] This version was not signed off in parliament, however, but was undertaken at the cabinet level and largely technocratic, a move that was criticized sharply by Renamo and several NGOs.

The improved macroeconomic picture and desire of the donors to make Mozambique a "success case" has also aided foreign direct investment (FDI) inflows. Stability and favorable policies led to marked increases in FDI following the country's liberation war. From 1989 to 1994, FDI averaged an anemic US$21 million per year, but increased to an average of US$153 million from 1995 to 2000 (EIU 2002a, 28). Indeed, in 1997 alone, US$1.8 billion in new foreign investment projects were approved, although US$1.3 billion alone was related to the Mozal aluminum smelter plant. Most FDI, including investment in the smelter project and the development of a major gas pipeline, historically has come from neighboring South Africa. South Africa is still the country's leading investor (and Mozambique's main source of imports), but two-way trade with the European Union (EU) is considerably larger (Eurostat 2010). However, new investment is coming from a range of diverse sources, including Australia, China, Brazil, India, Japan, and Vietnam. A Vietnamese company recently established Mozambique's third mobile phone network, and natural gas and especially coal mining are also attracting multinational interest. According to the EIU (2010b, 14): "This flurry of activity in Mozambique's coal sector is an indication that the country is on the verge of becoming a major new global coal producer."

Mozambique's economic achievements, while remarkable, must be viewed in their historical context. First, whereas the international debt reduction, for example, may be claimed as a victory for the World Bank, its global partners, and the HIPC and later MDRI, it is also a just result, considering that much of Mozambique's debt could be considered "odious debt" accumulated in the 1980s in the country's effort to resist destruction by first the Rhodesian armed forces and later by the SADF and its proxy, Renamo. Indeed, the economic costs of the war from 1977 to 1992 have been estimated at US$15 billion—including destruction of infrastructure and an estimated 1 million deaths and 5 million displacements (Vines 1996, 1).

Second, Mozambique was at the very bottom of the global economic ladder; thus, even at annual growth rates of 9 to 12 percent, it will still take many years to produce significant structural improvements in the lives of average citizens. The riots in 2010 are a stark reminder of this.

Third, as with its neighbors, Mozambique principally exports its primary commodities. In 2000, these were dominated by such basic commodities as prawns, cashew nuts, and cotton. Mozambique diversified its exports since then, yet the country's particular array of goods does not yet provide the necessary mix for sustainable development. Aluminum, which is principally exported to the European Union, accounted for nearly two-thirds of total exports in 2007. Given its hydropower resources, Mozambique also exports electricity to South Africa; the remaining 30 percent of exports comprises agricultural products such as cashews, cotton, tobacco, and fishery products (WTO 2009, 83), many of which are produced by poor fishermen and smallholders.

However ironic, Mozambique's economic performance and stability have transformed it into a major aid recipient: such foreign inflows amounted to 36 percent of GDP from 1994 to 1998 (Nordas and Pretorius 2000, 24), although they dropped to 10 to 20 percent of GDP in the first decade of the twenty-first century (IMF 2007, 24). In sum, Mozambique's primary commodities, its receipt of substantial debt relief, and inflows of international aid are all vital, if not necessarily sustainable, components of its near-term economic future. Mozambique still ranks among the world's—and even the region's—poorest countries. The economic boom that has brought such dramatic change and acclaim to Mozambique has been accompanied by deepening inequality. How the state, whose economic functions have been curtailed through liberalization, will address these concerns remains an open question (Pitcher 2003, 264).

Challenges of the Twenty-First Century

A generation after its historic peace agreement and a decade after its first multiparty elections, Mozambique would appear to be on a path of relatively democratic governance, political stability, and impressive economic growth that few might have predicted. The prelude to the December 2004 presidential elections represented a milestone in Mozambique's modern history. Initially it appeared that the retirement of President Chissano presented a genuine opportunity for *alternance* and for deepening democracy. Indeed, Chissano, the international laureate, set an important precedent by announcing in 2001 that he would step aside, allowing Renamo and other opposition groups to prepare for a competitive contest against a nonincumbent.

Clearly the outcome of the 2004 election obviated questions about Renamo's readiness to rule; 2009 rendered such questions moot. Yet the contemporary situation presents a number of other potential perils. Frelimo's resounding victories clearly set Mozambique on a path of sustained one-party dominance. Although this need not, in and of itself, imperil the polity or preclude a return to competitiveness in the future, Frelimo's style as the government of a legally multiparty system has been tailored toward exclusion rather than coalition, and this appears to have worsened under Armando Guebuza's presidency (Astill-Brown and Weimer 2010). Yet, as partly reflected in low voter turnouts since 2004, as well as by recent riots, Mozambique remains divided—by rural versus urban residency, by region, by ethnicity, and increasingly by wealth—and the ability of Frelimo alone to speak to the needs of this diverse populace is as much in question today as it was during the war. Hence Frelimo's domination at every level of politics is a potential source of conflict.

Renamo, though inconsequential in national elections, still commands a large following, which Dhlakama periodically threatens to mobilize in protest against the government; there is always the risk of violence. Yet time and again under Afonso Dhlakama's leadership, Renamo has dug in its heels where it should have compromised, bluffed where it should have cooperated. It is likely that Renamo will continue to fit quite uneasily, if at all, into the role of "loyal opposition," a role that may yet be assumed by the nascent MDM or some as yet unknown aspiring "third force."

After two decades of peace, competition has diminished, and the prospects for turnover have become remote. Perhaps more worryingly, key institutions such as the Constitutional Council, the electoral bodies, and local governments remain weak, lack autonomy, and appear ill equipped to manage social conflict effectively. At the same time, institutions of civil society do not yet consistently offer a meaningful bulwark against the misuse of state power. Although the strengthening of Mozambique's democratic institutions and the creation of a more equitable and sustainable economy must be top priorities, for the time being, such initiatives will have to be sourced from Frelimo alone.

Notes

1. Chissano's action played a part in the decision of the Mo Ibrahim Foundation to award Chissano its first ever African Leadership Prize in 2007. The citation for the prize, which included a US$5 million award, read in part: "President Chissano's achievements in bringing peace, reconciliation, stable democracy and economic progress to his country greatly impressed the committee. So, too, did his decision to step down without seeking the third term the constitution allowed" (Mo Ibrahim Foundation 2007).

2. Frelimo initially blamed the Portuguese for the assassination, but it is now widely accepted that his murder was part of a leadership struggle within Frelimo (Weinstein 2002, 145–146).

3. As of 1996, the new FADM had less than half its prescribed complement and represented one of the region's weakest armed forces (Vines 1996). Under United Nations guidance, the main failing was not the inability to recruit new troops but rather the failure to confiscate small arms, which are today widely available.

4. The country's main national languages are Elomwe, Emakhuwa, Xitsonga (Xichangana), Ciyao, Cisena, Cishona, Echuwabo, Cinyanja, Xironga, Shimaconde, Cinyungue, Cicopi, Bitonga, and Kiswahili. There is also a high degree of religious pluralism, including significant numbers of practitioners of traditional religions and Muslims. There have been Muslim majorities in Niassa and Cabo Delgado and a strong plurality (41.6 percent) in Nampula province (Baloi 1996, 487).

5. For example, the Supreme Court heard 298 cases in 2001; however, the number of cases still pending by year end totaled 1,126. Similar backlogs existed at lower levels of the judiciary as well, according to EIU (2002a, 17).

6. However, when Renamo expelled five of its MPs from the party, including, in 2000, former leader of the Renamo parliamentary bench and Rome negotiator Raul Domingos, the Frelimo majority argued that the constitution allowed them to keep their seats as independents until 2004. The other four former Renamo members were Almeida Tambara, Chico Francisco, Rachide Tayob, and José Henriques Lopes.

7. A 2007 law added representatives of civil society to the CNE, which perhaps should have helped with the transparency problems (Commonwealth Observer Group 2009, 20).

8. Indeed, in the late 1990s it became apparent that splits were emerging between the Frelimo "old guard" and younger members, although the party took some steps to address this divide at its 2002 congress (EIU 2002a).

9. Author interviews with the diplomatic and NGO community, Maputo, June 14–15, 2001.

10. PDD is actually still in existence, but it got a negligible share of the vote in 2009.

11. Author interview with Joachim Chissano, Maputo, June 14, 2001.

12. Author interview with Chico Francisco, Renamo secretary of external affairs, June 14, 2001.

13. Renamo's electoral strength lies in the rural areas, not the urban municipalities (Orre 2001, 85).

14. Francisco, interview.

15. Author interview with NGO coalition leaders, Maputo, June 16, 2001; author interview with IPADE leadership, Maputo, June 16, 2001.

16. Author interview with Department for International Development (UK) personnel, Mozambique office, Maputo, June 15, 2001.

6 Angola: Prosperity and Patronage Politics

In early January 2010, as host of the biennial African soccer competition for the Africa Cup of Nations, Angola was set to showcase to the world (and potential investors) its progress in overcoming a twenty-seven-year war that had ended in 2002. With peace finally achieved in the early twenty-first century, parliamentary elections conducted in 2008, and a new constitution adopted in 2010, the government of Angola and a population passionate about football had a lot to prove. Four brand-new Chinese-built stadia awaited fans in the cities of Luanda, Benguela, Lubango, and Cabinda; renovated roads and airports and rehabilitated hotels and restaurants awaited visitors from across the continent. And yet, just two days before the beginning of the games, a deadly attack upon the Togo team driving in from Congo Brazzaville seemed to suggest that Angola had not progressed very far at all. Indeed, three team staff members were killed, and two players were seriously injured in an ambush claimed by the Front for the Liberation of Cabinda (FLEC), a rebel movement fighting for the independence of Angola's oil-rich Cabinda province (which had signed a cease-fire with the government in 2006). The tournament went forward, though the Togo team withdrew, with the deadly attack bringing tragedy to what was supposed to be Angola's triumph—and providing a stark reminder of the many hurdles still facing the young African nation.

Only independent for thirty-five years by 2010, Angola and its people suffered through most of those years (as they also had during more than a decade of anticolonial struggle).[1] Like Mozambique, Angola only gained its independence from colonial Portugal in 1975 and, like Mozambique, was almost immediately plunged into further war.[2] That war continued, despite multiple attempts to end it, until early 2002, when National Union for the Total Independence of Angola (UNITA) leader Jonas Savimbi was assassinated and a cease-fire was signed between the ruling forces of the Popular Movement for the Liberation of Angola (MPLA[3]) and the rebel forces of UNITA. By mid-2004 peace had clearly taken hold. While problems persisted, the demobilization of UNITA troops had been completed, and as UNITA made the transition

Angola: Country Data

Land area   1,246,700 km²
Capital   Luanda
Date of independence   November 11, 1975
Population   13,068,161 (July 2010 estimate), 57% urban (2008 estimate)
Languages   Portuguese (official), several African languages
Ethnic groups   Ovimbundu 37%, Kimbundu 25%, Bakongo 13%, Mestíço 2%,
    European 1%, other 22%
Religions   indigenous beliefs 47%, Roman Catholic 38%, Protestant 15% (1998
    estimate)
Currency   kwanza (AOA); kwanza per US dollar: 77.17
Literacy rate   67.4% (male, 82.9%; female, 54.2% [2001 estimate]).
Life expectancy   38.48 years (male, 37.48 years; female, 39.52 years [2010
    estimate])
Infant mortality   178.13 per 1,000 live births
GDP per capita (PPP)   US$8,300
GDP real growth rate   –0.9%
Leaders since independence
    Agostino Neto, president, November 1975–September 1979
    José Eduardo dos Santos, president, September 1979–
Major political parties
    Ruling party   Popular Movement for the Liberation of Angola (MPLA)
    Other parties   National Front for the Liberation of Angola (FNLA), National
    Union for the Total Independence of Angola (UNITA), New Democracy
    Coalition, Social Renewal Party (PRS)
Women in parliament (lower/single house)   38.6% (2008 election)

Sources: Data derived from https://www.cia.gov; http://www.ipu.org/.
Note: Data from 2009 unless otherwise noted.

from a rebel movement to a political party, competition shifted slowly from the battlefield to the arena of party politics. National elections, the first in sixteen years, were held in late 2008, by which time a small group of civil society organizations were asserting themselves. Increased oil production contributed to unprecedented economic growth rates of around 15 percent by about 2008. Also, from 2005 on, billions of dollars in credit from China, Brazil, and several European countries were being deployed to rebuild Angola's broken infrastructure. Just as importantly, those funds allowed the Angolan government a certain autonomy vis-à-vis the international financial institutions and the more traditional bilateral donors.

And yet for the majority of Angola's more than 13 million people, life today remains precarious with only halting progress made in recovering from decades of war. Large parts of the country's social and economic infrastructure had been destroyed or had simply collapsed during the twenty-seven years of postindependence war. During those years about 1.5 million

Angolans had perished. Four million Angolans had been internally displaced by the war, 2.6 million since 1998, with most fleeing to urban areas. Among other things, Angolans had fled millions of land mines that littered the countryside, making cultivation of the land impossible and imperiling people's lives. As a result of the land mines, Angola ranked first in the world in number of amputees in the late 2000s.[4] As a result of the inability to cultivate the land, half of all Angolans were undernourished; indeed, many Angolans had relied upon international donors for their food during the many years of the conflict. The public health system in the country had been reduced to a shambles by war's end (Agadjanian and Prata 2001; Tvedten 2002). In 2010 life expectancy at birth in Angola (not yet hit by the AIDS crisis in the same way as other southern African countries) was barely thirty-nine years (better only than Haiti's), and the infant mortality rate was 178 per 1,000 live births, the highest in the world. In the education sector Angola had one of the lower overall adult literacy rates in southern Africa, around 67 percent, with a much lower rate for women at only 54 percent. Only 3 percent of Angola's budget was spent on education in the middle of the first decade of the twenty-first century.[5]

By some estimates, some Angolans in 2009 were living in conditions worse even than during the war. Inequality had increased dramatically in Angola during the 1990s and continued to rise (Hilhorst and Serrano 2010, 193). Moreover, these very poor socioeconomic indicators and rising inequality are found in what is potentially a tremendously wealthy country—endowed with vast oil reserves, gas, diamonds, fertile land on which to grow coffee and other agricultural products, and powerful rivers from which to generate hydroelectricity to sell to neighboring countries. Angola has a long coastline and a transport infrastructure that, once rehabilitated, will make it a transportation center for the region. Indeed, Angola's location ties it closely to economies in southern and central Africa and positions it well to become further integrated into and benefit from both. Finally, its capacity to wield military power abroad is also significant. Given these resources, Angola should vie with South Africa for regional superpower status in southern Africa. At the end of the first decade of the new millennium, it certainly did not.

Not counting Zimbabwe, Angola is the last country in southern Africa to attempt a transition from a very bleak past. Indeed, as Tony Hodges (2004, 199) has pointed out, Angola has been attempting "a quadruple transition: from war to peace and reconciliation; from humanitarian emergency to rehabilitation, recovery and development; from an authoritarian, one-party system of governance to pluralist democracy; and from a command economy to one based on the laws of the market." As many have observed, each of these transitions would be a tremendous challenge on its own—and Angola has been facing all four simultaneously. At the same time, Mozambique, with which

Angola shares so many common experiences, has made considerable progress since 1992 with these same transitions. Some have suggested that Angola's generous resource endowment, in stark contrast to Mozambique's relative lack of natural resources, goes a long way toward explaining its continued struggle to accomplish these transitions. As will be elaborated later in the chapter, the abundance of mineral resources in Angola, as in many other "resource-cursed" countries, clearly allowed war to continue as long as it did (long after other wars in the region had ceased)—on the one hand providing a powerful loot-seeking motive for fighting to win or to hold on to power, and on the other hand providing the means by which both sides could finance their war efforts. In addition, access to resources allowed the government to become and remain fully unaccountable to its people—revenues have been completely misman-aged and outright corruption has become rampant—with the result that a small elite thrives while the majority of Angolans struggle in chronic poverty, bereft of some the most basic social services and some of the most basic political rights.

Historical Origins of the Angolan State

As in a number of southern African countries, the first inhabitants of what is today Angola were the Khoisan peoples. From the eighth century onward, they were joined by Bantu-speaking peoples from western Africa, during two distinct waves—from the north and from the east—that were part of the great Bantu migrations east and south. The main influx of these peoples into Angola occurred during the fourteenth century, just before the arrival of the Portuguese. By 1500 most of Angola was populated by Bantu-speaking peoples, who first lived in peaceful coexistence with, and later largely absorbed, the original Khoisan population. According to Inge Tvedten (1997, 11), "most of the Bantu groups mixed and intermarried with each other and had contact through conquest and trade, but they still maintained distinct ethnic character-istics, including differences in dialect." Over time, villages joined together to form chiefdoms, which were later consolidated to form kingdoms. By the mid–fifteenth century, the Kongo kingdom—the most important of the Angolan kingdoms—stretched over large parts of northern Angola. Other important kingdoms included the Loango kingdom of the Vili in present-day Cabinda, the Mbundu kingdom of Ndongo, the Matamba and Kasanje king-doms, the Lunda kingdom, and the Kwanyama kingdom, on the border with Namibia. The Ovimbundu people arrived in the southern part of the territory between 1400 and 1600 but never developed a kingdom (Tvedten 1997, 14–16).

The first Europeans to arrive in Angola were the Portuguese, who reached the Angolan coast in 1483, where they encountered the Kongo kingdom. Initially, contacts between the Kongo and the Portuguese were to some extent mutually beneficial. Moreover, according to Tvedten:

> Kongo and Portugal were at this time in many respects on the same economic level. Both were monarchies ruled by kings and a class of nobles in which relations of kinship and clientage dominated the political system. Social indicators like life expectancy and infant mortality were roughly the same in both societies. Both societies had primarily agrarian economies, and both possessed general purpose money and were heavily involved in trade. (1997, 17–18)

The two groups were very different, however, in that the Portuguese possessed firearms and a superior transport technology that allowed them to move goods, including people, across oceans. Indeed, the Portuguese quickly became involved in a transatlantic slave trade transporting Angolans, first to sugar plantations in São Tomé and then, beginning in 1550, to sugar plantations in Brazil. Relations between the Portuguese and the Kongo quickly soured as Portuguese traders, missionaries, and officials began to interfere in internal Kongolese affairs. Moreover, the slave trade also began to weaken the Kongo kingdom, such that by the end of the sixteenth century "the authority and power of the Kongo kingdom had started to deteriorate" (Tvedten 1997, 18).

Indeed, Angola suffered a heavier loss than any other African country during the four centuries of the transatlantic slave trade. It is estimated that 4 million of the 12 million Africans who survived the Atlantic crossing to be enslaved in the Americas were from Angola—and that another 4 million Angolans died, either in being captured and held in captivity in Angola or on the journey to the Americas. This represents not only a severe population loss but also a profound loss in terms of the development of Angolan society in economic, political, and social terms.

In 1576 the Portuguese founded the city of Luanda and the colony of Angola. From that period onward they focused their efforts on conquering the interior of the territory. They met with significant resistance from Angolan kingdoms in the interior, a resistance epitomized by Queen Nzinga, who dominated the territory from the 1620s to the 1660s. A fierce anticolonial fighter and leader, Queen Nzinga "carried the flag of resistance to the verge of success" in the effort to stave off Portuguese domination (Birmingham 1992, 9). The Portuguese, meanwhile, also had to contend with incursions by other Europeans, including the Dutch, French, and British, who were eager for a share of the lucrative slave trade. After the Portuguese abolished slavery in all of their overseas territories in 1836 (although its practice continued until the 1880s), the Portuguese began to focus on the colonization and exploitation of the Angolan territory. To that end, from the late 1880s onward the Portuguese, bereft of revenues from the slave trade, enacted a brutal policy of forced labor. Moreover, they also implemented a system of local rule that played upon divisions among ethnic groups and weakened traditional political authorities. When all else failed, they engaged in intensive military campaigns to bring the territory under their control. The Portuguese launched their last major military campaign in 1917, stamping out the last vestiges of local resistance; after that "their occupation was complete" (Tvedten 1997, 19–25).

From 1915 onward, Portugal invested considerably in its colony, in order to better exploit it. The Benguela railway, linking mines in the Belgian Congo with the Angolan port city of Lobito, was built, and the Diamond Company of Angola was established and began mining Angolan diamonds in 1917. Coffee production was enhanced, and there was rapid development in a number of other industries, including fishing, manufacturing, and later, petroleum. Indeed, from the late 1950s on, oil production grew rapidly, and during the 1960s foreign oil companies from the United States, in particular, invested heavily in the oil sector. During this period the number of Portuguese settlers increased dramatically as well—from 40,000 in 1940 to 340,000 in 1974 (jumping from 2 to 6 percent of the Angolan population).[6] As in southern Africa's other settler colonies, the intensification of Portuguese settlement in the territory meant an intensification of the expropriation of land in the interior of the colony. Not only were indigenous Angolans expelled from their lands, but they were also forced to cultivate cash crops for export, such as coffee, maize, beans, and wheat, rather than produce food crops for their own consumption.

According to Tvedten (1997, 27–28), the African population in the Angolan colony was subject to a systematic policy of segregation in addition to the aforementioned land expropriation and forced labor. This system divided the population into *indígenas* (indigenous peoples), *assimilados* (assimilated nonwhites), and Europeans. For the vast majority of Africans— considered *indígenas*—the segregation consisted of "an elaborate system of social control (identification cards), economic requirements (payment of a head tax or, alternatively, an obligation to work for the government for six months a year), and lack of political and social rights." Unlike the situation in Botswana, traditional African institutions and leaders played little part in administering the colony; moreover, access to education and health services was extremely limited for the majority of the population. Angolans could be classified as *assimilados,* meanwhile, by meeting certain requirements related to level of educational attainment, proficiency in Portuguese, economic independence, and "abandonment of a traditional way of life." In general, it was *mestíços* in Angola who opted to qualify for *assimilado* status, though the number was always extremely small. Thus, whereas Angola had many of the same characteristics as the Anglophone settler societies in Namibia, South Africa, and Zimbabwe, the opportunity for assimilation and potentially citizenship, however negligible, made Angola more like the French colonial model than the British one (Davidson 1994).[7]

The common denominator of colonialism all over Africa, however, was the hardening of ethnic or "tribal" identities, even where only loose, ill-defined groupings had existed previously (Vail 1991). Within Angola, over time, ethnic identities among the indigenous population began to solidify and take on a greater salience as well, with three distinctive groupings emerging. The first was the Kongo people, who because of the once powerful Kongo kingdom had retained a distinctive identity; they also shared considerable ties with Kongo people across the border in Zaire (including a heavy use of the French language). The Mbundu were the second group. They were distinguished by their close interaction with the Portuguese colonists over the years (hence a greater degree of "Westernization" and urbanization) and were associated closely with the urban *mestiço* population. Finally, the third group was the Ovimbundu, who had once dominated the central highlands and were then forcibly removed to coffee plantations in the north, bringing them into potential conflict with both the Kongo and Mbundu (Tvedten 1997, 28–29). By the later years of the colonial period these three groups formed the basis for the three nationalist groups that would challenge Portuguese rule.

Nationalist movements organized somewhat later in Angola than they did in the other southern African colonies. The Portuguese harshly suppressed any kind of organized political activity, and the development of an effective leadership was hindered by lack of educational opportunities for most Angolans. Still, not just one but several nationalist movements did emerge. By 1956 the MPLA, led eventually by doctor and poet Agostino Neto, emerged with a support base among the Mbundu people and the *mestiço* population, particularly in the country's larger cities, especially Luanda. In 1962, the National Front for the Liberation of Angola (FNLA), led by Holden Roberto and supported primarily by the Kongo people in the north, was formed, with links across the border in Zaire. Finally, in 1966 UNITA was established by Jonas Savimbi, eventually drawing its main support from the Ovimbundu. The three movements were united in their demand for political independence for Angola but differed in ideological orientation and in terms of the support and resources each ultimately received from foreign backers. In brief, the MPLA, with a Marxist orientation, was the most radical of the three movements and drew international support eventually from Cuba and the Soviet Union. The FNLA was backed by Zaire, with US assistance, from the beginning; paradoxically, the FNLA was also supported by China (Vines 2000, 3). UNITA "never developed any clearly articulated political platform during the 15 years of [preindependence] struggle," although it did develop "ethnic Ovimbundu overtones" (Tvedten 1997, 30–31). Although initially supported by China, by the time of independence UNITA had turned to South Africa for support and later became a major recipient of US aid. Hodges (2004, 8) notes that the three independence movements "proved unable to mount a united front, and at times fought each other." Among other things, this seriously weakened the anticolonial effort in Angola such that by the early 1970s the divided anticolonial movement in Angola was "little more than an irritant to the Portuguese."

Among the European colonial powers in Africa, the Portuguese were the least willing to relinquish their colonies. Much less developed than the other European countries by the mid–twentieth century (and a military regime rather than a democracy), Portugal was determined to retain the economic benefits that colonialism provided. As a result, the people of Angola (and of Mozambique and Guinea-Bissau) were forced to resort to war to gain their independence. In Angola that war erupted violently in 1961 with uprisings in Luanda and the killing of white settlers in northern Angola (Minter 1994, 18). Over the next thirteen years the three different groups—the MPLA, the FNLA, and UNITA—fought the Portuguese (and at times each other) from exile bases from the north (Congo and Zaire) and east (Zambia) and from inside the country. The Portuguese fought back—indeed they were fighting the same battle in Guinea-Bissau and Mozambique—until the cost of the three colonial wars became too high. In April 1974 the regime that had been in power in Portugal for fifty years was overthrown by lower-level military officers fed up with the African wars, opening the door for independence in the country's African colonies.[8] In January 1975 the three nationalist movements in Angola and Portugal signed the Alvor Accord, providing for a transitional government and elections leading to independence in November 1975 (Minter 1994, 19). But the provisions of the Alvor Accord did not hold, and heavy fighting, aided and abetted by external supporters, quickly broke out among the three movements. Despite the continued fighting, on November 11, 1975, the MPLA declared Angola independent of Portuguese rule and installed itself as the new government. MPLA leader Agostino Neto was named the country's first president and remained so until his death four years later, when he was succeeded by José Eduardo dos Santos, who has held the office since.

Society and Development:
The Long War and Its Aftermath

Independence, however, did not bring peace to Angola. Rather, a war quickly erupted and continued largely unabated until 2002—despite two substantial attempts at peace in 1992 and 1994. After the MPLA gained power in 1975, the FNLA gradually disappeared as a contender in the fighting, and the war became one between the MPLA government and the rebel UNITA movement, which had quickly reorganized in the face of its 1975 defeat. As will be detailed below, two attempts to end the war in the early 1990s—when other regional wars were ending—failed, and with each failed attempt the war became more intractable and more brutal. In the end, it took the assassination of UNITA leader Jonas Savimbi to bring the violence and hostilities to an end. Ultimately, the prolonged conflict took an overwhelming toll on Angola. A number of factors have been identified as contributing to Angola's devastating postindependence conflict.

Ideological and Ethnic Divisions

As noted above, there were ideological and ethnic differences between the two movements that fed the conflict. In 1976 the MPLA, like its counterpart Frelimo in Mozambique, formally adopted Marxism-Leninism as its official ideology and set out to develop Angola along socialist lines. In 1977 the MPLA declared itself a "vanguard party" and commenced with a program of nationalizing abandoned Portuguese farms and businesses. By the second half of the 1970s the new government was attempting to manage a centrally planned economy (Hodges 2004, 9). But as in Mozambique, the obstacles were formidable. Both countries lacked skilled administrators and technicians who could replace the Portuguese who had fled at independence. Indeed, in each state, according to William Minter (1994, 24), "the post-independence governments took charge of economies in a state of collapse." And the political model that both governments relied upon—again highly centralized—was based upon the Marxist traditions of most of the countries and movements, mainly the Soviet Union and Eastern Europe, that supported them. Only in the mid-1980s did the MPLA government begin to move away from a centrally planned economy toward one based on market forces (in part due to the poor performance of the economy but also because of "emergent class interests" stymied by the planned economy [Hodges 2004, 11]). Political liberalization began in 1990 at the MPLA's third party congress.

UNITA, meanwhile, is described by many as not having had a clear ideological position, notwithstanding its eventual South African and US sponsorship. UNITA did have, especially over time, a more pronounced ethnic bias toward the Ovimbundu and other eastern and southern Angolan ethnic groups. Assis Malaquias (2000, 105–107) suggests that the Ovimbundu identification with UNITA was prompted in part by the MPLA government's failure over time to address the needs of most Angolans, particularly those from the southern and eastern regions. According to David Birmingham (2002, 156), Angola's southern elite, "who had not been dealt an equitable hand in the [post-independence] settlements of the late 1970s . . . remained isolated and aggrieved in their south-eastern guerrilla camps on the remote edge of the old Portuguese colonial world." More significant, perhaps, UNITA "relied on loyalty to a charismatic leader—Jonas Savimbi" (who was himself an Ovimbundu) (Minter 1994, 20). In the event, both ideological and ethnic differences were seized upon by a group of external actors with varying motives eager to intervene in the Angolan conflict.

The Cold War: Role of External Actors

A key factor fueling the war in Angola and helping to hone the ideological distinctions between the warring parties was the involvement of several external powers in the conflict, an involvement that had already begun before independence. Basically, as Steve Kibble (2002, 20) observes, by the 1980s "Angola was a pawn in Cold War politics." According to Birmingham:

> The role of the Soviet Union in Africa during its last ten years of existence is one factor that needs to be taken into consideration and it may be significant that Angola's second president, José Eduardo dos Santos, was an engineer in the petroleum industry who had been trained in Russia. Another long-distance factor that might be deemed important is the role of the United States which elected a president, Ronald Reagan, who adopted a virulently hawkish agenda during the Cold War confrontations of the 1980s. (2002, 155)

Aside from Zaire, which supported the Bakongo-dominated FNLA from the start, the first external power to become involved in the conflict was the United States, which allocated US$300,000 in January 1975 to provide support to the FNLA (thereby also undermining the Alvor Accord) (Ohlson and Stedman 1994, 81).[9] Shortly thereafter, the MPLA began to receive arms and equipment from Eastern European countries and, by the time of independence, from the Soviet Union. Around the same time the MPLA also enlisted the assistance of some foreign military advisers, including small numbers of Cubans. By mid-1975, South African and Cuban troops were involved in the conflict, on the sides of UNITA and the MPLA, respectively. Also around the same time, the United States embarked upon a US$32 million covert aid program to defeat the MPLA and to counter what was perceived as a Soviet and Cuban communist foothold in southern Africa (Ohlson and Stedman 1994, 81).

If the Angolan war had critical Cold War overtones, it contained a distinctly regional dimension as well. Indeed, regional politics also impinged upon the conflict in Angola, in many ways feeding the proxy war that was taking place between East and West.[10] In the years after independence, two regional liberation movements, the South West Africa People's Organization from Namibia and the African National Congress from South Africa, set up exile bases in Angola, thereby giving apartheid South Africa a pretext for greater military involvement in Angola. The scope of South Africa's involvement expanded considerably after about 1980. In 1981, moreover, the United States introduced the so-called linkage policy, linking Namibian independence to the withdrawal of Cuban troops from Angola and insisting that the MPLA government share power with UNITA. Throughout the rest of the 1980s the fighting and external involvement in Angola increased dramatically. By 1986 the United States was openly providing US$25 million to UNITA.[11] Similarly, South Africa publicly declared that it was also helping UNITA "in every possible way" (Tvedten 1997, 39). By 1985, meanwhile, 40,000 Cuban troops were on Angolan soil, and the Soviet Union was supplying large amounts of technical assistance and material aid. A major turning point in the war occurred in 1988, when Angolan government and Cuban troops defeated UNITA and South African forces at Cuito Cuanavale in southern Angola, allowing the government to regain control over large areas of the country previously dominated by UNITA. More important, the battle led to negotiations, beginning in May 1988, to end the thirteen-year war in Angola.

Paradoxically, then, just as external actors helped to prolong and magnify the conflict in Angola, they tried to bring it to an end. According to Minter (1994, 49), by the end of the 1980s the United States and the Soviet Union "were increasingly in accord on the need for settlements of 'regional conflicts.'" Moreover, antiwar sentiment was mounting in South Africa just as international economic sanctions and domestic political upheaval were wreaking havoc with the South African economy. Pressure for independence in Namibia was rising. As the fighting dragged on, the Soviet Union and Eastern European countries dissolved, Nelson Mandela was released from jail in South Africa, Namibia gained its independence, and the US interest in supporting UNITA waned. By the end of 1990 the MPLA accepted the notion of a new constitution and officially abandoned Marxism-Leninism in favor of democratic socialism.[12] A nominal multiparty political system emerged in the country by May 1991. Also in May 1991 the Bicesse Accord was signed between the government of Angola and UNITA. The agreement provided for an eighteen-month transition period during which some troops on both sides would be demobilized and eventually joined together to form a national army.[13] During this interim period, "the MPLA was to remain the legitimate and internationally recognized government of Angola, responsible for running the state until new elections could be held" (Vines 2000, 8). At the end of the period, elections for president and the National Assembly were to be held. The agreement was mediated by the United States, the Soviet Union, and Portugal, and the United Nations was charged with overseeing its implementation (Stedman 1997, 36).[14] Birmingham (2002, 171) writes that the period of eighteen months from May 1991 to September 1992 "was the most spectacular period of optimism and freedom that Angola had ever witnessed." When presidential and National Assembly elections were held in September 1992, 91 percent of the electorate participated, and the vote was deemed largely free and fair by international observers. Yet the results were not respected by the loser in the presidential ballot, UNITA's Jonas Savimbi, who won only 40 percent of the vote compared to Angolan president and MPLA leader José Eduardo dos Santos's 49 percent. Despite the apparent credibility of the electoral outcome, Savimbi immediately cried foul and returned to the bush to carry on UNITA's war against the Angolan government, which he was able to do since UNITA had demobilized very few troops (Stedman 1997, 38). By early 1993 UNITA had gained control of three-quarters of the Angolan countryside. By the end of the year, however, having used oil revenues to acquire additional arms, government forces were able to take back large tracts of territory from UNITA.

In the meantime, the United Nations had also imposed arms and fuel sanctions on UNITA, putting it on the defensive (EIU 2003d, 12). This led to another attempt to end the war in November 1994 with the signing by both parties of the Lusaka Protocol in Zambia. This agreement called for a new cease-fire, demobilization of UNITA troops, UNITA participation in the government, and the establishment of a UN peacekeeping force. But this effort also failed, despite the presence of 7,500 UN peacekeepers and a government of national unity and reconciliation (GURN) established in 1997.[15] When it became clear that UNITA was not disarming as required, its participation in the government was suspended, and in November 1998 President dos Santos decided to "resume the war in order 'to save the peace,' following the reluctance of UNITA to abide by the Lusaka Protocol" (le Billon 2001, 59; EIU 2003d, 12–13). When this happened, according to Philippe le Billon (2001, 59), "Angola became one of the worst conflict resolution failures of the 1990s." In 2001 the Angolan armed forces began to use controversial counterinsurgency tactics, moving civilians from the countryside to refugee camps in the urban areas in order to deny UNITA access to the support of the civilian population (EIU 2003d, 13). Eventually, the tide turned against UNITA. Jonas Savimbi was killed at the hands of government forces in February 2002, and Angola's protracted war was finally ended in April that same year.

Diamonds and Oil: Resource Curses?

Along with Savimbi's role as a "spoiler"[16] in the peace process (Stedman 1997), many have identified access to resources—in particular, oil and diamonds—as a key factor in prolonging the war and preventing a peaceful settlement in Angola in the 1990s (Cilliers 2000; le Billon 2001; Malaquias 2001; Munslow 1999), a phenomenon that has plagued the African continent. In brief, the Angolan government was able to rely upon the revenues generated by abundant oil supplies to continue fighting the war against UNITA; moreover, access to oil revenues meant that the decision to continue the war could be taken by the government alone, without consultation with the people. Similarly, UNITA's access to diamonds allowed, even encouraged, the movement to return to war in 1992 and again in the late 1990s. As le Billon notes, there is a clear relationship between abundant natural resources and armed conflicts:

> Rents generated by narrow and mostly foreign-dominated resource industries allow ruling groups to dispense with economic diversification and popular legitimacy, often resulting in rent-seeking, poor economic growth, and little social mobility outside politics and state patronage. . . . Indeed, quantitative analysis demonstrates that easily taxed or looted primary commodities

increase the likelihood of war by providing the motivation, prize, and means of a violent contest for state or territorial control. (2001, 56)

Oil is enormously important to the Angolan economy—with oil production and supporting activities contributing about 85 percent of gross domestic product late in the first decade of the twenty-first century. Moreover, given the potential political instability in African oil-producing countries such as Egypt, Libya, and Nigeria, and the interest of some Western countries to diminish their reliance on Middle Eastern oil, Angola has gained international significance as an oil producer. At the same time, the oil sector very much represents an "enclave economy"—one that has few linkages to other sectors of the economy and that, because it is capital- rather than labor-intensive, provides limited jobs. The oil industry in Angola is geographically isolated from the rest of the country as well—located in the tiny northern Cabinda enclave and offshore. In addition, although oil revenues could have been used over the years to diversify the Angolan economy (for which there is much potential), this has not happened. Finally, in Angola oil revenues were also used to make possible the government's war on UNITA (particularly through the purchase of more than US$5 billion worth of arms in the 1990s), to service debts, and to subsidize the lifestyle of a small elite. "Rather than mitigating the impact of the war and consolidating state governance, the oil revenue has thus reinforced distortions and undermined popular support for the government," le Billon asserted (2001, 63). Oil revenues have also provided enormous opportunities for corruption, which have been exploited. It has been asserted from many quarters that high-level government officials regularly embezzled part of the oil rent (le Billon 2001, 66), such that a popular slogan in Angola went "MPLA steals, UNITA kills."

Diamonds proved a very similar resource for UNITA. As with oil, Angola has an abundant supply of diamonds; together the two commodities account for 99 percent of the country's exports.[17] Angola's diamonds are located primarily in the northeastern part of the country—over vast and lawless areas far from government control—and some of them (alluvial deposits) are easily exploited. According to le Billon (2001, 67), diamonds were a revenue source for UNITA from the late 1970s on, when UNITA forces simply raided existing companies and freelance diggers. From 1983 on, UNITA professionalized its diamond operations, training its staff in diamond sorting and investing in mining equipment. UNITA's diamond exploitation was expanded considerably in the late 1980s and exponentially in the 1990s, as UNITA lost support from the United States and South Africa. According to le Billon (2001, 69), once war resumed in late 1998, UNITA developed new mines in central and southeastern Angola, and even in the southern Democratic Republic of Congo (DRC). From 1992 to 2000, it is estimated that diamonds produced under UNITA's control were worth between US$3 and $4 billion, with those revenues clearly enabling UNITA to return to war (le Billon 2001, 69–71). After 2000, however, the international campaign to halt the purchase of conflict diamonds reduced UNITA's diamond revenues, weakening the movement relative to the government. In the event, UNITA's war effort collapsed in the months following Jonas Savimbi's February 2002 assassination.

State Failure

A final factor contributing to the protracted struggle in Angola has been identified as state failure, defined by James Busumtwi-Sam (2002, 95) as "a situation where a state's claim to be the authoritative political institution over a population and territory is strongly contested." Moreover, state failure—as manifest in a weak domestic support base for a government—also contributes to leaders' seeking outside sources of support, even direct military assistance, as happened in Angola. According to Busumtwi-Sam (2002, 96), state failure in Angola occurred almost immediately after independence. From the start, the authority of the MPLA government was violently contested by UNITA. By the mid-1980s Angola had de facto dual sovereignty, with each side controlling large areas of the country. Further, as Kibble (2002, 20) observes, UNITA was aided in its quest to eliminate the MPLA by the lack of full legitimacy of the MPLA. This lack of legitimacy shaped Angola in the years after independence, according to Kibble: "The MPLA—though it controlled the capital and most of the country on independence day—was never granted the undisputed nationalist legitimacy which it aspired to and claimed."

Consistent with the conditions of state failure, the Angolan state was "no longer able to carry out vital functions associated with governance including forms of domination, the nature of surplus extraction, and the patterns of resource allocation." By 2000 most of those functions were formulated and carried out by powerful agents who were not accountable to the public (Malaquias 2000, 108). The vacuum created by the absence of the state and its institutions creates opportunities for "warlords," a term popularized by William Reno (1999, 79) to describe situations in which local "strongmen have used commerce to consolidate their political power within a coalition of interest among themselves, businesspeople, and local fighters." Indeed, state failure "serves the interests of 'warlords' in society to the extent that the disorder that ensues creates avenues for maintaining their power and profits" (Busumtwi-Sam 2002, 99). This, of course, describes well UNITA under Jonas Savimbi and the movement's involvement in the highly lucrative illicit diamond trade.

Thus a whole series of factors served to prolong Angola's deadly conflict that erupted with independence. These included early ideological and ethnic differences between the warring parties that were hardened over time; the external intervention of ideologically driven regional and international players who exaggerated the ideological dimension to justify their own actions and who exacerbated the two sides' ethnic bases; access to two highly profitable resources, oil and diamonds, that helped each side to finance the war and carry it out with impunity and without regard for the needs and wishes of the Angolan people; and a state failure bordering on warlordism that left the populace without access to the most basic services and the elite with enormous opportunities for accumulation. Finally, one individual agent in particular, Jonas Savimbi, has been identified by many as refusing to sanction or abide by any efforts to bring the conflict to an end (though in the case of the 1992 election, the United States and United Nations have also been held culpable for failing to prevent Savimbi from spoiling the process); indeed, it took Savimbi's death in early 2002 to finally bring an end to the war and allow peace to take hold.

Organization of the State

On April 4, 2002, the Angolan government and UNITA signed a memorandum of understanding, technically an addendum to the Lusaka Protocol, that formalized the cease-fire between the two parties in effect since Savimbi's February 2002 death. As set out in the memorandum, UNITA recommitted to the peace framework in the 1994 Lusaka Protocol, returned all remaining territory to Angolan government control, quartered all military personnel in predetermined locations, and relinquished all arms. In August 2002, UNITA demobilized all military personnel and in September 2002, together with the government, reconstituted the UN-sponsored joint commission to resolve all outstanding political issues under the Lusaka Protocol. As of late November 2002 the government and UNITA declared all outstanding issues resolved and the 1994 Lusaka Protocol fully implemented. Angola was thus in the early stages of the transition that other countries in the region had already completed.

In early 2004 the government announced that elections would be held in 2006; in the meantime a new constitution would be drafted, new electoral laws adopted, and a census conducted in order to register voters. Opposition political parties argued that a new constitution should be adopted by a new parliament, rather than in advance of parliamentary elections, and the government agreed. Elections were not held in 2006 as planned, but in September 2008. In early 2010 the new parliament adopted a new constitution.

Constitution

Political liberalization, it may be argued, began in the early 1990s in Angola, when hopes for peace and a resolution of decades of conflict were high. At its party congress in December 1990 the MPLA had formally renounced Marxism-Leninism as its guiding doctrine and in mid-1991 a law to revise the country's constitution was enacted. The constitutional revision law "proclaimed a democratic state based on the rule of law and respect for human rights, and introduced a multi-party political system" (Hodges 2004, 55). This new law was accompanied by others that loosened restrictions on associations, political parties, the right of assembly, the right to strike, and the media. A year later, in anticipation of September 1992 elections, further laws were passed that established a new electoral system, permitted private radio stations, set up a national press council, and made it easier to register political parties. A second constitutional revision law was passed in September 1992 dealing with decentralization and local government. At the same time, the name of the country was changed from the People's Republic of Angola to "the less ideologically charged" Republic of Angola (Hodges 2004, 55). In the end, however, the return to war threatened, though did not fully reverse, the attempted liberalization. As the Economist Intelligence Unit (EIU) noted (EIU 2003d, 14), the 1991 constitutional reform "nominally established Angola as a democratic state based on the rule of law, multiparty politics and guarantees of press freedom, right to assembly and right to strike." In practice, the EIU concluded, respect for these freedoms was weak, and the country remained a heavily centralized state under the political hegemony of the MPLA.

At war's end in 2002 a process of constitutional reform began anew, though ultimately a new constitution would only be adopted in early 2010—after a new parliament was elected in 2008. Angola's 2010 constitution contains a number of provisions that enhance the power of the president. The constitution eliminates the direct election of the president; rather, as in Botswana and South Africa, the president is selected by the political party with the most votes in the National Assembly.[18] The new constitution retains the president as head of state, the holder of executive power, and the commander of the armed forces. It replaces the prime minister with a vice president, thus assuring an even greater involvement of the president in the country's day-to-day affairs. Other provisions of the constitution are retained from the previous constitution, including: presidential appointment of judges to all courts; retention of Cabinda as a sovereign national territory; maintenance of a policy that all land belongs to the state, thus conferring only on the state the power to grant land concessions; freedoms of religion and the press; and a prohibition of the death penalty.[19]

Executive

In late 2010 José Eduardo dos Santos remained president of Angola after more than thirty continuous years in office. Dos Santos, who ascended to the presidency in 1979 upon the death of his predecessor, Agostino Neto, won the first round of the presidential election in 1992, the first—and perhaps the only—time a presidential election has been held in Angola. (As noted above, the election result was close, invoking a [never held] runoff election. Some observers have suggested that it is because dos Santos does not wish to experience a close election again that the new constitution eliminates the direct election of the president [Roque 2009, 147].) From 1998, when the position of prime minister was abolished, to 2002, the president of Angola was both chief of state and head of government. In December 2002 the post of prime minister was restored, although the president remained chief of state and head of government, and power remained highly concentrated in the executive, particularly the presidency. Following the September 2008 parliamentary election, Antonio Paulo Kassoma was named prime minister by the MPLA. But, as noted above, Angola's 2010 constitution eliminates the position of prime minister in favor of a vice president. In late 2010 Fernando da Piedade Dias dos Santos (the president's cousin) served as vice president of Angola and Kassoma as the president of the National Assembly.[20] The 2010 constitution limits the president's term to two five-year terms; dos Santos's three decades already in office are not counted, however; thus the first of two five-year terms for dos Santos could begin with the parliamentary election in 2012. This will likely ensure that dos Santos remains in power at least until 2022.

Birmingham (2002, 177) argued that after the failed 1992 elections and resumption of war, President dos Santos decided to concentrate still more power in his own hands: "From being a single-party state with a disaffected opposition thinly scattered in the provinces and abroad, Angola became a presidential state in which power emanated from the palace." From his presidential complex, known as the Futungo, dos Santos made decisions that bypassed "government ministries, party cells and state bureaucracies." This highly centralized presidential system represents a continuation of past practice in Angola. While the head of state, as president of the ruling party, president of the country, and commander of the armed forces, was a highly centralized role under President Neto, it became even more centralized after dos Santos came to power in 1979 (Hodges 2004, 52–53). In particular, in the face of the external threats outlined above, dos Santos was able to effect changes within the ruling MPLA that greatly enhanced his own position. His powers were further strengthened with the establishment of a defense and security council in 1984, chaired by the president, which quickly became the country's top decision-making body (Hodges 2004, 53). Within a short time, power became "increasingly personalized" around the person of the president, and a personality cult developed around dos Santos, though never quite on the scale as the one that emerged around Savimbi (Hodges 2004, 54).

Changes contained in the 2010 constitution confirm the concentration of power in the presidency. The executive branch is composed of the president, the vice president, and a council of ministers, all of whom are appointed by the president. Governors of the country's eighteen provinces are also appointed by the president and serve at the pleasure of the president. And the president remains the commander in chief of the armed forces. According to the US Department of State (2010a), in 2009 political power remained concentrated in the president and the council of ministers, through which the president exercised executive power. The council can enact laws, decrees, and resolutions, assuming most functions normally associated with the legislative branch. Further, the State Department noted, the ruling MPLA dominated all political institutions in the country. As David Sogge (2009, 14) observes, as Birmingham (2002) did some years earlier: "The reality is that Angolan politics pivot on the President's office, the '*Futungo.*' It manages clientelist systems through a state apparatus welded together at many points with the dominant party, the MPLA."

Judiciary

Just as with the other two branches, the judiciary in Angola is completely dominated by the Futungo, with the president holding the power to appoint or dismiss all officials of the judicial branch, from the Supreme Court to the Audit Court. On paper, at least, Angola appears to conform to many of the internationally accepted rules and norms of jurisprudence and has authorized the establishment of appropriate legal institutions and structures. In fact, however, the legal system is weak and fragmented. The Supreme Court heads the formal justice system and administers the eighteen provincial courts as well as a limited number of municipal courts. According to the US Department of State (2010a), during 2009 civil courts functioned in only some of the eighteen provinces and faced severe backlogs. During 2009 the Ministry of Justice worked with national and international agencies to improve human resource and technical capacity in provincial and municipal courts. Still, Sogge (2009, 14) charges that "a formal legal system has never been accessible to ordinary Angolans. Today the judicial branch remains weak and subordinated to central authorities." The US Department of State (2010a) concurs, finding in 2009 that the judiciary was subject to political interference and executive influence and was understaffed, inefficient, and corrupt.

As is the situation throughout southern Africa, the legal system in Angola is a dual one, based on Portuguese and customary law. For Angolans living in rural areas, informal courts remain the main institutions through which they attempt to resolve conflicts. Traditional leaders or *sobas* hear and decide local cases. These informal systems are inconsistent, however, with each community establishing its own rules (US Department of State 2010a).

In recent years, new offices have been established and new laws have been promulgated. Since March 2010 a Public Probity Law has been available to penalize corruption and require government officials to declare their personal wealth domestically and internationally. Sogge (2010) suggests that a judicial ombudsman's office, provincial human rights commissions, and mediation centers may provide opportunities for citizens to voice complaints, though "none has a mandate to enforce laws or impose legally binding outcomes." Still, he asserts, these bodies should not be dismissed out of hand as they may one day "provide sites for the powerless to gain a little leverage over, or at least embarrass, the powerful."

Military

The military in Angola, represented by the Angolan Armed Forces (FAA), is described as "competent" and "battle-hardened" after decades of war (Sogge 2009, 12).[21] At the end of the internal war, the national army and police force absorbed some of a total 130,000 demobilized combatants, including about 5,000 of an estimated 85,000 former UNITA soldiers (and generals). The incorporation of the latter was seen as an important (not to say prudent) gesture of reconciliation. Today, the FAA comprises three forces—army, navy, and air force. The largest of the three is the army, with 130,000 members. The navy has 3,000 personnel and the air force 7,000. There is a separate presidential guard, which reports directly to the office of the president. According to Sogge (2009), at mid-decade, nearly half a million people were on the payroll of the FAA, though less than a third of these were on active duty. Tens of thousands more served in regular and irregular police forces, the presidential guard, and secret services. In the intervening years, private security companies have grown as well, with nearly 200 private security agencies employing about 36,000 people, mainly in Luanda and in diamond mining zones around 2005.

The FAA is responsible for external security but also has internal security responsibilities for border security, expulsion of illegal immigrants, and actions against the FLEC in Cabinda. The national police are responsible for internal security and law enforcement. An internal intelligence service that reports to the office of the president investigates sensitive state security matters (US Department of State 2010a). Since independence, the armed forces and police have been the recipients of substantial government resources, making them, for a time, the "only real manifestation of a 'strong state'" in Angola, according to Hodges (2004, 72). Indeed, Christine Messiant (2001, 293) implicates the upper levels of the police force and the general staff of the armed forces in Angola in widespread corruption that has led to the massive personal enrichment of a small elite who provide the support base for the MPLA government.[22] FAA officers, for example, have exercised significant authority over legal and illicit concessions in the diamond fields, and many have arrayed vast forces of small prospectors in conditions of extreme exploitation (Dietrich 2000, 177–178). Hodges (2004, 74) identifies poor morale, discipline, and leadership as key problems of the FAA. These weaknesses derive, he suggests, from "low pay, arrears in wage payments, the lack of a motivating 'cause' and the preoccupation of much of the officer corps with business activities."

The security forces in Angola, including the police and the armed forces, have been accused of widespread abuses, including unlawful killings, extortion, beatings, torture, and rape (US Department of State 2010a). In May 2008 the government of Angola closed the United Nations Human Rights Office, thereby hampering efforts to better train army and police recruits. Still, professional training opportunities by law enforcement and military officials from the southern African region have been provided to Angolan security forces.

Sogge (2009, 12) estimates that relative to its population, Angola's military, paramilitary, and police forces are the largest in sub-Saharan Africa, with the possible exception of Eritrea. Given its size, experience, arms, and equipment, Angola's military can also be considered a regional superpower. It has been involved in wars outside Angola's borders, including the war in DRC. According to EIU (2003d, 13), the government of Angola became involved in the war in DRC (on the side of the DRC government) in an effort to deny UNITA territory from which to operate. By early 2003 the government of Angola claimed that all Angolan troops had been withdrawn from DRC. At the height of the conflict between FAA and UNITA troops, from late 1999 to late 2001, the war also spilled over into neighboring Namibia, whose government, much to the dismay of the populace, granted permission to the FAA to pursue UNITA onto Namibian soil.

Representation and Participation

Legislature

At the national level, Angola has a unicameral legislature, the 220-member National Assembly. For the first time in sixteen years, parliamentary elections were held in 2008—Angola's second multiparty elections ever. The MPLA experienced an overwhelming victory, winning 191 of 220 seats. UNITA won a mere 16 seats, the Social Renewal Party (PRS) 8 seats, the FNLA 3 seats, and the New Democracy Coalition 2 seats.[23] This result was in stark contrast to the preceding legislative election in 1992, when twelve parties won seats in the National Assembly, of which UNITA won 70 and the MPLA only 129. With the 2008 election, the MPLA is now able to govern, even change the constitution (as it has already done), without having to engage in political debate with anyone—opposition political parties, civil society organizations, or any such actors. The MPLA's near total dominance of the National Assembly, as a result of a national election, helps, according to Roque (2009, 137), "to transform Angola into a de facto one-party state while at the same time gaining long-elusive national and international legitimacy." Roque (2009, 147) echoes many other scholars over the years in suggesting in the wake of the 2008 election that Angola's National Assembly will continue "to serve not as a counterweight to the presidency but as a rubber stamp for the regime's policies, and President dos Santos will continue to be the arbiter of all political affairs of the country."

Nor has there been or is there likely to be any devolution of power to the provincial or local level. According to Tvedten (2002, 5), by 2000 there had been very little decentralization of political power to the regional and local level in Angola, and by 2010 that had not changed. Provisional governors are appointed by the president and not elected and so have little accountability to the populations in their provinces; there are no provincial legislative bodies. And while elected local authorities were provided for in the 1991–1992 constitution, they have yet to be established. Local and municipal elections were to be held after a presidential election, but now there will be no presidential election (Roque 2009, 146). The US Department of State (2010a) suggested in early 2010 that the right to elect local leaders (part of a broader right of citizens to change their government) remained a restricted right in Angola.

As in other countries in the region, women fared well in Angola's 2008 legislative election. Of 220 members elected, 82 are women; 77 of the women are members of the ruling MPLA, and the other women all belong to UNITA. With nearly 38 percent women in its National Assembly, Angola is ranked among the top fifteen countries worldwide. This is a dramatic increase over the representation of women in the National Assembly elected in 1992; at that time only 21 MPs, or 9.5 percent, were women. While there is no legal electoral gender quota in Angola, the MPLA has its own party quota, which requires that 30 percent of candidates on party lists be women.[24] As in other dominant-party countries in the region, a voluntary party quota by the ruling party is often more than enough to generate a significant portion of women in parliament. Angola also boasted a significant percentage of women in its cabinet in 2010—26 percent (Gender Links 2010a).

Elections in Angola: Not Yet a Tradition

The first democratic, multiparty elections in Angola, for National Assembly and president, were held on September 29–30, 1992. As noted, the results of the presidential election, which showed Jonas Savimbi trailing President dos Santos by a slight margin, were deemed fraudulent by Savimbi (though not by any of the international election observers) and resulted in UNITA's returning to war. A runoff election was supposed to be held between the two presidential candidates; it was officially canceled in February 1999 long after Savimbi refused to participate and war had begun anew.

As noted, it was not until September 2008 that National Assembly elections were again held in Angola; barring future changes to the constitution, a presidential election will never be held again in Angola. The MPLA government had set a number of preconditions for the elections that were eventually held in 2008, including improvements in basic infrastructure, to allow voter registration and voting, as well as the installation of an electoral commission. In August 2005 the National Assembly adopted new electoral laws pertaining to the electoral process, citizenship and identification, voter registration, election observation, and a code of conduct. The National Electoral Commission (CNE) was established as well as an intergovernmental commission to coordinate logistics.[25] According to Dorothea Hilhorst and Maliana Serrano (2010, 192), for many Angolans, the 2008 elections were "the marker of final peace."

Observers of the 2008 parliamentary elections cited many problems. As in so many dominant-party states in the region, the ruling MPLA enjoyed many advantages over other parties, including access to state resources and the state media. While campaign funding was to be made available to all parties ninety days before the election, it was not available until almost a month before the election. The MPLA also enjoyed the significant largesse of state-owned enterprises and foreign corporations. It is further suggested that the MPLA "packed" the CNE with its friends. Finally, once voting began logistical problems led to chaos, in particular in Luanda, with some alleging that the disorganization was "purposely created." In the rural areas, meanwhile, it is charged that the government engaged in a deliberate strategy of intimidation, threats of war, and the co-optation of *sobas* to secure a favorable vote. Civil service workers were allegedly told to vote for the MPLA if they wanted to keep their jobs, and the military and police were allegedly told that they should vote patriotically, meaning for the MPLA (Roque 2009, 143–144).

With a turnout of around 87 percent, national and international election observers reported that the election was "peaceful and generally credible," despite the ruling party's many advantages (US Department of State 2010a). In the end, according to Paula Roque (2009, 144), though Angola's opposition political parties considered the elections "a farce," they chose to accept the results rather than spark renewed conflict in the country. Ten political parties and four coalitions of parties contested the 2008 election, although only five parties won any seats in the National Assembly. In the 1992 election, eighteen parties had contested the election and twelve had won seats, though seven of those parties won only one seat each.[26]

Political Parties

Early in the twenty-first century, party politics in Angola remained largely dominated by the MPLA and UNITA—the two traditional "army parties" as Hodges (2004, 66) called them. By the 2008 parliamentary elections, however, UNITA could barely muster 10 percent of the vote. Roque (2009, 145) suggests that UNITA, "once a mammoth movement, is today politically weak, divided and lacking in technical and institutional capacity." Further, she notes, the party has been "intimidated, infiltrated and coopted by the MPLA," suffering significant well-rewarded defections. Part of the problem for UNITA may have been its participation in a government of national unity and reconciliation, which, as in South Africa in the early years after the transition, put the opposition party in an awkward position—part of the government and yet the main political opposition. Since June 2003, UNITA has been led by Isaias Samakuva, considered a more moderate and urbane figure than Jonas Savimbi and a person who, it was thought, would provide more constructive opposition for the country. And yet, according to Roque (2009, 145), Samakuva has largely failed to reconcile the provincial differences within the party or to provide it with a sufficient guiding vision. At the same time, it should be assumed that the MPLA—with its tremendous access to state and other resources, decades of experience as the governing party, a centrally directed patronage system, and multiple other advantages—has managed fairly easily to weaken the political opposition. Indeed, the MPLA was widely expected to win a majority of seats in the 2008 election. It campaigned on a platform of sustained economic growth and social programs. UNITA campaigned mostly in rural parts of the country, pledging to govern in the interest of all Angolans. UNITA accused the MPLA of failing to address widespread poverty and taking too long to reconstruct the country; it also charged that the ruling party intimidated UNITA supporters.[27]

Of the remaining three political parties with seats in the National Assembly following the 2008 election, the PRS with eight seats in the National Assembly is described by Roque (2009, 145) as well funded and well organized and perceived as a credible, nationwide opposition party, at least before the election. The FNLA, despite its historical importance as one of the early anticolonial movements, has been beset by significant internal divisions exacerbated by the death of leader Holden Roberto in 2007. The New Democracy Coalition, meanwhile, was only established in the months leading up to the 2008 election. Parties that observers thought might garner some seats in the election, but did not, included the Democratic Renewal Party and the Party of the Alliance of the Youth, Workers, and Farmers of Angola, both formed by former MPLA members, and the Angola Democratic and Progress Support Party, with its origins in Luanda's slums and its campaign focus on the urban youth. Like many opposition (and even some ruling) parties in the region, many of these parties were weakened by factionalism. After the election, in keeping with the 2005 election law, all parties that failed to win more than 0.5 percent of the national vote were dissolved. Whereas fourteen parties or coalitions of parties contested the 2008 election, in the aftermath of the election only six, which had met the minimum percentage, were officially registered (Roque 2009, 146).

Civil Society

In the early years after independence in Angola, civil spaces were "colonized ... with Soviet-type monopoly organizations for women, workers, peasants and youth," and only the women's organization reportedly ever attained any real legitimacy (Sogge 2010). In any event, with war the most prominent feature of life for decades in Angola, a "civil society" was hardly possible. As Fernando Pachecho (2002, 54) observed, "with a politically bipolarized society and with people's preoccupations essentially focusing on survival mechanisms, little time, energy and attention are left for associative life and collective action." Still, as part of the reforms of the early 1990s, previous restrictions on NGOs were lifted, with the result that, according to Hodges (2004, 88), "a more vibrant, active civil society came into being for the first time since the post-independence crackdown on independent organizations." At the same time, the growth and development of these organizations was hampered in the late 1990s by the "return to war, the politico-military division of the country and actions taken by the government to prevent these organizations, in particular the unions and the press, from posing a threat to its hold on power."

By 2001, Pachecho (2002, 55) found a range of civil society groupings in Angola. Among these were churches and religious organizations, which devoted themselves to issues of peace, national reconciliation, humanitarian and social assistance, protection of human rights, and so on; and a variety of issue-based NGOs dedicated to such diverse causes as education, health, development, women's emancipation, external debt forgiveness, and redemption of cultural values. Others included professional associations and trade unions, which represented member interests and sought to influence public policy, though with Angola's weak and disorganized formal sector, the labor movement has not been particularly strong. Still others were cultural groups, which contributed to the civic education of the population; the privately owned mass media, which promoted spaces for public debate and political pluralism; and peasant organizations, which have helped over the years to meet the needs of the population (unmet by the state) and have contributed to the population's autonomy. More recently, according to Hilhorst and Serrano (2010, 194–196), civil society organizations have been greatly hampered by a lack of funding. With few resources, national NGOs and church-based organizations are not able to serve well and protect the Angolan people. In Hilhorst and Serrano's view, Angola's civil society was actually stronger in the emergency and peace and reconciliation phases than it has been since 2005. Still, civil service organizations play an important role in delivering humanitarian assistance and voicing social concerns.

Roque (2009, 146) refers to a "veneer of democracy" in Angola in which most reforms by government are more about retaining power than creating inclusive processes. Observers such as Pachecho (2002, 57) noted that Angolan leaders failed to recognize that civil society could actually help to legitimatize the state. Instead civil society organizations were perceived as adversaries or enemies of the state. Roque (2009, 146) argues that civil society organizations, political parties, and the media are all allowed by the ruling party—so long as they "refrain from exposing inconvenient truths" and do not challenge the government. Like Messiant (2001) observed years earlier, Roque notes that the key strategy by government is the co-optation of its opposition by means of an extensive patronage network. In the mid-1990s a key mechanism for the dispersal of patronage was created—the Eduardo dos Santos Foundation (FESA). Indeed, Messiant (2001, 287) described the foundation as an attempt to take over civil society. Modeled on foundations in liberal democracies around the world, FESA is a fount of patronage, using its tremendous wealth and resources (principally from oil revenues) to centralize power within the presidential palace and to marginalize even the ruling MPLA (Messiant 2001, 287; Malaquias 2000, 111). Birmingham (2002, 178) referred to the creation of the FESA as "one of the small institutionalized steps on the road to totalitarian presidentialism in Angola." FESA remains robust to this day (Sogge 2010).

The media are typically considered to be an integral part of civil society. In Angola, though freedom of speech and of the press are enshrined in the constitution, government regulations and a small independent media—except in the capital city Luanda—limit these freedoms in practice (US Department of State 2010a). Indeed, Sogge (2010) suggests that vibrant digital and printed media are "alive and kicking" in Luanda but have yet to create, or indeed reach, a critical mass. The US Department of State (2010a) suggests that, as in other countries in the region, journalists (and human rights activists) practice self-censorship. In late 2009 there were twelve privately owned weekly newspapers in Angola and four Luanda-based commercial radio stations. In late 2008 a privately owned television station, TV Zimbo, began operating. The only national daily newspaper is the state-owned *Jornal de Angola*. While the government-owned national radio station, Rádio Nacional de Angola, is permitted to broadcast nationally, other radio stations are only permitted to broadcast in the provinces in which they are located. Journalists from both Rádio Nacional and the national television network, Televisão Popular de Angola, have been suspended for criticizing the government; other journalists, including foreign journalists, have been arrested, harassed, or intimidated (US Department of State 2010a). In general, state media organizations are given preferential treatment and access by the government.

Fundamentals of the Political Economy

In 2009 the estimated per capita GDP at purchasing power parity in Angola was US$8,300, up considerably from the low $2,000s at the beginning of the decade. While worldwide recession and lower oil prices led to a contraction in the economic growth rate in 2009, from 2004 to 2007 GDP grew at an annual rate of more than 15 percent. This high growth rate was driven by the country's oil sector and by high international oil prices. The bulk of national revenue comes from the petroleum sector, which contributes about 85 percent annually to GDP.[28] Diamonds are also a significant natural and financial resource, but their significance is dwarfed by oil, which supplies Angola's government with considerably greater and more consistent revenues (Reno 2000, 219). Much of Angola's oil production, conducted by multinational oil companies and overseen by the national oil company, Sonangol, finds its way to US markets—particularly as the United States tried in the first decade of the twenty-first century to diversify away from its dependence on oil from the Middle East. And yet, in 2009, more of Angola's exports went to China than anywhere else (with the United States a close second).

Angola's per capita GDP and oil wealth greatly disguise the true nature of the political economy in Angola today, however. Indeed, as noted earlier, on nearly every socioeconomic indicator Angola ranks at the very bottom among nations. Four decades of war took a devastating toll in Angola, and since the onset of peace the extent of the damage has been even more evident. Moreover, the nearly intractable conflict helped to spawn an astonishing level of predation and corruption in Angola, centered on the two resources that funded the war, diamonds and oil. That corruption, in turn, has exacerbated the already glaring discrepancies between rich and poor in Angola and has facilitated a centralization of power in Angola that threatens the country's recovery and future development.

It is not surprising, therefore, that there has been much criticism that the Angolan government is not doing enough to use its vast oil wealth responsibly and for the benefit of its own people. The United Kingdom–based organization Global Witness documented how "the progressive impoverishment of a country during almost four decades of war and civil conflict has gone hand-in-hand with rising oil revenues" (Global Witness 2002a). In brief, at the same time that Angola's socioeconomic indicators fell dramatically, the country's oil revenues rose markedly. And those revenues have largely "been diverted straight into parallel budgets of the shadow state." In 2001 alone, for example, up to US$1.4 billion in oil revenues was unaccounted for. And this at the same time that international aid agencies were scrambling to find funds to feed about a million internally displaced Angolans. Moreover, during this same period government officials were enriching themselves through their involvement in "a highly over-priced military procurement process" (Global Witness 2002a). In other words, as the Global Witness investigation documented, it was clear that the political and economic disorder brought about by the war had been deliberately exploited to enrich the ruling elite. At the same time the Angolan state blamed its failure to provide for its citizens on the years-long conflict.

Angola's undisclosed and unaccounted-for national revenues have been the main reason for a series of economic policy failures. At independence, in keeping with its Marxist-Leninist doctrine, the MPLA government sought to establish a centrally planned economy. From the late 1980s onward, the government announced a series of economic reform programs, though most were abandoned after failing to achieve their objectives. Then in 1990, as part of the larger liberalization effort, the government moved to adopt market-based reforms. After failing to carry out the conditions of some IMF-sponsored economic reform packages, however, the government announced in mid-2002 that it wanted no more of them. This stance had significant repercussions with potential donors, who were wary of giving aid to Angola unless the conditions existed to make that aid effective. From 2005 onward, most donors and aid agencies downsized or discontinued their operations (Hilhorst and Serrano 2010, 196). In an unprecedented move for an African country (and after years of negotiations), Angola canceled planned consultations with the IMF in early 2007, with the finance minister stating that an IMF program would not help the country to preserve the economic and social stability it had gained so far. In the view of some, the Angolan government was also not likely interested in the scrutiny that such a package would have required. Clearly, Angola was able to reject an IMF package because of its own significant oil wealth but also because of the generous aid from China that those oil resources have attracted (Ambrose 2007).

Alongside the egregious disparities in income and wealth in Angola are regional imbalances. Most of the development in the country since independence was concentrated in the coastal areas and large cities and towns under government control during the many years of war, particularly Luanda. Some agricultural activity was possible in southwestern Angola, which was less affected by the war, though agriculture represented only 10 percent of GDP in 2008 (with 85 percent of the population "employed" in agriculture).[29] Importantly, just four provinces—Cabinda and Zaire (oil) and Lunda Norte and Lunda Sul (diamonds)—account for 98 percent of export revenues. Nonetheless, like Nigerians in the Niger Delta, inhabitants of the four regions have benefited little from those revenues. Humanitarian needs in a province such as Bie, once controlled by UNITA, remain invisible or hidden (Hilhorst and Serrano 2010, 193).

Challenges of the Twenty-First Century

At the beginning of the twenty-first century, Angola was just embarking on the transitions that other countries in southern Africa had already completed, in some cases many years earlier. By 2010 some features of the transition had been accomplished. National legislative elections had been held in 2008, for the first time in nearly two decades, providing the MPLA, apparently, with a stunning mandate for continued rule. New laws around political parties had consolidated the total number of political parties to six in the aftermath of the election. A new constitution had finally been drafted and adopted by the new National Assembly in early 2010; among the other important provisions was one that precludes the direct election of the president by the people of Angola. Civil society organizations and an independent media struggled to have an impact, at least outside of Luanda. A highly centralized presidency tightly controlled the polity under a veneer of democracy.

To be sure, Angola faces enormous development challenges, greater than any in southern Africa today. In addition to devastating social conditions, shallow political institutions, and an economy that is marked by endemic corruption, Angola must also contend with healing a populace that has known little else but war, repression, and fear for decades. At the same time, Hodges has suggested somewhat optimistically (2004, 206) that the end of forty years of war should mean new opportunities for progress—removing justification for further mismanagement of resources and restrictions on democratic freedoms, raising expectations of better times ahead, easing the culture of fear, and changing the political landscape "by ending the bipolarism in Angolan politics that has barred the emergence of a credible civilian opposition with an agenda for progressive change." Now that Angola's many resources can be put to constructive rather than destructive purposes, the country is better placed to confront its significant challenges. Indeed, with its wealth of natural resources, its potential transport infrastructure, and its significant domestic and regional markets, Angola stands to become a country to be reckoned with in southern Africa and the continent as a whole—if the economic, political, and social challenges can be surmounted. After forty years of deadly conflict and unspeakable privation, the people of Angola deserve a chance to experience what should have been the fruits of independence.

Ricardo Soares de Oliveira (2007, 609) describes Angola as a "successful failed state"—a country that embodies at least two contradictory trends. On the one hand, despite (or perhaps because of) its abundant resource endowment, Angola is one of the worst-governed countries on the continent—among the lowest-ranked in the world on international transparency and development indexes—with inadequate social expenditure on its population and a public administration unable to deliver the most basic services or reach most of its territory. On the other hand, Angola is an enormously resource-rich country with enormously wealthy rulers who have successfully withstood internal and external challenges, created the armed forces of a regional superpower, and developed networks of support from a diverse group of emerging countries that are likely to guarantee the regime's incumbency for years to come. Like Mugabe in Zimbabwe, dos Santos in Angola has maintained a grip on political power for more than thirty years; in early 2011 that was a precarious position for a political leader in Africa.

Notes

1. As Sogge (2009, 1) notes, Angola experienced only about twenty years of peace during the twentieth century, from 1941 until 1961, between the last colonial military campaigns and the first open anticolonial revolts.

2. As Sogge (2009, 1) also notes, while many refer to the postindependence war as a civil war, it was very much a Cold War–era proxy war; specifically it was "a US led covert war to 'rollback' communism."

3. According to Sogge (2010) the MPLA formally renamed itself the MPLA (initials only) in December 2009, dropping terms from an earlier era such as *movement* and *liberation*. The South West Africa People's Organization (SWAPO) of Namibia did the same thing in the early years of independence.

4. According to David Birmingham (2002, 159), it has been estimated that 9 million mines were laid in Angola in order to deny farmers or their families access to land. "Such a number of mines made Angola's killing fields comparable to those of Cambodia."

5. Https://www.cia.gov/. Retrieved December 2010. See also Sogge 2010.

6. During the early colonial period very few Portuguese women had migrated to the colony, resulting in a significant *mestíço* population in the country (as Portuguese men "mixed" with indigenous women)—1.1 percent of the population by 1974. By then there were 31 *mestíços* for every 100 white Portuguese (Tvedten 1997, 26).

7. According to Inge Tvedten, personal e-mail communication, July 24, 2004: "A very important aspect of Portuguese colonialism (which partly explains why relations between Africans and whites are so different in the five former Portuguese colonies) is the presence of a large number of poor white Portuguese, who fought with Africans for jobs as maids, taxi drivers, bush traders, etc."

8. According to Hodges (2004, 8), "it was the success of liberation movements in Mozambique and Guinea-Bissau, not Angola, that eventually brought the downfall of the Salazarist regime of Marcello Caetano, thereby paving the way for the independence of all five Portuguese African colonies."

9. As Tvedten (1997, 37) notes: "The question of 'who came first' has been the subject of much debate"; this question is not pursued in full in this chapter.

10. In contrast, the postindependence conflict in Mozambique had only a limited East-West dimension. In fact, the unwillingness of the United States and the Soviet Union to insert themselves (or their official proxies) into the Mozambican conflict on a substantial scale may be one factor in its more rapid cessation.

11. In 1976, covert assistance to UNITA was prohibited by the Clark Amendment. However, the Clark Amendment was repealed by the US Congress in 1985, allowing the resumption of covert support to UNITA, totaling approximately US$250 million between 1986 and 1991 (Vines 2000, 7).

12. According to the Economist Intelligence Unit (2003d, 12), Marxist-Leninist ideology in Angola gradually softened after José Eduardo dos Santos came to power in 1979, following Agostino Neto's death in office.

13. A combined force, to be called the Angolan Armed Forces (FAA), was to number 50,000 troops. At the time of the Bicesse Accord, the government army numbered

120,000, whereas UNITA's army was 65,000. Both were expected to contribute equally to the new FAA (Vines 2000, 9).

14. According to Birmingham (2002, 170): "The peace, orchestrated by Portugal with help from the superpowers, was to be monitored by the United Nations, which sent Margaret Anstee to supervise Angola's first ever democratic election. Down in the Luanda slums the 1991 accord was gratefully known as Margaret's peace."

15. Birmingham (2002, 176) describes the GURN as a "political initiative designed to prevent a renewed outbreak of war. . . . As part of the search for a policy which would defuse the anger of the opposition and minimize the danger of a return to war the president created a 'government of national unity.'" The principle of a GURN was included in the Lusaka Accords (Vines 2000).

16. Many pages have been devoted to trying to figure out who was responsible for this failed attempt at a peaceful transition in 1992. Stephen John Stedman (1997, 5) suggests that the greatest risk to peacemaking endeavors is "spoilers"—"leaders and parties who believe that peace emerging from negotiations threatens their power, worldview, and interests, and use violence to undermine attempts to achieve it." What determines whether spoilers will succeed or fail, according to Stedman, is the role of international actors "as custodians of peace" (1997, 6). In the Angolan case in 1992, the consensus is that the United Nations and the United States, in particular, failed to prevent Savimbi from spoiling the outcome of the peace process. See also Anstee 1996 for a firsthand account of the process.

17. Http://www.upi.com/. Retrieved December 2010.

18. Http://www.eisa.org.za/. Retrieved December 2010.

19. Http://www.reuters.com/. Retrieved December 2010.

20. Http://www.angola.org/. Retrieved December 2010.

21. The government's armed forces were known as People's Armed Forces for the Liberation of Angola (FAPLA) prior to the Bicesse Accords. "By 1994, the army had been retrained and renamed under the banner of the FAA," which was originally intended to be the name given to the *combined* UNITA-MPLA armies, as stipulated in Bicesse (Vines 2000, 9).

22. According to Birmingham (2002, 184): "In the national army of the 1990s, officers dominated the now privatized trade in diamonds and invested their wealth in the Luanda housing market, earning large fortunes as landlords to the foreign employees of oil companies, diplomatic missions and international aid agencies."

23. Http://www.ipu.org/. Retrieved December 2010.

24. Http://www.eisa.org.za/. Retrieved December 2010.

25. Http://www.eisa.org.za/. Retrieved December 2010.

26. Http://www.ipu.org. Retrieved December 2010.

27. Http://www.ipu.org/. Retrieved December 2010.

28. Https://www.cia.gov/. Retrieved December 2010.

29. Https://www.cia.gov/. Retrieved December 2010.

7 Zimbabwe: State, Society, and Prolonged Crisis

Zimbabwe has gone from regional leader to international pariah at phenomenal speed. Zimbabwe, which achieved independence only in 1980, was not long ago regarded by observers as one of the most politically stable, prosperous, and indeed promising countries in Africa. Its postcolonial industrial and commercial agricultural development provided a solid base that augured positively for Zimbabwe's future economic performance (Stoneman and Cliffe 1989). The country was hailed as a model of postcolonial racial reconciliation for its apparent accommodation of blacks and white former settlers. Moreover, from a political standpoint, although never entirely democratic, Zimbabwe was nonetheless a *constitutional* polity, with an independent judiciary and largely protected civil liberties.

Within two decades of independence, Zimbabwe's promise had waned considerably, and the first decade of the twenty-first century saw it erode still further as the country slid into a deepening political, economic, and social crisis. By 2010, it appeared that the pace, at least, of economic and sociopolitical decline had slowed, though this was more a reflection of the precipitous collapse that had characterized the decade than of any semblance of recovery; indeed, there was little left to contract of the once vibrant Zimbabwean political economy. Zimbabwe's economic infrastructure has been severely degraded in all sectors, and the statistics paint a grim picture. GDP plummeted by an estimated 40 percent between 1998 and 2009 (EIU 2010c, 6). The once-heralded manufacturing sector, already battered by economic liberalization in the 1990s, declined by 17.2 percent in 2002 alone and thereafter faced widespread closures. Similarly, the mining sector, one of Zimbabwe's few remaining sources of foreign exchange, also suffered severely diminished capacity. The most glaring economic statistic, however, was inflation, which eventually reached a level so mind-bogglingly high that it was almost meaningless: 6.5×10^{108} percent (Hanke 2008), exceeding even Weimar Germany. Socioeconomic indicators were equally disturbing. The collapse of the health care sector means that the AIDS epidemic, which has ravaged Zimbabwe, continues

Zimbabwe: Country Data

Land area   386,847 km^2
Capital   Harare
Date of independence   April 18, 1980
Population   11,651,858, 37% urban (2008)
Languages   English (official), Shona, Sindebele, numerous but minor dialects
Ethnic groups   African 98% (Shona 82%, Ndebele 14%, other 2%), mixed and
    Asian 1%, European less than 1%
Religions   syncretic (part-Christian, part-indigenous beliefs) 50%, Christian
    25%, indigenous beliefs 24%, Muslim and other 1%
Currency   US dollar, since 2009, when use of the Zimbabwe dollar (ZWD) was
    suspended
Literacy rate   90.7% (male, 94.2%; female, 87.2%)
Life expectancy   47.55 years (male, 47.98 years; female, 47.11 years) (2010
    estimate)
Infant mortality   30.9 per 1,000 live births
GDP per capita (PPP)   Less than $100
GDP real growth rate   −1.3%
Leaders since independence
    Robert Mugabe, prime minister, 1980–1987
    Robert Mugabe, president, 1987–
Major political parties
    Ruling party   Zimbabwe African National Union–Patriotic Front (ZANU-PF)
    and Movement for Democratic Change (MDC-T, Tsvangirai faction)—
    nominal coalition government
    Other parties   MDC-M (Mutambara faction), Zimbabwe African People's
    Union (ZAPU)
Women in parliament (lower house)   15.0% (2008 election)

Sources: Data derived from https://www.cia.gov; http://www.ipu.org/.
Note: Data from 2009 unless otherwise noted.

with scant prospect for improvement, despite the fact that HIV prevalence rates have fallen elsewhere in the region. And new epidemics of cholera and tuberculosis have severely undermined the degraded capacity of the health system. A politically induced food shortage, combined with drought, meant that in 2003, 7.2 million Zimbabweans—or 60 percent of the population—needed emergency food aid; by 2010 nearly a million Zimbabweans still required food assistance (FEWS 2010). Another problem was that a decline in real wages of 28 percent between 1982 and 1997 (that is, *before* the onset of the recent crisis) contributed to a household poverty rate of over 75 percent of all households living in poverty in 2000; by 2010, Zimbabwe ranked last out of 169 countries on the Human Development Index (HDI) (Human Development Report 2010b). Finally, for political but mainly economic reasons, as many as 5 *million* Zimbabweans lived in exile in the first decade of the twenty-first century; the largest numbers are found in South Africa and in the region, with others in the United Kingdom, the United States, and elsewhere.

Zimbabwe's political situation deteriorated along with the socioeconomic one. The first decade of the twenty-first century was marked by political violence, repeated electoral fraud and intimidation of the opposition and its supporters, and deepening authoritarianism on the part of President Robert Mugabe and his party, the ZANU-PF. By contrast, by 2009 some slight glimmers of hope had appeared: the establishment of a coalition government, however dysfunctional, between ZANU-PF and the opposition Movement for Democratic Change (MDC); the substantial dollarization of the economy, which arrested the country's crippling hyperinflation; the presence of high-value commodities, including platinum deposits and the discovery of substantial diamond deposits in 2009 and 2010; and the end to the dispossession of Zimbabwe's white-owned commercial farms.[1]

Nonetheless, Zimbabwe's political deterioration is among the most striking developments. At a time when most of sub-Saharan Africa has made impressive strides and southern Africa in particular is home to some of the continent's most vibrant democracies, Zimbabwe is paired only with Angola as regional laggards. But Zimbabwe once had many democratic features. Although President Mugabe had revealed occasional authoritarian tendencies in the past, the country had generally had strong institutions that helped to constrain most autocratic impulses of the president and the ruling party.[2] In the first decade of the twenty-first century, the rule of law all but collapsed. The once famously independent judiciary was stocked with pliant judges who answered to the ruling party. Police no longer upheld the law, and sometimes participated in breaking it. Early in the decade, and particularly around the election cycles of 2000, 2002, 2005, and 2008, ruling-party militias roamed the country as formal and informal security forces and, acting as agents of the regime, frequently terrorized opposition supporters. As a result of the country's disregard for the rule of law; human rights violations, including torture; the forcible seizure of white-owned property (principally commercial farms); and abrogation of international agreements, Zimbabwe became an international pariah, at least outside of Africa. It was suspended from the Commonwealth in 2002 and was subsequently hit by economic ("smart") sanctions by the European Union, Japan, and the United States, among others; financial flows from Western countries, except urgent humanitarian assistance, slowed to a trickle. As traditional Euro-American partners have retreated, Zimbabwe has looked increasingly to Asian countries, such as China, Malaysia, and India, for aid and investment. At the household level, remittances from Zimbabweans now settled abroad have enabled the survival of hundreds of thousands of their kin back home. (Ironically, however, this has reduced pressure on the state.) Zimbabwe's southern African neighbors have also served as a lifeline: although Zimbabwe's status within Africa as a whole is somewhat ambiguous, criticism of the country is considerably more muted than in the West; South Africa, especially, is a vital trade partner, accounting for more than 45 percent of two-way trade in 2008, for example (EIU 2010c, 17). Yet precisely because of Zimbabwe's economic, political, and security importance to the region, the unresolved crisis certainly holds major implications for its neighbors and the continent.

Among the most striking features of Zimbabwe's decay is the rapidity with which it occurred. Admittedly, in 1997, the year generally regarded as the turning point in the country's recent collapse, Zimbabwe's prospects were somewhat tentative. The country was recovering from two debilitating droughts earlier in the decade, and although agricultural growth had returned impressively, the effects on the wider economy were still apparent. Moreover, an economic liberalization program (the economic structural adjustment program [ESAP]), which had been enacted in 1991, had concluded, and a successor program was under consideration. ESAP had contributed to considerable socioeconomic hardship for many Zimbabweans, and some scholars argue that there is a direct causal link between its impact and the economic decline that followed later (Bond and Manyanya 2002; Carmody and Taylor 2003). Nonetheless, there were still some indicators in early 1997 that a social partnership could emerge that might ameliorate some of the effects of a renewed ESAP (ZCTU 1996).

Linked to this situation, but perhaps of greater importance, was the fact that civil society had begun to play an increasingly active role in the political life of the country. Independent media outlets were expanding, and criticism of government was generally tolerated; labor unions and human rights organizations were gaining unprecedented influence; and cracks were beginning to appear in the de facto one-party state that had dominated since independence, providing some evidence of a maturing political culture (Sithole 2000). Conceivably, had these influences been utilized by the regime rather than marginalized and attacked, a more democratic path, rooted in strong social institutions, might have unfolded.

The fact that the country was in shambles scarcely half a decade later begs a number of questions, two of which preoccupy us in this chapter. First, is it possible to identify the factors that explain Zimbabwe's collapse? Second, given the country's myriad problems, what are its prospects for democracy and economic recovery? Although these questions defy easy answers, an examination of the various interactions between social and political actors and the context in which they operate in Zimbabwe can shed light on this inquiry.

There is disagreement among scholars and other observers about the root causes of Zimbabwe's "plunge" (Bond and Manyanya 2002). Among those who adhere to economic explanations, some blame it on structure, history, and uncorrected racial and socioeconomic imbalances that date from the independence agreement in 1979, or soon thereafter (Bond 1998; Bond and Manyanya 2002). Others, although still looking to structural factors, fix a more recent date and cite the international financial institutions, the World Bank and International Monetary Fund (IMF), as the principal culprits (Carmody 2001; Stoneman 1998). These authors suggest that the painful choices and harsh conditionalities of Zimbabwe's 1991–1995 ESAP undermined the socioeconomic fabric of Zimbabwe and destroyed the economic foundation on which its prior development and stability once rested. Conversely, economic liberals suggest that the government's *abandonment* of the neoliberal program in 1997 accounts for the collapse (World Bank 1995; Brett and Winter 2003). Advocates of the neopatrimonial paradigm, with its emphasis on the role of the "big man" in Africa, emphasize that weak state structures and institutions allow, indeed promote, the emergence of patrimonial leaders like President Robert Mugabe (Bratton and van de Walle 1997). Still others engage in what might be labeled a psychosocial analysis of history; these interpretations cite greed, power lust, corruption, and incompetence among the factors, but their common thread is a demonization of Mugabe and his political cronies (Rotberg 2000; Meredith 2007; Blair 2002). Such personalist approaches, however, tend to be the least analytically rigorous because they often discount the significant role of institutions, however weak, as well as interactions and the international context (Herbst 1990, 245–249).

In reality, the crisis in Zimbabwe requires an understanding of this complex mosaic of interlocking factors. Thus history, structure, and agency are essential components to consider. The framework employed in this book therefore allows examination of institutions and actors as well as material resources and the interactions among these factors. With this in mind, we may begin not only to make sense of the situation in Zimbabwe but also to determine the degree to which it is exceptional—or representative—in the region. Zimbabwe remains an important case study in the southern African region, and on the continent as a whole. In the late 1980s and early 1990s, Zimbabwe was seen as a bright light in the region; today its importance reflects negative concerns—that is, the threats that a moribund Zimbabwe poses to issues of regional health; security, including food security; development; and, importantly, perceptions of the region. The latter issue in particular inevitably raises an intriguing counterfactual question: instead of "contagion effects," what might a thriving Zimbabwe have contributed to a region otherwise buoyed by democratic progress, economic growth, and even World Cup euphoria? The future of Zimbabwe, which remains very much at stake, is therefore of grave concern to all of southern Africa.

Historical Origins of the Zimbabwean State: Context, Key Actors, and Issues

The area now known as Zimbabwe was established as territory of the British South Africa Company (BSAC) in 1890, under charter from the British crown.

Together with the territory to its north (modern-day Zambia), the area became known as Rhodesia around 1895, after Cecil Rhodes, the British-born magnate who headed the BSAC. At the time, Zimbabwe was inhabited by two principal ethnic groups: the Ndebele, who had arrived in the region only three generations earlier from South Africa, and the numerically dominant Shona, who were heirs to a once-vibrant trading empire that thrived between the eleventh and fifteenth centuries. In 1888, Rhodes's representatives signed the Rudd Concession with the Ndebele king, Lobengula, a treaty that granted them certain "legal" rights to explore mining opportunities in the region. Later, beginning in 1889 and 1890, Rhodes's men used several deceptions, including Lobengula's alleged subjugation of the Shona peoples to the north, as a pretext for violating the treaty and seizing control over all of Lobengula's kingdom, including the parts inhabited by both the Shona and Ndebele groups.

In 1896 and 1897, the Africans—both Shona and Ndebele—rebelled against their new colonial masters in what became known as the first *chimurenga* ("rebellion" in Shona). When the revolt was put down, with significant African loss of life, BSAC rule was secured. Thereafter, the white population of the territory steadily increased, although when the anticipated mining concessions proved to be far more limited than initially thought, most white settlers came as farmers. After evicting the indigenous Shona, whites established large farming tracts mainly in the central plateau and eastern highland regions of the country; in the southern Matabeleland region previously dominated by the Ndebele, mostly ranching activities were initiated.

The second phase of Zimbabwe's modern history can be dated from 1923, the last year of "company rule." Government of the territory, which by then had become known as Southern Rhodesia, was turned over to the settlers, whose population and self-interest had increased markedly since they began to arrive in the 1890s. This was a pivotal period in Southern Rhodesia. Not only were the settlers granted substantial self-government, but they also opted to remain semiautonomous (with some links to the colonial office) rather than accept an offer to amalgamate with South Africa. The decision to remain autonomous was based in part on Rhodesians' desire to avoid being swallowed up by their larger neighbor and its ascendant Afrikaner population. Hence, as Pierre du Toit (1995) notes, this was an important stage in the shaping of a distinctly Rhodesian nationalism, which was to set the stage for events that unfolded over the four-decades-long period from 1923 through 1964.

During that time, Southern Rhodesia experienced tremendous growth and the emergence of an efficient settler state apparatus that ensured the comfortable lifestyle of white residents. The federation with Northern Rhodesia and Nyasaland (Malawi) from 1953 to 1963 further fueled Southern Rhodesia's development, as Malawian labor and Northern Rhodesia's substantial copper wealth flowed almost unidirectionally toward Southern Rhodesia's far greater industrial base. Politically, although the federation's central government powers included defense, trade, industry, and finance, the members retained power over local government, African education, health, agriculture, and land policy. This left the authorities in each of the colonies a considerable degree of autonomy in determining "native policy," and Southern Rhodesia, with the highest number of settlers, had the most repressive native policy (Wills 1964; Sithole 1988). Indeed, in Southern Rhodesia, blacks were stripped of most of their land; forced into the wage economy but denied the right to strike; restricted in their livelihood, place of residence, and movement; and required to carry passes (du Toit 1995).

African nationalism in Southern Rhodesia gathered speed during the federal period, influenced both by the nature of settler rule and by the independence movements that had emerged elsewhere on the continent, including in federation partners Malawi and Zambia. Unlike those states, which gained their independence in 1963 and 1964, respectively, Southern Rhodesia's large settler population was highly resistant to the prospect of a transition to independence that would result in majority rule. In fact, in the face of mounting black nationalism throughout Africa, Southern Rhodesian politics had begun to shift sharply to the right in the late 1950s (Houser 1976, 5). A nascent African liberation movement, the Southern Rhodesia African National Congress, headed by Joshua Nkomo, was banned in 1959, and new repressive legislation was enacted.[3] Yet neither banning nor imprisonment could prevent the emergence of formal resistance movements in the African community. Nkomo subsequently played a leading role in the formation of the Zimbabwe African People's Union (ZAPU) in 1960, which was banned in 1962 but survived underground. A breakaway group, including Robert Mugabe, formed the Zimbabwe African National Union (ZANU) in 1963. ZANU was banned later that year but also continued underground.

As was the case elsewhere in the region where African nationalist movements encountered substantial settler populations, there was resistance to change, and eventually violence. Settlers' self-interest—defined by their social, political, and financial stake in the territory, both real and perceived—made compromise difficult.[4] The prospect of independence in Northern Rhodesia and Nyasaland provoked an even greater conservative backlash among Southern Rhodesia's settler population and resulted in a victory for the staunchly conservative Dominion Party (later the Rhodesia Front [RF]) in the 1962 legislative elections in the territory (Houser 1976).

In 1965, under pressure from London but opposed to making any concessions to its African population, Southern Rhodesia issued a unilateral declaration of independence (UDI) from Great Britain. Backed by the white population, RF premier Ian Smith vowed never to surrender to majority rule.[5] Zimbabwe's third historical phase thus dates from the UDI and continued until the advent of majority rule in 1979 and 1980. Despite the conditions under which the UDI was declared, including the imposition of UN sanctions in 1967, the Rhodesian economy flourished. After a small drop in national revenues immediately following the UDI, the economy underwent tremendous growth: real GDP increased nearly 40 percent between 1965 and 1970 and a further 35 percent by 1975 (Stoneman and Davies 1981, 97). In fact, in the face of sanctions, the Smith regime pursued an aggressive policy of import substitution industrialization that greatly enhanced the country's industrial base. Rhodesia also achieved self-sufficiency in a number of agricultural crops, including wheat, sugar, and maize, but despite international sanctions, trade relations continued with apartheid South Africa and, less openly, even with the United States and Great Britain. Still, the economy experienced sharp declines after 1975.

The African nationalist movements that emerged in the 1950s solidified during the 1960s and started to press for full independence. What began as scattered and disorganized attacks as early as 1966 led to full-scale war in 1972, when the Zimbabwe National Liberation Army (ZANLA) and the Zimbabwe People's Revolutionary Army (ZIPRA), sponsored by ZANU and ZAPU, respectively, commenced a primarily guerrilla war against the Rhodesian army (Stedman 1991, 37–39). The combination of gains by the African liberation movements and the prospect of a continued military stalemate and the exhaustion of the "easy" phase of import substitution that had helped to fuel the Rhodesian economy finally led the Smith regime to the negotiating table, although full negotiations with ZANU and ZAPU did not begin until September 1979 (Stedman 1991). After a brief interregnum in 1978 and 1979 in which the country was known as "Zimbabwe-Rhodesia" (a transparent attempt by Smith and the RF to maintain power by installing an African prime minister, Bishop Abel Muzorewa, which never gained popular legitimacy), the principal combatants reached a negotiated settlement in 1979 (Davidow 1984).

With the British acting as brokers, the negotiations took place at Lancaster House in London and included plans for a new constitution and a transition period and arrangements for a cease-fire (Stedman 1991, 177). Of these issues, the constitution was the most critical element, and its final version was extremely favorable to settler interests. Among its most noteworthy provisions were the establishment of a parliamentary constitutional model; the reservation of 20 seats for whites, elected on a separate roll, in the new 100-seat legislature; the protection of white property rights and land security, with the sale of land on a "willing buyer–willing seller" basis only; guaranteed pensions for white civil servants and military personnel; and a bill of rights (Stedman 1991, 177–183).[6] The final agreement, signed at Lancaster House on December 17, 1979, endorsed the constitution, formally ended hostilities between the warring parties, put in place a plan for the demobilization of armed forces on both sides, and set forth a timetable for a transition to majority rule beginning with national elections in February 1980.

The events of the fourth phase of Zimbabwe's history, from independence in 1980 to 1997, and the fifth, which marks the precipitous decline beginning in 1997 and continuing to the present, are addressed in greater detail in the remainder of the chapter. Nonetheless, a few key themes are worth highlighting here. ZANU, which claimed a "Marxist-Leninist" orientation, handily won the first independence elections and formed the first independence government. Despite its avowed socialist orientation, however, the new government pursued policies of relative economic and social moderation. Although the 1980–1997 period was marked by the emerging dominance of ZANU-PF[7] and the decline of white political power, the period was also characterized by continued white economic hegemony in the key commercial agriculture, manufacturing, and mining sectors. Scott Taylor (1999b) argues that a symbiotic relationship, of sorts, emerged between ZANU-PF and the white agroindustrial elite on whom ZANU-PF, and the country as a whole, were financially dependent. Hence, "Marxism-Leninism" figured more as a rhetorical device, although the development of an autonomous *black* middle class was discouraged by the state (with important later implications). The economy endured two major recessions in the 1980s, and given pressure from industrialists and the international financial institutions, Zimbabwe adopted a structural adjustment program in 1990 that ultimately had severe consequences.

After 1997, the country's overall economic situation did not improve, and the Mugabe government began to adopt an increasingly populist platform as it attempted to insulate itself from growing societal unrest and—after 1999—a serious political opposition. Mugabe also embroiled the country in the war in Democratic Republic of Congo (DRC) beginning in August 1998, which provided patronage opportunities for military and political elites but drained the national treasury of an estimated US$1 million *per day* for over three years (Nest 2001; United Nations Security Council 2002). At the same time, Zimbabwe's ever-worsening economic situation was matched by growing repression, aimed at political opponents and others. ZANU-PF's erstwhile white allies were among the principal targets of President Mugabe, who sought to blame white Zimbabweans, particularly commercial farmers, for pervasive landlessness among blacks and, by extension, the country's larger economic problems. As we demonstrate below, this was largely a search for scapegoats by Mugabe.[8] Nonetheless, by 2002 over 80 percent of Zimbabwe's 4,500 white-owned commercial farms had been forcibly seized by the government. By mid-decade, fewer than 300 white farmers remained active. The chaotic, corrupt, and violent "solution" to Zimbabwe's historical landownership disparities has precipitated economic collapse and contributed to the prevailing environment of lawlessness.

In response to growing international and domestic pressure, President Mugabe dug in his heels. The cooperation and patronage flows that once sustained the relationship between whites and ZANU-PF obviously have been irreparably fractured. Further, although elements in the military and some politically connected elites maintain access to certain rents in DRC, the regime's domestic sources of patronage became severely constrained due to the hemorrhaging of the local economy. With the state largely deprived of the resources to placate dissent through side payments to societal clients, it turned increasingly to "hard power" methods of coercion and repression. With both formal and informal resources drying up, growing dissent and fragmentation within the ruling party, and the society in chaos, it appeared by the middle of the first decade of the twenty-first century that the endgame was approaching for ZANU-PF, at least under Mugabe's direction. Yet Robert Mugabe has found a way to survive the challenges both within and outside his party. While Western and many Zimbabwean observers were writing his epitaph (see Gavin 2007), the savvy octogenarian managed to engineer his retention of the presidency, substantially neutralize an alleged power-*sharing* deal with the opposition MDC, and buy sufficient time for the discovery and exploitation of new sources of rents, provided by robust primary commodity prices and the massive diamond deposits identified in eastern Zimbabwe around 2009.

Many of these issues are elucidated below; however, three key junctures in this most recent period should be highlighted. The first was the crash of the economy in November 1997, heralded by the 75 percent loss in the Zimbabwe dollar's value—in one day—and the events that precipitated the currency's dramatic fall. The second began with the February 2000 constitutional referendum, in which the government's effort to change the constitution to increase presidential power and permit seizures of white farms was defeated by civil society. This marked the beginning of a new period of unprecedented electoral competition for ZANU-PF, which was met in turn by an increasingly violent and corrupt reaction, as the regime sought to cling to power. The June 2000 parliamentary election saw genuine interparty competition for the first time between ZANU-PF and a formidable new opposition party, the MDC. The March 2002 presidential election, in which the seventy-eight-year-old Mugabe won a controversial election against the MDC candidate, Morgan Tsvangirai, ushered in a new wave of violence and repression and saw the further erosion of ZANU-PF's popular legitimacy. These patterns were repeated in the November 2005 elections for the Senate, the newly reconstituted upper chamber; the 2005 parliamentary elections; and the 2008 tripartite elections.[9] The third key juncture begins with the achievement of the so-called Global Political Agreement in September 2008, which eventually led to the fragile coalition government between ZANU-PF and the opposition MDC in 2009. This uneasy and often dysfunctional partnership continues to the present and sets the prevailing political context for Zimbabwe today.

Chronology of the Crisis in Zimbabwe

March 1996   Mugabe wins presidential elections. Uncontested after Abel Muzorewa and Ndabaningi Sithole withdraw.

March 1997   War Victims Compensation Fund scandal breaks. Looting of ZW$4.5 billion in pensions is discovered (siphoned off by ministers and party hacks).

June/July 1997   Mugabe agrees (without cabinet approval) to compensate "war veterans" lump sums of ZW$50,000 each and stipends of ZW$2,000 per month.

November 1997   When Mugabe's plans emerge, donors balk, the economy slides: Zimbabwe dollar falls 75 percent against major currencies in one day.

November 1997   There are 1,503 farms (4.8 million hectares) listed for compulsory acquisition by the state.

September 1998   International Donors' Conference on Land: produces agreement to resettle just 118 farms over a two-year period (with international support).

February 1999   All designated farms are dropped by courts due to government inaction.

September 1999   Opposition party, Movement for Democratic Change, is launched.

February 2000   ZANU-PF referendum on constitution is defeated.

February 2000   Land invasions begin.

June 2000   MDC wins 57 seats of 120 contested.

September 2001   Abuja Agreement: Mugabe agrees to end land seizures.

February 2002   Land Acquisition Act (1992) is amended to allow any minister to order farms vacated. Legislation becomes effective May 2002.

March 2002   Presidential election: Mugabe defeats MDC candidate Morgan Tsvangirai with approximately 56 percent of vote. Result is widely condemned as illegitimate.

March 2002   In wake of election results, more international sanctions are applied; Zimbabwe is suspended from Commonwealth.

August 8–10, 2002   Eviction orders take effect against some 2,900 white farmers; defiant farmers are arrested.

August 12, 2002   In a series of speeches, Mugabe appears conciliatory toward whites but reverses course quickly.

September 2002   United States and donor countries continue to press South Africa, Nigeria, and other African states to place more diplomatic and economic pressure on Zimbabwe or risk aid reductions.

2003   Zimbabwe's decline continues. An estimated 600 white farmers remain on land, with only 300 actively farming. "Acquired" farms often lie fallow. Emergency food aid continues; ZANU-PF is accused of providing it only to partisan supporters.

May/June 2005   Operation Murambatsvina ("clear away trash"), the ZANU-PF initiative, bulldozes some 70,000 "squatter" residences and small informal sector businesses in Zimbabwe's urban areas. According to a UN special envoy, the operation displaces over 700,000 people and affects up to 2 million through destruction of livelihoods. Widely seen as targeting MDC's urban support.

2005   Elections for House of Assembly (March) and Senate (November).

2008   Elections for president, House of Assembly, and Senate.

2008   November inflation reaches 89.7 *sextillion* percent; December exceeds even that: 6.5×10^{108} percent.

2009   Economy grows at 3 percent, although data suggest the Zimbabwean economy shrank by 40 percent between 1998 and 2008.

February 2009   Coalition government is established (a provision of the September 2008 Global Political Agreement [GPA]), with Tsvangirai as prime minister; Mugabe continues to outmaneuver Tsvangirai politically.

Society and Development:
The Precarious Politics of Race and Ethnicity

Race Relations

From the time Europeans began settling in Zimbabwe, race has formed the principal cleavage in that society. White economic privilege was absolute in the colonial period. Africans were deprived of land, freedom of movement, and rights as they were forced into subservient positions in the Rhodesian economy. Ironically, the economic advantages that accrued to whites disproportionately before the liberation war continued through the 1990s (S. Taylor 2002).

The violence of the liberation struggle in Zimbabwe was considerable, a struggle that was very clearly defined in racial terms between white settlers and black nationalists.[10] When it became clear by the mid-1970s that the Rhodesian army would not defeat the liberation armies militarily and that some form of political settlement would be necessary, many white Rhodesians fled, going to apartheid South Africa among other destinations. In 1978, for example, over 13,000 whites emigrated (Stedman 1991, 162). Even more left the country in the aftermath of independence. However, some 130,000 whites remained in 1980, although they represented only about 2 percent of the population.

Notwithstanding the violence of the liberation struggle, the nature of the settlement at Lancaster, and the surprise—even fear—among whites and the international community over Mugabe's victory in the February 1980 elections, reconciliation of racial animosities quickly became the order of the day. The white population had fallen considerably from its peak of 270,000 in 1961 (Herbst 1990, 223) but remained significant. Whites still controlled virtually all industrial and commercial resources, the large-scale commercial farming sector, and most private managerial and senior bureaucratic positions (S. Taylor 2002). Indeed, in many ways the new government's policy of national reconciliation was a pragmatic one, forged out of concern for the country's economy:

> On 4 April 1980, Robert Mugabe addressed the nation as its new prime minister: "We will ensure that there is a place for everyone in this country. We want to ensure a sense of security for both the winners and the losers. There will be no sweeping nationalization; the pensions and jobs of civil servants are guaranteed; farmers will keep their land. Let us forgive and forget. Let us join hands in a new amity." (quoted in Nhema 2002, 101)

The speech was greeted with relief by most white residents and ushered in a period of rather astounding "reconciliation" in which even those who had been skeptical of the settlement *and* Mugabe's election victory were put at considerable ease. Indeed, despite their self-proclaimed "Marxist" sympathies,

ZANU and Mugabe quickly revealed through their policies that they would adhere to the provisions of Lancaster and safeguard white property rights.

This reconciliation was apparently so entrenched that Jeffrey Herbst (1990, 221) could argue less than a decade after independence that "the fact that 100,000 Whites live peacefully in Zimbabwe means that reconciliation can be called Zimbabwe's greatest success." Today we know that Herbst's account proved premature and overly optimistic: what passed for reconciliation was merely preservation of the preindependence status quo. For their part, whites used Mugabe's apparent nod to reconciliation as a basis for continued wealth accumulation and maintenance of their landholdings and relative tardiness about "affirmative action" in corporate and industrial ranks (Strachan 1986, 1989; S. Taylor 2002). Herbst claims this was part of an "implicit bargain" between the state and white residents: specifically, established farmers and businesspeople could stay, unmolested; however, their children would be discouraged from staying. Herbst thus saw blacks gaining control over economic resources through a process of attrition and demographic change (1990, 221, 223).

By definition, this bargain was implicit and "never discussed publicly" (Herbst 1990, 221); however, the existence of an "implicit" bargain like this presupposed that the Mugabe government was itself committed to black advancement. Subsequent research has called this assumption into question by suggesting that Mugabe and ZANU were content with continued white economic dominance because it could forestall the emergence of a black middle class that might present a challenge to ZANU's political hegemony (Raftopoulos 2001; Taylor 1999b). Moreover, what Herbst (and later du Toit [1995]) failed to recognize is that the implicit bargain, to the extent it truly existed, could be superseded or extended because of the mutually beneficial linkages between black political elites in ZANU and white economic elites. Therefore, although this relationship between "strange bedfellows" may not have continued indefinitely, its final collapse in 2000 is not adequately explained through the implicit bargain thesis.

In any event, one observation receives broad consensus: although the relationship between the races was substantially characterized by Mugabe's "new amity" for most of the independence era, many whites were able simply to continue a colonial lifestyle following independence (Herbst 1989, 1990; Raftopoulos 2001; Bond 1998; Meredith 2007). In fact, some whites remained unreconstructed and unapologetic racists (Weiss 1994; Godwin and Hancock 1993).[11] Many felt scant need to alter their behavior by integrating socially or politically, or through economic sacrifice, however limited (Bond and Manyanya 2002); indeed, this was an inherently rational strategy, since whites felt very little overt pressure from the new regime to adjust their behavior (S. Taylor 2002). Yet this also left them vulnerable to later attack by the state. Indeed, one can see how many whites would have been blindsided by Mugabe's resort to seemingly unbridled racism beginning in the 1996 presidential election. After all, amity *had* prevailed; the government had supported white economic interests consistently, even at the expense of black ones, and had only halfheartedly embraced "indigenization" (S. Taylor 2002).

Nonetheless, although race became a political smokescreen intended to distract the populace from the government's own failed policies on land, indigenization, economic redistribution, and general improvement of the black condition, it did gain some political traction for the ruling party in some quarters (Taylor 1999b). Moreover, some argue that following the assault on white farmers, mostly between 2000 and 2002, race largely ceased to be a major cleavage in Zimbabwe: many whites have abandoned commercial activities or fled the country altogether (Cooke, Morrison, and Prendergast 2003). Regardless of whether Zimbabwe's racial divisions have been "resolved" in this manner—that is, the coerced emigration of the vast majority of whites ipso facto obviates the racial conflict—the victimization of white Zimbabweans by their former collaborators in the government makes clear that Mugabe can no longer use whites as scapegoats for the country's mounting problems.[12]

Ethnic Relations

The departure of large numbers of whites refocuses attention on another major societal cleavage in Zimbabwe: ethnicity. The majority Shona, who compose approximately 82 percent of the population, have been the dominant black actors since independence. The remainder of the population is divided among the Ndebele (16 percent) and several other smaller groups. However, the Shona are also quite diverse, consisting of six subgroups who have recently shown signs of intraethnic competition as political and economic resources have become scarce (Maroleng 2003) and as representatives of each community jockey for position as possible successor to Mugabe.

Just prior to colonialism, the Shona, who arrived in modern-day Zimbabwe between the eleventh and fifteenth centuries, had been a subject people to the Ndebele, who settled in the area only in the 1830s, fleeing their own subjugation under the Zulu during the *mfecane* (the period during which the Zulu kingdom under Shaka Zulu was created). A century and a half later, interethnic friction contributed to the eventual division between the two liberation movements, ZAPU under Joshua Nkomo and ZANU under Ndabaningi Sithole (and later Robert Mugabe), where the former became identified with Ndebele and the latter with Shona.[13]

The level of contestation for resources in Zimbabwe between ethnic groups is itself a subject of debate (du Toit 1995). Importantly, the Shona and Ndebele have seen periods of conflict and cooperation. The ZAPU and ZANU parties together formed a loose "patriotic front" in 1976 as a basis for joint negotiations with the settler state. In 1980, Mugabe invited the predominantly Ndebele ZAPU to join his first cabinet. His rival Nkomo took the post of home affairs minister. Mugabe also appointed Canaan Banana, a Ndebele, to the then largely ceremonial position of president in the first independent government. Alfred Nhema (2002, 101) argues that this was part of an emergent "tradition" of ethnic balancing, which was earlier evidenced in the Muzorewa Zimbabwe-Rhodesia period.[14]

Interethnic relations also have been marked by great tension in the post-settler period. For example, when arms caches were discovered on ZAPU-owned property in February 1982, ZANU suspected a ZAPU plot to reconstitute its armed forces and to seize power. Nkomo and several other ZAPU ministers were sacked, and Nkomo subsequently fled to London in March 1983, where he remained until August 1983 (Nhema 2002, 114). When former ZIPRA soldiers rebelled in Matabeleland and the Midlands province beginning in 1982, the government responded by sending the army's Fifth Brigade to put down the disturbances. Between 1982 and 1985, 1,500 people, mostly Ndebele, were killed, according to the official estimate (du Toit 1995, 132); however, some estimates place the death toll as high as 20,000, including many innocent civilians (Meredith 2007). Debate about the period has resurfaced in recent years, as civil society organizations began to reexamine the roots of President Mugabe's authoritarianism. The leader of the Fifth Brigade, Air Marshal Perrence Shiri, became one of the most senior members of the Zimbabwean military, and some critics have called for Mugabe to be investigated for war crimes because of the actions of the army under his direction.

In part due to ongoing Ndebele resentment, some of the strongest zones of support for the leading opposition party, the MDC, are found in the two Matabeleland provinces, where Ndebele populations are numerous, in particular in the city of Bulawayo. Moreover, even though it was always quite inaccurate to label the MDC a Ndebele party, several senior positions in MDC were occupied early on by Ndebeles, although this concentration was diluted somewhat when the MDC itself split into two factions in 2004. Moreover, the ZAPU, the nationalist party long identified with the Ndebele, has been revived and plans to contest the next national elections.[15] It remains to be seen, however, whether substantial members of the Ndebele community will flock to the reconstituted ZAPU. Regardless of these political affinities, it is too simplistic to view intra-African relations in Zimbabwe through an exclusively ethnic lens. Ndebeles have served and continue to serve as prominent members of the government and cabinet, even during periods of great national tension. Indeed, Mugabe has demonstrated great skill at co-opting Ndebele nationalism and potential rivalry. For example, after several years of negotiations, the 1987 Unity Accord brought ZAPU and Nkomo back into government through a formal merger—absorption, really—into ZANU-PF. Nkomo remained in Mugabe's government as a vice president until his death in 1999. Moreover, a few Ndebeles occupy senior positions in government, perhaps most prominently John Nkomo, the current minister of state in the president's office.[16]

Among the most interesting aspects of Zimbabwe's ethnic politics is intra-Shona competition. Although a factor throughout the history of modern Zimbabwe, this competition has become increasingly pronounced as the debate accelerates over who will succeed Mugabe in ZANU-PF and, as would-be successors presume, the presidency. Mugabe himself appears to favor his own Zezuru group in recent appointments; however, he has in the past appeared to prefer Emmerson Mnangagwa, the former speaker of parliament and current defense minister who hails from the Karanga subgroup. Regardless, Mugabe has demonstrated his capacity to keep aspirants beholden to him and at bay.[17] Zezurus, including current vice president Joyce Mujuru and her husband, the powerful general Solomon Mujuru, are well placed to expand their power in the post-Mugabe future; at the same time, other groups, including the more numerous Karangas, believe it should be their turn; this raises the prospect for an intense struggle for control when Mugabe eventually leaves the scene.

Organization of the State

Executive

At independence, Zimbabwe was bequeathed a Westminster parliamentary model, courtesy of the Lancaster House agreement. Between 1980 and 1987, Mugabe was prime minister and the presidency was a ceremonial office. However, when the Lancaster provisions barring changes to the political system expired in 1987, Zimbabwe adopted an executive presidency, which provided for two vice presidents appointed by the president. Mugabe, who sought to adopt a presidential model even prior to independence, assumed the office. That same year, the post of prime minister was eliminated, although the position was reconstituted as part of the 2008 GPA that ended the standoff between ZANU-PF and the MDC following the controversial 2008 elections; Morgan Tsvangirai was named the new prime minister in 2009, ironically by his archrival Mugabe.

ZANU-PF enjoyed nearly unchallenged political hegemony from independence in 1980 to 2008. As we discuss below, opposition parties always existed during that period, at times garnering significant vote shares. Yet they were never able to penetrate ZANU-PF's dominance. ZANU's control of the executive branch and its functions (and of the pliant parliament until 2008) has been supported by the institutional architecture of the party's Central Committee and the Politburo; both policymaking bodies are vestiges of ZANU-PF's Marxist aspirations of the 1980s. Although the purviews of the Central Committee and Politburo lie in party affairs, historically party and state have been interchangeable in Zimbabwe. As a result, these entities serve to enhance and concentrate presidential power.

The Politburo is chaired by President Mugabe, and consists of Secretaries of the ten departments, their deputies, and 4 Committee members. It has 24 members who hold regular meetings once a month. This is a decision-making organ between the meetings of the Central Committee. The second organ is the Central Committee which has 150 members who meet once in three months. This is a decision-making body between [party] congresses.[18]

Thus the ZANU-PF party structure is also an important part of the government's executive functions and provides a mechanism to reward and punish individuals within the senior ranks of the party. The ZANU-PF Central Committee, for example, was enlarged from only 26 members in the early 1980s to 90 members by 1990 and to 280 members by 2000. The ZANU-PF Politburo is appointed by the president and key members of the Central Committee and deals with all regular party matters (Stoneman and Cliffe 1989, 79).

Under ZANU-PF domination, cabinet positions actually have been subordinated to these party organs (and in 2008, it appeared all were subordinate to the Joint Operations Command [JOC]). Nonetheless, the cabinet is equally bloated, especially since ministerial sinecures represent a critical outlet for regime patronage, and a coveted position for politicians.[19] Of course it would be unfair to label all ministers as ineffective talking heads—some, such as former finance minister Simba Makoni, for example, have been highly regarded—but the power, even of well-intentioned ministers, is ultimately subverted to the state and ZANU-PF party imperatives. In this vein, a long-standing hallmark of Mugabe's approach to governance has been the repeated reshuffling of cabinet members: ministers have been reassigned, demoted, or sacked altogether with increasing frequency. Again, this relates to threats and perceived threats to the president's authority: loyalty is rewarded, whereas those who are seen as "counterrevolutionaries," or as potential rivals to the president, are marginalized.

The adoption of the so-called Government of National Unity (GNU) in February 2009 only seemed to contribute to the dilution of ministerial power. In the early years of the twenty-first century, the executive was supported by a cabinet that consisted of 20 line ministries responsible for specific portfolios and 5 ministers of state. In addition, there were 12 deputy ministers as well as 8 provincial governors tasked with carrying out executive functions at the regional level. In the aftermath of the GPA, and the inauguration of the power-sharing government in early 2009, the number of ministers has ballooned to 40, backed up by an almost equally unwieldy group of 20 deputy ministers. ZANU-PF has a majority of the ministries, with 21, as well as 10 deputies, whereas Tsvangirai's faction of the MDC (MDC-T) has 16 and 10, respectively, and Arthur Mutambara's MDC-M holds 3 ministerial portfolios. Although the GPA was reached in September 2008, it took over five months to form the power-sharing government of the GNU; one of the main reasons for the lag was the inability to divide the cabinet in a way that satisfied all parties. MDC-T was particularly keen to end ZANU-PF domination of the security portfolios, which control military and police functions. In the end, however, although MDC gained control over the finance ministry (with some salutary impact on the economy), defense remains in the purview of Mugabe and ZANU-PF, as do the key resource-oriented ministries such as agriculture, mining, and energy—all sectors that generate considerable rents. Coupled with the Central Intelligence Organisation (CIO), the intelligence unit that reports directly to President Mugabe, ZANU-PF retains disproportionate strength within the "unity" government.

Constitutionalism: From Lancaster House to the Committee of Parliament on the New Constitution

The first decade of the twenty-first century saw constitutional principles subverted to executive authority in Zimbabwe, as the ruling ZANU-PF party began to ignore constitutional restrictions with impunity. Yet the earlier 1979 Lancaster House agreement provided a comprehensive constitutional blueprint for the independent state. Its more notable provisions have been enumerated above, including reserved parliamentary seats for whites, an independent judiciary, a bill of rights, a stipulation that land transfers could only be made on a "willing buyer–willing seller" basis rather than forcibly acquired, and a council of chiefs.[20] It was, in short, an inherently conservative document, intended to restrict the agenda of the new government and provide certain guarantees for white residents. Although the Lancaster House agreement stipulated that the constitution could only be changed with a 100 percent majority in the parliament, the constitution could be altered after ten years by a two-thirds majority. Many of the provisions agreed to at Lancaster had earlier expiry dates. The white seats, for example, were guaranteed only until 1987. It was believed that the ten-year expiration of the Lancaster constitution would give time for the new Zimbabwean state to become institutionalized and for constitutional protections to become entrenched.

In September 1987 the first of these changes took place. The 20 reserved white seats were abolished, and the 80 African members elected 20 new members to the lower house (11 of whom were white) (Nhema 2002, 117). The 10 white reserved seats in the upper house were abolished. In October 1987 the Westminster model was abandoned in favor of an executive presidency. Finally, by December the two-chamber parliament was abandoned in favor of a unicameral system, with a single, 150-member chamber, effective from the 1990 general election until a 66-member Senate was reconstituted in 2005.

Nonetheless, the 1979 constitution, with these and other amendments, has remained the basic legal framework in Zimbabwe. There have been numerous initiatives to create a new constitution, and in fact, the letter of the 2008 GPA mandates the enactment of a new constitution prior to more elections. Among the most robust initial efforts was the National Constitutional Assembly (NCA), a movement that emerged in mid-1997 and shortly thereafter began lobbying for a new constitution.

The NCA was a coalition of some ninety-six civil society organizations, including academics and legal experts, labor unions, churches, and human rights groups who argued that, at its core, the constitution of Zimbabwe still contained many colonial-era provisions and that numerous amendments had had the effect of reducing individual rights. The NCA successfully pressured the state to establish a constitutional commission in April 1999. To the dismay of the NCA, however, at least 300 members of the government's 400-member commission were also members of ZANU-PF. The NCA refused to accept the legitimacy of the process (Raftopoulos 2001, 15) and continued its own unofficial constitutional-drafting exercise in parallel.

On the one hand, the very emergence of the NCA was a striking example of the maturation of civil society in Zimbabwe, because a diverse range of interests and institutions came together around one goal. On the other hand, the NCA's exclusion from the drafting exercise was a reflection of the unwillingness of the ZANU regime to make the constitution a truly popular, *modern* document, appropriately reflective of people's concerns in the contemporary Zimbabwean state.

Confident of its ability to control the outcome, the government put the constitutional commission's version of the constitution to a national referendum. In Zimbabwe's first-ever plebiscite, held on February 12–13, 2000, 54.7 percent of the population voted to reject the government proposals. The NCA had rallied its supporters and others in the wider populace to vote no to the narrowly tailored, partisan document, which would have increased presidential powers and undermined property rights by abolishing the last vestiges of legal protections against state seizure of (largely white-owned) commercial farms. This marked the first electoral defeat President Mugabe had faced in twenty years of power, and later events revealed that he was unwilling to tolerate additional losses.

If it is possible retroactively to fix the start of Zimbabwe's collapse in November 1997, as suggested above, it is equally clear that the country took a sharp and irrevocable downward turn after the release of the referendum results in mid-February 2000. Prior to this date, most stakeholders and government opponents held firm to the belief that the economic and increasingly political crisis gripping the country could be addressed through popular means—including not only marches and periodic demonstrations but also mediation and consultation. Moreover, civic confidence that change might be possible via the ballot box was significantly boosted via the referendum process itself; indeed, President Mugabe appeared initially magnanimous in defeat when he announced the results (Raftopoulos 2001).

Very shortly after the referendum, however, the national environment became quite different. The defeat of the referendum ushered in a level of violence not seen in Zimbabwe in almost two decades, rising lawlessness, state disinterest in restoration of order, and government manipulation of race and the land issue for political ends. Since late February 2000, then, Zimbabwe has been characterized by an intolerance of dissent and gross human rights violations—including state-sanctioned torture, illegal imprisonment, the use of food aid as a weapon, and several hundred politically motivated deaths. Paradoxically, what began as a worthy effort to enshrine constitutionalism was so warped by the state that it succeeded in destroying its foundation. The "rule of law" was subverted to the caprices of President Mugabe and his allies in less than a decade.

The most recent attempt at constitution-making emerged out of the GPA. The select Committee of Parliament on the New Constitution (COPAC), comprising twenty-five members drawn from the three political parties in the GNU, began its work in June 2010; its proponents hoped that the COPAC could deliver a new constitution by 2011, which would then be subject to a national referendum. In some respects reminiscent of Zambia's constitutional reform committees, COPAC's mission is "to ensure the drafting of a new constitution through an inclusive, people-driven and democratic process." In addition, COPAC insists that the body will be "driven by the values of integrity, democracy, impartiality and transparency."[21] Yet because COPAC is situated in parliament itself, its capacity to incorporate societal input and values in a "people-driven" manner is open to question.

Moreover, notwithstanding the collegiality depicted on its official website, the COPAC process has been weighed down by the same divisions that have affected Zimbabwean politics for the better part of a decade. Andrew Arato (2010) argues that despite the flaws in the process, the end result, including limits on presidential power, would mark a substantial improvement for Zimbabwe. Yet he also notes that powerful actors are motivated "to distort [or] even block it altogether."

The GPA, which it had been agreed would only last for eighteen months, stipulated in Article 6 that new elections would not be held before the completion of a new constitution. As of early 2011, the GPA had formally expired, yet the MDC, civil society groups, and other critics were seeking to extend the constitutional review process, which would thereby push national elections to 2012. At the same time, however, it began to appear that rather than delay the constitution-drafting process, ZANU-PF would go forward with tripartite elections in 2011 under the 1979 constitution, as some observers had long predicted (see EIU 2010c). Such a maneuver would force MDC to make a difficult choice: boycott or compete in another election in which ZANU-PF would be poised to manipulate the process.

The Judiciary and Judicial-Presidential Relations

In a system of genuine balance of power, the judiciary should have been capable of mitigating Zimbabwe's slide toward authoritarianism. Zimbabwe had long had an autonomous judiciary, as enshrined in the Lancaster House agreement. Sections 11–26 of the 1979 Zimbabwean constitution included a "Declaration of Rights" that guaranteed freedom of expression, association, and assembly. Hence, government actions and decrees were regularly taken to the High Court, where it was not uncommon for the government to lose decisions, which it generally accepted, albeit grudgingly.[22]

However, starting with its defeat on the constitutional referendum in 2000, the executive branch pursued a strategy of intimidation and harassment, often simply ignoring judgments from the bench. More alarming, prominent jurists, including former Supreme Court chief justice Anthony Gubbay, were forced to retire under threat. In 2001, Gubbay was replaced by the more government-friendly Godfrey Chidyausiku. As noted above, presidential and executive authority has been increasingly dismissive of unfavorable judicial decisions, roughly since the 2000–2001 period. Whereas Mugabe was long chastened by judicial review of presidential directives, his administration no longer seems concerned about legal opinion. Indeed, the complicity of the bench in ZANU-PF's political machinations means that findings against ZANU have become rare, in any event. Thus, an artifice of checks and balances exists, but even this pretense is seldom maintained in an atmosphere increasingly characterized by lawlessness. ZANU-PF has become a law unto itself; in some cases, the response to unfavorable decisions from the bench has been to change the law. In other cases, however, the courts have simply been ignored.

The first decade of the twentieth century saw not only the erosion of constitutional protections but also an array of repressive legislation intended to consolidate the power of the ruling party and clamp down on dissent. Although passed with intent to influence the March 2002 presidential election, these laws have had sweeping ramifications well beyond that event. The notorious Public Order and Security Act (POSA) of 2002, for example, which contravenes Section 11 of the constitution, prescribed penalties of up to twenty years' imprisonment for any threat to organize civil disobedience and granted extraordinary powers to the police. Although MDC parliamentarians successfully introduced amendments to weaken the most egregiously draconian aspects of POSA in December 2010 (FES 2010), it remained unlikely at the time of writing that the changes would be enacted into law, given ZANU-PF control over the Senate.[23] The Citizenship Act of 2002 outlawed dual citizenship and was designed to prevent whites and the descendants of farm workers born in neighboring countries from voting for the MDC in the 2002 presidential election. The Access to Information and Protection of Privacy Act (AIPPA) of 2002 restricted the access of foreign reporters and imposed tight controls on local media. It also created a state-appointed commission to license journalists, with penalties of up to two years in prison for violating the regulations ("Zim Parliament" 2002). The already notorious AIPPA was made even more repressive through a 2005 amendment. Other proposed legislation has had a chilling effect on civil discourse, even though it was *not* ultimately signed by the president. The 2004 NGO Bill, for example, would have prohibited local NGOs from accessing foreign funds, thereby decimating and/or subjugating a host of civil society organizations. The mere *threat* of the law enabled the Mugabe government to assert its domination by inducing panic among NGOs.

The now pliant judiciary has largely concurred with the application of these repressive laws, though there have been interesting exceptions. David Blair (2002, 76) traces the breakdown of the rule of law to a single event: on March 17, 2000, as the land invasions were escalating and 630 farms were then occupied, the farmers' main representative body, the Commercial Farmers Union (CFU), sought and obtained a court order from High Court justice Paddington Garwe (who had ties to ZANU-PF himself) naming key agents of the regime as respondents.[24] The order, which was agreed to by the parties, stipulated that the farm occupations were illegal and that farms must be vacated. Garwe gave the police seventy-two hours to execute the order. However, encouraged by the president himself, at the end of the period the number of occupations had ballooned to 742, indicating the powerlessness of legal institutions in contemporary Zimbabwe. The turning point identified by Blair is compelling, and it was followed by numerous other assaults on judicial independence.[25]

The Military

Unlike the militaries of western Africa, which played a regular role in postcolonial politics in those countries (Clark 2007), the Zimbabwean military was not an overtly political actor after 1980, although the killing of noncombatants by the Fifth Brigade in the early 1980s was certainly an exception to this rule. Outside of that notorious unit, however, in general the military—which was established by merging ZANLA and ZIPRA forces and initially some members (especially senior officers) of the Rhodesian forces as well—was regarded as professional and apolitical. As in other southern African nations, military interventions have been uncommon, and coups unheard of. The post-1997 period, however, has witnessed the emergence of a newly politicized and enriched military establishment, which poses a looming threat to continued civilian rule in Zimbabwe. The military began to emerge as a political force following Zimbabwe's 1998 intervention in the war in DRC. Zimbabwe sent as many as 15,000 troops to Congo, severely stretching the country's deployment capacity.

Though the DRC intervention became a national economic disaster for Zimbabwe as a whole, military and political elites enriched themselves in DRC through mining and timber concessions, supply and transport contracts, and so on. Party- and military-owned and affiliated companies, such as Zimbabwe Defense Industries and Operation Sovereign Legitimacy (Osleg), managed to secure lucrative and controversial contracts in DRC, as well as joint ventures with the Congolese government (see Nest 2001; United Nations Security Council 2002; Global Witness 2002b). Thus the generals have become intricately linked within the ZANU-PF patronage web.

In addition to salary increases, security sector officials have received a range of gratuities. In mid-2007, for example, the government was reported to have "spent thousands of United States dollars acquiring luxurious Mazda 3 vehicles for army and police chiefs, at a time when the country has no foreign currency for essentials such as drugs." Each Mazda cost US$16,607, and beneficiaries received a then substantial Zimbabwe dollar top-up of $200 million as well. The army chiefs fared even better, receiving Toyota Prados or Mercedes Benzes depending on their rank; the government also acquired hundreds of Toyota Yaris vehicles for the CIO (Nkatazo 2007). Of course, senior military officials were also among the leading beneficiaries of land seizures (Smith 2010), and the state provided access to credit to support their various business interests, however they were acquired: "A special Reserve Bank fund gives cheap unsecured loans to top officers, politburo and central committee and central committee members, cabinet ministers, judges and parliamentarians to finance farming and business activities" (ICG 2007, 8). This transparent bias toward the active armed forces, as well as to the intelligence and security personnel and groups like the War Vets, while intended to bolster the strength of ZANU-PF, actually indicates its vulnerability. Indeed, in the aftermath of the 2008 election especially, the party and President Mugabe himself became thoroughly dependent on the military to retain power.

Perhaps more significant than the military's access to rents or penetration of the bureaucracy is that, prior to the GPA, political posts and institutions—including even the Politburo and the ZANU-PF Central Committee—were superseded by military ones. One such entity is the JOC, which comprises the heads of the army, the police, and the intelligence services and includes the ministers of defense, state security, the chief of prisons, and others. In the run-up to and aftermath of the 2008 presidential election, the International Crisis Group was one of many groups concluding that "the JOC has replaced the cabinet as the primary policy-making organ, briefed on and approving major measures before ministers implement them" (ICG 2007, 7). In October 2007, the JOC even took over the duties of the cabinet task force on Price Monitoring and Stabilisation (Chimakure 2007). Although this military presence has diminished somewhat in the wake of the détente between MDC and ZANU-PF, the military remains a key arbiter of politics in Zimbabwe for the foreseeable future. Military backgrounds are increasingly seen as a prerequisite to access the president's inner circle.

Whereas the rank and file have not fared particularly well—HIV/AIDS has been rampant in the armed forces; desertion has increased; and troops have been used for, at best, unconventional purposes[26]—senior officers have a vested interest in preserving ZANU-PF rule, which is an inherently political position; indeed, any threat to ZANU-PF power poses a corresponding threat to the military elite. The risk lies not only in the prospect of lost patronage but also in the potential of facing prosecution by a reformist, civilian government headed by the MDC or another opposition party. As a result, the military inserted itself into domestic political affairs (or was asked to do so). For example, "in an unprecedented display of strength and hubris prior to the 2003 presidential election, the military declared that it will be the final arbiter of who governs Zimbabwe" (Carmody and Taylor 2003, 13). Then commander in chief of the armed forces, Lieutenant-General Vitalis Zvinavashe, stated, in effect, that a Tsvangirai victory would not be tolerated and any presidential aspirant would be subjected to a liberation war "litmus test":

> We wish to make it very clear to all Zimbabwean citizens that the security organisations will pursue Zimbabwean values, traditions and beliefs for which thousands of lives were lost. . . . We will therefore, not accept, let alone support or salute, anyone with a different agenda that threatens the very existence of our sovereignty, our country and our people. (quoted in Carmody and Taylor 2003, 13; see also Zimbabwe Alert 202)

But the preservation of ZANU-PF domination does not necessarily equate to support for the Robert Mugabe–dominated status quo, and in fact, substantial fissures have emerged within the military elite. These became particularly pronounced in advance of the 2008 presidential election. General Zvinavashe came out publicly in support of Simba Makoni's long-shot, third-party candidacy for the presidency. Similarly, both liberation war hero and retired general Solomon Mujuru and his wife, Zimbabwe's vice president Joyce Mujuru, are alienated from President Mugabe. General Mujuru has long been considered a "kingmaker" in the military and in a faction of ZANU-PF. The Mujurus are extremely wealthy as businesspeople and owners of numerous farms (at least one of which was seized); General Mujuru has been linked periodically to Mugabe rivals and has thus run afoul of the president. Moreover, *both* Mujurus have long been suspected of having presidential ambitions of their own. Of course, one could argue that a partisan but divided military could be far more dangerous than a politicized one that supports only one side, but this endgame has yet to play out. In any event, it is clear there are divisions within the highly politicized military and security-related bodies. Both institutionally and individually, actors have interests they will strive to protect; genuine democratization in Zimbabwe, whether in the form of MDC or some other party that lacks the military/liberation war bona fides, represents a threat to those interests.

Representation and Participation

Legislature

As the ZANU-PF executive branch has concentrated authority and drawn on the military to solidify its power and insulate itself from challenges, the power of the legislature has remained marginal. This did not change with the ascendance of MDC as a parliamentary force after 2000. Between 1989, when the upper house of parliament (the Senate) was discarded, and 2005, when it was reconstituted, the unicameral parliament was composed of 150 members, 120 of whom were elected on the basis of a common voters' roll by a first-past-the-post, simple majority in single-member constituencies, and 30 members were appointed by the president (including the eight provincial governors, ten traditional chiefs, and twelve others). The president's capacity to appoint members—an anachronism also found in neighboring Botswana and Zambia—not only impedes the independence of the legislative branch but also vests extraordinary power in the president and potentially dilutes the will of the electorate by rendering opposition representation in the chamber less competitive.[27]

With effect from the 2008 election, the House of Assembly, the lower house, was expanded from 150 to 210 seats, all of which are now elected positions. The Senate, which was expanded from 66 to 93 seats, now includes 60 members who are directly elected (6 from each province), and the remaining members are appointed from among the chiefs and the ten provincial governors (including one each from the cities of Harare and Bulawayo, which have provincial status).[28] The ruling ZANU-PF decided to revive the Senate in 2005, not least because of the expanded patronage opportunities that a new chamber provides. In protest of the unfair electoral conditions and the violence perpetrated by ZANU-PF, Morgan Tsvangirai and his supporters within MDC opted to boycott the November 2005 Senate poll. However, this split the party, and a far smaller faction (now known as MDC-M) led by former professor Arthur Mutambara emerged to contest the Senate elections; MDC-M won just 7 of the 50 contested seats.

Until 2000, the year the MDC captured fifty-seven seats in the House of Assembly, the competitiveness of the chamber was unimportant; it was dominated by ZANU-PF, which served as a rubber stamp for President Mugabe's decisions. This is certainly no longer the case, as both the lower and upper chambers are now extremely competitive; indeed, together the two MDC factions have a majority in parliament, having won 109 of the 210 House of Assembly seats in the March 2008 election. The Senate is also evenly balanced, favoring ZANU-PF only with the addition of the appointed members. Yet these watershed developments in Zimbabwe's political history notwithstanding, the parliament effectively remains a stepchild to the executive branch; supported by the military and security apparatus, the latter has ensured ZANU-PF's dominance despite electoral defeat.

Party System and Elections

Zimbabwe has been a nominally multiparty state since independence in 1980. Although the country flirted with de jure single-party rule in the late 1980s, the ZANU-PF government, which had long pushed for such a change, abandoned the effort in 1990. In any event, a single-party option proved unnecessary: by the late 1980s, ZANU-PF had attained a virtual lock on elective office, cemented in the 1990 elections (Sylvester 1995). Not until the emergence of the Movement for Democratic Change in September 1999, and the parliamentary elections that followed in June 2000, was the dominant-party regime seriously challenged at the ballot box.

The country's two principal liberation movements, ZAPU, led by Joshua Nkomo, and ZANU, led by Mugabe, were the leading contenders in the first independence elections, held in February 1980 under the conditions agreed to at Lancaster House in December 1979. ZANU captured 57 of the 80 African seats, defeating ZAPU, which garnered 20 seats. Bishop Abel Muzorewa's United African National Council (UANC) picked up 3 seats. The Rhodesia Front, under Ian Smith, captured all 20 of the seats on the white voters' roll (Nhema 2002).

The elections in 1985, 1990, 1995, and 1996 each saw the steady consolidation of ZANU hegemony. In 1985, ZANU gained 64 seats in the 100-seat lower house; Muzorewa's UANC lost all its seats; ZANU-Sithole (later ZANU-Ndonga) gained one seat; and the RF (renamed the Conservative Alliance [CA] in 1983) gained 15 of the 20 white seats. A liberal RF breakaway group, the Independent Zimbabwe Group, could muster only 5 seats. Mugabe was publicly critical of whites for their continued support of Ian Smith's party, the CA, believing that "whites had spurned his government's hand of reconciliation" (Nhema 2002, 116).

The elections in 1990 were significant because they confirmed the consolidation of ZANU-PF political power after the 1987 Unity Accord. Former ZANU-PF secretary-general Edgar Tekere and his Zimbabwe Unity Movement party were defeated at the polls, and the opposition only managed to garner three seats. At the same time, however, this outcome also masked a latent discontent with ZANU-PF rule that was to escalate exponentially in the 1990s. Tekere's party actually received more than 19 percent of the vote nationally. Moreover, a turnout of just under 60 percent reveals that substantial numbers did not bother to vote, suggesting a reservoir of anti–ZANU-PF sentiment in the country (Sylvester 1995, 411). In any event, the ruling party was able to draw on the substantial resources of incumbency that it has exploited in every election before or since. These include virtually exclusive access to the state-owned media; the ability to dispense food in poor rural areas, typically in the form of maize or seed; and sole access to an electoral fund (amounting to ZW\$30 million annually in the elections of the 1990s, or about US\$4 million in mid-decade), which was not subject to public audit (ZimRights 1996). In addition, after the emergence of MDC as a credible electoral threat, ZANU-PF regularly utilized the state security apparatus to intimidate and often brutalize opposition supporters. Further, the plurality electoral system in single-member constituencies, which favors incumbents and underrepresents supporters of other parties, also worked in ZANU-PF's favor.

In the 1995 and 1996 elections, these factors as well as the deteriorating macropolitical and economic situation combined to produce apathy rather than voter mobilization. Although opposition parties gained 18 percent of the national vote in the parliamentary contest, turnout fell to 57 percent (Sylvester 1995, 411). In the 1996 presidential election, Zimbabwean NGOs claimed that the government engaged in rampant vote buying and distribution of maize, seed, and fertilizer to shore up rural support (ZimRights 1996, 9). The turnout for the 1996 elections was an anemic 31 percent of registered voters, which was interpreted in ZimRights (1996, 11–12) and by other domestic observers as a vote of no confidence in ZANU-PF.[29]

Despite ZANU-PF's substantial margins of victory in the 1990s, one important trend that emerged was the gradual evaporation of ZANU-PF support in the urban areas, where poverty, unemployment, and labor activism all were on the increase. This created legitimacy problems for ZANU-PF and exposed its growing vulnerabilities. Internal decay within the ruling party, declining living standards in the 1990s, and the emergence of a credible alternative to ZANU-PF all set the stage for major changes in the years that followed, culminating in the MDC's remarkable performance in the first decade of the twenty-first century, in which it swept the urban vote. The June 2000 election was a watershed event in modern Zimbabwe (see Alexander 2000; Kriger 2000; ICG 2000; Sithole 2001). Although fifteen political parties contested the June 24–25, 2000, parliamentary elections, ZANU-PF and the ascendant MDC were the principal contenders.[30] ZANU-PF captured 62 seats to the MDC's 57, but the results from over thirty constituencies were immediately challenged as fraudulent, albeit unsuccessfully, by the opposition. Yet considering the widespread irregularities, the harassment of MDC supporters—including the deaths of nearly thirty people, mostly MDC partisans—in election-related violence prior to the poll, and the benefits of incumbency, the MDC's achievement was impressive (Kriger 2000).

The March 2005 parliamentary (House of Assembly) elections occurred in a context of increased violence and uncertainty. Until just three weeks prior to the poll, the repressive POSA was utilized by the police to restrict campaigning by MDC and its supporters. On election day, the MDC, at that time still united behind Tsvangirai, won 41 seats (39.5 percent), some 16 fewer than it had five years earlier. ZANU-PF, by contrast, won 59.6 percent of the vote, or 78 seats; one independent candidate won the final seat. With the 20 members appointed by President Mugabe, and the 10 members drawn from the progovernment traditional chiefs, ZANU-PF actually enjoyed a significant majority. MDC and most international election observation groups immediately cried foul, claiming that all aspects of the election—voter registration, delimitation, freedom to organize (except in the last few weeks), electoral administration, and counting of the final votes—had been sufficiently compromised that the final result could not be considered an accurate reflection of voter preferences (International IDEA 2005).[31]

The traditional pattern for the subsequent legislative elections would have called for them to be held around March 2010; however, parliament altered the electoral schedule to harmonize elections for the Senate and the House of Assembly with the presidential elections scheduled for 2008. Even with a repetition of electoral violence orchestrated by ZANU-PF, its agents within the state and outside, and a corrupt election administration, MDC-T and MDC-M managed to capture a significant number of seats in both houses in 2008, as noted above.

The presidential elections, however, have been much more critical; indeed, in the context of Zimbabwe's presidentialist model, ZANU-PF rightly saw its continued domination of the executive branch as essential to its interests. The 2002 presidential election, therefore, took place in a context of rising repression and attacks on MDC supporters (this time over 100 people lost their lives). Despite ZANU-PF's intrinsic advantages, however, MDC candidate Tsvangirai garnered, officially, over 42 percent of the vote. Yet Mugabe was declared the winner, defeating Tsvangirai by an official margin of 1.6 million to 1.2 million votes. These results were immediately challenged by the MDC, its supporters, and much of the international community ("US Says Zim Election Fundamentally Flawed" 2002; Cowell 2002). Fraud was certainly a factor in the government's victory; by some estimates, it accounted for more than the 400,000-vote margin of Tsvangirai's defeat.[32] Indeed, these findings were consistent with the results of opinion polls conducted in the months prior to the election, which showed a substantial lead for Tsvangirai.[33]

By the time of the March 2008 presidential election, the economy had collapsed, and Mugabe appeared increasingly vulnerable. Only the instruments of repression and the assurances by military elites of their continued support conferred any advantage on the incumbent. Yet MDC and its supporters faced unspeakable harassment; Tsvangirai himself had endured trumped-up legal trials and personal tragedy, yet he renewed his quest for the presidency.[34] In fact, most observers believed that Tsvangirai actually won the first round of elections, and probably outright. Officially, however, he came just shy of receiving the 50 percent of the vote needed to avoid a run-off, which was eventually set for June 27, 2008. Predictably, between the first round of elections and the presidential run-off the government perpetrated massive violence against its own citizens. The US Department of State estimated that 50 Zimbabweans were killed, over 2,000 injured, and 30,000 displaced. The violence against MDC supporters and the repressive atmosphere led the MDC to pull out of the run-off poll just days before it was to occur. Mugabe became the only candidate, and he of course won the poll by a large majority.

Most Western observers—who were barred by the regime from monitoring the elections on the ground—did not see the process as legitimate. Yet, many African states recognized Mugabe as the victor. Despite African recognition of his political legitimacy, Mugabe and the ZANU-PF were compelled into power-sharing talks with the MDC, and the GPA was finally reached in September 2008 with substantial brokering by South Africa's Thabo Mbeki. Disputes over the allocation of cabinet positions in the new government led to delays in the implementation of the GPA, however.

Civil Society and Social Groups

The MDC's origins clearly lie in a civil society that became particularly energized in the late 1990s. Organized interest groups existed in the 1980s and before; however, they were able to strike an increasingly resonant chord with the wider society as the 1990s wore on, due to a confluence of factors. Prominent among these was the worsening economic situation for average Zimbabweans: real wages were declining, industrial closures were becoming commonplace, and the ability of the state to provide a social safety net was rapidly eroding. The economic structural adjustment program, which was intended to address many of these concerns, suffered from flaws in both design and implementation, and the program therefore contributed to deepening hardship (Carmody and Taylor 2003).

The trade unions, human rights organizations, and later the emergent MDC were able to capitalize on this discontent (ZCTU 1996; Bond and Manyanya 2002). Civil society's awakening, therefore, was both consequence and cause of ZANU-PF's declining hegemony. Civic organizations arose to challenge ZANU-PF's neglect of social, economic, and political concerns, and as more groups were emboldened, the regime no longer appeared impenetrable. In the Zimbabwe case, however, civic expression came at an enormous medium-term cost: the greater the voice of civic actors, the more repressive the regime response.

The MDC emerged partly out of the labor movement and partly out of the NCA, but it came to attract myriad other interests as well, including NGOs, human rights organizations, churches, and legal groups. The well-known linkage between civic organizations and the MDC is an important factor in explaining why groups from human rights NGOs, church and religious groups to women's organizations were targeted, intimidated, and frequently arrested by state authorities. Below we examine the role of several of these key "traditional" elements of civil society: labor, human rights organizations, and the media. It is important to note that Zimbabwe has a rich history of economic interest groups that play a critical mediating role in the economic arena as well. These actors have been the subject of numerous studies (e.g., Herbst 1990; Skalnes 1995; Taylor 2007) and have served as key societal partners, and sometime critics, of both the Rhodesian and Zimbabwean governments over the years. Since the role of these groups has been drastically curtailed, if not eliminated, as a result of the economic crisis, we instead concentrate on civil society actors who are more actively engaged in criticism or support of ZANU-PF's political agenda; hence this section includes examination of organizations that have been co-opted by the state. Among these, groups such as the liberation war veterans association and various local and national militia groups admittedly stretch our very conception of civil society, since they were regularly funded, organized, and utilized by the state for expressly political purposes.

Labor. Unlike the situation in some other African countries, including South Africa and Zambia, trade unions in Zimbabwe lacked strength historically. At independence, Zimbabwean labor was "weak, divided and had played no significant role in the discussions over the transition to majority rule at Lancaster House in 1979" (Raftopoulos 2001, 4). In the 1980s, labor was restrained as part of a state corporatist framework (Shaw 1989). Indeed, as Brian Raftopoulos argues (2001, 4), the main labor umbrella, the Zimbabwe Congress of Trade Unions (ZCTU), was effectively a wing of ZANU-PF in the 1980s; Robert Mugabe's brother, Albert, even served as ZCTU secretary-general until his death. Moreover, the nominally socialist government of ZANU-PF instituted repressive antilabor legislation, such as restrictions on shop floor organization, and dealt harshly with strikes in the early 1980s, even prohibiting the right to strike.[35] These measures were welcomed by employers, and the mostly white business community benefited. Beginning in 1987, however, new leadership emerged within the ZCTU, including Morgan Tsvangirai as secretary-general. With the familial link to ZANU broken, the ZCTU began to distance itself from the ruling party and actually represent worker interests. Despite the historical weakness of labor in Zimbabwe, the state was wary of its potential power, even in the early 1990s.[36] Thus, as relations between the state and the union federation grew more antagonistic, the state began to harass and arrest labor leaders, including Tsvangirai, who were later acquitted by the still autonomous High Court (Raftopoulos 2001, 8).

The early 1990s witnessed deepening hardship for the rank and file, and the decade marked a difficult time for the union movement generally in Zimbabwe and throughout the region. Patrick Bond and Masimba Manyanya (2002, 86) have disapprovingly stated that the ZCTU and Tsvangirai "sought an accommodation with neoliberalism." Arguably, this was the only way labor could avoid being marginalized, since economic policy decisions were being made chiefly between international donors and the state, and thus the parameters of economic policy "choice" were already set. In this vein, the ZCTU articulated a position in its 1996 *Beyond ESAP* report (ZCTU 1996) that largely accepted the hegemony of the neoliberal agenda.

But if the economic status of organized labor was increasingly constrained, paradoxically the modest political opening in the 1990s allowed bodies like ZCTU a new platform and nascent political clout. Hence, the second half of the decade saw the reemergence of strikes and stayaways called by the ZCTU. The ESAP deepened, if not caused, declines in real wages and sharp escalation in unemployment in all sectors except commercial agriculture (Carmody and Taylor 2003). In response, protests mounted, and the ZCTU gained a prominent role. Initially, it supported a strike by a previously unaffiliated union, the Public Sector Workers Union, over pay increases in early 1996. Later, the ZCTU called the first of its own strikes in December 1997 (Raftopoulos 2001, 10–12; Bond and Manyanya 2002, 88). The December 1997 action marked a critical turning point for the ZCTU. Called in response to a Mugabe-proposed tax that would severely undercut the already precarious position of workers, the threat of the strike induced the government to capitulate on the issue. However, the status of the unions as a genuine political force was ensured when the ZCTU went ahead with the successful strike anyway (Raftopoulos 2001, 13; Bond and Manyanya 2002, 88).

The events of this period in 1997, including but not limited to the role of the ZCTU, set off a chain of events that permanently altered the political and economic landscape in Zimbabwe. By early 1998 the ascendant ZCTU was playing a central role in the launch of the NCA, which was chaired by Tsvangirai. The "spectre of the Chiluba route to power," to quote Raftopoulos (2001, 8), was certainly apparent by September 1999, when much of the ZCTU leadership assumed prominent positions in the newly formed MDC. Tsvangirai became leader of the MDC, which gained the staunch support of not only labor unions but also business groups and the urban middle class. Ultimately, the ZCTU's ascendance was negated by an Icarus-like fall in the first decade of the twenty-first century, once inflation soared, the economy collapsed, and formal sector unemployment reached over 90 percent.

Human rights organizations. The mid- to late 1990s marked a period when ZANU-PF and Mugabe arguably were at their weakest. The economy over which they presided was under pressure from the combined effects of structural imbalances, two severe droughts, and the ESAP. The elections of 1995 and 1996, although swept by ZANU-PF, showed the party's vulnerabilities.

Finally, the regime's then latent authoritarianism permitted political and legal space in which to criticize the government.

In addition to the labor efforts noted above, a number of critical organizations arose in this period. Among these was the Zimbabwe Human Rights Association (ZimRights), which was actually established in 1992 but rose to prominence mid-decade as an outspoken government critic. By 1998 it claimed 15,000 members. In attempting to fulfill its organizational objectives, ZimRights clashed with ZANU-PF over many functions, including civic action, democracy and good governance, HIV/AIDS, victim support, and voter education and election monitoring as well as more "conventional" human rights concerns—lobbying the government to adopt international human rights norms (ZimRights 2002). One of the organization's most valued functions following the June 2000 parliamentary elections was to serve as an information conduit to international human rights organizations.

Finally, a host of other entities were established in response to the crisis. The aptly named Crisis in Zimbabwe Coalition was formed in 2001 as land invasions and political violence escalated, and it appeared that ZANU-PF would attempt to rig the 2002 presidential elections. The coalition initially included nine other entities, among them the NCA, the ZCTU, and the Media Institute, altogether representing some 350 NGOs. The coalition's main objectives center around the promotion of "freedom and democratic values through encouraging dialogue, tolerance and the shaping of ideas by Zimbabweans from all walks of life" (Crisis in Zimbabwe Coalition 2003). Although its success in this regard clearly has been limited, the existence of such bodies reveals both the resistance and resilience of Zimbabwe's civil society in the face of enormous challenges.

Other groups that have played a prominent role in this period include Women of Zimbabwe Arise (WOZA), which was founded in 2002 to advocate for women's rights and political reform; the Zimbabwe Lawyers for Human Rights; and the Zimbabwe Peace Project, headed by activist Jestina Mukoko. Many of these bodies and their supporters have faced repeated harassment, physical assaults, and wrongful imprisonment by state entities tied to ZANU-PF. Indeed, the party's hard-liners regard these civil society organizations as mere appendages of the MDC and a hostile international community. Certainly, a number of these civil society organizations (CSOs) do enjoy linkages with the international community as well as with vestiges of Zimbabwe's white elite; Mugabe has tried to use these ties, ineffectively, to undermine their local legitimacy. Yet these CSOs have been at the vanguard of local, *Zimbabwean* efforts to bravely, at times brazenly, challenge ZANU-PF and Mugabe. Importantly, organizations that lack an international profile have also persevered against great odds and with far more limited resources, although it is also necessary to note that many Zimbabweans have sought refuge in their families, churches, or abroad in the face of persistent hardship.

The media. As in most of Africa, the biggest player in Zimbabwe's media is the state, which has profound implications for the dissemination of ideas, the representation of alternative viewpoints, and the competitiveness of opposition parties and groups. The government-owned *Herald* newspaper and the *Sunday Mail* are among only three English-language dailies and have the widest circulation in the country. The government press, and the principal television broadcast company, Zimbabwe Broadcasting Corporation (ZBC), take an unapologetically ZANU-PF line. Similar progovernment views are espoused on state-run radio. Indeed, there are great risks for not doing so: the head of the state-owned press company, Zimpapers, was dismissed in the 1990s for not toeing the government line sufficiently.

By the same token, the independent media (especially print) long fought to publish dissenting viewpoints. Several weekly newspapers, such as the *Financial Gazette,* the *Zimbabwe Independent,* and the *Sunday Standard,* have criticized the government, at great risk to journalists, editors, and sellers of the papers.[37] The only independent daily newspaper, the *Daily News,* was established in April 1999 and immediately took an antigovernment position and attracted a wide readership. However, the *Daily News,* which developed a pro-MDC bias, paid a heavy price. Its press was bombed twice; both times army personnel were suspected, based on the devices used. Reporters and staff of the *Daily News,* like those from all the independent papers, have faced harassment and imprisonment, and numerous journalists have found asylum abroad. Even before the promulgation of the new media law, the AIPPA, journalists risked imprisonment, fines, or worse.

As noted above, the passage of AIPPA in January 2002 made it a criminal offense to publish certain kinds of stories, imposed licensing requirements on reporters—a privilege granted, and subject to revocation, by the state—and established registration procedures for news agencies. Given the hostile climate for journalists, it is a testament to the dedication of both local and foreign correspondents in Zimbabwe that they continued to publish stories in the wake of this legislation. However, the state continues to go to great lengths to control the dissemination and use of information. In September 2003 the government shut down the offices of the *Daily News* and confiscated its equipment, alleging company registry violations. The now pliant courts declined to overturn the draconian media law, despite local, regional, and international condemnation of Zimbabwe's failure to foster "an environment that protects the enjoyment of basic human freedoms" (MISA 2007, 40). It is not surprising, then, that some of the most compelling reporting on Zimbabwe today—by Zimbabwean journalists and bloggers—appears in online sources, often originating in the United Kingdom, South Africa, or the United States. Much of this reportage is not seen in Zimbabwe, however.

Progovernment groups: war veterans, militias, and mobs. The institutions and actors discussed above tended to coalesce around opposition to the regime and its policies. The Zimbabwe National Liberation War Veterans Association (the "war vets"), conversely, emerged as a significant player on the national stage beginning in July and August 1997 and provided an important plank in ZANU-PF's otherwise dwindling popular constituency. With the substantial completion of the land seizure project and the alienation of white farms, the war veterans have receded in prominence, yet continue to be influential. Moreover, given the organization's contribution as part of ZANU-PF's "shock troops" in previous national elections, it is likely that the war vets will reprise this role in the future.

Under Chenjerai Hunzvi, a Polish-trained doctor (who actually spent the liberation war in Eastern Europe), the war vets became a formidable organization. The black guerrillas of the liberation war had indeed been wronged. At the end of the war in 1979, they were demobilized and returned, sometimes quite uncomfortably, to civilian life. Their Rhodesian army counterparts were given substantial pensions, which were guaranteed by the Lancaster House agreement. Senior war veterans in the ruling party penetrated the highest ranks in the army, police, and state bureaucracy (Kriger 2003). However, for years after independence, many of the "rank and file" among the former guerrillas suffered from unemployment, landlessness, and homelessness, although collectively their contribution to independence was of course widely recognized (Bond and Manyanya 2002). "When it was discovered in 1997 that the War Victims Compensation Fund had been looted, to the tune of [ZW$450 million] by senior officials in ZANU-PF, war veterans organized mass demonstrations," including demonstrating against the president himself (Carmody and Taylor 2003, 10) at the Heroes Day celebration in August 1997.

Reportedly "shaken" by this threat from one of ZANU-PF's most vital constituencies, Mugabe unilaterally agreed on pension payments to the vets—all tax free. He also promised free education for dependents, free health care, free land, and interest-free loans of up to ZW$20,000 or approximately US$1,700 at then-prevailing exchange rates (Nhema 2002, 143–144). Shortly after this massive giveaway was announced, estimated at a total cost of some ZW$4.5 billion (approximately US$375 million at then-prevailing exchange rates), the Zimbabwe economy collapsed. Hunzvi, whose own war veteran credentials were dubious and who was believed to have been involved in a scheme to secure thousands of dollars for bogus compensation claims to war "injured," nonetheless was a skilled and charismatic leader who was able to put the war veterans on the center stage of national politics. However, revealing that the agreed payout was as much about contemporary politics and patronage as about compensation for the liberation war effort, "about 50,000 people were given the cash, even though fewer than 30,000 war veterans had been demobilized when the war ended in 1979" (Blair 2002, 39).

The liberation war vets were perhaps the only group with the standing to threaten President Mugabe, and he dared not respond with the repressive tactics he had so successfully used against his other societal foes. Indeed, the entirety of his revolutionary bona fides rested on accommodation of the fighters in the liberation struggle, with whom he identified politically, as well as the peasant farming community, on whose behalf the war was supposedly fought. Thus the promise of land reform, attained through the seizure of white-owned commercial farms, could shore up some much needed support for ZANU-PF among these essential constituencies. Raftopoulos (2001) argues that Mugabe rapidly capitulated to the war vets because he feared an alliance between labor and war vets that could undermine his government. Indeed, according to Raftopoulos (2001, 12), a potential alliance between the war vets and the ZCTU was discussed in 1996 but never came to fruition. Instead of an oppositional role, however, the war vets—many of whom were far too young to have fought in the actual independence war—became the shock troops of the farm invasions that began in February 2000 and continued unabated thereafter (ICG 2002). As such, they have been key players, and occasional pawns of the state, in the devastation of Zimbabwe's commercial farming-based economy. Ironically, though perhaps predictably, the rank and file among the war vets fared no better than in the post-1980 period; the bulk of the seized farms and best lands went to elites (Smith 2010).

Fundamentals of the Political Economy

At independence, Zimbabwe had a solid industrial infrastructure, an experienced commercial agriculture sector, and an internationally competitive mining industry. The combination of increased state spending after 1980, the impact of two recessions and regional droughts, and the burden of repaying Rhodesian-era war debts as well as the need to import vital industrial infrastructure led to the adoption of the ESAP in 1990. The program, which was implemented in 1991, was supposed to provide a foundation for growth. Instead, it helped precipitate a series of economic changes that had a devastating impact on the Zimbabwean economy (Gunning and Oostendorp 2002; Jenkins and Knight 2002). Determining who bears responsibility for the failure of ESAP depends on who one asks, although a strong case has been made that its flaws were principally of design rather than implementation (Bond and Manyanya 2002).

However, even if ESAP and the economic hardship it spawned pertain to structural factors, this is not to suggest that *agency* is not also important in the analysis. ESAP precipitated a series of events. How those events unfolded and were reshaped, however—including the rise of the opposition; the collapse of the relationship between ZANU-PF and the white economic community; the emergence of destructive populist economic policies, including land invasions and seizures; the massive authoritarian reaction of the regime to popular discontent; and finally, complete economic collapse—was the result of interactions and of *actors'* decisions, which were shaped by context. Particularly since the turn of the century, ZANU-PF's stewardship of the economy has been an unmitigated disaster. Only the takeover of key economic ministries—finance, industry and commerce, and economic planning—by MDC helped restore a modicum of stability and international legitimacy after 2008.

The 1990s witnessed a series of policy missteps that ultimately allowed the political space for opposition to emerge. The state struck back by targeting the politically weakest group in Zimbabwe—its former benefactors, the white farming community. By seizing the populist mantle of land reform, Mugabe thought he could cling to power. This strategy has called for the displacement of urban discontent and opposition support to the rural areas where ZANU-PF is traditionally strong (Carmody and Taylor 2003).

Government-sanctioned farm invasions began in February 2000 and escalated through 2002. As a consequence of targeting whites, a deliberate pattern of patronage flows, or "resource networks," between the ZANU-PF state and the white community has been permanently ruptured. To be fair, the land distribution under the status quo ante was grossly imbalanced in favor of a tiny white farming community, a dilemma that has been the subject of many comprehensive analyses (Bowyer-Bower and Stoneman 2000; Moyo 1995, 2000). Yet at the same time, the large-scale commercial sector unambiguously *produced,* contributing half a million formal sector jobs and more than 20 percent of GDP, and it contributed, if indirectly, to the ZANU-PF patronage base (Taylor 1999a). ZANU-PF attacked whites because it needed a *political* scapegoat, not because the maneuver made sense economically. Indeed, the predictable global condemnation and agroeconomic collapse that ensued are evidence that Mugabe's land seizures and demonization of whites were an economic cul-de-sac (Cooke, Morrison, and Prendergast 2003). Although more than 13 million hectares of white-owned farms were seized, recent studies reveal that at least 40 percent went to just 2,200 people—including President Mugabe and his political cronies (Smith 2010). Where poor black farmers and aspiring farmers have gained access to land, they have seldom been given the means to farm effectively or productively; the state, of course, itself destitute, lacks the ability to provide these resources. Agricultural production has fallen by some 60 percent since 2000 (Smith 2010).

The seizure of white farms and the corresponding declines in agricultural output did not begin until after the 2000 referendum, although some 1,471 farms were listed for acquisition as early as 1997. The ability to resist takeover for two and a half years is a reflection of the institutional capacity of the farming interest associations to resist the move, international carrots and sticks to prevent abrogation of property rights norms, and the fact that the white farmer presence (and performance) remained important to the state for some time (Taylor 2007). Even as late as 2001, it appeared as if Mugabe's so-called fast-track land reform program might be reversed. Indeed, at the special Commonwealth meeting in September 1997, the government even consented to halt the invasions, restore the rule of law, and initiate an orderly, internationally supported land reform process. However, Mugabe subsequently reneged on all commitments. The genie of land reform became impossible to put back in the bottle after February 2000; it was the only tool, however blunt, ZANU-PF could use to try to demonstrate its populist and "revolutionary" credentials against an ascendant MDC.

The Informalization of the Zimbabwean Economy

Economic policymaking became completely ad hoc once Zimbabwe faced the effects of international sanctions, disinvestment, and almost incalculable hyperinflation. As noted earlier in the chapter, by 2003 all formal sectors were in decline, with the exception of platinum mining. The country's GDP plummeted at a rate of approximately 13 percent per year in 2002 and 2003, slowing thereafter because there was little left to shrink. With inflation continuing to spiral out of control (in retrospect, a comparatively modest annual rate of around 350 percent in 2003), the currency collapsed; the government responded by instituting new price controls. Thereafter, inflation went from merely crippling, to unimaginable as the government simply printed money in an increasingly vain attempt to meet its obligations. The death of the Zimbabwe dollar came shortly after the Bank of Zimbabwe began issuing notes denominated at 100 *trillion* Zimbabwe dollars. The futility of this exercise was astounding: One hundred trillion Zimbabwe dollars were worth approximately thirty-three US *cents* in January 2009. Mercifully, the Zimbabwe dollar was discontinued in April that year, and regional and international currencies were officially allowed into use.

The collapse in the formal economic sectors, namely commercial agriculture and manufacturing, and of state-owned enterprises and their employment bases led to increasing informalization of the economy. For most Zimbabweans, survival has become increasingly difficult and shortages of even the most basic commodities are commonplace. International food aid, imported in 2002 and 2003 to prevent an estimated 6.2 million people from starving, was employed as a political weapon in the hands of the government, which denied food relief to MDC supporters. During the depths of the crisis, fuel was almost completely inaccessible and imported goods out of reach because of chronic foreign currency shortages. Barter, parallel market currency transactions, and elaborate schemes to find policy loopholes became the norm. Not surprisingly, millions of Zimbabweans have sought refuge abroad, principally in South Africa, for both economic and political reasons.

Zimbabwe was once among the world's top three producers of tobacco. Today, the industry is a shadow of its former self thanks to the decimation of the agricultural sector. At the same time, obligations to regional partners have also increased and caused tremendous unease. Mozambique and especially South Africa are owed enormous sums (Cooke, Morrison, and Prendergast 2003). Libya's Muammar Qaddafi stepped in to become the new international benefactor and a major supplier of Zimbabwe's fuel. However, even the Libyans have become increasingly uncomfortable due to Zimbabwe's nonpayment, and the country has been forced to mortgage state-owned assets to Libya and other foreign interests in return for services. China, which itself soured on Zimbabwe following the 2008 elections, began to reengage in 2011. Discussions centered around a potential Chinese loan of $3 billion or more in return for access to Zimbabwe's vast platinum deposits—widely condemned as an attempt to "grab the country's minerals for a song" (Muleya 2011). Thus, there is no small irony to Mugabe's railing against Western imperialists while succumbing to economic domination from new sources.

In the prevailing survivalist environment, it is difficult for those who oppose ZANU-PF to exert much pressure on it. Although MDC has helped stabilize the economy from its position inside the putative coalition government, MDC has not been able to effect substantial change in ZANU-PF control or its general policy direction. For example, the Indigenization and Empowerment Act enacted in early 2010 required all firms with investments valued at more than US$500,000 to be 51 percent owned by *indigenous* Zimbabweans. This potentially includes firms in some of the few sectors still performing in Zimbabwe, such as mining and financial services. Noncompliance could be punishable by imprisonment. According to John Robertson, a longtime Harare-based economist: "The news is very grim. It will effectively put a halt to any further investment in Zimbabwe, ironically just as the country is calling for investment" (quoted in Latham 2010). MDC's marginality has left northern countries unwilling to lift their limited sanctions against Mugabe and his allies, whereas the continuation of ZANU-PF's indigenization policies has discouraged potential investors.

Yet ZANU-PF could not maintain such domination of the political economy without a substantial basis of support from those who benefit from its policies. In fact, ZANU-PF's control may be challenged ultimately not by the MDC and civil society (both of which are under severe duress) but by dissatisfied clients in its own midst. For the time being, however, the regime has secured the support of military elites, first by awarding them lucrative contracts in the DRC and political influence via the JOC, and more recently through the distribution of farms and access to newly discovered diamond resources in eastern Zimbabwe. Within ZANU-PF, erstwhile challengers to Mugabe have been sidelined by frequent cabinet reshuffles. For those who remain, access to power and resources remains a considerable elixir: an incentive to maintain the status quo. Moreover, many senior military and party officials may harbor some fear of who comes next within ZANU; leading party officials long ago chose to cling to Mugabe as the "devil they know" (see Maroleng 2003).

In sum, the regime has momentarily placated the leadership (but perhaps not the rank and file) of its potentially most dangerous constituents, the "war vets," by empowering them through lawless militias and land occupations, and the military through the DRC. It has co-opted business interests not related to the military as well, awarding them business opportunities, shares of state companies, and various illegitimate contracts throughout the 1990s (S. Taylor 2002).

Nonetheless, the essential element in the maintenance of clientelism is continued access to resources; in short, patronage *costs*. For most of the decade ending in 2010, it appeared that ZANU would suffer from the effects of patronage compression, wherein the party would no longer be able to afford to buy the loyalty of potential *internal* opponents. Indeed, increasingly isolated internationally and resource deprived, Zimbabwe appeared to be sliding toward state failure. That the state has not failed is due both to changes in structural factors—the role of diamonds, China, South Africa, and others— and to the capacity of ZANU-PF and its octogenarian president to both reinvent themselves and substantially outflank their opposition.

In June 2006, substantial deposits of diamonds were discovered in Marange District, near the city of Mutare in Zimbabwe's east. Experts believe that the deposits stand to make Zimbabwe the world's largest diamond exporter. By some estimates, the production may yield as much as US$1.2 billion in annual revenue, perhaps more, and thus provide a substantial resource for ZANU-PF patronage (HRW 2009, 16). Initially, the diamonds were extracted by artisan miners; however, an effort in late 2006 to clamp down on "illegal" mining activity led to the substantial takeover of mining operations by police. The police themselves were involved in rampant corruption and numerous abuses. Thus, according to a report by Human Rights Watch, "with policing disintegrating into anarchy, the army operation called Operation Hakudzokwi (No Return), which started on October 27, 2008, appears to have been designed both to restore a degree of order and to allow key army units access to [these] riches" (HRW 2009, 4). Given the notorious history of diamond smuggling in Africa, the Marange fields represent an almost unlimited resource for the revitalized ZANU-PF patronage machine. Hence the party and its military allies have continued to exploit this new source of wealth for private purposes while excluding the larger population and employing brutal methods—including forced labor—when necessary. At bottom, a natural resource that could serve as a lifeline to Zimbabwe's embattled populace has instead provided a lifeline to ZANU-PF.

Challenges of the Twenty-First Century

ZANU-PF has been in power for three decades. It has presided over state consolidation, postwar reconstruction, and more recently, the near-dismantling of the state and economy under the aegis of largely exhausted nationalism. President Mugabe turned eighty-seven in February 2011, and succession strategies remain unsettled, at best.[38] Hence, the only certainty is that the current phase of the crisis in Zimbabwe will eventually reach an endpoint. The question concerns how this will come about and what will follow. Frighteningly, it is not difficult to imagine a scenario that is actually worse than the status quo. Among the considerations: there is no guarantee that a civilian ZANU-PF successor to Mugabe would be any less hostile to the opposition; a coup d'état by the increasingly politicized military, a popular uprising, or even a civil conflict also cannot be ruled out. At the same time, however, more positive alternative futures, spurred by interparty cooperation (whether through the existing GNU or some other body) and a modest economic recovery, are also not unimaginable.

It is unwise to locate all Zimbabwe's problems in the person of Mugabe, as some authors do, or to overstress the "personal rule." Yet individual leaders can be critically important in shaping—or misshaping—the histories of their countries: the death of Jonas Savimbi in Angola in March 2002 and the election of Levy Mwanawasa in Zambia in December 2001 or of Bingu wa Mutharika in Malawi in 2004 remind us of the instrumental role played by individual agents. Indeed, there is no denying that in Zimbabwe Mugabe has become a major obstacle to reaching an accord. However, as we have argued, one must not lose sight of structural factors as well: Zimbabwe is constrained by region and by its position in the international and regional political economy.

Many of the ruinous policies of the Mugabe government—for example, laws that repress civil and political liberties—can be repealed fairly quickly. A settlement will bring immediate relief from the international community, and efforts to repair Zimbabwe's industrial and commercial infrastructure could probably begin almost immediately, although their completion would take many years. Yet the country faces long-term problems as well, regardless of who holds the presidency and which party the president represents. Although Mugabe has claimed victory on the land problem, the issue is far from resolved. Other structural problems are no less daunting. A fifth of the adult population is infected with HIV, yet the social and medical system was ill equipped to deal with this population even before the current crisis. In addition, formal sector unemployment is estimated at a staggering 94 percent (AFP 2009) and an equal percentage of Zimbabweans live below the poverty line.

A successful post-Mugabe transition in Zimbabwe will require reengagement with the West and the region as well as considerable healing of deep domestic fissures (see Gavin 2007). The once enviable promise of Zimbabwe has now eroded almost completely—and in an astoundingly short period of time. Surely it will take far longer to restore Zimbabwe's position as an economic and political leader in the region.

Notes

1. The seizure of white-owned commercial farms was largely completed by mid-decade, yet by 2010 it appeared increasingly unlikely that the status quo ante would ever be restored. Thus, whereas understanding race relations is critical to understanding Zimbabwe's trajectory, and while the farm seizures will certainly remain controversial for years to come, "the land issue" has lost salience as an immediate, incendiary political matter.

2. One respected scholar even suggested that presidential and ruling-party authoritarianism was "eroding" as recently as 1999 (Sithole 2000).

3. This legislation included the Preventive Detention Act, the Unlawful Organizations Act, the Emergency Powers Act, the Native Affairs Amendment Act, and the Law and Order Maintenance Act. Never rescinded, the latter continues to be employed to repress dissent.

4. Rhodesia had had the status of a "self-governing colony" since 1923 and thus had long enjoyed considerable autonomy from the colonial office in London. This was something of an anomaly in the era of British imperialism, since the British in fact had little control or influence over the Southern Rhodesian polity (Stedman 1991, 36).

5. The UDI was declared in November 1965, following a referendum with 58,000 whites in favor and just under 7,000 opposed (Houser 1976).

6. According to Stephen John Stedman (1991, 182–183), it was the pledges from the British and US administrations to support the cost of land reform and pensions payments that enabled ZANU to agree to the draft constitution. The Lancaster House agreement preserved the landownership status quo, in which some 7,000 white farmers owned nearly a third of the country's agricultural land (Moyo 1995).

7. In 1987, former rivals ZANU and ZAPU merged to form ZANU-PF, thus resuscitating the old "patriotic front" title. Although the name came into use earlier, we use "ZANU-PF" in this text to refer to the merged entity.

8. It was also extremely hypocritical, since ZANU-PF had long tolerated marked disparities in landownership (Taylor 1999a). ZANU-PF also blamed the British for not fulfilling their commitment to finance land reform (Bond and Manyanya 2002).

9. The parliamentary election cycle had been every five years; hence the 2005 legislative election should have been followed by another in 2010. However, parliamentary elections were made concurrent with presidential terms effective from the March 2008 tripartite (president, senate, assembly) national elections.

10. The war cost between 30,000 and 40,000 lives, most of them black (Stedman 1991, vii).

11. Ian Smith remained in Zimbabwe unmolested following independence, and although also proclaiming the reconciliation mantra, he continued to spout racist, paternalistic invective, mostly directed at his black successors (see, for example, Smith 2002).

12. To some extent, Mugabe has tried to use the international community as a substitute, but demonizing the United Kingdom, and particularly the government of former Labour prime minister Tony Blair; the United States; and the United Nations, among others, carries little resonance within Zimbabwe.

13. ZAPU, which predated ZANU, was until the early 1970s a multiethnic organization. It was led by Nkomo, himself Ndebele. A series of Shona defections, based more on ideology than ethnic tensions, led the parties to be increasingly perceived as "Ndebele" or "Shona"; eventually reality came to reflect these perceptions (Sithole 1988).

14. Muzorewa, a Shona, appointed an Ndebele, Josiah Gumede, as ceremonial president in 1978.

15. ZAPU officially withdrew from the 1987 Unity Accord in December 2008; it relaunched as a party in February 2009 (http://www.zapu.org.zw).

16. In some circles Nkomo was actually viewed as a possible successor to Mugabe, although this was always highly unlikely, not least because of his Ndebele identity.

17. Mnangagwa was once nicknamed "son of God" because of his proximity to Mugabe. Although he was demoted to minister of housing in 2005 for his role in trying to establish himself as Mugabe's successor in the party without the latter's knowledge, he returned to Mugabe's good graces after the 2008 election and was appointed to the powerful post of minister of defense (Africa Confidential, n.d.).

18. Http://www.zanupfpub.co.zw.

19. Cabinet posts come with "fantastic perks." In addition to salaries of around US$1,000 per month, only "around 25 per cent of the ministers' income is treated as taxable. Cabinet ministers and their deputies [also] get a minimum of five security personnel and a couple of shiny new Mercedes Benz S-Class cars" (Sithole 2009).

20. The colonial-era chieftaincy structure was maintained despite the conflicts between chiefs and guerrillas during the war; many chiefs were seen as collaborationists with the Rhodesian state (see Nhema 2002, 99).

21. See COPAC Profile: http://www.copac.org.zw/.

22. For example, the government lost cases pertaining to its illegal acquisition of private land in the early 1990s (Taylor 1999a). It was also rebuffed by the courts in its efforts to use security laws to bar competition from a private mobile phone network (Taylor 1999b). In these and other cases, the government consented to the court's findings.

23. Even if the POSA amendments become law, the willingness of ZANU-PF–backed police and security forces to abide by the restrictions is also uncertain.

24. The CFU action named prominent ZANU-PF officials who were spearheading occupations of white-owned farms in order to intimidate their owners. Specifically, War Veterans Association leader Chenjerai Hunzvi, Minister of Youth and Sport Border Gezi, and Police Commissioner Augustine Chihuri were named as respondents.

25. In July 2002, for example, the top legal officer in the country, Minister of Justice Patrick Chinamasa, was found guilty of contempt of court. Chinamasa not only ignored the summons to appear but also publicly scoffed at it. In February 2003 the government ordered police to arrest sitting High Court judge Benjamin Paradza, at the courts, on trumped-up charges. The actual intention was to intimidate Paradza, who had issued several rulings unfavorable to the government, and any others who would follow his precedent (Meldrum 2003).

26. The troops that remained in DRC following the substantial pullout in October 2002 were charged with protecting Zimbabwean military-business investments—a far cry from the original mission, which was allegedly to protect Congo's sovereignty (EIU 2003l).

27. Namibia's president also appoints six members of parliament who are, unlike those in Botswana, Zambia, and Zimbabwe, nonvoting.

28. In the competitive electoral environment that now prevails, the president's ability to appoint members is highly contested. Indeed, despite an earlier agreement between Mugabe and Tsvangirai to share the selections between their parties, Mugabe unilaterally appointed ZANU-PF members.

29. The opposition in the 1996 elections was fragmented and poorly organized. The two other presidential candidates, Ndabaningi Sithole (ZANU-Ndonga) and Abel Muzorewa (United Parties), withdrew in the days before the election, although their names remained on the ballot.

30. Other parties were the reconstituted ZAPU, Muzorewa's United Parties, the Liberty Party, Margaret Dongo's Zimbabwe Union of Democrats, and ZANU-Ndonga. The latter four formed a "voting pact" prior to the elections (Commonwealth Observer Group 2000).

31. In contrast to those claims, only a few groups, such as SADC Election Observer Mission, made up of ministers of regional governments, echoed the ZANU-PF claim that the elections were free and fair.

32. Sources cited in Ignatius 2002 claim that, absent fraud, Mugabe would have lost by 466,000 votes.

33. R. W. Johnson (2000, 52) envisioned "a Tsvangirai landslide." An August–September 2001 poll of 3,013 people, conducted by Target Research for Zimbabwe's independent *Financial Gazette* and published in the *Financial Gazette* in November, revealed a narrower gap. It found that 52.9 percent of Zimbabweans supported Morgan Tsvangirai, while 47.1 percent favored Mugabe.

34. Tsvangirai was twice put on trial for treason, largely on specious grounds, by the ZANU-PF justice ministry. He was physically attacked on numerous occasions. More tragically, following the election, his wife Susan was killed in a car accident many believed to be suspicious.

35. As Raftopoulos (2001, 5) notes, the state arrested hundreds of striking workers in the 1980–1982 period and thereafter passed a new labor relations act in 1985 that severely restricted the right to strike. Of course, labor activism was further curtailed by the clientelistic relationship between the ruling party and main labor body, the ZCTU.

36. Interestingly, Raftopoulos (2001, 8) argues that since organized labor, and particularly Zambia's own Congress of Trade Unions (also known by the abbreviation ZCTU), played such an instrumental role in ending one-party rule in that country, ZANU-PF was clearly haunted in this period by "the spectre of the Chiluba route to political power" and thus sought to repress union activity even further.

37. These surviving papers have limited circulation within Zimbabwe and largely within elite circles; hence they may not be as threatening to the regime (Geoff Nyarota, personal comment, August 2006).

38. Rumors have persisted for a decade that President Mugabe might be considering retirement, a subject long regarded as taboo in ZANU-PF. Despite constant talk of his deteriorating health and energy, Mugabe remains firmly ensconced in office and unwilling to relinquish power. Whether he does so following the next presidential election in 2011 or 2012 is another source of immense, though ultimately idle, speculation.

8 Namibia: Liberation and Its Discontents

At independence in 1990, Namibia was viewed throughout Africa and the world as a potential exception on a continent wracked by ethnic violence, economic crisis, political decay, and social malaise. Despite a twenty-five-year war in the northern part of the country, Namibia boasted an enviable economic infrastructure and considerable resources—minerals, fish, and livestock—to match. Following a largely consensual process between previously antagonistic parties, Namibia had adopted a new constitution hailed as one of the most liberal and democratic in the world. And despite decades of South African–imposed apartheid rule, Namibia possessed a fairly educated and healthy society—notwithstanding major differences among groups—enhanced by tens of thousands of returning Namibian exiles, many of whom were highly educated and highly skilled. At independence in March 1990, President Sam Nujoma and his South West Africa People's Organization (SWAPO),[1] back after decades of exile, appeared ready to reconcile with their onetime adversaries and to commence with the business of governing their new country. Though some remained skeptical, the former adversaries—mostly white Namibians and a few others—seemed willing to give the new leader and government a chance. "Africa's last colony" was poised to set a new example for Africa. And with Namibian independence a product of the end of the Cold War, Namibia seemed to embody the hopes and aspirations of a continent for a new post–Cold War global order that would be friendlier to Africa.

In the intervening years, much of that promise has been realized. In more than twenty years of independence, Namibia's exemplary constitution has been largely respected. Since the first universal franchise elections for a constituent assembly in November 1989, largely free and fair elections have been held routinely, with all but the first election held under Namibian auspices. The rule of law has been maintained, and the rights of the Namibian populace have for the most part been upheld. Government commitments to health and education are manifest in a substantially expanded health infrastructure and

225

Namibia: Country Data

Land area   823,290 km²
Capital   Windhoek
Date of independence   March 21, 1990
Population   2,128,471 (July 2010 estimate), 37% urban (2008 estimate)
Languages   English 7% (official), Oshivambo about 50%, Rukavango 9%,
    Otjiherero 7%, and others; Afrikaans broadly spoken as lingua franca
Ethnic groups   Ovambo 50%, Kavango 9%, Herero 7%, Damara 7%, Nama
    5%, Caprivi 4%, San 3%, Baster 2%, Tswana 0.5%, European 6%, mixed race
    6.5%
Religions   Christian 80–90%, indigenous beliefs 10–20%
Currency   Namibian dollar (N$); Namibian dollars per US dollar: 8.54
Literacy rate   85% (male, 86.8%; female, 83.5% [2001 census])
Life expectancy   51.95 years (male, 52.25 years; female, 51.64 years)
Infant mortality   45.52 per 1,000 live births
GDP per capita (PPP)   US$6,600
GDP real growth rate   −0.8%
Leaders since independence
    Sam Nujoma, president, March 1990–March 2005
    Hifikepunye Pohamba, president, March 2005–
Major political parties
    Ruling party   South West Africa People's Organization (SWAPO)
    Other parties   Congress of Democrats (COD), Democratic Turnhalle Alliance
    (DTA), Rally for Democracy and Progress (RDP), United Democratic Front
    (UDF)
Women in parliament (lower/single house)   24.4% (2009 election)

Sources: Data derived from https://www.cia.gov; http://www.ipu.org.
Note: Data from 2009 unless otherwise noted.

improved school enrollment and literacy rates since independence. Women have made great strides in the electoral arena—reaching nearly 30 percent of the MPs in the National Assembly at one point, among the highest in Africa and the world, and more than 40 percent of local councilors, far above the world average. A fairly active civil society, including women's groups, churches, and human rights associations, has asserted itself since independence and has attempted to hold government accountable to the people. An independent media, operating alongside a government-owned one, has remained very vocal and very vigilant in the years since 1990. Economically, Namibia appears to have held its own as well. With an estimated per capita GDP of US$6,600 (at purchasing power parity) in 2009, Namibia is considered a lower-middle-income country by the World Bank, though this per capita income masks great wealth inequalities. The traditional primary sectors have continued to dominate Namibia's economy—with the country's fishing stocks considerably replenished after independence. And with major improvements made to the port at Walvis Bay and the completion of the Trans-Kalahari Highway, the opportunity has existed for Namibia to become a coastal "gateway to the Southern African Development Community"—and its 200 million people. In the intervening years, Namibia's tourism industry—targeted at the high-end tourist—has seen steady growth as well.

At the same time, there are indications that Namibia may be following old examples, rather than setting new ones. Though there have been regular elections at the local, regional, and national levels in Namibia since independence, there has been no alternation of power at the national level. While Namibia is still technically a multiparty democracy, with eight political parties represented in the National Assembly in 2010, the ruling SWAPO party holds at least a three-quarters majority in both houses of parliament and has done so since 1999. When a new political party emerged in 1999, largely from the ranks of disaffected SWAPO members, the ruling party engaged in a deliberate smear campaign against it and worked to ensure that the new party did not attain "official opposition" status in parliament, though it had clearly earned it. When another new party emerged in advance of the 2009 elections, also from disaffected SWAPO (leadership) ranks, the ruling party reacted in even more hostile fashion. Moreover, in a move reminiscent of one-party states around Africa, SWAPO managed to have the constitution amended in 1998 to allow President Nujoma (only) to stand for a third term of office in 1999. In another repetition of past practice among single-party states, SWAPO remains wedded to the model of political party and sectional affiliates. In a clear bid to forestall the emergence of a rival political movement with a readily mobilized base—à la the Movement for Multiparty Democracy in Zambia—the ruling party has held a tight rein over affiliates such as the country's largest trade union federation, the National Union of Namibian Workers (NUNW). The SWAPO government also managed to embroil Namibia in two foreign wars around century's end—in neighboring Angola and Democratic Republic of Congo (DRC)—and did so without consulting with the people's elected representatives first. In the view of many observers, Namibia's involvement in DRC stems at least in part from President Nujoma's close association with Zimbabwe's autocratic relic Robert Mugabe. The other trends reflect a pattern in a number of countries in the region—where a liberation movement steeped in authoritarian patterns of rule and undemocratic practices, arguably as a result of armed struggle and exile, is now the ruling political party.

Unfortunately, Namibia is also one of the countries in southern Africa hardest hit by the AIDS crisis, with significant consequences throughout the economy and society. But like governments in Botswana and eventually South Africa, the government in Namibia has been fairly proactive in responding to the AIDS menace. Additionally, like many countries in the region, semiarid Namibia faces recurrent drought, and the threat of water shortage remains a potential impediment to growth and development. The land question is another sensitive issue in Namibia, with overall land distribution still skewed to the advantage of a white minority—and increasingly an affluent black minority.

Like Botswana, Namibia is a very large country, very sparsely populated by just over 2 million people. With such a small population, Namibia will never be the economic powerhouse that neighboring South Africa is. Moreover, given its small market, Namibia will never attract a level of foreign investment comparable to that of South Africa or even Angola. But if it is able to resolve its land question peaceably, carefully cultivate existing natural resources, attract high-end visitors to its stunning landscapes and varied wildlife, become a trade and transport hub for the region, and create more jobs through export processing zones, Namibia may set a positive example for what a lower-middle-income country can accomplish. Similarly, if Namibia is able to transition to a new generation of political leaders, embrace more sincerely a multiparty political system in which opposition political parties are welcome, and witness the emergence of a more diversified and dynamic civil society, then it may again provide a model for what a postsettler society in Africa can achieve. This chapter explores the factors that will help to influence Namibia's future—whether as a progressive regional leader or as a continental hangover from a previous era.

Historical Origins of the Namibian State

Namibia has experienced a historical trajectory unlike any other in the region, though there are some important similarities with the other former settler colonies of South Africa and Zimbabwe. Namibia was the only colony in southern Africa to be colonized by the Germans, albeit only until World War I.[2] When the Germans arrived during the late 1880s in what is today Namibia, the territory was already occupied by several groups. In the northern part of the country (indeed extending into what is today Angola), the Ovambo people (the largest ethnic group in Namibia) practiced mixed farming, allowing for a greater concentration of people and for the evolution of more cohesive and centralized social and political structures. Indeed, precolonial Ovamboland was dominated by a series of independent kingdoms. Farther east along the Kunene River, the Kavango people, an Ovambo group who had developed independently of the main group in Ovamboland, lived less densely in a region of higher rainfall and therefore greater agricultural potential and fewer land pressures. Farther east still, in the contemporary Caprivi region, lived the Masubia and Mafue groups, both of which are related to communities in Zambia. The rest of Namibia, because of lack of rainfall, was, and remains, suitable only for livestock raising—large livestock in the central plateau and small livestock in the southern region of the country. When the Germans arrived, the Herero people, widely recognized as outstanding and dedicated cattle farmers, dominated the prime areas of the central and northern plateau. As pastoralists, the Herero experienced a wide dispersal of population and decentralized political authority. The Hereros had to contend with incursions from the Nama people from the south, who tended smaller stock in smaller herds and relied more heavily on strategies more commonly associated with hunter-gatherers—for example, raiding. There was a relative lack of social cohesion and centralized authority among Nama groups. Two other hunter-gatherer groups, the San and Damara, lived in much smaller numbers in central and southern Namibia and in some subjugation to the Nama and Herero (Emmett 1999, 42–45).

Much of Namibia then was characterized by a harsh, semiarid climate suitable only for raising small or large livestock, depending on the region of the country. At the same time, Namibia did posses a wealth of minerals of keen interest to early explorers and traders and, eventually, to European colonizers. These included diamonds in the southern part of the country, and copper, zinc, some gold, and several other minerals in the center and north of the country. Eventually, even uranium was discovered. Ultimately, Namibia's long Atlantic Ocean coastline would provide ample stocks of fish, though in the early colonial period the main interest was in collecting guano from offshore islands. Moreover, the cattle herds maintained by the Herero were greatly coveted by early visitors to the territory.

After initially being managed by German trading companies, South West Africa, as it was then called, became a settler colony of the Germans. Tensions over land between German settlers and especially the Herero, but also the Nama, led to the outbreak of wars in 1904 that lasted until 1907. The wars were conducted with such brutality on the part of the Germans that by the time of their end in 1907 an estimated 80 percent of the Hereros, 50 percent of the Namas, and 30 percent of the Damaras had perished. Moreover, at war's end the land and livestock of all black groups that had participated in the rebellions were confiscated. As in South Africa and Zimbabwe, regulations were put into place that required Africans to carry passes and "service books" that detailed any labor contracts they had entered into. Among other things, these regulations laid the groundwork for forced labor in the colony (Emmett 1999, 59).

German colonial rule in South West Africa ended less than a decade later when British forces defeated German forces in the territory during World War I. The 1919 Treaty of Versailles allowed the Allied powers to take over all of Germany's colonies, and South West Africa was entrusted as a "C Mandate" to the Union of South Africa by the League of Nations in December 1920. Between the two world wars, "native reserves" were established and "native commissioners" were appointed throughout the territory, including in the far northern Ovambo area, which had not fallen under direct German administrative rule before World War I. Also during this interwar period, South African authorities actively encouraged settlers from South Africa to take up farming in South West Africa. Finally, legislation introduced during these same years helped to regulate an emerging migrant labor system that would provide indigenous labor to the mines, commercial farms, and growing towns in the young colony.

With the creation of the United Nations in 1945 and the dissolution of the League of Nations in 1946, South West Africa's political status changed again as it became a trust territory of the UN, despite protestations from the South African government, which favored direct incorporation of the territory into South Africa. The UN General Assembly rejected direct incorporation in December 1946, however, and from then on South Africa sought to make South West Africa a de facto, but not de jure, fifth province of South Africa. A few years later the same legislation that began to formalize apartheid and the policy of separate development in South Africa was extended to the fifth province. This included, for example, the policy of transforming previous "native reserves" into "ethnic homelands," although none of Namibia's ethnic homelands was ever granted even nominal independence, as in South Africa.

South Africa's de facto incorporation of Namibia into its territory was not accepted by much of the population or the international community. From the 1940s and 1950s on, leaders such as Chief Hosea Kutako of the Herero Chiefs Council, Chief David Witbooi of the Nama, and others began petitioning the United Nations for an end to South African rule in the territory. By the end of the 1950s, moreover, an incipient nationalist movement had emerged, first among Namibian contract migrant workers in Cape Town (the Ovamboland People's Congress in 1957), and then among migrant workers in Windhoek (the Ovamboland People's Organization [OPO] in 1959). At the same time, ordinary Namibians continued to resist colonial rule and its oppressive regulations. When colonial authorities sought to forcibly remove residents from Windhoek's black township in 1959 and relocate them, the ensuing protest resulted in the shooting deaths of eleven and wounding of forty-four others. In the aftermath of the shootings, much of the nationalist leadership was imprisoned, banned, or restricted by the South African colonial authorities, with the result that many opted for exile. The activities of the OPO ground to a halt; then, in New York City in April 1960, OPO leader Sam Nujoma was elected president of the recently renamed nationalist movement, the South West Africa People's Organization.

In 1962 SWAPO leaders made the decision to take up arms against the South Africans and began training future combatants in Egypt. Armed struggle began when SWAPO's military base in Ongulumbashe in northern Namibia was discovered by the South Africans in 1966. More than 200 activists, most of the remaining internal SWAPO leaders, were arrested or fled into exile. In those early days SWAPO's exile base was in faraway Tanzania, though with independence in Zambia, and later Angola, the liberation movement shifted its exile camps closer to home. Tensions and unrest increased considerably inside Namibia, meanwhile, following two developments in the early 1970s: first, a massive general strike by contract migrant workers in 1971 and 1972 and the related imposition of emergency regulations in Ovamboland (to which most of the migrant workers returned during the strike), and second, South African efforts to grant self-government to the ethnic homelands, particularly Ovamboland. Protest rallies sponsored by the SWAPO Youth League and school boycotts by high school students were met with detentions and trials as well as the meting out of brutal punishments by tribal courts in the north. These factors, together with the proximity of new SWAPO exile camps in Zambia and Angola, led to an exodus of thousands of young Namibians from the territory from 1974 onward.

By then northern Namibia had become a war zone. Cross-border incursions by SWAPO combatants were more frequent as exile bases were established in Angola, and from late 1975 on South African Defense Force (SADF) troops were airlifted into the north. Civilians were ordered to withdraw from border areas of Ovamboland, and emergency regulations first imposed in Ovamboland in 1972 were extended to Kavango and the Caprivi in 1976. Martial law was declared throughout the north. In 1977 the SADF began recruiting Namibian volunteers for ethnic military units to fight the externally based nationalist movement and attempt to restore order in the north.

It was against this backdrop that the South Africans initiated the first of two attempts at an internal settlement of the Namibian situation in the form of an interim government established in 1980. This government lasted only three years before it collapsed amid charges of corruption and incompetence and was followed in 1985 by the second attempt, a transitional government of national unity. It lasted until 1989, when an internationally sanctioned and monitored transition to independence began. Indeed, by the 1980s international diplomatic efforts to rid Namibia of South African colonial rule, centered at the United Nations, began to bear fruit. These were further aided by the collapse of the Soviet Union and end of the Cold War in the late 1980s and were linked to a strong regional and international commitment to ending the war in Angola and achieving Namibian independence. The Brazzaville Accord, signed in December 1988, laid the groundwork for a year-long UN-supervised transition to independence that began in April 1989 under the auspices of Security Council Resolution 435. During that transition, SWAPO combatants—the People's Liberation Army of Namibia (PLAN)—as well as an indigenous force that had been created by the South Africans—the South West Africa Territorial Force (SWATF)—were demobilized by a UN Transitional Assistance Group, and SADF troops were sent home to South Africa. Tens of thousands of Namibian exiles from around the world, but mostly neighboring Angola, along with the former PLAN combatants, were repatriated to Namibia. In November 1989 UN-supervised elections were held for a constituent assembly to draw up a new constitution. On March 21, 1990, political independence was finally granted to Namibia.

Scholars have interpreted Namibia's transition to independence in different ways, with different implications for Namibia's future.[3] Michael Bratton and Nicolas van de Walle (1997), for example, view Namibia's transition to independence as one of many attempted democratic transitions across Africa in the late 1980s and early 1990s. They suggest that the prospects for a successful transition to democracy were likely somewhat better in Namibia than elsewhere in Africa because Namibia was one of a few African countries in which an "elite pact" provided the foundation for the democratic transition (Bratton and van de Walle 1997, 178).[4] It happened this way in Namibia, they contend, because Namibia was one of two remaining settler oligarchies in Africa at the time of its transition.[5] And while transitions from settler oligarchies were often violent and protracted, as in the Namibian case, they typically ended through negotiation (Bratton and van de Walle 1997, 178): "The contenders for power struck a series of political, military, and economic agreements that divided power (at least for an interim period) and protected minority interests." Moreover, settler oligarchies were also aided by the fact of having had some heritage of institutionalized political competition, albeit sharply restricted by race in the southern African context. Still, Bratton and van de Walle (1997, 179) argue that in such a situation, political liberalization becomes the somewhat easier task of expanding the franchise to allow greater political participation, rather than one of trying to institutionalize previously unknown principles of political pluralism.[6]

To a large extent Namibia conforms to Bratton and van de Walle's description of a settler oligarchy. In Namibia, as in South Africa, "the dominant group used the instruments of law to deny political rights to ethnic majorities, usually through a restrictive franchise and emergency regulations backed by hierarchically organized coercion" (1997, 81). From the beginning of colonial rule, black Namibians lost not only political but also economic and social rights through a series of laws and regulations governing nearly every facet of their lives. By the end of colonial rule, emergency regulations had been in effect in the northern Namibia war zone for decades. For the most part, in Namibia "settlers reproduced functioning democracies within their own microcosmic enclaves, with features like elections, leadership turnover, loyal opposition, independent courts, and some press freedom, all reserved exclusively for whites" (Bratton and van de Walle 1997, 81). For much of the twentieth century white Namibians had some form of elected representation, although their representatives often acted only in an advisory capacity or had jurisdiction over very limited areas. Namibia deviates from this characterization in that whites had no control over their executive; rather, he was appointed in South Africa.

Joshua Forrest describes Namibia's transition only slightly differently. In his view, the 1988 Brazzaville Accord may be considered "'a transitional pact' to which the nation's leading politicians lent their approval in the context of emerging from an authoritarian political system toward a democratic frame-work of government." Though the accord was signed by a number of countries external to the conflict in Namibia, it was made possible by a series of meet-ings outside Namibia during the 1980s between SWAPO and representatives of white political and economic interests inside the territory. Such a pact, according to Forrest (1998, 42), establishes "basic guidelines within which the country's political leaders can determine the exact nature of the constitution and decide on the democratic institutions to be established." Gerhard Erasmus (2000), moreover, focuses very heavily on Namibia's constitution, referring to the transition to independence as a "transition through constitutionalism"—a transition in which the constitution played a central role in the founding of an independent Namibia. Like Forrest, Erasmus (2000, 77) emphasizes the way in which the transition was "structured and guided by a prior agreement," which included a commitment to a "strong" constitution. "Thereafter, this con-stitution had to continue to fulfill other important functions. It had to constrain the inherent tensions in the Namibian body politic, and guide the young state along a path of constitutionalism and the rule of law. In this manner, it was hoped, stability and progress could be achieved and another 'African disaster' prevented."

These authors offer reasons to think that the perils of Africa's first wave of independence might be avoided in Namibia. Another group of authors (Bauer 1998; Dobell 1998; Leys and Saul 1995; Melber 2003), by contrast, worries that liberation without democracy could well be Namibia's fate, with the nature of the liberation struggle and the impact that it had on the liberation movement accounting for such an outcome. Indeed, Colin Leys and John Saul (1995, 5) suggest "the possibility exists that the very process of struggling for liberation, especially by resort to force of arms, almost inevitably generates political practices that prefigure undemocratic outcomes." This view contrasts markedly with a once popular view that proposed that "the logic of protracted struggle . . . made the politics of armed liberation movements more democratic and radical than those of other nationalist movements and more likely to lead to genuinely socialist [progressive] outcomes in the post liberation phase" (Leys and Saul 1995, 5). With hindsight, that view has evolved considerably. As Henning Melber (2003, 5) observes: "There is a growing insight that the armed liberation struggles were in no way a suitable breeding ground for establishing democratic systems of government after gaining independence. The forms of resistance against totalitarian regimes were themselves orga-nized on strictly hierarchical and authoritarian lines, otherwise they could hardly have had any prospect of success." In the case of SWAPO, there is ample evidence that while in exile in Zambia and in Angola in the 1970s and 1980s, hundreds if not thousands of SWAPO members were detained, starved, tortured, imprisoned in underground dungeons, and even killed—by the move-ment itself. Democratic voices within the movement were clearly silenced

(Leys and Saul 1995, 4). To make matters worse, since independence, SWAPO has steadfastly refused to account for or confront its policies and practices while in exile (Saul and Leys 2003). What does this legacy of authoritarianism in the liberation movement turned ruling party portend for Namibia's future? Moreover, the extent to which SWAPO was even a "liberation movement" with the goal of transforming Namibia in some meaningful way after independence, rather than simply a nationalist movement seeking political independence, has also been called into question (Bauer 1998; Dobell 1998). These issues have great significance for Namibia's political future and are revisited later in this chapter.

Organization of the State

Executive

As defined in Article 1 of its constitution, Namibia is a sovereign, secular, democratic, and unitary state. Government comprises the typical three branches (executive, legislative, and judicial), with a popularly elected president, who is both head of state and head of the executive, and an appointed prime minister. Executive power in Namibia vests in the president and the cabinet. The national legislature is a bicameral parliament consisting of a national assembly with 72 elected members and 6 nonvoting members appointed by the president, and a national council with 26 members elected from among thirteen regional councils. The constitution provides for the separation of powers and hence an independent judiciary. Judicial power in Namibia is exercised by a supreme court, a high court, and a number of lower courts.

According to Namibia's original constitution, the president was limited to two consecutive terms in office, with presidential and National Assembly terms running concurrently. Before the 1999 elections, however, the constitution was amended to allow President Nujoma (only) to run for a third term of office. The decision to amend the constitution to allow this change in presidential terms was taken by SWAPO at its May 1997 party congress. According to the *Namibian* of September 1, 1999, the party argued that President Nujoma was not popularly elected by the Namibian people in 1989 (he was elected by the Constituent Assembly in February 1990), so voters should be allowed a second opportunity—in 1999—to vote for him. Proponents of the change pledged that it would be applicable only to the 1999 elections and that future presidents would serve only two terms.[7] With a two-thirds majority for SWAPO in both houses of parliament, there was never any doubt that the amendment to the constitution would be approved, as happened in late 1998. In the December 1999 presidential elections, President Nujoma easily won a third term of office, polling 76.7 percent of the vote.[8] During his third term of office, President Nujoma sent mixed signals about his intention to stand for a fourth term. Then, as reported in the *Namibian* of May 31, 2004, in an extraordinary congress, SWAPO selected the party's vice president, Hifikepunye Pohamba, minister of lands, resettlement, and rehabilitation, to be the party's presidential candidate in 2004. Pohamba, Nujoma's age mate and comrade from the liberation struggle, was clearly Nujoma's personal choice to succeed him; indeed, Nujoma went so far as to dismiss from office two potential contenders for SWAPO presidential candidate: Prime Minister Hage Geingob in August 2002 and Foreign Minister Hidipo Hamutenya in May 2004.[9] Pohamba easily won the 2004 presidential race with 76.4 percent of the vote and a second presidential contest in 2009, again with 76.4 percent of the vote.

One implication of the third term for President Nujoma was an increasing concentration of power within the office of the president. Indeed, in the view of some observers, a "rising presidentialism" has existed for some time within Namibia's executive branch. This was evident, for example, in President Nujoma's practices of making cabinet-level appointments himself, keeping political rivals at bay through periodic cabinet reshuffles, choosing the first several of seventy-two candidates on SWAPO's party list for the National Assembly elections, and retaining much of the preindependence SWAPO leadership in key cabinet posts. President Pohamba has shown himself to be much less decisive; indeed, important positions have remained vacant while he considers whom to appoint.

Citing some of Nujoma's practices, Christiaan Keulder raised concerns as early as the late 1990s about the growing influence of the executive branch over the legislative branch in the first decade of independence. The situation was exacerbated, in Keulder's view (1999a, 6–7), by the existence of a "tight single party cabinet" (all members appointed from one party only) and by the fact that all cabinet members are appointed by the president. Moreover, because all of the ministers and deputy ministers are MPs in the National Assembly, they outnumber ordinary SWAPO MPs by a ratio of two to one. The result of this, according to Keulder (1999a, 7), is that "as far as the ruling party is concerned, the National Assembly is little more than the Executive in disguise." This of course has immediate negative implications for the autonomy of the National Assembly.

Constitution

Namibia's constitution was drawn up by the seventy-two-member Constituent Assembly elected during the special UN-supervised election held in November 1989. By many accounts, the drafting of the constitution was a remarkably consensual process.[10] Indeed, Forrest (1998, 43) marvels at the way in which SWAPO, "with its history of guerilla nationalism," and the main opposition group at the time, the Democratic Turnhalle Alliance (DTA), "with its history of collaboration," were able to work together to forge a national constitution. In Forrest's view, this represented "an impressive example of successful bargaining by opposing political elites in a transitional democratic context." This was possible, according to Forrest (1998, 43–44), because SWAPO and the opposition parties perceived it to be in their respective best interests to participate in the bargaining process "and forge a workable democratic framework." Forrest concedes that the commitment to democracy on the part of SWAPO and DTA elites may have been instrumental, "but even instrumental commitment may make possible the consolidation of democratic rule so long as both ruling and opposition politicians act as democrats and treat their opponents as democrats."

At the same time, it is important to note that much of what was ultimately included in the Namibian constitution was determined far in advance of the meetings of the Constituent Assembly in late 1989 and early 1990. In fact, a set of constitutional principles had been adopted in 1982 as part of the UN effort to bring about an international settlement of the conflict in Namibia. According to Erasmus (2000, 81), these principles go a long way toward explaining Namibia's remarkable constitution: "One of the most obvious explanations for the basic features of the Namibian Constitution and its liberal-democratic values lies in the framework that the Constitutional Principles comprised, and from which no deviation was permitted." Thus one might assert, as Erasmus does, "that Namibians actually did not enjoy a completely free hand in writing their own constitution." At the same time, Erasmus notes that while "the blueprint for the Constitutional Principles had originally been drafted by the Western Contact Group consisting of Canada, France, Germany, Great Britain and the USA," Namibian parties, including SWAPO, had accepted the principles as providing the basic framework for gaining independence.

When it was adopted in 1990, Namibia's constitution was hailed as one of the most liberal and democratic in the world. Indeed, some observers consider it to be the linchpin of Namibia's multiparty democracy. The Namibian constitution contains entrenched clauses guaranteeing fundamental human rights and freedoms, among which are freedoms of association and expression (including a free press) and peaceable assembly. The constitution also contains the proscription of arbitrary arrest, detention without trial, and the death penalty and enshrines the right of individual property ownership and the payment of just compensation for any expropriation of property. The constitution also provides for the establishment of two offices meant to protect democracy and promote accountability in Namibia, namely the offices of the ombudsman and the auditor general. Both offices were established in 1990 and have operated actively, albeit with limited resources, ever since.

As noted, Namibia's constitution has been largely respected since independence—the single, but significant, change was to allow a third term for President Nujoma—and the rule of law has largely prevailed during that same period. There were some concerns in the early twenty-first century about the government's respect for the human rights of its citizens, primarily in northern conflict areas. At the same time, there have been no reports of political prisoners being held, academic freedom being restricted, or journalists being subjected to harassment or violence by the police. There have been more recent reports of police use of excessive force, criticism of nongovernmental organizations, harassment and political intimidation of opposition members, and discrimination against women, ethnic minorities, and indigenous peoples, among other human rights concerns (US Department of State 2010d).

Judiciary

As noted above, judicial power in Namibia is vested in a supreme court, a high court, and lower courts presided over by magistrates. By 2002, thirty magistrate courts had been established in Namibia but none since. The Supreme Court serves as a court of appeals and a constitutional review court. In recent years, the greatest impediment to the administration of justice in Namibia has been inefficiency and lack of resources leading to prolonged pretrial detention and long delays in hearing cases within the court system, a problem afflicting other judiciaries in the region. According to the US Department of State (2010d), Namibia's right to a fair trial was limited during 2009 by long delays in hearing cases in the civil courts and the uneven application of constitutional protections in the customary courts. A lack of qualified magistrates and other court officials, the high cost of legal assistance, slow or incompetent police investigations, and the continued postponement of cases resulted in a considerable backlog of criminal cases and years between arrest and trial. In 2009 more than 100 "Caprivi treason detainees" remained imprisoned in Windhoek, detained since 1999 and awaiting the completion of a trial begun in 2003. The Caprivi treason trial is the longest and largest in Namibia's history and consists of 275 charges of murder, sedition, and treason against 132 people.

As in most of southern Africa, there is another set of courts in Namibia—customary courts. Namibia's constitution allows customary law in effect at the time of independence to remain in effect as long as that customary law does not conflict with the constitution or any other statutory law.[11] According to M. O. Hinz (1998, 10), this "constitutional recognition of both customary law, and through it, traditional government, has freed customary law and traditional government from its marginalization as an inferior way of living." It is likely that most of Namibia's rural residents first encounter the nation's legal system through customary law and the customary courts. Indeed, customary courts deal with most of the civil and petty criminal cases in the rural areas. One problem has been that within the customary courts there tends to be an uneven application of protections provided by the constitution (US Department of State 2010d).

Military

As in the rest of southern Africa, the military has played a minimal role in politics and society in Namibia to date. This despite the fact that the main military force, the Namibian Defense Force (NDF), was formed at independence by bringing together former combatants from both sides of the independence war: from SWAPO's People's Liberation Army of Namibia and the South African–sponsored South West Africa Territorial Force. NDF troops numbered about 16,000 in 2009. The Namibian Police Force (NAMPOL) numbered around 12,000 in 2009, of which half belonged to the Special Field Force (SFF), the paramilitary police unit recruited primarily from among former PLAN combatants in the mid-1990s.[12] The SFF, along with the rest of NAMPOL, are supervised by the Ministry of Safety and Security, and the NDF is supervised by the Ministry of Defense. Together the NDF and NAMPOL share responsibility for Namibia's internal security. The National Central Intelligence Service covers national security–related intelligence inside and outside the country (US Department of State 2010d).

Namibia's military was active outside its borders for about four years, from 1998 to 2002, participating in wars in two neighboring states. Namibia's involvement in the regional war in DRC and the rebel war in Angola caused considerable consternation among the populace and some opposition politicians. According to several reports, President Nujoma ordered the initial deployment of Namibian troops in DRC (in support of embattled DRC president Laurent Kabila) in August 1998 without first consulting his cabinet or parliament (Melber 2003, 15). According to the *Namibian* of October 19, 1998, opposition party MPs strongly condemned this "surreptitious" deployment of Namibian troops outside of the country's national borders. Moreover, this was one of the issues cited by Ben Ulenga when he resigned as Namibian high commissioner to the United Kingdom in August 1998; months later he would go on to form COD, the first significant opposition party to emerge in the country after independence.

Criticism of Namibia's involvement in the war mounted as, by the end of 1998, the government became increasingly reluctant to reveal any information about it. Indeed, in early 1999 it was reported by the *Namibian* of January 4 and 5 and by the *Daily Mail and Guardian* of January 6 that the minister of defense, backed by the prime minister, had instructed his staff in late 1998 to refuse further information to the media about Namibia's participation in the war. President Nujoma and SWAPO MPs justified Namibian involvement in the DRC war on the grounds of international solidarity and the need to secure Namibian peace, stability, and democracy. At the same time, many observers stressed the importance of close political ties between SWAPO and the ruling parties in Angola and Zimbabwe forged during the years of the armed liberation struggle and suggested that those ties led Namibia to join the two countries in the war in DRC.[13] By 2002 all NDF soldiers were withdrawn from DRC.

In December 1999 Namibia became involved in the internal war in Angola when the government gave permission to the Angolan Armed Forces to launch attacks from northern Namibia into southern Angola against troops of the National Union for the Total Independence of Angola (UNITA), as reported in the *Daily Mail and Guardian* on December 23, 1999. This decision by the Namibian government prompted retaliatory action by UNITA against Namibia, which in turn provoked NDF involvement in the conflict. By May 2, 2000, according to the *Namibian*, the NDF had set up military bases inside Angola in an attempt to prevent UNITA rebels from carrying out retaliatory attacks on Namibian soil. However, the expansion of the Angolan war into Namibia had swift and significant consequences, including the killing of several civilians. Coupled with the general fear caused by the fighting, losses to the tourism industry mounted as anxious potential visitors canceled trips to Namibia, as reported in the *Daily Mail and Guardian,* January 7, 2000, and the *Namibian,* February 15, 2000. The extension of Angola's civil war into Namibia also resulted in widespread charges of human rights abuses by NDF and SFF members in the Kavango and Caprivi regions, where the fighting was concentrated. Those abuses decreased significantly once cross-border fighting from Angola came to an end following the Angolan cease-fire in April 2002.

Finally, during this same period, Namibia's military and security forces became involved in an internal conflict. On August 2, 1999, separatist rebels, calling themselves the Caprivi Liberation Army and demanding independence for the Caprivi region, launched armed attacks on the police station, army base, and Namibian Broadcasting Corporation office at Katima Mulilo, Caprivi's largest town. According to the *Daily Mail and Guardian* of August 6, 1999, and the *Namibian* of August 2, 3, and 6, 1999, the Namibian government responded by declaring a state of emergency in the region and detaining hundreds of suspected rebel collaborators. The rebellion was led by onetime DTA leader and Caprivi native Mishake Muyongo, who subsequently fled to Botswana and then Denmark, where he was still living in exile in late 2010. Unrest in the region and the security forces' harsh response to the alleged secession attempt prompted thousands of ordinary Caprivians to flee to Botswana as well. By 2002 tension in the region had largely subsided; in 2010, however, more than 100 alleged Caprivian secessionists remained in prison in Windhoek.[14] In early 2007 a document, whose existence had long been denied by SWAPO leaders, surfaced in Namibia relating to the alleged Caprivi secession attempt. The 1964 document suggests an agreement by SWAPO leader Sam Nujoma that Caprivi would attain separate state status after Namibia attained its independence (Weidlich 2007).

Representation and Participation

Legislature

As noted above, Namibia's bicameral parliament consists of a national assembly (lower house) with 72 elected members of parliament and 6 nonvoting members appointed by the president, and a national council (upper house or house of review) with 26 members elected from thirteen regional councils. Members of the National Assembly are elected every five years under a closed list, proportional representation electoral system. Members of the National Council serve six-year terms, with two members from each regional council being elected to the National Council. Shortly after independence, the country was divided into thirteen geographic regions (as opposed to the ethnically based designations of the previous regime), each with a governor and council. For purposes of elections, each region is further divided into constituencies, with the number depending on the region's population. At the local level, municipalities, towns, and villages—in some cases newly proclaimed after independence—are governed by municipal, town, and village councils, respectively (Toetemeyer 2000, 118–123).

SWAPO easily dominates legislative bodies at all three levels in Namibia, from local to national, with its support ranging from roughly 60 percent at the local level to more than 75 percent at the national level from 1989 to 2009. In part, the choice of electoral system may be influencing electoral outcomes in SWAPO's favor. According to Keulder (1999b, 5), at the regional level at least, SWAPO is overrepresented in that the party's share of seats exceeds its share of votes. This can be attributed to the use of the first-past-the-post electoral system for regional elections, which requires a simple majority for the winner to take all. In addition, the prevalence of uncontested SWAPO constituencies has enhanced SWAPO's representation at the regional level.

Though SWAPO may be overrepresented at the regional level, Forrest (1998, 300–301) argued in the late 1990s that regional councils and the National Council, regardless of party composition, have the potential to make an important contribution to the consolidation of democracy in Namibia. He describes Namibia's national councilors, elected from among the country's regional councilors, as performing an important grassroots transmission role—serving as a "state-society connecting agency" to Namibia's predominantly rural areas. Against all odds and the expectations of the (then) Ministry of Local and Regional Government and Housing, regional councilors, regional governors, and national councilors managed to assert important roles for themselves and their institutions, tackling issues of significance to their largely rural, arguably neglected constituents. This is all the more interesting given that the ruling party, SWAPO, was initially strongly opposed to the notion of a second chamber of parliament, most likely because members would be elected (indirectly) on the basis of constituencies rather than party lists. SWAPO only agreed to the National Council on the condition that it would only review, and not veto, legislation passed by the National Assembly.

Electoral systems have other important implications for the National Assembly and the independence of the legislative branch. Indeed, the use of a closed list, proportional representation system in the National Assembly elections means that MPs are not elected directly by constituents; rather they are elected because their name is placed high enough on a party list to win a seat. What this also means is that MPs hold office at the pleasure of their party and are not accountable to anyone beyond the party. As Keulder (1999a, 9) notes, "members of the lower house are not turning to well-defined constituencies when seeking office, but rather to those that control the composition of the list. This undermines legislators' autonomy and restrains their potential to rebel against policy decisions taken in the executive." As in the Mozambican and South African proportional representation systems, the absence of genuine linkages to constituencies is a cause for concern.

A more benevolent result of Namibia's use of the closed list, proportional representation system for the National Assembly elections (combined with voluntary quotas on the part of political parties) has been a high percentage of women in the National Assembly—up to 29.2 percent in 2004 (falling to 24.4 percent after the 2009 election). Along with Angola, Mozambique, and South Africa (all with greater percentages of women), Namibia is in the top tier of countries in terms of women's representation in a national legislature in Africa and in the world. The representation of women is even greater at the local level in Namibia, where gender quotas are mandated by law. More than 40 percent of local councilors and many mayors and deputy mayors in Namibia are women.[15]

An additional level of representation exists in Namibia, in the form of traditional leaders and traditional authorities. This level can be extremely important, however, in countries that are predominantly rural, like Namibia, in that in many rural communities traditional leaders may "continue to control most of the important rural survival strategies: allocation of land, natural resources, communal labour practices and in some instances law and order" (Keulder 2000, 150). In Namibia, the Traditional Authorities Act of 1995 recognizes two types of traditional leadership: chieftainships and headmanships (but not kingships) and makes provision for remunerating both. In 1996 it was estimated that around 150,000 families, or 855,000 people (about half of Namibia's population), were living in communal areas under the jurisdiction of a traditional leader of some sort (Keulder 2000, 161). At the same time, however, the establishment of regional councils effectively transferred to the regional councils all of the administrative powers previously allocated to traditional authorities (Keulder 2000, 161). In general, traditional authorities have no role in local authorities, regional councils, or local land boards, except for an advisory role. The 1995 act also makes provision for a council of traditional leaders that would have an advisory role to the president; otherwise its sole jurisdiction would be over the traditional authorities at the local level. In her research on gender and traditional authorities in postcolonial Namibia, Heike Becker (2006) argues that traditional leaders and institutions in northern Namibia have been partially transformed by global and national gender discourses, reminding us of the ability of chiefs and ordinary people in the rural areas to continually reinvent "traditional" political practices.

Party System and Elections

Beginning with the Constituent Assembly elections in 1989, elections have been held on a regular basis in Namibia—every five years for the National Assembly and presidency, every six years at the local and regional level. Since 1989 all elections have been held under Namibian auspices and all have generally been deemed free and fair, although serious concerns were raised about the quality of the 1999 and 2009 National Assembly and presidential election campaigns. With the exception of the 1998 local and regional elections, voter turnout in Namibia has generally been fairly high, ranging from 98 percent in 1989 to 62 percent in 1999. By contrast, the voter turnout rate was only 33.75 percent in the February 1998 local elections and 40 percent in the December 1998 regional elections. In both cases, according to postelection analyses, low turnouts resulted from three broad factors: negative feelings toward political actors, special circumstances relating to the electoral process, and apathy or lethargy (Keulder 1999b, 18–19).

In the 1989 Constituent Assembly elections, 10 parties fielded candidates and 7 were represented in the first National Assembly. In the 2009 National Assembly elections, 9 parties won seats, up from 7 in 2004 and 5 in 1999. With 7 of the 9 parties winning only one or two seats, a fracturing of political parties rather than a consolidation of the opposition is suggested. With the exception of the 1998 local and regional elections, the ruling party, SWAPO, has steadily increased its share of the vote in each election, such that by 1999 (and again in 2004 and 2009) it received 75 percent of the vote. At the presidential level Nujoma won reelection overwhelmingly in 1994 and 1999, and his hand-picked successor, Pohamba, won easy victories in 2004 and 2009 as well, in all four cases winning around 75 percent of the vote. These trends have caused many observers to consider Namibia, like many countries in southern Africa, a dominant-party state.[16]

Indeed, institutionalizing strong multiparty political systems is one of the challenges facing many African countries today as they continue the transition from decades of authoritarian single-party rule to more democratic rule, and Namibia is no exception. The freedom to form and join political parties clearly exists in Namibia, and since independence dozens of political parties have come and gone, or reorganized themselves into coalitions or alliances with other parties. At the same time, none has managed to challenge effectively the ruling party or to encroach significantly upon its base of support. A number of reasons have been put forward to explain this, including SWAPO's role as the leading nationalist organization in the struggle for independence and (less so over time) other parties' continued association with preindependence "interim" governments, SWAPO's access to generous resources of the state, SWAPO's strong and unwavering support among the majority Ovambo ethnic group, SWAPO leader Sam Nujoma's continued appeal as "founding father" of the nation, a lack of significant ideological differences among nearly all political parties, and a lack of financial resources for the smaller opposition parties (despite public funding of political parties). In personally anointing a presidential successor (of his own generation, no less), Sam Nujoma continues to wield significant influence in Namibian and party politics.

Prior to the 1999 National Assembly and presidential elections there had been speculation that SWAPO's dominance might be seriously challenged by a new party, one that emerged from among the ranks of disaffected SWAPO members in the late 1990s (Kalenga 1999; Lodge 2000). That party, the COD, was formally launched in March 1999. The party was led by former SWAPO MP Ben Ulenga, deputy minister and high commissioner to the UK at the time of the party's formation. COD members, including Ulenga, explained their defection from SWAPO by "the failure of Swapo to transform itself from a secretive and exiled armed nationalist movement to a mass-based governing party." They complained that SWAPO allowed very little space for constructive dialogue within the party and accused President Sam Nujoma of copying "the tactics of his old ally and good friend, President Robert Mugabe of Zimbabwe" (Kalenga 1999, 26–27).

The new party quickly gained the attention of the SWAPO leadership; President Nujoma accused Ulenga and others of engaging in "rebellious activities" against the ruling party, as noted in the *Namibian,* March 31, 1999, and April 6, 1999. The attacks continued during the campaign for the 1999 national elections. For example, according to the *Namibian* of September 2, 1999, SWAPO issued a pamphlet that described the COD leadership as "political malcontents, who have been driven to their defection from the party by personal ambitions and infantile opportunism." In northern Namibia, the home affairs minister called the COD a group of "traitors and spies" who wanted to bring back "a white government like that of the Boers during the liberation struggle," echoing Robert Mugabe's verbal assaults on the opposition Movement for Democratic Change in Zimbabwe (Kalenga 1999, 25; Lodge 2000, 28). During the 2009 election, by which time yet another party had emerged from SWAPO (discussed below), the attacks and harassment by SWAPO supporters were even more vituperative and hostile (Melber 2010b; US Department of State 2010d).

The COD did not do as well as anticipated by many in the 1999 election, garnering only 9.9 percent of the vote in the National Assembly elections (translating to seven seats), compared to SWAPO's 76.3 percent. Moreover, the COD clearly lured votes away from the DTA, hitherto the strongest opposition party, rather than from the ruling party (Lodge 2000, 26). SWAPO's anti-COD campaign, historical dominance, and structural advantages as ruling party surely contributed to the final result as well. Following the election, the ruling party was successful in denying the COD its rightful place as the official opposition in the National Assembly. SWAPO played a role in the hasty formation of a coalition between the DTA and the United Democratic Front (UDF); with their combined nine seats the DTA-UDF coalition was regarded as the official opposition, according to the *Namibian* of April 13, 2000.[17] In the 2004 election, the COD won more votes than in the 1999 election but lost two seats in parliament; the DTA fared worse, losing votes and three seats in parliament.

The COD lasted for not even a decade, imploding, according to Melber (2010b), "over internal differences, power struggles and fights over resources" in late 2008; indeed in the 2009 election the COD gained less than 1 percent of the vote for only one seat in the National Assembly. In the meantime, however, another political party had emerged to challenge SWAPO's dominance. In late 2007 the Rally for Democracy and Progress (RDP) was formed by another group of disaffected SWAPO members belonging to the first generation of exiled political leaders. RDP leader and former cabinet member Hidipo Hamutenya had been both a contender and then loser in the struggle over who would succeed Sam Nujoma as SWAPO leader and president of Namibia a few years earlier. The RDP was considered a greater threat to SWAPO than the COD had been because of Hamutenya's potential following among his fellow Kwanyama, the largest of the Ovambo subgroups. Following the 2009 election, in which it garnered 11.3 percent of the vote and eight seats in the National Assembly, the RDP had clearly supplanted the COD as the strongest opposition to SWAPO in the country. At the same time, some observers such as Melber (2010a) consider that the RDP offers a scant alternative to SWAPO: "The RDP has seemed chiefly to promise more of the same, rather than any real alternative. For the most part, individuals promoting alternative political parties to SWAPO tend to campaign more to promote personal ambitions than political alternatives."

One consequence of the move toward a dominant-party political system has been a steady blurring of the distinction between party and state, a characteristic of one-party states throughout Africa. Party membership, for example, is essential for appointment to senior positions in government and parastatal organizations. Indeed, being a "loyal Namibian," according to the party, is essential for obtaining any government job. Cabinet reshuffles have been justified on the basis of "party discipline," and SWAPO party leaders rarely, if ever, articulate policy positions distinct from those of government (Bauer 1999, 433). It has been suggested that this blurring of the line between party and government has hampered the rooting out of corruption, which has become prevalent at both senior and junior levels. According to the US Department of State (2010d), government officials continued to engage in corrupt practices in Namibia during 2009. In 2010 Namibia was ranked fifty-fourth on Transparency International's Corruption Perceptions Index—but still the sixth least corrupt country in Africa.[18]

Some improvements to the electoral process in Namibia were made into law in 2009 with the passing of the Electoral Amendment Act. Among other things, the act accords Namibian citizens living abroad the right to vote, empowers the Electoral Commission of Namibia to accredit election observers, and provides that ballots be counted and results announced at polling stations immediately after the polls close. Additionally, the act provides for new political parties to be advertised in the *Government Gazette* (US Department of State 2010d).

Civil Society

While a "dense network" of voluntary associations may not yet fully exist in Namibia, civil society and its organizations have grown considerably in the years since independence. According to one survey there were about 220 NGOs in Namibia in the middle of the first decade of the twenty-first century: 160 NGOs and 60 community-based organizations (though many of these are very small, even inactive). The major areas of NGO intervention in Namibia are agriculture, rural development, education, and training. Organizations of civil society in Namibia work both with government, to address critical development needs, and on their own, identifying their own agendas for social, political, and economic action. NGOs in several sectors work in tandem with their relevant ministries; others collaborate with the National Planning Commission on development policy and programs or participate in the legislative process by attending committee hearings or meeting with legislators and their staffs. Several NGOs focus on independent organizing, constituency mobilization, and provision of information, all essential elements in expanding civil society's role and strengthening its voice. These include some of the larger, more prominent NGOs in Namibia, such as the Legal Assistance Centre, the Namibian Institute for Democracy (NID), the Namibian Society for Human Rights, Sister Namibia, the Institute for Public Policy Research, and the new local chapter of Transparency International. The Namibia NGO Forum, formed in 1991, acts as an umbrella body to many of Namibia's NGOs. For the first time, in the 2009 election, one Namibian NGO, the NID, served as a local monitor of the election.

Trade Unions, Churches, and Student Groups

Independent organizing is a relatively new phenomenon in Namibia. Before independence, both the South African–sponsored interim government and the externally based liberation movement worked hard to ensure that little in the way of independent organizing occurred outside their respective spheres of influence. During the 1970s and 1980s, a national trade union federation and affiliated unions, a church federation, and national student organization were all formed inside Namibia and have continued to exist, in different guises, up to the present. The emergence of trade unions from among the ranks of SWAPO supporters in the mid-1980s was only sanctioned by the exiled liberation movement when it became clear in the final days of the struggle that they had value as a mobilizing force (Bauer 1998). Indeed, upon independence SWAPO moved quickly to ensure that the recently formed federation—the National Union of Namibian Workers (NUNW)—affiliated itself formally with the party. In the early years of independence there were attempts on the part of some union members to move the unions away from the ruling party, but they were never successful. Such efforts were always met with great consternation, even threats, from SWAPO (Bauer 1999). As noted in the *Namibian* on October 1, 1998, the NUNW was one of the few organizations to state its "unequivocal" support for a third term for President Nujoma and for Namibian intervention in DRC. As noted earlier, the ruling party, cognizant of the role of labor movements in opposition politics in Zambia and Zimbabwe, has been very vigilant with respect to the nation's trade unions. A clear part of the government's co-optation effort has been the steady flow of trade union leaders into government, including as SWAPO members of parliament and deputy ministers.

The churches followed a slightly different trajectory with respect to the party. The Council of Churches of Namibia (CCN), representing about 80 percent of the Namibian population by the early 1980s, has a long-standing association with SWAPO; indeed, by the 1980s it was referred to by some as the party's "internal religious wing" (Steenkamp 1995, 99). The church had played an active part in early protests against South African rule in Namibia. In the urban areas, CCN offices tried to address the health, education, and economic development needs of the neglected majority population. After independence, however, the federation was rebuked by the ruling party for its demands that SWAPO address "the detainee issue"—those SWAPO members still missing from exile. The party even attempted to prevent the CCN from holding a national conference to address unresolved issues concerning the detainees. Ultimately, the conference was held in March 1998, though SWAPO pointedly sent no delegates, according to the *Namibian,* March 9, 1998. Moreover, during the Angola and DRC wars, the *Namibian* of February 10, 2000, reported that the CCN called for dialogue rather than war as a means for ending armed conflicts in the region. Thus, unlike the trade unions, the churches and their national federation have maintained some independence vis-à-vis the ruling party.

Organized youth have also wrestled with the ruling party since independence. First formed in 1984, the Namibian National Student Organization (NANSO) also considered itself part and parcel of the liberation movement inside the country in its early days (Maseko 1995, 120). Shortly after independence, however, in 1991, NANSO voted to disaffiliate from SWAPO, given concerns that affiliation prevented the organization from recruiting non-SWAPO students and youth, concern about preventing outside control of NANSO processes and structures, and a general desire to preserve the inner organizational democracy and autonomy of the student organization (Maseko 1995, 127–128). Leaders of the disaffiliation effort were labeled "foreign agents" by the SWAPO leadership and shortly thereafter a splinter student organization was formed with the assistance of the ruling party. Thereafter the original NANSO lost significant numbers of members and began to experience administrative, financial, and organizational difficulties (Bauer 1999, 437–438). The president and secretary general of NANSO from 1987 to 1990, Ignatius Shixwameni, currently serves as president of the All People's Party (APP), another new political party established in Namibia in 2008. Previously Shixwameni had served as secretary-general of the SWAPO Youth League and from there as a founding member of the COD, which he left in 2007 to form the APP.

This obvious reluctance on the part of the ruling party to sanction, never mind encourage, independent organization (and voices) outside of party structures is of great significance to the prospects for the consolidation of democracy in Namibia. As Leys and Saul (1995, 4) noted in the early years after independence: "While a formally democratic system has indeed emerged in Namibia, it seems fair to say that little popular empowerment has been realized." Melber (2003, 15) noted that criticism was not taken lightly by the ruling party: "Loyalty to Namibia is equated with loyalty to Swapo's policy and in particular the party's president. Dissenting views are marginalized." In the aftermath of the 2009 elections, according to Melber (2010b), the SWAPO website triumphantly proclaimed that "Namibia, SWAPO Party and Sam Nujoma are one."

Media

An integral part of an active civil society is a free and independent media. Indeed, a significant level of media freedom has existed in Namibia since independence. Namibia has an impressive array of government, private, and community media sources. The national radio station broadcasts throughout the country in every Namibian language. In recent years, there has been a proliferation of independent radio stations, including a community radio station in Katutura, the black township outside Windhoek. The national television network, the Namibian Broadcasting Corporation, is government owned, as are a number of newspapers and magazines, but operates with some measure of independence. Three independent dailies and a host of smaller, private newspapers and magazines vie with one another for readers from among the national populace. The privately owned and operated media in Namibia are fiercely independent, and editors and columnists freely voice their criticisms of government and other institutions. In 2008 and 2009, however, the government seemed to clamp down on the independent and state media, arresting foreign journalists and limiting topics on popular chat shows.

The Media Institute of Southern Africa (MISA), whose secretariat is based in Windhoek, monitors press freedom in the region. In its 2008 and 2009 annual reports, MISA issued six media freedom alerts for Namibia. Three concerned instances in which the government of Namibia had banned some journalists from covering specific events. Two concerned the passage of the 2009 Communications Act meant to regulate the media and other communications, and one other concerned the arrest of a South African journalist accused of working on a tourist visa (US Department of State 2010d). Surely in response, in August 2009 the Editors Forum of Namibia created the position of media ombudsman in Namibia, to which they appointed a highly respected human rights lawyer. The media ombudsman, along with a Media Complaints Committee and Media Appeals Board, is now available to receive and adjudicate grievances and complaints from the public against the media (US Department of State 2010d).

Society and Development: Enduring Cleavages

Politics of Race in Namibia

Namibia is a multiracial and multiethnic society. Most of the population is black, divided among several ethnic groups; just under 7 percent is mixed race or "Coloured"; and 6 percent of the population is white. About two-thirds of the white population are Afrikaans speakers, with the rest being German speakers descended from German colonists and English speakers of South African origins. After decades of colonial and apartheid rule, most white Namibians are far better off than their black counterparts—although the discrepancies are probably not as great as in South Africa. Indeed, the United Nations Development Programme (in UNDP 2000, 20) reported in 2000 that 55 percent of aggregate income in Namibia accrued to 10 percent of the population. A small minority of Namibians live like their middle-class counterparts in the industrialized world (or better) while the majority of Namibians live like their counterparts in the rest of sub-Saharan Africa. For this reason, it is very misleading to speak about a per capita income in Namibia and to rank the country on that basis. According to the UNDP, "in terms of its income and asset distribution, the Namibian economy is so extreme that the 'average' Namibian, in social and economic terms, is a rarity." At the same time Heidi Armbruster (2008, 611), who conducted research among German migrants to Namibia in the middle of the first decade of the twenty-first century, found them to be "evasive about the problematic inheritance of white privilege" and, many years after independence, yet to begin a process of critical self-reflection.

The persistence of disparities is reminiscent of the other postsettler societies in southern Africa and reflects, in part, the fact that each eschewed a policy of redistribution after independence. Namibia, like South Africa and Zimbabwe, turned to a policy of national reconciliation in an effort to move beyond the decades of apartheid rule and race-based oppression. Immediately upon his return to Namibia, Sam Nujoma was quoted in the *Namibian* of September 19, 1989, as stating his support for a policy of national reconciliation: "The first thing we have to do is pursue a policy of national reconciliation and open a new page of history, founded on respect for human life, human rights and equality, and build a new life for the whole society. Everybody has suffered; this war has affected everyone. Even whites." Nujoma's views were echoed repeatedly by other members of the new government after independence.

National reconciliation had a distinct economic component. The new government was keen not to antagonize the largely white private sector, whether local or foreign, which controlled commercial agriculture, the retail sector, and the mining industry. One of the National Assembly's very first acts was to pass a bill that provided generous conditions for foreign investment and various guarantees on the security of those investments. In the intervening years, however, it appears that the positions of the ruling party may have hardened. White commercial farms have not been invaded, businesses have not been nationalized or looted, white Namibians have not been given any indication that they are welcome but their children are not (as in Zimbabwe).[19] At the same time, verbal attacks on whites, in particular foreign whites (who in some cases are the owners of businesses or land in Namibia), have been growing. "Whites" are most typically criticized for attempting to intervene in internal Namibian affairs. For example, according to the May 29, 1997, *Namibian,* white Namibians and foreigners were accused of instigating the protests (for environmental and cultural preservation reasons) against building the Epupa dam in northern Namibia in the late 1990s. During his many years as president, Sam Nujoma railed against homosexuality in Namibia, labeling it a white or foreign import. At the World Summit on Sustainable Development in Johannesburg in September 2002, Nujoma publicly castigated foreign (European) donors, suggesting that Namibia did not need foreign aid.

Accordingly, there has been a trend away from including whites in senior positions in government. Whereas the SWAPO government that took power at independence in 1990 was a careful blend of party leaders from exile, party leaders from inside the country, and white Namibians, this mix gradually shifted in subsequent cabinet reshuffles such that by 2005 there were no longer any white ministers, although there were still several white deputy ministers and permanent secretaries. In some cases prominent whites in government have left of their own accord, while others have been asked to leave.

As indicated in President Nujoma's first words on the subject, national reconciliation in Namibia has always been about moving on, about burying the past rather than confronting it. Unlike South Africa, Namibia never established a truth and reconciliation commission that would have investigated past practices and atrocities of the South African administrations in Namibia and, perhaps more important, of the liberation movement. As Erasmus (2000, 78) charitably observes: Namibia "adopted a different policy of national reconciliation [from South Africa] by deliberately moving away from the unpleasant memories of the past and instead focusing on what was postulated as the building of a unified nation." This was not for lack of calls for such a commission in Namibia, but those calls went totally unheeded. To this day, the relatives of those young SWAPO members who never returned home from SWAPO exile camps in Angola call for the movement to be held accountable.[20]

Ethnic Conflict and the Politics of Pluralism

Since independence in 1990, Namibia has avoided significant overt ethnic conflict. Official government documents downplay ethnicity by presenting population and other statistics almost exclusively by region, rather than race or ethnicity, and only occasionally by "language group," the primary marker for ethnicity in southern Africa. The largest single ethnic group in the country comprises the Ovambo-speaking people, who constitute just over half of the population and live primarily in the four northern regions of Ohangwena, Omusati, Oshana, and Oshikoto and in some urban areas such as Windhoek and Oranjemund.[21] The Nama and Damara people together make up about another 12 percent of the population. Those speaking Otjiherero and Ruka-vango make up under 10 percent each of the population. Namibians of mixed-race origin compose less than 7 percent of the population and whites about 6 percent. Other groups include Lozi speakers, who live in the Caprivi, and the San, the most marginalized and deprived group in Namibia, who no longer have a territorial base. The Ovambo are further divided into eight subgroups, of which the Kwanyama are the largest and most significant.

There are clear reasons for the government of Namibia to avoid ethnic labels. Throughout colonial Africa perceived ethnicity was used by colonial authorities to divide, in order to more easily subjugate, colonial peoples.[22] This was even truer in apartheid South Africa and Namibia, where significant settler populations sought to deprive indigenous populations of even the most basic rights and did so on the basis of racial and ethnic classifications. Creating ethnic homelands, for example, was all about depriving black Namibians and black South Africans of Namibian and South African citizenship, respectively. In response, of course, the nationalist movement led the struggle for independence with the battle cry "One Namibia! One Nation!" and, like many other nationalist movements, sought to incorporate members of all ethnic groups into the movement, in particular into visible leadership positions.

At the same time, ethnic prejudice does appear to have reared its ugly head within SWAPO in exile. For example, it is charged by many that those most heavily persecuted by the movement in exile were predominantly Nama-Damara or Herero-speaking Namibians, or that they were "Ombuitis"[23]—Oshivambo speakers from the central and southern urban areas rather than the rural north. More often than not these might also have been the more educated and politically progressive SWAPO cadres (Bauer 1998, 165; Saul and Leys 2003, 54–55). Those accused of perpetrating the crimes in exile include Kwanyama speakers from the north. The EIU (EIU 2003f, 16) reported a Kwanyama bias within Namibia's military: "Kwanyama ex-PLAN commanders hold most senior NDF posts, and state security appointments have a similar ethnic bias." But the EIU also noted that there were few incidents of inter-ethnic tensions within the army.

Many people suggest that, as in other multiethnic societies, enduring ethnic allegiances in Namibia may prove a stumbling block to the consolidation of democracy. For example, SWAPO's long-standing and steadfast base of support has been from the Ovambo-speaking people. Since they compose more than half the population, should Ovambos continue to vote along ethnic lines for the ruling party, then no other party will ever defeat them. Similarly, if other political parties are organized largely along ethnic lines, then no other parties will ever garner more than about 10–12 percent of the vote. For the most part, political parties in Namibia do have an ethnic base, although there is significant crossover and some melding of ethnic allegiances into one political party. In the aftermath of the 2004 and 2009 elections, Melber (2010b) suggests that ethnicity has emerged more visibly and forcefully as a basis on which especially the smaller parties are formed, but also on which voters are mobilized.

Finally, there have been claims of an ethnic bias on the part of the SWAPO-led government. For example, during 2009 "some citizens continued to accuse the government of providing more development assistance and professional opportunities to the majority Ovambo ethnic group," the primary supporters of the ruling SWAPO party (US Department of State 2010d). Forrest (1998, 323) argued in the late 1990s that one of the reasons that significant ethnic tensions had not emerged in Namibia is that regional governments—by "contributing to the moderation of village-level tensions and providing an outlet for grievances against central government ministries"—helped to defuse the potential emergence of regional or ethnic challenges.

To date, the main exception to this appears to have been in the Caprivi, where long-standing ethnic concerns were seen by many to be at the heart of the alleged secession plot uncovered by the government in late 1998. Indeed, the movement was felt to have valid reasons (with certain ethnic overtones) for its disgruntlement with the Namibian government, including far fewer development projects in the Caprivi than in the more favored four northern regions, high levels of unemployment in the region, and the appointment of government and other officials from outside the region.

Fundamentals of the Political Economy

Since independence, the government's economic goals have focused on achieving a sustainable economic growth rate, achieving a real increase in per capita incomes, diversifying the economy, expanding employment opportunities, and improving education and health services. In recent years, there has been a heightened focus on reducing income inequalities and enabling black economic empowerment. During the 1995–2000 period, real GDP grew at about 3–5 percent per year, sometimes short of the targeted 5 percent. From 2005 to 2008, real GDP grew at a slightly higher 4–5 percent per year. In 2010 overall unemployment in Namibia was estimated at an unprecedented 50 percent, however. About 30-40 percent of Namibians are estimated to be employed in agriculture, primarily subsistence agriculture in the communal areas. The government had hoped to increase employment opportunities by promoting small- and medium-sized enterprises and by tripling manufacturing employment to 20 percent of all formal sector jobs. Whereas manufacturing in the past was primarily confined to the processing of fish and meat products, in recent years several large Asian-owned textile factories have opened in Namibia as part of a larger government strategy to attract foreign investment to the country. Indeed, legislation in 1995 provided for the establishment of export processing zones in the country, and by 2000 two dozen companies with such status were operating in the country. Textile companies, meanwhile, are seeking to take advantage of Namibia's eligibility under the Africa Growth and Opportunity Act to export textiles and clothing duty-free to the United States. Otherwise, mining, commercial agriculture, and fishing remain the mainstays of the Namibian economy. Significant effort has also been invested in building the tourism industry in Namibia.

Late in the first decade of the twenty-first century, a coalition of labor and church groups sought the widespread implementation of a Basic Income Grant (BIG) they had devised to offer monthly cash allowances to village residents as a means of empowering local communities. The program was completely rejected by government and eventually disavowed by the NUNW trade union federation—on the grounds of being a system of financial transfers that encouraged free riding (Melber 2010a). In the meantime Namibia's considerable income inequality continues.

As in the other postsettler southern African societies, the land issue remains a contentious one in Namibia. Like income, land remains very inequitably distributed in Namibia; about 4,000 white commercial farmers owned about 6,400 holdings on 30.5 million hectares, or about 37 percent of Namibia's land area in the early twenty-first century. Much of this is arid land devoted to livestock ranching. Much of the rest of Namibia's land, generally better watered, supports about 150,000 subsistence farm families in the overcrowded northern communal areas. So far, the redistribution of commercial farmland in Namibia has proceeded on a willing buyer–willing seller basis, as provided in the 1999 commercial land reform bill. The policy is also in keeping with Namibia's constitutional right to private property and reflects government's realization of "the importance of maintaining efficient commercial livestock ranching" (EIU 2003f, 7). The redistribution of land has been hampered, however, by the high prices of commercial farms and a lack of government funds to purchase them. In April 2003, a new land tax was imposed that was expected to raise significant funds to be used to purchase land for redistribution and resettlement. And in June 2003 new legislation provided government the right to acquire land for resettlement "in the public interest." Land still has to be purchased, but not at the market prices mandated by the willing buyer–willing seller policy (EIU 2003j). At the same time, as Melber (2010a) notes, the government's land policy in Namibia has been idling during the first two decades of independence with an apparent focus on securing farms for the country's new black elite rather than the black majority.

It has been suggested that the demands for land redistribution have not been as great in Namibia as in South Africa or Zimbabwe, because the majority of Namibians, the Ovambo-speaking people from the north, were not actually dispossessed of their land during the colonial period. Rather it was the Herero and Nama-Damaras from central and southern Namibia whose land and livestock were taken; moreover, these groups do not form the core of the ruling party's support base in the way that the Ovambo do. Indeed, in 2010 it was the leader of the South West Africa National Union (SWANU), a party with support predominantly among the Herero, who called for the convening of a second land conference in Namibia to once again consider land reform in the country. At the same time, there is also a crying need for land reform in the northern communal areas. There, the fencing of communal lands by the rich and politically powerful, as well as the historical neglect of the northern communal areas (in terms of agricultural extension services, access to credit and other inputs, environmental degradation, etc.), has limited access to land and income among subsistence households.

Challenges of the Twenty-First Century

And so we return to our original question: will Namibia set a new example of Africa's promise in the twenty-first century or will it follow the less inspiring example of some neighbors to the north? The structural constraints are numerous, and it seems that there is only so much that individual or even collective agents can do. Economically, the challenges abound. A generous resource endowment and healthy infrastructure are mitigated somewhat by a harsh climate marked by water shortages and recurring drought. Unemployment and lower-than-anticipated economic growth rates threaten continued improvements in living standards that are expected by the population and that are necessary to narrow the disparities across racial and ethnic groups. Remarkably, for nearly a decade, Namibia has had the highest Gini Index in the world, meaning it has the most unequal distribution of income in the world. Foreign investment, one source of jobs, remains the double-edged sword it has always been—damaging the environment and people's health, eroding hard-won labor standards, and yet providing some source of livelihood for many.

Socially, Namibia faces a continuing challenge, like other countries in southern Africa, from one of the highest HIV/AIDS adult prevalence rates in the world. At the same time, like other countries in southern Africa, Namibia has been at the forefront of efforts in Africa to provide universal access to treatment to all who need it and to put in place the prevention programs that seem to be finding a hearing among the youth, especially young women (UNAIDS 2008b). And while Namibia has made enormous strides in terms of primary health care and education provision since independence, both still need to reach large segments of the population, as do basic amenities such as electricity. Moreover, a very rapid rural to urban migration—as many as 600 people arrive in the capital city every month—puts a remarkable strain on local government resources and services, contributes to rising crime rates, and provides a ready reserve of disaffected people to threaten Namibia's hard-won political stability.

Finally, politically, the country faces the same challenges of many African and developing countries that have attempted recent democratic transitions: how to create a tolerant democratic political culture after decades of authoritarian colonial rule and decades of undemocratic practices within a liberation movement in exile; how to institutionalize a viable multiparty political system in which opposition political parties (with social bases that are other than ethnic) can thrive and not be labeled disloyal for daring to exist, let alone utter a criticism; how to carry out peaceful presidential successions on a continent where leaders were once removed only by force. Though President Sam Nujoma elected not to stand for an unconstitutional fourth term of office, he handpicked his successor—his "most loyal lieutenant," Hifikepunye Pohamba. Though Pohamba was "selected" by delegates at a SWAPO extraordinary congress in May 2004, his selection was clearly engineered by President Nujoma. Moreover, President Nujoma retains a significant behind-the-scenes role—having been ordained the founding father of the Namibian nation by SWAPO cadres. In the end, Namibia's first presidential succession (and Pohamba's subsequent reelection in 2009) was marked by far less than complete transparency and by the retention of power by the first, older generation of once-exiled liberation leaders. Presumably that will have to change for the 2014 election.

Notes

1. Once back in Namibia after exile, the name of the party was changed to simply SWAPO party of Namibia, http://www.swapoparty.org/. Retrieved January 2011.

2. For more on the history of Namibia, see Katjavivi 1990; Hayes et al. 1998; Dobell 1998; Ngavirue 1997; and Emmett 1999.

3. For more on the transition, see Cliffe et al. 1993 and Weiland and Braham 1994.

4. An elite pact is one in which "moderate factions in the government and opposition seek common ground through negotiations" (Bratton and van de Walle 1997, 178). In such a situation "incumbent and opposition leaders meet behind the scenes to provide mutual assurances that each would respect the vital interests of the other in a future democratic dispensation."

5. According to Bratton and van de Walle (1997, 81), settler oligarchies "resembled the bureaucratic-authoritarian regimes constructed by Europeans in those parts of the colonial world where white settlers gained *de facto* control of the state." They "approximate exclusionary democracies." Political competition was high but participation low—with settlers reproducing functioning democracies for themselves while fully excluding the indigenous majority.

6. "Where cultural and organizational contexts are unsupportive, the introduction of political contestation can lead to division, polarization, and instability. If this logic is correct, then the prospects for gradual, negotiated political opening are generally better in bureaucratic-authoritarian regimes, provided they display some heritage of political competition, than in neopatrimonial regimes" (Bratton and van de Walle 1997, 179).

7. Some observers also suggested that a "third term" for President Nujoma might not be such a bad thing, as the country would otherwise confront a potentially destabilizing presidential succession only ten years into independence.

8. In the 1994 presidential race, Sam Nujoma was reelected with 74.5 percent of the vote; rival candidate Mishake Muyongo of the Democratic Turnhalle Alliance (DTA) polled 23.1 percent of the vote. In the 1999 presidential race, according to the *Namibian* of December 7, 1999, Nujoma was again reelected, with 76.7 percent of the vote; Ben Ulenga of the Congress of Democrats garnered 10.6 percent of the vote, the DTA's Katuutire Kaura polled 9.7 percent of the vote, and the United Democratic Front's Justus Garoeb received 3.0 percent of the vote. In 2004 SWAPO's Hifikepunye Pohamba won 76.4 percent of the vote to Ben Ulenga's 7.3 percent and Katuutire Kaura's 5.1 percent of the vote, as reported in the *Namibian,* November 22, 2004.

9. In a cabinet reshuffle in August 2002, Geingob, who had served as prime minister since independence, was offered the post of minister of regional and local government and housing. Rather than accept this obvious demotion, Geingob resigned from office. Speculation about the reasons for Geingob's demotion centered around his campaign in early August 2002 to become the SWAPO party vice president. Instead, President

Nujoma's favored candidate, Pohamba, became the party's vice president. In early April 2004 a SWAPO Central Committee meeting selected Hamutenya, Pohamba, and long-time higher education minister Nahas Angula as contenders for SWAPO presidential candidate. Just days before the congress to select the candidate, Hamutenya was abruptly dismissed from office by President Nujoma.

10. Erasmus (2000, 81) calls it "a remarkable process of compromise and reconciliation."

11. According to F. M. d'Engelbronner-Kolff (1998, 62–63), "describing the essence of customary law is a controversial and complicated matter. The entire discourse about customary law, as well as the distinction between custom and law, relates to the autonomy, or for legal purposes, the sovereignty, of social groups outside the central government." Many seem to reconcile this contradiction by seeing customary law in terms of "society's semi-autonomy—the fact that it can generate rules and customs and symbols internally, but that it is also vulnerable to rules and decisions and other forces emanating from the larger world it is surrounded by." Importantly, customary law must also be understood as dynamic, "rather than being a static body of rules and principles."

12. Saul and Leys (2003, 338) assert that interrogators from SWAPO's detention centers in Lubango, Angola, during the 1980s have been "reincarnated as members of the Security Service or the President's Special Field Force."

13. In early 2011 the SWAPO party website had a laudatory front-page story about Zimbabwe's Mugabe "slamming" indigenous farmers for leasing land to white farmers, http://www.swapoparty.org/. Retrieved January 2011.

14. Thirteen of the alleged separatists were charged with high treason and the others with lesser offenses; of the thirteen, ten have been tried and convicted, two acquitted, and one passed away. The trial of the remaining defendants had not been concluded in 2010.

15. Retrieved December 2010 from www.ipu.org.

16. Retrieved December 2010 from www.eisa.org.

17. Certain privileges are accorded the official opposition, such as the leader's being able to respond first in major debates introduced by the ruling party and at times being able to speak for an unlimited period in the National Assembly. The leader of the official opposition also receives a higher salary than ordinary members of parliament.

18. Namibia followed Botswana, Mauritius, Cape Verde, Seychelles, and South Africa, among African countries; http://www.transparency.org/. Retrieved October 2010.

19. See Chapter 7 for a discussion of this issue in Zimbabwe.

20. See Saul and Leys 2003 for an account of "forgotten history" as politics in contemporary Namibia. As they observe (2003, 337): "Swapo's domestic critics have continued to make clear that, in their view, it is not differing philosophies and strategies of reconciliation but rather Swapo's desire to cover its own tracks that does indeed provide the most convincing explanation of the path the movement has chosen."

21. Most, though not all, of "historically disadvantaged Namibians"—those people particularly discriminated against under South African rule—live in these four regions plus the Kavango and Caprivi regions.

22. As Leroy Vail (1991, 7) reminds us, "ethnicity is not a cultural residue but a consciously crafted ideological creation." In southern Africa three variables were at play from the late nineteenth century onward: the need for a group of cultural brokers for the nationalist project, the practice of "indirect rule," and a reach toward "traditional values" in a period of rapid social change. European missionaries played a tremendous role in "creating" African ethnic identities.

23. Use of the term *Ombuiti*—as a slur—resurfaced during the 2009 election, with some supporters of the RDP labeled as Ombuitis.

9 South Africa: Hard Realities in the Rainbow Nation

In South Africa's first-ever, all-race election in 1994, the country achieved what only a short time before had seemed unthinkable: a peaceful transition of power from a white minority regime to a democratic, popularly elected black majority government. As a result of that election, the principal and long-standing liberation movement, the African National Congress (ANC), emerged as the leader of a new Government of National Unity (GNU). More astoundingly, the ANC was joined in the GNU by its erstwhile enemy, the National Party (NP), and its main black rival, the Zulu-based Inkatha Freedom Party (IFP). Accordingly, the election outcome and the new government were hailed around the world as a miracle; indeed, the election's importance is not to be underestimated. Prior to 1994, South Africa had been ruled by a racist white minority government under the brutally oppressive system of apartheid. It also faced a low-level guerrilla war and economic stagnation and was considered a pariah by the international community. The 1994 election allowed South Africa to reenter the community of nations and immediately claim a leadership position on the African continent.

Several of South Africa's attributes proved auspicious in its renewed promise and newfound legitimacy: the country's economic base, its leadership, and the nature of its negotiated transition to democracy. First, although the last years of apartheid and National Party rule had badly damaged the economy, South Africa could nonetheless claim a level of GDP and industrial development, as well as an economic infrastructure and degree of sectoral diversity, that is unsurpassed in Africa. Thus the country was poised to play a leading role on the continent economically as well as politically. Second, the new South Africa was substantially personified by the ANC's Nelson Mandela, the antiapartheid icon who became the first president of the democratic state. Mandela's lack of bitterness, despite twenty-seven years of imprisonment by the apartheid state, and his quest for reconciliation between the races brought him and his country worldwide acclaim and respect. More important, his leadership was essential in guiding South Africa through a very fragile

---

South Africa: Country Data

Land area   1,214,470 km²
Capital   Pretoria
Date of independence   May 31, 1961, declared a republic
Population   49,109,107, 61% urban
Languages   IsiZulu (official) 23.8%, IsiXhosa (official) 17.6%, Afrikaans (official) 13.3%, Sepedi (official) 9.4%, English (official) 8.2%, Setswana (official) 8.2%, Sesotho (official) 7.9%, Xitsonga (official) 4.4%, other 7.2% (2001 census)
Ethnic groups   black African 79%, white 9.6%, colored 8.9%, Asian 2.5% (2001 census)
Religions   Zion Christian 11.1%, Pentecostal/Charismatic 8.2%, Catholic 7.1%, Methodist 6.8%, Dutch Reformed 6.7%, Anglican 3.8%, Muslim 1.5%, other Christian 36%, other 2.3%, unspecified 1.4%, none 15.1% (2001 census)
Currency   rand (ZAR); rands per US dollar: 8.54
Literacy rate   86.4% (male, 87%; female, 85.7%) (2003 estimate)
Life expectancy   49.2 years (male, 50.08 years; female, 48.29 years) (2010 estimate)
Infant mortality   43.78 per 1,000 live births
GDP per capita (PPP)   US $10,300
GDP real growth rate   2.4% (2010 estimate)
Leaders since 1994
   Nelson Rolihlahla Mandela, president, May 1994–June 1999
   Thabo Mvuyelwa Mbeki, president, June 1999–September 2008
   Kgalema Petrus Motlanthe, president, September 2008–May 2009
   Jacob Zuma, president, May 2009–
Major political parties
   Ruling party   African National Congress (ANC)
   Other parties   Congress of the People (COPE), Democratic Alliance (DA), Inkatha Freedom Party (IFP)
Women in parliament (lower/single house)   44.5% (2009 election)

Sources: Data derived from https://www.cia.gov; http://www.ipu.org/.
Note: Data from 2009 unless otherwise noted.

---

period in its history. Third, the process of negotiation between former combatants, in which Mandela was instrumental, helped to establish the rules of the game for the democratic transition and set a positive and peaceful course for the future.

These accomplishments, however, mask a great number of problems. Notwithstanding the promise of majority rule, and indeed the promises of the ANC government itself, South Africa has failed to live up to many expectations both domestically and internationally. On the economic front, the growth anticipated in 1994 has not materialized. South Africa requires more than 6 percent annual GDP growth in order to achieve per capita increases in wealth and well-being. Yet owing to a variety of domestic and international forces, democratic South Africa averaged less than 3 percent in its first decade. More robust economic growth in the middle of the first decade of the twenty-first century allowed GDP per capita to grow at an average 2.4 percent per year between 2001 and 2009. Yet the country continues to be one of the most unequal in the world, measured by income disparities that still largely fall along racial lines. In the rural communities, a land reform program that dwarfs Zimbabwe's is behind schedule and below expectations. While a small number of blacks in the urban areas have joined the ranks of the new middle class, poverty remains entrenched and has deepened in many areas, with unemployment among nonwhites still running at nearly 40 percent.[1]

Not surprisingly, given the social demands on the state and its economic constraints, crime has skyrocketed, and South Africa today has the dubious distinction of having one of the highest and most violent crime rates on earth. Similarly, although the state has made gains in rural and urban health care provision, the AIDS crisis remains a threat to South Africa's fragile health and social infrastructure. With an astounding 5.6 *million* people living with AIDS in the country, South Africa has the highest number of infected persons anywhere in the world, notwithstanding indications that HIV prevalence rates are falling (UNAIDS 2010c).

The widely hailed reconciliation process that was embodied by President Mandela, Archbishop Desmond Tutu, and others—and was orchestrated by the Truth and Reconciliation Commission (TRC) from 1996 to 1998—revealed numerous shortcomings. Mandela retired from the presidency in 1999. More significant, although efforts at reconciliation have been far deeper than in Zimbabwe in 1980, black alienation, white resentment, and persistent divisions in the black community suggest renewed social conflict remains possible. This situation, coupled with a belief that the TRC failed to punish—or even identify—all the perpetrators of apartheid-era crimes, has led to bitterness and disillusionment in a substantial segment of the black community and among some members of the white population as well.

Finally, political challenges also threaten to undermine South Africa's meticulously negotiated transition. Thus, as Robert Mattes wrote in 2002, "if one looks at South Africa's new democracy in a comparative perspective, one's enthusiasm is greatly tempered, if not altogether removed" (Mattes 2002, 22). South Africa under the ANC has once again become a dominant-party system, albeit in the context of democratic institutions, including an impressive and inclusive constitutional structure and regular multiparty elections (Lodge 1999). The concentration of power, however, holds implications for governance, for these institutions, and for the country's still nascent democratic culture, which may be showing signs of decay (Mattes 2002).

Numerous theoretical and analytical approaches attempt to explain South Africa's performance in its first decades of independence. Critics on the left decry what they see as the ANC's abandonment of its social-democratic roots and its commitment to nationalization and economic redistribution in favor of a neoliberal, market-based development model (Saul 1999; Bond 2000, 2006). They argue that the ANC's unfettered embrace of market capitalism, which became apparent in the mid-1990s, has amounted to a betrayal of labor, and black interests more broadly, and has contributed to lasting social instability. Those on the right, to be sure, are generally less critical of the ANC's economic program, with its emphasis on property rights, supply-side policies, and an overall framework that promotes growth *before* redistribution. Nonetheless, the ANC has not escaped criticism from those on the right, who find fault with what are regarded as political choices, such as the enactment of affirmative action and labor legislation that they believe threatens corporate interests (Adam 1997). Thabo Mbeki, who succeeded Mandela as South African president, occasionally resorted to populist rhetoric that hinted at a penchant for redistribution. His successor, Jacob Zuma, who took office in 2009, has done likewise. While this occasionally causes some concern among capitalists, such allusions have yet to be taken seriously by those closest to the government (Bond 2000; I. Taylor 2002).

Many of the virtues attributed to South Africa, as well as the challenges it faced in the aftermath of its transition to democracy, are reminiscent of Zimbabwe in the same period (Herbst 1989; Stoneman 1988). Indeed, the countries have similar historical, economic, and political endowments. Although overstating those commonalities is unhelpful, some parallels warrant closer consideration. These include the nature and depth of reconciliation; the disparities in income, land, and resources between the black and white communities; the choice of economic development strategy; and the pitfalls of one-party dominance. Examination of these issues can shed light on the critical questions facing contemporary South Africa: What are the prospects for economic growth and social stability? How strong—or conversely, how fragile—is South Africa's democracy?

Historical Origins of the South African State

Formal European contact with South Africa dates to 1652, when the Dutch East India Company established a way station in the western Cape region for its Indian Ocean trade. Initially no settlement was intended, but the territory gradually attracted Dutch and French Huguenot farmers, and by 1672 a colony had been established (Omer-Cooper 1994). The area was not uninhabited, however, and white settlement led to the decimation of the local population, known as the Khoi. Many of these indigenous peoples died, and miscegenation between white men and Khoi women was also common.[2] Dutch hegemony eventually gave way to the superior military and commercial capacity of the British, who established control in the Cape colony between 1795 and 1803. In 1828 the British annexed the other South African territory of Natal, to the east. The arrival of the British in South Africa gave rise to centuries of tension between English speakers and the descendants of the original Dutch-French settlers, who became known as Afrikaners.

Cultural and economic clashes between the European populations—over, among other things, the modestly more liberal British policies toward indigenous peoples—led a significant portion of the Afrikaner population to push farther into South Africa's hinterland, and in 1836 many of them migrated from the principal areas of European settlement in the British-controlled Cape and Natal colonies. This "Great Trek," as it came to be known, led to the establishment of the Transvaal Republic and the Orange Free State. One of the great foundation myths of the Afrikaner people was that the vast territories of the country that they settled were empty and uninhabited; in fact they were home to several hundred thousand Khoisan and several million Bantu-speaking peoples, including Xhosa on the eastern frontier and Sotho speakers and Zulu subgroups to the north and northeast.[3] These early nineteenth-century migrations set the stage for more than a century of racial conflict (Omer-Cooper 1994).

By the late 1870s, most of the African populations had been conquered or subdued, and white South Africa was essentially divided into two British colonies, Cape and Natal, and two Afrikaner-led republics, Transvaal and the Orange Free State, on which the British and English-speaking economic interests long had designs. The discovery of significant deposits of diamonds at Kimberley in the late 1860s, and gold in 1886 in the Transvaal, greatly exacerbated existing tensions between the British and Afrikaner populations. These came to a head with the outbreak of the 1899–1903 Anglo-Boer War. In the course of the war, the Boers (literally, "farmers" in Afrikaans) were brutally defeated by the British forces, suffered an estimated 25,000 deaths of women and children in British concentration camps, and ultimately lost the Transvaal and Orange Free State to British control. Although the prosecution of the war contributed to an enduring enmity between the two groups, the formation of the Union of South Africa in 1910—which joined the Cape colony, Natal, Transvaal, and Orange Free State into a single, self-governing political entity—actually placed Afrikaners on equal legal and political footing with the British for the first time.

The nineteenth century was a period in which South Africa's black populations, including kingdoms, chiefdoms, and less hierarchical communities, lost their autonomy to white control and faced escalating oppression by both British and Afrikaner populations. By the time of the union in 1910, the foundations for the violent, destructive policies that were to become apartheid had all been laid. As indicated in Table 9.1, a series of increasingly restrictive pieces of legislation began the process of forcing blacks into the labor economy, particularly after the discovery of gold in the 1880s spurred the development of a substantial mining industry. These laws served to deprive blacks of their limited franchise (which in any event existed previously only in Cape

Table 9.1   Key Pieces of Preapartheid and Early Apartheid-Era Legislation

	Year Enacted	Function
Preapartheid Laws		
Glen Grey Act 1	1894	Restricted black landholdings (principally in the Cape)
Mines and Works Act	1911	Barred Africans from skilled positions
Native Lands Act	1913	Limited African landownership to 7 percent of land (all in "native reserves")
Natives Trust and Land Act	1936	Limited African landownership to 13 percent of land
Natives (Urban Areas) Consolidation Act	1945	Mandated carrying of passes in urban areas
Apartheid-Era Laws		
Prohibition of Mixed Marriages Act	1949	Outlawed interracial marriages
Population Registration Act	1950	Classified South Africans by "race"
Group Areas Act	1950	Outlawed interracial communities and created racially defined residential areas
Suppression of Communism Act	1950	Granted state broad police powers to prevent "communist" activity
Bantu Education Act	1953	Consigned Africans to menial education
Reservation of Separate Amenities Act	1953	Outlawed integration of public facilities
Native Labor (Settlement and Disputes) Act	1953	Made African strikes illegal

province), the right to organize, and the choice of where to live as well as land and capital ownership.

The Union of South Africa enjoyed autonomous status vis-à-vis London as a self-governing entity, and the period between 1910 and 1948 witnessed the alternation in power of political parties that represented a mix of Afrikaner and British influences, though pro-British, English-speaking politicians predominated. Nonetheless, the racial policies of the Anglophile governments were hardly progressive and mirrored those of other British settler colonies such as Rhodesia (Zimbabwe). For example, during this period, laws were passed that regulated sexual relations between blacks and whites, mandated a pass system for black males, deprived blacks of most jobs in an effort to eliminate economic competition for "poor whites," and eliminated the vestiges of black franchise in the Cape. In 1948 the Afrikaner-dominated National Party won the elections, and for the first time a non-British-influenced party gained control over the South African state. The National Party had campaigned on a platform of racial separation known as apartheid and immediately began to institute its policy, which called for total social and territorial separation of the races. Having consolidated control of the South African state by the 1958 elections, the National Party's hegemony lasted until 1994. In the process, the nationalists created a system of gross inequality and unchecked brutality, whose legacy continues to affect South African state and society.

Apartheid and Its Legacy:
Enduring Cleavages in Politics and Society

The four-decade history of apartheid has been extraordinarily well chronicled: activists and scholars, the victims of apartheid as well as its architects, all provide thorough documentation (Luthuli 1962; Carter 1980; Mandela 1995; O'Meara 1996; de Klerk 1999). In short, it is well known that the apartheid-era policies were brutally repressive. In broad strokes, apartheid entailed an economic program intended to advance the interests of Afrikaners, undergirded by hypernationalism, maintained by a system of repression, and rationalized by strict Calvinist religious convictions and a belief that the Afrikaners were "God's chosen people" (Dubow 1995, 258–260). Although scholars differ as to the degree to which any of these factors deserves greater consideration, it is clear that they are not mutually exclusive (O'Meara 1983; Giliomee 1983; Dubow 1995, 259–260). The Afrikaner-dominated state after 1948 therefore sought to serve class, ethnic, and religious interests and did so by enacting a draconian and ever more intricate web of laws, some of which are highlighted in Table 9.1.

An essential pillar of apartheid was the notion of racial "purity." This required an elaborate racial classification scheme codified in the 1950 Population Registration Act. Without any scientific basis, racial categories were prescribed: white, black, Asian (predominantly those from the Indian subcontinent), and "Coloured" or mixed race (the very existence of such people might have undermined any notion of race purity). Somewhat ironically, these categories persist today.[4]

Nonwhite groups emerged to resist oppression. Initially, their objectives were quite modest and their methods conservative, but opposition grew more radicalized after 1948. The African National Congress was the largest as well as the oldest such organization. Formed in 1912 by educated African elites who sought inclusion *within* the existing political framework at the time, the ANC eventually attracted a mass following and became one of the most racially inclusive black nationalist organizations. A critical step in the ANC's transformation to a more radical organization seeking to fundamentally change the status quo was the establishment of the ANC Youth League in 1944. Originally committed to nonviolence, the ANC formally adopted a policy of armed struggle in 1961 when it became clear that its methods of peaceful resistance and civil disobedience were being met with the slaughter of its people. Many of the ANC's leaders, including Nelson Mandela and Walter

Sisulu, were caught, charged with treason, and sentenced to life in prison at the Rivonia Trial in 1964. From there they were sent to Robben Island, where they remained for more than two decades in some cases, until they were released or sent to other prisons.

The resistance to apartheid continued, however, and both the struggle and efforts to contain it became decidedly more lethal in the 1970s and 1980s. Domestically, mass actions protesting apartheid policies were met with state violence, as well as the imposition of states of emergency curtailing the already limited rights of blacks. Beginning in the late 1960s, the state developed a massive security apparatus designed to crush dissent in the form of black "subversive" activity. However, this had mixed results and may have contributed to the mass mobilization throughout the country over the years, in which one antiapartheid movement after another surfaced to replace or supplement its predecessor. Over time, the black urban townships, to which South African blacks had been forcibly relocated, became ungovernable.

With the ANC and other African nationalist movements banned, and their leaders exiled or in prison, a number of multiracial movements emerged. The United Democratic Front, for example, which was formed in 1983 by an alliance of some 565 civic, political, and religious organizations, mobilized townships in such activities as rent, consumer, and school boycotts (du Toit 1995). Later in the 1980s, trade unions became more directly involved in antiapartheid activities; in 1989 the Congress of South African Trade Unions (COSATU), the black trade union umbrella body, joined with the United Democratic Movement to form the Mass Democratic Movement, which then initiated a nationwide campaign of civil disobedience designed to weaken the apartheid state.

Internationally, occasional armed incursions from outside the country from the military wings of the ANC and the Pan-Africanist Congress (PAC), regional instability, and global sanctions against South Africa also contributed to the state's "manpower shortages, declining resources, and a weakening resolve" (du Toit 1995, 194). Hence the exponential increase in the human and material cost of state repression, economic crisis, international condemnation, and domestic stalemate contributed to the negotiated end of apartheid (du Toit 1995; Sisk 1995). The negotiated settlement, of course, culminated in the historic ANC victory and ascension of Mandela to the national presidency in 1994.

Given its successful transition to democracy and majority rule—though many had predicted a bloodbath[5]—South Africa is fondly referred to as the "Rainbow Nation" today, a designation it wore proudly and demonstrated with resounding success during the 2010 World Cup. However, this label obscures the fact that the colors of this rainbow are in many respects as separate and distinct as ever. Many if not most of South Africa's contemporary problems are rooted in its racist history; thus it is impossible to discount its past experiences and the structural, social, and historical inheritance of the contemporary regime. However, whereas many of the choices made and policies enacted by the ANC government since 1994 were constrained by the domestic and international environment, such structural constraints fail to explain the whole of contemporary South African politics. Indeed, individuals and institutions have, in the words of Bruce Magnusson (2002), "endogenized the exogenous" by shaping external norms to fit the local context.

The Politics of Transition and Negotiation

Faced with both domestic and international pressures, the South African state was "substantially weakened" by the late 1980s and early 1990s (du Toit 2001, 20). As Pierre du Toit (2001, 21) notes, many activities were beyond the reach of state control: corruption, dirty tricks, and clandestine murder among them. Thus the prospect of a negotiated settlement brought great risk (the potential loss of hegemony) as well as opportunity (the prospect of stemming economic losses and maintaining political control) for the government, as it did for the ANC. Nonetheless, both parties anticipated that they might use their positions and the perceived weakness of the other party to gain from negotiation.

In fact, the negotiations began as early as 1985, when secret meetings commenced between the imprisoned Nelson Mandela and NP justice minister Kobie Coetsee at the behest of then president P. W. Botha. These meetings, which were later branded "talks about talks" to reflect their preliminary and exploratory nature, actually lasted several years and coincided with the rapidly deteriorating economic and political environment in South Africa at the time. Mandela and Botha finally met in July 1989, although the two men were unable to arrive at a mutually acceptable program (Mandela 1995). Mandela insisted on a number of state actions, including the unbanning of the ANC and other organizations, the unconditional release of political prisoners, and a plan for majority rule. Botha also sought more concessions than Mandela was willing to grant, such as the renunciation of the armed struggle (Mandela 1995; Sisk 1995).

When Botha suffered a stroke in 1989, the elevation of Frederik W. de Klerk to the South African presidency in September 1989 proved to be a watershed event. De Klerk, previously education minister, and a devoted member of the National Party, was an unlikely candidate for change, yet he proved instrumental in paving the way for the transition to majority rule. With only limited consultation with his party, de Klerk removed the nearly three-decade-old bans on the Pan-Africanist Congress, the ANC, and the South African Communist Party (SACP) on February 2, 1990. He released Mandela unconditionally on February 11, 1990, after twenty-seven years of imprisonment, having earlier released most of Mandela's compatriots (du Toit 2001, 58).

What followed was more than three years of negotiations between, principally, the ANC and the NP, although other parties joined in these discussions (du Toit 2001, 61). The negotiations between the ANC and NP were punctuated by repeated clashes and suspensions and occasionally public accusations that one or the other party was acting in bad faith. Moreover, this very fragile period was overshadowed by a worsening security environment, growing community violence, and accusations, later substantiated, that the state was instigating conflicts in the black community, especially between the ANC and the Inkatha Freedom Party, the Zulu nationalist organization based in the KwaZulu "homeland."

Various explanations have been advanced for why the parties initiated—and more important, continued with—negotiations, despite the considerable hurdles. Hermann Giliomee (1997, 126) argues that demographic pressures (namely the growing black population relative to whites), economic stagnation, and swelling black resistance undermined the prior stability of the apartheid state beginning in the 1980s, thereby forcing the regime to capitulate in the early 1990s. Thus, as things began to unravel, NP elites such as President de Klerk and Minister of Constitutional Development and of Communication Roelf Meyer (who served as the National Party's chief negotiator in the constitutional negotiations) became less interested in the ethnic entrepreneurship that had underpinned apartheid's logic and more interested in negotiating a position for themselves; indeed, de Klerk and Meyer, among others, retained government positions after the transition (Giliomee 1997, 130).

Taking a less personalist approach, du Toit (2001, 63) contends that "both the NP and the ANC saw themselves as the ascendant power in the negotiating process. . . . Neither considered the other to be an equal." In other words, in the initial period, both parties thought they could *win:* the ANC because of its numerical superiority, and the NP because of its control over the state apparatus and later its perception that it could counter ANC support by appealing to the predominantly Afrikaans-speaking Coloured community and building tacit alliances with the IFP. Conversely, Timothy Sisk (1995, 15, 27) argues that power symmetries actually existed between the parties and that de Klerk in particular recognized that neither side could impose its solution on the other; he was simply more pragmatic than his predecessors.

In any event, while perceived power symmetries may explain the willingness of both the ANC and the NP to enter into negotiations, the balance of power eventually shifted quite clearly to the ANC. The National Party sought, for example, a guaranteed white veto in the legislature (similar to that assured in Zimbabwe's 1979 negotiations) and a leading role in writing the final constitution. However, when the "Record of Understanding" that would guide the transition process was signed by the ANC and NP on September 26, 1992, it was on terms overwhelmingly favorable to the ANC: it rejected the white veto and stipulated that the final constitution was to be written by an elected assembly (du Toit 2001, 65). Having failed to gain concessions from its numerically superior rival that might preserve elements of white power, the NP's electoral defeat was already ensured by 1993, when the election date was set for April 27, 1994. Clearly, de Klerk and his negotiators did not intend to lose power for the Afrikaner population. Indeed, as Giliomee (1997, 139–140, 188) suggests, they simply lost control of the process in the face of superior ANC tactics.[6]

The importance of Mandela and de Klerk as individual agents should not be underestimated. Although negotiations with the ANC were initiated under de Klerk's predecessor, it is unlikely that P. W. Botha could have carried them through. Both by demeanor and by professional background in the government's security and defense arms, Botha was scarcely a conciliator. Moreover, in the view of some analysts, the conflict was insufficiently "ripe" for resolution until the early 1990s, when domestic and international circumstances necessitated movement (Zartman 1989, cited in Sisk 1995).

Mandela, for his part, was indispensable in the negotiation and transition. He compromised where necessary, such as by agreeing to "suspend" the ANC's armed struggle; however, he refused to renounce violence until the NP's commitment to the process was clear. Mandela was also implacable when it came to other dimensions of the negotiations, such as setting the dates for the election and the writing of the constitution. Other individuals were also instrumental in achieving a peaceful outcome. Indeed, the finer details of the negotiation were hammered out not by Mandela and de Klerk, but by their subordinates. The ANC's Cyril Ramaphosa and the NP's Roelf Meyer held some forty meetings between June and September 1992 when wider interparty negotiations had stalled (du Toit 2001, 64). Thus, at multiple levels, leadership was essential to keeping the project on track. The ANC won the April 1994 elections overwhelmingly with 62.65 percent of the vote, against 20.31 percent and 10.54 percent for the NP and IFP, its nearest rivals, respectively. With that, South Africa witnessed a remarkable transfer of power to majority rule.

The first postapartheid government, as stipulated in the 1993 interim constitution, was to be a government of national unity. The GNU was an essential, if largely *symbolic,* aspect of the negotiated settlement. The ANC formed the majority, and seven of the twenty-seven cabinet posts were awarded to the NP (in addition, F. W. de Klerk was appointed second deputy president), and three to the IFP, proportionally on the basis of each party's electoral performance. The GNU offered to both the population and the international community a picture of peaceful transfer of power, of power sharing and cooperation, and of reconciliation between former adversaries. In other words, it was a vision of the country, and its future, that all members of the new government were desperate to present to the wider populace, particularly following the violence that had accompanied the 1990–1994 transition period.[7]

However, the three-party GNU endured for only two of its anticipated five years; in June 1996 the National Party withdrew from the government over disagreements with the ANC. Following the passage of the "final" constitution by the Constituent Assembly, and feeling dissatisfied with the ANC refusal to extend the GNU beyond the 1999 elections, the National Party determined that its prospects were better as a formal opposition party than as a member of the GNU. As discussed below, the NP never regained its strength or its share of the vote and eventually passed into history. Nonetheless, its withdrawal from the GNU helped to usher in a period of more conventional opposition politics in South Africa and a period in which observers began to look more critically at the nature of the "miracle" and the country's prospects for reconciliation, for growth and economic revitalization, and for good governance in South Africa's fragile but much heralded democracy.

Organization of the State

Constitutionalism

Postapartheid South Africa has had two constitutions. The first was the 1993 interim constitution, which established the framework for the transition and the initial years of the new state and came into effect following the elections on April 27, 1994. In 1996, a new, "final" constitution was ratified (effective February 1997), entrenching many of the provisions of the interim version, although it made some important changes. The 1993 document, and its 1996 successor, had a number of international influences and were modeled on the Canadian, German, and Indian constitutions as well as the International Covenant on Civil and Political Rights and the European Convention for Human Rights (Dugard 1998, 25). Enshrining many of the protections long denied to black South Africans, the interim constitution guaranteed equality before the law; freedom from torture and degrading punishment; freedom of speech, assembly, and association; and the right to a speedy and fair trial as well as electoral rights, such as universal adult franchise and the right to political choice (Jeffery 1998, 32). The new constitution also contained provisions for freedom of speech and a constitutional court, the latter intended to provide a "clean slate" for judicial oversight of constitutional matters, given the tainted status of the apartheid-era judiciary (Dugard 1998, 27).

Given its scope, the 1996 South African constitution is celebrated in many circles as one of the most comprehensive and inclusive constitutions in the world. Its preamble clearly establishes the constitution as a means to promote both healing and democracy in South Africa. Its preamble states: "We, the people of South Africa, Recognise the injustices of our past; Honour those who suffered for justice and freedom in our land; Respect those who have worked to build and develop our country; and Believe that South Africa belongs to all who live in it, united in our diversity." "Widely seen as a 'state of the art' document," according to Robert Mattes (2002, 24), "it contains a wide array of classic political and socioeconomic rights, institutional innovations . . . and an activist Constitutional Court." Nonetheless, the constitution has also attracted some criticism, including, surprisingly, from many liberals.

For example, committed liberals decry the *qualified* freedom of speech provisions in the constitution (Dugard 1998, 27), although given the abuses by state and society during apartheid it is difficult to condemn South African constitutionalists for banning hate speech and speech advocating violence. Also controversial were aspects of the Bill of Rights, which establishes not only "vertical rights"—that is, protections for the individual from the state—but also "horizontal rights" that extend to relations between individuals (Dugard 1998, 26). This sets up a potential "clash between [individuals'] competing rights, for example, between the right to free speech and [another's] right to dignity" (Jeffery 1998, 34). In the same vein, the Bill of Rights attracts criticism because it is *too* inclusive—containing provisions about the right to housing and health care, for example, which many regard as governmental rather than constitutional functions (Jeffery 1998, 38). In South Africa, however, it may have proved impossible to exclude such elements from the constitution. Mattes (2002, 24), conversely, criticizes the constitution for what it leaves out, "particularly with regard to the interaction among party politics, voter representation, and legislative-executive relations."[8]

South Africa's 1994 and 1996 constitutions each affirmed the country's status as a federal state and acknowledged the role of the nine provinces (expanded from the original four provinces as part of the transition) in this structure. Among the most controversial aspects of the negotiated settlement was the issue of "minority rights" in the new South Africa. Many whites, even those who never supported the National Party, remain concerned about their place in the new South African society. At the extreme, many members of the white far right continue to harbor dreams of an independent Afrikaner *volkstaat* ("homeland").[9] In the 1990s especially, many blacks too, notably the supporters of the IFP in KwaZulu-Natal, sought some degree of autonomy from ANC dominance. Indeed, the dissatisfaction with the range of powers granted the provinces under the interim constitution led the IFP and others initially to refuse to participate in the 1994 election. Paradoxically, though the interim constitution did not grant territorial autonomy, it did help to alleviate some of these concerns, in part by suggesting that federalism would be a component of a future South African polity.[10]

In fact, however, federalism was weakened in the 1996 document, which centralized many government functions and institutions and strengthened the position of the national parliament vis-à-vis provincial legislatures.[11] The federal senate was replaced as the upper house by the National Council of Provinces (NCOP), which was intended to have greater contact with the provinces. Critics saw these steps as evidence of continued consolidation not only of central government power but also of ANC power specifically (Jeffery 1998, 39–41; Mattes 2002). And in many respects these constitutional changes mirrored centralization of ANC power. Nevertheless, the 1996 constitution was presumed to be relatively insulated from political interference, since constitutional changes required a two-thirds majority, which the ANC did not have at that time.[12]

Concerns about ANC dominance and minority rights were heightened further when the Constitutional Court approved an amendment (signed into law in 2003) that lifted the constitutional prohibitions on party mergers and "floor-crossing" by MPs between elections. This immediately resulted in a two-thirds parliamentary majority for the ANC, allowing it to change the constitution unilaterally. Ironically, as James Myburgh (2003, 36) notes, this "greatly diminishes the status of the Constitutional Court," the institution charged with protecting democracy in South Africa. "If the court strikes down legislation, the ANC now has the choice of altering the law to make it comply, or changing the constitution." The ANC cemented its super majority by taking 279 seats (69.7 percent) in the 2004 national elections; however, fears of constitution tampering appear to have been exaggerated. Besides, the ANC lost seats in the 2009 election, falling to 264 (Independent Electoral Commission of South Africa 2009).

Judiciary

The 1993 constitution established the principle of constitutional supremacy in South Africa; this was reaffirmed in the "final" constitution. In this sense, the constitution is the supreme law, and "all government bodies, including parliament, were subjected to it, and any action, including parliamentary legislation, inconsistent with the constitution was invalid" (Malherbe 1998, 86). Thus the newly created Constitutional Court became the highest court in South Africa for adjudication of constitutional matters. The Constitutional Court consists of the chief justice, who also presides over the Supreme Court; a deputy; and nine other judges, each of whom serves a single twelve-year term. Below the Constitutional Court are the Supreme Court of Appeal, the High Courts, and the Magistrate Courts.[13] "High Courts have jurisdiction in all constitutional matters," except those exclusively reserved to the Constitutional Court (Malherbe 1998, 91). The Supreme Court hears, at its discretion, appeal cases, including constitutional cases. It consists of the president, a deputy president, and eighteen judges of appeal. By 2010, nearly two decades after apartheid, the court remained disproportionately white—nearly half its members—and male; the court's five women members all joined beginning in 2003.

As a creation of the new South Africa, the Constitutional Court is multiracial. More important, its members are guided by the principal functions of the 1996 constitution, which in its preamble include the desire to "heal the divisions of the past and establish a society based on democratic values, social justice and fundamental human rights; Lay the foundations for a democratic and open society in which government is based on the will of the people and every citizen is equally protected by law; Improve the quality of life of all citizens and free the potential of each person." In contrast, in the lower courts, white judges, predominantly apartheid-era appointees, outnumbered nonwhites by a two-to-one margin well into the first decade of the twenty-first century; not all of them subscribed to these values. Judicial tenure and civil service protections meant that many members of the judiciary were in fact staunch supporters of apartheid laws. It is a further irony, then, that changes in the South African judicial and political system granted judges far more autonomy and independence than they had enjoyed under the previous system. Absent a jury system model, South African law rests squarely with judges. In situations where judges may lack objectivity, this can foster a crisis of jurisprudence and loss of faith in the system.[14]

Only about 62 percent of South Africans have confidence in the judicial system, although on the whole South Africans appear to have comparably low levels of trust in all national institutions (Mattes 2008). Questions certainly have been raised about the level of political interference in the judicial system, most notably concerning high-profile cases involving ANC officials and corruption. The present president, Jacob Zuma, was implicated in a corruption scandal as early as 2003 but not prosecuted until two years later. After considerable delays on the part of prosecutors, the case against Zuma was eventually dropped in 2008 on procedural grounds; the judge himself accused the state prosecuting authority of politicizing the cases against Zuma.

On the other hand, the courts have also been the site of confidence-restoring verdicts. For example, the 2010 conviction of former police head and ANC stalwart Jackie Selebi, on bribery charges, helped send a signal that "high profile figures are not completely immune" from criminal prosecution (EIU 2010d). It is very likely that South Africa's judicial system, and criminal justice system as a whole, will continue to navigate this course between criticisms of its practices, both those deemed too passive and pro-ANC and those that go against the government or its officials.

Executive

The presidency. Most of the countries in southern Africa adopted direct elections for their presidents shortly after independence as a means of centralizing executive power. South Africa's president, by contrast, is elected by the National Assembly immediately after its seating. The South African president is required to be an elected member of the National Assembly; he or she must vacate his or her seat upon being elected president, which is then filled from the party list. Although this does not ensure legislative oversight, at the very least it preserves some of the linkages between the executive and the legislature found in the parliamentary model. In spite of these institutional constraints, however, the executive is unquestionably the dominant actor in the South African system, and "few mechanisms exist with which the legislature may check executive action" (Mattes 2002, 24). Executive power became more concentrated, in practice if not in law, under President Thabo Mbeki, who was first elected to succeed Mandela in 1999.

At first glance, this is somewhat surprising, since some constraints exist on the institutional powers of the presidency. For example, the South African president does not have veto power but can refer bills back to parliament or to the Constitutional Court. The president chairs meetings of the cabinet, but this body, which attempts to reach decisions by consensus, is ultimately accountable to parliament. However, whereas cabinet members—and the larger parliament through the vote-of-no-confidence maneuver—are theoretically able to impose constraints on presidential authority, postapartheid new South Africa is a place of strong parties and party loyalties. More precisely, it remains a dominant-party system, much like the apartheid-era system, but with the ANC replacing the NP at its apex. Thus, when President Mbeki was held to account, it was to the national ANC leadership to a far greater degree than to the legislature, which the party dominates. Despite his power within the ANC, Mbeki's successor, Jacob Zuma, operates within similar party-institutional strictures. In practice, however, the party's strength and rigid hierarchy generally redound to the state president's benefit, since he is also president of the ANC. Both party leaders and rank and file are generally loathe to risk a challenge to the authority or legislative initiatives of the president, since doing so risks expulsion from the party and parliament.

This logic was turned on its head, however, in 2007 when, with nearly two years left in his second term, Thabo Mbeki was ousted from the ANC presidency at a tumultuous party congress. Mbeki's removal was actually set into motion in 2005, when he sacked Jacob Zuma, who was then his deputy president. Zuma had been a longtime ally of Mbeki's and was Mbeki's presumed successor; he was a hero of the antiapartheid movement, not least among his own ethnic Zulus. However, Zuma was implicated in a corruption scandal, which allowed Mbeki both to distance himself from his erstwhile comrade and to sideline an emergent rival for the leadership of the ANC. Although Zuma's alleged involvement in a corrupt transaction with a French arms company dating back to 1999 had long been part of South Africa's political chatter, it came to a head when Zuma's financial adviser, Schabir Shaik, was sentenced to fifteen years in prison for soliciting bribes. Zuma was alleged to have helped shield the company from investigators. In fact, from at least 2003 on the ANC and legal authorities believed there to be a case against Zuma but declined initially to seek prosecution. When prosecutors only took up the Zuma case in 2005, the timing suggested that the ANC was motivated more by politics than by the pursuit of justice.

Although Mbeki's maneuver was initially effective, his increasing detachment from the base—owing to his unpopular economic policies and alienation
from key party supporters—served to isolate him within the party. In the meantime, Zuma came increasingly to be seen as a populist martyr, particularly by
the working class, the unemployed, and Zulu nationalists. When the charges
against Zuma were dropped in September 2008 on technical grounds—in
another highly politicized legal environment—Mbeki's downfall as president
was sealed. He resigned the state presidency in September 2008.

Mbeki had lost control of the party in December 2007 at a congress at
Polokwane but had been expected to continue in office as a lame duck to the end
of his term. Yet when the court declared in September 2008 that the charges were
improperly brought against Zuma, Zuma's rise was assured. Mbeki resigned the
presidency, and the parliament elected Kgalema Motlanthe, a Zuma ally, as a
caretaker president. Upon the ANC's election victory in April 2009, Zuma was
elected to the presidency.

The Mbeki presidency is particularly intriguing because despite its igno-
minious end, throughout most of his nearly two terms, critics were regularly
preoccupied with concerns about his concentration of power in the wake of the
magnanimous Mandela. For instance, constitutionally, the president is limited
to two five-year terms. Yet this long failed to allay the concerns of the ANC's
rivals that with a two-thirds majority in parliament (which it achieved in 2004)
the ANC would simply change the constitution to allow its president more
time in office, as the ruling party did (for one election only) in Namibia. While
such criticisms are unpersuasive, President Mbeki did occasionally display an
intolerance of dissent and a paranoia about threats both real and imagined
(Mattes 2002; Gevisser 2009). Moreover, although there is no evidence to suggest that Mbeki sought a constitutional amendment to extend his term, he was
determined to seek an extraordinary third term as ANC *party* president
(Hamill 2008). All in all, though both Presidents Mbeki and Zuma have displayed at times imperious behavior, it appears that the principle of presidential
term limits has been institutionalized at the national level.

The cabinet. Cabinet ministers are appointed by and serve at the discretion of
the president and are selected from among sitting MPs. The president may also
appoint up to two ministers who are not members of parliament, and the size
of the cabinet is not constitutionally prescribed; it numbered 27 or 28 members in the first several governments. And although this was a fairly large
grouping even by regional standards, the cabinet in the current Zuma government numbers 34 ministers.

Even the original GNU cabinet, which had a compelling mandate for
inclusion, had just 27 members (excluding deputy ministers, who are not
members of the cabinet), including 7 and 3 positions apportioned to the NP
and IFP, respectively. Although the GNU effectively collapsed with the

National Party's withdrawal in June 1996, the IFP continued its governing partnership with the ANC. Mbeki's 1999–2004 cabinet included 3 members of the IFP who held the arts and culture, corrections, and home affairs portfolios; the latter was held by IFP party leader Mangosuthu Buthelezi. The cabinet reshuffle following the April 2004 election saw the dismissal of Buthelezi and the refusal of 2 IFP members of parliament to assume deputy ministerial posts, while the New National Party (NNP) and the left-wing Azanian People's Organization party were awarded 2 ministerial appointments. The practice of appointing opposition members to the cabinet, so essential during the early years of the transition, is today nearly moribund. In President Zuma's cabinet, reshuffled in October 2010, 3 ministers are affiliated with the SACP; however, given the party's long-standing electoral alliance with ANC, this distinction is not especially meaningful in practice. Interestingly, Zuma has reached across party lines in certain deputy ministerial appointments: Pieter Mulder, the leader of the far right Freedom Front–Plus party that has 4 seats in parliament, is deputy minister of agriculture.

Each of South Africa's four postapartheid presidents has also used cabinet appointments to reflect the gender, racial, and ethnic diversity of the country. Mandela's 28-member post-GNU 1996–1999 cabinet included 18 Africans (14 men and 4 women), 4 Indians, 3 Coloureds, and 2 whites (Venter 1998, 64). Although Mbeki initially appeared somewhat less inclined to mimic the inclusiveness of Mandela, he too sought ethnic, racial, and gender balance in his cabinet appointments, which included 4 Indians and 3 whites; in 2004, 5 women were placed at the helm of ministries. Zuma, with his expanded cabinet, has appointed 14 women (more than 40 percent—the highest in the region), although the racial composition, which in early 2011 included 4 Indians, 2 whites, and 1 Coloured, is similar to the past.

The president may also appoint a deputy president from the sitting MPs. In the first postapartheid government, Mandela selected as deputy presidents Mbeki, who had been part of the ANC's leadership in exile during apartheid, and the former state president F. W. de Klerk. The appointment of de Klerk was part of the arrangement for the GNU, in which the NP's second-place finish entitled it to the position.[15] In Mandela's administration, Mbeki effectively ran most of the day-to-day activities of the government as deputy president, while Mandela tended to more symbolic functions. Since the constitutional changes in 1996 and de Klerk's subsequent withdrawal of the National Party from the GNU, only one deputy president remains. Thus, when Mbeki became president himself in 1999, he appointed Jacob Zuma as his deputy. The powers and functions of the deputy president are as limited or expansive as those assigned him by the president. Indeed, the constitution (Chapter 5, Sections 91–92) simply states that "the Deputy President must assist the President in the execution of the functions of government."

Military

Transformation of the armed forces. South Africa's apartheid-era military, the South Africa Defense Force (SADF), was notorious for its role in destabilizing the region as part of then prime minister (and later president) P. W. Botha's Total Strategy. Begun in 1977, the Total Strategy linked domestic security and intelligence efforts with a program of regional destabilization designed to root out the ANC and other antigovernment groups operating externally, increase the economic dependence of regional neighbors on South Africa, and ultimately maintain South Africa as a preserve of apartheid and capitalism. As part of this strategy, the SADF intervened militarily in Angola on behalf of that country's UNITA allies, conducted bombing campaigns in Mozambique and elsewhere, and engaged in clandestine activities throughout the region (Minter 1994). Operating with other intelligence and security arms of the state, the military was also involved in gross human rights violations, including torture and biological warfare experimentation (TRC 1999). In short, notwithstanding Botha's insistence that South Africa in the 1970s and 1980s faced a "total communist onslaught," the actions of the SADF could only be seen as "defensive" by this perverse logic.

The transition to majority rule necessitated fundamental changes in the way South Africa's military conducted its affairs. Symbolically, the armed forces were renamed the South African *National* Defense Force (SANDF) to reflect the domestic and defensive nature of the new military, rather than its being a source of regional destabilization.[16] Moreover, the armed forces faced the formidable task of integration. Since the SADF had literally been on the "front lines" of apartheid, and numerous senior civilian and military leaders of the armed forces were later implicated in apartheid-era crimes, this was an exceedingly complex task. The integration imperative also impacted the liberation movements, whose soldiers and paramilitaries were expected to be combined into the new national force. In addition to the SADF, the liberation movements had armed forces, as did several of the former "black homelands" (although they lacked sovereignty). The process of integrating these former rivals swelled the size of the armed forces well beyond the target of a combined force of 70,000 by May 1997. Indeed, by the late 1990s there were 100,000 military personnel, including 18,300 former members of Umkhonto we Sizwe (Spear of the Nation; the ANC's armed wing), 5,700 former members of the Azanian People's Liberation Army (the PAC's armed wing), and 11,500 former members of the homeland armies (du Toit 2001, 119). As of 2005, the SANDF was around 70 percent black (a designation including Indians and Coloureds). Whereas the senior ranks are mixed, whites continued to represent 41 percent of officers as of 2009, whereas black Africans represented 47 percent, Coloureds 12 percent, Indians 0.5 (Heinecken and van der Waag-Cowling 2009: 520).[17]

The military as economic actor. South Africa's apartheid-era military-industrial complex was extensive. It was not only a major purchaser of weaponry but also a major arms manufacturer as well. The state-owned weapons manufacturer, Armscor, was established in 1968. According to HRW (2000): "By 1994 South Africa had established itself as the tenth largest arms producer in the world, with approximately 800 arms and arms component manufacturers employing a workforce of 50,000 (down from 160,000 in the 1980s)." Weapons were produced for both domestic and international purposes. Consistent with the National Party's regional strategy, Armscor "was virtually given a free hand in pursuing lucrative markets that often turned out to be located where gross human rights abuses were taking place." However, an arms export scandal exposed in 1994 led to the appointment of an independent commission and subsequently the adoption of major reforms to and restrictions on the arms export regime. The new policies included a strong human rights plank.

As in nearly all developing countries, military spending is controversial; states that are unable to provide basic needs nonetheless spend heavily on militaries. Moreover, these forces are seldom used in defense of national sovereignty, but instead perform domestic police functions, often repressively (Ball 1988). Like the state it replaced, postapartheid South Africa faces no perceptible external military threats. Hence the role of the military in the posttransition environment demanded a reevaluation of its budget allocation. The 1995–1996 Strategic Defense Review suggested that military expenditure would remain more or less constant in the 1990s, at 9.7 billion rand per year. Yet military expenditures continued to increase through the early part of the first decade of the twenty-first century; these included a highly controversial arms purchase in 1999.[18] Despite improved security conditions and declines in the offensive *and* defensive capacity of the South African military,[19] spending reached 6.74 percent of government expenditure in 1999. The peak was 6.45 percent of government expenditure (1.78 percent of GDP) in 2002; from there the figure declined measurably, to 4.42 percent of spending in 2008 (World Bank Data Bank, nd).

Representation and Participation

Legislature

South Africa has a bicameral parliament consisting of a 400-member lower house, the National Assembly, whose members are elected directly every five years, and a 90-member upper house, the National Council of Provinces, whose members are elected from the nine provinces. The NCOP, which "is subordinate to the National Assembly because it has less formal power" (Calland 1999, 22), is intended to represent provincial interests. However, as noted above, the NCOP is only a partial substitute for the broad federal powers anticipated during the transition and in drafting the 1993 constitution. Thus the purpose of the NCOP is to provide "a national forum for public consideration of issues affecting the provinces" (Taljaard and Venter 1998, 36). When the National Assembly passes a bill, it goes to the NCOP, which can then pass the bill, pass it subject to amendments, or reject it; in the latter cases, it goes back to the National Assembly for reconsideration (Taljaard and Venter 1998, 44). However, the National Assembly is clearly the superior legislative body in this framework.[20] Further, the NCOP is actually several steps removed from its provincial constituents: NCOP members are not popularly elected; rather they are nominated by the elected members of the provincial assemblies and represented proportionally, on the basis of their party's share of provincial legislative seats. Since the ANC dominates eight of nine provincial governments, as well as the national parliament, power remains concentrated instead in the party and in the executive (Rapoo 2001).

While lacking single-member constituencies, even these "local-regional" bodies have little local orientation (Lodge 1999). Indeed, for both houses, the legislative-constituency link is quite weak; this is the result of a structural constraint of the party list proportional representation electoral system, which privileges party loyalty. Combined with the lack of single-member constituencies, voters have very limited actual influence over their designated legislators (Mattes 2002, 24).

In South Africa, the proportional representation system is used without minimum electoral thresholds (for example, requiring a party to receive 5 percent of the vote before obtaining any seats in parliament); thus the number of parties represented in the National Assembly increased from 7 in 1994 to 13 in 1999. Although the number dropped slightly, to 10, in 2004, by 2009 there were again 13 parties represented. The number of seats held by most parties declined, however, while the ANC increased its numerical advantage. Following the historic 1994 elections (shown in Table 9.2), the ANC held a 62.65 percent majority (or 252 seats) in the National Assembly. In the 1999 election it reached 66.36 percent (266 seats), or just one seat short of a two-thirds majority. In 2004 the ANC's 289 seats reflected nearly 70 percent of the vote. Although the ANC's seat total dropped to 264 in 2009, this hardly represents a meaningful flight from the party. All in all, the ANC's continued electoral dominance since 1994 has come at the cost of the diversity of opinion and debate in parliament (Independent Electoral Commission 2009).

As noted above, parliament is supposed to have oversight over the executive as in the traditional parliamentary model. In practice, South Africa's executive is the dominant institution, contributing to a trend of executive concentration of power. Indeed, this is so severe that, as Mattes (2002, 27) notes, "parliament may continue to play an active role in developing and amending legislation in areas of no great interest to the executive, but when there is a dif-

Table 9.2   South African National Election, 1994

Party	Number of Valid Votes	Percentage	Number of Seats
African Christian Democratic Party	88,104	0.45	2
African Democratic Movement	9,886	0.05	0
African Moderates Congress Party	27,690	0.14	0
African Muslim Party	34,466	0.18	0
African National Congress	12,237,655	62.65	252
Democratic Party	338,426	1.73	7
Dikwankwetla Party of South Africa	19,451	0.10	0
Freedom Front	424,555	2.17	9
Federal Party	17,663	0.09	0
Inkatha Freedom Party	2,058,294	10.54	43
Keep It Straight and Simple	5,916	0.03	0
Luso-SA Party	3,293	0.02	0
Minority Front	13,433	0.07	0
National Party	3,983,690	20.39	82
Pan Africanist Congress	243,478	1.25	5
Soccer Party	10,575	0.05	0
Women's Rights Peace Party	6,434	0.03	0
Workers List Party	4,169	0.02	0
Ximoko Progressive Party	6,320	0.03	0
Total	19,533,498	99.99[a]	400

Source: Independent Electoral Commission 2003.
Notes: Registered voters: 22,709,152; total ballots (nonvalid included): 19,726,610; voter turnout: 86.87 percent.
a. Total does not equal 100 due to rounding.

ference of opinion on matters that are important to the executive, it will always prevail."

In sum, three clear trends are observed. First, the promise of devolution of power to local and regional governments has not been realized. On the contrary, South Africa has seen a growing centralization of authority in the national governing structures. Second, power in the South African system is vested in the executive, notwithstanding the existence of formal checks and balances. Third, it is critical to note, therefore, that the check on the executive comes not from government but from *party* institutions; hence, Mbeki's downfall came at the hands of the ANC rather than of the National Assembly. South Africa has acquired all the trappings of the dominant-party state observed elsewhere on the continent and in the region; the ANC has successfully consolidated power across all levels of government in South Africa: local, regional, and national.

Party System and Elections

By some measures, and certainly in popular discourse, South Africa is frequently regarded as a robust democracy (Freedom House 2010), although other observers are more cautious (Friedman 1999; Mattes 2002). The global euphoria sparked by the peaceful transfer in 1994 notwithstanding, South

Africa's historic election did not transform it instantly into a flourishing democracy, and little appreciated is that the election itself was beset by substantial irregularities (Lodge 1999). While many of the electoral problems have since been addressed,[21] elections are but one component of democratization. Although Staffan Lindberg (2006) suggests that iterative elections themselves habituate polities in the practice of democracy, others contend that they are insufficient to achieve democracy (Carothers 2002).

Alternation in power is also an important aspect of democratization, but this prospect appears unlikely in South Africa for the foreseeable future in the face of ANC dominance. Indeed, South Africa under the ANC bears many of the hallmarks of a one-party state. Yet the risks of such a state, even a nominally democratic one, are not insubstantial and include lack of representation or, more serious, repression of dissent. South Africa's proportional representation system, of course, was designed to alleviate the former problem, and the increased number of parties in parliament is encouraging in this regard. But an emerging popular disconnect from political life, in part related to the ANC, is a matter of great concern (*Afrobarometer* 2003b).

Yet it is unreasonable to fault the ANC alone. In the 1999 election, for example, the opposition parties were incapable of mounting a credible campaign against the popular ruling party; their principal rallying cry was the claimed need to block the ANC from gaining the constitution-changing two-thirds majority in the National Assembly, rather than substantive policy alternatives. In the 2009 election opposition parties saw perhaps their best opportunity to dilute ANC domination (see Table 9.3). In the wake of Mbeki's ouster, several ANC leaders loyal to Mbeki, including former defense minister Mosiuoa Lekota, split from the ruling party and established a new party, which they called the Congress of the People (COPE). COPE leaders believed they could make substantial headway among the anti-Zuma elements within the party; some observers believed the split could mark the end of ANC hegemony. Yet, if ANC is at all vulnerable, it is to the left wing of South African politics: dissatisfaction runs deep among the poor, for example, and the ANC's labor allies. Aligned mainly with Mbeki's legacy of center-right economic policies, however, COPE garnered a mere 7.42 percent of the vote in 2009 and attained thirty seats in parliament (see Table 9.3).

The Democratic Alliance (DA) is led by former journalist and onetime mayor of Cape Town Helen Zille. Representing mostly white and mixed-race South Africans, the DA has struggled to appeal to black South Africans, but it nonetheless significantly outperformed COPE with 16.7 percent of the vote in 2009. The DA, with its origins in the historically liberal, white, and predominantly English-speaking Democratic Party, has clearly supplanted other opposition parties as the party of choice for most white South Africans, including Afrikaners. Together with its strong backing among Coloureds, the DA captured the Western Cape provincial government in 2009—the only parliament governed

Table 9.3   2009 National Assembly Election Results

Party	Number of Votes	Percentage of Votes	Seats
African National Congress (ANC)	11,650,748	65.90	264
Democratic Alliance (DA)	2,945,829	16.66	67
Congress of the People (COPE)	1,311,027	7.42	30
Inkatha Freedom Party (IFP)	804,260	4.55	18
Independent Democrats (ID)	162,915	0.92	4
United Democratic Movement (UDM)	149,680	0.85	4
Vryheidsfront Plus	146,796	0.83	4
African Christian Democratic Party (ACDP)	142,658	0.81	3
United Christian Democratic Party (UCDP)	66,086	0.37	2
Pan Africanist Congress (PAC)	48,530	0.27	1
Minority Front (MF)	43,474	0.25	1
Azanian People's Organization (AZAPO)	38,245	0.22	1
African People's Convention	35,867	0.20	1
Others[a]	134,614	0.76	0
Total	17,680,729	100.01[b]	400

Source: Www.elections.org.za.
Notes: Registered voters: 23,181,997; total ballots: 17,919,966; spoiled ballots: 239,237; voter turnout: 77.30 percent.
   a. Thirteen other parties won marginal votes and did not win any seats in parliament.
   b. Total does not equal 100 due to rounding.

by an opposition party. Yet nationally, only about an eighth of the DAs MPs are black; as long as the ability to attract both black candidates and constituents remains a challenge, the electoral demographics will prevent the party from moving far beyond its current vote share.

The once formidable Afrikaner-oriented National Party (subsequently renamed the New National Party, NNP) was in steep decline by the time it left the GNU in 1996. In 2000 the NNP joined an electoral partnership with the liberal DA, but the union proved short-lived. The NNP reemerged a year later when the alliance collapsed, only to enter subsequently into a curious electoral alliance with its old archenemy, the ANC, in late 2001. The National Party's near-constant attempts to reinvent itself merely cemented the perception that it had lost both its ideological and racial compass—the twin sources of its former appeal—in the wake of apartheid's collapse. The National Party was awarded just seven parliamentary seats following the 2004 election. With its dwindling electoral influence confined to the Western Cape province, the party determined in mid-2004 that it would shut down entirely.

As noted above, notwithstanding ANC's impressive hold on power, there appears to be ideological and policy space in which to challenge the party's hegemony. Thus far, however, none of the established larger parties has sought to occupy it with conviction. Indeed, the ANC's unmistakable rightward shift on economic issues in the 1990s co-opted much of the neoliberal economic agenda of the Democratic Alliance and the NNP. (Other parties represent even narrower racial, ethnic, or religious agendas.) The ANC's own neoliberal economic stance would appear to make it vulnerable to a challenge by a left-wing party; however, the ANC has been able to effectively block any leftist-populist insurgency. Indeed, the only measurable split, which precipitated the founding of COPE in 2008, was a defection of centrists who had supported Mbeki and his agenda. Thus the ANC maintains its "tripartite" electoral alliance with the trade union umbrella body COSATU and the South African Communist Party, notwithstanding the fact that ANC economic policies frequently have been antithetical to leftist interests. This continues to be the case under Zuma's presidency. Although friction increased noticeably during Mbeki's tenure, particularly with the labor unions, the president and the party's dexterity at "talking left, but acting right" (Bond 2000; I. Taylor 2002) enabled them to successfully co-opt and confuse would-be opposition supporters on either side of the ideological spectrum.

There are limits to this strategy, however, and the labor movement has grown increasingly restive, particularly in the face of the economic downturn that began in 2008. In 2007, even before the downturn began, public sector unions shut down hospitals and schools, and autoworkers, mine workers, and others also went on strike, winning modest pay increases. In 2010, the country saw a series of strikes and threatened strikes that rattled the political coalition. A country-wide strike by public sector employees, who fall under the umbrella of COSATU, began in August that year over pay increases and housing allowances. Although they eventually reached a compromise settlement with the government, public sentiment was reported in the *New York Times* of September 7, 2010, to have turned against the unions both because of their violent methods and because of the sense that the unions were too little concerned with the mass of South Africans who have no jobs whatsoever. President Zuma was also criticized for his handling of the crises.

Although labor has been repeatedly outflanked by Mbeki and the ANC's prevailing neoliberalism, the unions' political clout should not be underestimated (Taylor 2009). Nevertheless, despite the periodic and occasionally volatile dissension in the ranks, thus far the ANC has proved adept at consolidating its hold on power and maintaining its partners on the left. Moreover, it has skillfully retained its MPs and found ways to attract members of smaller parties into its orbit.[22]

Beyond the intraparty dynamics of the ANC, however, there have been several indications at the popular level of growing disaffection with party politics, and perhaps democracy, as practiced in South Africa. As many as 40 percent of individuals surveyed before the 2004 election indicated that they might not vote *at all* in that election (*Afrobarometer* 2003b; Mattes 2002). Surveys conducted in 2002 had indicated an overall drop in support for all political parties, including the ANC (votes for the ANC declined to 42 percent from 56 percent two years earlier) (*Afrobarometer* 2003b). Actual voter turnouts foreshadowed this growing problem of political apathy: turnout has steadily declined "from between 86 and 92 percent of all eligible voters in 1994 to 68 percent in 1999. In 2000, turnout in local government elections stood at 48 percent of registered voters and 37 percent of all eligible voters" (*Afrobarometer* 2003b, 2–3). National turnouts since 2004 have stabilized somewhat at around 77 percent, possibly reflecting the modest improvements in the economy. A linkage of economic trends with enthusiasm for politics, coupled with the decline of party competition, continues to be a cause for concern about the direction of South Africa's democracy.

The Truth and Reconciliation Commission

The TRC was in many ways postapartheid South Africa's most remarkable achievement; it was also its greatest disappointment. When the TRC was established by the Promotion of National Unity and Reconciliation Act (1995) and began its hearings in 1996, it was widely hailed as a model for postconflict reconciliation. In contrast to regional precedent, as in Zimbabwe or Namibia, where no formal reconciliations were ever conducted, and in contrast to trials, such as those at Nuremberg following World War II, the TRC was a unique institution (Minow 1998). It consisted of three related activities. The Human Rights Violations Committee was charged with taking written statements and hearing oral testimonies in an attempt to establish a record of apartheid-era crimes and determine a narrative truth about perpetrators and victims of crimes. The Amnesty Committee determined whether or not applicants would be granted amnesty in return for their testimony—"truth telling"—to the TRC about their involvement in an act that was deemed to be *political;* nonpolitical criminal activity was ineligible and a matter for the legal system. The applicant was not required to show contrition, and the victims or their families were not required to grant forgiveness, although clearly this was desired by some of the principals on the TRC (Tutu 1999). Finally, the Reparations and Rehabilitation Committee was charged with ascertaining who should be compensated as victims of apartheid-era violence and with determining appropriate restitution.

The most prominent of the TRC's three committees was the Human Rights Violations Committee, which was chaired by the retired Anglican archbishop and Nobel Peace Prize winner Desmond Tutu. Tutu saw the work of the commission as an essential component of the postapartheid healing process and argued that South Africa could not move forward unless its citizens came to grips with its past through full disclosure of the horrors of apartheid. Supporters of the process believed that, in contrast to punitive trials, the TRC would encourage national healing through forgiveness; unlike in postwar Germany, for example, in South Africa both victims and perpetrators would have to live among one another in the postconflict environment. Punishment, TRC advocates argued, would lead to a cycle of hostilities that might irreparably tear the fabric of the new nation (Minow 1998).

The TRC, which held hearings from 1996 to 1998, is now recognized as a sincere if deeply flawed process (Minow 1998; Krog 1999; Wilson 2001; Graybill 2002). Among other problems, its scope may have been too limited. For example, the commission limited its inquiry to the period from March 1960 (the date of the Sharpeville Massacre, arguably the onset of apartheid-era violence) to April 1994 (the date of the transition). In addition, the TRC investigated only 9,980 deaths. Yet between September 1984 and May 1994 alone there were some 20,500 deaths directly related to apartheid policies and the transition process, indicating that the TRC barely scratched the surface (du Toit 2001, 33). From the start, as du Toit (2001, 32) notes, the number of potential cases meant that the TRC faced "an unattainable task." Another problem was that the TRC received 21,298 submissions or testimonies, but held only 700 public hearings. As a result, many individual victims for whom public truth *telling* might have proved cathartic indeed were merely able to present their stories to a lone TRC representative (Wilson 2001).

In addition, the TRC failed to secure the testimony of, or in many cases even identify, the principal architects of apartheid. While policemen and agents of the security and intelligence services were an occasional presence, very few of apartheid's leaders were ever called to account. Former president P. W. Botha defied the TRC's demand to appear. His successor, F. W. de Klerk, simply denied any knowledge of or responsibility for political killings carried out under his presidency—even though his denials directly contradicted testimony of subordinates. Moreover, the prosecutorial mechanism largely failed to convict, and in many cases to even try, alleged perpetrators like biological weapons scientist Wouter Basson, former defense minister Magnus Malan, Botha, and others who refused to cooperate with the TRC.[23] On the other side, Nelson Mandela's former wife and chair of the ANC Women's League, Winnie Mandela, downplayed her culpability in political murders of ANC rivals in the late 1980s and early 1990s. In short, "truth" was not always attainable, even in the absence of punishment.

In terms of the prospects for healing generated by the TRC, these too must be questioned. Most white South Africans failed to buy into the process, whether or not they were directly involved in the perpetration of apartheid (Tutu 1999; Wilson 2001). Similarly, the reparations committee, tasked with arguably one of the most important functions of the TRC, proved inadequate. It was not until 2003 that one-time payments of 30,000 rand (roughly US$4,000) each were determined and allocated to some 22,000 victims and their families. The delay and the amount of the restitution were a source of considerable bitterness.

Thus it appears that, at best, the TRC was a vehicle for initiating a national dialogue and in that sense had additive value. Du Toit (2001, 35) argues that the TRC made "a modest contribution to the factual knowledge on the subject of political violence." However, it is not clear what impact it had on popular attitudes. In a 2003 survey (Institute for Justice and Reconciliation 2003), for example, 73.6 percent of black respondents saw whites as having profited *and continuing to profit* from apartheid, whereas just 22.4 percent of whites felt the same way. Indeed, 90 percent of white respondents thought that South Africans should just move on with their lives. In the context of southern Africa, "forgive and forget" is a better method for *deferring* rather than preventing conflict. Conversely, *durable* institutional solutions can help create channels for mediation, communication, and future resolution of conflicts. If South Africa is any more "healed" for having gone through the TRC process, the degree of healing may ultimately prove shallow. This realization, along with South Africa's festering problems with crime, inequality, AIDS, and so forth, continues to threaten to undermine the democratic experiment. To some degree, South Africa's civil society organizations help to preserve the democratic tendencies and compensate for the state's shortcomings.

Civil Society and Social Groups

South Africa has a plethora of civic organizations and a vibrant civil society. It has sophisticated media in multiple languages, activist NGOs, and a historically powerful labor movement. Many of these organizations can trace their development as centers of power outside the state to the apartheid era. Despite the draconian nature of the apartheid state, including its restrictions on movement, labor, association, and so forth, many groups honed their skills in that social context. Indeed, the constraints of apartheid, in which society was tightly circumscribed, and the state was only a tool of repression, compelled the creation of alternative means of interest articulation within communities.

Editors and journalists of black and liberal white media faced harassment and banning during the apartheid years, and many publications were closed by the state. Similarly, political organizations were banned and forced to operate underground. Trade unions, key players in anticolonial movements around the continent, were legalized much later in South Africa than elsewhere in Africa. Initially resistant, the apartheid state gradually acquiesced with many of the demands of organized labor as the significance of an increasingly skilled black labor force to the white South African economy could no longer be ignored. Business associations also became key players in the apartheid era, and a number of them arguably have as great an influence today (Taylor 2007). In addition, religious organizations provided both the greatest supporters and the staunchest opponents of apartheid. The various churches in the South African Council of Churches (SACC), for example, played an instrumental role in attacking apartheid both domestically and internationally in the 1980s, whereas the Dutch Reformed Church supplied apartheid's theological foundations. Similarly, cultural groups such as Inkatha (which later established the political party IFP) helped solidify Zulu nationalism and opposition to apartheid, though

Inkatha supporters eventually came into conflict with ANC supporters between the dismantling of apartheid in 1992 and the 1994 elections, with deadly results. Long-standing groups like the Afrikaner Broederbond helped cement Afrikaner nationalism and were part of a class project to elevate the status and socioeconomic position of Afrikaners (Dubow 1995; du Toit 1995).

Many of the other civil society organizations that began to emerge in the late 1980s and early 1990s also helped to unravel apartheid. Policy advocacy organizations especially thrived in this period. Amid great uncertainty, many of these groups attempted to promote a particular type of democratic and political reform and lobbied both domestically and internationally for change. Among these were organizations that continue to this day, including the Institute for a Democratic Alternative in South Africa (IDASA), the South African Institute of Race Relations, and the Center for Policy Studies, which generally support a liberal democratic model and liberal to progressive economic policies.

In the wake of the successful transition, the number of NGOs expanded further and many altered their mandates. Included among those civic organizations are those actively engaged in the fight against HIV/AIDS. Such organizations have persevered despite an initial resistance in South African political and social circles to discussing the disease and providing access to antiretroviral drugs (see Chapter 10). The South African government has been rather Janus-faced about the issue of AIDS. President Mandela, especially in retirement, has been an outspoken advocate for those facing the disease; his government, led by Thabo Mbeki, aggressively and successfully challenged World Trade Organization rules, multinational pharmaceutical companies, and their Western governments for the right to distribute generic AIDS drugs in South Africa. As president, however, Thabo Mbeki actually led the charge against antiretroviral drugs, questioned the etiological links between HIV and AIDS, and appointed a health minister, Manto Tshabalala-Msimang, who advocated beet root as a legitimate treatment for the disease. President Jacob Zuma and his government have been far more proactive in the dual campaigns to prevent and provide treatment for HIV/AIDS.

Thus, in a national environment in which leading government officials were initially uncooperative and the wider society in denial, civil society organizations (CSOs) have overcome tremendous obstacles. A noteworthy victory came in 2003, for example, when the Treatment Action Campaign (TAC) enlisted the support of the South African Medical Association and religious organizations and compelled the government to make antiretrovirals available to HIV-positive pregnant women and others at risk from the virus.

South African civil society's mobilization clearly reached its zenith late in the struggle against apartheid and in the transition period. The culture of civic activity and organization flourished, at least initially, in the new liberal postapartheid environment, but that activity is more erratic and diverse today as the transition to democracy, which served as a catalyst for mobilization, has passed. This is not to say, however, that the policies of the new South African state do not engender protest, as well as support, among societal actors. Yet whereas civil society organizations such as the unions, AIDS activists, and religious groups have each found ample grounds to challenge the state, particularly on policies perceived as hostile to the poor and labor, their activity generally has lacked the coordination seen in the past.

Whereas South Africa is undeniably "procedurally" democratic under the ANC government (Bratton and van de Walle 1997), it lacks many of the *substantive* aspects of democracy, which are concerned with delivery—access to resources, improved quality of life, and the like (Mattes 2002; Friedman 1999). Although these shortcomings might be expected to form an area of coordinated, intense, and sustained debate, this has not materialized. This has led critics on the left to call for a remobilization of churches, NGOs, and even the unions to oppose the ANC's continued embrace of neoliberal economic policies and an agenda seen as "anti-poor" (Saul 1999, 39; Bond 2006).

The media. South Africa's print and broadcast media are among the most vibrant on the continent. Newspapers have a long tradition. Television broadcasts were introduced only in 1976, but today the country has half a dozen free channels and five subscription stations, making it one of Africa's most diverse markets. Its satellite broadcasters, Mnet, DSTV, and TopTV, have made inroads throughout the African continent. In the old days of apartheid, the English-language press was one of the few media voices that spoke out against the system, though this was limited to one or two newspapers. Most, in fact, supported the National Party fairly consistently. The Afrikaans-language press, of course, was unabashedly pro-NP (Williams 1998, 192). Today the Afrikaans- and English-language presses both are more outspoken in their criticism of the ANC state than they were of apartheid governments. On the one hand, this stems from the democratization process itself and the fact that press freedoms are enshrined in the constitution. On the other hand, the ANC resents press criticism, and some analysts argue that English-language editors in particular have responded to ANC pressures by being less outspoken (Williams 1998, 195). Nonetheless, the sheer diversity of print outlets today provides far more opportunities for a vigorous fourth estate in South Africa.

The broadcast media have also diversified, though the publicly owned South African Broadcasting Corporation (SABC) remains the dominant actor. The SABC is a state-owned enterprise, but the Broadcasting Act of 1999 seeks to fully commercialize its operation. This is in marked contrast to the state-dominated broadcast networks in other countries in the region, however. In 2009 a draft broadcasting bill proposed giving the communications minister control over SABC finance and its board. The bill was withdrawn following sustained criticism ("South Africa Padayachie Pulls Plug" 2010), but it and other attempts to curb South Africa's media indicate a reactionary impulse on the part of the ANC. A corresponding risk is that of self-censorship. As Tom Lodge (1999, 204) argues, the SABC gained considerable praise as even-handed and impartial in the 1994 election. However, in the 1999 election, "a series of contentious staff changes at the SABC in early 1999 . . . effectively placed journalists with strong ANC affiliations in charge of the news," a maneuver that led to accusations that radio and television broadcasts were biased toward the ANC and eroded the national broadcaster's credibility.

For their part, South African media critics have expressed concerns about further media *commercialization:* that it will only deepen the corporation's reliance on advertising revenues. Such private sector "dependence means that programming continues to be marked in many ways by racism, sexism and classism, as advertisers skew programming mainly towards white middle-class men" (Duncan 2000). The commercialization strategy has progressed, in any event. As of 2009, some 64 percent of the SABC's revenue derived from advertising ("South Africa Padayachie Pulls Plug" 2010).

Religious communities. According to the 2001 census, the population of South Africa is just under 80 percent Christian. The Muslim and Hindu populations are negligible as a percentage of the population, but represent significant minorities—654,064 and 551,669—in absolute terms (Statistics South Africa 2001, 27). In the 1990s, there were 30,000 Christian churches in South Africa, representing some 130 denominations (Tingle 1998), and this number has continued to increase, particularly among charismatic or pentecostal Christian churches (Pew Forum on Religion and Public Life 2006).

Despite its overwhelmingly Christian orientation, as noted earlier, the churches have played an ambiguous role in South African history. The Dutch Reformed Church (DRK) actually provided a religious justification for apartheid, seeking to explain the subjugation of blacks under apartheid in biblical terms. In fact, the first prime minister elected under apartheid in 1948, Daniel Malan, was a DRK minister (Dubow 1995). However, when the DRK declared racism to be a sin in 1986, its declaration helped create a basis for the reform and eventual demise of apartheid among the deeply religious Afrikaner population (Tingle 1998, 200).

In contrast to the DRK, many of the other Protestant churches were important actors in the antiapartheid struggle as members of the South African Council of Churches and the Institute for Contextual Theology. The SACC, which was a prominent platform for antiapartheid theologians such as Archbishop Tutu and the Reverend Allan Boesak, was seen as aligned with the ANC by the late 1980s (Tingle 1998, 204).

In the contemporary period, certain ties of "solidarity" persist between the ANC and the church umbrella body. These linkages were strained when the ANC firmly embraced a neoliberal economic model in 1996 (the Growth, Employment, and Redistribution program; GEAR), which the churches believed hostile to the poor, ostensibly the ANC's (and the churches') primary constituency. Despite South Africa's poverty rates, however, the SACC has not resumed the "oppositional" role it assumed in the 1980s. Other denominations, such as the evangelical churches (which have gained an enormous foothold in the wider region), began to affiliate with the SACC only in the late 1990s. Yet they tend to be concerned with the perceived decline of social mores under ANC rule, following the legalization of abortion, pornography, and gambling, for example (Tingle 1998, 219). As is the case throughout sub-Saharan Africa, so-called renewalist (pentecostal and charismatic) churches are growing in South Africa at a rapid pace. The Pew Forum on Religion and Public Life (2006) found that the percentage of the country's population that self-described as renewalists exceeded 34 percent.

Trade unions. Although it got a comparatively late start, the trade union movement was instrumental in bringing about an end to apartheid. Through such umbrella bodies as the Congress of South African Trade Unions, the black unions organized strikes, mobilized community boycotts, and engaged in mass protests at a time when the core leadership of the various liberation movements was either in jail or in exile. In recognition of that role and the close alliance between the 1.7 million–member COSATU and the ANC, the two left-leaning bodies joined together with the ANC's longtime ally the South African Communist Party to form a governing partnership in the postapartheid government. Despite these ties, labor (like the SACP) is, at best, a junior partner in the alliance and has long complained that the ANC simply dictates policies rather than engaging in consultation. As noted earlier, however, South Africa's labor bodies have begun to flex their considerable, if long dormant, muscle—first, through their role in undermining Mbeki and, second, through escalating strike activity that paralyzed numerous sectors, particularly after 2008.

Many of those in labor and on the left assumed that the ascendance of Jacob Zuma—who comfortably adopted the mantle of a populist outsider following his split with Mbeki—would improve these relations. Despite occasional rhetoric, however, Zuma, much like his predecessors, has largely governed from the center. Hence, the government's economic policies have tended to run afoul of its putative labor allies.

Labor's disaffection with ANC economic policy actually began shortly after the 1994 transition. The adoption of the GEAR program in 1996, with its inherent hostility to labor interests, was the first egregious example of what COSATU considered ambush tactics by the ANC (Mattes 2002, 26). As discussed in the following section, the ANC refused to negotiate any aspect of the GEAR program, despite labor objections (Bond 2000). However, the fact that SACP and COSATU MPs sit in parliament as ANC members severely curtails their ability to challenge the party (Mattes 2002, 26).

In the meantime, South Africa's economy faces a labor crisis that has been exacerbated by deindustrialization in key sectors. Unemployment was already extremely high in 1994—31.5 percent by the so-called broad measure. Expectations that overall economic conditions, especially jobs, would improve as envisioned in the initial ANC development strategy, the Reconstruction and Development Program (RDP), were a key part of COSATU concessions to and compromise with its ANC partners in the early 1990s. Yet, the moderately more labor-friendly RDP was replaced by GEAR in 1996, following which jobless levels increased to around 40 percent among blacks, who make up the bulk of union membership. Some 500,000 formal sector jobs were lost between 1994 and 1997, putting a rapid and severe strain on South Africa's "miracle." Black South Africans are disproportionately affected by retrenchments, followed by the Coloured community.

Nevertheless, despite numerous disagreements within the tripartite alliance,[24] any unraveling will not be orchestrated by the ANC. Indeed, the ANC has every incentive to attempt to placate its leftist partners, and it has variously attempted to do so through a range of concessions—on wages, for example (S. Taylor 2009)—albeit not on the overall macroeconomic strategy. Notwithstanding recent tensions, the ANC has more control over the political direction of the union federation only while ANC remains in a close, formal relationship with the labor body. The experience of Zambia's and Zimbabwe's dominant-party states, which saw the rapid rise of formidable, electorally successful labor-based parties, is not lost on ANC elites (Bond and Manyanya 2002). Hence, despite the ouster of Mbeki that cheered the unions, the ANC will continue to "talk left" even as it "acts right." As the following section shows, however, the ANC appears to have abandoned nearly all but its rhetorical claim to the left; therefore it is unclear if the party will be able to co-opt, and thereby contain, labor interests ad infinitum.

Fundamentals of the Political Economy

Labor friction and deindustrialization have not prevented South Africa from boasting the strongest, most diversified economy on the African continent. Indeed, South Africa's recent (and long-hoped-for) invitation to join the BRICS nations—Brazil, Russia, India, China, and now South Africa—is a confirmation of its status as a potentially major emerging economy (Wooldridge 2011). Yet South Africa (like several of its regional neighbors) is also one of the most unequal societies, in terms not only of distribution of wealth but also of industry and landownership. Analysts have acknowledged that 6–7 percent annual growth is required to combat unemployment and inequality (Mattes 2002, 23). Although the economy grew at more than 5.5

percent between 2005 and 2007 and a slower but still encouraging rate of 3.7 percent in 2008, it fell into negative growth in 2009; growth rates of 3–4 percent are forecast through about 2015 (EIU 2010d). Although this would be better than recent history, forecasts are unreliable, and even 3–4 percent for several years would barely offset the country's average of approximately 3 percent per year in the first decade after apartheid.

Early in its tenure, the ANC was in search of the right policy mix, but clearly driven by structural constraints of globalization as well. It moved from a socialist perspective calling for nationalization and redistribution, to one promising "growth with equity," to staunch neoliberalism, all within the span of six years. In exile, and until 1992, the ANC advocated a program of democratic socialism, including the redistribution of wealth through nationalization. However, the ANC's letter of intent to the IMF in 1993 agreeing to pay apartheid's US$20 billion external commercial bank debt cemented the ANC as a firm adherent of "globalization" (Saul 1999, 19). The RDP was briefly tried, but the global and South African capitalist influences on the ANC soon prompted the state to abandon even this modestly statist economic program (I. Taylor 2002).

The GEAR program, adopted in 1996, was fundamentally a neoliberal structural adjustment program, although it was "homegrown" and not "imposed" on South Africa by the international financial institutions (IFIs) (I. Taylor 2002). Yet where similar structural adjustment programs have earned criticism elsewhere on the continent (Mkandawire and Soludo 1999), the initiation of the program caused some puzzlement in its application to South Africa. Not only did GEAR call for austerity at a time when society was demanding a *greater* state role in the economy, but it was not mandated by the IFIs, nor was it, critics charge, even necessary, as economic alternatives had yet to be fully explored (Bond 2000; Taylor and Nel 2002).

The manner in which GEAR was adopted by the ANC was also a source of considerable controversy. With its market orientation, calls for corporate tax reductions, low government spending, and privatization, GEAR won the full endorsement of business and the international financial institutions. However, it was presented to parliament and to the ANC's governing "partners"—the SACP and COSATU—as a fait accompli and deemed "nonnegotiable." Objections to the method of GEAR's announcement and adoption were summarized by leftist scholar John Saul (1999, 22), who noted that "it is this kind of coolly self-satisfied, self-righteous, and profoundly ideological thrust on the part of the new ANC elite . . . that is the single most depressing attribute of South Africa's transition." By and large, this neoliberal tilt has continued, both after GEAR and after Mbeki.

Although neoliberalism's critics cannot claim complete vindication, neither can the government; in fact, neoliberal policies have had a mixed record.

On the negative side, a major problem was government disingenuousness about what GEAR specifically would deliver. Targets such as employment, as noted above, were off sharply, yet GEAR predicted that the economy would *add* 400,000 new jobs by 2000. Moreover, other key indicators, such as investment and GDP growth, fell substantially below their targets (Bond 2000, 78). These shortfalls came on top of the government's failure to meet its overly optimistic and ambitious goals enshrined in the RDP,[25] thereby deepening the disillusionment of the populace. More fundamentally, however, the government's neoliberal direction raises substantial questions about equity, the social tenets upon which the ANC was founded, and which constituencies the party primarily serves. The fact that the programs failed to deliver new jobs, sufficient investment in human and physical infrastructure, or a halving of the deficit, but have accommodated the interests of predominantly white business and facilitated the emergence of a privileged black economic elite has sparked searing critiques (Mbeki 2009; Bond 2004, 2006).

On the positive side, the overall stability of the South African economy has defied naysayers who once predicted ANC rule would spell ruin. In international circles especially, the stewardship of fiscal and monetary policy by South Africa's finance ministry and central bank (the Reserve Bank of South Africa), specifically under the leadership of Trevor Manuel and Tito Mboweni, respectively (each of whom served until 2009), has won plaudits. Moreover, some economic problems, such as the 60-plus percent decline in the value of the rand in 2001—which later substantially reversed—and the drop in foreign direct investment, were substantially outside the control of South Africa's economic team. Ultimately, what is unknowable is the counterfactual, that is, what might have been the impacts on growth, investment, infrastructure development, business environment, and social stability had the ANC eschewed neoliberal policies instead? In a review of Patrick Bond's *Talk Left, Walk Right,* Pádraig Carmody (2006) writes, "The decommodification of basic human rights such as 'lifeline' water and electricity supplies and access to antiretrovirals that Bond advocates are eminently sensible and just. However economic growth could facilitate such expenditures, whereas ineffective economic delinking [from the Western neoliberal world order] à la Zimbabwe would bring the worst of both worlds—a contracting economy and worsening social conditions."

Indeed, while not all attributable to GEAR per se, a number of South Africa's economic targets were later reached, and when a new economic strategy, the Accelerated and Shared Growth Initiative (ASGI), was launched in 2006, a decade after GEAR, the economic picture looked less bleak—and by some measures, even substantially positive (AsgiSA n.d.).[26] In fact, even as early as 2004 some analysts pointed out that South Africa was "in the longest cyclical upturn since World War II" and that "even with population growth since

1994, the GDP growth has been consistently higher" (Marud 2004). Similarly strong indicators were noted for inflation, interest rates, and the exchange rate of the rand.[27] Hence, ASGI's ambitious goal, inspired by the MDGs, was to halve poverty by 2014 (AsgiSA n.d.).[28]

Regardless of periodic successes, however, the ANC's important political alliance with COSATU and the SACP remains under strain as long as the ruling party pursues centrist-neoliberal policies. More critically, the South African populace as a whole remains deeply skeptical of programs, like GEAR, that lack meaningful provisions for social development, human resource development, public sector transformation, crime prevention, or infrastructure development, even on the modest level prescribed by the ill-fated RDP (Bond 2000, 83). Judith Streak (2004, 286) argued that "whether we will eventually begin to see redistribution will depend largely on the extent to which the government stays true to [its] promises" of using its improved capacity, gained through budget deficit reduction, to deliver services and adequate resources to the poor.

Yet to be fair, although social grants expenditure declined following GEAR's enactment, it actually grew from 2.2 percent of GDP in the 2001–2002 period to 3.3 percent of GDP in the 2006–2007 period, which "represents a major step in the fight against poverty" (Pauw and Mncube 2007, 14). In fact, spending on social assistance grew at a real annual rate of 20.2 percent between 2002 and 2006. Though such high levels were not sustained—and a United Nations Development Programme study (Pauw and Mncube 2007) actually recommended against increasing social cash transfers further to avoid harming other social programs—the government clearly expanded its social security grants to protect poorer South Africans ("Social Security Spending" 2008).

These somewhat contradictory findings bring us full circle: to the 2010 World Cup, whose enormous cost necessarily reignited these essential debates about South Africa's national priorities. Government expenditure on the World Cup exceeded US$4 billion (28 billion rand). Although the government claimed it was "using its investment in the World Cup to speed up growth and development in the country so that it leaves behind a proud legacy that will benefit generations of South Africans to come," more than a third of the monies (approximately US$1.4 billion or 9.8 billion rand) were allocated to the construction of stadiums and precinct development. At the same time, approximately US$1.6 billion; $42 million; and $500 million (11 billion, 300 million, and 3.5 billion rand) were contributed to transport, telecommunications, and ports, respectively.[29] Yet while these are doubtless beneficial investments in the long term, their capacity to affect the immediate priorities of most South Africans—persistent poverty and structural unemployment—is necessarily more limited.

The ANC, the Business Community, and Black Economic Empowerment

The ANC's critics argue that the business community has been the biggest beneficiary of government. The ANC's noteworthy realignment from a platform of redistribution to a free market orientation is in large part a reflection of the influence of South Africa's leading firms. Representing South Africa's leading mining, industrial, and financial services companies, many of these have roots in the last century and were deeply involved in apartheid. They were supporters of the state and helped provide the economic infrastructure that enabled the apartheid government to endure and indeed thrive, both domestically and internationally (Nattrass 1999). Paradoxically, however, it was many of these same firms that began to chip away at apartheid in the 1980s and may have accelerated its demise.

Eventually, apartheid became an extra tax on business. The Physical Planning and Utilization of Resources Act of 1967, for example, blocked industries from expanding their black labor force without state approval. By 1978 there were over 4,000 laws and 6,000 regulations affecting business (du Toit 1995, 160). In short, apartheid produced uncompetitive labor laws, international sanctions, and a worsening domestic economy that led South African business to support its dismantling by the mid-1980s.

Among the leading firms in South Africa today are Anglo-American Corporation, Liberty Life, SAB-Miller, Old Mutual, Remgro, and Sanlam, the same conglomerates that have dominated the business scene for a century.[30] Although their principal businesses are in mining, manufacturing, and financial services, these companies are multisectoral conglomerates (they have substantial "concentration," or vertical integration, as well) that formed the backbone of the South African economy for generations. Through a process of unbundling after 1994 (including through the mechanism of Black Economic Empowerment, discussed below), however, some firms no longer have as many diverse, multisectoral business lines. Moreover, while three—Anglo, Liberty, and SAB-Miller—have become truly global corporations and moved their headquarters to London (not without controversy, as noted above) and delisted from the principal bourse, the Johannesburg Stock Exchange, they remain important actors in the local economy as employers and taxpayers. The leading corporations collectively associate in the South Africa Foundation, a business chamber that provides one of several avenues for business to influence government policy. Both individually and collectively, the large South African firms have been successful in this regard (Taylor 2007).

Although the business impact on government is noteworthy given the ANC's history, it is also not surprising, given the national dependence on this handful of firms. The emergence of a small but well-connected coterie of black businesspeople through a state-initiated process of Black Economic Empowerment (BEE) has also played a key role in the development of the ANC's relationship with business and markets. Moreover, there have been synergies between the government, emergent "BEE companies," and the country's large, historically white firms. Notwithstanding their onetime direct or indirect complicity with policies of racial discrimination, the latter have played a key role in the growth of BEE companies (Taylor 2007; Handley 2008). The latter lack the deep financial roots of their white counterparts. BEE companies typically involve a black ownership stake (at least 50 percent was required under the legislation to be considered black-*owned*) in a holding company created for the purpose of acquiring shares, though the underlying operating company, or companies, remain mostly white. Nevertheless, BEE executives have cultivated extraordinary influence with the state. Having joined the ranks of the "super rich," many of these black elites have class interests commensurate with those of the white senior executives with whom they regularly interact (Seekings and Nattrass 2005, 43–45).

Many of the ANC's labor allies, including COSATU, condemned the Black Economic Empowerment process as enriching only a "few politically connected figures," such as ANC stalwarts Cyril Ramaphosa and Saki Macozoma (Reed 2004). Aware of this growing resentment among much of its labor and urban constituents in particular, the ANC moved toward a new strategy. In 2007 it adopted "Broad-Based" BEE (BB-BEE), which endeavored to expand the beneficiaries and contained stricter enforcement mechanisms; compliance has been mixed, however.

Race and the Economy: Whither Redistribution?

Since large residual white populations remained in southern Africa after independence, a considerable degree of accommodation has been required to reduce conflict between the owners of the resources and the new majority "owners" of the state. Two decades after majority rule, South Africa's 4.5 million white citizens continue to dominate industry, commercial agriculture, the financial sector, mining, and the vast majority of agricultural lands and resources. Hence the abandonment of the RDP in 1996, so early in the transition, was a concern to many both within and outside South Africa. Rather than rely solely on an unpredictable market mechanism that might cement the socioeconomic status quo, the RDP explicitly sought to shift some of the responsibility for redress onto the beneficiaries of apartheid, as well as to address specific social needs. In fairness, both before and since GEAR's enactment, the state has made improvements in some areas among the urban and rural poor. Since 1994, infant mortality has declined, and some black household incomes have increased. By December 1997 the ANC government had constructed 250,000 new houses, provided electricity to 1.4 million homes, built or upgraded 560 health clinics, and completed 1,020 new water projects that provided access to clean water for 8.9 million people (du Toit 2001, 123–124). These improvements are cited in survey data as the most recognizable achievements of the ANC government (*Afrobarometer* 2003a). Yet, in spite of additional investment in infrastructure and social welfare spending cited earlier, glaring inequities continue to exist, not only in regard to basic needs but also in employment, ownership, and opportunities for advancement.

Some assert that a new black middle class has emerged, which offsets some of the concerns about the macroeconomic framework. Estimates of the size of this grouping vary, though some have placed it between 2.2 million to as high as 3 million, expanding by some 15 percent annually, with average annual incomes of about US $12,000 or 84,000 rand in 2008 (Cohen 2008). This upwardly mobile cohort has adopted expensive consumer spending habits and is increasingly the target of both domestic companies and foreign investors (Goyal 2010). Indeed, the spending power of the "Black Diamonds" increased by 39 percent between 2007 and 2008 (Cohen 2008), although spending was curtailed somewhat by the 2009 recession. At the apex of this emergent black middle class is a far smaller group of elites, including the current and former ANC stalwarts who have benefited disproportionately from empowerment programs but now are established business magnates in their own right. Clearly, they have a vested interest in preserving their considerable personal and corporate economic gains, and in this respect they find themselves closely aligned with the economic interests of both white business and the ANC government.

In any event, while the new black middle class has facilitated important interracial economic and political alliances, the size and stability of this "class" are not sufficient to insulate South Africa from a possible backlash against the perceived slow pace of socioeconomic progress. Too much triumphalism about the middle class fails to give sufficient attention to the magnitude of South Africa's poverty; it has impressively fallen some 10 percentage points, but a massive 64 percent of South African households remain below the poverty line and the state is the only institution suited to address it. The state has taken some proactive steps to stimulate black advancement through its BEE and BB-BEE legislation. In addition, companion legislation including changes to the Labor Relations Act, the Employment Equity Act requiring white-run firms to meet specific black employment targets or face fines, and so on also have been promulgated. Yet many of these policies suffer from erratic enforcement or too many loopholes. And in any event, they affect more urbanized, relatively more educated blacks—still a comparatively small portion of the population. Meanwhile, the mass of poor, uneducated, or undereducated black South Africans face few solutions and declining household incomes. They therefore find themselves increasingly desperate, and as some surveys indicate, disillusioned with the ANC and democracy (Mattes 2002) and perhaps turning to crime.

The latter tendency reached epic proportions in May 2008, when several weeks of anti-immigrant violence killed more than 50 people and displaced some 40,000. Immigrant residents of South Africa, both legal and illegal, were driven from their homes as violence raged, particularly in the townships surrounding the major urban centers of Johannesburg and Cape Town. The catalyst was apparently a clash between immigrant shopkeepers and residents in Alexandra township that set off a wave of violence around the country (Gurney 2008).

Even under colonialism and apartheid, South Africa was a magnet in the southern Africa region, drawing those seeking jobs, particularly in the mining industry. Since 1994, Africans from all over the continent have flocked to South Africa, drawn by the country's stability, economy, and the prospects for jobs. As many as 5 *million* Zimbabweans have sought refuge there since the collapse of Zimbabwe's economy began in 2000. Many of the Zimbabweans, Somalis, Congolese, and others are legal immigrants to South Africa and occupy some of the highest rungs of their adopted country's socioeconomic ladder. However, far more are poor, undocumented, and often highly visible in the communities in which they reside. The South African attackers blamed immigrants for increased crime and for taking jobs from poor South Africans.

The Mbeki government responded by establishing, in effect, refugee camps for those fleeing the violence, including many who had lived in South Africa for years. For the South African government, particularly for the self-styled pan-Africanist Mbeki, this episode was a tremendous embarrassment, and the xenophobia was a repudiation of the "rainbow nation."[31] Although eventually (if impermanently) quelled, the violence was also a stark reminder of the deep, unresolved tensions and frustrations embedded in South Africa's impoverished communities.

The violence that shook South Africa in 2008 was directed at a vulnerable and relatively powerless community—immigrants, who were perceived to be taking jobs and resources from black South Africans—rather than at the state or its economic backers. Yet economic deprivation in the black community remains the Achilles' heel of the postapartheid state: it makes plain the absence of substantive democracy and imperils the genuine gains of the 1994 "miracle."

Challenges of the Twenty-First Century

The economy and poverty remain, in our view, the principal obstacles to future stability in South Africa. As noted, growth has only recently reached levels sufficient to meet population needs, and the controversial neoliberal policies have to a considerable extent removed the state from the direct provision of economic resources to the poor in terms of redistribution, instead placing much of this critical role in the purview of "the market." Although the business community has responded to some degree, through contributions to BEE and the practice of corporate social responsibility, and state spending recently has increased, the long-term impact on poverty is uncertain. The failure to mitigate poverty, crime, the AIDS crisis, corruption, and public discontent over access to basic human needs reveals that South Africa's highly vaunted democracy remains fragile in "substantive" terms.

If the economy is South Africa's Achilles' heel, however, there are many other areas of concern in the body politic. By substantial majorities, South Africans of all races profess an interest in forgetting about the past, although whites are more likely to want to "just move on" than blacks. While this is in one sense an encouraging phenomenon, the now many intensive studies of the TRC and its aftermath may suggest otherwise. Indeed, many analyses suggest that the wounds of apartheid remain substantially unhealed and that, in many ways, the TRC, despite its enormous efforts and considerable goodwill, has proved to be little more than a palliative in the end (Wilson 2001; Graybill 2002). Certainly the economic reminders of apartheid are everywhere apparent. Evidence from within the region itself tells us that it is far more difficult to simply "forgive and forget," as Zimbabwe's Robert Mugabe pledged in 1980. Such instructions, whether well meaning or cynical, are particularly challenging to follow if the bulk of the populace lacks the material basis to move forward, let alone the psychological one (Minow 1998; Chua 2003). Ominously, it is not impossible to foresee an "antimarket backlash" against the ANC's embrace of economic liberalism in general, and whites in particular, if the economy and general living standards do not improve markedly (Chua 2003). The Zimbabwe example, however cynical and hypocritical Mugabe's manipulations of race have been, is simply too proximate to ignore. "Reconciliation" is inherently fragile where the inequalities of the past persist and are so visible.

Procedural democracy, too, stands at a crossroads. The regularization of elections and the institutionalization of the Independent Electoral Commission appear to have been substantially achieved. Indeed, the establishment of procedures and improvements in the conduct of elections and respect for their results indicate that "South Africa has traveled quite far along the road to democratic consolidation" (Lodge 1999, 210). Conversely, the concentration of power in the ANC and the party's increasing centralization of authority are matters of concern, as is the corresponding erosion of federalism. The ANC dominates virtually every level of government in South Africa with the exception of the Western Cape. The absence of a nationally competitive opposition party, or parties, is also problematic "when a governing party sees less and less need to respond to public opinion because it is assured of re-election" (*Afrobarometer* 2003b).

Many factors augur positively for South Africa, and the achievements of both its government and society in the years since the end of minority rule cannot be diminished. In many respects, both the awarding and the successful hosting of the 2010 World Cup were part of a global celebration—joined by the international community and South Africans themselves—of the country's enormous progress. Yet with the crowds departed and the stadiums quiet, South Africa now returns its focus to the enormous challenges facing its economy, its society, and its democracy.

Notes

1. South Africa uses both a broad definition of unemployment, which includes those no longer actively looking for work, and a narrow definition, which is comparable to International Labour Organization (ILO) standards and more frequently cited in government statistics. In 2010, the latter stood at 29.5 percent for blacks, 22.5 percent for Coloureds, and 10.1 percent for Asians (Statistics South Africa 2010, Appendix p. 4).

2. This miscegenation was generally prior to the arrival of large numbers of European women, after which mixed public unions declined (Omer-Cooper 1994). Nonetheless, it does raise some questions about the "purity" of white Afrikaner culture, which was to become a key part of the Afrikaner foundation myth and of apartheid (Dubow 1995).

3. Many African peoples had been displaced just prior to and during the Great Trek as a result of a series of conflicts, known as the *mfecane,* that resulted in the consolidation of the Zulu kingdom. Not only did the *mfecane* disrupt existing African political structures, but it also made weaker peoples more likely to seek alliances with whites against their African enemies (Omer-Cooper 1994, 68; Hamilton 1998).

4. Although in official discourse the term *black* has come to encompass all nonwhites, much of the contemporary research, including polling data, continues to utilize the traditional classifications. While we acknowledge their arbitrariness, we nonetheless employ the narrower, more common understanding of *black* in this chapter (unless otherwise specified).

5. As late as 1989, more than 40 percent of Afrikaners said that they would physically resist an ANC-led government (Giliomee 1997, 114).

6. Several other parties from both the right and left walked out of the negotiations, most prominently the IFP, which had only agreed to participate in the elections several weeks before they were held.

7. A total of 13,546 deaths, or more than 3,000 per year, resulted from political violence in the four-year period 1990 through 1993 (du Toit 2001, 41).

8. Although these elements are typically components of electoral rather than constitutional law, it is worth noting that these are issues of major contention, especially since the 1999 election.

9. One of the long-standing white extremist, right-wing political parties, the Freedom Front (recently referred to as FF+), dropped the desire for an independent Afrikaner state from its manifesto in the 2009 elections, though it continues to advocate the devolution of power to independent communities and even the potential redrawing of the South African map.

10. The interim constitution also established twelve official languages, which was, at the very least, an acknowledgment of cultural pluralism.

11. Compare Chapter 6, Section 146, of the 1996 constitution to Chapter 90, Section 126, of the 1993 constitution, in which legislative competence of provincial assemblies was considerably less circumscribed. The 1993 constitution (Chapter 11A) also contained provisions for the consideration of a *volkstaat,* a proposition that was rejected by 1996.

12. The party was fifteen seats short following the 1994 election, but just one seat short after the 1999 election.

13. The Supreme Court of Appeal is "below" the Constitutional Court only in terms of the ultimate findings on constitutional matters. "The Supreme Court of Appeal: functions only as a court of appeal; may decide any matter on appeal; and is, except for constitutional matters, the highest court of appeal" ("Supreme Court of Appeal of South Africa" n.d.).

14. One prominent example was the widely criticized April 2002 verdict by an apartheid-era High Court judge, Willie Hartzenberg, exonerating biological weapons expert Wouter Basson. Basson was found not guilty, notwithstanding substantial evidence implicating him in the deaths of hundreds of black South Africans during apartheid. Judge Hartzenberg repeatedly frustrated the state's attempts to introduce evidence, dismissed a number of charges, and refused to recuse himself despite apparent conflicts of interest. Blacks, and the government, were justifiably outraged. An interesting early account of the case was written by William Finnegan (2001).

15. A high-profile member of the government, de Klerk lacked any real authority, although other NP members of the GNU headed line ministries, including finance. Indeed, the retention of National Party finance minister Derek Keys helped bolster the credibility of the new government's economic program in the international marketplace, which had feared redistributive policies from the ANC (I. Taylor 2002).

16. However, this domestic defensive emphasis does not rule out engagement in regional or global peacekeeping operations, and the military is committed as well to the creation of a potential African rapid response force.

17. There have been, however, a number of defections at all levels. Many white members of the former SADF retired from the service shortly before and after 1994 rather than serve the new black government led by the ANC. Some of these enlisted in private army operations, most prominently Executive Outcomes, a company that has engaged in controversial mercenary operations in Angola, Sierra Leone, and elsewhere. South Africa adopted a constitutional provision prohibiting "South African citizens from participating in armed conflict either nationally or internationally" (HRW 2000). In May 1998 this provision was given enforcement teeth when "the government passed the Foreign Military Assistance Act, a law unique in the world, that limits and controls the activities of mercenaries," including those in private military companies like Executive Outcomes. Established in 1989, Executive Outcomes closed business in South Africa in 1999.

18. In 1999 a scandal broke when the government announced a US$5 billion (29.9 billion rand) arms purchase, an extraordinary sum that was immediately greeted with allegations of corruption and conflicts of interest (Mattes 2002). A parliamentary report found no evidence of "improper or unlawful conduct" by government in the arms procurement (Parliament of South Africa 2001).

19. Interview with Richard Cornwell, senior research fellow, Institute for Security Studies, Pretoria, conducted by Scott Taylor, June 13, 2001.

20. On bills not affecting the provinces, the National Assembly passes legislation over an NCOP veto with a simple majority. However, even on ordinary bills affecting the provinces, "the National Assembly can ignore the NCOP's wishes if it can muster a two-thirds majority in favor of the measure" (Calland 1999, 23).

21. Elections are overseen by the Independent Electoral Commission, which was restructured and professionalized after 1994. Although considerably more independent than, say, its counterparts in Zambia and Zimbabwe, the commission also relies on the state for financial support. This has led to protracted budget disputes with the Ministry of Home Affairs (Lodge 1999).

22. The 2003 constitutional amendment that permitted floor-crossing during prescribed periods in the legislative session, for example, allowed the ANC delegation to the National Assembly to immediately gain 9 new members, who saw better opportunities with the ruling party. The change decimated some opposition parties, such as the United Democratic Movement, whose delegation went from 14 to 4, and resulted in a 275-seat supermajority for the ANC.

23. In 2005, however, the Constitutional Court ruled that a criminal case against Basson could be reopened.

24. There was a public exchange of insults between cabinet members, including the president and union leaders, in August 2001, leading to the calling of massive strikes (Mattes 2002, 26).

25. Among other things, RDP pledged to guide the delivery of 1 million new housing units, 2.5 million electrifications, clean water and sanitation, and the redistribution of 30 percent of quality agricultural land, most of which was to be completed within the first five years of ANC rule (Bond 2000, 92).

26. Many of the deficit and GDP target ratios were met or exceeded: the deficit was 6.5 percent in 1994 but reduced to just 2.1 percent of GDP in 2001 (surpassing the budget target of 2.5 percent) (Marud 2004).

27. This information is from George Kershoff of the Bureau for Economic Research in Stellenbosch, quoted in Marud (2004).

28. Ironically, history will almost certainly repeat itself here, as the economic slowdown of 2008 and 2009 virtually ensured.

29. South African Government Information, http://www.info.gov.za/.

30. Remgro is the contemporary incarnation of the apartheid-era company Rembrandt, which split into Remgro, now an investment company, and Richemont, a luxury goods group actually based in Switzerland (Taylor 2007).

31. Eighty-three percent of South Africans responded that they trust foreigners in South Africa "not at all" or "just a little" (*Afrobarometer* 2010, 2).

10 Living with HIV/AIDS in Southern Africa

In 2009 sub-Saharan Africa remained the world region most heavily affected by HIV/AIDS. Although comprising only 10 percent of the world's population at the end of 2008, sub-Saharan Africa accounted for more than two-thirds (67 percent) of all people living with AIDS, an estimated 22.5 million people. In addition, sub-Saharan Africa accounted for nearly three-quarters (72 percent) of all AIDS-related deaths in late 2009, an estimated 1.3 million people. Sub-Saharan Africa also accounted for about 69 percent of all new HIV infections, with an estimated 1.8 million adults and children in sub-Saharan Africa newly infected during 2009. Finally, an estimated 14.1 million children in sub-Saharan Africa were considered to be AIDS orphans for having lost one or more parents to the disease. And yet the good news was that the number of people living with AIDS in sub-Saharan Africa in 2009 was up slightly (from 19.7 million in 2001), due in part to people's improved access to HIV treatment. In addition, the number of AIDS-related deaths represented a 20 percent decline in annual HIV-related mortality in the region between 2004 and 2009. Finally, the rate of new infections was also on the decline; between 2001 and 2009, twenty-two countries in sub-Saharan Africa experienced a decline of more than 25 percent in new HIV infections. Those countries with the largest epidemics in sub-Saharan Africa, countries in southern Africa, were leading the drop in new HIV infections (UNAIDS 2009a, 2010a, 2010b, 2010c). Still, despite the recent good news, it may be assumed that the social, economic, and political toll on the continent, directly or indirectly as a result of AIDS, will take some time to reverse.

In early 2010 the worldwide HIV/AIDS crisis remained the most severe in southern Africa, with about 34 percent of all people living with AIDS living in ten southern African countries (UNAIDS 2010c). Countries in southern Africa continued to bear a disproportionate share of the global AIDS burden—except for Angola, each of them had adult HIV prevalence rates of greater than 10 percent. At the same time, as across the continent, significant progress could be detected in southern Africa. For example, in 2001 four southern

African countries had adult HIV prevalence rates that were "higher than thought possible," exceeding 30 percent: Botswana (38.8 percent), Lesotho (31 percent), Swaziland (33.4 percent), and Zimbabwe (33.7 percent) (UNAIDS 2002a, 17). By 2009, by contrast, the adult HIV prevalence rates seemed to have stabilized at lower rates: 24.8 percent in Botswana, 25.9 percent in Swaziland, and 23.6 percent in Lesotho—though still extremely high compared to other parts of Africa and the world (UNAIDS 2009a, 27) (see Table 10.1). In 2009 South Africa still had the highest absolute number of people living with HIV of any country in the world—5.6 million, up from 5.3 million in 2002 (UNAIDS 2003, 9; 2010c). In 2009, UNAIDS (2009a, 27–28) concluded that the HIV incidence for southern Africa as a whole had peaked in the mid-1990s, and then stabilized, though still at extremely high levels. Across the region in the first decade of the twenty-first century, significant drops in HIV incidence were detected among specific groups: for example, young pregnant women in Lusaka and all women in Zambia, young pregnant women in Botswana, and young people in South Africa. The rate of new infections was down by more than 25 percent in South Africa, Zambia, and Zimbabwe, three of the five countries with the largest epidemics in sub-Saharan Africa (UNAIDS 2010c).

The scale of the HIV/AIDS epidemic in southern Africa makes it still one of the most serious issues confronting the region, with implications for many aspects of economic, political, and social life. This chapter considers those implications in detail. Our intention is to move beyond the statistics that have become so familiar in the international discourse on AIDS. What do the numbers *mean* for southern Africa's development and governance? While once

Table 10.1   HIV/AIDS Estimates for Southern Africa, 2009

	People Living with AIDS				
	Adult Percentage Rate (age 15–49)	Adults (ages 15 and up)	Children (ages 0–14)	Deaths, Adults and Children	AIDS Orphans
Angola	2	180,000	22,000	11,000	140,000
Botswana	24.8	300,000	16,000	5,800	93,000
Lesotho	23.6	260,000	28,000	14,000	130,000
Malawi	11	800,000	120,000	51,000	650,000
Mozambique	11.5	1,400,000	130,000	74,000	670,000
Namibia	13.1	160,000	16,000	6,700	70,000
South Africa	17.8	5,300,000	330,000	310,000	1,900,000
Swaziland	25.9	180,000	14,000	7,000	69,000
Zambia	13.5	980,000	120,000	45,000	690,000
Zimbabwe	14.3	1,000,000	150,000	83,000	1,000,000

Sources: "Report on Global AIDS 2009," http://www.unaids.org/en/regionscountries/countries/; http://www.unaids.org/documents/20101123_FS_SSA_em_en.pdf.

considered much more than a health crisis—transcending economic, political, and social boundaries and issues—HIV/AIDS is now something with which the people of southern Africa are *living*. Efforts at providing universal access to HIV treatment across the region are clearly having an impact, and HIV prevention strategies are clearly finding resonance among broad swathes of the population. With funds and resources from a range of international, regional, and national partners, a global response to HIV/AIDS is making a difference. Through the collaboration of such efforts as the Joint United Nations Programme on HIV/AIDS (UNAIDS), the Global Fund, the US President's Emergency Plan for AIDS Relief (PEPFAR), and the Millennium Development Goals, HIV/AIDS is being tackled head on in southern Africa (see Ngoasong 2009). Leadership from presidents, former presidents, and other government leaders across the region is contributing significantly to the transformation of the AIDS epidemic in the region as well.

The Impact on the Region

Since the early 1990s, the HIV/AIDS crisis in southern Africa has had an impact on nearly every facet of life, affecting sectors as diverse as agriculture, defense, education, health, and industry. Early in the twenty-first century, there were great fears about the enduring impacts of the epidemic on economies and polities. There was fear that the HIV/AIDS crisis would act as a drag on national economies, contributing to sharp declines in household income and purchasing power and thereby reducing the demand that fuels economic growth. There was concern that the growing inability of many children to attend school would lead to greater social problems and a loss of competitiveness in a global economy increasingly dependent on knowledge. There was worry that the region's fragile polities—in the sense of having experienced recent political transitions of one type or another—would be destabilized if individuals or groups were to blame each other or scapegoat minorities for their increasing economic deprivation (USIP 2001, 7). Another worry was that, to the extent that governments did not respond to people's demands for treatment and care, electorates would respond by ousting them from power. In the event, these more staggering impacts have not come to pass. The following sections explore some of the impacts to date.

Demographic Impact

The demographic impact of the HIV/AIDS epidemic is revealed by a series of socioeconomic indicators such as life expectancy and infant and child mortality. In 2000 the United Nations Development Programme (UNDP) predicted that life expectancy in the region would return to levels from half a century earlier because of HIV/AIDS: "Life expectancy at birth in southern Africa, which rose from 44 years in the early 1950s to 59 in the early 1990s, was set to drop to just 45 years between 2005 and 2010 because of AIDS" (UNDP 2000, 10). And indeed by 2000, according to the *Human Development Report 2002*, life expectancy at birth was already as low as 40 years for Botswana and Malawi, 41 for Zambia, 43 for Zimbabwe, and 44 for Namibia and Swaziland (UNDP 2002, 151–152). For Botswana, this drop represented a level "not seen in the country since before 1950" (UNAIDS 2002d). For Botswana and Zambia, the dire predictions were that by 2010, life expectancy would fall to 30 years (Osei Hwedie 2001a, 56; Poku and Cheru 2001, 42).

And yet the remarkable story is that the most dire predictions have not come to pass. Life expectancy did not dip to 30 years for Botswana or Zambia by the end of the first decade of the twenty-first century. Rather, life expectancy in Botswana, where AIDS deaths had peaked in about 2000 and new HIV infections and incidence rates in the mid-1990s, had recovered to about 53 years by 2007. In Namibia, where AIDS deaths had peaked a few years later than in Botswana, life expectancy had recovered to about 60 years in 2007 after a low of around 45 years in 2000. In South Africa, where deaths from AIDS had peaked only in about 2006, the 2007 life expectancy rate was about the same as that in 2000.[1] These numbers no doubt reflect the alacrity and comprehensiveness (or not) with which national governments responded to the HIV/AIDS epidemics in their countries. And while the recovery is very encouraging, without an AIDS epidemic many socioeconomic indicators would surely be much better than they are.

AIDS Orphans

The AIDS epidemic has also affected infant and child mortality rates.[2] And the crisis has impacted children in another way, namely that they are being orphaned as their mothers and fathers die of the disease. Officially defined as children who have lost their mothers or both parents to AIDS, AIDS orphans numbered just over 14 million in Africa in 2008 (UNAIDS 2009a, 21). A study released in Namibia in 2003 found that half of all orphans in that country had lost their parents or guardians to AIDS-related illnesses. In South Africa in 2002 an estimated 330,000 children had been orphaned by AIDS, with that number expected to grow to 1.72 million by 2010 (Delius and Walker 2002, 10). For southern Africa as a whole, it was estimated in 1999 that AIDS orphans composed nearly 10 percent of the total population (Delius and Walker 2002, 43). Here again, though, recent developments are encouraging. Between 2004 and 2009 AIDS-related deaths among children in southern Africa declined by 26 percent; in addition the number of children in southern Africa who became newly infected with HIV fell by 32 percent (UNAIDS 2010c).

For AIDS orphans, it is grandparents and other extended family members, often with very limited resources, who are typically called upon to provide. In Zambia, for example, three of every four households had taken in at least one AIDS orphan by the turn of the century (UNAIDS 2002d). In many cases, however, the burdens simply become too great for surviving relatives. Therefore, many AIDS-affected children, including large numbers of girls, find themselves on the streets. Some resort to prostitution in order to survive, thereby putting themselves at very high risk of HIV transmission (HRW 2002). Another concern is that increasing numbers of AIDS orphans could contribute to a growing child soldier population that has, however, so far bypassed southern Africa. In rural areas, the premature deaths of parents disrupt the transfer of skills and knowledge from one generation to another, putting future generations at risk. "Children growing up as orphans have fewer opportunities to learn how to use and sustain land and to prepare nutritious food for family members" (UNAIDS 2002a, 28). Similarly, AIDS orphans have significantly fewer opportunities to attend school than their non-AIDS counterparts.

The Household

For most southern Africans, the impact of HIV/AIDS is felt first at the level of the household. In the late 1990s, Gabriel Rugalema (2000, 538) investigated the impact of HIV/AIDS on rural households in southern Africa and concluded that the epidemic was having "significant adverse effects on household composition, labour, and income," which were then having "knock-on effects on the ability to produce food, schooling of children, cropping patterns, livestock production, labour allocation, access to productive assets and consumption of goods and services essential for household maintenance and reproduction." More concretely, Rugalema observed that the death of key adult household members often resulted in a dissolution of the household, forcing remaining household members to leave and join other households. One study in Zambia found that 65 percent of households in which the mother died of HIV/AIDS had dissolved (UNAIDS 2002e). Another study in Zimbabwe found that a similar percentage of households that lost "a key adult female" during 2000 had "disintegrated and dispersed" (UNAIDS 2002a, 28).

Household responses to illness of a key member due to HIV/AIDS include disposing of household assets; curtailing the number and quality of meals, resulting in poor nutrition or even malnutrition; withdrawing children (mostly girls) from school, thereby contributing to increasing illiteracy levels and a diminishing ability to participate in the global economy; and a general household insecurity and vulnerability, undermining the capacity of households and communities to cope and recover, in the long term. Another coping strategy found in Lesotho and Malawi has been for families to employ children's migration as a way of addressing the impacts of HIV/AIDS (Ansell and van Blerk

2004). Decisions to have children migrate are aimed both at meeting children's needs and using their capacities to meet wider household needs. According to Rugalema (2000, 542–543), the fact that "AIDS kills strong people and leaves behind the weak . . . renders households more vulnerable to future shocks than, say famine" or other disasters do.

A number of factors, including loss of income, increased care-related expenses, the reduced ability of caregivers to work outside the home, and mounting medical and funeral expenses, come together to push AIDS-affected households more deeply into poverty. In Zambia, research has shown that "in two-thirds of families where the father died, monthly disposable income fell by more than 80 percent." Typically, the burden of coping with the impact of HIV/AIDS on households falls on women "as the demands for their income-earning labour, household work, child-care and care of the sick multiply. As men fall ill, women often step into their roles outside the homes; in parts of Zimbabwe, women are moving into the traditionally male-dominated carpentry industry, for example" (UNAIDS 2002e). And yet, despite this, when men fall ill with HIV/AIDS, more money will be spent on their health care than on women's care when they fall ill.

Education

At one time it was feared that the impact of HIV/AIDS on education in southern Africa would be to deplete the ranks of students and teachers alike. School enrollments were dropping because children were being removed from school to care for ill parents or family members, HIV-affected households could no longer afford school fees and other school-related expenses, children themselves were becoming infected and therefore not able to complete their schooling, and the number of children was falling due to AIDS-related infertility and falling birthrates (UNAIDS 2002e). In parts of South Africa's KwaZulu-Natal province, for example, enrollments in the first year of primary school were 20 percent lower in 2001 than in 1998. In part this was due to AIDS-imposed economic hardship, but enrollments also dropped because children themselves were dying of the disease (UNAIDS 2002e).

Teachers are another casualty of the HIV/AIDS epidemic, with significant consequences for classroom size and overall quality of education. This is an even greater hardship for rural schools that often rely on only one or two teachers. In Zambia, it was estimated at the turn of the century that more than 30 percent of teachers were already infected with the virus. The number of teacher deaths in 1998 in Zambia was the equivalent of two-thirds of the annual output of newly trained teachers at all teacher training institutions combined (Poku and Cheru 2001, 42). Indeed, large numbers of skilled teachers are difficult to replace in southern Africa even under the best of circumstances.

Education is a cornerstone of a society's development. In southern Africa, improvements to the educational system constituted one of the most important achievements of political independence. However, education at all levels, already damaged by economic liberalization, has faced further devastation by AIDS. Moreover, in many southern African countries there is a very real concern that resources may be diverted from the education sector to other sectors, such as health and welfare, where the HIV/AIDS-induced needs are more immediate.[3] Severe budget constraints, only partly due to AIDS, force hard choices on governments.

Health

Clearly, health sectors throughout southern Africa have been adversely impacted by HIV/AIDS. The demands due to HIV/AIDS on already overburdened and underfunded health care systems are manifold: "extending prevention and care for sexually transmitted infections, counseling and testing, prevention of mother to child transmission services, and HIV treatment and care." Moreover, just as the demand for care increases, so too does the toll on health care workers. Malawi and Zambia, for example, were experiencing five- to sixfold increases in health-worker–related illness and death rates in the early 2000s. To compensate, the training of doctors and nurses would have had to increase by an estimated 25 to 40 percent during the rest of the decade in southern Africa (UNAIDS 2002b).

While much care is provided to family members in the home and the community, hospitals and clinics are also feeling the burden of the AIDS epidemic. Although care for AIDS patients in southern Africa is typically inadequate, AIDS threatens to swamp all other medical services, including hospital space. In 2001 it was estimated that half of all beds in some health care centers in Swaziland were occupied by people living with AIDS. Similarly, in Zimbabwe half of all inpatients at health care centers studied were people living with AIDS. In South Africa, the health care system was said to be "reeling under the impact of the epidemic" in the early twenty-first century (Delius and Walker 2002, 10). There is also immense pressure on health care budgets and health insurance schemes as a result of the epidemic.

Agriculture

Agriculture, the source of livelihood for about 70 percent of southern Africans, is also being hard hit by the HIV/AIDS crisis, with serious implications for food security in the region. As farmers fall ill or die, their labor and that of family members assigned to care for them is lost. In Namibia in 2001, 60 percent of commercial and smallholder farmers reported that they had suffered labor losses due to HIV/AIDS (UNAIDS 2002a, 27). Labor losses mean that households are not able to produce enough food for their own consumption, or for sale, with implications for household nutrition and household income. In some instances, farmers have reported switching to less labor intensive but also less nutritious food crops. In the quest to pay for much-needed medicines and to meet household expenses in the face of income loss, farm equipment and other household assets may be sold off, thereby rendering household recovery more difficult. Similarly, in the face of lost labor power and lost income, farm infrastructure may fall into disrepair, and agricultural inputs such as pesticides may become too expensive. The situation is all the more dire when, as is frequently the case, drought threatens the region.

In the early twenty-first century, Alex de Waal and Joseph Tumushabe (2003, 2) suggested that the HIV epidemic was disproportionately affecting agriculture relative to other sectors. This is not because HIV infection rates are higher among agricultural workers than other workers but because "the structure of the agriculture sector, especially the smallholder subsector, is such that it is much less able to absorb the impacts of the human resource losses associated with the pandemic." The impact of the epidemic on the agricultural sector, according to the authors, would be to intensify labor bottlenecks, increase widespread malnutrition, add to the problems of rural women, and reduce agricultural exports. The reasons that the impact would likely be so severe included "the pre-existing fragility of most African farming systems . . . and the role of the agrarian sector in most African countries as an unacknowledged social safety net." The authors concluded that under the strain of HIV/AIDS, more vulnerable farming systems were simply breaking down, "threatening a social calamity on a scale not witnessed before on the continent."

There is a continuing fear that HIV/AIDS erodes the few coping mechanisms that households have at their disposal. "It reduces households' capacities to produce and purchase food, depletes their assets, and exhausts social safety nets" (UNAIDS 2002a, 27). A study conducted in Malawi in 2002 found a range of links between the HIV/AIDS epidemic and the onset of household food insecurity. These included "the loss of able-bodied labour in the households, the loss of remittances from working family members, the additional challenge of caring for orphans, child-headed families, and increased expenditures on health care and funerals" (UNAIDS 2002a, 27).

National Security

Early in the twenty-first century there was concern that national security could also be at risk in southern Africa due to the high HIV/AIDS prevalence. According to UNAIDS (2002f), early in that decade in African countries where HIV/AIDS had been present for more than a decade, the HIV prevalence rate among soldiers was as high as 50 to 60 percent; in other hard-hit countries the rate was about 20 to 40 percent. A 2001 report (USIP 2001, 5) also indicated that 40 percent of the military in South Africa and up to 60 percent in Angola and Democratic Republic of Congo (DRC) were HIV-positive at that time. More recent scholarship, however, suggests that the threat to militaries in Africa may not be as dire as originally predicted. Whiteside, de Waal, and Gebre-Tensae (2006) suggest that, as a rule, military populations do not necessarily have higher HIV prevalence rates than civilian populations and that a number of other factors—demographics, deployment patterns, national disease burden, and preventive measures taken by militaries—will have an important bearing on overall military prevalence rates. Also, with a few exceptions, national militaries across the continent have shown themselves able to withstand the potential HIV threat. Further, there is little evidence that war per se contributes to new HIV infections; rather, factors such as population mobility and changing sexual networks—often resulting from conflict—may be the more important factors. Finally, Whiteside, de Waal, and Gebre-Tensae (2006) conclude that the overall hypothesis that HIV/AIDS "has the potential to disrupt national, regional and international security remains speculative."

The Industrial Sector

A number of countries in southern Africa, in particular Zambia and Zimbabwe, have already experienced substantial deindustrialization as a result of years of structural adjustment programs. Still, industry in southern Africa stands to be further undermined by HIV/AIDS, and perhaps for that reason some of the most progressive early responses to the disease were found in industry, in particular in the mining sector in Botswana and South Africa. Of course the vast majority of those affected by HIV/AIDS—fifteen- to forty-nine-year-olds—are precisely a country's economically active population and the most productive segment of that population. At one time a host of factors combined to reduce labor productivity and industry profits—and to act as a disincentive to investment, especially foreign investment—throughout the region. Early on, Namibia's bulk water supplier, NamWater, reported that HIV/AIDS was hindering its operation as worker absenteeism rates rose and labor productivity rates fell. In Zambia, dozens of businesses reported dramatic increases in annual mortality rates of their employees as well as marked increases in absenteeism among workers. Increased absenteeism resulted from the declining health of HIV-infected workers but also from time off spent at the funerals of other workers. High employee turnover rates mean increased training costs for businesses. Additional costs to businesses include more medical care, salary compensation for the families of deceased workers, and funeral grants (Poku and Cheru 2001, 42).

As noted above, mining companies in South Africa and Botswana were among the first to respond to the HIV/AIDS crisis, worried that if early trends continued they would incur significant costs and expenditure of resources from the presence of the disease among their workers. A number of companies, such as South Africa's largest, the mining giant Anglo-American Corporation, joined together to make antiretroviral drugs available to their workers, long before the South African government made treatment available to all who needed it. Even at greatly reduced prices, these drugs were prohibitively expensive to the average South African worker, and so company decisions to provide them to their workers were highly significant (Hunter-Gault 2001). In Botswana, the mining company Debswana also moved early on to provide antiretrovirals to its workers and their families. Debswana's policy was in keeping with national policy in Botswana, the first country in Africa to make antiretrovirals available to the entire population (Rollnick 2002).

The situation may be even more critical in the informal sector, which provides a source of livelihood for more than three-quarters of workers in countries like Zambia and Mozambique. In informal enterprises, when the lead entrepreneur is no longer able to work, there is a high risk that the entire enterprise will collapse. With the collapse of the enterprise, the incomes of others are in turn lost, as are the goods or services produced. Indeed, a recent study in Zambia (International Labour Office 2009a) found HIV/AIDS to be having a major impact on the informal sector where stigma and discrimination remain widespread: for example, in informal markets. A number of possible interventions were identified in the study, including linking informal sectors to Zambia's national policy to provide free antiretroviral drugs to all who need them. In Mozambique around 2005 the national association of informal sector workers began working with outside agencies on a regular program of HIV activities: HIV prevention, strategies to fight discrimination and exclusion, and access to services providing condoms and antiretroviral drugs. In the first two years of the program, 6,000 vendors and their clients were reached (International Labour Office 2009b).

Taken together, the interrelated effects of HIV/AIDS on all of these sectors suggest a huge burden for southern African economies and polities. But why has the HIV/AIDS crisis been so severe in Africa in general and southern Africa in particular? Many of the factors are common to all the states of the region.

Factors Contributing to the HIV/AIDS Epidemic

In 2008 southern Africa was described as experiencing "a perfect storm of HIV-related risks" (Piot et al. 2008, 853). Shula Marks (2002, 17) had suggested that in South Africa HIV had spread with such alarming speed because "in many ways, HIV/AIDS was a pandemic waiting to happen." Marks cited A. B. Zwi and A. J. Cabral (1991) and their definition of a "high-risk situation"—a term that describes "the range of social, economic, and political forces that place groups at particularly high risk of HIV infection." According to Zwi and Cabral, a number of features—impoverishment and disenfranchisement, rapid urbanization, the anonymity of urban life, labor migration, widespread population movements and displacements, social disruption, and wars, especially counterinsurgency wars—characterize these high-risk situations. According to Marks (2002, 17), in the 1980s South Africa's black population experienced nearly every one of these features. "Given its underlying health conditions and its levels of social dislocation in that decade," she continued, "it took no great prescience to predict that AIDS would wreak havoc in South, indeed Southern, Africa if and when it entered the region."

The set of factors that accounted for the rapid spread of the virus in Botswana, which lacked the conflict and the entrenched poverty of South Africa, were nonetheless similar. According to Bertha Osei Hwedie (2001a, 56), in the early twenty-first century, these included

> the extreme mobility of the population and good communication systems; a high rate of sexually transmitted diseases [STDs]; the accepted norm of sexual behaviour that allows multiple partners and frequent change of partners prevalent in both rural and urban areas; the breakdown of traditional ways of regulating sexual behaviour due to rapid urbanization which currently stands at 45 percent; poverty, which, among other factors, forces women to engage in risky sexual behaviour; and gender relations which are biased in favour of males who dominate social and sexual relations leaving females powerless.

It is important to recognize that some of these variables are grounded in individual behaviors and cultural norms (agency). However, as evidenced from the country case studies in this volume, other factors, such as male living and migration patterns, are a result of historical and structural factors and thus cannot be divorced from apartheid and colonialism. Similarly, the condition of southern Africa's health care systems can only be explained with reference to both international and national policies. Given the scope of the disease in southern Africa, the specific factors fueling the epidemic in the region warrant closer examination.

Mode of Transmission

In southern Africa, HIV transmission occurs primarily within long-term and occasional heterosexual partnerships (Piot et al. 2008, 853). The fact that in Africa as a whole the virus is transmitted primarily by heterosexual intercourse has meant, among other things, that many more women than men are infected in Africa. In nearly all countries in sub-Saharan Africa the majority of people living with HIV are women; indeed 76 percent of all HIV-positive women in the world live in Africa (UNAIDS 2010c).[4] A higher percentage of women infected with the virus leads directly to more children becoming infected with the virus. Indeed, 87 percent of the children infected with the virus worldwide live in Africa. This is because there are more women of child-bearing age infected in Africa than elsewhere and because African women, on average, have more children than women elsewhere in the world.[5] According to a United Nations Development Fund for Women (UNIFEM) report, more than 85 percent of the cases of pediatric infection in Africa have resulted from perinatal transmission (UNIFEM n.d.). Moreover, nearly all children in Africa are breast-fed, and breast-feeding is another transmission route for the virus. The result is that most of the world's mother-to-child transmission of HIV occurs in Africa.

More recently, researchers have come to recognize the importance of par-ticular patterns of sexual behavior. Surveys from across Africa have found that lifetime numbers of sexual partners in African countries tend to be similar to those in Europe and the Americas and much lower than those in Asia. But while African people may not have more sexual partners than people in other coun-tries, they are more likely to have two or three partners concurrently—what has been termed long-term concurrency—rather than two or three or more partners serially (Epstein 2008, 1265–1266). Long-time concurrency has been shown to give rise to "an interlocking network of sexual relationships that creates a superhighway for HIV" in a way that serial monogamy does not. According to Helen Epstein (2008, 1266) and mentioned also by Peter Piot and colleagues (2008, 848), long-term concurrency "probably explains why HIV in Africa has spread so rapidly beyond typical 'high risk groups' such as sex workers."

Lack of Male Circumcision

One factor distinguishing southern, and to a lesser extent eastern, Africa from the rest of the continent (and some other parts of the world) is the low rate of male circumcision. In 2000 John Caldwell (2000, 120) noted that "whole eth-nic groups" in the two parts of Africa do not practice male circumcision and posited that this may have contributed to the rapid spread of the virus. Indeed, recent studies have found that circumcised men are 60 to 70 percent less sus-ceptible to HIV than uncircumcised men (Epstein 2008, 1266). Over the years, this factor in particular has been identified as one that could be relatively eas-ily rectified, with programs to increase circumcision in uncircumcised men growing across the region.

The Status of Women

A lower status for women in most African societies has contributed to a higher HIV prevalence among African women and therefore in Africa as a whole. According to UNAIDS (2009a, 22), "women's vulnerability to HIV in sub-

Saharan Africa stems not only from their greater physiological susceptibility to heterosexual transmission, but also to the severe social, legal and economic disadvantages that they often confront." Women are often infected at a younger age than are men. In many southern African countries, young women (in their teens and twenties) are many times more likely to be infected with the virus than are young men of the same age. This is due to several factors. In situations of poverty, for example, "relationships with men (casual or formalized through marriage) can serve as vital opportunities for financial and social security, or for satisfying material aspirations. Generally, older men are likely to be able to offer such security. But, in areas where HIV/AIDS is widespread, they are also more likely to have become infected with HIV" (UNAIDS 2002a, 19). Moreover, in southern Africa and other parts of Africa, up to 80 percent of women aged fifteen to twenty-four have been shown to lack sufficient knowledge about HIV/AIDS. Finally, young women and girls are more biologically prone to HIV infection (UNAIDS 2002a, 19).[6]

To make matters worse, HIV-positive women are typically discriminated against when they attempt to access care and support for themselves. Men are more likely to be admitted to health care facilities than are women, and family resources, in the form of medicine and care, are more likely to be devoted to AIDS-infected men than to AIDS-infected women members of a household (UNAIDS 2001). Reflecting their lower status in society, women often have limited access to health care, meaning that their symptoms may also go unrecognized and untreated (UNIFEM n.d.). HIV-positive women may be physically and emotionally abused when their status is revealed. In South Africa in the early part of the first decade of the twenty-first century, a woman named Gugu Dlamini was brutally killed by young men in her community shortly after publicly announcing her HIV-positive status (Power 2003, 59). In Zimbabwe, AIDS widows have been accused of causing the deaths of their husbands (UNIFEM n.d.).

Moreover, women are largely responsible for an invisible and unaccounted-for "care economy" that has emerged in many parts of the world, including southern Africa. This care economy is dominated by older women and young girls who sacrifice their lives to fill the HIV/AIDS care gap left by governments and the global community. This happens when young girls are pulled out of school to care for sick and dying parents or siblings, or when grandmothers take on the burden of caring for sick and dying family members or for orphaned children. With no information and training and few resources at their disposal, these female caregivers are looking after HIV-positive family members, often at great risk to themselves (Urdang 2006).[7]

In addition, according to UNAIDS (2001), there is growing evidence that a large share of new cases of HIV infection are due to gender-based violence in homes, schools, the workplace, and other social settings. A recent study in Lesotho found that sexual and physical violence was a key determinant in the country's HIV epidemic (UNAIDS 2009a, 22). Coerced sex, because of increased tearing, increases the likelihood of HIV transmission. Unwilling sex with an infected partner also increases the likelihood of HIV transmission, because a condom is not likely to be used (UNIFEM n.d.). In situations of political strife, civil disorder, or war, women and girls are often systematically targeted for abuse, including sexual abuse, thereby dramatically increasing their chances of acquiring HIV or other sexually transmitted infections. In situations of political conflict and war one also finds poverty, famine, destruction of health and other infrastructure, large population movements, and the breakdown of families. All of this means a breakdown in the institutions and services that normally protect women and girls (USIP 2001, 8). Fortunately, since the early 2000s, southern African has not experienced much political conflict or war.

War and Conflict

At one time, however, widespread conflict certainly contributed to the spread of HIV/AIDS in the region. Soldiers, with their often high infection rates, have been a vector of the disease in southern Africa and other parts of Africa (USIP 2001, 8). They can be responsible for spreading HIV/AIDS not only within situations of conflict and war but also once back in their home towns, villages, and communities upon demobilization. War and other conflicts contribute to persons being displaced from their homes internally and even becoming refugees across national borders. Displaced persons and refugees, the bulk of whom are women and children, are susceptible to harassment and exploitation by soldiers and others and usually have no recourse to any legal or social protections. In actual conflict situations, according to the USIP (2001, 8–9), "law enforcement, judicial, religious, and other state systems that protect individual rights break down. Within this set of circumstances the vulnerability of women to sexual intimidation is greatly increased." Indeed, the incidence of rape and other forms of sexual coercion skyrockets in conflict settings as witnessed in appalling numbers in Democratic Republic of Congo throughout the first decade of the twenty-first century.

Indeed, from 1998 to late 2002, several southern African countries, including Angola, Namibia, and Zimbabwe, were embroiled in the war in DRC. Congolese soldiers are said to be heavily infected with HIV, as well as up to 70 percent of Zimbabwe's armed forces, according to some estimates. In Angola, a long-standing war only ended around the same time, in 2002, and in Mozambique only a decade earlier. In South Africa, the province that has seen the highest levels of HIV infection is KwaZulu-Natal. This is also the part of South Africa that "witnessed the most prolonged, bloodiest and dirtiest of the conflicts that marked the last days of the apartheid government, as well as some of the most rapid and disorderly urbanization in the subcontinent"

(Marks 2002, 19–20). Finally, as Joe Collins and Bill Rau (2000) note, "warfare presents major opportunity costs for Third World countries." In other words, money spent on military equipment and personnel is money not spent on HIV/AIDS treatment and prevention.

Labor Migration

Southern Africa's migrant labor system—involving the internal migration of men from the rural areas to mines and other places of employment in Botswana, Namibia, South Africa, or Zambia, or the cross-border migration of men from any number of southern African countries into South Africa—has proved to be the perfect setting for an HIV/AIDS epidemic. In a similar case decades ago, according to Marks (2002, 17), South Africa's migrant labor system was implicated in the spread of syphilis, another sexually transmitted infection. According to health practitioners at the time, treatment of the disease could not be successful in the context of a widespread migrant labor system. In addition to depleting the rural areas of young men, with implications for food security and family stability, the migrant labor system had "vast repercussions on public health control as 'the process of continuous movement of large numbers of people spread a variety of communicable diseases'" (Marks 2002, 18).

In South Africa and Namibia significant population movements accompanied the demise of apartheid, further facilitating the spread of infectious diseases. As influx controls were lifted, huge numbers of the rural poor and unemployed flocked to urban areas seeking greater opportunities. Instead, according to Marks (2002, 19), many found themselves in "urban shacklands" where they were "easy prey to the diseases of poverty like malnutrition and tuberculosis, to parasitic infections and to sexually transmitted diseases. All of these diseases also lower resistance to HIV infection."

The epidemiological relationship between labor mobility or migration and HIV has been established in study after study (Collins and Rau 2000). Male migrants typically leave impoverished rural areas that offer little or no hope of employment for lengthy stays at mines or other work sites far from home. Once there, removed from family and other support systems, men often spend hard-earned wages on alcohol and high-risk sex, sometimes even starting families at the work site.[8] When migrant workers return home to rural areas, they act as another vector of HIV transmission (Collins and Rau 2000; Poku and Cheru 2001, 45). And as the male migrants themselves fall prey to the disease, their remittances home become less frequent, thereby adding to the hardships already facing women and children in rural areas (Upton 2003, 317). Moreover, not only do women lose their husbands and their remittances, but they also often lose secure access to land, thereby jeopardizing their livelihoods and those of their children. While somewhat diminished in southern Africa today, the migrant labor system, in facilitating the spread of HIV/AIDS, contributes to a vicious cycle of poverty and need.[9]

The Constraints of Poverty

Another factor contributing to the HIV/AIDS epidemic in southern Africa today is high levels of poverty. While the South African economy is the most advanced in sub-Saharan Africa, and Botswana, Angola, and Namibia have relatively high per capita incomes by African standards, other countries such as Malawi, Zambia, Zimbabwe, and Mozambique are among the poorest countries in the world. And poverty in the region has been exacerbated in recent decades by economic reform programs that have mandated large cutbacks to many social services. Indeed, poverty underlies a number of AIDS cofactors in the region. In general, poverty is associated with weak endowments of human and financial resources, such as low levels of education, including literacy and numeracy; few marketable skills; generally poor health; and low labor productivity (Poku 2001, 195). Poverty certainly contributes to higher levels of labor mobility and to women's entering into commercial sex work.[10] Poverty in the rural areas means that households are much less able to cope with drought, famine, health emergencies, and other disasters.

One aspect of high poverty levels is overburdened and inadequate health care systems, which in turn facilitate the epidemic. Most health care systems in southern Africa are not easily able to cope with existing health care problems, let alone an epidemic of the magnitude of HIV/AIDS. Underfunded and understaffed health care systems mean that countries are not able to keep their blood supplies as clean as they might otherwise do, making available another transmission route for the virus. They also mean that countries are less able to diagnose the disease, allowing people to avoid knowing their HIV status.[11] Such health care systems also mean that people are less likely to be effectively treated for the opportunistic infections that accompany HIV/AIDS, thereby contributing to early deaths from HIV infection. Finally, countries with inadequate health care systems are less able to diagnose or treat the sexually transmitted infections that greatly amplify the chances of HIV transmission.

The Political Dimension

A final factor fueling the HIV/AIDS epidemic in southern Africa has been the failure of some governments to respond adequately to the epidemic, though this has evolved considerably with time. In some ways, it should come as no surprise that governments anywhere might take a long time to respond appropriately. As Marks (2002, 16) notes, unlike other "plagues," because HIV "is transmitted sexually, it makes government and indeed public health intervention particularly fraught. Perhaps no other single human behaviour is as surrounded by cultural sensitivities." One early response to the crisis in many countries was simply to deny the existence of an HIV/AIDS crisis or to refuse to acknowledge its magnitude and gravity.

The initial response to HIV/AIDS by Thabo Mbeki, president of South Africa from 1999 to 2008, has been well documented (Power 2003); indeed, it attracted widespread condemnation, both within South Africa and internationally. For some time Mbeki refused to acknowledge the link between HIV and AIDS; in a public statement in 2000, Mbeki declared that extreme poverty rather than AIDS was "the world's biggest killer." "Since poverty also broke down people's immune systems, Mbeki said, 'we could not blame everything on a single virus'" (Power 2003, 63). As discussed above, poverty is clearly a cofactor for AIDS in southern Africa; in a very real sense, poverty can contribute to the spread of AIDS and the lack of resources to combat it. However, as observers noted, "by attributing the AIDS epidemic to mass poverty and malnutrition, Mbeki sidestepped difficult questions about sex and responsibility" (Power 2003, 63). Mbeki also refused to consider government sponsorship of antiretrovirals in the public sector, charging that the drugs were too dangerous and were being proposed for widespread use in an effort "to poison blacks" (Power 2003, 62). Indeed, it took a court ruling in mid-2001 to force the South African government to make available to pregnant women the drug nevirapine, which has proved so effective worldwide in reducing mother-to-child transmission of the virus.

Mbeki's response contrasts markedly with that of his successor Jacob Zuma, who in early 2010 launched a national HIV counseling and testing drive in South Africa aimed at testing 15 million South Africans by 2011. UNAIDS executive director Michel Sidibe called it the "biggest national mobilization in South Africa around any one single issue since the end of apartheid." Another goal of the campaign was to expand access to antiretroviral treatment to 80 percent of those in need in South Africa by 2011 (UNAIDS 2010f); indeed already by 2008 South Africa had the largest antiretroviral therapy program in the world (UNAIDS 2009a, 16). Another early response was for leaders to stigmatize HIV and to punish those associated with it. In late 2000 Malawi's then-president Bakili Muluzi reportedly called upon police to "intensify swoops on known brothels to slow down the spread of AIDS. So convinced was the president of the relationship between high prevalence and the sex industry that he proposed to give police greater powers to restrict the 'civil liberties' of known prostitutes and their clients" (Poku 2001, 199–200). In Swaziland, King Mswati III displayed both ignorance and a penchant for barbarism when, during a parliamentary debate, he called for HIV-positive citizens to be "sterilized and branded" (Poku 2001, 200). In Zimbabwe, according to Catherine Boone and Jake Batsell (2001, 10), AIDS remained a "closeted issue in Zimbabwean politics throughout the 1990s," despite a growing epidemic. According to the authors, *The Herald,* the government daily newspaper, consistently denied any government obligation to respond to the AIDS crisis and berated young people "who contract AIDS because they insist on indulging in risky sexual experimentation."

Caldwell (2000, 121) suggests that, in some respects, governments cannot be condemned for not doing more. He argues that for many African leaders there is a "fear of alienating their followers by intruding into sexual matters and by speaking aloud on such subjects. There is [also] a fear of failure." At the same time, as Marks (2002, 13) notes in her article on HIV in southern Africa, quoting A. M. Brandt (1998, 148): "The way a society responds to problems of disease reveals its deepest cultural, social and moral values." Not to mention that the willingness or unwillingness of leaders to act forcefully in combating HIV/AIDS can be the difference in the life or death of thousands of citizens, as the examples of Yoweri Museveni in Uganda and Festus Mogae in Botswana and, increasingly now, others have shown (UNAIDS 2008a).

Stemming the Tide of HIV/AIDS

As everywhere, two issues dominate the discussion of combating HIV/AIDS in southern Africa: treatment and care for those already infected, and prevention for those not yet infected. In both areas, significant gains have been recorded in southern Africa over the past decade—as in the rest of Africa. Some of these significant gains reflect a more concerted effort on the part of the global community toward HIV/AIDS: making AIDS a major global health priority, scaling up universal access to treatment, focusing on HIV prevention, and integrating and combining resources and responses as in the collaborative efforts of UNAIDS, the Global Fund, PEPFAR, and the Millennium Development Goals, among others. But the gains surely also reflect a heightened recognition among southern African governments and leaders of the need to act forcefully and the tremendous benefits—on all fronts—of doing so.

Treatment

Remarkably, by the end of 2008, 44 percent of adults and 35 percent of children in sub-Saharan Africa in need of antiretroviral therapy had access to such treatment. Five years earlier, only 2 percent of those in need of such treatment had received it. There are regional differences within sub-Saharan Africa, and antiretroviral therapy coverage is notably higher in eastern and southern Africa (48 percent) than in west and central Africa (30 percent) (UNAIDS 2009a, 25). In 2009, the largest increase in one year in the number of people receiving antiretroviral therapy worldwide was recorded. Remarkably again, the greatest increase in the absolute number of people receiving treatment during 2009 was in sub-Saharan Africa—nearly 1 million people (WHO/UNAIDS/UNICEF

2010, 4). Moreover, as noted in a recent UNAIDS report (2009a, 25), "the rapid scaling-up of antiretroviral therapy in sub-Saharan Africa is generating considerable public health gains."

Treatment and care for those already infected with the virus had once been a highly contentious issue in southern Africa, played out very publicly in South Africa. Given the cost of antiretroviral drugs, most Africans were never going to be able to pay for them themselves. In the developing world, two options were initially open to countries seeking to reduce the cost of the anti-retrovirals—producing generic versions of the drugs locally or importing them from third parties abroad (Akukwe and Foote 2001).[12] In South Africa, the Treatment Action Campaign (TAC) took the lead in challenging the multinational pharmaceutical companies that produced the antiretroviral drugs and that sought to prevent South Africa from producing cheaper, generic versions of them. After initially filing a suit against the South African government, thirty-nine pharmaceutical companies withdrew the suit under intense local and international pressure (Akukwe and Foote 2001). Instead, the companies pledged to facilitate the flow of lower-priced antiretrovirals to Africa. By 2010 universal access to treatment for South Africans was identified as one of the top priorities of the South African government by Deputy President Kgalema Motlanthe. In seeking to achieve universal access, the government pledged to work with development partners and civil society, to support the regional and global AIDS response, and to advocate for a fully funded Global Fund (UNAIDS 2010e).

In January 2002, Botswana became the first country in Africa to make antiretrovirals and other medicines available, through the public health system, to all Batswana who needed them (Rollnick 2002). The government targeted 19,000 people (out of Botswana's total population of 330,000 HIV-positive adults) for enrollment in the first year of the program. Initial reports showed very high drug regimen adherence rates—90 to 100 percent—suggesting that the program was faring much better than anticipated (IRIN 2003). Free counseling and testing formed another component of the treatment program, as well as increasing the number of health care professionals and facilities. The effort in Botswana is a country-led public/private development partnership, known as the African Comprehensive HIV/AIDS Partnership, established in 2000 among the government of Botswana, the Bill and Melinda Gates Foundation, and the pharmaceutical business Merck and Company. Only five years after beginning to make medicines available through the public health system, Botswana was able to achieve near universal access to antiretroviral treatment, delivering HIV treatment to more than 90 percent of those who needed it (with Rwanda, Botswana is one of only two countries in Africa to have reached this milestone). Since 2004 the offer of HIV testing has been routine in all health facilities in Botswana (WHO/UNAIDS/UNICEF 2010; UNAIDS 2007, 2008a).

In 2003 the government of Namibia began implementing an antiretroviral therapy program through the public sector and was quickly able to provide coverage to thirty-five health facilities around the country. In 2002 the Namibian government had already made nevirapine available to pregnant women, on a trial basis, in two large urban centers, Windhoek and Oshakati. In 2007 the government announced the launching of a National HIV/AIDS Policy. In general in Namibia, access to treatment remains a challenge due to the sparsely distributed population and long distances between clinics. While Namibia is doing very well in treatment initiatives, prevention remains a greater hurdle (UNAIDS 2008b).

Initially, a number of arguments were made against the widespread use of antiretrovirals in Africa. One of the strongest was that Africa's generally very poor health infrastructures and high levels of poverty would make it very difficult for ordinary Africans, especially in the rural areas, to adhere to the strict regimens that are part and parcel of antiretroviral therapy (Rollnick 2002).[13] So far, however, this has not proved to be the case—far from it. In the first public clinic in South Africa to begin offering antiretroviral therapy—in the Cape Town township of Khayelitsha—380 men and women have adhered to the complex drug regimens, even more "fastidiously" than people in the United States, with the result that in 92 percent of cases "the virus had been suppressed to the point of being undetectable" (Power 2003, 56). Similarly, in Botswana in 2002, drug regimen adherence rates ranged between 90 and 100 percent (IRIN 2003). In a measure of how much progress has been made, discussion among governments, international organizations, and nongovernmental organizations in 2010 was about achieving universal access to treatment; removing stigma, discrimination, and gender and human rights abuses; strengthening of human resources and health care systems; and preventing any more infections—rather than worry over adherence rates that always seemed somewhat of a red herring anyway.

Prevention

Across the world, activism for HIV prevention has been much less pronounced than mobilization for HIV treatment (Piot et al. 2008, 851). If treatment programs are to remain viable and the impact of the epidemic is to be mitigated, then priority must be given to HIV prevention, according to UNAIDS (2009a, 26). Prevention programs are increasingly common throughout southern Africa. Several different prevention programs have been undertaken in Botswana. Prevention efforts have emphasized awareness campaigns targeted at all educational levels—primary, secondary, and tertiary. The most conspicuous has been the "ABC" campaign, successfully used in Uganda, which calls upon Batswana to "Abstain, Be Faithful, and Condomize." Widespread distribution of condoms is another part of overall prevention efforts (Osei Hwedie

2001a, 59). The aim of Botswana's multisectoral approach to HIV/AIDS prevention is to have no new infections in the country by 2016 (IRIN 2003).

Botswana's national policy for fighting HIV/AIDS has been in place since 1993 (UNAIDS 2004). The policy, issued by presidential directive, is a comprehensive one: "stipulating roles for everyone involved; designing control strategies; facilitating ways of mobilizing resources to cover costs; developing structures for implementation, and mechanisms for coordination and evaluation; and promoting the rights of both the infected as well as those not infected to enable them to live healthy and responsible lives" (Osei Hwedie 2001a, 57). Moreover, the policy includes roles for national leaders, government ministries, the private sector, NGOs, community-based organizations, and AIDS-infected people and their communities in the response to the epidemic. The policy, involving both prevention and care, aims to reduce the transmission of AIDS and its impact at all levels of society. "What is commendable about the policy," according to Osei Hwedie (2001a, 58), is that it has been followed by successive national strategic plans that build upon, but also revise as necessary, previous policy.[14]

Indeed, a number of governments in southern Africa have recognized the advantages, if not the necessity, of working together with local and international NGOs. Zambia has proposed a multidonor debt relief program to enhance its national response to the HIV/AIDS crisis. For Zambia, this proposal provides a way for the government to address the crisis, despite the country's very high external debt. Under the plan, "scarce national funds which now go to service the debt would be set aside for investment into activities that will control the spread of HIV/AIDS" (Poku and Cheru 2001, 51). The funds are available to Zambian NGOs as well as to the government for use in implementing national programs that help to prevent HIV/AIDS transmission, manage existing cases, and address the country's growing population of AIDS orphans. The program is part of an overall national HIV/AIDS strategy developed by Zambia's HIV/AIDS Council and Secretariat (Poku and Cheru 2001, 51).

According to Epstein (2008, 1266), wherever infection rates have fallen in Africa (and the causes have been properly investigated), "reductions in sexual partners have been the dominant factor." UNAIDS (2009a, 30) reports that in southern Africa "a trend towards safer sexual behavior was observed among both young men and young women (15–24 years old) between 2000 and 2007." Increased condom use has also contributed to recent declines, although partner reduction is still the much more effective way of decreasing overall infection rates. Epstein argues that school-based AIDS education programs often fail to warn young people of the dangers of long-term concurrency, focusing instead on abstinence and condom use, thereby failing to make clear the dangers of even a few concurrent relationships. UNAIDS (2009a, 26) argues that in much of Africa, prevention strategies are failing "to address the key drivers of national epidemics"; those over age twenty-five (and involved in stable relationships) may account for more than two-thirds of adult infections, and yet few programs target adults, married couples, or people in long-term relationships.

Male circumcision is important, but only partially effective, in preventing HIV infection. Moreover, depending upon how it is done, male circumcision can also be risky, as attested by dozens of deaths in the past few years due to botched bush circumcisions in South Africa, among other places. Among southern African countries, Botswana and Namibia have taken steps to increase medical male circumcision for HIV prevention. Additionally, South Africa is considering strategies for neonatal circumcision, concluding that painless circumcision for nearly all newborn boys within a week of birth would be feasible (UNAIDS 2009a, 32).

Mother-to-child transmission continues to account for a substantial, though decreasing, share of new HIV infections in many African countries (UNAIDS 2009a, 35). As such, preventing mother-to-child transmission is a critical component of an overall prevention strategy. As with antiretroviral therapy, significant progress has been made in expanding access to services to prevent mother-to-child transmission. In eastern and southern Africa, 64 percent of HIV-infected pregnant women received antiretroviral therapy in 2008 as compared to a much lower percentage in 2004, with positive results. In Botswana, Namibia, and South Africa, coverage of antiretrovirals for preventing mother-to-child transmission of HIV reached more than 80 percent by 2009 (UNAIDS 2010c). With such increases in services to prevent mother-to-child transmission in Botswana, the number of new HIV infections among children fell precipitously from 4,600 in 1999 to 890 in 2007. In general, the services that can be provided in antenatal clinics mean that not only can newborns be prevented from becoming infected, but the health of HIV-infected women can be better monitored and women as a group are more likely than men to know their HIV status (UNAIDS 2009a, 35).

The solutions to southern Africa's AIDS crisis are evolving markedly. As alluded to earlier, political leadership has certainly played a critical role in combating AIDS at the national level. Few African leaders realized early in the epidemic the severity of the disease and the calamity of inaction. Southern Africa had no leaders who immediately aggressively championed an anti-AIDS platform, though former president Festus Mogae came very close. Indeed, while president of Botswana from 1998 to 2008, Mogae made the government AIDS response the priority of his administration—with results to show. Since leaving office he has continued to work to halt the spread of AIDS around Africa and beyond (UNAIDS 2008a). In the interim, many leaders and former leaders have become actively engaged in the struggle against HIV/AIDS. Former South African president Nelson Mandela and former Zambian president Kenneth Kaunda have organized charitable foundations to address

AIDS and AIDS-related issues. Former Mozambican president Joachim Chissano and his prime minister, Pascal Mocumbi, a medical doctor, have taken strong and public stands against HIV/AIDS.[15] In Namibia in 2009, President Hifikepunye Pohamba urged representatives of more than fifty-five countries to heed a renewed call to work together to fight the AIDS pandemic (UNAIDS 2009b). In South Africa in 2010, President Jacob Zuma and his deputy president were highly visible advocates for greater HIV testing, the adoption of HIV prevention strategies, and the achievement of universal HIV treatment. National leadership, especially at the presidential level, is not only symbolic but also demonstrates that combating the disease is a part of the political agenda of African states.[16]

"Striving for Normality in a Time of AIDS"

HIV/AIDS has become part of the fabric of life in southern Africa. For a time in countries like Botswana, it seemed that people were attending funerals each and every weekend; more recently that pattern has altered notably. (That is not just anecdote; from 2003 to 2007 the estimated number of AIDS-related deaths fell by more than half in Botswana; additionally, the estimated number of newly orphaned children declined by 40 percent [UNAIDS 2009a, 25].) Fears of the most dire economic and political consequences of HIV/AIDS have been revised, though even the mitigated impacts are not to be ignored. In a recent article on Malawi, Pauline Peters, Peter Walker, and Daimon Kambewa (2008) found that at least some Malawians were "trying to control the abnormal circumstances of the rising toll of HIV-related illness and death." While 40 percent of households in one sample had experienced at least one AIDS-related death, only 10 percent of the same households were found "to be suffering acute or serious livelihood stress." As Peters, Walker, and Kambewa conclude, people are "striving for normality in a time of AIDS."

Notes

1. See UNDP 2002, 224–225; UNAIDS, *Country Fact Sheets 2010,* http://cfs .unaids.org/. Retrieved January 2011.

2. According to the US National Intelligence Council (2000), "infant mortality is a good indicator of the overall quality of life, which correlates strongly with political instability . . . high infant mortality has a particularly strong correlation with the likelihood of state failure in partial democracies."

3. For example, according to UNAIDS (n.d.), "the cost of treatment for one AIDS patient for one year is about equal to the cost of providing education to 10 children for one year."

4. According to Caldwell (2000), in otherwise healthy persons, a woman is about three times as likely as a man to be infected through vaginal intercourse. According to UNAIDS (2002a, 6), 55 percent of HIV-positive adults are women in North Africa and

the Middle East, and 50 percent in the Caribbean. For all other regions of the world, the percentage is 36 percent (South and Southeast Asia) or lower.

5. Early in the first decade of the twenty-first century, the fertility rate for women in sub-Saharan Africa was 5.8 children per woman, the highest in the world. This compared to 4.1 for the Arab states, 3.6 for South Asia, and 2.7 for Latin America and the Caribbean (UNAIDS 2002a, 165).

6. As noted, women are more susceptible to HIV infection than men during vaginal intercourse because of a larger mucosal surface and because microlesions that can occur during intercourse may be entry points for the virus. Very young women or girls, with immature genital tracts, are even more vulnerable in this respect. This risk is elevated by the common practice of early marriage for girls, often to older men, in parts of Africa. The problem has been further compounded by the belief in some places that intercourse with a virgin will cure HIV, meaning that younger girls are being forced into unsafe sex with HIV-positive men (UNIFEM n.d.).

7. According to UNIFEM (n.d.), older women are sometimes looking after thirty to forty grandchildren orphaned by AIDS. UNIFEM studies in Zimbabwe show that girls are increasingly pulled out of school to take on the burden of health care and that there is a decrease in school enrollment of girls. The survey showed that 70 percent of the children pulled out of school were girls.

8. A number of authors, such as Peter Delius and Liz Walker (2002, 6) and Catherine Campbell and Brian Williams (2001, 138), note the link between constructions of masculine identity among migrant workers and risk-taking behaviors in the mines. Campbell and Williams assert that to help cope with harsh, potentially life-threatening conditions in the mines, "mineworkers constantly appeal to masculine identities reminding one another that as men they need to have the courage to deal with the stresses and dangers of underground work in order to fulfil their roles as breadwinners. While this concept of masculinity serves as a key coping mechanism at work, it also has other sexual associations: a rampant sexual desire driving men to seek out multiple casual partners; the representation of a biological male need for pleasures of 'flesh-to-flesh sex'; the desire to father many children; high levels of risk-taking which cause men to scorn the alleged dangers of a mysterious disease which may kill them in five to ten years time."

9. Delius and Walker (2002, 7), based upon the work of Mark Lurie (2000), suggest that the portrayal of migrant workers as transmitting HIV to the rural areas may be overdrawn. They write: "The idea that rural areas represent a haven from unsafe practices was also shown [in a recent conference] to be an illusion. Research presented at the conference suggests that people are having sex even younger in rural than in urban areas. . . . The image of returning workers being the main source of infection in rural communities was also called into question by data, which suggested that women in rural areas often have higher rates of HIV infection than their migrant husbands."

10. Not only does poverty drive women into commercial sex work, but it also "makes it difficult for women to refuse sex if a client refuses to use a condom and this is exacerbated by women's lack of confidence in a male-dominated community that accords them little social status or respect" (Campbell and Williams 2001, 138).

11. In many cases people are reluctant to know their HIV status anyway, because of the stigmatization and even violence that often greet a known HIV-positive status. Moreover, in the absence of available antiretroviral drugs, the incentive for knowing one's status is greatly diminished.

12. Such a system of importing is otherwise known as "compulsory licensing"—an international trade mechanism by which countries can instruct a patent holder to license the right to use a patent to any national company or government agency. It is

also known as "parallel importing"—whereby a country imports goods for resale without authorization from the original seller.

13. The fear was that lack of proper adherence to such regimens, brought on by poor nutrition, lack of access to clean water, long distance to health clinics, and so on, would result in the development of drug-resistant strains of HIV. Another argument was that rather than "wasting" resources on those who were already ill and could likely not properly utilize the drugs, resources should be expended on preventing new infections.

14. In fact, as far back as 1985, when the first HIV-infected person in Botswana was diagnosed, the government of Botswana had developed programs to address HIV/AIDS. These included a national AIDS control program, a one-year emergency response, a short-term plan, and then a medium-term plan (Osei Hwedie 2001a, 58).

15. Author interview, Harare, June 11, 2001.

16. In an interesting article about the role of executive time horizons in state responses to AIDS in east and southern Africa, Kim Yi Dionne (2011) finds that while lengthening the executive time horizon increases the level of government spending on health, executives with shorter time horizons tend to have more comprehensive AIDS policies than their counterparts with longer time horizons.

11 Women Remaking Politics in Southern Africa

In most countries in southern Africa, women are more than half the population. And yet they remain underrepresented at nearly all levels of politics and decisionmaking, in many sectors of the formal economy, and in leadership positions throughout society.[1] In a number of southern African countries where white minority rule continued into the 1980s and 1990s, women contend with the legacy of a triple oppression based on race, class, and gender. But even where independence was achieved sooner, women remain disadvantaged with regard to a variety of socioeconomic indicators, and they bear the burdens of an increasing feminization of poverty clearly exacerbated by decades of harsh economic reforms (see Table 11.1). Everywhere in the region women are subject to discrimination in the areas of land tenure and customary law. And throughout the region women face spiraling levels of violence and an HIV/AIDS crisis that is affecting them, in many diverse ways, even more harshly than it is men.

At the same time, southern African women have achieved some of the highest levels of legislative representation in the world, and they have organized vibrant women's movements across the region. In many countries they fought side by side with their male comrades in the struggle for independence, and in other countries they were part and parcel of efforts to end years of authoritarian, single-party rule in favor of a more democratic, multiparty rule. In a few countries in the region, women easily outnumber men at universities, and they are at the forefront of efforts to stem the tide of HIV/AIDS and to care for those already afflicted. For decades women have cared for families and communities in the rural areas while men have migrated out in search of work.

In a region in which a resort to arms was necessary to win independence in more cases than not, in which local struggles were framed in larger Cold War terms, in which minority white settler populations ruled over exploited and disenfranchised majority black populations, race and class oppression have received particular attention. But especially for the more than half the population in the region who are women, gender-based oppression has had a significance that cannot be ignored.

327

Table 11.1 Gender Inequality Index and Other Indicators

| | Gender Inequality Index, 2008 | | Life Expectancy at Birth, 2010 | | Adult Literacy Rate, 1999–2007 (percentage age 15 and above) | | Combined Primary, Secondary, and Tertiary Gross Enrollment Ratio, 2007 (%) | | Estimated Earned Income, 2007 (PPP US$) | |
	Rank	Value	Female	Male	Female	Male	Female	Male	Female	Male
Angola	91	.663	39.52	37.48	54.2	82.9			4,212	6,592
Botswana	126	.758	60.75	61.11	82.9	82.8	71.3	70.0	9,961	17,307
Malawi	111	.718	51.64	50.22	64.6	79.2	61.7	62.1	646	877
Mozambique	75	.615	40.68	42.05	33.0	57.2	50.2	59.4	759	848
Namibia	82	.635	51.64	52.25	87.4	88.6	68.2	66.3	4,006	6,339
South Africa	124	.752	48.29	50.08	87.2	88.9	77.3	76.3	7,328	12,273
Zambia	105	.705	53.28	50.81	60.7	80.8	60.7	66.0	980	1,740
Zimbabwe			47.11	47.98	88.3	94.1	53.4	55.5		

Sources: "Human Development Report, 2009," 2010, http://hdr.undp.org/en/reports; CIA World Factbook, 2010, https://www.cia.gov.

Women in the Precolonial and Colonial Periods in Southern Africa

As in all of Africa, the position of women in precolonial southern African societies varied considerably from one group to another and over place and time. Toward the end of the precolonial period, women fulfilled many important roles in their societies, as Iris Berger notes:

> During the nineteenth century, women in most societies remained central to production, trade, and other economic pursuits and had considerable autonomy in controlling the products of their labor. In centralized kingdoms, queen mothers and members of royal families wielded significant power and authority. As healers, priestesses, and spirit mediums, other women addressed individual and communal afflictions, while older women directed life-cycle rituals for girls that helped to create cohesion in values and institutions. Substantial variation remained, however, in the levels of women's political and legal authority and in the degree of submissiveness and deference demanded of them. (1999, 24)

For example, at one end of the spectrum, among the Tswana, women remained legal minors all their lives. "Access to land depended on the goodwill of their husband's family. Women were barred from the ward or chiefly court and thus rendered politically powerless. Severe beatings by husbands and fathers received no social censure. Although nominally protected by a web of obligations and dependencies, women who opposed male dominance lived in fear of abandonment and poverty" (Parpart 1988, 209). Xhosa women, like Tswana women, controlled the crops that they produced but could not own cattle and also remained legal minors subject to male control throughout their lives. Zulu women "experienced similar forms of subordination, intensified by the development of a highly militaristic state in the early nineteenth century" (Berger 1999, 27). Among the Tonga of southern Zambia, by contrast, "although a woman's wealth was often in her brothers' custody, she had her own fields and granary as well as control over grain production. This control over land enabled women to command the labor and allegiance of sons and sons-in-law and facilitated a degree of access to political power. Some women even became village headwomen" (Parpart 1988, 209). Other women even held high political office—for example, among the Zulu (and other groups in Africa) as queen mothers. These positions could be inherited or elected. Yet the fact that most Zulu women were mainly in subordinate roles reveals that there were clear limits to women's political power. Nonetheless, women who enjoyed relatively high status often "had important ritual roles, especially those concerned with fertility and social survival" (Parpart 1988, 210).

A number of factors likely account for such differences in women's access to political and economic power at the time. For example, when women controlled certain economic tasks or, as in the case of the Tonga, had security of tenure over land, they were more likely to wield some political authority or power within their group. So, in agricultural societies "where women controlled certain productive areas, such as farming, marketing or trading, their power and authority seem to have been largely based on this very control." Indeed where women were allowed to accumulate wealth they were most likely to have political institutions "which not only protected them but also enabled them to exert influence" (Parpart 1988, 209). Those societies that were matrilineal societies usually allowed greater land security for women thereby placing them in a more favorable position. In the case of the Tswana, the position of women "may have been connected with the society's great vulnerability to drought and economic scarcity" (Berger 1999, 27).[2] In general, according to Berger, many southern African societies combined cattle-keeping, state systems, and a greater domination of women. Age also played a significant role in determining women's access to power and authority.

Indeed, age was just as important as gender in many African societies, and as women aged they achieved positions of greater power and authority in the family and community.[3] All social relationships in a community reflected the idea that older members of the group (women and men) commanded the respect of younger members of the group. While this principle structured relations between rulers and family heads, patrons and clients, and husbands and wives, it also meant that "mothers-in-law held authority over wives, as did older over younger co-wives" (Berger 1999, 6). Thus women were able to wield public power and authority as members of older women's "age grades," in addition to positions as queen mothers, royal wives, priestesses, healers, and spirit mediums (Berger 1999, 6). So, for example, during the nineteenth century, "although Shona women exercised considerable influence in their households and lineages, only a few women, through their religious and political positions, occupied a status equivalent to that of men. . . . Women's status increased over the course of their life cycles, however, first as they married and bore children, and later as they exercised authority over co-wives and daughters-in-law" (Berger 1999, 25). According to Berger (1999, 6), women's access to greater power within the family and community as they aged makes it "hazardous to generalize about their status in society." As noted above, there was considerable variation in the level of women's political access and influence between, and in some instances within, societies. In any case, despite the critical role of women, the bulk of political power in southern Africa's precolonial societies was held by men.

With the onset of formal colonialism in the late nineteenth century in most of southern Africa, the peoples of the region became increasingly integrated into a European-dominated global economic and political system, and the relative positions of women and men were transformed in many ways. For women, most scholars suggest, colonialism brought about an overall decline in their position—particularly relative to that of men (Berger 1999; Parpart 1988; Staudt 1987). As Jane Parpart writes:

> For most African women (with the exception of some urban women) the colonial period was characterized by significant losses in both power and authority. Colonial officials accepted Western gender stereotypes which assigned women to the domestic domain, leaving economic and political matters to men. As a result, although many African men suffered under colonialism, new opportunities eventually appeared for them, while women's economic and political rights often diminished. Colonial officials ignored potential female candidates for chiefships, scholarships and other benefits. Many female institutions were destroyed, often more out of ignorance than malice. (1988, 210)

Women's loss of political power during this period was often associated with, if not a result of, losses in access to land and labor power. In the view of colonial officials, men were the farmers and producers of food in Africa, and when land rights were commercialized, men, considered to be the heads of households, received the titles to the land. In Zimbabwe and South Africa, according to Parpart (1988, 210–211), women's land was often transferred to men as land was commercialized. Moreover, while women were considered mere subsistence farmers, men were identified as potential cash crop farmers and therefore were eligible for technical and other assistance. Indeed, new technologies, such as the plow, introduced in South Africa in the nineteenth century, often affected women negatively. "Both in the ethnically diverse northeastern Cape and among the Tswana, the plow increased men's work in food production, granting them rights to the crops they grew, and sometimes expanding their control over women's labor" (Berger 1999, 29). As a result, male farmers were better able to accumulate a surplus and came increasingly to dominate the rural areas.

Under such circumstances, some rural women were motivated to seek opportunities in emerging urban areas. But here again, women's efforts were often thwarted, for in the urban areas, "all but the most unskilled and irregular wage labor remained a male preserve," with the result that women moved largely into the informal sector (Parpart 1988, 211). Over time, colonial authorities attempted to close off that venue for women as well, passing laws that made it difficult for them to subsist independently in urban areas. For example, such laws restricted women's ability to brew and sell homemade beer, one of the main informal income-generating opportunities for women in the urban areas. In some South African towns and cities at the turn of the twentieth century, many black women found employment as domestic workers. In Zambia around the same time some women were targeted to be trained as "children's nurses" or "girl domestic servants," thereby releasing men (who also worked as domestics) for the mining industry (Staudt 1987, 200). In Cape Town, as clothing production took hold by the onset of World War I, some women began working in factories, preferring this to domestic service in white households (Berger 1999, 34).

In controlling women's migration to the urban areas, colonial authorities were attempting to control the production and reproduction of labor, perhaps the critical ingredient in the emerging regionwide mineral economy. Indeed, a steady flow of low-wage male labor was essential to the exploitation of mines throughout southern Africa, as well as for building the associated infrastructure and for working the commercial farms and plantations. As many scholars have observed, rural women subsidized the regional mineral economy: "Women's continuing presence in the rural areas was necessary to subsidize the low wages of African men, to reproduce a new generation of laborers, and to provide the care to ill and aged workers that capital and parsimonious colonial states were equally unwilling to fund" (Berger 1999, 32). By continuing to produce food and provide care in the rural areas, women enabled male migrant workers to be paid less than a family, or living, wage.

Rural women not only enabled male outmigration from the rural areas during the colonial period but were also meant to encourage it, according to Kathleen Staudt (1987, 197): "The colonial state laid the foundation for societies to conform with its cultural notions of appropriate gender relations in industrializing class society, in which women enable and stimulate male work force productivity through home labor (which in Africa includes food production and water and fuel collection) and consumer demand as well as serve as a low skill reserve labor force. In this conception, women are also politically conservative and thus help maintain a given political order."[4]

Christian missionaries played a significant role in molding indigenous populations in the service of the colonial state. Certainly for most of the colonial period, mission schools provided the bulk of the education in African colonies.[5] And the Christian missionaries, like the colonial authorities, brought with them from overseas their own conceptions about gender roles and gender relations. Indeed, according to Staudt (1987, 197), the Christian missionaries' "ideology and activities also prescribed an extreme dichotomization of gender along the lines of antiquated Victorian norms." For African women, the missionaries established home and marriage training programs, which set a standard for women as "helpmates, appendages, and financial dependents on men as well as moral guardians of the home, family, and children." As Otrude Moyo and Saliwe Kawewe (2002, 170) note, "missionaries believed that education was an opportunity to 'improve' the status of African women; also, African women themselves saw education as a route to better their life chances." Indeed, some African women were able to take advantage of the opportunities offered by mission educations and move into otherwise unattainable positions as teachers or nurses.

Over time, however, with some notable exceptions, the losses to women's position became more pronounced. In the late colonial period, following

World War II, efforts to modernize African agriculture accelerated, again at the expense of women farmers. Continued greater access for men to credit, technology, extension services, and markets made many rural women increasingly dependent on their husbands. Likewise, a continued commercialization of land, with land titles invariably going to men, undermined women's autonomy in the economy and the family. Faced with hard times in the rural areas, men at least could usually leave in search of wage labor elsewhere. For example, in Malawi during the 1950s, "the failure of the peasant cotton economy, in which women and men had shared equally left women limited to precarious subsistence production, while men became increasingly involved in the cash economy, including migrant labor" (Berger 1999, 44).

But women, too, increasingly sought to leave the rural areas. Indeed, by the postwar period, the numbers of men and women in many urban areas began to equalize. Though most women continued to work in the informal sector, as petty traders, beer brewers, and prostitutes, some formal sector jobs were becoming increasingly available to women. Many urban women continued to be employed as domestic workers while others worked in factories processing food and tobacco and producing textiles. Some of the few women who had gained access to formal education entered "acceptably female professions" such as teaching, nursing, and social welfare. In many colonies, the authorities still balked at the increasing movement of women from the rural to urban areas, associating "urban women with prostitution, venereal disease, adultery, alcoholism, divorce, and high illegitimacy rates" (Berger 1999, 46). In an effort to stem the flow of women to the urban areas, South Africa took the most drastic step, extending pass laws to women in the 1950s and thereby severely curbing their freedom of movement (Berger 1999, 45). As the colonial state took over an increasing share of African education from the 1950s onward, colonial authorities imbued their educational efforts for girls and women with "a morally laden message emphasizing women's primary place in the home and family," combining academic subjects at school with a heavy emphasis on "domestic science" (Berger 1999, 46–47).[6]

Women in Nationalist Movements:
The Struggle for Independence

In the 1950s in southern Africa (sometimes earlier), nationalist and labor movements emerged to challenge the colonial state and demand independence. In southern Africa and throughout the continent these movements "drew initially from educated, urbanized World War II veterans and from the wage-earning populace, most of whom were men" (Staudt 1987, 202). But women quickly became active participants in nationalist struggles as well, engaging in anticolonial protest activities in some cases, and in other cases, in armed resistance and war. Independence came in three or four waves to southern Africa, and for the latter two waves, independence was achieved much later than on the rest of the continent. For countries such as Botswana, Malawi, and Zambia, however, independence was achieved relatively peacefully in the 1960s, following a trajectory similar to that of other sub-Saharan African countries. In Malawi and Zambia, women participated in the independence struggle by joining the women's branches of newly organized nationalist parties. In Zambia, women joined women's wings of, first, the (Zambian) African National Congress and, later, the United National Independence Party (UNIP), organizing protests in the rural and urban areas. "The UNIP Women's Brigade participated in literacy drives to aid voter registration and helped organize town funerals, mass demonstrations, rallies and boycotts to prove UNIP's power" (Parpart 1988, 214). In Botswana, by contrast, with no independence struggle to speak of, women were hardly involved in political parties at all. Indeed, it was not until well after independence that the two main political parties in Botswana even organized women's wings (Ntseane 2005). In the early years after independence, the main association available to women was the Botswana Council of Women, organized by the president's wife. This was an organization of the wives of politicians and chiefs who engaged primarily in social welfare activities.

Once independence was attained in these countries, as elsewhere on the continent, women and their concerns were dealt with primarily through the women's wings of newly elected ruling political parties or national women's associations firmly controlled by government. Such organizations were often headed by the wives of national presidents and other prominent male politicians and their tasks were often ceremonial—celebrating the president and the ruling party and greeting visiting foreign dignitaries.[7] With the rapid consolidation of single-party rule, moreover, a separate female agenda outside of the women's wings of political parties became even more unlikely, as Gwendolyn Mikell observes:

> The new society was represented by the single political party—a symbol of the idealized classless African society, which was above ethnicity, traditional status distinctions, traditional political domination of one group over another, gross male dominance over women, and social exploitation in any form. The massive state commitment to social services—the guarantees of health provisions and universal education as well as water, sanitation, and roads—were seen as benefiting women as well as men. The post-independence national goals were portrayed as negating the necessity for a separate female agenda. (1997, 23)

In Malawi, for example, the League of Malawi Women and the National Council for Women in Development were two of several organizations affiliated with the ruling Malawi Congress Party and therefore precluded from articulating any positions independent of the ruling party. These two, like the other affiliated organizations, were "subjected to centralized presidential decision-making and they lacked meaningful influence in determining national development policies" (Kaunda 1992, 71). Wiseman Chirwa suggests that Hasting Banda's control over the two organizations was central to his "grip on the country's political life" with women members' dancing and praise singing vital to reinforcing his position as Malawi's leader (2001, 14). In Botswana, meanwhile, according to Judith Van Allen (2001), the main gain for women from independence was the right to vote: independence had been achieved "through a generally peaceful, colonially-mediated process, with no particular commitment to the emancipation of women beyond the right of suffrage and the same ambiguities about women's status embedded in its constitution as could be found elsewhere in southern Africa."[8] After independence in Zambia, according to Parpart (1988, 215), "Women's Brigade organizers in UNIP [were] mainly backstage supporters for male politicians. The few women in high level politics . . . clustered in traditional female areas, such as welfare and health."

In Angola and Mozambique, a resort to arms was necessary to oust the Portuguese colonial rulers, and independence was not attained until the mid-1970s. In both countries, according to Mikell (1997, 24), "women staged their own demonstrations, fought alongside men to oppose colonial domination, and sustained the rural resistance that supported liberation fighters." In Mozambique women participated in the armed struggle as porters and, occasionally, even as combatants. As David Birmingham (1992, 62) recounts, they "headloaded ammunition, and occasionally perhaps even fired a gun, during the war of liberation." But once the Portuguese were defeated and independence attained, the results for women were mixed. On newly formed agricultural cooperatives they won for themselves "prestige posts," such as tractor drivers. They were outspoken members of community committees, in a way "they never had done in traditional society," and they even became magistrates at the local level with "unheard-of powers to order men to obey them." But at the same time that they established their own political organizations, "women were excluded from the real conclaves of power-broking and decision-making. The only government ministry given to a woman was in the caring field of education rather than in the mainstream of economics or national security." Stephanie Urdang (1989, 24–25) describes a similar paradox in Mozambique—women having been made equal before the law and in the constitution and even taking on tasks previously confined to men, but at the same time being subject to an enduring subordination in the form of a rigid sexual division of labor within the household. Moreover, any suggestion that such subordination should be contested was seen as threatening "the male leadership, more than a little." Rather "women are actively called upon to leave aside such struggle, not to use women's liberation as a 'weapon,' and to wait."

Finally, in Zimbabwe, Namibia, and South Africa, independence came much later and only after a resort to arms. In those countries women's participation in nationalist struggles began long before armed struggle commenced. Indeed, women's resistance activities may not always have been linked directly to nationalist movement efforts but nonetheless formed part of a broader protest against colonial rule. Often, women's actions were quite spontaneous, as in South Africa in the late 1950s. "Rural women, enraged at forced removals, stock control, and a new system of land allocation under which women no longer were guaranteed their own fields, smashed dipping trucks, burned fields, and attacked available symbols of the state. Women in Durban, responding to restrictions on domestic beer brewing and to government support for municipal beer halls, clashed with police, picketed, and engaged in ribald gestures" (Berger 1999, 48). In Namibia, Anna Mungunda is considered the first person to have died in the "modern period" of Namibia's anticolonial struggle—killed in December 1959 as she led a group of township residents protesting their forced removal from one location to another (Bauer 2004). Township women in Namibia had also earlier organized themselves to resist South African colonial policy that sought to deprive them of their primary income-generating opportunity, the brewing of beer. Female food and clothing workers in South Africa were among the early organizers of the Federation of South African Women, the group that led protests against passes for women in the late 1950s (Berger 1999, 47).[9] According to Gisela Geisler (2000, 608), the federation was distinctive during this period in that "it represented a broad based women's organization that was not conceived of as an auxiliary to a male-dominated body, such as other women's organizations at the time, and that it was thus 'a real and serious attempt to incorporate women into the political programme of the national liberation movement on an equal footing with men.'"

In all three countries, women participated in crucial ways in their national liberation struggles from both inside and outside the country. In Namibia, an armed struggle against South African colonial rule began with the first military incursion of the South West Africa People's Organization (SWAPO) into the country in 1965.[10] Over the years, women made up between 20 and 40 percent of Namibian exiles in neighboring countries, primarily Angola. From 1974 onward, at their insistence, young women exiles who were unmarried and had no children received the same military training as their male counterparts—and they participated in military combat. Moreover, young women in exile, in equal or greater numbers to men, also had access to many study and training opportunities at UN-sponsored institutions in Angola and Zambia and at universities and polytechnics abroad. According to Heike Becker (1995, 149–150, 153), this participation on the part of women had a significant impact on men and women alike. On the one hand, "the participation of women in the armed fighting caused men to revise their perception of women and added much to women's self-confidence," while on the other hand, as a result of their various educational opportunities, by the time of independence "many educated young Namibian women were no longer prepared to be subordinate to male dominance but claimed equality and power-sharing, with men on all levels, including politics." In Zimbabwe, too, from 1972 onward women joined the armed struggle, "first as carriers of military equipment and later as front-line fighters" (Geisler 1995, 551). In the military camps, gender differences were suspended as men and women cooked, fought, and trained together. Those differences quickly resurfaced after independence, however, according to Geisler:

> Because women had lived side by side with men, they were now labeled "loose" women: parents would not allow their "clean sons" to marry an ex-combatant, thinking they would not make good wives. In "real" life the virtues of being an independent woman were again undesirable, to parents, to men and it seemed to the new government. Against expectations and hopes, very few women were brought into the new government. (1995, 552)

When not actually fighting for independence themselves, women often played supportive roles to those who were. In rural northern Namibia, which was the literal battleground in that country's war for independence, women joined the resistance effort by playing a supportive role to SWAPO combatants or those sought after by the police (Soiri 1996, 58–59). Iina Soiri (1996, 91) identifies these women as "radical mothers." According to her, the radical motherhood is marked by "family-mothers" taking an active part in political struggle based on their responsibilities and capabilities as members of a community under threat. The women "acted as mothers, daughters and sisters, utilizing the potential opportunities given by their traditional role. They were not aware of or even interested in feminism or its analysis of their situation, but were still empowered as women." Women in rural Zimbabwe—"mothers of the revolution," according to Irene Staunton (1990, xii)—repeatedly risked their lives to serve and protect the "freedom fighters," their common children, who were fighting to end minority white rule. "Without the women," Staunton concludes after interviewing dozens of them, "the war could not have been won." At the same time, according to Geisler (1995, 552), some rural women "used the change of gender ideologies that took place during the war to renegotiate relationships within the household." In South Africa as well, according to Geisler (2000, 608), "motherism" helped propel women into politics: "In South Africa, as elsewhere, women forced their way into political activism against male resistance on the basis of practical gender needs, namely as mothers who were to secure a better future for their children. . . . Motherhood served as a unifying factor across rural-urban, class and race boundaries . . . but also allowed for women's continued subordination to the broader nationalist project."

Indeed, while nationalist and liberation movements throughout the world often relied heavily on women and espoused laudable emancipatory goals with respect to them, they almost universally subordinated gender concerns to the larger nationalist struggle. This became especially evident once independence was achieved and the results for women were often found to be limited at best. The experience of women in nationalist movements in Zambia and Malawi largely confirms this observation. In other cases, it has been argued that violent conflict, which results in major disruptions to gender relations, can provide "new opportunities to articulate debate about gender politics as well as for individual women to live in a different way." This may be all the more true when "liberation movements" have been part of that conflict (Pankhurst 2002, 127). Zimbabwe, Namibia, and South Africa took this pathway to independence, and the outcome for women appears, at least initially, to have been somewhat different as a result.

In Zimbabwe, although few women were brought into government at independence, major legal gains for women did follow independence, in the form of new laws to redress past discrimination and enhance women's status in society. The most significant of these was the Legal Age of Majority Act (LAMA) of 1982, which conferred legal adult status on both men and women at age eighteen and provided women with a range of legal rights not recognized in customary law: to marry without parental consent or payment of bridewealth, inherit property, own a passport or business, open a bank account, enter into legal contracts, and vote (Van Allen 2001). Other legislation containing provisions beneficial to women included a labor relations act, a matrimonial causes act, a maintenance act, and a finance act (Moyo and Kawewe 2002, 171). Interestingly, the LAMA was overturned in a 1999 Supreme Court ruling that found that "'the nature of African society' dictates that women are not equal to men, and that 'women should never be considered adults within the family, but only as a junior male, or teenager'" (Van Allen 2001, 60). Of all of the provisions of the LAMA, only the right to vote was retained. According to Van Allen (2001, 60), "the Court justified its ruling on the grounds that 'the majority of Africans in Zimbabwe still live in rural areas and still conduct their lives in terms of customary law.'" In addition, despite bitter protests from the Zimbabwean Women's Bureau, the government refused, in the course of introducing a land resettlement scheme, to change customary land-tenure practices that continue to discriminate against women (Parpart 1988, 219).[11]

In Zimbabwe, then, women proved unable to retain some of the early gains of independence. In the late 1990s Sita Ranchod-Nilsson (1998, 274) attributed this to an increasing consolidation of power by a single-party state: "As access to state power has become more narrow and exclusive, the state's gender ideology has been transformed." Indeed, those with access to change power have changed. "Since independence," argued Ranchod-Nilsson (1998, 274), "the cast of state insiders and outsiders has drastically changed, as young, educated women and ex-combatants have been replaced by co-opted key women as regime insiders." In her more recent work on gender politics in Zimbabwe, Ranchod-Nilsson (2006, 49) argues that "the state's commitment to women's issues was always ambivalent, at best." Ranchod-Nilsson (2006, 66) suggests that from the mid-1980s onward, as the government of Robert Mugabe failed to meet targets for economic growth and land resettlement, it began "to shift its stance on women's issues as a way to appease those who were increasingly dissatisfied." As the economic crisis deepened, a government rhetoric of women's rights shifted to one of women's responsibilities and "controlling the activities of women became more important than ever."

Namibia and South Africa are different cases altogether, with independence and black majority rule attained only in the 1990s. In both cases, women's extensive participation in the liberation efforts from inside and outside the country had significant implications for the postindependence gender dispensations. As Jo Beall (2001, 135) observes for South Africa, in the 1990s the African National Congress (ANC), "by taking gender seriously," appeared to "reverse the trend set by many liberation movements elsewhere: namely, women being mobilized as agents in struggle around class and race, yet denied the imperative of addressing gender subordination." Gender-progressive constitutions in both countries are evidence of this (Scribner and Lambert 2010). Though women's struggles have been long and hard in Namibia and South Africa, there have not been the same reversals as in Zimbabwe.

Women in the Political Transitions of the 1990s

The 1990s witnessed dramatic political transitions across the African continent, including in southern Africa as, in many countries, decades of authoritarian single-party rule gave way to a more democratic multiparty rule. For a number of countries it may be argued that the promise of initial democratic transitions is still to be fully realized. Nonetheless, as Aili Tripp (2001, 143) suggests, "it is important to note that the democratization efforts of the 1990s, despite their limitations, gave women the impetus to make bolder strides in the political arena." Indeed, women and their organizations, like student groups, trade unions, and human rights associations, were often at the forefront of such democratization efforts, openly opposing "corrupt and repressive regimes through public demonstrations and other militant actions" (Tripp 2001, 142). Moreover, the demise of single-party states and powerful ruling parties often freed women of their obligations to the women's wings of those parties and national women's associations and coincided with a rise in independent women's organizations seeking to take advantage of the opening of new political space. Leaders of these new women's organizations moved beyond previous preoccupations with development and pushed for constitutional and legislative changes as well as greater access for women to political office at all levels (Tripp 2001, 143).

Women were actively involved in Zambia's democratic transition. According to Tripp (2001, 148), "women from NGOs, churches, and political parties formed a nonpartisan National Women's Lobby Group (NWLG) in 1991, with the goal of increasing the representation of women in decisionmaking positions in government and the political parties. The NWLG encouraged women to compete in local elections, worked to repeal discriminatory legislation, and conducted human rights training and civic education seminars. By 1995, the organization had grown to 2,000 dues-paying members." Together with other NGOs, the NWLG also pressed to have a section on women's rights included in Zambia's new constitution. Despite heavy protest from a number of quarters, the groups were successful in including in the constitution sections on women's reproductive rights and equal opportunities for women in education (Tripp 2001, 149). During the early part of the first decade of the twenty-first century, the Nongovernmental Organization Coordinating Committee (NGOCC), an umbrella organization of women's lobby groups, played an instrumental role in national legal and political affairs. The NGOCC was a central player in the Oasis Forum, which in 2001 mobilized civil society to block President Frederick Chiluba's effort to seek an extraconstitutional third term in office.[12] The body also took a leading role in Zambia's 2003 constitutional review process. Geisler (2006, 76, 79) argues that the NWLG served as a model for other women's movements in the region that "took note of the group's efforts and tried to improve on the approach." Enduring challenges for the NWLG included ongoing mistrust and animosity between women politicians and women activists and an inability for a partisan political climate to accommodate a nonpartisan lobbying group.

In Malawi women were also actively involved in the political transition. In subsequent years, the National Commission on Women and Development worked together with women's organizations for a greater representation of women in local and national political office. They also pressed for the adoption of laws against domestic violence and for the protection of women's property in the event that their husbands die (Tripp 2001, 150–151). According to Linda Semu (2002, 77), however, the political will to implement such new laws was lacking in the early years following the transition. In her view, women's continued participation in civil society offered the best mechanism for women to gain access to the political process and to attempt to effect legal changes in the country.

Indeed, results for women of the political openings offered by the region's democratic transitions appear to be mixed. For Zambia, Anne Ferguson and Beatrice Katundu (1994, 24–25) found "continuities and change" with regard to women's participation in politics following the 1991 transition. On the one hand, "the powerful gatekeeping role of women's wings of political parties" was found to be declining, "thus allowing for the representation of women with more diverse interests in politics and government." On the other hand, Ferguson and Katundu (1994, 24–25) found that women involved in politics confronted a "persistent gender discrimination" reinforced by a constitution and legal code that "denies women equal rights with men in areas of family law, maintenance and inheritance rights, and thus contributes significantly to making participation in politics costly for many women." Despite the efforts of the National Commission on Women and Development, in Malawi's first posttransition local government elections held in 2000, women fared surprisingly poorly, winning only 69 of 842 wards, a worse representation of women than at the national level (Patel et al. 2007, 77). Lisa Gilman (2001, 2004) notes that women in Malawi continue to be exploited by political parties as dancers and praise singers at party rallies and events; whereas the Banda regime coerced women into this role, more recent administrations compensate women monetarily.

In Namibia and South Africa, meanwhile, a number of factors came together to make for more enduring and more significant changes for women than elsewhere in the region in the posttransition period. Indeed, both countries adopted constitutions that are very progressive with respect to women and gender relations. For example, Namibia's constitution, written entirely in gender-neutral language, states that all people shall be equal before the law and prohibits discrimination based on sex, race, color, ethnic origin, and a number of other factors. It also notes that women have traditionally suffered special discrimination in Namibia and need to be encouraged and enabled, through affirmative action measures, to participate more fully in every aspect of life in Namibia. Finally, customary or common law (often discriminatory toward wives and women in general) is allowed to remain in effect in Namibia but only to the extent that it does not conflict with the constitution or any other laws (Bauer 2004).

In addition, both countries adopted a host of new laws that prohibit discrimination and harassment in the workplace on the basis of sex, marital status, family responsibilities, and sexual orientation; aim to ensure that women and other disadvantaged persons have equal access to employment opportunities; prescribe minimum sentences for rape and place more emphasis on the rights of rape victims; and treat women and men equally in the allocation of communal land and protect widows against dispossession, among other things. Finally, in both countries a number of offices and national policies—official "national machineries" for women—were established to monitor the progress of women and to ensure the representation of their interests (Bauer and Britton 2006).

Except for Angola, Namibia, and South Africa, national machineries for women had been established by governments across the region sometime during the United Nations Decade for women (1975–1985)—and were established following transitions in those three countries respectively in 1991, 1990, and 1997.[13] Beginning in the 1990s, as political transitions unfolded, nearly all southern African countries upgraded their early machineries to fully fledged ministries. Gender ministries were formed in Angola in 1997, Malawi in 1992, Mozambique in 2000, Namibia in 1995, South Africa in 1997, Zambia in 2006, and Zimbabwe in 1997 (Tripp et al. 2009, 168–172). Botswana was joined only by Swaziland in the region in not having a dedicated women's ministry in 2010, although its women's affairs unit was upgraded to a division in 1989 and a department in 1996 (Tripp et al. 2009, 169, 172). Moreover, following the Fourth United Nations Conference on Women in Beijing in 1995, under pressure from national women's movements, government across the region (and continent) began to adopt gender mainstreaming and gender focal points as strategies for advancing women's interests.[14]

Increasing Women's Political Representation

One of the main areas of progress for women in South Africa, Angola, Mozambique, and Namibia has been political representation. Indeed, these four countries were among the top thirty-five worldwide in terms of women's representation in single or lower houses of parliament in late 2010, with women constituting nearly one-third or more of the MPs of either lower or single houses: 45 percent in South Africa, 39 percent in Angola and Mozambique, and 27 percent in Namibia (see Table 11.2). This is a notable achievement given that 30 percent has been considered to constitute the critical mass necessary to promote the recruitment of still more women officeholders as well as

Table 11.2   Women's Political Participation

	Year Women Received Right to Vote and to Stand for Election[a]	Year First Women Elected (E) or Appointed (A) to Parliament	Women in Government at Ministerial Level (2010)	Parliament Seats Held by Women— Lower House or Single House (2010)
Angola	1975	1980 E	25.7	38.6
Botswana	1965	1979 E	21.1	7.9
Malawi	1961	1964 E	22.7	21.2
Mozambique	1975	1977 E	32.1	39.2
Namibia	1989	1989 E	18.2	26.9
South Africa	1930, 1994	1933 E	41.2	44.5
Zambia	1962	1964 E,A	13.0	15.2
Zimbabwe	1957, 1978	1980 E,A	17.1	15.0

Sources: Inter-Parliamentary Union 2010; Gender Links 2010a.
Note: a. White women first received the right to vote in South Africa and Zimbabwe in 1930 and 1957, respectively, and the right to stand for election in 1994 and 1978, respectively.

to develop new legislation and institutions beneficial to women (Lovenduski and Karam 2002). In Namibia, Mozambique, and South Africa women have been represented in greater numbers since founding or transitional elections in the early 1990s; for Angola only since the most recent election—the first in 16 years—in 2008. With each election the momentum has been maintained with the percentage of women continuing to increase even if only slightly.

In the other four countries in the region, the representation of women in national legislatures hovered around the sub-Saharan African average—around 19 percent (which also happened to be the world average in 2010). Botswana ranked lowest among countries with 8 percent women in its National Assembly since elections in 2009, followed by Zambia and Zimbabwe with 15 percent and Malawi with 21 percent. In the four southern African countries in which women have achieved the highest levels of political representation, a proportional representation electoral system and voluntary party quota (by the dominant party) are used. The other four countries, by contrast, all utilize a first-past-the-post electoral system and no form of electoral gender quota. In general, proportional representation systems are considered more friendly to women while plurality-majority systems are much less friendly to women (Laserud and Taphorn 2007); moreover, gender quotas are more seamlessly used with a proportional representation than a first-past-the-post electoral system. The use of an electoral gender quota is the single most important determinant worldwide of women's access to political office (Tripp and Kang 2008). This finding is borne out by the experiences of women seeking political office throughout southern Africa (Bauer 2008).

The promise of women's increased representation in legislatures is that women's enhanced descriptive representation will be matched by significant substantive and symbolic representation. In their book on women in African parliaments, Bauer and Britton (2006) identified significant legislative accomplishments for women in South Africa, Namibia, and Mozambique, especially in the areas of family law, land rights, and gender-based violence. In her study of the first women members of parliament in a new South Africa, Hannah Britton (2005) found that at least in the first parliament women members succeeded in changing parliamentary culture to make the institution more women friendly and in incorporating gender issues into legislative debates and policy creation. Even in a country such as Botswana with few women in the National Assembly, those women MPs who are there claim a significant impact on the introduction and passage of legislation of broad concern to women and children (Bauer 2010). In Botswana symbolic representation effects of women in parliament and cabinet have also been identified; one of four women chiefs in Botswana, Balete paramount chief Kgosigadi Mosadi Seboko, suggests that others were convinced to accept her right to become chief by the women they saw in government, including the minister of local government, to whom chiefs report.[15]

At the local level, women have been making similar gains. Lesotho, which uses an electoral gender quota at the local level, led the region with more than 58 percent of members of local councils being women in late 2010. In Namibia, where a different type of quota is used at the local level, 44 percent of members of local councils across the country were women in 2010, as were many mayors and deputy mayors. Namibia was followed by South Africa with 40 percent and Mozambique with more than 30 percent women in local councils (Gender Links 2010a).

Women in southern Africa are making inroads not just into the legislative but also the executive branch of government. In early 2010 Luísa Días Diogo was one of only two women executives in all of sub-Saharan Africa; she served as prime minister of Mozambique from 2004 until she stepped down in 2010. More than 40 percent of cabinet members in South Africa were women in early 2010, followed by 32 percent in Mozambique, 26 percent in Angola, and 23 percent in Malawi. The remaining countries lagged somewhat behind with 21 percent in Botswana, 18 percent in Namibia, 17 percent in Zimbabwe, and 13 percent in Zambia (Gender Links 2010a). Moreover, as has been observed as a trend worldwide (Bauer and Tremblay 2011), women are increasingly leading previously male-dominated portfolios in cabinets. So, for example, in South Africa in late 2010, women were ministers of international relations and cooperation; defense and veterans; mining; and science and technology, among many others. In Angola, women were the ministers of planning and of water and energy, and in Malawi they served as ministers of foreign affairs and of trade and industry. In all countries women continued to dominate those ministries typically held by women as well, such as women's affairs, education, arts and culture, and so on. In several countries in the region, such as Malawi, Zimbabwe, and South Africa, women have served or continue to serve as vice or deputy presidents.

In southern Africa a number of regional initiatives have supported women's increased political representation. In 1997, southern African heads of state and government signed a Declaration on Gender and Development in the Southern African Development Community (SADC) that, among other things, called very clearly for women to occupy 30 percent of positions of power and decisionmaking in national governments by 2005 (only three countries met the goal). This goal was repeated in an SADC gender action plan that was approved by the SADC Council of Ministers in 1998 (SADC Gender Unit 1999, 5). In making this demand, women activists and politicians in the region targeted decisionmaking posts at all levels of government as well as positions in the public sector more generally, the private sector, and the professions (SADC Gender Unit 1999, 6). Around the region (and continent), 50-50 campaigns have also emerged in several countries. These campaigns—linked to a global effort by the same name—have been launched to achieve a 50 percent representation of women at all levels of politics and decisionmaking. The same goal was endorsed by southern African heads of state as part of the SADC Protocol on Gender and Development, which calls for the same 50 percent representation by 2015; Botswana was the only country not to sign on to the protocol by 2010 (see Gender Links 2010a).

In 1998 the SADC Gender Unit was established in the SADC Secretariat in Gaborone, Botswana, with the mandate to coordinate the mainstreaming of gender issues throughout SADC programs and initiatives. Another SADC initiative to support those women already elected to national office has been the SADC Regional Women's Parliamentary Caucus, launched in Luanda, Angola, in April 2002. This organization brings together the members of parliamentary women's caucuses throughout the region to provide an additional empowering strategy for women MPs. The SADC women's caucus works with women MPs to identify important issue areas for women and to propose strategies for addressing them. Another aspect of the regional body is skills development for women MPs, particularly in regard to introducing gender-sensitive legislation and ensuring a gender component to all laws and bills passing through parliaments.[16]

Women's Movements in the Region

The critical importance of women's movements to the success of women politicians and women's agendas is well documented. Though a number of sources suggest that women in southern Africa have not historically been as "highly organized" (Berger 1999, 56; Mikell 1997, 28) as women in other parts of Africa, recent experience suggests otherwise. In some countries, such as Botswana, early women's movements emerged in the wake of women's participation in the Third United Nations Conference on Women, held in Nairobi in 1985, one (though not the only) catalyst for women's organization all over Africa (Tripp et al. 2009), and in response to a specific issue in that country. In countries such as Malawi and Zambia, women took advantage of political openings and transitions to press their own as well as broader agendas. In countries such as South Africa and Namibia, women had organized for decades as part and parcel of the struggle to overcome white minority rule. Across the region today, women's movements at various stages of mobilization and vibrancy contend with a range of issues and challenges (Essof 2009; Van Allen 2007; Hassim 2006; Geisler 2004).

In Botswana, a group of women activists coalesced in the mid-1980s, initially around a single issue, namely a change to the nation's Citizenship Law. As a result of the change, citizenship in Botswana was no longer determined by birth in the country but rather by birth descent, and for married women, the citizenship of the father only thereafter determined the citizenship of a child. Thus a Motswana woman married to a foreigner could no longer pass her citizenship, with its significant educational and economic benefits, on to her own child (Van Allen 2001, 42). Within a few years of the new law's passage, a women's rights group, Emang Basadi, emerged to challenge the law through a test case—the Unity Dow case. The challenge to the citizenship law was ultimately victorious, though it took more than a decade (Leslie 2006). In the meantime, Emang Basadi succeeded in persuading government to undertake a comprehensive review of existing laws with an eye toward eliminating gender discrimination. Further, as the Unity Dow case dragged on, Emang Basadi, working together with other organizations, began to focus on increasing the number of women in political office; during the 1990s and the early part of the first decade of the twenty-first century Emang Basadi offered workshops for women candidates at local and national level and launched a Women's Manifesto with the aim of influencing political party manifestos. In drawing lessons from the Botswana case, Judith Van Allen (2001, 57) highlights the importance of a "working liberal democratic system" and an autonomous women's movement—one that can "generate its own agenda and priorities." In the mid-1990s Botswana's women's movement was considered to be the strongest among civil society actors and to have contributed significantly to changing the character of politics in the country (Good 1996, 57; Holm, Molutsi, and Somolekae 1996, 62–63). By 2010, however, the movement had waned significantly, perhaps as a result of its own successes but also as a result of overall challenges to civil society; the emergence of newer, more intractable issues such as HIV/AIDS; and an executive much less receptive to women's activism.

In Namibia women similarly galvanized early after independence around a single issue—electing more women to political office—such that one could even identify a unified women's movement in the country for a time. Around 1999 a number of women activists and women's organizations joined together under the guise of the Namibian Women's Manifesto Network to demand the 50 percent representation of women at all levels of decisionmaking in the country.[17] In an unprecedented manner, this network mobilized women across the country to attend workshops; visit schools and churches; meet with traditional leaders, local and regional councilors, and party leaders; and participate in marches demanding a greater representation of women in politics in Namibia. The campaign garnered the support of major women's organizations and women politicians alike as well as the support of much of the populace (Bauer 2004). It also seemed to verify Mikell's observation (2003, 104) that "the pragmatics of political representation in the 1990s [were] shaping the emerging African women's movement." Despite the 50-50 movement, women in Namibia have not made quite the same strides in women's political representation as in a few other countries in the region.

For South Africa, Gay Seidman (1999, 289) attributed some of the gains for women of the early posttransition years to an increasingly articulate women's movement that was able to challenge the antiapartheid movement's previous subordination of gender concerns to nationalist goals. This was accomplished in part, according to Seidman, through the discussion of how apartheid had actually treated black women and men differently and the realization that unless gender concerns were considered during the course of democratization, new political institutions would re-create and reinforce inequality. Moreover, in the years before the transition, antiapartheid activists began to develop separate women's groups in which women began to analyze their lives in terms not only of race and class oppression but also of gender oppression (Seidman 1999, 292). Strongly influencing these developments, according to Seidman (1999, 295), were a new global discourse around gender issues that had emerged in the 1990s and a global feminist movement, manifest in part in the United Nations conferences mentioned above.

Despite the long tradition of women's organizing, women's posttransition political successes may have had a negative impact on the women's movement in South Africa. Geisler (2000, 626) argues that women politicians' successes in South Africa—avoiding the mistakes of women elsewhere on the continent by being an integral part of the transition process from the beginning and in "numbers too large to be easily reversed"—may have come at a price. That price, according to Geisler (2000, 627) may have been "the weakening [of] the mass-based movement that was the driving force behind South African women's move into parliament." In the new South Africa, according to Geisler (2000, 605), the women's movement lost its strongest leaders to government, and once in government women politicians lacked the support of a strong women's movement. Shireen Hassim (2005) describes the situation somewhat differently, as a tension between the twin goals of inclusion and transformation. In her view, in South Africa a strategy focused on the inclusion of women in formal political institutions of state and party has tended to displace transformatory goals of structural and social change. Further, Hassim (2006) warns that the increased representation of women in and of itself is not as important as the increased representation of poor women; the role of a vibrant women's movement then is to ensure accountability to the interests of large vulnerable populations.

Women in Southern Africa: Present and Future Challenges

What have these political gains meant for the socioeconomic status of the majority of ordinary women in southern African countries today? What of the status of women in those countries where they remain excluded from positions of political power? These are vexing questions, as women in the whole of southern Africa continue to struggle for equality at the levels of the family, society, and state. For women in South Africa, Namibia, Angola, and Mozambique, the challenge lies in consolidating the gains of formal political representation;

for women elsewhere in the region, it lies in creating an environment in which a higher degree of women's political participation is possible. Given the inter-connectedness of the countries in the region and the role of regional organizations active around gender and politics, there may be some cause for optimism that the advances in formal political representation in some countries may eventually take root in the whole of southern Africa.

As Table 11.3 reveals, there are no simple correlations between women's enhanced political representation and their socioeconomic status across the region. While Botswana ranks at the bottom in nearly all measures of formal political representation, it had among the best socioeconomic indicators for women in 2009—a reflection, no doubt, of the country's long track record of political stability, good governance, and steady economic growth. For most other countries in the region, the seemingly intractable economic crises, debilitating droughts, and AIDS pandemic continue to have a disproportionate impact on women's lives and livelihoods. Decades of economic reform measures have been especially harmful to the most vulnerable sections of the population, typically women and children (see Table 11.3). Whether structural adjustment programs implemented from outside or economic recovery programs adopted from within, the reforms of the past couple of decades have meant that women have longer work days, decreased access to basic resources such as land and labor, reduced opportunities in formal sector employment and education, increased costs of basic social services, greater family responsibilities (often without the support of a male partner), increased rural to urban migration, and a growing number of female-headed households.

Table 11.3   Survival: Progress and Setbacks

	Life Expectancy at Birth, 2010		Total Fertility Rate (births per woman), 2010 Estimate	Maternal Mortality Rate[a] (2003–2008)
	Female	Male		
Angola	39.52	37.48	6.05	1,400
Botswana	60.75	61.10	2.54	380
Malawi	51.64	50.22	5.55	1,100
Mozambique	40.68	42.05	5.13	520
Namibia	52.25	51.64	2.57	210
South Africa	50.08	48.29	2.33	400
Zambia	53.28	50.81	6.07	830
Zimbabwe	47.98	47.11	3.66	880
World	68.07	64.29	2.56	273

Sources: "Human Development Report, 2009," 2010, http://hdr.undp.org/en/reports; CIA World Factbook, 2010, https://www.cia.gov.
Note: a. Defined as maternal deaths per 100,000 live births.

Women's struggles also take place against the background of the world's worst AIDS epidemic. While data from 2009 show a decline in the HIV infection rate in Africa as a whole, well over half of those infected with the virus in southern Africa are still women (UNAIDS 2010c). In the region and in Africa as a whole, women and children are particularly vulnerable to HIV infection, since the primary methods of transmission are through heterosexual intercourse and from mother to child. Women and girls are further vulnerable because of their lack of knowledge about and power over their sexuality and their reproductive functions and because of limited access to economic opportunities and autonomy. Throughout the region, young and older women alike have became the primary actors in an emerging "care economy" that has them caring for the AIDS-afflicted and dying, often at great risk to themselves (Urdang 2006). In the case of both economic reform and HIV/AIDS, women have taken over the tasks, now burdens, abandoned by states and governments.

These crises rob women and states of incentives and resources to deepen the commitment to gender equality. Moreover, they threaten democratic transitions and, therefore, the constitutional protections that these fragile polities might offer to women. Clearly, the political advances such as those achieved by women in Angola, Mozambique, Namibia, and South Africa need to be cemented by corresponding changes at the grassroots level. Women politicians and women activists across the region are taking on the challenge. There is no doubt, as Geisler (2004, 216) concludes in her book on women remaking politics in southern Africa, that women's engagement with the state—so prominent in the region in the past couple of decades—whether as a woman politician or as a women's movement activist "has changed the life of many women and changed the face of politics."

Notes

1. Gisela Geisler first alerted us to the idea of women remaking politics in southern Africa in her 2004 book, *Women and the Remaking of Politics of Southern Africa: Negotiating Autonomy, Incorporation, and Representation.*

2. According to Berger (1999, 29): "In Tswana society, the ever present threat of drought helped to shape local forms of male domination and female submissiveness."

3. Meredith McKittrick (1998, 244) argues that it was actually seniority rather than age that mattered and that "seniority is in fact more than age; it is a status which can be achieved only in certain circumstances." Especially as the colonial period progressed, not everyone was guaranteed senior status simply by becoming physically old. "Young people recognized this, and looked to new ideas and systems of authority that might hold a strong promise of increased status and economy power"—for example, migrant labor or Christianity.

4. Staudt (1987, 200) writes of a deliberate policy in colonial Kenya "to create competition and jealousy" in an effort to spur men to work. Wrote one colonial official of the rural woman in colonial Kenya: "She must be educated to want a better home,

better furnishings, better food, better water supplies, etc. and if she wants them she will want them for her children. In short, the sustained effort from the male will only come when the woman is educated to the stage when her wants are never satisfied."

5. According to Staudt (1987, 197): "Early colonial governments put little or no energy into public education, especially for girls, but they did support and cooperate with mission education. As late as the 1950s, mission stations still controlled 80 to 90 percent of schools, with supplementary government grants-in-aid provided."

6. Gwendolyn Mikell (1997, 17) identifies four factors as significant in establishing a new form of gender bias during the colonial period: "1) Christianity, with its notions of monogamy and female domesticity and subordination; 2) Westernized education, which gave men advantages over women; 3) differential marriage systems, with Western marriage guaranteeing women access to property rights that women married under traditional rites could not claim; 4) alternative legal systems that supposedly acknowledged African women's independent rights, although colonial magistrates often treated women as jural minors needing male guardians."

7. Aili Tripp (2001, 146) writes: "Former dictator Hastings Banda of Malawi required members of the League of Malawi Women to be present at all official functions, dress in party uniforms, singing and dancing in praise of him. Such women's organizations were tied to the party's dictates and its overriding interest in securing women's votes. Similarly the women's leagues were unable to fight forcefully for women's interests if these were at odds with the priorities and goals of the ruling party."

8. According to James Zaffiro (1997, 20): "The Botswana constitution is silent regarding unfair or unequal treatment of citizens based on gender. Women still lack essential legal protections. Since patriarchy was a significant element of traditional Tswana society, nationalists who drafted key documents consciously omitted language outlining rights and protections of women." See also Scribner and Lambert 2010.

9. According to Gisela Geisler (2000, 608), the formation of the Federation of South African Women was "premised on the observation that the existing male dominated political organizations were unlikely to meet women's specific needs . . . and although the organization claimed full gender equality . . . its membership 'wanted to expand the scope of women's work within nationalist liberation.'"

10. In Namibia, three women were among the first members of SWAPO to flee the country, establish an exile base in Tanzania, and commence military training in the 1960s (Bauer 2004).

11. According to Berger (1999, 60): "When a rural woman in 1994 suggested that land permits in resettled areas be registered jointly in the names of both spouses, President Robert Mugabe retorted, 'If women want property, then they should not get married.'"

12. Author interview with the Oasis Forum Executive Committee, Lusaka, June 9, 2001.

13. Beall (2001, 137–138) writes that official national machineries for women are a direct result of the United Nations Decade for Women (1975–1985). They include women's units, bureaus, desks, and ministries that, however, often lack sufficient status, resources, and influence. Over time national machineries have sought to focus more on linking gender issues and national policy and involving women's organizations from civil society. See also Tripp et al. 2009.

14. Tripp et al. (2009, 172) note that gender mainstreaming is a contested concept; generally, they suggest, "the term refers to pragmatic efforts to eliminate gender-based discrimination and adopt measures to promote gender equality at all stages of policy making."

15. Author interview, Ramotswa, Botswana, June 15, 2009.

16. Author interview with Rumbi Nhundu, SADC Parliamentary Forum gender officer, Windhoek, Namibia, June 22, 2002.

17. In a clear sharing of resources and strategies across the region, Namibian women activists from the Namibian Women's Manifesto Network acknowledged that their manifesto was modeled on the manifesto drawn up by women activists in Botswana. Author interview, Elizabeth Khaxas, Windhoek, Namibia, June 28, 2002.

12 Southern Africa's International Relations

Southern Africa is a land of enormous contradictions. Along major development indicators, it leads the continent. It has the wealthiest population per capita, the most urbanized population, the greatest industrial base, and the leading commercial agriculture output. It is also endowed with ample natural resources, including vast mineral deposits, natural gas, and petroleum; to aid in the exploitation of this natural and human capacity, the region boasts a vast transportation network and advanced communications systems that also work to boost trade and ensure the interconnectedness of the region. Yet southern Africa's promise is counterbalanced by numerous challenges, as described in the previous chapters of this book. The region is home to two of the world's fifteen poorest countries; and it has millions of internally displaced persons from old conflicts, such as that now ebbing in Angola, and refugees fleeing newer conflicts, such as the crisis in Zimbabwe. Southern Africa also has the highest HIV/AIDS infection rates in Africa and the world, though they have fallen dramatically in recent years. Indeed, the issues of trade, economic relations, the Zimbabwe crisis, and AIDS pose both short- and long-term challenges for the stability of the region and threaten to undermine the many positive developments from the region's comparatively strong economic performance, its investment opportunities, political stability, and even the regional identity on display at the World Cup. There are, in short, many issues in the realm of international relations worthy of examination, as well as multiple perspectives through which to examine those issues in the southern Africa context.

This chapter emphasizes international concerns that can broadly be described as economic, rather than political, although they too are clearly important. In the absence of the war and interstate conflict that prevailed in the previous decades, the key to regional development lies in the region's ability to master international and intraregional economic relations. Economic as well as political issues at the state and substate level have been addressed in the country chapters. The AIDS crisis, though recently mitigated, is clearly a transborder phenomenon with implications for regional development but has been treated in Chapter 10. This chapter, meanwhile, speaks to the regional, continental, and "global" levels of analysis. There is also a growing tension, of sorts, between regionalism and internationalism—that is, between southern African states' identities as regional players and their identity and roles as global actors (Khadiagala and Lyons 2001, 2). As a result, at each level of analysis, there is not only a discernible tension between the role of structures and that of agents, but there are also forces at play that impact the coherence of southern Africa *as a region.*

The remainder of the chapter is divided into five sections. The first section examines southern Africa's principal regional institutions. The most prominent among these is the fourteen-member Southern African Development Community (SADC), although there are two other entities that warrant examination—the Southern African Customs Union (SACU) and the Common Market for Eastern and Southern Africa (COMESA)—which at times complement SADC but often duplicate it. Despite the plethora of regional unions, the history of regional integration efforts in Africa is not very encouraging. Harmonizing trade and sectoral policies, a prerequisite for more comprehensive integration, has been difficult, as most of the states in the region have competing rather than complementary products and resources to offer the global marketplace. Moreover, with the exception of Botswana, Namibia, and South Africa, the countries in the region are still weak states, lacking bureaucratic capacity and autonomy. As Gilbert Khadiagala (2001, 149) observes, "weak states furnish fragile bases for regionalism. . . . This is why the debilitating conflicts in Angola, the DRC [Democratic Republic of Congo], Lesotho, and Zimbabwe nullify institution building and postpone the creation of sturdy mechanisms for both economic development and security."[1] Nevertheless, it is also the case that greater promise for regional integration and development exists in southern Africa than in other regions on the continent.

The second section builds on this notion of regional strength, in terms of both economic clout and leadership, to address southern Africa's position within Africa as a whole. Southern Africa's relative economic development, its concentration of democratically elected governments, its regional hegemon South Africa, all combine to give the region a leading profile on the continent. Indeed, led by the former South African president, Thabo Mbeki, and South Africa, southern Africa has emerged as something of a focal point for pan-African initiatives, such as the African Union (AU) and the New Partnership for African Development (NEPAD). Admittedly, the success of these has been mixed, and President Jacob Zuma has been much more inwardly focused; however, few other countries in Africa are in a position to lead such continental initiatives.

The third section of the chapter addresses the impact of globalization on southern Africa. In the 1980s, Africa's ties to the international community turned increasingly negative, as southern Africa became a hub of Cold War proxy battles, the continent became increasingly marginalized, and austerity programs in the form of structural adjustment programs (SAPs) were first imposed. In recent years, although Africa's structural dependency has not decreased, and in fact has worsened by some measures, the relationship with the outside world has become more complex than simplistic structuralist accounts allow. Moreover, neoliberal economic policies and the global trade regime have created important opportunities for some states while severely undermining others. The arrival of China as a significant player in the region has also had a mixed impact.

Chapter 7 focused on Zimbabwe but treated the crisis largely in terms of its domestic characteristics, albeit one with both political and economic origins. In the fourth section of this chapter, we reexamine the crisis in Zimbabwe at the international level of analysis. Specifically, we consider the economic and political problems the country poses for southern Africa, both within the region and for the region's relations with the developed world. By and large, African states, particularly in the south, have tended to close ranks around Zimbabwe, at least publicly.[2] This solidarity is puzzling, given that the devastation in Zimbabwe—from diseases like cholera, to refugees and migrants, to economic contagion effects—wrought mostly by the ruling party, has negative regional and continental implications. Furthermore, it has damaged southern Africa's relations with the international community, by contributing to a view that the region is unstable, cannot enforce collective security concerns, and is not fully committed to transparent, democratic governance.

The final section concludes with some perspectives on the direction of the region as a whole.

Southern African Regional Institutions and Issues

The region has three principal organizations that represent different levels of economic integration: the Southern African Customs Union, the Common Market for Eastern and Southern Africa, and the Southern African Development Community. This discussion focuses chiefly on SADC, which is the most comprehensive in scope and encompasses all of the states of the region, though it treats the other two organizations briefly.

SACU

SACU has a narrow membership, which consists of only Botswana, Lesotho, South Africa, Swaziland, and Namibia. For these states, however, SACU has fulfilled a number of positive functions. Established in the early twentieth century, SACU "serves as the best example of a customs union in sub-Saharan

Africa. Except for agricultural products, the movement of goods within SACU countries is duty free, and member countries have a common external tariff" (Mshomba 2000, 177). SACU is a revenue-sharing arrangement. Given its origins in the colonial era, SACU overwhelmingly favored South Africa and created greater dependency on that country by its putative partners in the agreement. Some of these imbalances were subsequently addressed in renegotiations to the agreement in 1969 and again in 2004 (Sidaway and Gibb 1998, 173; Gibb 2006).

COMESA

COMESA warrants examination as much for its historical intersections with SADC and other regional groupings as for its current footprint in southern Africa, which has diminished markedly in recent years. Nonetheless, COMESA's challenges also illustrate the challenge of regional organization in Africa. COMESA came into being in December 1994, but its origins lay in the Preferential Trade Area (PTA) for Eastern and Southern Africa, which was established in 1981. By 1999, COMESA had seventeen members, including eight SADC states, which then grew to nineteen members by 2006 with the addition of Libya and Comoros. The number of SADC members, however, declined in the twenty-first century. Under apartheid, South Africa was excluded from both bodies. Prior to 1992, SADC and COMESA complemented one another: "SADC pursued a strategy of regional cooperation via sectoral development and the PTA/COMESA a strategy of trade integration" (Lee 2003, 88). After 1992, however, SADC decided to transform itself into a development community, thereby essentially duplicating COMESA's functions, including the removal of all nontariff barriers and free movement of goods and services (Khadiagala 2001, 137).

The advent of majority rule in South Africa in 1994, therefore, was met with considerable anxiety by both SADC and COMESA adherents, as it was clear that the institution favored by South Africa, with an economy that dwarfs its neighbors, would be most likely to endure. South Africa's decision not to join COMESA severely undermined its prospects and certainly appears to have proved nearly fatal to the body's reach in southern Africa. Initially, SADC leaders wanted the trade functions claimed by COMESA to be incorporated into SADC, but this became unnecessary as SADC advised its members to quit COMESA in 1994 (Mshomba 2000, 186).[3]

Among the problems plaguing COMESA is its unwieldiness. Whereas "SADC is massively heterogeneous in terms of economic and political conditions, most of its members are linked through a certain functional unity, derived from the (colonial) network of labour migration, trade and communications that was centered on the industrial, minerals-energy economy of South Africa. . . . COMESA does not enjoy even this asymmetric and uneven set of linkages" (Sidaway and Gibb 1998, 171). Margaret Lee (2003, 88–89) suggests that COMESA continued to claim members in southern Africa solely for political reasons, namely states' resentment of South African domination within SADC. This proved to be insufficient incentive; between the late 1990s and 2006, Mozambique, Namibia, Lesotho, Tanzania, and Angola—all SADC member states—withdrew from COMESA.

SADC

SADC has a very different origin than its counterparts and an orientation that extends beyond the objective of economic integration to political and military cooperation and development functions. SADC's origins lie in the Frontline States, the regional political body established in 1975 to counteract apartheid South Africa. The hostile international and regional context in which the Frontline States emerged prompted its members to adopt something of a siege mentality, which also affected domestic institutions, such as the development of strong presidencies. "With the decolonization of Zimbabwe in 1980, the [Frontline States] moved to incorporate the more economically vulnerable regional states into an inclusive alliance, SADCC, that sought economic integration and dependence reduction through sectoral coordination" (Khadiagala 2001, 133).

The original Southern Africa Development Coordination Conference (SADCC) was established by the 1980 Lusaka Declaration, to which there were nine signatories: Angola, Botswana, Lesotho, Malawi, Mozambique, Swaziland, Tanzania, Zambia, and Zimbabwe. Namibia joined upon its independence in 1990. SADCC was a less "defensive" structure than the Frontline States, aiming chiefly to reduce economic dependence on South Africa, foster regional integration, and promote resource mobilization (Sidaway and Gibb 1998, 166). In none of these goals was SADCC particularly successful, however. When black majority rule appeared imminent in South Africa, SADCC was transformed into SADC (in 1992). When the African National Congress (ANC) was elected to power in 1994, South Africa joined SADC.

SADC seeks to move beyond the sectoral coordination efforts that preoccupied its predecessor organization, into deeper cooperation that would facilitate true regional integration, such as the creation of a common market including currency and labor integration, elimination of trade barriers, and so on (Khadiagala 2001, 136). However, the failure of SADCC generated great skepticism that the new organization would be able to deliver development or regional integration either. Even SADC's small secretariat in Gaborone, Botswana, was undersupported, and the organization was highly dependent upon donors for project assistance (Sidaway and Gibb 1998, 166).

By the mid-1990s, SADC included twelve member states: Angola, Botswana, Lesotho, Malawi, Mauritius, Mozambique, Namibia, South Africa, Swaziland, Tanzania, Zambia, and Zimbabwe; Democratic Republic of Congo and Seychelles joined in 1997. South Africa, it was assumed, "would serve as the locomotive of recovery, growth and development for the region and the rest of [sub-Saharan Africa]" (Tsie 2001, 133).[4] As Balefi Tsie (2001, 133) noted at the turn of the century, South Africa "has the most sophisticated manufacturing industry in SSA, the best infrastructure, a highly developed mining industry, a relatively advanced agricultural sector . . . a robust service sector." South Africa's GDP is four times that of the other thirteen SADC countries combined, and its manufacturing value-added is five times that of the others combined, "and nearly 15 times that of the second biggest manufacturer," which was Zimbabwe prior to its collapse. South Africa exports finished manufactured goods to the region, imports raw materials from its neighbors, and exports four times as much as it imports from the region (Tsie 2001, 133).

In contrast to the other countries in the region, then, South Africa is a developed country, able to play the role of regional hegemon to foster development. But as Tsie (2001, 141) observed, South Africa has declined to play that role. "Unfortunately, available evidence suggests that South Africa is reluctant to assume the role of benign hegemon. . . . Instead, South Africa has increasingly displayed a neo-realist regional economic policy in which it uses its economic power to address domestic problems at the expense of the rest of the region. . . . As a result the previous neocolonial pattern of regional economic relations [i.e., under apartheid] is being reinforced, this time more and more by South African corporate capital."[5] The consequences of South Africa's pursuit of a neorealist strategy vis-à-vis its neighbors rather than a more idealist "developmental regionalism" (Hettne 1990) are addressed below.

The inclusion of war-torn DRC in SADC, at the insistence of South Africa, was clearly an error, analysts argue (Sidaway and Gibb 1998, 170; Khadiagala 2001, 145). According to James Sidaway and Richard Gibb (1998, 170), South Africa was anxious to include DRC in SADC in part to access its resources, particularly its hydroelectric power. Yet the infrastructure of Congo had been decimated by three decades of misrule and then by two years of war; it lacked a functioning formal economy. Moreover, its connection to southern Africa was always tenuous, at best. Indeed, DRC had almost none of the approved criteria for admission to the body, namely proximity to southern Africa, democratic government, and a sharing of SADC's ideals (Sidaway and Gibb 1998, 170). Of even greater concern, DRC's membership in SADC provided SADC members Angola, Namibia, and Zimbabwe with a plausible excuse for their intervention in the Congo war in 1998: support of a regional ally (Nest 2001).

Stretching Southern Africa: SADC in DRC

Even with its defensive origins in the Frontline States, SADC's principal function is as an economic body. Yet the emergence of security issues in the region, including in Lesotho in 1994, contributed to the establishment of the SADC

Organ on Politics, Defense, and Security, which was launched at an extraordinary summit in Botswana on June 28, 1996. It was intended as a separate structure that would not only ensure high-level attention to matters of security, peacekeeping, and conflict management and prevention, but would permit greater flexibility and a more timely response (Cilliers 1999). According to Khadiagala (2001, 141), the organ was to function as the security arm of SADC, concerned with regional stability, political cooperation (including on issues of democracy and human rights), conflict prevention and resolution, and peacekeeping and collective security and defense.[6] However, the organ did not work as planned, especially as it was effectively captured by President Robert Mugabe of Zimbabwe.

Upon its launch, the organ was administered by Zimbabwe's Ministry of Foreign Affairs and headed by Mugabe, who was elected by his SADC counterparts. However, there was some debate in SADC as to the permanence and place of the organ. This led to considerable ambiguity about intervention whereby assistance *could* be rendered to another member state provided it was requested by the government. The result was an ad hoc practice in the interventions in both DRC and Lesotho, when few if any collective controls were exercised (Khadiagala 2001, 143).

Mugabe, of course, used his position as head of the organ to rationalize Zimbabwe's intervention in DRC in August 1998. Similarly, the September 1998 intervention by 900 South African and Batswana troops in Lesotho (where they remained until April 1999) was also poorly conducted and revealed a lack of institutionalization of policies and procedures, although the action was immeasurably less violent and exploitative than the DRC intervention (Nest 2001). In fact, Angola's and Zimbabwe's involvement in DRC was driven not by regional concerns and collective responsibility but by far narrower *national* political and security interests, as well as economic opportunity. According to Khadiagala, Mugabe in particular used the "SADC Organ as a unilateral instrument for his own aggressive foreign policy" (Khadiagala 2001, 145). A new Protocol on Politics, Defense, and Security Cooperation was enacted in 2001 in an attempt to rein in some of the functions of the organ (and perhaps of Mugabe, who then rotated out of the chairman's role). To a certain degree, the Organ on Politics created—or deepened—fault lines in SADC. Some observers, however, suggest that differences between Mugabe and other SADC heads of state stemmed more from legitimate political debate than from the former's personalization of the Organ on Politics (Fisher and Ngoma 2005, 1, 8).

In any event, given SADC's competing and duplicative structures, overexpansion, and diversion to DRC, among other issues, it is not surprising that it has had scant success as a development body (Khadiagala 2001, 139). Partly to address these shortcomings, SADC underwent a restructuring in 2000 and 2001 to streamline a conflicting and redundant set of issues and institutions into four directorates: trade, industry, finance, and investment; infrastructure and services; food, agriculture, and natural resources; and social and human development and special programs (Fisher and Ngoma 2005). Nevertheless, it would appear that the regional institutions and their member states have yet to make regionalism benefit most southern Africans. Indeed, "southern African integration . . . still tends to have a plot from which the mass of the people are excluded" (Sidaway and Gibb 1998, 179). The African Union, in the launch of which South Africa played an instrumental role, has attracted similar criticism.

Southern Africa in Africa

The African Union

In 2002 the African Union was officially launched in Durban, South Africa, replacing the nearly forty-year-old Organization of African Unity (OAU). Established at Addis Ababa in 1963, the OAU "sought to establish a normative order that would permit the continent's sovereign states to live alongside one another in peace and amity" (Rothchild and Harbeson 2000, 13). Among the principal objectives of the OAU was to assert and protect the sovereignty of Africa's fragile new states; thus territorial integrity and the principle of non-interference were sacrosanct. Unable to project power themselves to defend their borders, weak states needed these assurances of security. However, the inviolability of national borders had disastrous consequences as well, as countless abuses were perpetrated against domestic populations by autocratic regimes that faced little sanction from OAU counterparts. Perhaps the most extreme example of this was the 1994 genocide in Rwanda. The slaughter of nearly 1 million ethnic Tutsis and Hutu sympathizers in just 100 days provided a stark illustration that the extant "institutions of interstate amity and cooperation were inadequate to cope with impending state and interstate dangers" (Rothchild and Harbeson 2000, 13).

Yet as long as the norms were mutually reinforcing and states respected each other's sovereignty, the OAU could persist. The war in DRC, however, which at one stage involved some eight countries—Angola, Chad, Namibia, Rwanda, Uganda, Zimbabwe, and, briefly, Burundi and Sudan—marked an unprecedented degree of interstate conflict in Africa and claimed millions of lives.[7] "Africa's world war" in Congo, then, decimated the noninterference norm and hastened the demise of the old order symbolized by the OAU (Khadiagala 2000, 98). It bears noting also that the OAU was largely incapable of fulfilling even its basic functions. Chronically underfunded, for example, the OAU was "unable to collect its dues and gripped with immobilism" as well as "unable to offer effective leadership on interstate matters envisaged in the Charter" (Rothchild and Harbeson 2000, 13).

In September 1999 the Sirte Declaration formally proposed that a new African Union should be established to foster continental unity and development and eventually integration along the European Union model. In this early period, Muammar Qaddafi, the controversial Libyan leader, played a leading role in financing and promoting the formation of a union (Huliaras 2001). Qaddafi was determined that the new parliament should be in the Libyan capital, Tripoli, and that he should serve as the initial president of the new body. Drawing on Libya's substantial oil wealth, Qaddafi was able to cultivate support among sub-Saharan African leaders; one way was to pay their countries' dues to the OAU. Qaddafi would have been a controversial and problematic choice to lead the new body, however, and strong resistance emerged from South African president Thabo Mbeki, among others. In contrast to others, especially Qaddafi, Mbeki enjoyed continental and international legitimacy. Moreover, his profile as a new leader and his role in the development of the well-received development initiative—the Millennium Africa Program (MAP)—made him an attractive choice to serve as the AU's first chairperson. It is worth noting, however, that Qaddafi was in fact elected AU president in 2009 for a one-year term. As Mbeki supporters predicted a decade earlier, his controversial term damaged the already fragile reputation of the body ("Malawi's President to Succeed Gaddafi" 2010).

The AU replicates some of the OAU's more problematic structures, including the fact that its chief representation remains at the presidential level. The main body of the AU is its assembly body, which is composed of the heads of state of the fifty-two AU members. Its executive council, which is responsible to the assembly, is a subordinate body composed of ministers designated by the governments of member states. In turn, there are eight commissioners, each of whom is responsible for a portfolio.[8] Where the AU attempts to depart from its predecessor organization is in its effort to better institutionalize governing structures, along the lines of the European Union model. Hence a pan-African parliament was launched in 2004 to "ensure the full participation of African peoples in governance, development and economic integration of the Continent." Other administrative bodies include a peace and security council, which was established in 2004; an economic, social, and cultural council; and a court of justice.[9] As OAU adherents learned in the past, however, the problem is not the existence of such institutions. Rather it is that they are not endowed with appropriate resources and the legitimacy that would enable them to carry out their mandate. The paucity of resources on the continent for interstate institution building continues to undermine the autonomy and the capacity of the AU.

NEPAD

NEPAD had several fathers, but its emergence perhaps became most closely associated with South Africa's Thabo Mbeki, who was therefore connected as well to the initiative's shortcomings. Those who championed the establishment of the AU, including Mbeki, argued that it marked the beginning of a mature pan-Africanism and a new era of collective identity, responsibility, and development on the African continent. In this vein, perhaps the biggest test of the AU's capacity to deliver is NEPAD, which was launched in July 2001, endorsed by the outgoing OAU, and eventually adopted by the AU. NEPAD was the result of the merger between two competing visions of Africa's continental future. The first, articulated by Mbeki, was the Millennium Africa Plan; the other was the Omega Plan, advocated by Senegalese president Abdoulaye Wade. Mbeki, who held the first AU chairmanship and whose MAP proposal became the principal basis for NEPAD, is perhaps most closely associated with "New Africa" globalization and the effort to promote an "African Renaissance."[10] Although NEPAD is a continental rather than exclusively southern African initiative, its origins— and some of its greatest obstacles to its efficacy—reside in southern Africa.

As its name implies, NEPAD is intended to herald a new era of partnership in Africa, both with the global North, symbolizing an end to exploitation and neocolonialism, and within the continent. The latter marks an unambiguous departure from the norm of noninterference that characterized the OAU; NEPAD insists that African countries should take interest in what goes on *inside* each other's borders. Toward this end, NEPAD contained the following among its goals: good governance; democracy, peace, and security; sound economic policy; "smart partnerships" with donors that will "reward achievers"; and domestic ownership of the programs enacted (Hope 2002). NEPAD embodied "a pledge by African leaders . . . that they have a pressing duty to eradicate poverty and place their countries, both individually and collectively, on a path of sustainable growth and development. . . . [Further,] the Programme is anchored on the determination of *Africans to extricate themselves* and the continent from the malaise of underdevelopment and exclusion in a globalising world" (UNECA 2001; emphasis added).

In the developed world, therefore, NEPAD was greeted more favorably than previous initiatives had been because it adopted a new and seemingly aggressive framework that advanced a uniquely intra-African collective responsibility. Similarly, its principal architects—particularly Mbeki, Wade, and Nigerian president Olusegun Obasanjo—all democratically elected, were then hailed as exemplars of responsible leadership in Africa (Taylor and Nel 2002) and regarded by some as enlightened free marketeers and staunch advocates of democracy, good governance, human rights, and the rule of law (Hope 2002, 402).

NEPAD rejects withdrawal from the "world system" (Wallerstein 1974). Indeed, it fundamentally *opposes* exclusion and seeks greater integration into the global economy. Hence the envisioned integration embraces and affirms the dominant neoliberal paradigm. Critics of this approach argue that NEPAD's intention to "participate in the globalisation process" (UNECA

2001) amounts to business as usual (Taylor and Nel 2002). Problematically, as evidenced by its sponsors' appeals for financing to the Group of Eight (G8) countries, NEPAD relies substantially on the developed nations and is not, practically speaking, a program of Africans solely extricating *themselves.* In this sense, NEPAD was not appreciably different from previous proposals, such as the African Alternative Framework, that also relied on donor states to get off the ground (Lancaster 2000).[11] At the same time, NEPAD's appeal to the global North is neither unrealistic nor unreasonable: whereas African agents bear great responsibility, the continent's malaise is hardly exclusively self-imposed; therefore, neither should its solutions be (Mkandawire and Soludo 1999). Yet because NEPAD duplicates many of the same donor dependencies of its predecessor strategies—a point sometimes obscured in the NEPAD policy documents—its proponents should expect similar problems ahead.[12]

Indeed, even as early as one year after its official launch, NEPAD appeared to be languishing. First was the 2002 G8 summit in Alberta, Canada. International terrorism dominated almost exclusively, despite the expectation that a substantial portion of the agenda would be dedicated to Africa and the developing world. Africa sought some US$64 billion from the G8 for NEPAD, but only US$6 billion was committed, sparking considerable outcry and disappointment ("G-8 Guilty" 2002). The 2003 G8 meeting, in Evian, France, yielded developed country support for fighting AIDS (a subject omitted, inexplicably, from NEPAD), but not through the NEPAD mechanism. These setbacks were anticipated by Ian Taylor and Philip Nel (2002, 164), who argued that the "New Africa" project of Mbeki and others "play[ed] into the hands of the [G8] strategists."

Where NEPAD does attempt to substantially depart from previous African-led approaches is in its African Peer Review Mechanism (APRM), which insists, essentially, that Africa must police itself, particularly on issues of governance and democracy. At the launch of NEPAD, it appeared that this mechanism would give the AU power to impose various sanctions on errant member states. But the peer review system only gradually began to materialize by the end of 2003, and in any event, participation—including a report on conditions in a given state done within six months of a visit by an "eminent persons" team—is on a voluntary basis. As of September 2010, fourteen AU member states had undergone the APRM, including only Mauritius, Lesotho, Mozambique, and South Africa in southern Africa.[13] These states, and the others, include only a few of Africa's poor political performers, which suggests that the states that most need the oversight manage to evade it. More problematic, the notion of peer review also reveals another major fault line in NEPAD: the persistence of conflict (including internal strife and political repression) anywhere on the continent poses tremendous legitimacy problems for it. As these challenges have continued unabated, NEPAD's credibility has suffered.

This dilemma is particularly acute in southern Africa, which saw itself as the centerpiece of Mbeki's "African Renaissance"[14] but instead plays host to an intractable Zimbabwe problem. In direct contradiction to the spirit, if not the letter, of NEPAD, African countries like South Africa opted for quiet, or passive, diplomacy in relation to Robert Mugabe. For former South African president Thabo Mbeki, however, these positions would appear to be irreconcilable. The elite stance on Zimbabwe, led by Mbeki, was disparagingly labeled as his "softly-softly" approach and forestalled any prospect of a deepening partnership with the West, at least via NEPAD and the AU. Under Jacob Zuma's presidency, South Africa has not taken as much of a leading role in continental institutions. Zuma's electoral mandate—certainly how he interpreted it—was far more inward looking than Mbeki's.

Globalization and Southern Africa

The Neoliberal Prescription

As each of the country chapters in this book reveals, the neoliberal model is as predominant in southern Africa as it is throughout the continent. Thus globalization, for our purposes, involves liberal or market-driven policies on trade, investment, employment, government spending, and so on. In theory, such policies are expected to undergird development; at worst, they may spark a "race to the bottom" with respect to labor, the environment, social spending, and poverty levels (Korten 2001). The vehicle for the neoliberal agenda in the 1980s and 1990s was some version of the structural adjustment program, although several countries in southern Africa, namely Botswana, Namibia, and South Africa, avoided the SAPs prescribed by the International Monetary Fund and World Bank. None, however, has escaped the effects of globalization on economic life, and none is disconnected from the global economy; a complete delinking, though occasionally advocated by some on the left, is not feasible.

South Africa's "Growth, Equity, and Redistribution" program (GEAR), for example, was very much a structural adjustment program that was as rigorous as, if not more so than, one the international financial institutions (IFIs) might have drawn up themselves (I. Taylor 2002), although its effects were mediated somewhat, in more recent years, by increased social programs (Ferguson 2007). Moreover, Botswana, with its diamond export–dominated economy, is highly dependent on global markets for this single commodity. Only Zimbabwe has turned its back on the international financial institutions and on its Western bilateral donors. Yet Zimbabwe is scarcely autarkic: it remains substantially dependent on food aid, for example, as well as on its regional counterparts for energy and other essential imports; it relies increasingly on nontraditional partners such as China and Libya. Further, there is a widespread expectation that

Zimbabwe will return to the global capitalist system, including, especially, IFI-sponsored adjustment, when the Mugabe regime is defeated or collapses. In short, although some states, notably South Africa, have embraced economic globalization to a greater degree than others, by and large globalization is not a *choice* for southern Africa. The countries of the region are embedded in the global political economy, albeit to highly variable degrees.

The connectedness of the global economy to southern Africa is revealed through trade relations, investment, the international debt regime, and international aid. Since aid is largely a bilateral function, we can dispense with that discussion here and instead refer the reader to the individual country chapters. The international finance regime, on the other hand, is multilateral and not only affects how individual states in the region deal with the IFIs but also conditions the nature of their relationship with each other, such as through SADC, COMESA, or SACU. Moreover, with the exception of Zimbabwe, countries in the region are engaging more with the forces of globalization rather than delinking from them.

In a similar vein, South Africa's ascension to membership in the so-called BRICS (Brazil, Russia, India, China, and South Africa) group of emerging country powerhouses—ironically occurring under the less auspiciously internationalist Zuma—is evidence of the embrace of the region's global aspirations. Certainly it is evidence of South Africa's. The scope and impact of this nascent alignment with the BRICS remain to be seen (as does Zimbabwe's "look east" policy that aims to embrace Asian nations rather than its traditional western partners Britain and the United States). Yet the BRICS themselves, deeply enmeshed in world trade, finance, resources, and investment, can hardly be considered "apart" from globalization in any measurable sense. Indeed, though some analysts have suggested that the presence of South Africa's far smaller economy could distort the BRICS, it could make South Africa more attractive for investment. But the "globalized" interests of the existing group cannot be overlooked: "What China above all—but also India, Brazil and Russia—are interested in is South Africa as an engine for development and a gateway for investment in Africa as a whole" (Wooldridge 2011).

Regardless of the intent of the BRICS, however, it is certainly the case that neoliberal SAPs, delivered by Western states and international financial institutions, and the wider globalization of which they are a part, have themselves had an uneven effect on southern Africa. Most states appear to have been harmed by the austerity measures that accompanied SAPs, but what is not known—or knowable—is what the region would look like in the absence of such programs.[15] Privatization and foreign investment, for example, are regarded as essential corollaries to a neoliberal agenda. Yet critics have noted that under globalization, developing states tend to facilitate transnational investment with shallow and transient ties, leading them to become what James Mittelmann (2000) calls "courtesan states." Flows of foreign direct investment (FDI), especially into the extractive sectors on which most of southern Africa relies, have proved fickle in the past.

Indeed, it is clear that such concessions to global capitalism have consequences for states, not only externally, but in their internal relations as well. As Béatrice Hibou (1999, 97) observes, "the unending quest to satisfy the donors' financial requirements has particularly pernicious consequences. Since the survival of the government depends increasingly on its external resources, it is increasingly led to concern itself more with its exterior respectability than its interior legitimacy." Thus, as Pádraig Carmody and Scott Taylor (2003) note, this dependence on transnational forces impels the state to shift its priorities away from a domestic agenda. In southern Africa, the embrace of the market-led model of development has contributed to increased social dislocation, as states struggle to reduce government spending in line with donor prescriptions. Indeed, Malawi, South Africa, Zambia, and Zimbabwe, each of which has undergone an adjustment program, have experienced the consequences of these contradictory policies (Bond 2000; I. Taylor 2002; Carmody and Taylor 2003). However, to some degree the region's dependence on "transnational forces" has expanded since 2001, and beneficially. Debt relief under HIPC and MDRI freed up considerable budgetary capacity, whereas high commodity prices, driven largely by Chinese and other international demand for industrial inputs, have contributed to a decade of sustained economic growth.

Ultimately, only Zimbabwe experimented with a measure of "delinking" (Brecher, Costello, and Smith 2000, 135) from the global economy (or at least from the Western-dominated one), and the results have been catastrophic. Driven in part by sanctions, expulsion from the Commonwealth, and suspension of aid, Zimbabwe's decision to go it alone has resulted in chronic shortages and near-total economic collapse (Carmody and Taylor 2003). Perhaps ironically, then, the Bank of Zimbabwe's abandonment of the Zimbabwean dollar in 2009 in favor of a US-dollarized economy can be seen as a failure of delinking and a capitulation to US monetary policy.

At the regional level too, the countries of southern Africa appear to have adopted a Western liberal model as well, with the idea that a larger regional market becomes "attractive to global operators"; larger trading blocs, the thinking goes, are likely to be more successful in coping with the challenges of globalization than individual states (Ajulu 2001, 38). Scholars such as Tsie (2001, 136–137) reject this idea of a benign "neoliberal regionalism"—which focuses on reducing tariffs to facilitate trade, financial market liberalization, and currency convertibility—because it is "premised on the contestable assumption that is what is good for local and foreign capital is good for society as a whole or in this specific instance, for regional economies."

Tsie (2001, 142) and others argue that this approach will merely further impoverish the African countries—including South Africa, albeit to a slightly lesser extent—as their dependence on inequitable world trade and investment flows deepens. Yet advocates of liberalized trade and free trade agreements, whether with the United States through the Africa Growth and Opportunity Act (AGOA), or with the European Union, argue that such frameworks redound to the benefit of *each* of the countries of the region. This is not necessarily the case, however, as an examination of two major recent trade initiatives makes clear.

The International Trade Regime

The Africa Growth and Opportunity Act. Signed into law by US president Bill Clinton in May 2000, AGOA began as an eight-year pact designed to permit duty-free imports of certain African goods, particularly clothing and textiles, into the United States. The agreement was eventually expanded to include a wider range of goods under the US Trade Act of 2002, and in 2004 it was extended to 2015 by the George W. Bush administration.[16] The preferential trade agreement allows up to 3.5 percent of these imports to come from sub-Saharan Africa. Within its first few years, however, despite AGOA's having been touted "as the success story of US economic policy towards Africa, it [had] not increased aggregate African exports to the US. Instead, the value of total exports to the US from the 38 countries [shrank] by almost a quarter (in dollar terms) since AGOA's inception" (Naumann 2003).[17] What happened instead in the first few years is that AGOA supplanted non-AGOA exports to the United States from African countries.

Today, AGOA applies to more than 6,400 items, including textiles. Yet whereas textiles and clothing accounted for between 3 and 7 percent of the total by 2008, energy products—seemingly far removed from the original intent of the legislation—accounted for 90 percent of African imports to the United States ("US-African Trade Profile" 2009).[18]

Under AGOA, sub-Saharan Africa receives more preferential access to the US economy than any other region without a free trade agreement, although African nations must meet several eligibility requirements. According to the AGOA legislation, the US president may designate sub-Saharan African countries eligible to receive the benefits of AGOA "if they are making progress in such areas as the establishment of market-based economies; development of political pluralism and the rule of law; elimination of barriers to US trade and investment; protection of intellectual property; efforts to combat corruption; policies to reduce poverty; increased availability of healthcare and educational opportunities; protection of human rights and worker rights; and elimination of certain practices of child labour" (du Toit 2003). The legislation also requires recipient countries to refrain from activities that undermine US national security. Along many of these parameters, the situation in Zimbabwe, therefore, bars that country's participation in AGOA.

A number of studies suggest that, after a decade in force, the overall impact of AGOA is limited. Since 2001, total trade between the two regions has nearly tripled (Páez et al. 2010, 103). Total imports to the United States increased significantly from US$5 billion in 2000 to over US$25 billion in 2005. From 2005 to 2010 total imports fluctuated, reaching as high as US$86 billion in 2008, but in 2009 imports dropped by nearly 50 percent from the preceding year to US$47 billion, as a result of the global financial crisis. Nonetheless, it has been estimated that over 300,000 jobs were created since AGOA's enactment, with Lesotho being by far the largest beneficiary ("U.S. Trade with Sub-Saharan Africa, January–December 2010" 2011; I. Taylor 2009, 85).

Although oil imports to the United States swamp all other African products, one of the factors contributing to the anemic contribution of textiles—except from the southern African countries of Mauritius and Lesotho—was the expiration of the Multi-Fibre Arrangement (MFA) in early 2005, which governed rules of origin and the global textile trade. Although administered by General Agreement on Tariffs and Trade (GATT) and later the WTO, the MFA was actually "a major departure from the basic GATT rules and particularly the principle of non-discrimination" because it served as a protectionist mechanism for textile producers in the developed world (WTO n.d.). Once the MFA expired, however, African producers were ill-positioned to compete with Chinese firms. China, which is the world's lowest-cost textile and clothing producer, overwhelmed what remained of Africa's fragile, high-cost producers; they simply could not compete. The preferences provided under AGOA provide some room for African producers to maneuver, though many components are actually transshipped from China (Africa's poorest producers, which includes all of the AGOA-eligible countries *except* South Africa, have been granted a waiver on rules of origin). Because South Africa cannot compete with Chinese imports, nor can it assemble clothing and textiles made of Chinese fabrics and yarns and export them to the United States duty free under AGOA, its sector has been decimated (I. Taylor 2009, 74–77).

Hence, AGOA is at best an unreliable vehicle for the expansion of southern African export-oriented sectors (energy and minerals excepted). In the first five years prior to the expiration of the MFA in 2005, US imports of textiles and apparel produced in Africa increased fourfold, from US$355 million in 2001 to US$1.6 billion in 2004. The leading sources of those exports were Kenya, Lesotho, Madagascar, South Africa, Mauritius, Swaziland, and Botswana ("Apparel Trade Under AGOA" n.d.). Owing to the MFA expiration, textile and apparel imports fell to US$1.4 billion in 2005; they fell further to US$918 million in 2008 ("US-African Trade Profile" 2009). Beyond the enclave state of Lesotho and the island country of Mauritius, the benefits for southern Africa's textile sector have been illusory.

In sum, AGOA offers opportunities for African states to export goods to the United States at no tariff. However, the structure of AGOA favors petroleum producers and the handful of countries that have competitive or reasonably competitive textile sectors. Whereas South Africa was prominent among these at AGOA's inception, it has been eclipsed by tiny Lesotho and long-established producer Mauritius.[19] For most of the remainder of sub-Saharan Africa and southern African countries, AGOA has not generated the degree of trade and investment envisioned by its early champions. Further, the existence of AGOA notwithstanding, the region is not all moving in the same direction regarding trade with the North; one of the initial criticisms of AGOA was that the poorest, least-developed nations in Africa would lack the industrial and export infrastructure to be able to take advantage of AGOA's provisions. Indeed, they certainly have not been able to benefit to the degree Angola has, for example, as the region's only oil producer and the second largest source of petroleum exports to the United States from Africa.

South Africa and China: Fellow BRICS and competitors. Since the end of apartheid, all of the southern African countries have increased their dependence on South Africa and, increasingly, on China. China is an important source of investment and is now one of Africa's leading trade partners, with two-way trade exceeding US$107 billion in 2008; Africa is China's second largest export recipient. This trade consists primarily of petrochemicals, metals, minerals, and other primary commodities. Whereas Chinese exports to Africa include consumer goods, heavy equipment, and other useful materials, imported Chinese goods have also earned a reputation for being cheaply made, low-cost consumables. These imports have not only put African competition out of business; their quality has generated considerable hostility (I. Taylor 2009, 75).

South Africa, therefore, is in many ways a much more credible and tested partner in the region. South African companies enjoy business and trade relations that they began to exploit intensely almost immediately after the fall of apartheid (Taylor 2007). Yet South Africa's partnership with its neighbors is fairly one-sided. Whereas other countries have run substantial trade deficits with South Africa and have experienced heavy investment by South African firms and heavy South African imports, South Africa instead has looked increasingly to the European Union as well as the United States. Richard Mshomba (2000, 197) suggests that free trade partnerships between Europe or the United States and Africa tend to "divert (rather than direct)" African attempts at regional economic cooperation, as the African states compete among themselves for attention and assistance from the developed "partners." This appears to have been the case with South Africa's October 1999 trade pact with the EU, which in fact "chagrined" other SADC members (Khadiagala 2001, 139).

Southern Africa and the European Union. In 1999, South Africa signed a trade, development, and cooperation agreement (TDCA) with the EU, its main trading partner, following three years of negotiations. The agreement stipulated the creation of a free trade area to be implemented over a twelve-year transition period in accordance with World Trade Organization rules ("South Africa Signs" 1999). Pursuant to the agreement, South Africa will offer duty-free access to 86 percent of its EU imports over the twelve-year period. Conversely, the EU is to grant duty-free status to 95 percent of South African exports. On paper, the EU was to open its market at a much faster pace and was scheduled to complete most liberalization by 2002, but progress moved more slowly than anticipated. The EU is to eliminate all tariffs on exports of industrial goods from South Africa over time, as well as on 75 percent of agricultural products, including "sensitive products" like cut flowers and fruit. However, since the bulk of South African exports are primary goods, including coal (14 percent) and diamonds (14 percent) as well as other metals and minerals, it is hard to see the major benefits accruing to South Africa as a result of this pact, which threatens its already embattled industry. Moreover, South Africa enjoyed greater access to EU markets than the EU did to South Africa prior to the trade agreement, thereby suggesting that South Africa may have gained more before its enactment (Lee 2003, 219). Still, thanks largely to primary commodities, South Africa ran a US$559 million trade surplus with the EU in 2008 (EIU 2010d).

Nonetheless, another complication, Margaret Lee (2003, 209) writes, is that "although the EU is a major trading partner for South Africa, South Africa is not a major trading partner for the EU." Hence, fully liberalized trade with South Africa scarcely threatens the EU, but in South Africa deindustrialization and unemployment are a possible result (Lee 2003, 219), although "sensitive products" (for South Africa, industrial goods) were supposed to take until 2012 to free up ("South Africa Signs" 1999).

In part stemming from South Africa's perceived neglect of the region and its own protectionism vis-à-vis neighboring states, the agreement with the EU generated resistance in the region, as well as within South Africa itself.[20] South Africa's SACU partners, for example, were unenthusiastic about the agreement (Wadula and Maletsky 1999). Not only does the agreement threaten serious repercussions for Botswana, Lesotho, Namibia, and Swaziland, but these countries were not consulted about its establishment, even though their approval is required by SACU treaty (Lee 2003, 220). Moreover, as a de facto EU-SACU free trade area (Lee 2003, 220), the agreement effectively governed the trade policies of other SACU members, and these countries risked losing their own preferential, *nonreciprocal* benefits with the EU as a result.[21]

In 2003 the United States renewed a push for a new free trade agreement of its own with the SACU countries. Although by 2008 the parties had only reached the point where a formal *mechanism* was established to negotiate a free trade agreement ("US Signs" 2008), such an agreement would substantially replace the preferential access to US markets that SACU countries currently enjoy under AGOA but make such access more permanent. Yet while it would presumably open new markets in the United States for SACU countries, a SACU-US free trade agreement potentially would also expose southern Africa to a far greater flow of US imports, including US-subsidized agricultural production and superior US-manufactured goods. These changes could reverse even the modest benefits achieved thus far under AGOA for nonenergy or mineral products.

In sum, a number of countries have done well in recent years, despite the presumptively hostile global neoliberal order, running at times substantial surpluses with their trade partners in the United States, the EU and, increasingly, China. For the most part, however, this growth is commodity driven, which subjects southern African economies to the vicissitudes of global commodity prices—much like the situation in the 1970s. AGOA has helped at the margins, particularly in places like Lesotho and Mauritius, small southern African countries that have not been focal points in this book. At the level of regional institutions, however, the results have been more ambiguous. Regional subgroups like SACU or SADC have yet to achieve the level of integration and development necessary to establish a free trade agreement that truly generates widely shared benefits. Yet in South Africa's headlong rush to consummate such deals, it serves to undermine the region as a whole.

The Zimbabwe Dilemma

Zimbabwe remains a significant obstacle to further economic and political integration in the region. Since Zimbabwe's decline accelerated beginning in 2000, the country has maintained its linkages to regional institutions such as SADC and, at a wider level, the AU; however, Zimbabwe plainly has become a liability for its erstwhile regional partners.

Zimbabwe's present condition is ironic. It was a key actor in the creation of SADCC in 1980; served as an anchor of stability in the region, especially in the tumult of the 1980s; and was regarded by some as a model for the successful transition from late settler rule (Herbst 1990).[22] Today, however, Zimbabwe is a laggard in a region that is generally marked by political stability, improving economic performance, and some democratic promise. Indeed, some of the previous worst performers in the region have experienced remarkable turnarounds. Yet, Zimbabwe's distinguishing features include an economy in disarray, thinly veiled political repression under the veneer of a coalition, and a debilitating public health crisis. What is perhaps most striking about the Zimbabwe case is the rapidity of its collapse and the fact that its fall did not precipitate the corresponding collapse—economic, political, social— of its better-performing but nonetheless fragile neighbors.

The structural similarities between Zimbabwe and its regional counterparts, particularly Namibia and South Africa, have been noted by numerous authors; indeed, we have emphasized them in this book. Both Namibia and South Africa have small but powerful white minorities who enjoy disproportionate economic privilege and landownership vis-à-vis blacks, and race and class covary in highly destabilizing ways. It is less important that what precipitated Zimbabwe's collapse was not racial divisions per se; of prominence is the fact that President Mugabe could draw on those divisions in an attempt to score political points. If Zimbabwe is not a model for Namibia and South Africa, we should at least regard it as a cautionary tale for the future of the two other postsettler societies in the region.

Importantly, Mugabe himself has escaped widespread or sustained condemnation (certainly publicly) from his counterparts in the region for his destruction of the economy, subversion of the rule of law, and persecution of the opposition, white and black. In fact, as early as May 2000 Mugabe urged his SADC neighbors in Namibia and South Africa to adopt the same approach, at least in regard to race relations: "It is a simple solution. If the other neighboring countries have problems similar to the ones we have encountered, why not apply the same solution as Zimbabwe. If the white commercial farmers are ready to discuss with you and give land then there is no need for a fight. But in Zimbabwe the British are not ready and we are making them ready now" (quoted in Khadiagala 2001, 152).

Mugabe's regional counterparts came under repeated criticism from domestic activists and international observers for their inaction on Zimbabwe. Perhaps no one has attracted more attention than South Africa's former president Thabo Mbeki, whose position was no doubt complicated by the high expectations that accompanied his ambitious international programs or his democratic legitimacy. Mbeki's behavior was all the more surprising considering that Zimbabwe's situation negatively impacted both the AU and NEPAD, two projects in which he had a major personal and political stake (ICG 2002). Indeed, Western critics, whose economic support is essential to the success of NEPAD and the AU, argue that "the unwillingness to confront the Mugabe policies more robustly has almost single-handedly destroyed the credibility of the nascent NEPAD" (ICG 2003b, 11). Of course, the ultimate irony was that it was Mbeki more than anyone who helped orchestrate the Global Political Agreement (GPA) signed between Mugabe and opposition Movement for Democratic Change (MDC) leaders in September 2008. For awhile it appeared that Mbeki's "softly-softly" approach had been vindicated. Yet as Chapter 7 indicates, Mugabe and ZANU-PF have bested their MDC "partners" at virtually every turn; the coalition is virtually devoid of international or domestic credibility. At the time of the GPA, Mbeki had already lost control of the African National Congress and within two months would lose his presidency: Mugabe was able to outlast the regional president who had the most at stake by his staying in office.

Other members of SADC have been as muted in their criticism as Mbeki. This includes the organization itself, despite the fact that Zimbabwe contravened various SADC directives before and during its March 2002 presidential election.[23] Moreover, SADC-sponsored election teams, made up of regional parliamentarians, concurred with ZANU-PF that the 2006 and 2008 election contests were also "free and fair." And now Jacob Zuma has inherited Thabo Mbeki's legacy—and his Zimbabwe liability.

Some international observers of the Zimbabwe scene advocated placing pressure on South Africa, which is responsible for 50 percent of Zimbabwe's imports and a significant portion of its electrical power, to use this economic leverage to compel Mugabe to reach a political solution with the opposition and to restore some semblance of democracy in the country.[24] Such pressure repeatedly backfired, however, as SADC countries appeared unwilling to take actions that would unleash even greater chaos in Zimbabwe.

There is also a political loyalty issue at play that is admittedly difficult for analysts to dissect. In power since 1980, Mugabe is an elder statesman in the region and one of the few remaining leaders of the independence and anti-apartheid eras. This legacy affords him a certain degree of deference in the region—not solely among liberation movement leaders, who are a dying breed, but by younger politicians as well. Further, for their own domestic legitimacy and credibility, leaders like Mbeki have been highly reluctant to be seen as carrying out a British or US agenda with regard to Zimbabwe.

In sum, the region is effectively paralyzed over Zimbabwe. Mugabe has deftly used the issues of race and regional solidarity to forestall any action against him, "the AU has largely deferred to SADC on Zimbabwe" (ICG 2003c, 13), and SADC has shown great reluctance to act, either jointly or individually. It is abundantly clear that Zimbabwe has done grave damage to the institutions such as SADC and NEPAD; moreover, it has placed the region under increasing stress. The violent attacks against Zimbabwean and other immigrants around South Africa in 2008 are in part a manifestation of that clearly *regional* strain. Refugees numbering as high as 5 million have fled Zimbabwe, 60 percent of them to South Africa, straining fragile services there and elsewhere. The International Crisis Group estimated that the Zimbabwe crisis cost South Africa some US$1.9 billion, claimed 30,000 jobs, and cut its economic growth rate by 0.4 percent, between 2000 and 2003 alone. As mentioned above, tens of millions of dollars are owed to South African public and private firms (ICG 2003b). At the end of the day, even if Zimbabwe's crisis has not been "externalized" to the degree feared by some observers, regional performance, growth, and advancement require stability in the region. Given Zimbabwe's geographic centrality, its large population, and its once significant wealth and economic output, genuine regional advancement cannot take place as long as the crisis continues.

Conclusions on the Direction of the Region

Southern Africa appears to be headed in multiple directions at once. On the one hand, economic giant South Africa continues to anchor the region and lead in the development of trade initiatives with the developed countries that aim to place it on an equal footing with its new partners. Hence South Africa is generally regarded as having the capacity to act as regional hegemon in southern Africa, promoting and underwriting development and integration between itself and its neighbors, although South Africa itself is not always equipped to do so, given its own deep-seated economic, social, and political problems. Notwithstanding the potentially detrimental impacts of free trade, other economies in the region are performing well macroeconomically, although their populations remain quite poor. Further, norms of democracy, albeit favoring dominant parties, and development appear to have become entrenched throughout most of the region. Each of these factors augurs positively for efforts to develop a regional political economy.

On the other hand, South Africa's global aspirations may come at the *expense* of its neighbors, as it has shown disregard for the consequences of its own trade and investment strategies within the region or of the regional impact of its trade relations with the developed world. As numerous scholars have noted, such actions threaten to leave the region worse off; indeed, South Africa itself is best served by a blossoming regional economy, regardless of its successes at the "international" level. The crisis in Zimbabwe also undermines genuine economic integration within the region and capital flows from without, as everything from investment to tourists, to donors leaves the region or avoids it altogether. These dilemmas suggest that southern Africa, and South Africa in particular, must reconsider its internal challenges and establish a cohesive foundation for development at the regional level before turning its attentions inexorably toward the global arena.

Notes

1. Democratic Republic of Congo is a member of SADC; the addition of this (geographically) central African nation presents a number of problems for SADC, as discussed in this chapter.

2. Only Botswana, led by President Ian Khama, and Zambia's late president Levy Mwanawasa have offered substantial public criticism, and in neither case was it sustained.

3. Only three SADC countries—Lesotho, Mozambique, and Tanzania—later quit COMESA, and none as a result of the rivalry (Lee 2003, 89).

4. See Nathan (2006) for an analysis of SADC's difficulties in establishing a common security regime playing a peacemaking role in the region.

5. South African conglomerates are covering the continent in terms of investment, and these transcend the regional environment, from Egypt to Ghana. South African capital is increasingly mobile: "For instance from March 1995 until September 2000, the South African Reserve Bank approved 7.85 billion rand worth of direct investment in southern Africa while globally South African corporations received approval for 74.5 billion rand in foreign direct investment overseas" (Taylor and Nel 2002, 170). See also Hentz (2005).

6. The organ bore many similarities to the peacekeeping body established by its West African counterpart, the Economic Community of West African States, whose peacekeeping and peace-monitoring force, the Economic Community of West African States Monitoring Group (ECOMOG), was deployed in Liberia in the 1990s.

7. A study by the International Rescue Committee revealed that between the start of the war in 1998 and 2004, 3.9 million people had died, "arguably making DR Congo the world's deadliest crisis since World War II" (IRC 2007, ii). Some 90 percent of these deaths were from preventable diseases rather than direct violence, but they were nonetheless indirect consequences of the conflict. IRC determined that a total of "5.4 million excess deaths [had] occurred between August 1998 and April 2007. An estimated 2.1 million of those deaths have occurred since the formal end of war in 2002" (IRC 2007, ii).

8. According to the home page of the AU's official website, the African Union Commission is regarded as "the key organ playing a central role in the day-to-day management of the African Union. Among others, it represents the Union and defends its interests; elaborates draft common positions of the Union; prepares strategic plans and studies," and so forth. Its eight portfolios are available at http://www.africa-union.org/.

9. For more information, see the AU home page: http://www.africa-union.org/.

10. Mbeki's "voice has been among the loudest in promoting the New Africa project . . . in elite circles around the globe" (Taylor and Nel 2002, 164). The New Africa Initiative—resulting from the merger of the Omega Plan and MAP—was renamed NEPAD in October 2001.

11. The 1989 Africa Alternative Framework—an African proposal for a model of "independent" development meant to challenge SAPs—was never fully acted upon, in large part because of its (paradoxical) overreliance on Western financing.

12. NEPAD "centres on African ownership and management" (UNECA 2001). The October 2001 NEPAD document does address the bilateral and multilateral role, but in a secondary way: the pertinent sections are Section 6, "A New Global Partnership," and Section 7, "Implementation of the New Partnership for Africa's Development."

13. See NEPAD/APRM (New Partnership for African Development/African Peer Review Mechanism), http://www.nepad.org/; Transparency International, "NEPAD's African Peer Review Mechanism," http://www.transparency.org/.

14. See Van Ameron and Buescher (2005) for an analysis of how "peace parks" in southern Africa may further an African Renaissance.

15. For conflicting interpretations of SAPs, compare, for example, adjustment critics Patrick Bond (2000) and John Saul (1999) to Nicolas van de Walle (2001) and Patrick Chabal and Jean Pascal Daloz (1999).

16. "AGOA builds on existing US trade programs, and expands the benefits previously available only under the Generalised System of Preferences (GSP). . . . The number of products qualifying for duty-free access to US market under AGOA presently stands at over 7,000, including the 4,600 GSP products, approximately 1,800 products that have been added under AGOA (including footwear, wine, motor vehicle components etc.) and approximately 600 apparel products (subject to restrictions)" ("About AGOA" n.d.).

17. Total exports to the United States from sub-Saharan Africa declined by 18 percent, to US$18.2 billion, between 2000 and 2003, although AGOA exports increased (US International Trade Commission 2003).

18. Energy, mainly petroleum, and other unprocessed goods attract little or no import tariff in any event, hence their inclusion under AGOA is misleading. Although imports from AGOA-eligible nations have significantly increased, the framework has failed to achieve its diversification agenda. In 2008, energy-related products accounted

for over 90 percent of imports, the next leading industry being transportation equipment, accounting for 4.2 percent or US$1.4 billion. Textiles and apparel only account for 2.7 percent of imports, valued at US$918 million in 2008, while minerals and metals accounted for 1.2 percent. Non-oil imports have doubled since 2001, reaching US$5.1 billion in 2008 ("US-African Trade Profile" 2009).

19. In 2002, Lesotho accounted for 28 percent of all apparel imports under AGOA; the two next largest, South Africa and Mauritius, accounted for 18 percent and 23 percent, respectively. As "middle-income" countries, South Africa and Mauritius were subject to more stringent rules of origin requirements than Lesotho, hence the lower totals ("Apparel Trade Under AGOA" n.d.).

20. Licensing requirements instituted by the EU in 2000 for importers of dairy products, however, eliminated benefits on these goods to South African producers (Cook 2001).

21. The Lomé Accord, initiated in the 1970s and renegotiated in four rounds, gave certain trade preferences to African, Caribbean, and Pacific countries doing business with the EU. In the case of SACU countries, this meant duty-free manufactured exports to the EU and preferential treatment for agricultural goods.

22. Clearly the inclusive processes followed in Namibia and South Africa were far more comprehensive and resulted in liberal and democratic constitutions. Jeffrey Herbst's assessment (1990) preceded Namibian independence by a year.

23. Several provisions of SADC electoral norms and standards were violated, including those governing the impartiality of the electoral commission, the role of security forces, and the presence of SADC observers (ICG 2002, 2).

24. In 2003, the South African electrical power company Eskom and Mozambique's Cahorra Bassa were reportedly owed US$150 million by Zimbabwe's bankrupt state power authority, the Zimbabwe Electricity Supply Authority (ZESA) (Cooke, Morrison, and Prendergast 2003, 4).

13 Conclusion

We began this book by suggesting that the 2010 World Cup in South Africa was a signal event in the region. We conclude by returning to that event, although not the tournament per se (which was by nearly all accounts a rousing success), but to the symbolic importance of the first truly global sporting event to be held in Africa. That symbolism was captured by the totality of the one-month competition, but it was also evident early in the kickoff concert that marked the opening of the World Cup games. The show in Johannesburg featured world pop star Shakira performing a compelling ballad called "Waka Waka," perhaps better known by its subtitle "This Time for Africa."[1] Although reviews of the song and choice of a Colombian singer were mixed,[2] the song certainly caught on throughout Africa. Its ubiquity made "This Time for Africa" a particularly fitting anthem for a region, if not a continent.[3]

The notion of "This Time for Africa" was reinforced not only by the stunning spectacle of the month-long tournament, which defied the expectations of the naysayers—many of whom insisted that Africans, even relatively advantaged South Africans, could not pull off such a riveting world event—but also by the developments that have occurred throughout southern Africa since the twenty-first century began. Indeed, "this time for Africa" connotes a sense of *arrival*, albeit not at a particular democratic destination (which Thomas Carothers [2002] would suggest does not exist in any event) or flourishing free market economies, per se. Instead, it speaks to the region's visibility, importance, its *acceptance* as part of the world rather than on the margins of it, and its renewal. It indicates also that it is time that we recognize the political, social, and economic transformations occurring on the continent. These latter dimensions are demonstrated powerfully in a recent book by Steven Radelet, *Emerging Africa: How 17 Countries Are Leading the Way.* Along five dimensions—including democratization, economic policy reform, debt, technology, and technocratic leadership—Radelet (2010, 16–20) confirms that it is time for Africa, at least as represented by these seventeen dynamic countries. Fully seven of the seventeen are located in southern Africa—including five of the eight we analyzed in this book.[4] "It's time for Africa," then, can also be seen as a clarion call for Africa to move ahead in more concrete terms: on constitutionalism and the rule of law; on peace and democracy; on poverty reduction and social equity/access. In each of these dimensions, too, as Radelet indicates, southern Africa is leading.

The 2010 World Cup showcased South Africa, southern Africa, and Africa (in that order), dispelling many stereotypes. Even so, the enthusiasm and optimism generated by the games cannot mask the tremendous challenges that still plague many countries in southern Africa two decades after the transitions of the early 1990s.[5]

In fact, the picture remains mixed in the region, thereby suggesting cautious optimism rather than irrational exuberance. Yet there are many laudable achievements. Consider first the issues of peace and security. Most of southern Africa has been at peace since the early 1990s, although in Angola, peace was secured only in 2002 after two failed attempts in the early 1990s.[6] And Zimbabwe, which has not suffered from war since the 1970s, certainly has been wracked by periodic social conflict that has claimed several hundred lives since 2000. Each of these struggles, both the forty-year war in Angola and ten years of periodic state-sponsored violence in Zimbabwe, was prolonged by access to resources or the promise of access to resources of one type or another—whether oil, diamonds, mineral concessions, or land. But even more commonplace issues such as poverty, the availability of food, and price hikes led to riots, indicating that these countries are hardly immune to social conflict, even on a significant scale, as the examples of South Africa, Mozambique, and Zimbabwe amply demonstrate. Importantly, however, with the partial exception of Zimbabwe, southern African states have remained firmly under civilian control,[7] even at a time when the coup has remained a tool in parts of western Africa, which has seen military takeovers in Niger, Guinea, and Mauritania since 2008.[8]

Hence, constitutionalism is becoming entrenched, and South Africa remains the gold standard in the region (and perhaps the world), given its enshrinement of protections of human rights, minorities, civil liberties, and so on. Among the eight countries featured in this book, only two have not adopted new constitutions since the early 1990s. Notably, these lie at opposite ends of the spectrum: Botswana, which still abides by its democratic, although admittedly not very innovative independence constitution, and Zimbabwe, whose constitution has long been regarded as abetting the ruling party and presidential power. Constitutional reform processes now under way in several countries, including Zambia and Mozambique, as well as Zimbabwe, suggest some prospect exists for the creation of more inclusive, consensus-driven laws of the land.[9] The new constitutions are progressive in terms of civil liberties, individual freedoms, women's rights, and so on, but the true test remains the states'—and their courts'—willingness to uphold and protect these rights.[10]

Nonetheless, the institutionalization of constitutionalism is no small feat on a continent that has experienced the extraconstitutional seizure of power by militaries, or parliamentary majorities that have done the bidding of their parties and presidents to unilaterally alter constitutions in their favor (Diamond 2008). Indeed, despite the fact that in several southern African countries ruling parties enjoy more than two-thirds majorities in parliament and could change these founding documents unilaterally, constitutions largely have been respected. The most significant challenge has been the occasional effort to undo presidential term limits. Yet only in Namibia did the ruling SWAPO party successfully amend the country's constitution in 1999 to allow President Nujoma—and only Nujoma—a third presidential term. Institutional and popular resistance to such machinations appears to be firm: in Malawi, Bakili Muluzi tried repeatedly to get around the constitution's two-term limit but was ultimately prevented from doing so by the judiciary; in Zambia, Frederick Chiluba's attempt for a third term was thwarted by a party and popular revolt against the idea; and in Mozambique, Joachim Chissano himself resisted the urgings of some in his party to seek a constitutionally dubious third term. In a wholly different way, Botswana *added* a two-term limit to its constitution in 1998, a restriction that has been respected ever since.

All of the region's constitutions call for separation of powers among the three branches of government, with the intended result being at least some semblance of a balance of power among the branches. And yet throughout the region the executive clearly remains dominant in highly centralized structures. This power is exercised and maintained in myriad ways. For example, in three countries—Angola, Botswana, and South Africa—this concentration of power begins with presidents who are not directly elected by the people. Moreover, in famously democratic Botswana, an automatic succession of the vice president to the presidency—in advance of an election cycle—ensures that the president handpicks his successor. Such institutional design separates executives from the populations they purport to serve. South Africa, meanwhile, provides an example of both executive power and detachment; when Thabo Mbeki fell out of favor with his African National Congress political party, his term as president of the country was also brought to an end.

In the Mbeki example, the ruling *party* briefly proved more powerful than the president himself; this, admittedly, is an unusual occurrence. In all cases, however, legislatures remain subverted to executives. This executive dominance manifests itself in different ways. In two countries—Botswana and Zambia—presidents have the prerogative of appointing additional members of parliament, from 4 in Botswana to 8 in Zambia. In Namibia the president does likewise, although there the 6 additional members are at least nonvoting. Zimbabwe's president appoints 20 members to the less powerful but nonetheless influential upper chamber (an additional 10 seats are filled by traditional chiefs, typically loyal to the president). Further, in most of the parliamentary systems in the region, cabinets are drawn from among members of parliament, thereby ensuring that parliament as a body clearly represents executive interests. Thereafter, the use of frequent cabinet reshuffles to keep potential rivals at bay is a tool in the president's arsenal that tends to produce supplicants rather than independent voices. Another method of concentrating power in or around the office of the president is through the establishment of institutions, with or without a constitutional basis, that accrete all power to the themselves, including legislative (and frequently other executive) functions. Angola's Futungo is perhaps the most extreme example of this in the region, although Zimbabwe's national security apparatus has engaged in a similar usurpation of legislative *and* judicial power.

These continued problems notwithstanding, most countries in the region are characterized by presidential term limits, at least a modicum of accountability to the people or parliament, and respect for the constitution—a far cry from the presidents-for-life and central committee–anointed leaders of the past. This is partly a function of the institutionalization, throughout the region, of competitive presidential and parliamentary elections. In Namibia, Malawi, Zambia, Mozambique, and South Africa, national elections have been held every five years since their respective founding elections in the early 1990s and in Botswana since the year before independence in 1965. Angola's first such election was held in 2008; although perhaps not "transitional" in the sense conveyed by the political science literature of that genre, some observers believe that the 2008 election provided the final marker of peace in the embattled nation (Hilhorst and Serrano 2010). In all countries national election commissions are now in place to oversee electoral processes; although not all of these are fully autonomous of political actors, they are increasingly supported—and where necessary checked—by the emergence of vibrant election monitoring groups in civil society.

A striking achievement of southern Africa's democracies is the percentage of women in parliament in those countries that utilize proportional representation (PR) electoral systems. In fact, the four countries that use a PR system have representations of women that are among some of the highest in Africa and the world—as high as 45 percent in South Africa—while the four that use plurality systems have much lower percentages, as astonishingly low as 8 percent in Botswana. In the four countries that use the PR system, the ruling parties have all adopted voluntary party quotas to increase women's participation, which can be seamlessly utilized in party list systems. The only real quota option for plurality systems, by contrast, is some kind of reserved or special seat, which is much more controversial and—while such systems have been used with great success in other African countries (Bauer 2008)—they are not used in any of the four countries examined in this book. Women in Malawi have made the most progress among those four countries, in part because of an active 50-50 campaign that aims for parity in political office. In South

Africa, Mozambique, and Angola, women have also made great inroads into cabinets, as high, again in South Africa, as 41 percent of members. Throughout the region, women's movements both in and outside politics have been actively striving to reshape politics and decisionmaking in their respective countries.

Elections in southern Africa since 2000 have scarcely been flawless, yet many have had a high degree of legitimacy. Notably, in not one country has an election result been thrown out, though several elections have been challenged. Zimbabwe's elections since 2000 have involved substantial fraud, and Zambia's 2000 presidential election was challenged in court. In Angola in 2008, opposition parties ultimately decided to accept disputed election results so as to save the peace, whereas in Zimbabwe, the disputed election ultimately led to the establishment of a coalition government. Without a doubt, ruling parties hold tremendous advantages over opposition parties, in terms of access to state resources, state media, and so on, even in those few countries such as Namibia where public funding of political parties is available. Nonetheless—although Zimbabwe and Angola, as authoritarian states, are somewhat exceptional— even where elections are flawed, the process of holding them helps to inculcate democratic norms over time (Lindberg 2006).

Still, institutionalizing vibrant multiparty political systems remains one of the biggest challenges facing all of Africa's nascent democracies, southern Africa's included. Indeed, every one of the eight countries covered in this book may be considered a dominant-party political system. Even in countries which saw turnover as a result of founding elections, namely, Malawi and Zambia, although South Africa and Namibia could be added to this group, dominant parties emerged. Although this is a potentially problematic concentration of power, it does not preclude *alternance*. Indeed, many analysts suggest Zambia's government could turn over in 2011, thereby ending the ruling Movement for Multiparty Democracy's two-decade hold on power (whether such a change might result in the eventual domination by a new party, of course, is impossible to divine). In addition, Malawi effectively experienced turnover following the 2004 election. At that time, no party had a clear majority, and a ruling coalition was necessary. But since the 2009 election a new party, the Democratic Progressive Party (DPP) has dominated,[11] reflecting the region's—and the continent's—propensity toward dominant-party systems. While dominant-party political systems (but not single-party political systems) may provide a needed measure of stability and continuity in these fragile polities, it is also the case that their natural tendency toward exclusion is harmful to dissenting voices in these young democracies. At the same time, so long as opposition parties (and some ruling parties) remain beset by persistent factionalism or engage in the constant shuffle of alliances and coalitions, the emergence of genuinely competitive multiparty systems—in which opposition parties have bona fide opportunities to win and where such parties can provide a bulwark against executive domination by the incumbent party—will be difficult in southern Africa.

Fortunately, southern Africa's nascent and at times embattled opposition parties are not the only forces that offset executive and ruling-party domination. Since the early 1990s, civil societies, including independent media sources, religious and human rights organizations, women's groups, and a host of others, have matured and played increasingly visible and critical roles throughout the region. They often have been united within ad hoc coalitions; from the Oasis Forum in Zambia, to the valiant fight of the endangered press in Zimbabwe, to AIDS activists from the Treatment Action Campaign in South Africa, civil society frequently finds avenues of expression. Moreover, civil society watchdog groups, although still often donor dependent, are developing local capacity for such diverse activities as election monitoring, civic education, poverty reduction, AIDS prevention and treatment, and so forth; these are essential in enhancing and undergirding fragile democracies. Moreover, these laudable efforts must be encouraged further, lest societies find expression in more destructive form. Indeed, the violent riots in Mozambique in 2010 and in South Africa in 2008, and the proliferation of militias (with or without the express role of the state) in Zimbabwe, for example, reveal some of the persistent fault lines in society and, in these cases at least, the incapacity of civil society organizations to sufficiently capture and productively channel popular discontent into action.

One area in which civil society organizations, especially the Treatment Action Campaign in South Africa, have had a substantial impact is through their role in attacking HIV/AIDS, the prevention and treatment of which has seen stunning success in the region. As recently as the early 2000s, dire predictions were being made about the likely devastating impact of the disease on the region (de Waal 2003). Yet whereas the region remains the most AIDS-affected in the world (although this, too, is changing), today the conversation centers around people *living* with AIDS and indeed "striving for normality" in a time of AIDS (Peters, Walker, and Kambewa 2008). Across the region, HIV prevalence rates, once higher than thought possible, have stabilized at much lower levels. By 2009, the rate of new infections was down by more than 25 percent in the three southern African countries with the largest epidemics. Across the region, prevention strategies appear to be working, and access to treatment has expanded markedly (UNAIDS 2010c). The AIDS crisis presented the region with the potential loss or incapacitation of an entire generation of workers, managers, consumers, and caregivers; slowing the progress of the disease provides new hope, not only at a societal level but at the economic level as well. Indeed, the AIDS epidemic has long represented a major liability for the region's economies, from the standpoint of both associated costs and the loss of productivity; this liability has abated somewhat.

Fortunately, the southern African region has experienced remarkable economic growth in the first decade of the twenty-first century, at levels not seen in a generation or more. Within southern Africa, the World Bank recently identified Angola, Mozambique, Botswana, Zambia, and Malawi as having particularly robust economic growth prospects in the years ahead.[12] This potential for future growth builds upon the promising economic growth of nearly 6 percent seen since 2000. Angola's economic growth of close to 15 percent per year was made possible by oil exports, making Angola one of the fastest-growing economies on the continent in the period. Regionwide, much of the growth was resource driven, which means southern Africa remains subject to the vagaries of international commodity markets or, to put it another way, to many of the same structural constraints that have plagued the region (and the continent) for generations. Yet these too are expected to remain robust until the 2020s. It is not beyond the pale to expect that the vicissitudes of electoral politics may impel the region's more democratic regimes to better utilize these resources to benefit their populations.

Four countries now enjoy "middle-income" status—namely Angola, Botswana, Namibia, and South Africa. Yet their status and higher economic growth rates have not been enough to eliminate chronic poverty. Some have argued that the predominantly neoliberal economic policies adopted throughout the region have contributed to growing income inequality. Although some states, such as South Africa, have belatedly begun to address these disparities through increased social spending, and some governments, such as Zambia, have utilized commodity windfalls to reduce fees on schools and healthcare, the wide gaps remain a potential source of social instability.[13] Although Anthony Leysens (2006) suggests that marginalized groups do not in fact pose a threat to political stability, the recent unrest in South Africa (2008) and Mozambique (2010) certainly raises questions about state responses, societal cohesion, and the capacity of these states to use their resource bases to measurably improve the lives of their citizens. Ultimately, this is inextricably linked to the quality of democracy in these societies.

As noted, structural factors, global commodity prices, and increased trade, long a constraint on regional progress, have moved in the region's favor. Particularly since 2000, the role and influence of external economic actors have expanded considerably in the region. First and foremost among these are Chinese interests, both public and private, which have been among Africa's most aggressive investors. Chinese firms have built or rebuilt infrastructure in exchange for resources, whether these are deep-water drilling rights in Angola, an expanded international airport in Botswana, or special economic zones in Zambia. Yet in some countries, the influx of Chinese workers and companies has led to tremendous friction with African residents, perhaps most infamously in Zambia, where Chinese managers have, on more than one occasion, fired upon protesting Zambian workers or have been responsible for unsafe work conditions and have violated employment laws by exceeding the limits on expatriate employees.

Conversely, Chinese interests bring with them new opportunities for the region, by constructing essential infrastructure and providing an alternative source of funding to countries long dependent on Western donors and the international financial institutions; this ability to broker national interests with a broader set of partners represents newfound leverage for some countries. Yet this too has a potential dark side for democracy and transparency that otherwise differentiates southern Africa from many other regions. For example, Angola has been able to snub the international financial institutions and traditional donors and also fully avoid accountability and scrutiny of its financial practices. With the Chinese attention, however, has also come new interest from Western companies as well as those from elsewhere in the global South. Indeed, whereas Brazil has long played a role in Angola and Mozambique, given the historical connections, it is now increasingly active in trade and investment activities in South Africa. At the same time, South Africa itself remains the leading regional player, as both partner to its neighbors and as hegemon.[14] South Africa has long been the leader in the regional economy and will surely continue to play this role well into the future. The problems and the prospects of the region are certainly shared by South Africa, however. Thus the country must remain vested in the region and not solely as an economic actor; unlike other external partners, the political and social stability of South Africa's neighbors has a direct bearing on its own domestic harmony.

Each of the issues discussed above returns us to the prospects for democratic stability in the region. All are critical to democracy's success or failure. The evolution of these processes—constitutionalism, constraints on executive power, electoral legitimacy, and the like—suggests that democratic transformation is only to be achieved slowly, and even then in occasionally violent fits and starts, as the Zimbabwe case discussed in Chapter 7 reveals. In less than a decade, that country underwent low-intensity conflict, utter economic collapse, and the unraveling of its once impressive political, legal, and social institutions. At the same time, however, although Zimbabwe is a "cautionary tale," Zimbabweans and their regional counterparts may also note that opposition voices have persevered against immense odds, suggesting that there remains a deep-seated desire for peace, security, and stability that a genuine democratic transformation could provide.

Yet, while Zimbabwe trends negative and Angola remains substantially undemocratic, six of the eight countries examined in this book are proceeding, if haltingly, in a more democratic direction (McFerson 2010). While it may be "time" for southern Africa, the region stands only at the very beginning of the economic and social transformations that will ensure a deepening of democracy.

Notes

1. The fact that the show in Johannesburg featured Colombian singer and world pop star Shakira on a spectacular stage adorned with African imagery and filled with South African dancers and musicians as "background" struck some as ironic. Yet the choice of a multicultural global performer symbolized Africa's inclusiveness and reinforced the idea of a *World* Cup.

2. See http://www.mg.co.za/.

3. In our own travels in the region in 2010, we found this song to have a resonance throughout, played over and over again in cafés and malls, nightclubs and bars. Although it is certainly possible to read too much symbolism into pop culture, in a way the song was pan-African and even global. It was sung by a Colombian headliner backed up by the South African group Freshlyground to a chorus and melody sampled from a twenty-five-year-old Cameroonian hit ("Zangalewa"). "This Time for Africa" also used lyrics in English, Spanish, and various African languages.

4. The others are Lesotho and Mauritius.

5. For a more wistful assessment of liberated southern Africa, see Saul (2007).

6. Of course, Angola and Zimbabwe were deeply involved in the war in neighboring DRC, a fellow SADC member.

7. This generally civilian control is notwithstanding the presence of a lieutenant general, Ian Khama, as president in Botswana.

8. As a consequence of the civilian control, the countries of southern Africa have avoided the African growth tragedy described by Beaulier and Subrick (2006) whereby militaries have wreaked havoc with polities and enormous expenditures on militaries have starved economies.

9. In Botswana recently, there have been calls from the opposition for a constitutional review process, among other things to address the underrepresentation of women in the National Assembly and to alter an electoral system that severely disadvantages the opposition.

10. Indeed, in Zimbabwe and Angola—clearly the region's democratic laggards— even the extant protections of human rights, for example, have not been honored consistently,

11. Importantly, this new party is unique in Malawi in not drawing its base exclusively from one of the country's three regions as has been the case to date. Indeed, observers suggest (VonDoepp 2010; Smiddy and Young 2009) that the DPP's remarkable success in the 2009 election may be attributed to the favorable economic policies of President Mutharika, who created the DPP after breaking with the United Democratic Front (UDF) and former president Muluzi. This is a significant development in Malawian and perhaps even regional party politics.

12. For further information, see http://www.africafocus.org.

13. Since diamonds were discovered in Botswana after independence, that country has been a model of how a government should utilize its natural resources to build its human resource base and physical infrastructure for development. See also Robinson 2009.

14. Indeed, South Africa has long aspired to join the group of Brazil, Russia, India, and China (BRIC) and was invited to do so in early 2011, adding an S to the acronym.

Acronyms and Abbreviations

ACDP	African Christian Democratic Party (South Africa)
AFORD	Alliance for Democracy (Malawi)
AGOA	Africa Growth and Opportunity Act (United States)
AIDS	acquired immunodeficiency syndrome
AIPPA	Access to Information and Protection of Privacy Act (Zimbabwe)
ANC	African National Congress (South Africa)
ANP	African National Party (Zimbabwe)
APP	All People's Party (Namibia)
APRM	African Peer Review Mechanism
ASGI	Accelerated and Shared Growth Initiative (South Africa)
AU	African Union
AZAPO	Azanian People's Organization (South Africa)
BAM	Botswana Alliance Movement
BB-BEE	Broad-Based BEE (South Africa)
BCP	Botswana Congress Party
BDF	Botswana Defense Force
BDP	Botswana Democratic Party
BEE	Black Economic Empowerment (South Africa)
BIG	Basic Income Grant (Namibia)
BIP	Botswana Independence Party
BNF	Botswana National Front
BPP	Botswana People's Party
BRICS	Brazil, Russia, India, China, and South Africa
BSAC	British South Africa Company
CA	Conservative Alliance (Zimbabwe)
CCC	Committee for a Clean Campaign (Zambia)
CCN	Council of Churches of Namibia
CEEC	Citizens Economic Empowerment Commission (Zambia)
CFU	Commercial Farmers Union (Zimbabwe)

CIO	Central Intelligence Organisation (Zimbabwe)
CKGR	Central Kalahari Game Reserve (Botswana)
CNE	National Electoral Commission (Angola, Mozambique)
COD	Congress of Democrats (Namibia)
COMECON	Council for Mutual Economic Cooperation
COMESA	Common Market for Eastern and Southern Africa
COPAC	Committee of Parliament on the New Constitution (Zimbabwe)
COPE	Congress of the People (South Africa)
COSATU	Congress of South African Trade Unions
CPI	Corruption Perceptions Index
CRC	constitutional review commission (Zambia)
CSO	civil society organization
DA	Democratic Alliance (South Africa)
DIS	Directorate of Intelligence and Security (Botswana)
DPP	Democratic Progressive Party (Malawi)
DRC	Democratic Republic of Congo
DRK	Dutch Reformed Church
DTA	Democratic Turnhalle Alliance (Namibia)
ECOMOG	Economic Community of West African States Monitoring Group
ECZ	Electoral Commission of Zambia
EIU	Economist Intelligence Unit
ESAP	economic structural adjustment program (Zimbabwe)
ESKOM	Electricity Supply Company of South Africa
EU	European Union
FAA	Angolan Armed Forces
FADM	Armed Forces for the Defense of Mozambique
FAM	Armed Forces of Mozambique
FAPLA	People's Armed Forces for the Liberation of Angola
FDD	Forum for Democracy and Development (Zambia)
FDI	foreign direct investment
FESA	Eduardo dos Santos Foundation (Angola)
FF+	Freedom Front (South Africa)
FIFA	International Federation of Association Football
FLEC	Front for the Liberation of Cabinda (Angola)
FLS	Frontline States
FNLA	National Front for the Liberation of Angola
Frelimo	Front for the Liberation of Mozambique
G8	Group of Eight
GDP	gross domestic product
GEAR	Growth, Employment, and Redistribution program (South Africa)

GNU	Government of National Unity (South Africa)
GNU	Government of National Unity (Zimbabwe)
GPA	general peace agreement (Mozambique)
GPA	Global Political Agreement (Zimbabwe)
GURN	government of national unity and reconciliation (Angola)
HIPC	highly indebted poor countries
HIV	human immunodeficiency virus
HP	Heritage Party (Zambia)
ID	Independent Democrats (South Africa)
IDA	International Development Association
IDASA	Institute for Democracy in Africa
IFI	international financial institution
IFP	Inkatha Freedom Party (South Africa)
ILO	International Labour Organization
IMF	International Monetary Fund
IPADE	Institute for Peace and Democracy (Mozambique)
ISI	import substitution industrialization
ITU	International Telecommunications Union
JOC	Joint Operations Command (Zimbabwe)
LAMA	Legal Age of Majority Act (Zimbabwe)
MAP	Millennium Africa Program
MBC	Malawi Broadcasting Corporation
MCP	Malawi Congress Party
MDC	Movement for Democratic Change (Zimbabwe)
MDC-M	MDC—Mutambara (Zimbabwe)
MDC-T	MDC—Tsvangirai (Zimbabwe)
MDM	Democratic Movement of Mozambique
MDP	Malawi Democratic Party
MDRI	Multilateral Debt Relief Initiative
MELS	The Marx, Engels, Lenin, and Stalin Movement of Botswana
MF	Minority Front (South Africa)
MFA	Multi-Fibre Arrangement
MISA	Media Institute of Southern Africa
MMD	Movement for Multiparty Democracy (Zambia)
MNC	multinational corporation
MNR	Mozambique National Resistance (known as Renamo after 1981)
MP	member of parliament
MPLA	Popular Movement for the Liberation of Angola
NAC	Nyasaland African Congress
NAMPOL	Namibian Police Force
NANSO	Namibian National Student Organization
NCA	National Constitutional Assembly (Zimbabwe)

NCC	National Constitutional Convention (Zambia)
NCOP	National Council of Provinces (South Africa)
NDA	National Democratic Alliance (Malawi)
NDF	National Democratic Focus (Zambia)
NDF	Namibian Defense Force
NEPAD	New Partnership for African Development
NGO	nongovernmental organization
NGOCC	Nongovernmental Organization Coordinating Committee (Zambia)
NID	Namibian Institute for Democracy
NNP	New National Party (South Africa)
NP	National Party (South Africa)
NUNW	National Union of Namibian Workers
NWLG	National Women's Lobby Group (Zambia)
OAU	Organization of African Unity
ONUMOZ	United Nations Operation in Mozambique
OPO	Ovamboland People's Organization (Namibia)
Osleg	Operation Sovereign Legitimacy (Zimbabwe)
PAC	Pan-Africanist Congress (South Africa)
PARPA	Action Plan for the Reduction of Absolute Poverty (Mozambique)
PDD	Party for Peace, Development, and Democracy (Mozambique)
PEPFAR	President's Emergency Plan for AIDS Relief (United States)
PF	Patriotic Front (Zambia)
PLAN	People's Liberation Army of Namibia
PLD	Liberal Democratic Party (Angola)
PMU	Police Mobile Unit (Botswana)
POSA	Public Order and Security Act (Zimbabwe)
PPP	purchasing power parity
PR	proportional representation
PRE	Economic Rehabilitation Program (Mozambique)
PRS	Social Renewal Party (Angola)
PRSP	Poverty Reduction Strategy Paper (Mozambique)
PTA	Preferential Trade Area
RDP	Rally for Democracy and Progress (Namibia)
RDP	reconstruction and development program (South Africa)
Renamo	Mozambique National Resistance (known until 1981 as MNR)
RF	Rhodesia Front (Zimbabwe; known as the Conservative Alliance after 1983)
SABC	South African Broadcasting Corporation
SACC	South African Council of Churches
SACP	South African Communist Party

SACU	Southern African Customs Union
SADC	Southern African Development Community
SADCC	Southern African Development Coordination Conference
SADF	South African Defense Force
SANDF	South African National Defense Force
SAP	structural adjustment program
SEZ	Special Export Zone
SFF	Special Field Force (Namibia)
SMS	short message service
STAE	Technical Secretariat for Electoral Administration (Mozambique)
STD	sexually transmitted disease
SWANU	South West Africa National Union (Namibia)
SWAPO	South West Africa People's Organization (Namibia)
SWATF	South West Africa Territorial Force (Namibia)
TAC	Treatment Action Campaign (South Africa)
TDCA	trade, development, and cooperation agreement (South Africa)
TRC	Truth and Reconciliation Commission (South Africa)
UANC	United African National Council (Zambia)
UCDP	United Christian Democratic Party (South Africa)
UDA	United Democratic Alliance (Zambia)
UDF	United Democratic Front (Malawi)
UDF	United Democratic Front (Namibia)
UDI	unilateral declaration of independence (Zimbabwe)
UDM	United Democratic Movement (South Africa)
UE	Electoral Union (Mozambique)
UK	United Kingdom
ULP	United Liberal Party (Zambia)
UN	United Nations
UNAIDS	Joint United Nations Programme on HIV/AIDS
UNDP	United Nations Development Programme
UNIFEM	United Nations Development Fund for Women
UNIP	United National Independence Party (Zambia)
UNITA	National Union for the Total Independence of Angola
UPND	United Party for National Development (Zambia)
UPP	United Progressive Party (Zambia)
VOP	Voice of the People (Zimbabwe)
WOZA	Women of Zimbabwe Arise
Zanaco	Zambia National Commercial Bank
ZANLA	Zimbabwe National Liberation Army
ZANU	Zimbabwe African National Union
ZANU-PF	Zimbabwe African National Union—Patriotic Front
ZAPU	Zimbabwe African People's Union

ZAR	rand (South Africa)
ZBC	Zimbabwe Broadcasting Corporation
ZCCM	Zambian Consolidated Copper Mines
ZCTU	Zimbabwe Congress of Trade Unions
ZESCO	Zambia Electricity Supply Corporation
ZimRights	Zimbabwe Human Rights Association
ZIMT	Zambia Independent Monitoring Team
ZIPRA	Zimbabwe People's Revolutionary Army
ZPA	Zambia Privatization Agency
ZPP	Zambia Progressive Party
ZRA	Zambia Revenue Authority
ZUDP	Zambia United Development Party

Bibliography

"About AGOA." N.d. http://www.agoa.info/.

Adam, Kanya. 1997. "The Politics of Redress: South African Style Affirmative Action." *Journal of Modern African Studies*. 35: 231–249.

ADB and OECD [African Development Bank and the Organization for Economic Cooperation and Development Investment Centre]. 2011. *African Economic Outlook*. Country Overview: Zambia. http://www.africaneconomicoutlook.org/.

AFP [Agence France Presse]. 2009. "Zimbabwe Unemployment Soars to 94%."

Africa Confidential. N.d. "Who's Who Profile: Emmerson Dambudzo Mnangagwa." http://www.africa-confidential.com/.

Afrobarometer. 2003a. "The Changing Public Agenda? South Africans' Assessments of the Country's Most Pressing Problems." Afrobarometer Briefing Paper, no. 5. Cape Town: IDASA.

———. 2003b. "Trends in Political Party Support in South Africa." Afrobarometer Briefing Paper, no. 6. Cape Town: IDASA.

———. 2010. "Tolerance in South Africa: Exploring Popular Attitudes Toward Foreigners." Afrobarometer Briefing Paper, no. 82. March.

Afronet. 1998. "The Dilemma of Local Courts in Zambia: A Question of Colonial Legal Continuity or Deliberate Customary Law Marginalisation?" http://afronet.org.za/.

Agadjanian, Victor, and Ndola Prata. 2001. "War and Reproduction: Angola's Fertility in Comparative Perspective." *Journal of Southern African Studies*. 27, 2: 329–347.

Ajulu, Rok. 2001. "Thabo Mbeki's African Renaissance in a Globalising World Economy: The Struggle for the Soul of the Continent." *Review of African Political Economy*. 28, 87: 27–42.

Akukwe, Chinua, and Melvin Foote. 2001. "HIV/AIDS in Africa: Time to Stop the Killing Fields." *Foreign Policy in Focus Policy Brief*. 6, 15. April.

Alden, Chris. 2001. *Mozambique and the Construction of the New African State: From Negotiations to Nation Building*. Basingstoke, UK: Palgrave.

Alexander, Peter. 2000. "Zimbabwean Workers, the MDC, and the 2000 Election." *Review of African Political Economy*. 27, 85: 385–406.

Ambrose, Soren. 2007. "The Decline (& Fall?) of the IMF or, Chronicle of an Institutional Death Foretold." *Focus on the Global South*. http://focusweb.org/.

Ansell, Nicola, and Lorraine van Blerk. 2004. "Children's Migration as a Household/ Family Strategy: Coping with AIDS in Lesotho and Malawi." *Journal of Southern African Studies*. 30, 3: 673–690.

Anstee, Margaret Joan. 1996. *Orphan of the Cold War: The Inside Story of the Collapse of the Angolan Peace Process, 1992–93.* New York: St. Martin's.

"Apparel Trade Under AGOA." N.d. http://www.agoa.info/.

Arato, Andrew. 2010. "Dispelling Myths of a People-Driven Constitution." *Zimbabwe Independent.* December 16.

Armbruster, Heidi. 2008. "'With Hard Work and Determination You Can Make It Here': Narratives of Identity Among German Immigrants in Postcolonial Namibia." *Journal of Southern African Studies.* 34, 3: 611–628.

AsgiSA [Accelerated and Shared Growth Initiative for South Africa]. N.d. http://www.info.gov.za/.

Astill-Brown, Jeremy, and Markus Weimer. 2010. *Mozambique: Balancing Development, Politics and Security.* London: Chatham House.

Ayittey, George. 1998. *Africa in Chaos.* New York: St. Martin's.

Ba, Alice, and Matthew J. Hoffman. 2003. "Making and Remaking the World for IR 101: A Resource for Teaching Social Constructivism in Introductory Classes." *International Studies Perspectives.* 4, 1: 15–33.

Ball, Nicole. 1988. *Security and Economy in the Third World.* Princeton, NJ: Princeton University Press.

Baloi, Obede. 1996. "Conflict Management and Democratic Transition." In Brazão Mazula, ed., *Mozambique: Elections, Democracy and Development.* Translated by Paul Fauvet. Maputo: Embassy of the Kingdom of the Netherlands.

Barei, Geoffrey. 2008. "Parliament." In Zibani Maundeni, ed., *Transparency, Accountability and Corruption in Botswana.* Gaborone: Democracy Research Project; and Cape Town: IDASA.

Bates, Robert. 1981. *Markets and States in Tropical Africa.* Berkeley: University of California Press.

Bauer, Gretchen. 1998. *Labor and Democracy in Namibia, 1971–1996.* Athens: Ohio University Press.

———. 1999. "Challenges to Democratic Consolidation in Namibia." In Richard Joseph, ed., *State, Conflict, and Democracy in Africa.* Boulder: Lynne Rienner.

———. 2004. "'The Hand That Stirs the Pot Can Also Run the Country': Electing Women to Parliament in Namibia." *Journal of Modern African Studies.* 42, 4: 479–509.

———. 2008. "50/50 by 2020: Electoral Gender Quotas for Parliament in East and Southern Africa." *International Feminist Journal of Politics.* 10, 3: 348–368.

———. 2010. "'Cows Will Lead the Herd into a Precipice': Where Are the Women MPs in Botswana?" *Botswana Notes and Records.* No. 42: 56–70.

Bauer, Gretchen, and Hannah Britton, eds. 2006. *Women in African Parliaments.* Boulder: Lynne Rienner.

Bauer, Gretchen, and Manon Tremblay, eds. 2011. *Women in Executive Power: A Global Overview.* London: Routledge.

Bayart, Jean-François, Stephen Ellis, and Béatrice Hibou. 1999. *The Criminalization of the State in Africa.* Bloomington: Indiana University Press.

Baylies, Carolyn, and Morris Szeftel. 1984. "The Rise to Political Prominence of the Zambian Business Class." In Cherry Gertzel, ed., *The Dynamics of the One-Party State in Zambia.* Manchester, UK: Manchester University Press.

———. 1992. "The Fall and Rise of Multiparty Politics in Zambia." *Review of African Political Economy.* 19, 54: 75–91.

———. 1997. "The 1996 Zambian Elections: Still Awaiting Democratic Consolidation." *Review of African Political Economy.* 24, 71: 113–128.

Beall, Jo. 2001. "Doing Gender from Top to Bottom? The South African Case." *Women: A Cultural Review.* 12, 2: 136–146.

Beaulier, Scott, and Robert Subrick. 2006. "The Political Foundations of Development: The Case of Botswana." *Constitutional Political Economy.* 17: 103–115.

Becker, Heike. 1995. *Namibian Women's Movement 1980 to 1992: From Anti-Colonial Resistance to Reconstruction.* Frankfurt: IKO.

———. 2006. "'New Things After Independence': Gender and Traditional Authorities in Postcolonial Namibia." *Journal of Southern African Studies.* 32, 1: 29–48.

Berger, Iris. 1999. "Women in East and Southern Africa." In Iris Berger and Francis White, eds., *Women in Sub-Saharan Africa: Restoring Women to History.* Bloomington: Indiana University Press.

Berman, Eric. 1996. *Managing Arms in Peace Processes: Mozambique.* Geneva: United Nations Institute for Disarmament Research, Disarmament and Conflict Resolution Project.

Beveridge, Andrew, and Anthony Oberschall. 1979. *African Businessmen and Development in Zambia.* Princeton, NJ: Princeton University Press.

Birmingham, David. 1992. *Frontline Nationalism in Angola and Mozambique.* Trenton, NJ: Africa World Press.

———. 2002. "Angola." In Patrick Chabal, ed., *A History of Postcolonial Lusophone Africa.* Bloomington: Indiana University Press.

Blair, David. 2002. *Degrees in Violence: Robert Mugabe and the Struggle for Power in Zimbabwe.* London: Continuum.

Bond, Patrick. 1998. *Uneven Zimbabwe: A Study of Finance, Development, and Underdevelopment.* Trenton, NJ: Africa World Press.

———. 2000. *Elite Transition: From Apartheid to Neoliberalism in South Africa.* London: Pluto Press.

———. 2004. *Talk Left, Walk Right: South Africa's Frustrated Global Reforms.* Scottsville, South Africa: University of KwaZulu Natal Press.

———. 2006. *Talk Left, Walk Right: South Africa's Frustrated Global Reforms.* 2nd ed. Pietermaritzburg: University of KwaZulu Natal Press.

Bond, Patrick, and Masimba Manyanya. 2002. *Zimbabwe's Plunge: Exhausted Nationalism, Neoliberalism, and the Struggle for Social Justice.* Trenton, NJ: Africa World Press.

Boone, Catherine, and Jake Batsell. 2001. "Politics and AIDS in Africa: Research Agendas in Political Science and International Relations." *Africa Today.* 48, 2: 3–33.

Bowen, Merle. 2000. *The State Against the Peasantry: Rural Struggles in Colonial and Postcolonial Mozambique.* Charlottesville: University Press of Virginia.

Bowyer-Bower, T.A.S., and Colin Stoneman, eds. 2000. *Land Reform in Zimbabwe: Constraints and Prospects.* Aldershot, UK: Ashgate.

Brandt, A. M. 1998. "AIDS: From Social History to Social Policy." In E. Fee and D. M. Fox, eds., *AIDS: The Burdens of History.* Berkeley: University of California Press.

Bratton, Michael. 1989. "Beyond the State: Civil Society and Associational Life in Africa." *Comparative Politics.* 24, 4: 407–430.

———. 1992. "Zambia Starts Over: The Rebirth of Political Pluralism." *Journal of Democracy.* 3, 2: 81–94.

Bratton, Michael, and Daniel Posner. 1999. "A First Look at Second Elections in Africa, with Evidence from Zambia." In Richard Joseph, ed., *State, Conflict, and Democracy in Africa.* Boulder: Lynne Rienner.

Bratton, Michael, and Nicolas van de Walle. 1997. *Democratic Experiments in Africa: Regime Transitions in Comparative Perspective.* Cambridge: Cambridge University Press.

Bräutigam, Deborah. 2009. *The Dragon's Gift: The Real Story of China in Africa.* New York: Oxford University Press.

Bräutigam, Deborah, Lise Rakner, and Scott Taylor. 2002. "Business Associations and Growth Coalitions in Sub-Saharan Africa." *Journal of Modern African Studies.* 40, 4: 519–547.

Brecher, Jeremy, Tim Costello, and Brendan Smith. 2000. *Globalization for Below: The Power of Solidarity.* Boston: South End Press.

Brett, Tedy, and Simon Winter. 2003. "The Origins of the Zimbabwe Crisis." *Focus.* 30: 10–14. Johannesburg: Helen Suzman Foundation.

Britton, Hannah. 2005. *Women in the South African Parliament: From Resistance to Governance.* Urbana-Champaign: University of Illinois Press.

Burnell, Peter. 2001. "The Party System and Party Politics in Zambia: Continuities Past, Present, and Future." *African Affairs.* 100: 239–263.

————. 2002. "Parliamentary Committees in Zambia's Third Republic: Partial Reforms, Unfinished Agenda." *Journal of Southern African Studies.* 28, 2: 291–323.

Busumtwi-Sam, James. 2002. "Sustainable Peace and Development in Angola." *Studies in Comparative International Development.* 37, 3: 91–118.

Caldwell, John. 2000. "Rethinking the African AIDS Epidemic." *Population and Development Review.* 26, 1: 117–135.

Calland, Richard, ed. 1999. *The First Five Years: A Review of South Africa's Democratic Parliament.* Cape Town: IDASA.

Campbell, Catherine, and Brian Williams. 2001. "Briefing: Riding the Tiger: Contextualizing HIV Prevention in South Africa." *African Affairs.* 100: 135–140.

Carmody, Pádraig. 2001. *Tearing the Social Fabric: Neoliberalism, Deindustrialization, and the Crisis of Government in Zimbabwe.* Portsmouth, NH: Heinemann.

————. 2006. "Review of 'Talk Left, Walk Right: South Africa's Frustrated Global Reforms,' by Patrick Bond." *African Studies Quarterly.* 9, 1 and 2. http://www.africa.ufl.edu/.

Carmody, Pádraig, and Scott Taylor. 2003. "The Decline of the Industrial Sector in Zimbabwe." *African Studies Quarterly.* 7, 2. http://www.africa.ufl.edu/.

Carothers, Thomas. 2002. "The End of the Transition Paradigm." *Journal of Democracy.* 13, 1: 5–21.

Carrilho, Norberto. 1996. "The Electoral Legislation in Mozambique and the Political and Social Achievement." In Brazão Mazula, ed., *Mozambique: Elections, Democracy, and Development.* Maputo: Embassy of the Kingdom of the Netherlands.

Carter, Gwendolen M. 1980. *Which Way Is South Africa Going?* Bloomington: Indiana University Press.

Carter Center. 2000. *Observing the 1999 Elections in Mozambique: Final Report.* Atlanta: Carter Center.

————. 2002. *Observing the 2001 Zambia Elections: Final Report.* Atlanta: Carter Center.

Chabal, Patrick, and Jean Pascal Daloz. 1999. *Africa Works: Disorder as Political Instrument.* Bloomington: Indiana University Press.

Chan, Stephen. 1999. "Troubled Pluralisms: Pondering an Indonesian Moment for Zimbabwe and Zambia." *Round Table.* 349: 61–76.

Chazan, Naomi, Peter Lewis, Robert Mortimer, Donald Rothchild, and Stephen John Stedman. 1999. *Politics and Society in Contemporary Africa.* 3rd ed. Boulder: Lynne Rienner.

Cheeseman, Nic, and Marja Hinfelaar. 2010. "Parties, Platforms and Political Mobilization: The Zambian Presidential Elections of 2008." *African Affairs.* 109, 434: 51–76.

Chimakure, Constantine. 2007. "JOC Takes Over Price Controls." *Zimbabwe Independent.* October 6.

Chinamining.org. 2010. "Zambia's Copper Output Up 5% in May: Bank of Zambia." June 29. http://www.chinamining.org.

Chinsinga, Blessings. 2002. "The Politics of Poverty Alleviation in Malawi: A Critical Review." In Harri Englund, ed., *A Democracy of Chameleons: Politics and Culture in the New Malawi.* Stockholm: Nordiska Afrikainstitutet.

Chirwa, Wiseman. 1994a. "Elections in Malawi: The Perils of Regionalism." *Southern Africa Report.* December: 17–20.

———. 1994b. "The Politics of Ethnicity and Regionalism in Contemporary Malawi." *African Rural and Urban Studies.* 1, 2: 93–118.

———. 2001. "Dancing Toward Dictatorship: Political Songs and Popular Culture in Malawi." *Nordic Journal of African Studies.* 10, 1: 1–27.

"Chona Report." 1972. *Report of the National Commission on the Establishment of a One-Party Participatory Democracy in Zambia.* Lusaka: Government Printers.

Chua, Amy. 2003. *World on Fire: How Exporting Free Market Democracy Breeds Ethnic Hatred and Global Instability.* New York: Doubleday.

Cilliers, Jakkie. 1999. *Building Security in Southern Africa: An Update on the Evolving Architecture.* Monograph No. 43. Pretoria: Institute for Security Studies. http://www.iss.co.za/.

———. 2000. "Beyond the Stalemate." In Jakkie Cilliers and Christian Dietrich, eds., *Angola's War Economy: The Role of Oil and Diamonds.* Pretoria: Institute for Security Studies.

Clapham, Christopher. 1982. *Private Patronage and Public Power: Political Clientelism in the Modern State.* London: Pinter.

Clark, John F. 2007. "The Decline of the African Military Coup." *Journal of Democracy.* 18, 3: 141–155.

Cliffe, L., with R. Bush, J. Lindsay, B. Mokopakgosi, D. Pankhurst, and B. Tsie. 1993. *The Transition to Independence in Namibia.* Boulder: Lynne Rienner.

Cohen, Mike. 2008. "South Africa Has Black Middle Class of 3 Million, Study Finds." *Bloomberg Business News.* October 11.

Collins, Joe, and Bill Rau. 2000. "HIV/AIDS and Failed Development." Africa Policy Information Center Working Paper. March.

Commonwealth Observer Group. 2000. "The Parliamentary Elections in Zimbabwe: 24–25 June 2000."

———. 2009. "Report of the Commonwealth Observer Group: Mozambique National and Provincial Elections." October 28. London: Commonwealth Secretariat.

Cook, Louise. 2001. "European Union Trade Deal Brings Out Mixed Reaction." *Business Day* (South Africa). January 12.

Cooke, Jennifer, Steven Morrison, and John Prendergast. 2003. "Averting Chaos and Collapse in Zimbabwe: The Centrality of South African and US Leadership." *CSIS Africa Notes no. 15.* April.

Cowell, Alan. 2002. "Angry at Vote, Commonwealth Bars Zimbabwe." *New York Times.* March 20.

Crisis in Zimbabwe Coalition. 2003. http://www.kubatana.net/.

Crocker, Chester. 1992. *High Noon in Southern Africa: Making Peace in a Rough Neighborhood*. New York: W. W. Norton.

da Silva, Aida Gomes. 1996. "The Mozambican Press: A Historical Overview and a Political Analysis." Occasional Paper no. 54. Nijmegen, Netherlands: Catholic University of Nijmegen, Third World Center, July.

Davidow, Jeffrey. 1984. *A Peace in Southern Africa: The Lancaster House Conference on Rhodesia, 1979*. Boulder: Westview.

Davidson, Basil. 1994. *Modern Africa: A Social and Political History*. New York: Longman.

de Brito, Luis. 1996. "Voting Behaviour in Mozambique's First Multiparty Elections." In Brazão Mazula, ed., *Mozambique: Elections, Democracy, and Development*. Maputo: Embassy of the Netherlands.

DeGrassi, Aaron. 2008. "Neopatrimonialism and Agricultural Development in Africa: Contributions and Limitations of a Contested Concept." *African Studies Review*. 51, 3: 107–133.

de Klerk, F. W. 1999. *The Last Trek: A New Beginning—The Autobiography*. New York: St. Martin's.

Delius, Peter, and Liz Walker. 2002. "AIDS in Context." *African Studies*. 61, 1: 5–12.

d'Engelbronner-Kolff, F. M. 1998. "The People as Law-Makers: The Juridical Foundation of the Legislative Power of Namibian Traditional Communities." In F. M. d'Engelbronner-Kolff, M. O. Hinz, and J. L. Sindano, eds., *Traditional Authority and Democracy in Southern Africa*. Windhoek: New Namibia Books.

de Waal, Alex. 2003. "How Will HIV/AIDS Transform African Governance?" *African Affairs*. 102, 406: 1–23.

de Waal, Alex, and Joseph Tumushabe. 2003. "HIV/AIDS and Food Security in Southern Africa." A Report for DFID. http://tacilim.com/emergencies/deWaalFood.pdf.

Diamond, Larry. 2008. "The Rule of Law Versus the Big Man." *Journal of Democracy*. 19, 2: 138–149.

Dietrich, Christian. 2000. "Power Struggles in the Diamond Fields." In Jakkie Cilliers and Christian Dietrich, eds., *Angola's War Economy: The Role of Oil and Diamonds*. Pretoria: Institute for Security Studies.

Dionne, Kim Yi. 2011. "The Role of Executive Time Horizons in State Response to AIDS in Africa." *Comparative Political Studies*. 44, 1: 55–77.

Dobell, Lauren. 1998. *SWAPO's Struggle for Namibia, 1960–1991: War by Other Means*. Basel Namibia Studies Series no. 3. Basel: P. Schlettwein.

Dowden, Richard. 2010. *Africa: Altered States, Ordinary Miracles*. New York: Public Affairs.

Dubow, Saul. 1995. *Scientific Racism in Modern South Africa*. Cambridge: Cambridge University Press.

Dugard, John. 1998. "The New Constitution: A Triumph for Liberalism? A Positive View." In R. W. Johnson and David Welsh, eds., *Ironic Victory: Liberalism in Post-Liberation South Africa*. London: Oxford University Press.

Duncan, Jane. 2000. "Now on SABC: Ode to Thatcher." *Business Day* (South Africa). November 23.

du Toit, Jacques. 2003. "SA Enjoying Benefits of US Trade Largesse." *Business Day* (South Africa). September 1.

du Toit, Pierre. 1995. *State Building and Democracy in Southern Africa: Botswana, Zimbabwe, and South Africa*. Washington, DC: US Institute of Peace.

———. 2001. *South Africa's Brittle Peace: The Problem of Post-Settlement Violence*. New York: Palgrave.

EISA [Electoral Institute of Southern Africa]. 2005. "Observer Mission Report: Regional Observer Mission, Mozambique Parliamentary and Presidential Elections, 1–2 December 2004." Johannesburg: EISA.

"EISA and SADC Join Chorus of Critics." 2009. *AllAfrica Media*. October 31. http://allafrica.com/stories/200910310004.html.

EIU [Economist Intelligence Unit]. 2002a. *Country Report: Mozambique*. London: EIU, July.

———. 2002b. *Country Report: Zimbabwe*. London: EIU.

———. 2003a. "Angola: Economy: Outlook." *EIU Viewswire*. August 20.

———. 2003b. "Botswana: Politics: Political Structure." *EIU Viewswire*. July 3.

———. 2003c. *Country Profile: South Africa*. London: EIU, June.

———. 2003d. *Country Profile Angola*. London: EIU.

———. 2003e. *Country Profile Malawi*. London: EIU.

———. 2003f. *Country Profile Namibia, Swaziland*. London: EIU.

———. 2003g. *Country Profile Zambia*. London: EIU.

———. 2003h. *Country Profile Zimbabwe*. London: EIU, October.

———. 2003i. *Country Report Malawi*. London: EIU.

———. 2003j. *Country Report Namibia*. London: EIU, July 14.

———. 2003k. *Country Report Zambia*. London: EIU, September.

———. 2003l. *Country Report Zimbabwe*. London: EIU.

———. 2008. *Country Profile Zambia*. London: EIU.

———. 2010a. *Country Report Zambia*. London: EIU, September.

———. 2010b. *Country Report Mozambique*. London: EIU, December.

———. 2010c. *Country Report Zimbabwe*. London: EIU, December.

———. 2010d. *Country Report South Africa*. London: EIU, December.

Emang Basadi. 1999. *Emang Basadi's Political Education Project: A Strategy that Works*. Gaborone: Lentswe La Lesedi.

Emmett, Tony. 1999. *Popular Resistance and the Roots of Nationalism in Namibia, 1915–1966*. Basel Namibia Studies Series no. 4. Basel: P. Schlettwein.

Englund, Harri. 2002. "Introduction: The Culture of Chameleon Politics." In Harri Englund, ed., *A Democracy of Chameleons: Politics and Culture in the New Malawi*. Stockholm: Nordiska Afrikainstitutet.

Epstein, Helen. 2008. "AIDS and the Irrational." *British Medical Journal*. 337: 1265–1267.

Erasmus, Gerhard. 2000. "The Constitution: Its Impact on Namibian Statehood and Politics." In Christiaan Keulder, ed., *State, Society, and Democracy: A Reader in Namibian Politics*. Windhoek: Gamsberg Macmillan.

Essof, Shereen. 2009. "She-murenga: Challenges, Opportunities and Setbacks of the Women's Movement in Zimbabwe." *Feminist Africa*. Issue 13. www.feminist africa.org.

European Union. 2001. *European Union Election Observation Mission: Zambian Elections 2001, Final Statement*. http://europa.eu.int/.

Eurostat Statistical Regime 4. 2010. http://trade.ec.europa.eu/doclib/.

Fawcus, Peter, and Alan Tilbury. 2000. *Botswana: The Road to Independence*. Gaborone: Pula Press and Botswana Society.

Ferguson, Anne, and Beatrice Liatto Katundu. 1994. "Women in Politics in Zambia: What Difference Has Democracy Made?" *African Rural and Urban Studies*. 1, 2: 11–30.

Ferguson, James. 2007. "Social Assistance in Neoliberal South Africa." *African Studies Review*. 50, 2: 71–86.

FES [Friedrich Ebert Stiftung] Media. 2010. "Zimbabwe: POSA Amendments Sail Through Parliament." December 14. http://fesmedia.org/.

FEWS [Famine Early Warning System]. 2010. "Zimbabwe Food Security Outlook, per EIU." December.

Finnegan, William. 2001. "The Poison Keeper." *New Yorker.* January 15.

Finnemore, Martha, and Kathryn Sikkink. 2001. "Taking Stock: The Constructivist Research Program in International Relations and Comparative Politics." *Annual Review of Political Science.* 4: 391–416.

Fisher, L. M., and N. Ngoma. 2005. "The SADC Organ Challenges in the New Millennium." Pretoria: Institute for Security Studies, Paper 114 (August).

Fisher-French, Maya. 2010. "Making Sure the World Cup Is Money Well Spent." *Mail and Guardian.* June 10.

Forrest, Joshua. 1998. *Namibia's Post-Apartheid Regional Institutions: The Founding Year.* Rochester, NY: University of Rochester Press.

Forster, Peter. 1994. "Culture, Nationalism, and the Invention of Tradition in Malawi." *Journal of Modern African Studies.* 32, 3: 477–497.

Franklin, Harry. 1963. *Unholy Wedlock: The Failure of the Central African Federation.* London: Allen and Unwin.

Freedom House. 1999. "Freedom in the World Survey: 1998–99." http://www.freedom house.org/.

———. 2002. "Mozambique." http://www.freedomhouse.org/.

———. 2010. "Freedom in the World." http://www.freedomhouse.org/.

"Frelimo Wins Huge Electoral Victory." 2004. Mozambique News Agency. AIM Report no. 289. December 22.

Friedman, Steven. 1999. "South Africa: Entering the Post-Mandela Era." *Journal of Democracy* 10, 4: 3–18.

Gann, L. H. 1964. *A History of Northern Rhodesia, Early Days to 1953.* London: Chatto and Windus.

Gavin, Michelle D. 2007. "Planning for Post-Mugabe Zimbabwe." CSR [Council Special Report], no. 31 (October). New York: The Council on Foreign Relations.

"G-8 Guilty of 'Moral Default,' Says UN Envoy on HIV/AIDS." 2002. *Africa News.* July 2.

Geisler, Gisela. 1995. "Troubled Sisterhood: Women and Politics in Southern Africa." *African Affairs.* 94: 545–578.

———. 2000. "Parliament Is Another Terrain of Struggle: Women, Men, and Politics in South Africa." *Journal of Modern African Studies.* 38, 4: 605–630.

———. 2004. *Women and the Remaking of Politics of Southern Africa: Negotiating Autonomy, Incorporation, and Representation.* Uppsala: Nordic Africa Institute.

———. 2006. "'A Second Liberation': Lobbying for Women's Political Representation in Zambia, Botswana and Namibia." *Journal of Southern African Studies.* 32, 1: 69–84.

Gender Links. 2010a. "50/50 by 2015? Women in Politics in Southern Africa." Policy Brief 2. www.genderlinks.org.za/.

———, ed. 2010b. *This Seat Is Taken: Elections and the Under-representation of Women in Seven Southern African Countries.* Johannesburg: Gender Links.

Gertzel, Cherry. 1984. Introduction to Cherry Gertzel, ed., *The Dynamics of the One-Party State in Zambia.* Manchester. UK: Manchester University Press.

Gevisser, Mark. 2009. *A Legacy of Liberation: Thabo Mbeki and the Future of the South African Dream.* New York: Palgrave Macmillan.

Gibb, Robert. 2006. 'The New Southern African Customs Union Agreement: Dependence with Democracy." *Journal of Southern African Studies.* 32, 3: 583–603.

Giliomee, Hermann. 1983. "Constructing Afrikaner Nationalism." *Journal of Asian and African Studies.* 18, 1–2: 83–98.

———. 1997. "Surrender Without Defeat: Afrikaners and the South African 'Miracle.'" *Daedalus.* 126, 2: 113–146.

Gilman, Lisa. 2001. "Purchasing Praise: Women, Dancing, and Patronage in Malawi Party Politics." *Africa Today.* 48, 4: 43–64.

———. 2004. "The Traditionalization of Women's Dancing, Hegemony, and Politics in Malawi." *Journal of Folklore Research.* 41, 1: 33–60.

Global Witness. 2002a. *All the President's Men: The Devastating Story of Oil and Banking in Angola's Privatised War.* March. http://www.globalwitness.org/.

———. 2002b. *Branching Out: Zimbabwe's Resource Colonialism in Democratic Republic of the Congo.* 2nd ed. London: Global Witness.

Godwin, Peter, and Ian Hancock. 1993. *Rhodesians Never Die: The Impact of War and Political Change on White Rhodesia.* Oxford: Oxford University Press.

Good, Kenneth. 1996. "Towards Popular Participation in Botswana." *Journal of Modern African Studies.* 34, 1: 53–77.

———. 2010. "The Presidency of General Ian Khama: The Militarization of the Botswana 'Miracle.'" *African Affairs.* 109, 435: 315–324.

Good, Kenneth, and Skye Hughes. 2002. "Globalization and Diversification: Two Cases in Southern Africa." *African Affairs.* 101: 39–59.

Good, Kenneth, and Ian Taylor. 2008. "Botswana: A Minimalist Democracy." *Democratization.* 15, 4: 750–765.

Gordon, April A., and Donald L. Gordon. 2001. *Understanding Contemporary Africa.* 3rd ed. Boulder: Lynne Rienner.

Goyal, Malini. 2010. "Black Diamonds." *Forbes India.* June 18. http://www.forbes.com/.

Graybill, Lyn. 2002. *Truth and Reconciliation in South Africa: Miracle or Model?* Boulder: Lynne Rienner.

Grunwald, Michael. 2002. "A Small Nation's Big Effort Against AIDS." Washington Post Foreign Service. December 2.

Gunning, Jan, and Remco Oostendorp. 2002. Introduction to Jan Willem Gunning and Remco Oostendorp, eds., *Industrial Change in Africa: Zimbabwean Firms Under Structural Adjustment.* Basingstoke, UK: Palgrave.

Gurney, Kim. 2008. "Collapsed Hopes: Can Thabo Mbeki Find a Way to Stop the Killing of Foreigners in South Africa?" *Newsweek,* May 29. http://www.newsweek.com/.

Hall, Richard. 1966. *Zambia.* London: Pall Mall Press.

Hamill, James. 2008. "'Not with a Bang but a Whimper': The Fall of Thebo Mbeki." *Contemporary Review.* 290, 1691: 409–419.

Hamilton, Carolyn. 1998. *Terrific Majesty: The Powers of Shaka Zulu and the Limits of Historical Invention.* Cambridge: Harvard University Press.

Handley, Antoinette. 2008. *Business and the State in Africa.* Cambridge, MA: Cambridge University Press.

Hanke, Steve. 2008. "The Printing Press." *Forbes Magazine.* December 22.

Harrison, Graham. 1996. "Democracy in Mozambique: The Significance of Multiparty Elections." *Review of African Political Economy.* 23, 67: 19–35.

Hassim, Shireen. 2005. "Voices, Hierarchies, and Spaces: Reconfiguring the Women's Movement in Democratic South Africa." *Politikon.* 32, 3: 175–193.

———. 2006. *Women's Organizations and Democracy in South Africa: Contesting Authority.* Madison: University of Wisconsin Press.

Hayes, Patricia, Jeremy Silvester, Marion Wallace, and Wolfram Hartmann, eds. 1998. *Namibia Under South African Rule: Mobility and Containment, 1915–46.* Oxford: James Currey.

Heinecken, Lindy, and Noëlle van der Waag-Cowling. 2009. "The Politics of Race and Gender in the South African Armed Forces: Issues, Challenges, Lessons." *Commonwealth and Comparative Politics.* 47, 4: 517–538.

Hentz, James. 2005. "South Africa and the Political Economy of Regional Cooperation in Southern Africa." *Journal of Modern African Studies.* 43, 1: 21–51.

Herbst, Jeffrey. 1989. "Racial Reconciliation in Southern Africa." *International Affairs.* 65: 43–54.

———. 1990. *State Politics in Zimbabwe.* Harare: University of Zimbabwe Press.

———. 2000. *States and Power in Africa: Comparative Lessons in Authority and Control.* Princeton, NJ: Princeton University Press.

Hettne, Björn. 1990. *Development Theory and the Three Worlds.* Harlow, UK: Longman.

Hibou, Béatrice. 1999. "The 'Social Capital' of the State as an Agent of Deception, or The Ruses of Economic Intelligence." In Jean-François Bayart, Stephen Ellis, and Béatrice Hibou, *The Criminalization of the State in Africa.* Bloomington: Indiana University Press.

Hilhorst, Dorothea, and Maliana Serrano. 2010. "The Humanitarian Arena in Angola, 1975–2008." *Disasters.* 43, 2: 183–201.

Hillbom, Ellen. 2008. "Diamonds or Development? A Structural Analysis of Botswana's Forty Years of Success." *Journal of Modern African Studies.* 46, 2: 191–214.

Hinz, M. O. 1998. "The 'Traditional' of Traditional Government: Traditional Versus Democracy-Based Legitimacy." In F. M. d'Engelbronner-Kolff, M. O. Hinz, and J. L. Sindano, eds., *Traditional Authority and Democracy in Southern Africa.* Windhoek: New Namibia Books.

Hodges, Tony. 2004. *Angola: Anatomy of an Oil State.* Oxford: James Currey.

Holm, John. 1988. "Botswana: A Paternalistic Democracy." In Larry Diamond, Juan Linz, and Seymour Martin Lipset, eds., *Democracy in Developing Countries,* vol. 2, *Africa.* Boulder: Lynne Rienner.

Holm, John, and Staffan Darnolf. 2000. "Democratizing the Administrative State in Botswana." In York Bradshaw and Stephen Ndegwa, eds., *The Uncertain Promise of Southern Africa.* Bloomington: Indiana University Press.

Holm, John, Patrick Molutsi, and Gloria Somolekae. 1996. "The Development of Civil Society in a Democratic State: The Botswana Model." *African Studies Review.* 39, 2: 43–69.

Hope, Kempe Ronald, Sr. 2002. "From Crisis to Renewal: Towards a Successful Implementation of the New Partnership for Africa's Development." *African Affairs.* 101: 387–402.

Horowitz, Donald. 1985. *Ethnic Groups in Conflict.* Berkeley: University of California Press.

Houser, George M. 1976. "Rhodesia to Zimbabwe: A Chronology, 1830 to 1976." New York: Africa Fund.

HRW [Human Rights Watch]. 2000. "South Africa: A Question of Principle—Arms Trade and Human Rights Report." http://www.hrw.org/.

———. 2002. "HIV/AIDS and Human Rights." *World Report 2002.* http://www.hrw .org/.

———. 2009. "Diamonds in the Rough: Human Rights Abuses in the Marange Diamonds Fields of Zimbabwe." New York: Human Rights Watch.

Huliaras, Asteris. 2001. "Qadhafi's Comeback: Libya and Sub-Saharan Africa in the 1990s." *African Affairs*. 398: 5–25.

Human Development Report. 2010a. "Explanation Note on 2010 HDR Composite Indices: Zambia." http://hdrstats.undp.org/.

———. 2010b. "Explanation Note on 2010 HDR Composite Indices: Zimbabwe." http://hdrstats.undp.org/.

Hunter-Gault, Charlayne. 2001. "AIDS: 20 Years of an Epidemic—In South Africa, AIDS Sparks Fears of Devastation." http://www.cnn.com/.

———. 2006. *New News Out of Africa: Uncovering Africa's Renaissance*. New York: Oxford University Press.

ICG [International Crisis Group]. 2000. "Zimbabwe: At the Crossroads." *Africa Report* no. 22. July 10.

———. 2002. "Zimbabwe's Election: The Stakes for Southern Africa." January 11. http://www.crisisweb.org/.

———. 2003a. "Angola's Choice: Reform or Regress?" *Africa Report* no. 61. April 7.

———. 2003b. "Decision Time in Zimbabwe." Africa Briefing Paper. July 8.

———. 2003c. "Zimbabwe: Danger and Opportunity." *Africa Report* no. 60. March 10.

———. 2007. "Zimbabwe: A Regional Solution?"*Africa Report* no. 132. September 18.

Ignatius, David. 2002. "New Doubts Cast on Mugabe Victory: Fearing Defeat, Zimbabwe Aides Said to Have Inflated Vote Totals." *International Herald Tribune*, April 3.

Ihonvbere, Julius. 1995. *Economic Crisis, Civil Society, and Democratization: The Case of Zambia*. Trenton, NJ: Africa World Press.

———. 1997. "From Despotism to Democracy: The Rise of Multiparty Politics in Malawi." *International Studies*. 34, 2: 193–219.

IMF [International Monetary Fund]. 2007. "Republic of Mozambique: Selected Issues." *IMF Staff Country Reports*. July. Washington, DC: The International Monetary Fund.

Independent Electoral Commission, Government of South Africa. 2003. *Atlas of Results*. http://www.elections.org.za/.

———. 2009. *National and Provincial Elections, 2009*. http://www.elections.org.za/.

Institute for Justice and Reconciliation. 2003. "The SA Reconciliation Barometer." Rondebosch, South Africa. http://www.ijr.org.za/.

International IDEA [Institute for Democracy and Electoral Assistance]. 2005. "Regional Assessment of Elections: Controversy for Southern Africa." March. Stockholm: International IDEA.

International Labour Office. 2009a. "Getting the Facts on HIV in Zambia's Markets." http://data.unaids.org/.

———. 2009b. "Street Vendors Lead the HIV Response in Mozambique's Markets." http://data.unaids.org/.

Internet World Stats. 2010. http://www.internetworldstats.com.

Inter-Parliamentary Union. 2010. Women in Politics. January 1. http://www.ipu.org/pdf/publications/wmnmap10_en.pdf.

IRC [International Rescue Committee]. 2007. "Mortality in the Democratic Republic of Congo: An Ongoing Crisis." New York: The International Rescue Committee.

IRIN [Integrated Regional Information Networks]. 2003. "Botswana: A Model for Combating HIV/AIDS." *Science in Africa*. http://www.scienceinafrica.co.za/.

Jackson, Robert, and Carl Rosberg. 1982. *Personal Rule in Black Africa: Prince, Autocrat, Prophet, Tyrant*. Berkeley: University of California Press.

Jeffery, Anthea. 1998. "The New Constitution: A Triumph for Liberalism?" In R. W. Johnson and David Welsh, eds., *Ironic Victory: Liberalism in Post-Liberation South Africa*. London: Oxford University Press.

Jenkins, Carolyn, and John Knight. 2002. *The Economic Decline of Zimbabwe: Neither Growth nor Equity*. New York: Palgrave.

Johnson, R. W. 2000. *Public Opinion and the Crisis of Zimbabwe*. Johannesburg: Helen Suzman Foundation.

———. 2003. "Botswana: Success Breeds Its Own Problems." *Focus*. 30. June. Helen Suzman Foundation. http://www.hsf.org.za/.

Joseph, Richard. 1992. "Zambia: A Model for Democratic Change." *Current History*. 91, 565. May: 199–203.

———. 1997. "Democratization in Africa After 1989: Comparative and Theoretical Perspectives." *Comparative Politics*. 29, 3: 363–382.

Kalenga, Paul. 1999. "The Congress of Democrats." *Southern Africa Report*. 15, 1: 25–27.

Kalungu-Banda, Martin. 2009. *It's How We End That Matters: Leadership Lessons from an African President*. London: AuthorHouse.

Kamkwamba, William, and Brian Mealer. 2009. *The Boy Who Harnessed the Wind: Creating Currents of Electricity and Hope*. New York: HarperCollins

Kamwendo, Gregory. 2002. "Ethnic Revival and Language Associations in the New Malawi: The Case of Chitumbuka." In Harri Englund, ed., *A Democracy of Chameleons: Politics and Culture in the New Malawi*. Stockholm: Nordiska Afrikainstitutet.

Kaplan, Robert. 1994. "The Coming Anarchy." *Atlantic Monthly*. 273, 2. February: 44–76.

———. 2000. *The Coming Anarchy: Shattering the Dreams of the Post Cold War*. New York: Random House.

Kaspin, Deborah. 1995. "The Politics of Ethnicity in Malawi's Democratic Transition." *Journal of Modern African Studies*. 33, 4: 595–620.

Katjavivi, Peter. 1990. *A History of Resistance in Namibia*. Trenton, NJ: Africa World Press.

Kaunda, Jonathan. 1992. "The Administrative Organisation and Processes of National Development Planning in Malawi." In Guy C.Z. Mhone, ed., *Malawi at the Crossroads: The Post-Colonial Political Economy*. Harare: SAPES Books.

Kayizzi-Mugerwa, Steve. 2003. "Privatization in Sub-Saharan Africa: On Factors Affecting Implementation." In S. Kayizzi-Mugerwa, ed., *Reforming Africa's Institutions: Ownership, Incentives, and Capabilities*. New York: United Nations University Press.

Keim, Curtis. 2008. *Mistaking Africa: Curiosities and Inventions of the American Mind*. 2nd ed. Boulder: Westview Press.

Keulder, Christiaan. 1998. *Traditional Leaders and Local Government in Africa: Lessons for South Africa*. Pretoria: Human Sciences Research Council.

———. 1999a. "A Review of the Namibian Budget Process." Report Prepared for the National Democratic Institute (NDI). Windhoek: NDI.

———. 1999b. *Voting Behaviour in Namibia II: Regional Councils 1998*. Windhoek: Friedrich Ebert Stiftung.

———. 2000. "Traditional Leaders." In Christiaan Keulder, ed., *State, Society, and Democracy: A Reader in Namibian Politics*. Windhoek: Gamsberg Macmillan.

Khadiagala, Gilbert. 2000. "Europe in Africa's Renewal: Beyond Postcolonialism?" In John Harbeson and Donald Rothchild, eds., *Africa in World Politics: The African State System in Flux,* 3rd ed. Boulder: Westview.

———. 2001. "Foreign Policy Decisionmaking in Southern Africa's Fading Frontline." In Gilbert Khadiagala and Terrence Lyons, eds., *African Foreign Policies: Power and Process.* Boulder: Lynne Rienner.

Khadiagala, Gilbert, and Terrence Lyons. 2001. "Foreign Policy Making in Africa: An Introduction." In Gilbert Khadiagala and Terrence Lyons, eds., *African Foreign Policies: Power and Process.* Boulder: Lynne Rienner.

Khapoya, Vincent B. 2009. *The African Experience: An Introduction.* 3rd ed. Saddle River, NJ: Prentice Hall.

Kibble, Steve. 2002. "Options for Peace and Reconciliation." In Inge Tvedten, ed., *Angola 2001/2002: Key Development Issues and Aid in a Context of Peace.* Report R 2002: 8. Bergen: Christian Michelsen Institute.

Korten, David. 2001. *When Corporations Rule the World.* 2nd ed. San Francisco: Kumarian Press.

Kriger, Norma. 2000. "Zimbabwe Today: Hope Against Grim Realities." *Review of African Political Economy.* 27, 85: 443–450.

———. 2003. *Guerrilla Veterans in Post-war Zimbabwe: Symbolic and Violent Politics, 1980–1987.* Cambridge: Cambridge University Press.

Krog, Antjie. 1999. *Country of My Skull: Guilt, Sorrow, and the Limits of Forgiveness in the New South Africa.* New York: Times Books.

Lancaster, Carol. 2000. "Africa in World Affairs." In John Harbeson and Donald Rothchild, eds., *Africa in World Politics: The African State System in Flux,* 3rd ed. Boulder: Westview.

Laserud, Stina, and Rita Taphorn. 2007. *Designing for Equality: Best-fit, Medium-fit and Non-favourable Combinations of Electoral Systems and Gender Quotas.* Stockholm: International Idea.

Latham, Brian. 2010. "Zimbabwe Government Passes Law on 51% Black Ownership." *Business Week.* February 9. http://www.businessweek.com/.

le Billon, Philippe. 2001. "Angola's Political Economy of War: The Role of Oil and Diamonds, 1975–2000." *African Affairs.* 100: 55–80.

Lee, Margaret. 2003. *The Political Economy of Regionalism in Southern Africa.* Boulder: Lynne Rienner.

Legum, Colin. 2000. "The Balance of Power in Southern Africa." In York Bradshaw and Stephen Ndegwa, eds., *The Uncertain Promise of Southern Africa.* Bloomington: Indiana University Press.

Lekorwe, Mogopodi. 2005. "Organisation of Political Parties." In Zibani Maundeni, ed., *40 Years of Democracy in Botswana, 1965–2005.* Gaborone: Mmegi Publishing House.

Lekorwe, Mogopodi, Mpho Molomo, Wilford Molefe, and Kabelo Moseki. 2001. "Public Attitudes Toward Democracy, Governance, and Economic Development in Botswana." Afrobarometer Paper no. 14. Cape Town: IDASA.

Leslie, Agnes Ngoma. 2006. *Social Movements and Democracy in Africa: The Impact of Women's Struggle for Equal Rights in Botswana.* New York: Routledge.

Leys, Colin. 1994. "Theoretical Perspectives." In Colin Leys and Bruce Berman, eds., *African Capitalists in African Development.* Boulder: Lynne Rienner.

Leys, Colin, and Cranford Pratt, eds. 1960. *A New Deal in Central Africa.* London: Heinemann.

Leys, Colin, and John Saul. 1995. Introduction to Colin Leys and John Saul, eds., *Namibia's Liberation Struggle: The Two-Edged Sword.* London: James Currey.

Leysens, Anthony. 2006. "Social Forces in Southern Africa: Transformation from Below?" *Journal of Modern African Studies.* 44, 1: 31–58.

Lijphart, Arend. 1977. *Democracy in Plural Societies: A Comparative Exploration.* New Haven, CT: Yale University Press.

Lindberg, Staffan. 2006. *Democracy and Elections in Africa.* Baltimore: Johns Hopkins University Press.

Lodge, Tom. 1999. *Consolidating Democracy: South Africa's Second Popular Election.* Johannesburg: Witwatersrand University Press.

———. 2000. "Heavy-Handed Democracy: SWAPO's Victory in Namibia." *Southern Africa Report.* 15, 2: 26–29.

Logan, Carolyn. 2009. "Selected Chiefs, Elected Councillors, and Hybrid Democrats: Popular Perspectives on the Co-existence of Democracy and Traditional Authority." *Journal of Modern African Studies.* 47, 1: 101–128.

Lovenduski, Jone, and Azza Karam. 2002. "Women in Parliament." In International IDEA, *Women in Parliament.* Stockholm. http://www.idea.int.

Lurie, Mark. 2000. "Migration and AIDS in Southern Africa: A Review." *South African Journal of Science.* 96, 6: 343–346.

Lute, Aubrey. 2011. "2011–2015: 8 Percent Growth Rate for Mining Sector." *Botswana Gazette.* January 31. http://www.gazettebw.com.

Luthuli, Albert. 1962. *Let My People Go.* New York: McGraw Hill.

Lwanda, John. 2002. "Tikutha: The Political Culture of the HIV/AIDS Epidemic in Malawi." In Harri Englund, ed. *A Democracy of Chameleons: Politics and Culture in the New Malawi.* Stockholm: Nordiska Afrikainstitutet.

MacLean, Sandra J. 1999. "Peacebuilding and the New Regionalism in Southern Africa." *Third World Quarterly.* 20, 5: 943–956.

Magnusson, Bruce. 2002. "Transnational Flows, Legitimacy, and Syncretic Democracy in Benin." In Daniel M. Green, ed., *Constructivism and Comparative Politics.* Armonk, NY: M. E. Sharpe.

Malaquias, Assis. 2000. "Ethnicity and Conflict in Angola: Prospects for Reconciliation." In Jakkie Cilliers and Christian Dietrich, eds., *Angola's War Economy: The Role of Oil and Diamonds.* Pretoria: Institute for Security Studies.

———. 2001. "Diamonds Are a Guerrilla's Best Friend: The Impact of Illicit Wealth on Insurgency Strategy." *Third World Quarterly.* 22, 3: 311–325.

"Malawi President Gains Majority." 2004. June 18. http://news.bbc.co.uk.

"Malawi's President to Succeed Gaddafi as AU Chairman." 2010. *France24.* January 2. http://www.france24.com/.

Malherbe, Rassie. 1998. "The Legal System and the Judiciary." In Albert Venter, ed., *Government and Politics in the New South Africa.* Pretoria: Van Schaik.

Malupenga, Amos. 2009. *Levy Patrick Mwanawasa: An Incentive for Posterity.* Grahamstown, South Africa: National Inquiry Services Centre (NISC).

Mandela, Nelson. 1995. *Long Walk to Freedom.* Boston: Little, Brown.

Manning, Carrie. 2001. "Competition and Accommodation in Post-Conflict Democracy: The Case of Mozambique." *Democratization.* 8, 2: 140–168.

Marks, Shula. 2002. "An Epidemic Waiting to Happen? The Spread of HIV/AIDS in South Africa in Social and Historical Perspective." *African Studies.* 61, 1: 13–26.

Maroleng, Chris. 2003. "Zimbabwe: Smoke Screens and Mirrors." African Security Analysis Programme, Situation Report. Pretoria: Institute for Security Studies.

Marshall, Monty G., and Keith Jaggers. 2001. "Polity IV Country Report 2001: Mozambique." CIDCM. http://www.cidcm.umd.edu/.

Martin, Matthew. 1993. "Neither Phoenix nor Icarus: Negotiating Economic Reform in Ghana and Zambia, 1983–92." In Thomas Callaghy and John Ravenhill, eds., *Hemmed In: Responses to Africa's Economic Decline.* New York: Columbia University Press.

Marud, Maureen. 2004. "A Long, Sure Walk to Economic Stability." *Cape Argus.* February 18.

Maseko, Sipho. 1995. "The Namibian Student Movement: Its Role and Effects." In Colin Leys and John Saul, eds., *Namibia's Liberation Struggle: The Two-Edged Sword.* London: James Currey.

Masire, Quett Ketumile Joni. 2006. *Memoirs of an African Democrat: Very Brave or Very Foolish?* Gaborone: Macmillan Botswana.

Matemba, Jonah. 2005. "A Chief Called 'Woman': Historical Perspectives on the Changing Face of Bogosi (Chieftainship) in Botswana, 1834–2004." *JENDA: Journal of Culture and African Women Studies.* Issue 7.

Mattes, Robert. 2002. "South Africa: Democracy Without the People?" *Journal of Democracy.* 13, 1: 22–36.

———. 2008. "South Africans' Views of Parliament and MPs: A Comparative Perspective." Presentation to Panel for Assessment of Parliament. February 12. http://www.pmg.org.za/.

Maundeni, Zibani. 2005. "Succession to High Office: Tswana Culture and Modern Botswana Politics." In Zibani Maundeni, ed., *40 Years of Democracy in Botswana, 1965–2005.* Gaborone: Mmegi Publishing House.

———. 2008. "The Executive." In Zibani Maundeni, ed., *Transparency, Accountability, and Corruption in Botswana.* Gaborone: Democracy Research Project; and Cape Town: IDASA.

Mbeki, Moeletsi. 2009. *Architects of Poverty: Why African Capitalism Needs Changing.* Johannesburg: Pan Macmillan.

McCarthy, Colin. 1999. "Regional Integration in Sub-Saharan Africa: Past, Present, and Future." In T. Ademola Oyijide, B. Ndulu, and D. Greenaway, eds., *Regional Integration and Trade Liberalization in Sub-Saharan Africa,* vol. 4, *Synthesis and Review.* London: Macmillan.

McFerson, Hazel. 2010. "Developments in African Governance Since the Cold War: Beyond Cassandra and Pollyanna." *African Studies Review.* 53, 2: 49–76.

McGowan, Patrick. 2003. "African Military Coups d'Etat, 1956–2001: Frequency, Trends, and Distribution." *Journal of Modern African Studies.* 42, 3: 339–370.

Mchombo, Sam. 1998. "Democratization in Malawi: Its Roots and Prospects." In Jean-Germain Gros, ed., *Democratization in Late Twentieth Century Africa.* Westport, CT: Greenwood Press.

McKittrick, Meredith. 1998. "Generational Struggles and Social Mobility in Western Ovambo Communities, 1915–1954." In Patricia Hayes, Jeremy Sylvester, Marion Wallace, Wolfram Hartmann, with Ben Fuller, eds., *Namibia Under South African Rule: Mobility and Containment, 1915–46.* Oxford: James Currey.

Melber, Henning. 2003. "From Anti-Colonial Resistance to Government: A Sociology of Former Liberation Movements as Political Parties." Paper presented at the Institute of African Affairs. University of Hamburg, Germany.

———. 2010a. "Namibia: A Trust Betrayed Again?" AfricaFiles. Online.

———. 2010b. "Namibia's National Assembly and Presidential Elections 2009: Did Democracy Win?" *Journal of Contemporary African Studies.* 28, 2: 203–214.

Meldrum, Andrew. 2003. "The Observer." *Guardian Special Report.* March 30.

Meredith, Martin. 2006. *The Fate of Africa.* New York: PublicAffairs.

———. 2007. *Mugabe: Power, Plunder, and the Struggle for Zimbabwe's Future.* New York: PublicAffairs.

Messiant, Christine. 2001. "The Eduardo Dos Santos Foundation, or How Angola's Regime Is Taking Over Civil Society." *African Affairs.* 100: 287–309.

Mfundisi, Adam. 2008. "Local Governance." In Zibani Maundeni, ed., *Transparency, Accountability, and Corruption in Botswana*. Gaborone: Democracy Research Project; and Cape Town: IDASA.

Mikell, Gwendolyn. 1997. Introduction to Gwendolyn Mikell, ed., *African Feminism: The Politics of Survival in Sub-Saharan Africa*. Philadelphia: University of Pennsylvania Press.

————. 2003. "African Feminism: Toward a New Politics of Representation." In Carole McCann and Seung-Kyung Kim, eds., *Feminist Theory Reader: Local and Global Perspectives*. New York: Routledge.

Minow, Martha. 1998. *Between Vengeance and Forgiveness: Facing History After Genocide and Mass Violence*. Boston: Beacon Press.

Minter, William. 1994. *Apartheid Contras: An Inquiry into the Roots of War in Angola and Mozambique*. London: Zed Books.

MISA [Media Institute of Southern Africa]–Zimbabwe. 2007. "The Access to Information and Protection of Privacy Act: Five Years On." http://www.zimbabwejournalists.com/.

Mittelmann, James. 2000. *The Globalization Syndrome: Transformation and Resistance*. Princeton, NJ: Princeton University Press.

Mkandawire, Thandika, and Charles Soludo. 1999. *Our Continent, Our Future: African Perspectives on Structural Adjustment*. Trenton, NJ: Africa World Press.

MNA [Mozambique News Agency]. 2001. "President Chissano to Step Down in 2004." AIM Report no. 207. May 15. http://www.poptel.org.uk/.

Mo Ibrahim Foundation. 2007. "Citation of the Prize Committee for President Chissano." http://www.moibrahimfoundation.org/.

Mogotsi, Vance. 1995. "Is the Centre Willing to Share Power? The Importance of Regional and Local Government." In Carrie Marais, Peter Katjavivi, and Arnold Wehmhoerner, eds., *Southern Africa After Elections: Towards a Culture of Democracy*. Windhoek: Friedrich Ebert Stiftung.

Mokomane, Zitha. 2008. "Civil Society." In Zibani Maundeni, ed. *Transparency, Accountability, and Corruption in Botswana*. Gaborone: Democracy Research Project; and Cape Town: IDASA.

Molomo, Mpho. 2001. "Civil Military Relations in Botswana's Developmental State." *African Studies Quarterly*. 5, 2.

————. 2005. "Electoral Systems and Democracy in Botswana." In Zibani Maundeni, ed., *40 Years of Democracy in Botswana, 1965–2005*. Gaborone: Mmegi Publishing House.

Molutsi, Patrick. 2005. "Botswana's Democracy in a Southern African Regional Perspective: Progress or Decline?" In Zibani Maundeni, ed., *40 Years of Democracy in Botswana, 1965–2005*. Gaborone: Mmegi Publishing House.

Morton, Fred, Jeff Ramsay, and Part Themba Mgadla. 2008. *Historical Dictionary of Botswana*. Lanham, MD: Scarecrow Press.

Motshipi, Michael. 2010. "The Future of the DIS." *Botswana Gazette*. April 7.

Moyo, Otrude, and Saliwe Kawewe. 2002. "The Dynamics of a Racialized, Gendered, Ethnicized, and Economically Stratified Society: Understanding the Socioeconomic Status of Women in Zimbabwe." *Feminist Economics*. 8, 2: 163–181.

Moyo, Sam. 1995. *The Land Question in Zimbabwe*. Harare: SAPES Books.

————. 2000. "The Political Economy of Land Acquisition and Redistribution in Zimbabwe, 1990–1999." *Journal of Southern African Studies*. 26, 1: 5–28.

"Mozambique Adopts New Constitution." 2004. *Mail and Guardian Online*. November 16. http://www.mg.co.za/.

"Mozambique Govt Suspends SMSes." 2010. *Mail and Guardian Online.* September 11. http://www.mg.co.za/.

"Mozambique Launches Constitutional Reform." 2010. *Johannesburg Star.* December 24.

Mozambique Political Process Bulletin. 2004. Issue 26. December 15.

"Mozambique's Former Rebel Peace Negotiator Forms Political Party." 2003. South African Press Agency (SAPA). June 27. http://www.anc.org.za/.

Mshomba, Richard E. 2000. *Africa in the Global Economy.* Boulder: Lynne Rienner.

Mulemba, Humphrey. 1992. Speech delivered at the conference "Democracy and Economic Recovery in Africa: Lessons from Zambia." Reprinted in *Proceedings of the Zambia Consultation, June 11–12, 1992.* Atlanta: Carter Center.

Muleya, Dumisani. 2011. "US $3 Billion Offer for Platinum Raises Tension." *Zimbabwe Independent.* February 3.

Munslow, Barry. 1999. "Angola: The Politics of Unsustainable Development." *Third World Quarterly.* 20, 3: 551–568.

Mutharika, A. Peter. 1996. "The 1995 Democratic Constitution of Malawi." *Journal of African Law.* 40, 2: 205–220.

Myburgh, James. 2003. "Floor Crossing Adds New Muscle to ANC." *Focus.* 30. Helen Suzman Foundation. http://www.hsf.org.za/.

Nathan, Laurie. 2006. "SADC's Uncommon Approach to Common Security, 1992–2003." *Journal of Southern African Studies.* 32, 3: 605–622.

Nattrass, Nicoli. 1999. "The Truth and Reconciliation Commission on Business and Apartheid: A Critical Evaluation." *African Affairs.* 98: 373–391.

Naumann, Eckhart. 2003. "A Stitch in Time: US Deal Will Open New Markets for SACU but There Are Pitfalls." (South Africa) *Financial Mail.* August 1.

Negi, Rohit. 2008. "Beyond the 'Chinese Scramble': The Political Economy of Anti-China Sentiment in Zambia." *African Geographical Review.* 27: 41–63.

Nengwekhulu, Ranwedzi. 1979. "Some Findings on the Origins of Political Parties in Botswana." *Pula: Botswana Journal of African Affairs.* 1, 2: 47–76.

Nest, Michael. 2001. "Ambitions, Profit, and Loss: Zimbabwean Economic Involvement in the Democratic Republic of the Congo." *African Affairs.* 100, 400: 469–490.

Ngavirue, Zedekia. 1997. *Political Parties and Interest Groups in South West Africa (Namibia): A Study of a Plural Society.* Basel Namibia Studies Series no. 1. Basel: P. Schlettwein.

Ngoasong, Michael Zisuh. 2009. "The Emergence of Global Health Partnerships as Facilitators of Access to Medication in Africa: A Narrative Policy Analysis." *Social Science and Medicine.* 68: 949–956.

Nhema, Alfred. 2002. *Democracy in Zimbabwe: From Liberation to Liberalization.* Harare: University of Zimbabwe.

Nkatazo, Lebo. 2007. "New Wheels for Mugabe's Army, Police Bosses." August 8. http://newzimbabwe.com/.

Nordas, Hildegunn, and Leon Pretorius. 2000. "Mozambique: A Sub-Saharan African NIC?" CMI Working Paper no. 10. Bergen: Christian Michelsen Institute.

Northern Rhodesia Constitutional Conference. 1961. "Northern Rhodesia: Proposals for Constitutional Change." Presented to Parliament by the Secretary of State for the Colonies by Command of Her Majesty. London: HM Stationery Office.

Ntseane, Dolly. 2005. "Women in Party Politics." In Zibani Maundeni, ed., *40 Years of Democracy in Botswana, 1965–2005.* Gaborone: Mmegi Publishing House.

Oasis Forum. 2001. "The Oasis Declaration." Lusaka, Zambia. February 21.

Oden, Bertil. 2001. "South African Benevolent Hegemony in Southern Africa: Impasse or Highway?" In Peter Vale, Larry Swatuk, and Bertil Oden, eds., *Theory, Change, and Southern Africa's Future*. Hampshire, UK: Palgrave.

Ohlson, Thomas, and Stephen John Stedman. 1994. *The New Is Not Yet Born: Conflict Resolution in Southern Africa*. Washington, DC: Brookings Institution.

O'Meara, Dan. 1983. *Volkskapitalisme: Class, Capital, and Ideology in the Development of Afrikaner Nationalism*. Johannesburg: Ravan Press.

———. 1996. *Forty Lost Years: The Apartheid State and the Politics of the National Party, 1948–1994*. Athens: Ohio University Press.

Omer-Cooper, J. D. 1994. *A History of Southern Africa*. 2nd ed. Portsmouth, NH: Heinemann.

"Opposing Chiluba's Encore: Pressure Mounts in Zambia to Prevent an Unconstitutional Bid for Power." 2001. *Africa Analysis*. January 26.

Orre, Aslak. 2001. "Local Government Reform in Mozambique: Does It Matter?" MA thesis, Department of Comparative Politics, University of Bergen, Norway.

Osei Hwedie, Bertha. 2001a. "HIV/AIDS and the Politics of Domestic Response: The Case of Botswana." *International Relations*. 15, 6: 55–68.

———. 2001b. "The State and Development in Southern Africa: A Comparative Analysis of Botswana and Mauritius with Angola, Malawi, and Zambia." *African Studies Quarterly*. 5, 5.

Pachai, B. 1973. *Malawi: The History of the Nation*. London: Longman Group.

Pachecho, Fernando. 2002. "The Role of Civil Society in the Social Reconstruction of Angola." In Inge Tvedten, ed., *Angola 2001/2002: Key Development Issues and Aid in a Context of Peace*. Report R 2002: 8. Bergen: Christian Michelsen Institute.

Padayachee, Vishnu. 1997. "The Evolution of South Africa's International Economic Relations." In Jonathan Michie and V. Padayachee, eds., *The Political Economy of South Africa's Transitions*. London: Dryden Press.

Páez, Laura, Stephen Karingi, Mwangi Kimenyi, and Mekalia Paulos. 2010. "A Decade of African-US Trade Under the African Growth and Opportunities Act (AGOA): Challenges, Opportunities, and Framework for Post AGOA Engagement." United Nations Commission for Africa.

Pankhurst, Donna. 2002. "Women and Politics in Africa: The Case of Uganda." In Karen Ross, ed., *Women, Politics, and Change*. Oxford: Oxford University Press.

Parliament of South Africa. 2001. "Joint Investigation Report into the Strategic Defence Procurement Packages." November 14. http://www.parliament.gov.za/.

Parpart, Jane. 1988. "Women and the State in Africa." In Donald Rothchild and Naomi Chazan, eds., *The Precarious Balance: State and Society in Africa*. Boulder: Westview.

Parsons, Neil. 1985. "The Evolution of Modern Botswana: Historical Revisions." In Louis Picard, ed., *The Evolution of Modern Botswana*. London: Rex Collings.

Parsons, Neil, Willie Henderson, and Thomas Tlou. 1995. *Seretse Khama 1921–1980*. Gaborone: The Botswana Society.

Patel, Nandini, Richard Tambulasi, Bright Molande, and Andrew Mpesi. 2007. "Consolidating Democratic Governance in Southern Africa: Malawi." EISA Research Report No. 33. http://www.eisa.org.za/.

Pauw, Kalie, and Liberty Mncube. 2007. "Expanding the Social Security Net in South Africa: Opportunities, Challenges, and Constraints." United National Development Programme (UNDP), International Poverty Center (IPC) Country Study No. 8: 14. July.

Peters, Pauline, and Daimon Kambewa. 2007. "Whose Security? Deepening Social Conflict over 'Customary' Land in the Shadow of Land Reform in Malawi." *Journal of Southern African Studies*. 45: 447–472.

Peters, Pauline, Peter Walker, and Daimon Kambewa. 2008. "Striving for Normality in a Time of AIDS in Malawi." *Journal of Modern African Studies*. 46: 659–687.

Pew Forum on Religion and Public Life. 2006. "Historical Overview of Pentecostalism in South Africa." October 5. http://pewforum.org/.

Picard, Louis. 1985. "From Bechuanaland to Botswana: An Overview." In Louis Picard, ed., *The Evolution of Modern Botswana*. London: Rex Collings.

Piet, Bame. 2009. "DIS Is a Terror Squad—Saleshando." *Mmegi Online*. December 3. http://www.mmegi.bw.

Piot, Peter, Michael Bartos, Heidi Larson, Debrework Zewdie, and Purnima Mane. 2008. "Coming to Terms with Complexity: A Call to Action for HIV Prevention." *The Lancet*. 372: 842–859.

Pitcher, Anne, Mary H. Moran, and Michael Johnston. 2009. "Rethinking Patrimonialism and Neopatrimonialism in Africa." *African Studies Review*. 52, 1: 125–156.

Pitcher, M. Anne. 2003. *Transforming Mozambique: The Politics of Privatization, 1975–2001*. Cambridge: Cambridge University Press.

Poku, Nana. 2001. "Africa's AIDS Crisis in Context: 'How the Poor Are Dying.'" *Third World Quarterly*. 22, 2: 191–204.

Poku, Nana, and Fantu Cheru. 2001. "The Politics of Poverty and Debt in Africa's AIDS Crisis." *International Relations*. 15, 6: 37–54.

Posner, Daniel. 1995. "Malawi's New Dawn." *Journal of Democracy*. 6, 1: 131–145.

———. 2005. *Institutions and Ethnic Politics in Africa*. Cambridge: Cambridge University Press.

Power, Samantha. 2003. "Letter from South Africa: The AIDS Rebel." *New Yorker*. May 19.

"Presidential Candidate's Adoption Is an Act of Desperation." 2001. *(Zambia) Post*. August 27.

Radelet, Steven. 2010. *Emerging Africa: How 17 Countries Are Leading the Way*. Washington, DC: Center for Global Development.

Raftopoulos, Brian. 2001. "The Labour Movement and the Emergence of Opposition Politics in Zimbabwe." In Brian Raftopoulos and Lloyd Sachikonye, eds., *Striking Back: The Labour Movement and the Post-Colonial State in Zimbabwe*. Harare: Weaver Press.

Rakner, Lise. 1998. "Reform as a Matter of Political Survival: Political and Economic Liberalisation in Zambia, 1991–96." PhD diss. University of Bergen, Norway.

———. 2001. "The Pluralist Paradox: The Decline of Economic Interest Groups in Zambia." *Development and Change*. 32, 3: 521–543.

Rakner, Lise, Nicolas van de Walle, and Dominic Mulaisho. 2001. "Zambia." In S. Devarajan, David Dollar, and T. Holmgren, eds., *Aid and Reform in Africa*. Washington, DC: World Bank.

Ramsay, Jeff. 1993. "The 1962 BPP Split." *Botswana Notes and Records*. 25: 79–86.

Ranchod-Nilsson, Sita. 1998. "Zimbabwe: Women, Cultural Crisis, and the Reconfiguration of the One-Party State." In Leonardo Villalon and Phillip Huxtable, eds., *The African State at a Critical Juncture: Between Disintegration and Reconfiguration*. Boulder: Lynne Rienner.

———. 2006. "Gender Politics and the Pendulum of Political and Social Transformation in Zimbabwe." *Journal of Southern African Studies*. 32, 1: 49–67.

Rapoo, Thabo. 2001. "In Poor Voice: NCOP's Weakness Flows from the Westminster System." Center for Policy Studies, CPS Policy Brief no. 22. April.

Reed, John. 2004. "Black Elite Faces a Backlash over South Africa Wealth Reform." *Financial Times* (London). October 14.

"Renamo Boycotts and Marginalization." 2000. http://www.mozambique.mz/awepa/eawepa25/corpo.htm.

Reno, William. 1999. *Warlord Politics and African States*. Boulder: Lynne Rienner.

————. 2000. "The Real (War) Economy of Angola." In Jakkie Cilliers and Christian Dietrich, eds., *Angola's War Economy: The Role of Oil and Diamonds*. Pretoria: Institute for Security Studies.

"Report of the Committee on Economic Affairs and Labour on the Privatisation of Zambia Consolidated Copper Mines Limited for the Fourth Session of the Eighth National Assembly. Appointed on 10th February 2000." Lusaka.

Roberts, Andrew. 1976. *A History of Zambia*. New York: Africana Publishing.

Robinson, James. 2009. "Botswana as a Role Model for Country Success." Research Paper No. 2009/40. UN University World Institute for Development Economics Research.

Rodney, Walter. 1974. *How Europe Underdeveloped Africa*. Washington, DC: Howard University Press.

Rollnick, Roman. 2002. "An African Test Case for Wide Distribution of Life-Prolonging Medicines." *Africa Recovery*. September 1. http://allafrica.com/.

Roque, Paula Cristina. 2009. "Angola's Façade Democracy." *Journal of Democracy*. 20, 4: 137–150.

Rotberg, Robert. 2000. "Africa's Mess: Mugabe's Mayhem." *Foreign Affairs*. 79, 5: 47–61.

Rothchild, Donald, and John Harbeson. 2000. "The African State and State System in Flux." In John Harbeson and Donald Rothchild, eds., *Africa in World Politics: The African State System in Flux*. 3rd ed. Boulder: Westview.

Rugalema, Gabriel. 2000. "Coping or Struggling? A Journey into the Impact of HIV/AIDS in Southern Africa." *Review of African Political Economy*. 27, 86: 537–545.

Rupiya, Martin. 1998. "Historical Context: War and Peace in Mozambique." In Alex Vines and Dylan Hendrickson, eds., *The Mozambican Peace Process in Perspective*. London: Conciliation Resources.

SADC [Southern African Development Community] Gender Unit. 1999. *Women in Politics and Decision Making in SADC: Beyond 30 Percent in 2005*. Conference proceedings. Gaborone: SADC Gender Unit.

Saleshando, Dumelang. 2010. "The State of the Nation—A Response (part 2)." *Mmegi Online*. December 3. http://www.mmegi.bw.

Samatar, Abdi Ismail. 1999. *An African Miracle: State and Class Leadership and Colonial Legacy in Botswana Development*. Portsmouth, NH: Heinemann.

Saugestad, Sidsel. 2001. *The Inconvenient Indigenous: Remote Area Development in Botswana, Donor Assistance, and the First People of the Kalahari*. Stockholm: The Nordic Africa Institute.

Saul, John. 1999. "Cry for the Beloved Country: The Post-Apartheid Denouement." *Monthly Review* 52, 8: 1–51.

————. 2007. "The Strange Death of Liberated Southern Africa." *Transformation*. 64: 1–26.

Saul, John, and Colin Leys. 2003. "Lubango and After: 'Forgotten History' as Politics in Contemporary Namibia." *Journal of Southern African Studies*. 29, 2: 333–353.

Schwab, Peter. 2002. *Africa: A Continent Self-Destructs*. New York: Palgrave Macmillan.

Scribner, Druscilla, and Priscilla Lambert. 2010. "Constitutionalizing Difference: A Case Study Analysis of Gender Provisions in Botswana and South Africa." *Politics and Gender.* 6, 1: 37–62.

Sebudubudu, David, and Bertha Osei Hwedie. 2006. "Pitfalls of Parliamentary Democracy in Botswana." *Africa Spectrum.* 41, 1: 35–53.

Seekings, Jeremy, and Nicoli Nattrass. 2005. *Class, Race, and Inequality in South Africa.* New Haven, CT: Yale University Press.

Seidman, Gay. 1999. "Gendered Citizenship: South Africa's Democratic Transition and the Construction of a Gendered State." *Gender and Society.* 13, 3: 287–307.

Selolwane, Onalenna. 2000. "Civil Society, Citizenship and Women's Rights in Botswana." In Shirin Rai, ed., *International Perspectives on Gender and Democratization.* New York: St. Martin's Press.

Semu, Linda. 2002. "Kamuzu's Mbumba: Malawi Women's Embeddedness to Culture in the Face of International Political Pressure and Internal Legal Change." *Africa Today.* 49, 2: 77–99.

Sevenzo, Farai. 2011. "Is Malawi Reverting to Dictatorship?" BBC News Africa. www .bbc.co.uk. May 3.

Shafer, D. Michael. 1994. *Winners and Losers: How Sectors Shape the Developmental Prospects of States.* Ithaca, NY: Cornell University Press.

Shaw, Timothy. 1989. "Corporatism in Zimbabwe." In Timothy Shaw and Julius Nyangoro, eds., *Corporatism in Africa: Comparative Analysis and Practice.* Boulder: Westview.

Sidaway, James, and Richard Gibb. 1998. "SADC, COMESA, SACU: Contradictory Formats for Regional Integration in Southern Africa?" In David Simon, ed., *South Africa in Southern Africa: Reconfiguring the Region.* Athens: Ohio University Press.

Simon, David. 2005. "Zambia." Freedom House Countries at the Crossroads. http:// www.freedomhouse.org/.

Simpson, Mark. 1993. "Foreign and Domestic Factors in the Transformation of Frelimo." *Journal of Modern African Studies.* 31, 2: 309–337.

Simutanyi, Neo. 2010. "The 2008 Presidential Elections in Zambia: Incumbency, Political Contestation and Failure of Political Opposition." Paper presented to the CMI/IESE conference on Election Processes, Liberation Movements and Democratic Change in Africa. Maputo. April 8–11.

Sindima, Harvey. 2002. *Malawi's First Republic: An Economic and Political Analysis.* Lanham, MD: University Press of America.

Sisk, Timothy. 1995. *Democratization in South Africa: The Elusive Social Contract.* Princeton, NJ: Princeton University Press.

Sithole, Chipo. 2009. "Zimbabwe: New Government Comes at a Price." *Institute for War and Peace Reporting* (London). February 12. http://allafrica.com/stories/ 200902120771.html.

Sithole, Masipula. 1988. "Zimbabwe: In Search of a Stable Democracy." In Larry Diamond, Juan Linz, and Seymour Martin Lipset, eds., *Democracy in Developing Countries,* vol. 2, *Africa.* Boulder: Lynne Rienner.

———. 2000. "Zimbabwe: The Erosion of Authoritarianism and Prospects for Democracy." In York Bradshaw and Stephen Ndegwa, eds., *The Uncertain Promise of Southern Africa.* Bloomington: Indiana University Press.

———. 2001. "Fighting Authoritarianism in Zimbabwe." *Journal of Democracy.* 12, 1: 160–169.

Skalnes, Tor. 1995. *The Political Economy of Economic Reform in Zimbabwe: Continuity and Change in Development.* New York: St. Martin's.

Sklar, Richard. 1975. *Corporate Power in an African State.* Los Angeles: University of California Press.

Smiddy, Kimberly, and Daniel Young. 2009. "Presidential and Parliamentary Elections in Malawi, May 2009." *Electoral Studies.* 28: 662–666.

Smith, David. 2010. "Mugabe and Allies Own 40% of Land Seized from White Farmers—Inquiry." November 30. Guardian.co.uk.

Smith, Ian Douglas. 2002. *Bitter Harvest: The Great Betrayal and the Dreadful Aftermath.* London: Blake.

Soares de Oliveira, Ricardo. 2007. "Business Success, Angola-style: Postcolonial Politics and the Rise and Rise of Sonangol." *Journal of Modern African Studies.* 45, 4: 595–619.

"Social Security Spending Increased." 2008. October 22. http://www.southafrica.info/.

Sogge, David. 2009. "Angola 'Failed' Yet 'Successful.'" April. http://www.tni.org/.

———. 2010. "Angola Reinventing Pasts and Futures." June. http://www.tni.org/.

Soiri, Iina. 1996. *The Radical Motherhood: Namibian Women's Independence Struggle.* Research Report no. 99. Uppsala: Nordiska Afrikainstitutet.

"South Africa Padayachie Pulls Plug on Broadcasting Bill." 2010. *Balancing Act.* 93. November 23. http://balancingact-africa.com/.

"South Africa Signs Historic Trade Deal with EU." 1999. *African Review of Business and Technology.* December 31.

Soyinka-Airewele, Peyi, and Rita Kiki Edozie. 2009. *Reframing Contemporary Africa: Politics, Economics, and Culture in the Global Era.* Washington, DC: CQ Press.

Statistics South Africa. 2001. "Primary Tables, South Africa Census 2001: Census '96 and 2001 Compared." http://www.statssa.gov.za/census01/html/RSAPrimary.pdf.

———. 2010. Quarterly Labour Force Survey [Q3 2010]. http://www.statssa.gov.za/publications/P0211/P02113rdQuarter2010.pdf.

Staudt, Kathleen. 1987. "Women's Politics, the State, and Capitalist Transformation in Africa." In Irving Leonard Markovitz, ed., *Studies in Power and Class in Africa.* Oxford: Oxford University Press.

Staunton, Irene, ed. 1990. *Mothers of the Revolution.* Harare: Baobab Books.

Stedman, Stephen John. 1991. *Peacemaking in Civil War: International Mediation in Zimbabwe, 1974–1980.* Boulder: Lynne Rienner.

———. 1997. "Spoiler Problems in Peace Processes." *International Security.* 22, 2: 5–53.

Steenkamp, Philip. 1995. "The Churches." In Colin Leys and John Saul, eds., *Namibia's Liberation Struggle: The Two-Edged Sword.* London: James Currey.

Stoneman, Colin. 1998. "Lessons Unlearned: South Africa's One-Way Relationship with Zimbabwe." In David Simon, ed., *South Africa in Southern Africa: Reconfiguring the Region.* Cape Town: David Philip.

———, ed. 1988. *Zimbabwe's Prospects.* London: Macmillan.

Stoneman, Colin, and Lionel Cliffe. 1989. *Zimbabwe: Politics, Economics, and Society.* London: Pinter.

Stoneman, Colin, and Rob Davies. 1981. "The Economy: An Overview." In Colin Stoneman, ed., *Zimbabwe's Inheritance.* New York: St. Martin's.

Strachan, Brigid. 1986. "Report on Job Creation and Black Advancement, Part II: Black Advancement." Confederation of Zimbabwe Industries Job Creation/Black Advancement Subcommittee of the Labour and Manpower Committee. Harare.

————. 1989. "Black Managerial Advancement in a Sample of CZI Member Companies." Unpublished internal report for the Confederation of Zimbabwe Industries. Harare.

Streak, Judith. 2004. "The Gear Legacy: Did Gear Fail or Move South Africa Forward in Development?" *Development Southern Africa*. 21, 2: 271–288.

"Supreme Court of Appeal of South Africa (About)." http://www.justice.gov.za/.

Sylvester, Christine. 1995. "Whither Democracy in Zimbabwe?" *Journal of Modern African Studies*. 33, 3: 403–423.

Taljaard, Raenette, and Albert Venter. 1998. "Parliament." In Albert Venter, ed., *Government and Politics in the New South Africa*. Pretoria: Van Schaik.

Taylor, Ian. 2002. *Stuck in Middle GEAR: South Africa's Post-Apartheid Foreign Policy*. New York: St. Martin's.

————. 2009. *China's New Role in Africa*. Boulder: Lynne Rienner.

Taylor, Ian, and Gladys Mokhawa. 2003. "Not Forever: Botswana, Conflict Diamonds, and the Bushmen." *African Affairs*. 102: 261–283.

Taylor, Ian, and Philip Nel. 2002. "'New Africa' Globalisation and the Confines of Elite Reformism: 'Getting the Rhetoric Right, Getting the Strategy Wrong.'" *Third World Quarterly*. 23, 1: 163–180.

Taylor, Scott D. 1999a. "Business and Politics in Zimbabwe's Commercial Agriculture Sector." *African Economic History*. 27: 177–215.

————. 1999b. "Race, Class, and Neopatrimonialism in Zimbabwe." In Richard Joseph, ed., *State, Conflict, and Democracy in Africa*. Boulder: Lynne Rienner.

————. 2002. "The Challenge of Indigenization, Affirmative Action, and Black Empowerment in Zimbabwe and South Africa." In Alusine Jalloh and Toyin Falola, eds., *Black Business and Economic Power*. Rochester, NY: University of Rochester Press.

————. 2006. "Divergent Politico-Legal Response to Presidential Corruption in Zambia and Kenya: Catching the 'Big Fish' or Letting Him off the Hook." *Third World Quarterly*. 27, 2: 281–301.

————. 2007. *Business and the State in Southern Africa: The Politics of Economic Reform*. Boulder: Lynne Rienner.

————. 2009. "Labor Markets in Africa: Multiple Challenges, Limited Opportunities." *Current History*. 108, 718: 214–220.

Thompson, Alex. 2001. *An Introduction to African Politics*. New York: Routledge.

Tingle, Rachel. 1998. "What Role for the Churches in the New South Africa?" In R. W. Johnson and David Welsh, eds., *Ironic Victory: Liberalism in Post-Liberation South Africa*. London: Oxford University Press.

Toetemeyer, Gerhard. 2000. "Decentralisation and State-Building at the Local Level." In Christiaan Keulder, ed., *State, Society, and Democracy: A Reader in Namibian Politics*. Windhoek: Gamsberg Macmillan.

Tordoff, William. 1980. Introduction to William Tordoff, ed., *Administration in Zambia*. Madison: University of Wisconsin Press.

Tranberg Hansen, Karen. 2000. *Salaula: The World of Second Hand Clothing and Zambia*. Chicago: University of Chicago Press.

Transparency International. "NEPAD's African Peer Review Mechanism." http://www.transparency.org/.

TRC [Truth and Reconciliation Commission]. 1999. *Truth and Reconciliation Commission of South Africa Report*. New York. Distributed by Grove's Dictionaries.

Tripp, Aili Mari. 2001. "The New Political Activism in Africa." *Journal of Democracy*. 12, 3: 141–155.

Tripp, Aili Mari, Isabel Casimiro, Joy Kwesiga, and Alice Mungwa. 2009. *African Women's Movements: Changing Political Landscapes.* Cambridge: Cambridge University Press.

Tripp, Aili Mari, and Alice Kang. 2008. "The Global Impact of Quotas: On the Fast Track to Increased Female Legislative Representation." *Comparative Political Studies.* 41, 3: 338–361.

Tshosa, Onkemetse. 2008. "The Judiciary." In Zibani Maundeni, ed., *Transparency, Accountability, and Corruption in Botswana.* Gaborone: Democracy Research Project; and Cape Town: IDASA.

Tsie, Balefi. 1996. "The Political Context of Botswana's Development Performance." *Journal of Southern African Studies.* 22, 4: 599–616.

———. 2001. "International Political Economy and Southern Africa." In Peter Vale, Larry A. Swatuk, and Bertil Oden, eds., *Theory, Change, and Southern Africa's Future.* London: Palgrave.

Tutu, Desmond. 1999. *No Future Without Forgiveness.* New York: Doubleday.

Tvedten, Inge. 1997. *Angola: Struggle for Peace and Reconstruction.* Boulder: Westview.

———, ed. 2002. *Angola 2001/2002: Key Development Issues and Aid in a Context of Peace.* Report R 2002: 8. Bergen: Christian Michelsen Institute.

UNAIDS [Joint United Nations Programme on HIV/AIDS]. 2001. *Special Session Fact Sheets: Gender and HIV/AIDS.* http://www.unaids.org/.

———. 2002a. *AIDS Epidemic Update: December 2002.* http://unaids.org/.

———. 2002b. *Epidemiological Fact Sheets on HIV/AIDS and Sexually Transmitted Infections: South Africa.* http://www.unaids.org/.

———. 2002c. "A Global Overview of the Epidemic." *Report on the Global HIV/AIDS Epidemic 2002.* http://www.unaids.org/.

———. 2002d. "Join the Fight Against AIDS in Zambia." Menu of Partnership Options. Geneva: UNAIDS.

———. 2002e. "Mounting Impact." *Report on the Global HIV/AIDS Epidemic 2002.* http: www/unaids/org/.

———. 2002f. "UNAIDS Releases New Data Highlighting the Devastating Impact of AIDS in Africa." Press release. http://www.unaids.org/.

———. 2003. *AIDS Epidemic Update: December 2003.* http://www.unaids.org/.

———. 2004. *AIDS Epidemic Update: December 2004.* http://www.unaids.org/.

———. 2007. "Progress and Challenges for Botswana." http://unaids.org/.

———. 2008a. "Leadership and Aids: Festus Mogae." http://www.unaids.org/.

———. 2008b. "Namibia Country Situation." http://data.unaids.org/.

———. 2009a. *AIDS Epidemic Update: December 2009.* http://data.unaids.org/.

———. 2009b. "HIV Prevention Central to the AIDS Response." http://www.unaids .org/.

———. 2010a. "At Least 56 Countries Have Either Stabilized or Achieved Significant Declines in Rates of New HIV Infections." http://www.unaids.org/.

———. 2010b. "Global Report Fact Sheet: The Global AIDS Epidemic." http://www .unaids.org/.

———. 2010c. "Global Report Fact Sheet: Sub-Saharan Africa." http://www.unaids .org/.

———. 2010d. "Twenty-Two of the Most Affected Countries in Sub-Saharan Africa Have Reduced New HIV Infections by More than 25%." http://unaidstoday.org/.

———. 2010e. "South Africa Committed to Achieving Universal Access." http://www .unaids.org/.

————. 2010f. "UNAIDS Executive Director Joins President Zuma to Launch National HIV Counselling and Testing Drive in South Africa." http://www .unaids.org/.

————. N.d. *Gender and AIDS Fact Sheets.* http://unaids.org.

UNDP [United Nations Development Programme]. 2000. *Namibia: Human Development Report.* Windhoek: UNDP.

————. 2002. *Human Development Report 2002.* New York: Oxford University Press.

————. 2003. *Human Development Report 2003.* "Human Development Indicators." http://www.undp.org/.

UNECA [United Nations Economic Commission for Africa]. 2001. "The New Partnership for African Development" (NEPAD). http://www.uneca.org/.

UNIFEM [United Nations Development Fund for Women]. N.d. *Women's Human Rights: Gender and AIDS.* http://www.unifem.undp.org/.

United Nations Security Council. 2002. *Final Report of the Panel of Experts on the Illegal Exploitation of Natural Resources and Other Forms of Wealth of the Democratic Republic of Congo* (S/2002/1146). New York: United Nations Security Council.

Upton, Rebecca. 2003. "'Women Have No Tribe': Connecting Carework, Gender, and Migration in an Era of HIV/AIDS in Botswana." *Gender and Society.* 17, 2: 314–322.

Urdang, Stephanie. 1989. *And Still They Dance: Women, War and the Struggle for Change in Mozambique.* New York: Monthly Review Press.

————. 2006. "The Care Economy: Gender and the Silent AIDS Crisis in Southern Africa." *Journal of Southern African Studies.* 32, 1: 165–177.

"US-African Trade Profile 2009." 2009. US Department of Commerce. International Trade Administration. http://agoa.gov. (July).

US Department of State. 2010a. *2009 Human Rights Report: Angola.* Washington, DC: Bureau of Democracy, Human Rights, and Labor. http://www.state.gov/.

————. 2010b. *2009 Human Rights Report: Botswana.* Washington, DC: Bureau of Democracy, Human Rights, and Labor. http://www.state.gov/.

————. 2010c. *2009 Human Rights Report: Malawi.* Washington, DC: Bureau of Democracy, Human Rights, and Labor. http://www.state.gov/.

————. 2010d. *2009 Human Rights Report: Namibia.* Washington, DC: Bureau of Democracy, Human Rights, and Labor. http://www.state.gov/.

————. N.d. "Background Note: Zimbabwe." http://www.state.gov/r/pa/ei/bgn/5479 .htm.

Usher, Ann Danaiya. 2010. "Donors Lose Faith in Zambian Health Ministry." *The Lancet.* 376, 9379: 403–404.

US International Trade Commission. 2003. "Sub-Saharan Africa: US Exports, Imports, GSP Imports, and AGOA Imports, by Major Commodity Sectors, Annual and Year to Date Jan.–Jun." http://reportweb.usitc.gov/.

USIP [US Institute of Peace]. 2001. *AIDS and Violent Conflict in Africa.* Special report. Washington, DC: USIP.

US National Intelligence Council. 2000. *The Global Infectious Disease Threat and Its Implications for the United States.* January. http://www.cia.gov/nic/pubs/index .htm.

"US Says Zim Election Fundamentally Flawed." 2002. *Harare Financial Gazette.* Reuters, March 14.

"US Signs Commercial Pact with SACU, Says Free Trade Agreement Still Possible." 2008. *BNA.* July 17.

"U.S. Trade with Sub-Saharan Africa, January–December 2010." 2011. www.agoa.gov.

Vail, Leroy, ed. 1991. *The Creation of Tribalism in Southern Africa*. Berkeley: University of California Press.

Vale, Peter. 1997. "Backwaters and By-passes: South Africa and 'Its' Region." In L. A. Swatuk and D. R. Black, eds., *Bridging the Rift: The New South Africa in Africa*. Boulder: Westview.

———. 2001. "Dissenting Tale: Southern Africa's Search for Theory." In Peter Vale, Larry Swatuk, and Bertil Oden, eds., *Theory, Change, and Southern Africa's Future*. Hampshire, UK: Palgrave.

Van Allen, Judith. 2001. "Women's Rights Movements as a Measure of African Democracy." *Journal of Asian and African Studies*. 36, 1: 39–64.

———. 2007. "Feminism and Social Democracy in Botswana." *Socialism and Democracy*. 21, 3: 97–124.

Van Ameron, Marloes, and Bram Buescher. 2005. "Peace Parks in Southern Africa: Bringers of an African Renaissance?" *Journal of Modern African Studies*. 43, 2: 159–182.

van de Walle, Nicolas. 2001. *African Economies and the Politics of Permanent Crisis, 1979–1999*. Cambridge: Cambridge University Press.

van Donge, Jan Kees. 1995. "Kamuzu's Legacy: The Democratization of Malawi." *African Affairs*. 94: 227–257.

———. 2009. "The Plundering of Zambian Resources by Frederick Chiluba and His Friends: A Case Study of the Interaction Between National Politics and the International Drive Towards Good Governance." *African Affairs*. 108, 430: 69–90.

Venter, Albert, ed. 1998. *Government and Politics in the New South Africa*. Pretoria: Van Schaik.

Vines, Alex. 1996. *Renamo: From Terrorism to Democracy in Mozambique?* Rev. ed. London: James Currey.

———. 2000. "Angola: 40 Years of War." Track Two Occasional Paper no. 9. Cape Town: Centre for Conflict Resolution.

VonDoepp, Peter. 2001a. "Patterns of Judicial Activism in Malawi and Zambia: A Comparison and Initial Exploration." Paper presented at the annual meeting of the African Studies Association. Houston, Texas.

———. 2001b. "The Survival of Malawi's Enfeebled Democracy." *Current History*. 100, 646: 232–237.

———. 2002. "Malawi's Local Clergy as Civil Society Activists? The Limiting Impact of Creed, Context, and Class." *Commonwealth and Comparative Politics*. 40, 2: 21–46.

———. 2006. "Politics and Judicial Assertiveness in Emerging Democracies: High Court Behavior in Malawi and Zambia." *Political Research Quarterly*. 59, 3: 389–399.

———. 2010. "Malawi." Freedom House Countries at the Crossroads 2010. http://www.freedomhouse.org/.

Wadula, Patrick, and Christof Maletsky. 1999. "SA's Neighbours Lose Out." *South Africa Business Day*. October 15.

Wallerstein, Immanuel. 1974. *The Modern World System*. New York: Academic Press.

Wass, Peter. 2004. "Initiatives to Promote Civil Society in Botswana in the 1960s: A Personal Memoir." *Botswana Notes and Records*. 36: 74–81.

Weidlich, Brigitte. 2007. "Secret Nujoma Muyongo Document Surfaces." *Namibian*. January 24.

Weiland, H., and M. Braham, eds. 1994. *The Namibian Peace Process: Implications and Lessons for the Future*. Freiburg: Arnold-Bergstraesser-Institut.

Weinstein, Jeremy. 2002. "Mozambique: A Fading UN Success Story." *Journal of Democracy.* 13, 1: 141–156.

Weiss, Ruth. 1994. *Zimbabwe and the New Elite.* London: St. Martin's.

Wendt, Alexander. 1999. *Social Theory of International Politics.* Cambridge: Cambridge University Press.

Whiteside, Alan, Alex de Waal, and Tsadkan Gebre-Tensae. 2006. "AIDS, Security and the Military in Africa: A Sober Appraisal." *African Affairs.* 105, 419: 201–218.

WHO/UNAIDS/UNICEF [World Health Organization/Joint United Nations Programme on HIV/AIDS/United Nations Children's Fund]. 2010. "Towards Universal Access: Scaling Up Priority HIV/AIDS Interventions in the Health Sector." http://www.who.int/.

Widner, Jennifer A. 2001. *Building the Rule of Law: Francis Nyalali and the Road to Judicial Independence in Africa.* New York: W. W. Norton.

Williams, David. 1978. *Malawi: The Politics of Despair.* Ithaca, NY: Cornell University Press.

Williams, Martin. 1998. "The Press Since 1994." In R. W. Johnson and David Welsh, eds., *Ironic Victory: Liberalism in Post-Liberation South Africa.* Oxford: Oxford University Press.

Williams, Susan. 2007. *Colour Bar: The Triumph of Seretse Khama and His Nation.* London: Penguin Books.

Wills, A. J. 1964. *An Introduction to the History of Central Africa.* Oxford: Oxford University Press.

Wilson, Richard. 2001. *The Politics of Truth and Reconciliation in South Africa: Legitimizing the Post-Apartheid State.* Cambridge: Cambridge University Press.

Wiseman, John. 1998. "The Slow Evolution of the Party System in Botswana." *Journal of Asian and African Studies.* 33, 3: 241–265.

———. 2000. "Presidential and Parliamentary Elections in Malawi, 1999." *Electoral Studies.* 19, 4: 615–646.

Wooldridge, Mike. 2011. "Will Brics Strengthen South Africa's Economic Foundations?" *BBC News.* http://www.bbc.co.uk/news/world-africa-12113830.

World Bank. 1981. *Accelerated Development in Sub-Saharan Africa.* Washington, DC: World Bank.

———. 1995. *Zimbabwe: Achieving Shared Growth.* Country Economic Memorandum, 2 vols. Washington, DC: World Bank.

———. 2003a. *Sustainable Development in a Dynamic World: Transforming Institutions, Growth, and Quality of Life.* New York: Oxford University Press.

———. 2003b. *World Development Report 2003.* New York: Oxford University Press.

———. 2011. *World Bank Data Indicators.* http://data.worldbank.org.

WTO [World Trade Organization]. 2009. "Trade Policy Review: Mozambique." Statistical Appendix. WT/TPR/209. http://www.wto.org/.

———. N.d. "Textiles Monitoring Body (TMB); The Agreement on Textiles and Clothing." http://www.wto.org.

Zaffiro, James. 1997. "Women and Democratization of Politics in Botswana." Paper presented at the fortieth annual African Studies Association meeting. Columbus, Ohio.

"Zambia's Ruling Party Approves Third Term for Chiluba." 2001. Agence France Presse. April 30.

Zartman, I. William, ed. 1989. *Ripe for Resolution.* 2nd ed. New York: Oxford University Press.

———. 1995. *Collapsed States: The Disintegration and Restoration of Legitimate Authority.* Boulder: Lynne Rienner.

ZCTU [Zimbabwe Congress of Trade Unions]. 1996. *Beyond ESAP.* Harare: ZCTU.
Zimbabwe Alert. 2002. "Army General Warns Independent Media and Foreign Journalists." Windhoek: Media Institute of Southern Africa.
"Zim Parliament Passes Media Bill." 2002. Reuters. January 31.
ZimRights [Zimbabwe Human Rights Association]. 1996. "1996 Presidential Election Monitoring Report." Harare: Zimbabwe Human Rights Association.
————. 2002. Home page. http://www.kubatana.net/.
Zwi, A. B., and A. J. Cabral. 1991. "Identifying 'High Risk Situations' for Preventing AIDS." *British Medical Journal.* 303: 1527–1529.

Index

About the Book

The developments of the past six years are reflected throughout this thoroughly revised edition of *Politics in Southern Africa*.

Gretchen Bauer and Scott Taylor systematically examine politics and society in the region. After introducing the themes that guide their analysis, in each of eight country studies they trace the country's historical origins and then analyze state institutions, political parties and civil society, fundamentals of the political economy, and the major challenges faced by state and society. In the final chapters of the book, they investigate issues that transcend regional borders: living with HIV/AIDS, women and politics, and southern Africa's role on the continent and in the world.

Gretchen Bauer is professor and chair in the Department of Political Science and International Relations at the University of Delaware. She is the author of *Labor and Democracy in Namibia, 1971–1996* and coeditor of *Women in African Parliaments*. **Scott D. Taylor** is associate professor and director of African Studies in the School of Foreign Service at Georgetown University. He is the author of *Business and the State in Southern Africa: The Politics of Economic Reform* and *Culture and Customs of Zambia*.